COLLINS GUIDE
TO ENGLISH PARISH CHURCHES

COLLINS GUIDE TO
ENGLISH PARISH
CHURCHES

INCLUDING
THE ISLE OF MAN

EDITED BY
JOHN BETJEMAN

COLLINS

ST JAMES'S PLACE, LONDON

1958

To the memory of

ST. AGNES', KENNINGTON, 1877
CHRIST CHURCH, SALFORD, 1830

*fine churches of unfashionable date
demolished since the war*

Acknowledgments

Apart from his immense debt to country contributors, the Editor's thanks are due to Mr. John Piper for causing this book to be compiled and to Mr. E. T. Long, F.S.A. for providing the basis of it (*see The Purpose of this Book, Page 13 et seq.*); to Dr. N. Pevsner, F.S.A. and to Penguin Books Ltd, for permission to use their glossary in abbreviated form from *The Buildings of England* and to the former for help in the text; to Messrs. Faber and Faber; to Messrs. B. T. Batsford Ltd; to the Cambridge University Press; to the Central Council for the Care of Churches and to the following: The Rev. Canon G. W. O. Addleshaw, F.S.A., Robin Atthill, Hope Bagenal, F.R.I.B.A., Peter Bayley, The Very Rev. R. A. Beddoes, Provost of Derby, L. H. Bond, L.R.I.B.A., The Rev. Anthony Bridge, Howard Colvin, Sir Ninian Comper, The Rev. Dennis Cooper, W. Croome, F.S.A., The Rev. Victor Davies, The Misses Dennistoun, The Rt. Rev. Colin Dunlop, Dean of Lincoln, The late Dr. F. C. Eeles, Frederick Etchells, F.R.I.B.A., Miss Joan Evans, F.S.A., H. S. Goodhart-Rendel, F.S.A., P.P.R.I.B.A., The Rev. Max Gregory, Rupert Gunnis, H. L. Honeyman, F.S.A., A.R.I.B.A., Graham Hutton, O.B.E., The Rev. G. Irvine, Francis Johnson, F.S.A., F.R.I.B.A., Sir Thomas Kendrick, F.S.A., Osbert and Kareen Lancaster, F. W. Lloyd, Esq., Arthur Mackenzie, H. Meynall, The Very Rev. E. Milner White, Dean of York, Lord Mottistone, F.S.A., and Mr. Paul Paget, Ian Nairn, The late Sir Charles Nicholson, Bt., F.R.I.B.A., The Hon. Humphrey Pakington, F.R.I.B.A., Miss Petersen, Mrs. John Piper, F. I. G. Rawlins, Sir Albert Richardson, K.C.V.O., P.P.R.A., F.S.A., F.R.I.B.A., A. E. Royser, L.R.I.B.A., Miss Judith Scott, F.S.A., Dr. Thomas Sharp, W. B. Stonebridge, F.R.I.B.A., Sir John Summerson, F.S.A., A.R.I.B.A., Gordon Sutcliffe, A.R.I.B.A., Bishop Taylor, Miss Joan Wake, F.S.A., Harold White, Sir Harold Wilberforce-Bell, Paul Wilson, The Rev. Christopher Woodforde, F.S.A., J. T. Yates, Wayland and Elizabeth Young.

The Editor is finally grateful to Mr. Herbert Rees who spent many hours with him correcting proofs and keeping files in order and also to the numerous Bishops, Deans, Archdeacons and Incumbents, Squires, Peers, local historians and architects who helped him and his contributors over the twelve years during which the material for this book was assembled. Their name is many and their letters make excellent reading.

CONTENTS

LIST OF PLATES

11

Drawings by John Piper

*Plans of Churches adapted by Zena Flax from
'The Ground Plan of the English Parish Church'
by A. H. Thompson, Cambridge University Press*

THE PURPOSE OF THIS BOOK

IT HAD long bothered my friend Mr. John Piper and me that there was no selective list of English parish churches, judging the buildings by their atmosphere and aesthetic merit. For instance, when motoring through a district we had not hitherto explored, we would see a church on some nearby hill or in a valley and wonder whether it was worth diverting our journey to go and see it. If it were an old church, would it be ruined inside by Victorian 'restoration'? If it were a 19th or early 20th century church, who was the architect? The answers to these questions can be found, by reading between the lines in Kelly's admirable county directories. But these are bulky things to carry about and do not describe churches in large cities. Other answers can be found in Dr. Pevsner's Penguin *Buildings of Britain*, but these are not yet complete and one passes, in a motor car or train, quickly from one county to another, nor does one always need quite so much information as he gives for a cursory visit. Of one thing we could be quite certain and that was that the more old fashioned guide books and works on church architecture would give no information about the look of a church from the point of view of artists and Anglicans. They are concerned, primarily, with the search for style or with particular details which interested their authors such as brasses, bells or church plate or woodwork. Very learned and painstaking these books are. We both possess hundreds of them. Then there was no work which listed the better of the many hundreds of 19th and early 20th century churches. Because we felt the need for such a book, this work was undertaken.

There are over 16,000 parish churches in England and, as editor, I had to decide the limitations of the work. I therefore excluded all cathedrals except a few which, though they might contain a bishop's throne, were originally built as parish churches and had only recently been ennobled, e.g. Derby and Leicester. I also had to exclude the many fascinating college, almshouse and hospital chapels, often unknown and difficult of access. Even so there was probably no one who had visited every parish church in England and could undertake the task – and the task as first envisaged was this:

1. Churches should be listed under counties.

2. Only Church of England parish churches should be included.

3. No church should be included which did not have one or more of these qualifications:

   a. Wholly un-'restored' by the Victorians with box-pews, clear glass and three-decker pulpit,

   or

13

   b. so well-restored as to have preserved the atmosphere of the past.

   c. though heavily restored by Victorians, still magnificent as *architecture*, e.g. the parish churches of Louth and Newark.

   d. containing one object which, regardless of date, was aesthetically worth bicycling twelve miles against the wind to see. This, I thought, ought to rule out objects of 'antiquarian interest' like banner-stave lockers and squints.

   e. not built later than 1930 as it is an invidious task to distinguish between the works of living architects often obliged to use cheap mass-produced materials.

We have been unable to deal with essentially specialist subjects such as bells, organs and brasses in a book of so large a scope.

Discussion with friends put me in touch with Mr. E. T. Long, F.S.A., who was the one person qualified to produce such lists because he has visited more old churches in the country than most and made notes. Mr. Long's lists when compiled, exactly complied with the conditions. But, after much heartburning, I decided that they needed expansion and extension for the following reasons – they were written as I had originally suggested, in the shortest terms just giving approximate dates of styles and, where necessary, the name of the objects to be seen under (d). But I thought the language might be too technical and unexplanatory for those who were uninitiated in the terms of ecclesiology: they left out some 19th-century churches: they were inevitably one man's judgment and consequently had a certain impersonality when applied to the whole of England. But these lists by Mr. Long, together with his brief accounts of the architectural characteristics of the churches of each county, were the basis of this book and without them it could never have been written, for they proved a stimulant and source of information to each of the writers in the next stage of the task.

The next stage was to find, in every county of England, an enthusiast for its churches to whom Mr. Long's texts could be sent and who, reading them, would make his own additions and expansions. I had decided that each English county was so different and that there were so many aspects of aesthetic judgment, that variety in style and choice was essential; such variety would anyhow never let slip the most splendid churches in each county.

When the authors had been discovered and persuaded to write, and the lists arrived, I found there were still parts of the book missing. First, architecture does not consist of buildings themselves, but also of their setting. Authors were asked to write 'setting' after a church where the site or village was attractive. I found it necessary to supply brief prefaces to each county and large city, describing its characteristics in scenery and building materials and houses. Some of them I wrote myself, others were supplied by contributors. Both owe much to Mr. Long's original notes.

Finally, I had to presume that there were some readers who would want to know about the history of the growth of our churches (never better expressed than by Professor K. Hamilton Thompson in his two short monographs on *The Growth of the English Parish Church*, and *The Ground Plan of the English Parish Church*), and so I wrote two preliminary chapters compiled, I fear, in overpopular terms and dangerously resembling the well-known advertisements of Mr. Kirkland Bridge, giving the pre- and post-Reformation stories of parish churches in terms of their buildings, fittings and adjuncts and methods of worship.

So here at last is gathered into one volume an aesthetic and atmospheric assessment of English and Manx parish churches. I do not think that any really outstanding church will have escaped the sieve of the contributors, though there must be many borderline cases which might have been included and are not. Obviously counties like Norfolk, Suffolk and Somerset, where old churches are thick on the ground, had to have a larger quota given to them than, let us say, Middlesex or Westmorland. The standards contributors set themselves were influenced by the churches in the county as a whole. Tastes change and personal opinions vary and this volume is the expression of many. It is inevitable that it will have more detractors than friends; some will say the 19th century is overstressed. I would remind these last that the majority of our parish churches are 19th century. Others will be disappointed at some favourite church being omitted. I now ask them to send me the information about the church and the reasons why they think it should be included. Still more may find inaccuracies and omissions in the descriptions. To all who would like this book to be as complete and accurate as it can be within the limits prescribed, I appeal for information to me, c/o the publishers, in case there should ever be another edition.

J.B.

Note on Abbreviations

It is hoped every church listed in this book
is worth seeing. Most are medieval unless
otherwise marked. By way of amplification
the following abbreviations have been used
in the county lists:

*	*Exceptionally attractive church*
GS	*Gothic Survival*
CL	*Classical*
GR	*Gothic Revival*

INTRODUCTION

by John Betjeman

PART ONE

THE OLD CHURCHES

TO ATHEISTS inadequately developed building sites; and often, alas, to Anglicans but visible symbols of disagreement with the incumbent: 'the man there is "too high", "too low", "too lazy", "too interfering" ' – still they stand, the churches of England, their towers grey above billowy globes of elm trees, the red cross of St. George flying over their battlements, the Duplex Envelope System employed for collections, schoolmistress at the organ, incumbent in the chancel, scattered worshippers in the nave, Tortoise stove slowly consuming its ration as the familiar 17th-century phrases come echoing down arcades of ancient stone.

Odi et amo. This sums up the general opinion of the Church of England among the few who are not apathetic. One bright autumn morning I visited the church of the little silver limestone town of Somerton in Somerset. Hanging midway from a rich-timbered roof, on chains from which were suspended branched and brassy-gleaming chandeliers, were oval boards painted black. In gold letters on each these words were inscribed:

TO GOD'S

GLORY

&

THE HONOR OF

THE

CHURCH OF

ENGLAND

1782

They served me as an inspiration towards compiling this book.

17

The Parish Churches of England are even more varied than the landscape. The tall town church, smelling of furniture polish and hot-water pipes, a shadow of the medieval marvel it once was, so assiduously have Victorian and even later restorers renewed everything old; the little weather-beaten hamlet church standing in a farmyard down a narrow lane, bat-droppings over the pews and one service a month; the church of a once prosperous village, a relic of the 15th-century wool trade, whose soaring splendour of stone and glass subsequent generations have had neither the energy nor the money to destroy; the suburban church with Northamptonshire-style steeple rising unexpectedly above slate roofs of London and calling with mid-Victorian bells to the ghosts of merchant carriage folk for whom it was built; the tin chapel-of-ease on the edge of the industrial estate; the High, the Low, the Central churches, the alive and the dead ones, the churches that are easy to pray in and those that are not, the churches whose architecture brings you to your knees, the churches whose decorations affront the sight – all these come within the wide embrace of our Anglican Church, whose arms extend beyond the seas to many fabrics more.

From the first wooden church put up in a forest clearing or stone cell on windy moor to the newest social hall, with sanctuary and altar partitioned off, built on the latest industrial estate, our churches have existed chiefly for the celebration of what some call the Mass, or the Eucharist and others call Holy Communion or the Lord's Supper.

Between the early paganism of Britain and the present paganism there are nearly twenty thousand churches and well over a thousand years of Christianity. More than half the buildings are medieval. Many of those have been so severely restored in the last century that they could almost be called Victorian – new stone, new walls, new roofs, new pews. If there is anything old about them it is what one can discern through the detective work of the visual imagination.

It may be possible to generalise enough about the parish church of ancient origin to give an impression of how it is the history of its district in stone and wood and glass. Such generalisation can give only a superficial impression. Churches vary with their building materials and with the religious, social and economic history of their districts.

THE OUTSIDE OF THE CHURCH – GRAVESTONES

See on some village mound, in the mind's eye, the parish church of today. It is in the old part of the place. Near the church will be the few old houses of the parish, and almost for certain there will be an inn very near the church. A lych-gate built as a memorial at the beginning of this century indicates the entrance to the churchyard. Away on the outskirts of the town or village, if it is a place of any size, will be the arid new cemetery consecrated in 1910 when there was no more room in the churchyard.

Nearer to the church and almost always on the south side are to be found the older tombs, the examples of fine craftsmanship in local stone of the Queen Anne and Georgian periods. Wool merchants and big farmers, all those not entitled to an armorial monument on the walls inside the church, generally occupy the grandest graves. Their obelisks, urns and table tombs are surrounded with Georgian ironwork. Parish clerks, smaller farmers and tradesmen lie below plainer stones. All their families are recorded in deep-cut lettering. Here is a flourish of 18th-century calligraphy; there is reproduced the typeface of Baskerville. It is extraordinary how long the tradition of fine lettering continued, especially when it is in a stone easily carved or engraved, whether limestone, ironstone or slate. The tradition lasted until the middle of the 19th century in those country places where stone was used as easily as wood. Some old craftsman was carving away while the young go-aheads in the nearest town were busy inserting machine-made letters into white Italian marble.

The elegance of the local stone carver's craft is not to be seen only in the lettering. In the 18th century it was the convention to carve symbols round the top of the headstone and down the sides. The earlier examples are in bold relief, cherubs with plough-boy faces and thick wings, and scythes, hour glasses and skulls and cross-bones diversify their tops. You will find in one or another country churchyard that there has been a local sculptor of unusual vigour and perhaps genius who has even carved a rural scene above some well-graven name. Towards the end of the 18th century the lettering becomes finer and more prominent, the decoration flatter and more conventional, usually in the Adam manner, as though a son had taken on his father's business and depended on architectural pattern-books. But the tops of all headstones varied in shape. At this time too it became the custom in some districts to paint the stones and to add a little gold leaf to the lettering. Paint and stone by now have acquired a varied pattern produced by weather and fungus, so that the stones are probably more beautiful than they were when they were new, splodged as they are with gold and silver and slightly overgrown with moss. On a sharp frosty day when the sun is in the south and throwing up the carving, or in the west and bringing out all the colour of the lichens, a country churchyard may bring back the lost ages of craftsmanship more effectively than the church which stands behind it. Those unknown carvers are of the same race as produced the vigorous inn signs which were such a feature of England before the brewers ruined them with artiness and standardisation. They belong to the world of wheelwrights and wagon-makers, and they had their local styles. In Kent the chief effect of variety was created by different-sized stones with elaborately-scalloped heads to them, and by shroud-like mummies of stone on top of the grave itself; in the Cotswolds by carving in strong relief; in slate districts by engraved lettering. In counties like Surrey and Sussex, where stone was rare, there were many wooden graveyard monuments, two posts with a board between them running

down the length of the grave and painted in the way an old wagon is
painted. But most of these wooden monuments have perished or decayed out of recognition.

'At rest', 'Fell asleep', 'Not dead but gone before' and other equally
non-committal legends are on the newer tombs. In Georgian days it
was the custom either to put only the name or to apply to the schoolmaster or parson for a rhyme. Many a graveyard contains beautiful
stanzas which have not found their way to print and are disappearing
under wind and weather. Two of these inscriptions have particularly
struck my fancy. One is in Bideford and commemorates a retired sea-
captain Henry Clark, 1836. It summarises for me a type of friendly and
pathetic Englishman to be found hanging about, particularly at little
seaports.

> For twenty years he scarce slept in a bed;
> Linhays and limekilns lull'd his weary head
> Because he would not to the poor house go,
> For his proud spirit would not let him to.
>
> The black bird's whistling notes at break of day
> Used to awake him from his bed of hay.
> Unto the bridge and quay he then repaired
> To see what shipping up the river stirr'd.
>
> Oft in the week he used to view the bay,
> To see what ships were coming in from sea,
> To captains' wives he brought the welcome news,
> And to the relatives of all the crews.
>
> At last poor Harry Clark was taken ill,
> And carried to the work house 'gainst his will:
> And being of this mortal life quite tired,
> He lived about a month and then expired.

The other is on an outside monument on the north wall of the church
at Harefield, near Uxbridge, one of the last three country villages left in
Middlesex. It is to Robert Mossendew, servant of the Ashby family,
who died in 1744. Had he been a gentleman his monument would at
this time have been inside the church. He was a gamekeeper and is
carved in relief with his gun above this inscription.

> In frost and snow, thro' hail and rain
> He scour'd the woods, and trudg'd the plain;
> The steady pointer leads the way,
> Stands at the scent, then springs the prey;
> The timorous birds from stubble rise,
> With pinions stretch'd divide the skies;
> The scatter'd lead pursues the sight
> And death in thunder stops their flight;

His spaniel, of true English kind,
With gratitude inflames his mind;
This servant in an honest way,
In all his actions copied Tray.

The churchyard indeed often contains cruder but more lively and loving verses than the polished tributes inscribed on marble tablets within the church to squires and peers and divines of the county hierarchy. The Dartmoor parish of Buckland Monachorum displays this popular epitaph to a blacksmith which may be found in other parishes:

My sledge and hammer both declin'd,
My bellows too have lost their wind.
My fire's extinct, my forge decay'd,
And in the dust my vice is laid,
My coal is spent, my iron's gone,
My nails are drove, my work is done.

Though such an epitaph can scarcely be called Christian, it is at least not an attempt to cover up in mawkish sentiment or in crematorial good taste the inevitability of death.

THE OUTSIDE

The church whose southern side we are approaching is probably little like the building which stood there even two centuries before, although it has not been rebuilt. The outside walls were probably plastered, unless the church is in a district where workable stone has long been used and it is faced with cut stone known as ashlar. Churches which are ashlar-faced all over are rare, but many have an ashlar-faced western tower, or aisle to the north-east or south-east, or a porch or transept built of cut stone in the 15th century by a rich family. Some have a guild chapel or private chantry where Mass was said for the souls of deceased members of the guild or family. This is usually ashlar-faced and has a carved parapet as well, and is in marked contrast with the humble masonry of the rest of the church.

Rubble or uneven flints were not considered beautiful to look at until the 19th century. People were ashamed of them and wished to see their churches smooth on the outside and inside walls, and weatherproof. At Barnack and Earl's Barton the Saxons have even gone so far as to imitate in stone the decorative effects of wooden construction. Plaster made of a mixture of hair or straw and sand and lime was from Saxon times applied as a covering to the walls. Only the cut stone round the windows and doors was left, and even this was lime-washed. The plaster was thin and uneven. It was beautifully coloured a pale yellow or pink or white according to the tradition of the district. And if it has now been stripped off the church, it may still be seen on old

*Norfolk 15th-century flint flushwork, typical of Norwich. The
East Anglian way of decorating outside walls with flint and stone
in districts where building stone was scarce*

cottages of the village if any survive. The earlier the walls of a church
are, the less likely they are to be ashlar-faced, for there was no widespread use of cut stone in villages until the late 14th century when
transport was better, and attention which had formerly been expended
on abbeys was paid to building and enlarging parish churches.

And this is the place to say that most of the old parish churches in
England are building rather than architecture. They are gradual growths,
as their outside walls will shew; in their construction they partake of
the character of cottages and barns and the early manor house, and not
of the great abbey churches built for monks or secular canons. Their
humble builders were inspired to copy what was to be seen in the
nearest great church. The styles of Gothic came from these large buildings, but the village execution of them was later and could rarely rise to

more than window tracery and roof timbering. Even these effects have a local flavour, they are a village voluntary compared with the music played on a great instrument by the cathedral organist. Of course here and there, when the abbeys declined, a famous mason from an abbey or cathedral might rebuild the church of his native place, and masons were employed in rich wool districts of East Anglia, the Midlands and parts of Yorkshire and Devon to build large churches which really are architecture and the product of a single brain, not the humble expression of a village community's worship. Much has been discovered about the names and work of medieval architects by Mr. John Harvey in his book *Gothic England* and in the researches of Messrs. Salzman, and Knoop and Jones.

These outside walls on which the sun shews up the mottled plaster, the sudden warm red of an 18th-century patching of brick, the gentle contrast with the ashlar, the lime-washed tracery of the windows, the heating chimney-stack in local brick climbing up the chancel wall or the stove pipe projecting from a window, these are more often seen today in old watercolours in the local museum, or in some affectionate and ill-executed painting hanging in the vestry shewing the church 'before restoration in 1883'. Most of our old churches have been stripped of their plaster, some in living memory. The rubble has been exposed and then too often been repointed with grey cement, which is unyielding and instead of protecting the old stones causes them to crack and flake in frosty weather, for cement and stone have different rates of expansion. To make matters worse the cement itself has been snail pointed, that is to say pointed in hard, flat lines, so that the church wall looks like a crazy pavement.

Old paintings sometimes shew the external roofs as they used to be. The church roof and chancel are scarcely distinguishable from the cottage roofs. If the original steep pitch survives, it is seen to be covered with the local tiles, stones or thatch of the old houses of the district. 15th-century and Georgian raisings or lowerings of the roof and alterations to a flatter pitch generally meant a re-covering with lead, and the original pitch may be traced on the eastern face of the tower. Victorian restorers much enjoyed raising roofs to what they considered the original pitch, or putting on an altogether new roof in the cathedral manner. The effect of those re-roofings is generally the most obviously new feature on the outside of an old church. Red tiles and patterned slates from Wales or stone tiles which continually come down because they are set at a pitch too steep for their weight, are the usual materials. Instead of being graded in size, large at the eaves and getting smaller as they reach the ridge, the stone tiles are all of the same size so that the roof is not proportioned to the walls. The ridges are usually crowned with ridge tiles of an ornamental pattern which contrast in colour and texture with the rest. The gable ends are adorned with crosses. The drainage system is prominent and there will be pipes running down the wall to a gutter. On the rain-water heads at the top of these pipes there

will probably be the date of the restoration. The old way of draining a
roof was generally by leaden or wooden spouts rushing out of the fearsome mouths of gargoyles and carrying the water well beyond the
walls of the church into the churchyard. If the water did drip on to the
walls the plaster served as a protection from damp. Butterfield, a comparatively conservative and severely practical Victorian restorer, in his
report on the restoration of Shottesbrooke church (1845) remarks of
the flint walls of that elegant building 'There are no parapets to any
part of the Church, and the water has continued to drip from the eaves
for five centuries without any injury to the walls'. On the other hand the
water has continued to drip from the eaves of Sir Edwin Lutyens' fine
church of St. Jude-on-the-Hill, Hampstead Garden Suburb, London,

*Blythburgh, Suffolk. A 15th-century church with Victorian gate
to the churchyard*

and over its Portland stone cornice with considerable injury to the brick walls in less than half a century. The nature of the wall surface, the pointing, and the means devised for draining the water clear from the wall foundations once it has reached the ground, have much to do with keeping out the damp.

Sometimes we may find on the outside walls a variety of scratches, marks and carvings. The only ones of any beauty will probably be the consecration crosses, where the Bishop anointed the walls with oil when the church was newly built. They are high up so that people should not brush them in going past. Similar crosses may be seen on stone altars inside the church. The small crosses which are cut roughly in the jambs of doorways were, according to the late E. A. Greening Lamborn, an angry antiquarian with a good prose style, probably put there not for consecration but 'to scare away evil spirits and prevent them crossing the threshold'. There is a whole literature devoted to masons' marks on the walls of churches, outside and in, and to the 'scratch dials' or 'mass clocks' which look like sundials lacking a gnomon, to be found on the outside south walls of many churches. The masons' marks are triangles, diamonds, bent arrows, circles, squares and other shapes looking rather like boy scout signs, cut into ashlar in some churches, notably the large ones, and surviving where stone has not been re-tooled by the Victorians. Often they may be only scribbles. But they seem to help some antiquaries to give an exact date to buildings or portions of a building. Scratch dials or mass clocks were used generally to show the time when Mass was to be said (usually 9 a.m. in medieval England). Others are primitive clocks. But they, like the parish registers, belong to the non-visual side of church history and it is with the look of a church that this book is primarily concerned.

Finally there are on the outsides of churches the gargoyles spouting water off the roof and the carved heads to be found either side of some windows and the figures in niches on tower or porch. Gargoyles can be fearsome, particularly on the north side of the church, and heads and statues, where they have survived Puritan outrage and Victorian zeal, are sometimes extremely beautiful or fantastic.

The church porch flapping with electoral rolls, notices of local acts, missionary appeals and church services (which will occupy us later) gives us a welcome. Though the powers of the parish vestry have been taken over by parish councils and local government, church doors or the porches which shelter them are often plastered with public announcements. Regularly will the village policeman nail to the church door some notice about Foot-and-Mouth Disease when the British Legion Notice Board has been denied him or the Post Office is shut. Most church porches in England are built on the south side, first as a protection for the door from prevailing south-west gales. Then they were used as places for baptism, bargains were made there, oaths sworn, and burial and marriage services conducted. Above some of them, from the 14th century onwards, a room was built, usually for keeping parish chests and records. In these places many a village school was started. At first they may have been inhabited by a watchman, who could look down into the church from an internal window. In counties where stone is rare there are often elaborate wooden porches, notably in Sussex, Surrey and Essex.

Professor E. A. Freeman, the great Victorian ecclesiologist, thought little of a man who went up the churchyard path to the main door, which is more or less what we have done, and did not go round the whole building first. But he was an antiquary who took his churches slowly, speculated on them and did detective work about dates of extensions. On a day when the wind is not too cold and the grass not too long and wet, a walk round the outside of the church is always worth while. On the farther side, which is generally the north, there may well be extensions, a family mausoleum for instance, of which there is no sign inside the church beyond a blocked archway. Mr. John Piper and I had a peculiar experience through not going round the outside of the derelict church of Wolfhamcote near Daventry in Warwickshire. The lovely building was locked, the windows smashed, and the sun was setting on its lichened stone. There was only one cottage near and we could make no one hear. So we climbed through a window in the south aisle. Bat-droppings were over rotting floors and damp stains on the ochre-plastered walls, and in the fading light we saw that the altar cloth had been raised and revealed a black tunnel with light at the end, a most peculiar thing to see beyond an altar. We approached and saw there were stairs going down under the table leading to a passage in which brass-studded coffins lay on shelves. When we went round the outside of the church we saw that beyond the east end was a Strawberry Hill Gothick extension, the mausoleum of the Tibbits family. Vestries are more usual on the north side of churches than mausolea, and very ugly most of them are, hard little stone sheds leant against the old walls. There will be almost for certain a north door blocked or bricked-up long ago, with the trace of its arch mouldings still there. There may even be a north porch. But unless the village and manor house are to the north of the church this side of the churchyard will be gloomy and its tombs will be, at the earliest, 19th century, except for a very few near the east end. And so round by the sexton's tool-shed and the anthracite dump and the west door of the tower, we return to the south porch.

Notice the stonework round the outside doors. Often it is round-headed and of Norman date, an elaborate affair of several concentric semi-circles of carved stone. It may even be the only Norman work left in the church and may originally have been the chancel arch before the chancel was enlarged and a screen put across its western end. The later medieval rebuilders respected the Norman craftsmanship and often kept a Norman door inside their elaborate porches.

There is often difficulty in opening the door. This gives the less impatient of us a chance of looking at the door itself. Either because the business of transferring the huge church lock was too difficult, or because here was a good piece of wood older than any of the trees in the parish, church doors have survived from the middle ages while the interiors on to which they open have been repaired out of recognition. The wood of the door may be carved or be decorated with old local ironwork. If it is an old door it will invariably open inwards. So first turn the iron handle and push hard. Then if the door seems to be locked, turn the handle the other way and push hard. Then feel on the wall-plate of the porch for the key. Then look under the mat. Then lift the notice-board from the porch wall and look behind that. Then look inside the lamp bracket outside the porch. Church keys are usually six or eight inches long and easy to find. If there is no sign of the key and all vestry doors are locked, call at a house. If the path leading through the churchyard to a door in the vicarage wall is overgrown and looks unused, you may be sure the vicarage has been sold to wealthy un-believers and there is no chance of getting the key from there. The houses to choose are those with pots of flowers in the window. Here will be living traditional villagers who even if they are chapel will probably know who it is who keeps the church key. Men are less likely to know than women, since men in villages are more rarely church-goers. Villagers are all out on Saturday afternoons shopping in the local town. Only an idiot and the dog remain behind.

THE PORCH AND BELLS

Down one step – for the churchyard will have risen round an old building – and we are in the church itself.

The practised eye can tell at a glance how severe the restoration has been, and often indeed who has done the damage. For instance almost every other church in Cornwall, beside many farther east, was restored by Mr. J. P. St. Aubyn late in the last century, and he has left his mark at the church porch in the form of a scraper of his own design, as practical and unattractive as his work. We must remember, however much we deplore it, that the most cumbersome bit of panelling bought from a Birmingham firm without regard for the old church into which it is to go, the sentimental picture from the Art Shop, the banner with the dislocated saint, the Benares ware altar vases, the brass commemorative tablet, the greenish stained-glass window with its sentimental Good Shepherd – often have been saved up for by some devout and penurious communicant. It must be admitted that spirituality and aesthetics rarely go together. 'Carnal delight even in the holiest things,' says Father R. M. Benson, founder of the Cowley Fathers '(habits of thought and philoso-phy, acquisition of knowledge, schemes of philanthropy, aesthetic pro-priety, influence in society) hinders the development of the Christ-life by strengthening the natural will.' So when one is inclined to lament lack of taste and seemingly wilful destruction of beauty in a church, it is wise to remember that the incumbent, even if he be that rarity a man of aesthetic appreciation, is probably not to blame for modern blemishes to the fabric. He is primarily a missioner and he cannot offend his parishioners on so unspiritual a matter. The reader who casts his mind back to his early worship as a child will remember that a hymn board, or a brass cross or a garish window were, from his customary gazing on them Sunday after Sunday, part of his religious life. If as an older and more informed person his taste and knowledge tell him these things are cheap and hideous, he will still regret their passing with a part of him which is neither his intellect nor his learning. How much more will an uninformed villager, whose feeling always runs higher where the church is concerned than a townsman's, cling to these objects he has known as a boy, however cheap they are. When the vicar or rector felt himself entitled to be a dictator, he could with more impunity and less offence than now, 'restore' the old church out of recognition. He could hack down the box-pews, re-erect a screen across the chancel, put the choir into surplices and move it from the west gallery to the chancel, and substitute a pipe organ for the old instruments. Even in those days many a disgruntled villager left the church to try his voice in chapel or to play his instrument in the old village band. It is a tribute to the hold of our church that congregations continued to use their churches after restorations in Victorian times. Perhaps the reason for the continued hold is that the more ritualistic performance of the Church Services made church more interesting. There is no doubt that Evangelicals were worried at the success of Tractarian methods. But picture your own childhood's church whitewashed on the advice of the Diocesan Advisory Committee, your pew gone and a row of chairs in its place, the altar different, and the chancel cleared of choir-stalls and the choir non-existent as a consequence. Were it not your childhood's church, you would consider this an improvement. One part of you may consider it an improvement despite associations, but not the other. Conservatism is innate in ecclesiastical arrangement. It is what saves for us the history of the village or town in wood and glass and metal and stone.

Let us enter the church by the tower door and climb to the ringing chamber where the ropes hang through holes in the roof. Nowhere outside England except for a very few towers in the rest of the British Isles, America and the Dominions, are bells rung so well. The carillons of the Netherlands and of Bourneville and Atkinson's scent shop in London are not bell ringing as understood in England. Carillon ringing is done either by means of a cylinder worked on the barrel-organ and musical box principle, or by keyed notes played by a musician. Carillon bells are sounded by pulling the clapper to the rim of the bell. This is called chiming, and it is not ringing.

Bell ringing in England is known among ringers as 'the exeroise', rather as the rearing and training of pigeons is known among the pigeon fraternity as 'the fancy'. It is a class-less folk art which has survived in the church despite all arguments about doctrine and the diminution of congregations. In many a church when the parson opens with the words 'Dearly beloved brethren, the Scripture moveth us in sundry places . . .' one many hear the tramp of the ringers descending the newel stair into the refreshing silence of the graveyard. Though in some churches they may come in later by the main door and sit in the pew marked 'Ringers Only', in others they will not be seen again, the sweet melancholy notes of 'the exercise' floating out over the Sunday chimney-pots having been their contribution to the glory of God. So full of interest and technicality is the exercise that there is a weekly paper devoted to it called *The Ringing World*.

A belfry where ringers are keen has the used and admired look of a social club. There, above the little bit of looking-glass in which the ringers slick their hair and straighten their ties before stepping down into the outside world, you will find blackboards with gilded lettering proclaiming past peals rung for hours at a stretch. In another place will be the rules of the tower written in a clerkly hand. A charming Georgian ringers' rhyme survives at St. Endellion, Cornwall, on a board headed with a picture of ringers in knee-breeches:

> *We ring the Quick to Church and dead to Grave,*
> *Good is our use, such usage let us have*
> *Who here therefore doth Damn, or Curse or Swear,*
> *Or strike in Quarrel thogh no Blood appear,*
> *Who wears a Hatt or Spurr or turns a Bell*
> *Or by unskilful handling spoils a Peal,*
> *Shall Sixpence pay for every single Crime*
> *'Twill make him careful 'gainst another time.*
> *Let all in Love and Friendship hither come,*
> *Whilst the shrill Treble calls to Thundering Tom,*
> *And since bells are our modest Recreation*
> *Let's Rise and Ring and Fall to Admiration.*

Many country towers have six bells. Not all these bells are medieval. Most were cast in the 17th, 18th or 19th centuries when change-ringing was becoming a country exercise. And the older bells will have been re-cast during that time, to bring them into tune with the new ones. They are likely to have been again re-cast in modern times, and the ancient inscription preserved and welded on to the re-cast bell. Most counties have elaborately produced monographs about their church bells. The older bells have beautiful lettering sometimes, as at Somerby, and South Somercotes in Lincolnshire, where they are inscribed with initial letters decorated with figures so that they look like illuminated initials from old manuscripts interpreted in relief on metal. The English love for Our Lady survived in inscriptions on church bells long after the Reformation, as did the use of Latin. Many 18th and even early 19th-century bells have Latin inscriptions. A rich collection of varied dates may be seen by struggling about on the wooden cage in which the bells hang among the bat-droppings in the tower.

Many local customs survive in the use of bells. In some places a curfew is rung every evening; in others a bell is rung at five in the morning during Lent. Fanciful legends have grown up about why they are rung, but their origin can generally be traced to the divine offices. The passing bell is rung differently from district to district. Sometimes the years of the deceased are tolled, sometimes the ringing is three strokes in succession followed by a pause. There are instances of the survival of prayers for the departed where the bell is tolled as soon as the news of the death of a parishioner reaches the incumbent.

Who has heard a muffled peal and remained unmoved? Leather bags are tied to one side of the clapper and the bells ring alternately loud and soft, the soft being an echo, as though in the next world, of the music we hear on earth.

I make no apology for writing so much about church bells. They ring through our literature, as they do over our meadows and roofs and few remaining elms. Some may hate them for their melancholy, but they dislike them chiefly, I think, because they are reminders of Eternity. In an age of faith they were messengers of consolation.

The bells are rung down, the ting-tang will ring for five minutes, and now is the time to go into church.

THE INTERIOR TODAY

As we sit in a back pew of the nave with the rest of the congregation – the front pews are reserved for those who never come to church – most objects which catch the eye are Victorian. What we see of the present age is cheap and sparse. The thick wires clamped on to the old outside wall, which make the church look as though the Vicar had put it on the telephone, are an indication without that electric light has lately been introduced. The position of the lights destroys the effect of the old mouldings on arches and columns. It is a light too harsh and bright for an old building, and the few remaining delicate textures on stone and walls are destroyed by the dazzling floodlights fixed in reflectors from the roof, and a couple of spotlights behind the chancel arch which throw their full radiance on the brass altar vases and on the Vicar when he marches up to give the blessing. At sermon time, in a winter evensong, the lights are switched off, and the strip reading-lamp on the pulpit throws up the vicar's chin and eyebrows so that he looks like Grock. A further disfigurement introduced by electrical engineers is a collection of meters, pipes and fuses on one of the walls.* If a church must be lit with electricity – which is in any case preferable to gas, which streaks the walls – the advice of Sir Ninian Comper might well be taken. This is to have as many bulbs as possible of as low power as possible, so that

* I have even seen electric heaters hung at intervals along the gallery of an 18th-century church and half-way up the columns of a medieval nave.

they do not dazzle the eye when they hang from the roof and walls. Candles are the perfect lighting for an old church, and oil light is also effective. The mystery of an old church, however small the building, is preserved by irregularly placed clusters of low-powered bulbs which light service books but leave the roof in comparative darkness. The chancel should not be strongly lit, for this makes the church look small, and all too rarely are chancel and altar worthy of a brilliant light. I have hardly ever seen an electrically lit church where this method has been employed, and we may assume that the one in which we are sitting is either floodlit or strung with blinding pendants whose bulbs are covered by 'temporary' shades reminiscent of a Government office.

Other modern adornments are best seen in daylight, and it is in daylight that we will imagine the rest of the church. The 'children's corner' in front of the side altar, with its pale reproductions of water-colours by Margaret W. Tarrant, the powder-blue hangings and un-stained oak kneelers, the side altar itself, too small in relation to the aisle window above it, the pale stained-glass figure of St. George with plenty of clear glass round it (Diocesan Advisory Committees do not like exclusion of daylight) or the anaemic stained-glass soldier in khaki – these are likely to be the only recent additions to the church, excepting a few mural tablets in oak or Hopton Wood stone, much too small in comparison with the 18th century ones, dotted about on the walls and giving them the appearance of a stamp album; these, thank goodness, are the only damage our age will have felt empowered to do.

THE INTERIOR IN 1860

In those richer days when a British passport was respected throughout the world, when 'carriage folk' existed and there was a smell of straw and stable in town streets and bobbing tenants at lodge gates in the country, when it was unusual to boast of disbelief in God and when 'Chapel' was connected with 'trade' and 'Church' with 'gentry', when there were many people in villages who had never seen a train nor left their parish, when old farm-workers still wore smocks, when town slums were newer and even more horrible, when people had orchids in their conservatories and geraniums and lobelias in the trim beds beside their gravel walks, when stained glass was brownish-green and when things that shone were considered beautiful, whether they were pink granite, brass, pitchpine, mahogany or encaustic tiles, when the rector was second only to the squire, when doctors were 'apothecaries' and lawyers 'attorneys', when Parliament was a club, when shops competed for custom, when the servants went to church in the evening, when there were family prayers and basement kitchens – in those days God seemed to have created the universe and to have sent His Son to redeem the world, and there was a church parade to worship Him on those shining

Sunday mornings we read of in Charlotte M. Yonge's novels and feel in Trollope and see in the drawings in *Punch*. Then it was that the money pouring in from our empire was spent in restoring old churches and in building bold and handsome new ones in crowded areas and exclusive suburbs, in seaside towns and dockland settlements. They were built by the rich and given to the poor: 'All Seats in this Church are Free.' Let us now see this church we have been describing as it was in the late 1860s, shining after its restoration.

Changed indeed it is, for even the aisles are crowded and the prevailing colours of clothes are black, dark blue and purple. The gentlemen are in frock coats and lean forward into their top hats for a moment's prayer, while the lesser men are in black broad-cloth and sit with folded arms awaiting the rector. He comes in after his curate and they sit at desks facing each other on either side of the chancel steps. Both wear surplices: the Rector's is long and flowing and he has a black scarf round his shoulders: so has the curate, but his surplice is shorter and he wears a cassock underneath, for, if the truth be told, the curate is 'higher' than the rector and would have no objection to wearing a coloured stole and seeing a couple of candles lit on the altar for Holy Communion. But this would cause grave scandal to the parishioners, who fear idolatry. Those who sit in the pews in the aisles where the seats face inward, never think of turning eastwards for the Creed. 'Hymns Ancient and Modern' has been introduced. The book is ritualistic, but several excellent men have composed and written for it, like Sir Frederick Ouseley and Sir Henry Baker, and Bishops and Deans. The surpliced choir precede the clergy and march out of the new vestry built on the north-east corner of the church. Some of the older men, feeling a little ridiculous in surplices, look wistfully towards the west end where the gallery used to be and where they sang as youths to serpent, fiddle and bass recorder in the old-fashioned choir, before the pipe organ was introduced up there in the chancel. The altar has been raised on a series of steps, the shining new tiles becoming more elaborate and brilliant the nearer they approach the altar. The altar frontal has been embroidered by ladies in the parish, a pattern of lilies on a red background. There is still an alms dish on the altar, and behind it a cross has been set in stone on the east wall. In ten years' time brass vases of flowers, a cross and candlesticks will be on a 'gradine' or shelf above the altar. The east window is new, tracery and all. The glass is green and red, shewing the Ascension – the Crucifixion is a little ritualistic – and has been done by a London firm. And a smart London architect designed all these choir stalls in oak and these pews of pitch-pine in the nave and aisles. At his orders the new chancel roof was constructed, the plaster was taken off the walls of the church, and the stone floors were taken up and transformed into a shining stretch of red and black tiles. He also had that pale pink and yellow glass put in all the unstained windows so that a religious light was cast. The brass gas brackets are by Skidmore of Coventry. Some antiquarian remains are carefully preserved. A Norman capital from the old aisle which was pulled down, a pillar piscina, a half of a cusped arch which might have been – no one knows quite *what* it might have been, but it is obviously ancient. Unfortunately it was not possible to remove the pagan classical memorials of the last century owing to trouble about faculties and fear of offending the descendants of the families commemorated. The church is as good as new, and all in the medieval style of the middle-pointed period – the best period because it is in the middle and not 'crude' like Norman and Early English, or 'debased' like Perpendicular and Tudor. Nearly everyone can see the altar. The Jacobean pulpit has survived, lowered and re-erected on a stone base. Marble pulpits are rather expensive, and Jacobean is not wholly unfashionable so far as woodwork is concerned. The prevailing colours of the church are brown and green, with faint tinges of pink and yellow.

Not everyone approved of these 'alterations' in which the old churches of England were almost entirely rebuilt. I quote from Alfred Rimmer's *Pleasant Spots Around Oxford* (c. 1865), on the taking down of the body of Woodstock's classical church.

'Well, during the month of July I saw this church at Woodstock, but unhappily, left making sketches of it till a future visit. An ominous begging-box, with a lock, stood out in the street asking for funds for the "restoration". One would have thought it almost a burlesque, for it wanted no restoration at all, and would have lasted for ever so many centuries; but the box was put up by those "who said in their hearts, Let us make havoc of it altogether". Within a few weeks of the time this interesting monument was perfect, no one beam was left; and now, as I write, it is a "heap of stones". Through the debris I could just distinguish a fine old Norman doorway that had survived ever so many scenes notable in history, but it was nearly covered up with ruins; and supposing it does escape the general mêlée, and has the luck to be inserted in a new church, with open benches and modern adornments, it will have lost every claim to interest and be scraped down by unloving hands to appear like a new doorway. Happily, though rather late in the day, an end is approaching to these vandalisms.'

THE CHURCH IN GEORGIAN TIMES

See now the outside of our church about eighty years before, in, let us say, 1805, when the two-folio volumes on the county were produced by a learned antiquarian, with aquatint engravings of the churches, careful copper-plates of fonts and supposedly Roman pieces of stone, and laborious copyings of entries in parish rolls. How different from the polished, furbished fane we have just left is this humble, almost cottage-like place of worship. Oak posts and rails enclose the churchyard in

B

which a horse, maybe the Reverend Dr. Syntax's mare Grizzel, is grazing. The stones are humble and few, and lean this way and that on the south side. They are painted black and grey and the lettering on some is picked out in gold. Two altar tombs, one with a sculptured urn above it, are enclosed in sturdy iron rails such as one sees above the basements of Georgian terrace houses. Beyond the church below a thunderous sky we see the elm and oak landscape of an England comparatively unenclosed. Thatched cottages and stone-tiled farms are collected round the church, and beyond them on the boundaries of the

An unrestored church with Norman chancel arch. Old Bradwell,
Buckinghamshire

parish the land is still open and park-like, while an unfenced road winds on with its freight of huge bonnetted wagons. Later in the 19th century this land was parcelled into distant farms with significant names like 'Egypt', 'California', 'Starveall', which stud the ordnance maps. Windmills mark the hill-tops and water-mills the stream. Our church to which this agricultural world would come, save those who in spite of Test Acts and suspicion of treachery meet in their Dissenting conventicles, is a patched, uneven-looking place.

Sympathetic descriptive accounts of unrestored churches are rarely found in late Georgian or early Victorian prose or verse. Most of the writers on churches are antiquarians who see nothing but ancient stones, or whose zeal for 'restoration' colours their writing. Thus for instance Mr. John Noake describes White Ladies' Aston in Worcestershire in 1851 (*The Rambler in Worcestershire*, London, Longman and Co., 1851). 'The church is Norman, with a wooden broach spire; the windows, with two or three square-headed exceptions, are Norman, including that at the east end, which is somewhat rare. The west end is disgraced by the insertion of small square windows and wooden frames, which, containing a great quantity of broken glass, and a stove-pipe issuing therefrom impart to the sacred building the idea of a low-class lodging house.' And writing at about the same time, though not publishing until 1888, the entertaining *Church-Goer* of Bristol thus describes the Somerset church of Brean. 'On the other side of the way stood the church – little and old, and unpicturesquely freshened up with whitewash and yellow ochre; the former on the walls and the latter on the worn stone mullions of the small Gothic windows. The stunted slate-topped tower was white-limed, too – all but a little slate slab on the western side, which bore the inscription:

JOHN GHENKIN
Churchwarden
1729

Anything owing less to taste and trouble than the little structure you would not imagine. Though rude, however, and old, and kept together as it was by repeated whitewashings, which mercifully filled up flaws and cracks, it was not disproportioned or unmemorable in aspect, and might with a trifling outlay be made to look as though someone cared for it.'

Such a church with tracery ochred on the outside may be seen in the background of Millais' painting *The Blind Girl*. It is, I believe, Winchelsea before restoration. Many writers, beside Rimmer, regret the restoration of old churches by London architects in the last century. The despised Reverend J. L. Petit, writing in 1841 in those two volumes called *Remarks on Church Architecture*, illustrated with curious anastatic sketches, was upbraided by critics for writing too much by aesthetic and not enough by antiquarian standards. He naturally devoted a whole chapter to regretting restoration. But neither he nor many poets who preceded him bothered to describe the outside appearance of unrestored village churches, and seldom did they relate the buildings to their settings. 'Venerable', 'ivy-mantled', 'picturesque' are considered precise enough words for the old village church of Georgian times, with 'neat', 'elegant' or 'decent' for any recent additions. It is left for the Reverend George Crabbe, that accurate and beautiful observer, to recall the texture of weathered stone in *The Borough*, Letter II (1810):

> But 'ere yon enter, yon bold tower survey
> Tall and entire, and venerably grey,
> For time has soften'd what was harsh when new,
> And now the stains are all of sober hue;

and to admonish the painters:

> And would'st thou, artist! with thy tints and brush
> Form shades like these? Pretender, where thy blush?
> In three short hours shall thy presuming hand
> Th' effect of three slow centuries command?
> Thou may'st thy various greens and greys contrive
> They are not lichens nor like aught alive.
> But yet proceed and when thy tints are lost,
> Fled in the shower, or crumbled in the frost
> When all thy work is done away as clean
> As if thou never spread'st thy grey and green,
> Then may'st thou see how Nature's work is done,
> How slowly true she lays her colours on . . .

With the precision of the botanist, Crabbe describes the process of decay which is part of the beauty of the outside of an unrestored church:

> Seeds, to our eye invisible, will find
> On the rude rock the bed that fits their kind:
> There, in the rugged soil, they safely dwell,
> Till showers and snows the subtle atoms swell,
> And spread th' enduring foliage; then, we trace
> The freckled flower upon the flinty base;
> These all increase, till in unnoticed years
> The stony tower as grey with age appears;
> With coats of vegetation thinly spread,
> Coat above coat, the living on the dead:
> These then dissolve to dust, and make a way
> For bolder foliage, nurs'd by their decay:
> The long-enduring ferns in time will all
> Die and depose their dust upon the wall
> Where the wing'd seed may rest, till many a flower
> Show Flora's triumph o'er the falling tower.

Yet the artists whom Crabbe admonishes have left us better records than there are in literature of our churches before the Victorians restored them. The engravings of Hogarth, the water-colours and etchings of John Sell Cotman and of Thomas Rowlandson, the careful and less inspired records of John Buckler, re-create these places for us. They were drawn with affection for the building as it was and not 'as it ought to be'; they bring out the beauty of what Mr. Piper has called 'pleasing decay'; they also shew the many churches which were considered 'neat and elegant'.

It is still possible to find an unrestored church. Almost every county has one or two.

THE GEORGIAN CHURCH INSIDE

There is a whole amusing literature of satire on church interiors. As early as 1825, an unknown wit and champion of Gothic published a book of coloured aquatints with accompanying satirical text to each plate, entitled *Hints to Some Churchwardens*. And as we are about to enter the church, let me quote this writer's description of a Georgian pulpit: 'How to substitute a new, grand, and commodious pulpit in place of an ancient, mean, and inconvenient one. Raze the old Pulpit and build one on small wooden Corinthian pillars, with a handsome balustrade or flight of steps like a staircase, supported also by wooden pillars of the Corinthian order; let the dimensions of the Pulpit be at least double that of the old one, and covered with crimson velvet, and a deep gold fringe, with a good-sized cushion, with large gold tassels, gilt branches on each side, over which imposing structure let a large sounding-board be suspended by a sky-blue chain with a gilt rose at the top, and small gilt lamps on the side, with a flame painted, issuing from them, such Pulpits as these must please all parties; and as the energy and eloquence of the preacher must be the chief attraction from the ancient Pulpit, in the modern one, such labour is not required, as a moderate congregation will be satisfied with a few short sentences pronounced on each side of the gilt branches, and sometimes from the front of the cushion, when the sense of vision is so amply cared for in the construction of so splendid and appropriate a place from which to teach the duties of Christianity.'

And certainly the pulpit and the high pews crowd the church. The nave is a forest of woodwork. The pews have doors to them. The panelling inside the pews is lined with baize, blue in one pew, red in another, green in another, and the baize is attached to the wood by brass studs such as one may see on the velvet-covered coffins in family vaults. Some very big pews will have fire-places. When one sits down, only the pulpit is visible from the pew, and the tops of the arches of the nave whose stonework will be washed with ochre, while the walls will be white or pale pink, green or blue. A satire on this sort of seating was published by John Noake in 1851 in his book already quoted:

> '*O my own darling pue, which might serve for a bed,*
> *With its cushions so soft and its curtains of red;*
> *Of my half waking visions that pue is the theme,*
> *And when sleep seals my eyes, of my pue still I dream.*
> *Foul fall the despoiler, whose ruthless award*
> *Has condemned me to squat, like the poor, on a board,*
> *To be crowded and shov'd, as I sit at my prayers,*
> *As though my devotions could mingle with theirs.*
> *I have no vulgar pride, oh dear me, not I,*
> *But still I must say I could never see why*
> *We give them room to sit, to stand or to kneel,*
> *As if they, like ourselves, were expected to feel;*
> *'Tis a part, I'm afraid, of a deeply laid plan*
> *To bring back the abuses of Rome if they can.*
> *And when SHE is triumphant, you'll bitterly rue*
> *That you gave up that Protestant bulwark – your pew.*'

The clear glass windows, of uneven crown glass with bottle-glass here and there in the upper lights, will shew the churchyard yews and elms and the flying clouds outside. Shafts of sunlight will fall on hatchments, those triangular-framed canvasses hung on the aisle walls and bearing the arms of noble families of the place. Over the chancel arch hang the Royal Arms, painted by some talented inn-sign artist, with a lively lion and unicorn supporting the shield in which we may see quartered the white horse of Hanover. The roofs of the church will be ceiled within for warmth, and our boxed-in pew will save us from draught. Look behind you; blocking the tower arch you will see a wooden gallery in which the choir is tuning its instruments, fiddle, base viol, serpent. And on your left in the north aisle there is a gallery crowded under the roof. On the tiers of wooden benches here sit the charity children in their blue uniforms, within reach of the parish beadle who, in the corner of the west gallery, can admonish them with his painted stave.

The altar is out of sight. This is because the old screen survives across the chancel arch and its doors are locked. If you can look through its carved woodwork, you will see that the chancel is bare except for the memorial floor slabs and brasses of previous incumbents, and the elaborate marble monument upon the wall, by a noted London sculptor, in memory of some lay-rector of the 18th century. Probably this is the only real 'work of art' judged by European standards in the church. The work of 18th-century sculptors has turned many of our old churches into sculpture galleries of great interest, though too often the Victorians huddled the sculptures away in the tower or blocked them up with organs. No choir stalls are in the chancel, no extra rich flooring. The Lord's Table or altar is against the east wall and enclosed on three sides by finely-turned rails such as one sees as stair balusters in a

A medieval church with Renaissance altar furnishings. Lockington, Leicestershire

country house. The Table itself is completely covered with a carpet of plum-covered velvet, embroidered on its western face with IHS in golden rays. Only on those rare occasions, once a quarter and at Easter and Christmas and Whit Sunday when there is to be a Communion service, is the Table decked. Then indeed there will be a fair linen cloth over the velvet, and upon the cloth a chalice, paten and two flagons all of silver, and perhaps two lights in silver candlesticks. On

Sacrament Sundays those who are to partake of Communion will leave their box-pews either at the Offertory Sentence (when in modern Holy Communion services the collection is taken), or at the words 'Ye that do truly and earnestly repent you of your sins, and are in love and charity with your neighbours', and they will be admitted through the screen doors to the chancel. They will have been preceded by the incumbent. Thereafter the communicants will remain kneeling until the end of the service, as many as can around the Communion rails, the rest in the western side of the chancel.

The only object which will be familiar from the Victorian church is the font, still near the entrance to the church and symbolical of the entrance of the Christian to Christ's army. Beside the font is a large pew whose door opens facing it. This is the christening pew and here the baby, its parents and the god-parents wait until after the second lesson, when the incumbent will come forward to baptise the child in the presence of the congregation. Some churches had Churching pews where mothers sat.

Our churches were, as Canon Addleshaw and Frederick Etchells have pointed out in *The Architectural Setting of Anglican Worship*, compartmented buildings. So they remained from 1559 (Act of Uniformity) until 1841 onwards when Tractarian ideas about the prominence of the altar, the frequent celebration of Holy Communion and adequate seating for the poor – for the population had suddenly increased – caused a vital replanning of churches. What we see in 1805 is a medieval church adapted to Prayer Book worship. The object of having the Prayer Book in our own language was not so doctrinal and Protestant, in the Continental sense, as is often supposed, but was to ensure audible and intelligible services. The compartments of the building were roughly three. There is the font and christening pew which form a Baptistry. There is the nave of the church with the pews facing the pulpit which is generally half-way down the church against one of the pillars, and the nave is used for Mattins, Litany and Ante-Communion, and Evensong. There is the chancel which is used only for Holy Communion. Some of the larger churches have one end of an aisle or a transept divided off with the old screens which used to surround a Chantry chapel in this part. This the parson might use for weekday offices of Mattins and Evensong when the congregation was small and there was no sermon.

The lime-washed walls form a happy contrast with the coloured baize inside the box-pews, the brown well-turned Stuart and Georgian woodwork and the old screens, the hatchments which hang lozenge-shaped on the wall above family pews, and the great Royal Arms in the filled-in tympanum of the chancel arch. Behind the Royal Arms we may see faintly the remains of a medieval painting of the Doom, the Archangel Michael holding the balance, and some souls going to Heaven on one side of him, others to Hell on the other side. In other parts of the church, too, the pale brick-red lines of the painting which once covered the church may be faintly discernible in sunlight. Mostly the walls will be whitewashed, and in bold black and red, with cherubs as decorative devices, will be painted admonitory texts against idolatry. The Elizabethan texts will be in black letters; the later and less admonitory Georgian ones will be in the spacious Roman style which we see on the gravestones in the churchyard. In the Sanctuary on either side of the altar are the Lord's Prayer and the Commandments painted in gold letters on black boards, and perhaps Moses and Aaron flank these, also painted on boards by a local inn-sign painter. An oil painting of the *Crucifixion* or *the Deposition of our Lord* or some other scriptural

A medieval church refurnished in 1815 in Gothick style to conform with the requirements of the Book of Common Prayer. Mildenhall, Wiltshire

subject may adorn the space above the altar table. Far more people could read than is generally supposed; literacy was nearly as rife as it is today. There was not the need to teach by pictures in the parish church that there had been in the middle ages.

The lighting of the church is wholly by candles. In the centre of the nave a branched brass candelabrum is suspended by two interlocking rods painted blue, the two serpent heads which curl round and interlock them being gilded. In other parts of the church, in distant box-pews or up in the choir gallery, light is from single candles in brass sconces fixed to the woodwork. If the chancel is dark, there may be two fine silver candlesticks on the altar for the purpose of illumination. But candles are not often needed, for services are generally in the hours of daylight, and the usual time for a country evensong is three o'clock in the afternoon, not six or half-past six as is now the custom.

Outside the church on a sunny Sunday morning the congregation gathers. The poorer sort are lolling against the tombstones, while the richer families, also in their best clothes, move towards the porch where the churchwardens stand with staves ready to conduct them to their private pews. The farm-workers do not wear smocks for church, but knee breeches and a long coat and shoes. Women wear wooden shoes, called pattens, when it is wet, and take them off in the porch. All the men wear hats, and they hang them on pegs on the walls when they enter the church.

> 'How still the morning of the hallowed day!
> Mute is the voice of rural labour, hushed
> The ploughboy's whistle, and the milkmaid's song.
> The scythe lies glittering in the dewy wreath
> Of tedded grass, mingled with fading flowers,
> That yester morn bloomed waving in the breeze.
> Sounds the most faint attract the ear, – the hum
> Of early bee, the trickling of the dew,
> The distant bleating, midway up the hill.
>
> With dove-like wings, Peace o'er yon village broods:
> The dizzying mill-wheel rests; the anvil's din
> Hath ceased; all, all around is quietness.
> Less fearful on this day, the limping hare
> Stops, and looks back, and stops, and looks on man
> Her deadliest foe. The toilworn horse, set free,
> Unheedful of the pasture, roams at large;
> And as his stiff unwieldy bulk rolls on,
> His iron-armed hoofs gleam in the morning ray'.

So the Scottish poet James Graham begins his poem *The Sabbath* (1804). All this island over, there was a hush of feudal quiet in the country on a Sunday. We must sink into this quiet to understand and tolerate, with our democratic minds, the graded village hierarchy, graded by birth and occupation, by clothes and by seating in the church. It is an agricultural world as yet little touched by the machines which were starting in the mills of the midlands and the north. The Sabbath as a day of rest and worship touched all classes. Our feeblest poets rose from bathos to sing its praises. I doubt if Felicia Hemens ever wrote better than this, in her last poem (1835), composed less than a week before she died.

> 'How many blessed groups this hour are bending,
> Through England's primrose meadow paths, their way
> Towards spire and tower, midst shadowy elms ascending,
> Whence the sweet chimes proclaim the hallowed day:

The halls from old heroic ages grey
Pour their fair children forth; and hamlets low,
With whose thick orchard blooms the soft winds play,
Send out their inmates in a happy flow,
Like a freed rural stream.

                I may not tread
With them those pathways, – to the feverish bed
Of sickness bound, – yet, O my God, I bless
Thy mercy, that with Sabbath peace hath filled
My chastened heart, and all its throbbings stilled
To one deep calm of lowliest thankfulness.'

One is inclined, seeing the pale whites and ochres and greys, relieved here and there with the warm brown red of local bricks, which we associate today with Georgian England, to forget how highly coloured were the clothes of the people. Thomas Hood's early poem *The Two Peacocks at Bedfont* (1827) describes with the colours of an aquatint the worshippers entering that then countrified Middlesex church:

'*So speaking, they pursue the pebbly walk*
    That leads to the white porch the Sunday throng,
Hand-coupled urchins in restrained talk,
    And anxious pedagogue that chastens wrong,
And posied churchwarden with solemn stalk,
    And gold-bedizened beadle flames along,
And gentle peasant clad in buff and green,
Like a meek cowslip in the spring serene;

And blushing maiden – modestly array'd
    In spotless white, – still conscious of the glass;
And she, the lonely widow that hath made
    A sable covenant with grief, – alas!
She veils her tears under the deep, deep shade,
    While the poor kindly-hearted, as they pass,
Bend to unclouded childhood, and caress
Her boy, – so rosy! – and so fatherless!

Thus as good Christians ought, they all draw near
    The fair white temple, to the timely call
Of pleasant bells that tremble in the ear, –
    Now the last frock, and scarlet hood and shawl
Fade into dusk, in the dim atmosphere
    Of the low porch, and heav'n has won them all . . .

The Lord of the manor and his family have entered their private pew, hidden in a transept and with a separate entrance. Their liveried servants sit on a bench behind them. All round the church is an array of hats hanging on pegs on the walls above the pews. The parson, who has entered the church in his long white surplice and red silk hood of an

Oxford Master of Arts, takes his place in the second desk of the three-decker. The parish clerk is below him to say 'Amen'. He begins Morning Prayer, facing the congregation. He then mounts to the pulpit and preaches a sermon, which is usually read. Extempore preaching was a sign of 'enthusiasm'. The Devon poet N. T. Carrington well describes a morning service in *My Native Village* (1830):

> '*Ah, let me enter, once again, the pew*
> *Where the child nodded as the sermon grew;*
> *Scene of soft slumbers! I remember now*
> *The chiding finger, and the frowning brow*
> *Of stern reprovers, when the ardent June*
> *Flung through the glowing aisles the drowsy noon;*
> *Ah admonitions vain! a power was there*
> *Which conquer'd e'en the sage, the brave, the fair, –*
> *A sweet oppressive power – a languor deep,*
> *Resistless shedding round delicious sleep!*
> *Till closed the learned harangue, with solemn look*
> *Arose the chaunter of the sacred book, –*
> *The parish clerk (death-silenced) far-famed then*
> *And justly, for his long and loud – Amen!*
> *Rich was his tone, and his exulting eye*
> *Glanced to the reedy choir, enthroned on high,*
> *Nor glanced in vain; the simple-hearted throng*
> *Lifted their voices, and dissolved in song;*
> *Till in one tide, deep welling, full and free*
> *Rung through the echoing pile, old England's psalmody.*'

The singing is from metrical psalms which are bound with every prayer book. The versions used were generally those awkward quatrains by Tate and Brady. They are easily committed to memory. The minister or clerk reads out the stanzas and then the congregation sings, stanza by stanza, those few who cannot read committing the lines to memory. The custom, still prevailing in some Evangelical churches and many chapels, of the minister's proclaiming the first verse of the hymn, is doubtless a survival of these days. Two of Tate and Brady's metrical psalms, 'Thro' all the changing scenes of life' and 'As pants the hart for cooling streams', survive, cut down, in modern hymn books. An appendix to the Psalms was also printed, consisting of rhyming doxologies and a few hymns for special occasions such as 'While Shepherds watched'. From this appendix grew the separate hymn book, of which the most famous and successful was *Hymns Ancient and Modern* (1861), which consisted first of 273 hymns.

The parson's sermon is the end of the service unless it is 'Sacrament Sunday'. For the sermon has come after the Nicene Creed and not at the end of the office of Morning Prayer. It was the custom to have Morning Prayer, Litany and Ante-Communion. The whole service lasted about two hours. As the time of eating was at three o'clock, this was no great inconvenience. But one can understand where the deep-rooted English idea that church worship is boring had its origin. The layman was asked to take part in the monkish offices of Morning and Evening Prayer (an anglicised and potted version of the daily offices of monks and nuns) as well as in the celebration of Communion, always the central act of worship of the Church. The English habit of attending but not receiving Communion was the origin of the Ante-Communion service alone being read, and 'Sacrament Sundays' being special and rare occasions; for it was ordered in the Prayer Book that two or three people must be willing to partake of the Sacrament before it could be celebrated. This order was made with the intention of encouraging people to communicate. But the habit of abstaining was too strong, hence the diminution of the service to Ante-Communion.

THE CHURCH IN THE FIFTEENTH CENTURY

There will be no end to books on the Reformation. It is not my intention to add to them. Rather I would go back to the middle of the 15th century, when the church we have been describing was bright with its new additions of tower, porch, aisles and clerestory windows, and to a medieval England not quite so roseate as that of Cardinal Gasquet, nor yet so crime-ridden as that of Dr. Coulton.

The village looks different. The church is by far the most prominent building unless there is a manor-house, and even this is probably a smaller building than the church and more like what we now think of as an old farm. The church is so prominent because the equivalents of cottages in the village are at the grandest 'cruck houses' (that is to say tent-like buildings with roofs coming down to the ground), and most are mere hovels. They are grouped round the church and manor-house and look rather like a camp. There is far more forest everywhere, and in all but the Celtic fringes of the island agriculture is strip cultivation, that is to say the tilled land is laid out in long strips with no hedges between and is common to the whole community, as are the grazing rights in various hedged and well-watered fields. There are more sheep than any other animals in these enclosures. The approaches to the village are grassy tracks very muddy in winter. Each village is almost a country to itself. Near the entrance to the churchyard is the church house where the churchwardens store beer or 'church ales' for feasts. This is the origin of so many old inns being beside the churchyard in England. The graveyard has no tombstones in it. The dead are buried there but they are remembered not in stone but in the prayers of the priest at the altar at mass. Everyone goes to mass, people from outlying farms stabling their horses outside the churchyard. The church itself looks much the same. The stone tower gleams with new cut ashlar; the walls of the church when they are not ashlar are plastered.

Not only does everyone go to church on Sunday and in his best clothes; the church is used on weekdays too, for it is impossible to say daily prayers in the little hovels in which most of the villagers live. School is taught in the porch, business is carried out by the cross in the market where the booths are (for there are no shops in the village, only open stalls as in market squares today). In the nave of the church on a weekday there are probably people gossiping in some places, while in others there are people praying. There was no privacy in the middle ages, when even princes dined in public and their subjects watched them eat. The nave of the church belonged to the people, and they used it as today we use a village hall or social club. Our new suburban churches which are used as dance halls during the week with sanctuary partitioned off until Sunday, have something in common with the medieval church. But there is this difference: in the middle ages all sport and pleasure, all plays and dancing were 'under God'. God was near, hanging on his Cross above the chancel arch, and mystically present in the sacrament in the pyx hanging over the altar beyond. His crucifixion was carved on the preaching cross in the churchyard. People were aware of God. They were not priest-ridden in the sense that they bowed meekly to whatever the priest said. They had decided opinions and argued about religion and the clergy, and no doubt some went to church reluctantly. But no one thought of not going to church. They believed men had souls and that their souls must be exercised in worship and customed by sacraments.

Let us go in by its new south porch to our parish church of five-hundred years ago. Many of the features which were there when we last saw it are still present, the screen and the font for instance, but the walls are now painted all over. Medieval builders were not concerned with 'taste'. But they were moved by fashion. If the next village had a new tower, they must have one like it. If the latest style at the nearest big abbey or bishop's seat made their own building seem out of date, then it must be rebuilt. At the time of which we are writing, the style would be Perpendicular. Only the most shewy features of earlier building – a Norman chancel arch removed in a few instances to the south door, a 'decorated' window with rich tracery, and perhaps a column with sculptured foliage capital of Early English times – might be spared if they could be made to look well. The builders were chiefly concerned with making the interior of the church as rich and splendid as possible, something to bring you to your knees. Most parish churches, even the smallest, had three altars, one in the chancel and one on either side of the chancel arch.

Where we go in, there is a stoup made of stone or metal, containing Holy Water. And somewhere near, very prominent, is the font. Over it is a painted wooden cover, rising like a church steeple and securely clasped down to the basin of the font and locked. This is because the font contains Baptismal Water, which is changed only twice a year at Easter and Whitsun when it is solemnly blessed. The cover is raised by

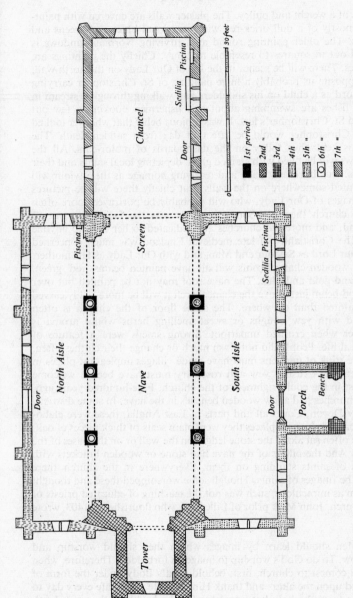

0   30 feet

1st period ■
2nd "
3rd "
4th "
5th "
6th " ○
7th "

Chancel

Sedilia

Piscina

Door

Screen

Piscina

North Aisle

Door

Nave

South Aisle

Sedilia Piscina

Door

Porch

Bench

Tower

The growth of a medieval church: 'At Harringworth in Northamptonshire there had been an aisleless church, to which a tower had been added at the end of the 12th and aisles early in the 13th century. In about 1300 a new north aisle had been built, with a new altar at the east end. Soon after the whole of the south aisle and arcade were built. The work was done in a very conservative spirit. During the next few years, the north arcade was entirely rebuilt so as nearly to match that on the south. Thus the work, beginning with the north aisle, and extending over some 30 or 40 years, finished on the side on which it began.' (From 'The Ground Plan of the English Parish Church')

means of a weight and pulley. The plaster walls are covered with paintings, mostly of a dull brick-red with occasional blues and greens and
blacks. The older painting round any surviving Norman windows is
picked out in squares to resemble masonry. Chiefly the paintings are
pictures. There will be scenes in the life of Our Lady on the north wall,
and opposite us probably a huge painting of St. Christopher carrying
Our Lord as a child on his shoulders and walking through a stream in
which fishes are swimming about and fishermen hooking a few out
around St. Christopher's feet. It was a pious belief that whoever looked
at St. Christopher would be safe that day from sudden death. The
belief is kept alive today on the dashboards of motor-cars. All the
windows will be filled with stained glass, depicting local saints and their
legends. Our Lord as a baby and receiving homage as the Saviour will
be painted somewhere on the walls. But chiefly there will be pictures
and images of Our Lady, who will probably be portrayed more often
in the church than her Son. Our Lady was the favourite saint of
England, and more old churches are dedicated to her than to anyone
else. The Christianity of late medieval England was much concerned
with Our Lord as Saviour and Man, and with Our Lady as His mother.
  The wooden chancel roofs will all have painted beams, red, green,
white and gold and blue. The nave roof may not be painted but over
the rood-beam just above the chancel arch it will be more richly carved
and painted than elsewhere. The stone floor of the church is often
covered with yew boughs or sweet-smelling herbs whose aroma is
stronger when crushed underfoot. Strong smells were a feature of
medieval life. People did not wash much or change their clothes often,
and the stink of middens must have made villages unpleasant places in
hot weather. Crushed yew and rosemary must have been a welcome
contrast in the cool brightness of the church. Five-hundred years ago,
most churches had a few wooden benches in the nave. In some districts,
notably Devon, Cornwall and parts of East Anglia, these were elaborately carved. In most places they were plain seats of thick pieces of oak.
People often sat along the stone ledges on the wall or on the bases of the
pillars. And the pillars of the nave had stone or wooden brackets with
statues of saints standing on them. Everywhere in the church there
would be images of saints. Though some worshipped these and thought
of them as miraculous, such was not the teaching of educated priests of
the Church. John Mirk prior of Lilleshall, who flourished *c.* 1403, wrote
thus:

'Men should learn by images whom they should worship and
follow. To do God's worship to images is forbidden. Therefore, when
thou comest to church, first, behold God's Body under the form of
bread upon the altar; and thank Him that He vouchsafe every day to
come from the holy heaven above for the health of thy soul. Look
upon the Cross, and thereby have mind of the passion he suffered
for thee. Then on the images of the holy saints; not believing on

them, but that by the sight of them thou mayest have mind on them
that be in heaven: and so to follow their life as much as thou mayest.'

And here in the nave, the people's part of the church, we have not yet
looked eastward to Our Lord upon the Cross. His figure hanging on a
wooden cross over the chancel arch, with St. Mary and St. John weeping
on either side of Him at the foot of the cross, looks down from above
the screen. This dominates the nave, and behind it or above it, painted
on the east wall, is the depiction of the Doom. There, above His Body
on the Rood, is a painting of the Resurrected Christ, the severe judge.
His wounds are shewn, His hands are raised with the nail prints in them,
and His eyes fix you as you stare up. Angels blow trumpets around
Him, and there rising from their graves are naked souls, painted as
naked bodies but wearing head-dresses, tiaras, crowns and mitres to
shew their rank in life. On one side they enter rather joylessly the gates
of heaven. On the other, with terrible imagery, are shewn devils with
sharks' teeth and rolling eyes, hauling off the helpless souls to the gaping
mouth of hell, a yawning cauldron in the bottom corner of the picture.
The artists had a far more enjoyable time drawing devils and hell than
angels and heaven. For one sweet-faced saint or tender portrait of Our
Lady surviving in the wall-painting in our islands, there must be two or
three alarming devils.

It is appropriate that here in the nave, with Our Lord looking down
sadly from the Cross and sternly from His glory, people should be
reminded of how to live while on earth if they wish to escape hell. And
while we look at the judgement on the wall, let us listen to John Bromyard, a Dominican Friar of c. 1390, preaching against the rich:

'Their souls shall have, instead of palace and hall and chamber, the
deep lake of hell, with those that go down into the depth thereof. In
the place of scented baths, their body shall have a narrow pit of
earth; and there they shall have bath more black and foul than any
bath of pitch and sulphur. In place of a soft couch, they shall have a
bed more grievous and hard than all the nails and spikes in the
world; in place of inordinate embraces, they will be able to have there
the embraces of the fiery brands of hell . . . Instead of wives, they shall
have toads; instead of a great retinue and throng of followers, their
body shall have a throng of worms and their soul a throng of demons.
Instead of large domain, it shall be an eternal prison house cramped
for both.'

Heaven is represented in the chancel beyond that richly-painted
screen, where the priest murmurs scarcely audible Latin and where the
Body of Our Lord under the form of bread, hangs above the altar in a
shrouded pyx. Much chatting goes on in the church during sermon and
Mass, and we may now approach the screen to examine it and the
jewel-like blazing richness beyond, in the holiest part of the church.

Through the screen which runs across the whole width of the church, you may glimpse the richest part of all this teaching imagery. The altars at the end of the aisles are either guild chapels, or family chapels, each with their paid priests. The Shoemakers may have an altar dedicated to Crispin, and will subscribe for its upkeep and to keep its lights burning. Another chapel may be kept up by a guild which pays a priest to say Mass for the Souls of its departed members. The secular descendants of these guilds are the trade unions and burial societies of today. The big town churches such as those at Coventry, Stamford and Bristol, had many guild chapels with priests maintained to serve them. And many altars contained a relic of a saint. The walls round the altars were painted, the roofs above them were richer and more elaborately painted than those in the people's part of the church, the altar hangings were of the richest silks and threaded with jewels, the fair linen-cloth laid upon the altar itself a white, plain contrast with the elaborate hangings. The floors of the chancel are of marble or tiles. Brasses of dead priests shone bright among them. You may see what they looked like in illuminated missals. The ornaments on the altar were few, candles perhaps, and if a cross, then a small one to help the priest in his devotions – for here in the chancel we meet the risen Lord. Only in the nave is He dead on the cross, as large as life.

Few people will make their communion at Mass. Indeed it is rare for anyone to make his communion except at Easter. People think of the Mass as something offered for them rather than something of which they partake the sacred elements.

On a hot summer Sunday morning in the country, when I have been reading Chaucer to the sound of bells pouring through the trees, I have been able dimly to imagine this late medieval religion. Life is short for everybody. It is matter of fact. The pictures on the church walls are not thought of as 'art', but are there to tell a story. Small parish churches were not consciously made beautiful. They were built and decorated for effect, to be better than the church in the next village, to be the best building in the village itself, for it is the House of God, and God become Man – that was the great discovery – offered here upon the altar. All sorts of miraculous stories were invented about Him, and even more about His mother. Because He was Man born of woman, he becomes within the grasp of everyone. Few of the extravagances of German and Spanish late medieval art are found in English representations of the scourging, the crucifixion and the deposition. Jesus is thought of as the baby of poor people who received the tributes of a king. His mother is the most beautiful woman in the world – and how many lovely, loving faces of Our Lady we may see in the old glass, wall-paintings and statues which survive in England. And she bore a Spotless Son who was God and Judge of all. No wonder she was loved by the pious English.

The miracles of Our Lord were not so interesting to these peoples as the miracles they ascribed to His saints. Here extravagancy knew no bounds. St. Petroc sailed in a silver bowl from Cornwall to an isle in the Indian Ocean. St. Winifred was beheaded by an angry lover, but her head was reunited to her body and she became an abbess. There were saints like St. Quintin who cured dropsy, saints for toothache, and for colds and fever, and for finding things. There were patron saints for every craft and trade. There were miraculous images which winked, or flew to bedsides; there were statues of saints that had never been, like the Maid Uncumber in old St. Paul's Cathedral.

Though for the everyday things of life there were friendly saints who helped, life itself must have been terrifying, a continual rush to escape hell. Our Lord and His Mother were the loving and human part of it; hell was the terrifying part. The Devil was seen. His fellow devils yawned as gargoyles with bats' wings on the north walls of the church, black against the evening sky. The white teeth of devils and their red eyes gleamed out of the darkness. Evil spirits lurked behind stones on lonely moors and ranged the deep woods. Good and evil fought together in the roar of the storm. All thought, all sight, every breath of the body, was under God. The leaping sciapod, the man-eating mantichora, the unicorn, might easily be met in the forest by men with imaginations, which as easily would expect to see Our Lady flying through the air, or the local saint, for centuries enshrined in his altar, walking down the street. The witch cast her evil spells, blood and death lay around everywhere, the entrails of a man hung, drawn and quartered, shone black with flies in the sun, silvery lepers tinkled their bells, creating loneliness around them. The fear that men felt is expressed in the grotesque carvings over the north walls of churches, and in the corbels and bosses of roofs, and in bench-ends, screens and miserere stalls. Their humour is shewn there too. Chiefly in the figure of Our Lady do we see the tenderness and sweetness of this late religion.

So when we walk down a green lane like an ancient cart track towards the ringing church-bells, we can see the power of God in the blossom and trees, remember legends of the saints about birds and stones, and recall miracles that happened in the parish at this or that spot. And on a feast day we can see the churchyard set out with tables for the church ale when mass is over, and as we enter the nave we can see it thronged below the painted roof and walls with people in the village, young and old, and the rest of the parish crowding in with us. Human nature may not have been better. Life was as full, no doubt, of wrong and terror as it is today. How different it was is expressed in the words of Froude:

'For, indeed, a change was coming upon the world, the meaning and direction of which even still is hidden from us, a change from era to era. The paths trodden by the footsteps of ages were broken up; old things were passing away and the faith and the life of ten centuries were dissolving like a dream. Chivalry was dying; the abbey and the castle were soon together to crumble into ruins; and all the forms, desires, beliefs, convictions of the old world were passing away never to return. A new continent had risen up beyond the western sea. The floor of heaven, inlaid with stars, had sunk back

into an infinite abyss of immeasurable space; and the firm earth itself, unfixed from its foundations, was seen to be but a small atom
in the awful vastness of the universe. In the fabric of habit which they
had so laboriously built for themselves, mankind were to remain no
longer.

And now it is all gone – like an unsubstantial pageant faded; and
between us and the old English there lies a gulf of mystery which the
prose of the historian will never adequately bridge. They cannot
come to us, and our imagination can but feebly penetrate to them.
Only among the aisles of our cathedrals, only as we gaze upon their
silent figures sleeping on their tombs, some faint conceptions float
before us of what these men were when they were alive; and perhaps
in the sound of church bells, that peculiar creation of medieval age,
which falls upon the ear like the echo of a vanished world.'

THE CHURCHES BEFORE THE FIFTEENTH CENTURY

To imagine our church in earliest times of Christian England is, alas, to
enter the controversial world of archaeology. There was a Christian
Church in the Roman settlement at Silchester, Berkshire, and its remains have been excavated. It had an apse at the west end instead of the
east where one would expect it to be, and the altar which is supposed to
have been wooden and square, was also in the west. The east end was
square. The church is said to be 4th century. Only the foundations
remain. The form of worship was probably more like that of the
Orthodox church today than the western rite.

But there are enough later pre-Conquest churches remaining to give
us an idea of the architecture of those times. They are called Saxon.
There are two types. The southern, of which the earliest churches are
found in Kent – three in Canterbury, St. Mary Lyminge, Reculver, and,
most complete, Bradwell, Essex, all of which are 7th century – were the
result of the Italian mission of St. Augustine, and were reinforced
after the coming of St. Theodore in 669. In plan and style they
resembled certain early Italian churches. The northern group found in
Northumberland and Durham are survivals of the Celtic church, and
their architecture is said to have come from Gaul, and is more barbaric
looking than that of their southern contemporaries. Their three distinctive features were, according to Sir Arthur Clapham, an unusual
length of nave, a small chancel, less wide than the nave, and very high
side walls. In the northern group, the most complete is Escombe,
Durham (7th and early 8th century?), a stern building, nave and chancel
only, with squared rubble walls, small windows high up and square or
round headed, and a narrow and tall rounded chancel arch. We have a
picture of the interiors of these northern churches from near contemporary accounts. The walls and capitals and arch of the sanctuary were

adorned 'with designs and images and many sculptured figures in relief on the stone and pictures with a pleasing variety of colours and a wonderful charm'. We learn, too, of purple hangings and gold and silver ornaments with precious stones. Elsewhere in England the most considerable remains of pre-Conquest work are those at Monkwearmouth (Durham), Jarrow (Durham), Brixworth (Northants), Deerhurst (Glos), Bradford-on-Avon (Wilts.), the tower of Earls Barton (Northants), Barton-on-Humber (Lincs), Sompting (Sussex), the Crypts at Repton (Derby), Wing (Bucks), and Hexham (Northumberland). From the pre-Conquest sculpture, like the crosses at Bewcastle and Ruthwell, and the carvings at Langford (Oxon), Romsey (Hants), Bexhill (Sussex), St. Dunstan's Stepney (London), and the moving relief of the Harrowing of Hell in Bristol Cathedral, and from such enrichment as survives in such objects as St. Cuthbert's stole (Durham), the Alfred Jewel in the Ashmolean Museum, Oxford, the beautiful drawing in the Winchester Psalter and Lindisfarne Gospel in the British Museum, we know that

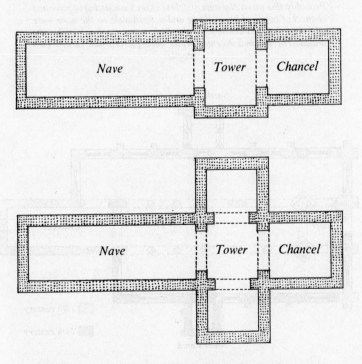

Anglo-Saxon and Norman. Two aisleless plans with central tower. (1) tower between nave and chancel; (2) tower over crossing of transepts with nave and chancel

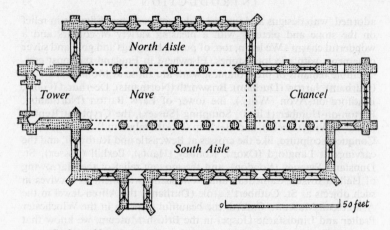

Gothic additions to a Norman plan. Raunds, Northamptonshire. Probably this was a Norman aisleless church consisting of nave and chancel of equal width. A tower and a north aisle to the nave were added in the 13th century. In the 14th century a south aisle was added. The original Norman walls were pierced and turned into arcades

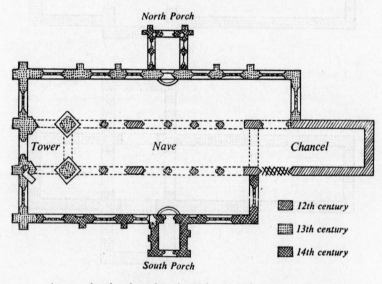

A town church enlarged in the 13th and 14th centuries so as to provide guild chapels. Grantham, Lincolnshire

these Romanesque masons, sculptors and illuminators were very fine artists, as fine as there have ever been in England.

However, it is safer to try to imagine our parish church as it was in Norman times, as far more of our old churches are known to be Norman in origin than pre-Conquest, even though as in the church of Kilpeck (Herefordshire) the pre-Conquest style of decoration may have continued into Norman times. It is narrow and stone built. Let us suppose it divided into three parts. The small, eastward chancel is either squared-ended or apsidal. Then comes the tower supported internally on round arches. The nave, west of the low tower, is longer than the chancel. The windows are small and high up. The church is almost like a fortress outside. And it is indeed a fortress of Christianity in a community where pagan memories and practices survive, where barons are like warring kings and monasteries are the centres of faith. These small village churches are like mission churches in a jungle clearing.

There are no porches, and we enter the building by any of the three doors to the nave on the north, south or west. Inside, the walls of the nave are painted with red lines to look like blocks of stone. The raftered roof is hidden by a flat wooden ceiling which is painted with lozenges. The floor of the nave is paved with small blocks of stone or with red tiles. There are no pews. We can only see the chancel through a richly moulded round arch, that very arch which is now the South Door of your parish church. Above this chancel arch is a painted Doom, not quite so terrifying as that of the 15th-century church, for all the painting here is in the manner of the mosaics still seen in basilicas of Italy and eastern Europe.

The splays of the windows in the nave have figures of saints painted on them. But it is through the chancel that we see the greatest riches. Stained glass is rare. If there is any it is in the sanctuary and black with much leading and giving the impression of transparent mosaics. The walls are painted everywhere with figures, also recalling mosaic pictures. There are bands of classic style, patterns dividing them. The altar is of stone, small and box-like, recalling the tombs of Christians in the catacombs of Rome in the very earliest days of Christianity. The altar stands well away from the eastern, semi-circular end of the apse. It is covered with a cloth hanging over its four sides, decorated with vertical bands.

Our Lord is depicted on the cross as a King and Judge, not as a man in anguish as in later crucifixions. The religion of the time was less concerned with Him and Our Lady as human beings, more concerned with the facts of Judgement, Death and Hell. It was more ascetic and severe.

PART TWO

THE NEWER CHURCHES

O F THE 16,000 parish churches in England more than half have been
built since the 17th century, and the majority of these were erected
in the last and present centuries. Guide books, almost wholly antiquarian in outlook, still dismiss even 18th-century churches as 'modern',
while Victorian buildings are usually beneath their consideration. Yet
some of the noblest churches are post-Reformation, from cathedrals
like St. Paul's and Truro and Liverpool, to the great town churches
designed by such architects as Hawksmoor, Gibbs, Street, Butterfield,
Pearson, Brooks, Bodley, Nicholson and Comper.

The first post-Reformation churches differed little in plan from those
of medieval times. Wren in some of his churches for the City of London
seems to have tried to build uncompartmented churches, where Baptism, Morning and Evening Prayer and Holy Communion could all be
conducted in an undivided space, without the priest and his assistants
moving out of sight and earshot.

Usually the plan was of nave with three-decker pulpit dominating for
Mattins, Litany and Evensong, a screen through which the congregation passed for Communion, and a Baptistry at the west end. The
earliest post-Reformation churches usually had west galleries for organ
and choir and also side galleries, because by the 17th century the population had begun to increase, especially in the towns where many new
churches were built. The churches of the 17th and 18th centuries were
mostly built on the English medieval plan. The only noticeable new
feature in the more traditional churches was that the chancels were
shallower and broader than those surviving from earlier times.

The style of tracery and decoration and wood-carving certainly
changed. Windows were square-headed in the 16th century, and thereafter became round-headed. Grapes and cherubs and a cornucopia of
fruit cascaded down the sides of altar-pieces, wreathed round the
panelling of pulpits, and flattened themselves into patterns on the
ceiling. The Renaissance style of Italy became the fashion. But it was an
English version. Wren's Portland stone steeples and lead spires, so
happily clustering round St. Paul's Cathedral, are a recollection of
Gothic architecture, though most of them are Renaissance in detail.

The interior of even the most room-like classic church of the 17th and
early 18th centuries generally differs from its contemporary Dissenting
interior. In the former there is provision for the expounding of the
Word, and for the two chief sacraments; in the latter there is provision
for the Word, but there is no suggestion of an altar about the table that
is set for Communion. There may be some significance in the hour-
glasses so often found beside the Anglican pulpits. They were intended

as a check on the length of the sermon, and perhaps as a reminder to parson and people that there were other offices of the Church to be performed than preaching. Only for the short period when the Commonwealth ejected ordained priests of the Church, who returned with the Restoration, can these interiors have resembled Dissenting meeting houses.

Some of our finest sculpture is to be found in the monuments erected in all parish churches new or old during the 17th, 18th and early 19th centuries. A whole illustrated literature of this has been developed by the late Mrs. Esdaile and Mr. Rupert Gunnis. The work of great sculptors ignored or despised by the Victorians, such as Roubiliac, Rysbrack, Stone, Wilton, the Bacons, Hickey and Paty, has received recognition owing to their writings.

17th-century furnishings. Langley Chapel, Shropshire. Altar in middle of chancel facing north and south. Communicants' pews along wall. Pew for saying daily offices on left facing nave

From the middle of the 18th century until its end, new churches were Classic, usually in the manner of the Brothers Adam, with chaste decorations in low relief in interior plaster and woodwork, and comparatively plain exteriors. The individuality of architects was beginning to assert itself over traditional plan and local styles. Cross-shaped churches were built with altar at the eastern axis and there were square and octagonal churches as well as proprietary chapels with the pews all

Mid-18th-century Classic. Langton-by-Partney, Lincolnshire. The family church of the Langton family, rebuilt c. 1750. Two-decker pulpit on south wall on right

Mid-18th-century 'Rococo Gothick' Shobdon, Herefordshire. Rebuilt for Lord Bateman, 1753. Prevailing colours white, pale blue and grey with crimson hangings. Coloured glass of same date.

arranged for a view of the occupier of the pulpit. These last buildings came as near to a Dissenting chapel as Anglicanism permitted.

Gothic never died. The style was driven by the Renaissance out of churches and houses into barns, farms and cottages. It was revived in a romantic form, suggesting Strawberry Hill (1733), even in the 17th century. And a slender case might be made for its never having died even in ecclesiastical building. There are Stuart churches which are Tudor Gothic, such as Low Ham in Somerset (1624), and Staunton

Harald in Leicestershire (1653), which are like late Perpendicular
medieval churches, and not a conscious revival but a continuance of the
old style. St. Martins in the Fields, London, until its rebuilding by
Gibbs in 1721, had been continuously rebuilt in the Gothic style since
the time of Henry VIII. There are churches like St. John's, Leeds (1632),
and Compton Wynyates (1663), which are a mixture of Classic and
Tudor Gothic. Then there are the first conscious imitations of old forms
by architects, such as Sir William Wilson's tower of St. Mary's, Warwick
(1694), and Wren's tower and steeple to St. Dunstan's-in-the-East
(1698), and his towers of St. Mary Aldermary (1711) and St. Michael

*Classic and Gothick. King's Norton, Leicestershire. By Wing the
younger of Leicester, 1760–75. The exterior and window tracery
are very early Gothic Revival. The oak furnishings in Classic style
divide this rectangular church into compartments for worship
according to the Book of Common Prayer. Pulpit in nave for
Morning and Evening Prayer. Choir in West gallery, not shown in
picture. Altar for Communion and communicants' pews in chancel
behind pulpit. Clear 18th-century glass throughout*

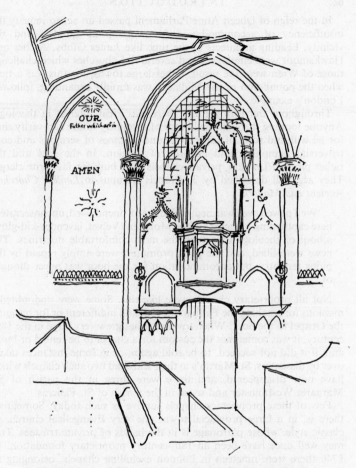

A Liturgical experiment. Teigh, Rutland. Rebuilt 1782 by the Rev. Robert Sherard, Earl of Harborough, and one of his three rebuildings in the neighbourhood. Pulpit over West door; reading desks flank door. Behind pulpit a painted representation of a window with trees beyond

Cornhill (1721). There is an interesting and well-illustrated chapter on this subject of the earliest revival of Gothic in M. Whiffen's *Stuart and Georgian Churches*. The plan of these buildings was almost always traditional with an emphasised chancel. Now and then a Lutheran element crept in. In the Gothic church of Teigh in Rutland (1783), the small font is fixed by a brass bracket to the Communion rails. But the seats face north and south and the pulpit is at the west end.

In the reign of Queen Anne Parliament passed an act to remedy the insufficiency of accommodation for worship in London and the vicinity. Leading architects of the time like James Gibbs, Archer and Hawksmoor were employed, and several fine churches which challenge those of Wren were the result. Other large towns, for this was a time when the population of the Midlands was rapidly expanding, followed London's example.

Throughout the 18th century there was great interest in theology. Anyone looking through the library of a country house can verify this, for he will find rows of superbly bound volumes of sermons and controversial pamphlets and histories of religion. In the spas and the richer parts of London, private chapels were built for favourite clergy. They are well described by T. Francis Bumpus in *London Churches, Ancient and Modern*:

> 'Well pewed, well warmed, undedicated, unendowed, unconsecrated, here captivating preachers of the Morphine Velvet, lavender-kid-glove school of theology dispensed the most comfortable doctrines. The pews were filled, and the good promoters were amply repaid by the pious tenantry, but accommodation for the poor was never thought of.'

Not all proprietary chapels were like this. Some were undoubtedly missions for teaching the Faith to the rich and indifferent or for bringing the Gospel to the poor. When town parishes grew very large in the 18th century, it was sometimes the custom for a chapel to be rented or built, and, if it did not succeed, to be sold again, or in some instances taken over by dissenters. St. Martin's in the Fields had two such chapels which have now disappeared, and there were three in the parish of St. Margaret Westminster and seven in the parish of St. Pancras.

Few of these proprietary chapels survive as such today. Sometimes there is, in a large provincial town, one very Evangelical church, in classic style, whose patronage is in the hands of private trustees. This may well once have been an 18th-century proprietary foundation. In 1746 there were nineteen in London excluding chapels, belonging to Royal and Episcopal Palaces, Almshouses, Prisons, Livery Companies and Inns of Court. Those which have not been pulled down or become Dissenting places of worship, have been consecrated and turned into parish churches. I remember one in Bath called Kensington Chapel, which was Calvinistic yet Anglican, but which is now a furniture store. At another in Homerton, London, known as Ram's Episcopal Chapel, I attended worship, and the clergyman wore a black gown and bands for preaching. This charming 18th-century chapel is now, alas, demolished. At Christ Church, North Brixton, London, is an extremely original and impressive episcopal chapel re-erected in 1904 in the Byzantine style from designs by Professor Beresford Pite. It was built privately and in it the black gown was still used in 1952.

Another reason for the erection of new churches in the 18th century was the inadequacy of medieval buildings. They could sometimes hold galleries erected in the aisles and at the west end, but no more. Old prints shew us town churches which have almost the appearance of an opera house, galleries projecting beyond galleries, with the charity children away up in the top lighted by dormers in the roof, pews all over the aisles and in the chancel, and only here and there a pointed arch or a bit of window tracery to shew that this was once a gothic medieval church. Walls began to bulge, stone decayed, structures were unsound and ill-behaved children could not be seen by the beadle and clerk. The only thing to do was to pull down the building. A surviving interior of this sort is the parish church of Whitby. To go into it is like entering the hold of a ship. There are box-pews shoulder high in all directions, galleries, private pews, and even a pew over the chancel screen. Picturesque and beautiful as it is, with the different colours of baize lining the pews, and the splendid joinery of varying dates, such an uneven effect cannot have pleased the 18th-century man of taste. Therefore when they became overloaded with pews, these old churches were taken down and new ones in Classic or Strawberry Hill Gothick style were erected on the sites.

In the country there can have been little need to rebuild the old church on the grounds of lack of accommodation. Here rebuilding was done at the dictates of taste. A landlord might find the church too near his house, or sited wrongly for a landscape improvement he was contemplating in the park, or he might simply dislike the old church on aesthetic grounds as a higgledy-piggledy, barbarous building. Most counties in England have more than one 18th-century church, now a sad relic in a park devastated by timber merchants, still crowning some rise or looking like a bit of Italy or ancient Greece in the pastoral English landscape.

Eighteenth-century churches are beautiful primarily because of their proportions. But they were not without colour. Painted hatchments adorned the walls, gilded tables of the Commandments were over the altar, with Moses and Aaron on either side, the Royal Arms on painted wood or coloured plaster was above the chancel opening, coloured baize lines in the pews, rich velvets of all colours were hanging from the high pulpit and the desks below it, an embroidered velvet covering decked the altar in wide folds, gilded candles and alms dish stood on the altar. The art of stained glass was not dead in the 18th century as is often supposed. East windows were frequently coloured, with pieces of golden-yellow 16th-century foreign glass brought back from a Grand Tour, and gold, blue and dark green glass, partly pot-metal and partly coloured transparency, such as went on being made in York until late in the century. Another popular kind of window was the coloured transparency – a transparent drawing enamelled on to glass, like the Reynolds' window in New College, Oxford, by such artists as Eginton of Birmingham, Peckitt of York, James Pearson and Jervais.

After 1760 country churches were often rebuilt in the Gothick taste.

Pointed windows, pinnacled towers and battlemented walls were considered ecclesiastical and picturesque. They went with sham ruins and amateur antiquarianism, then coming into fashion. The details of these Gothick churches were not correct according to ancient examples. Nor do I think they were intended to be. Their designers strove after a picturesque effect, not antiquarian copying. The interiors were embellished with Chippendale Gothick woodwork and plaster-work. Again nothing was 'correct'. Who had ever heard of a medieval box-pew or an ancient ceiling that was plaster moulded? The Gothick taste was but plaster deep, concerned with a decorative effect and not with structure. The supreme example of this sort of church is Shobdon, Herefordshire (1753).

Amid all this concern with taste, industrialism comes upon us. It was all very well for the squire to fritter away his time with matters of taste in his country park, all very well for Boulton and Watt to try to harness taste to their iron-works at Soho, as Darby before them had tried at Ironbridge; the mills of the midlands and the north were rising. Pale mechanics, slave-driven children and pregnant women were working in the new factories. The more intelligent villagers were leaving for the towns where there was more money to be made. From that time until the present day, the country has been steadily drained of its best people. Living in hovels, working in a rattling twilight of machines, the people multiplied. Ebenezer Elliott the Corn Law Rhymer (1781–1849) was their poet:

> The day was fair, the cannon roar'd,
> Cold blew the bracing north,
> And Preston's mills, by thousands, pour'd
> Their little captives forth . . .

> But from their lips the rose had fled,
> Like 'death-in-life' they smiled;
> And still, as each pass'd by, I said,
> Alas! is that a child? . . .

> Thousands and thousands – all so white! –
> With eyes so glazed and dull!
> O God! it was indeed a sight
> Too sadly beautiful!

A Christian himself, Ebenezer called out above the roar of the young industrial age:

> When wilt thou save the People?
> O God of mercy, when?
> The people, Lord, the people,
> Not thrones and crowns, but men!
> Flowers of thy heart, O God, are they;
> Let them not pass, like weeds, away, –
> Their heritage a sunless day.
> God save the people!

The composition of this poem was a little later than the Million Act of 1818, by which Parliament voted one million pounds towards the building of churches in new districts. The sentiments of the promoters of the Bill cannot have been so unlike those of Elliott. Less charitable hearts, no doubt, terrified by the atheism consequent on the French Revolution and apprehensive of losses to landed proprietors, regarded the Million Act as a thank-offering to God for defending them from French free-thinking and continental economics. Others saw in these churches bulwarks against the rising tide of Dissent. Nearly three hundred new churches were built in industrial areas between 1819 and 1830. The Lords Commissioner of the Treasury who administered the fund required them to be built in the most economical mode, 'with a view to accommodating the greatest number of persons at the smallest expense within the compass of an ordinary voice, one half of the number to be free seats for the poor'. A limit of £20,000 was fixed for 2,000 persons. Many of these 'Commissioners' or 'Waterloo' churches, as they are now called, were built for £10,000. The most famous church of this date is St. Pancras in London, which cost over £70,000. But the money was found by private subscription and a levy on the rates. For other and cheaper churches in what were then poorer districts the Commissioners contributed towards the cost.

The Commissioners themselves approved all designs. When one reads some of the conditions they laid down, it is surprising to think that almost every famous architect in the country designed churches for them – Soane, Nash, Barry, Smirke, the Inwoods, the Hardwicks, Rickman (a Quaker and the inventor of those useful terms for Gothic architecture, 'Early English', 'Decorated' and 'Perpendicular'), Cockerell & Basevi and Dobson, to name a few. 'The site must be central, dry and sufficiently distant from factories and noisy thoroughfares; a paved area is to be made round the church. If vaulted underneath, the crypt is to be made available for the reception of coals or the parish fire engine. Every care must be taken to render chimneys safe from fire; they might be concealed in pinnacles. The windows ought not to resemble modern sashes; but whether Grecian or Gothic, should be in small panes and not costly. The most favourable position for the minister is near an end wall or in a semicircular recess under a half dome. The pulpit should not intercept a view of the altar, but all seats should be placed so as to face the preacher. We should recommend pillars of cast iron for supporting the gallery of a chapel, but in large churches they might want grandeur. Ornament should be neat and simple, yet variable in character.'

In short, what was wanted was a cheap auditorium, and, whether Grecian or Gothic, the solution seems always to have been the same. The architects provided a large rectangle with an altar at the end in a very shallow chancel, a high pulpit on one side of the altar and a reading desk on the other, galleries round the north, west and south walls, an organ in the west gallery, and lighting from two rows of

windows on the north and south walls, the lower row to light the aisles
and nave, the upper to light the galleries. The font was usually under
the west gallery. The only scope for invention which the architect had
was in the design of portico and steeple, tower or spire.

Most large towns have at least one example of Commissioners'
Churches, particularly in the north of England, where they were usually
Gothic. None to my knowledge except Christ Church, Acton Square,
Salford (1831) survived exactly as it was when its architect designed it.
This is not because they were badly built. But they were extremely un-
popular with the Victorians, who regarded them as cheap and full of
shams and unworthy of the new-found dignity of the Anglican liturgy.
The usual thing to do was to turn Grecian buildings into 'Byzantine' or
'Lombardic' fanes, by filling the windows with stained glass, piercing
the gallery fronts with fretwork, introducing iron screens at the east
end, adding a deeper chancel and putting mosaics in it, and of course
cutting down the box-pews, thus ruining the planned proportions of the
building and the relation of woodwork to columns supporting the
galleries. The architect, Sir Arthur Blomfield, was a specialist in spoiling
Commissioners' Churches in this way. Gothic or Classic churches were
'corrected'. In later days side chapels were tucked away in aisles
originally designed for pews. Organs were invariably moved from the
west galleries made for them, and were fitted awkwardly alongside the
east end.

One can visualise a Commissioners' Church as it was first built, by
piecing together the various undisturbed parts of these churches in
different towns. The Gothic was a matter of decoration, except in St.
Luke's new church, Chelsea, London, and not of construction. A
Commissioners' Church will be found in that part of a town where
streets have names like Nelson Crescent, Adelaide Place, Regent
Square, Brunswick Terrace and Hanover Villas. The streets round it
will have the spaciousness of Georgian speculative building, low-
terraced houses in brick or stucco with fanlights over the doors, and,
until the pernicious campaign against Georgian railings during the
Nazi war, there were pleasant cast-iron verandahs on the first floor and
simple railings round the planted square. Out of a wide paved space,
railed in with Greek or Gothic cast iron according to the style of the
building, will rise the Commissioners' Church, a brick structure with
Bath stone dressings, two rows of windows and a noble entrance
portico at the west end. Such churches are generally locked today, for
the neighbourhood has often 'gone down'; the genteel late Georgian
families who lived there moved into arboured suburbs at the beginning
of this century, and their houses have been sub-let in furnished rooms.

But Commissioners' Churches, which provided worship for nearly
five million people, had a dignity and coherence which we can appreciate today now that the merits of Georgian Architecture are recognised.
They were the last auditory buildings of the Establishment to be erected
for about a century. Through the rest of the 19th century, most new

churches might be considered inauditory buildings, places where the ritual of the service could best be appreciated, where sight came first and sound second.

By 1850 began a great period of English church building, which is comparable with the 15th century. Much as we regret the Victorian architect's usual 'restoration' of an old building, when he came to design a new one, he could produce work which was often original and awe-inspiring. To name only a few London churches, All Saints', Margaret Street; St. Augustine's, Kilburn; St. James the Less, Victoria; St. Columba's, Haggerston; Holy Trinity, Sloane Street; Holy Redeemer, Clerkenwell; St. Michael's, Camden Town; and St. Cyprian's, Clarence Gate, are some large examples of the period which have survived Prussian bombing. To understand the inspiration behind these churches, we must leave architecture for a while and turn to the architects and the men who influenced them; architects such as Pugin, Street, Butterfield, Pearson, Gilbert Scott, Bodley and the Seddings, and priests such as Newman, Keble, Pusey, Neale, Wilberforce, and later Lowder, Mackonochie and Wainwright.

The Commissioners' Churches were built to provide more space for the worship of God. But in what way was God to be worshipped? And even, who was God? Those 19th-century liberals who survived the shock of the French Revolution took up a line which we can still find today in the absurd Act inaugurated by R. A. Butler (1944) about the teaching of religion in State Schools. The liberal view was, as Newman described it, 'the doctrine that there is no positive truth in religion, but that one creed is as good as another.' This view commended itself to Dissenters in the beginning of the last century, since they saw in it the liberty to expound their doctrines, and perhaps to win the world to believe them. It commended itself to those whom scientific discovery was driving to unwilling agnosticism. And, of course, it commended itself to materialists who had not yet made a dogma of materialism.

In the late Georgian Church there was little of such liberalism. People were divided into Low Church Evangelicals and old-fashioned 'High and Dry'. By the 1830s the great Evangelical movement was, as W. S. Lilly says, 'perishing of intellectual inanition. Beginning, in Apostolic wise, with 'the foolishness of preaching, it had ended unapostolically in the preaching of foolishness.' The evangelical tea-parties, revelations, prophecies, jumping, shaking and speaking in strange tongues which went on in England in those days within and without the Church, make fascinating reading. But they have left no enduring architectural monument, except for some of buildings belonging to the Catholic Apostolic Church. The other party in the Church of England, the 'high and dry', was orthodox and uninspiring. Once a quarter, after preparing themselves by means of those Queen Anne and Georgian manuals of devotion which we sometimes find bound up in old prayer books, its members moved through the chancel screen on Sacrament Sunday to partake of the outward and visible signs of inward and spiritual grace. Their parsons wore the surplice and the wig, and abhorred change. They were not quite so negative as they are made out to be. There are several instances in the late 18th and early 19th centuries of screens being erected across chancels to shut off from the nave the place where the Sacrament was partaken.

The Church of England at this time drew its ministers from men who were scholars or gentlemen, usually both. Harriet Martineau's acid biography of Bishop Blomfield (1786–1857) in her *Biographical Sketches*, rather cattily says:

'In those days, a divine rose in the Church in one of two ways, – by his classical reputation, or by aristocratic connection. Mr. Blomfield was a fine scholar; . . .'

Let us try to put ourselves into the frame of mind of somebody living in the reign of King William IV. Let us suppose him just come down from Oxford and still in touch with his University. The grand tour was no longer so fashionable. A squire's son usually went abroad for sport. Few came back with works of art for the adornment of their parks or saloons. Most country house libraries stop at the end of George IV's reign, except for the addition of sporting books and works of reference on husbandry, law and pedigrees of family and livestock. A studious man, such as we have in mind, would have turned his attention to antiquity and history. The novels of Scott would have given him a taste for England's past. The antiquarian publications of Britton would have reinforced it. In Gothic England he would have found much to admire. And the people of his village were still the product of agricultural feudalism. Tenantry bobbed, and even artisans touched their hats. Blasphemy shocked people, for many believed that Christ was the Incarnate Son of God.

Our young man would undoubtedly read *The Christian Year* by the Reverend John Keble (1827). It is hard to see today how this simple and unexciting, oft-reprinted book could have fired so many minds. Perhaps the saintly life of the author, who had thrown up academic honours and comfort to live among simple villagers as their minister, had something to do with it. At any rate, Newman regarded that book as the foundation of the Tractarian movement. The verses of *The Christian Year* were a series composed to fit in with the feasts, fasts and offices of the Book of Common Prayer. They drew people back to the Prayer Book's Catholic teaching, and emphasised the sacramental nature of the Established Church. And the *Tracts for the Times* which followed, from Keble's Assize Sermon of 1833 up to Tract XC by Newman on the Thirty-nine Articles in 1841, would certainly influence him greatly. In these he would learn how the Church was finding herself part of the Catholic Church. Although many great men, greatest of all Newman, have left her for the Church of Rome, others remained faithful. Their witness in England in the last century is apparent in the hundreds of churches which were built on Tractarian principles in new suburbs and towns, in the church schools, public and elementary, in the Sisterhood buildings, in the houses of rest erected by good people of the kind one reads about in the novels of Charlotte M. Yonge, who was herself a parishioner and friend of Keble.

English architecture was also beginning a new phase of professionalism in the reign of William IV. Architects had in the past been regarded either as builders or as semi-amateurs who left the details of their designs to masons and plasterers. There had been great architects since the time of Wren. There was also a host of lesser men who in domestic work were pursuing their local styles and imitating the splendid designs of the metropolis, rather as village builders in monastic times had tried to reproduce in village churches the latest styles at the abbeys. But for years now architecture had been becoming a profession. Architects designed buildings and produced their own beautiful, detailed drawings. Less was left to the builder and the gifted amateur. In 1837 the Institute of British Architects was incorporated by Royal Charter. Architects were by now rather more like doctors and lawyers than artists.

The most influential was Augustus Welby Northmore Pugin (1812–52), who was said by his doctor to have crammed into his forty years of existence the work of a hundred years. Pugin's life has been entertainingly described by his contemporary Benjamin Ferrey in *Recollections of Augustus Welby Pugin*, 1861, and lately his life has been written by Michael Trappes-Lomax, who stresses his Roman Catholicism. Sir Kenneth Clark in *The Gothic Revival*, the Revd. B. F. L. Clarke in *Nineteenth Century Churchbuilders*, and John Summerson in an essay in *The Architectural Review* (April 1948), have all written most illuminatingly about him.

In 1841 Pugin published his *Contrasts* and his *True Principles of Christian Architecture*. Herein he caricatured in skilful drawings the false Gothick of the Strawberry Hill type, and lampooned everything that was classical. To contrast with these he made beautiful shaded drawings of medieval buildings, particularly those of the late 14th century. He did not confine his caricatures to architecture, and peopled the foregrounds with figures. In front of pagan or classical buildings he drew indolent policemen, vulgar tradesmen and miserable beggars; before the medieval buildings he drew vested priests and pious pilgrims. He idealised the middle ages. His drawings were sincere but unfair. The prose accompaniment to them is glowing and witty.

Pugin's own churches, which were almost all Roman Catholic, are attempts to realise his dreams. But for all the sincerity of their architect, the brass coronals, the jewelled glass by Hardman of Birmingham, the correctly moulded arches and the carefully carved woodwork have a spindly effect. St. Chad's Roman Catholic Cathedral at Birmingham, St. Augustine's Church, Ramsgate, and St. Giles's, Cheadle, are exceptions. It is not in his buildings but in his writing that Pugin had so great an influence on the men of his time.

Pugin is sometimes supposed to have joined the Church of Rome for aesthetic reasons only. It is true that he saw in it the survival of the Middle Ages to which he desired the world to return. But the Roman Catholics of his time were not whole-heartedly in favour of the Gothic style he advocated, and to his annoyance continued to build in the classic style of the continent or else in the plaster-thin Gothick he despised. The Church of England, newly awakened to its Catholicism, took more kindly to his doctrines, so that although he came in for some mild criticism from *The Ecclesiologist* (the organ first of the Cambridge Camden Society, and from 1845 of Catholic-minded Anglicans in general), Pugin contemplated writing an essay called: 'An Apology for the separated Church of England since the reign of the Eighth Henry. Written with every feeling of Christian charity for her Children, and honour of the glorious men she continued to produce in evil times. By A. Welby Pugin, many years a Catholic-minded son of the Anglican Church, and still an affectionate and loving brother of the true sons of England's church.'

I do not think it was solely for aesthetic reasons, or even for doctrinal reasons, that Pugin joined the Church of Rome. He possessed what we now call a 'social conscience'. He deplored the slums he saw building round him. He abhorred the soullessness of machinery, and revered hand craftsmanship. His drawings of industrial towns contrasted with a dream-like Middle Ages, his satire on the wealthy ostentation of a merchant's house – 'On one side of the house machicolated parapets, embrasures, bastions, and all the show of strong defence, and round the corner of the building a conservatory leading to the principal rooms, through which a whole company of horsemen might penetrate at one smash into the heart of the mansion! – for who would hammer against nailed portals when he could kick his way through the greenhouse?' – are summed up in the two principles of Gothic or Christian architecture which he delivered to the world. These are they. 'First, that there should be no features about a building which are not necessary for convenience, construction, or propriety; second, that all ornament should consist of enrichment of the essential construction of the building.' Pugin's principles, and his conviction that the only style that was Christian was Gothic, are fathered by popular opinion on Ruskin. But Ruskin was not fond of Pugin. He disliked his Popery, and he thought little of his buildings. If one must find a successor to Pugin, it is the atheist William Morris. Both men liked simplicity and good craftsmanship. Both had a 'social conscience'. Pugin dreamed of a Christian world, Morris of a Socialist world, but both their worlds were dreams.

Let us imagine our young man again, now become a Tractarian clergyman. His convictions about how best to honour the God he loves, and how to spread that love among the artisans in the poorer part of his parish, are likely to take form in a new church. And, since he is a Tractarian, it must be a beautiful church. His reading of Pugin, the publications of the Cambridge Camden Society and *The Ecclesiologist*, will have inspired him. He will have no truck with the cheap Gothic or Norman Revival of the Evangelical school. A pamphlet such as that of the Revd. W. Carus Wilson's *Helps to the Building of Churches, Parsonage Houses and Schools* (2nd Edition, Kirby Lonsdale, 1842) will have disgusted him. Here we find just the sort of thing Pugin satirised: 'A very neat portable font has been given to the new church at Stonyhurst, which answers every purpose; not requiring even the expense of a stand; as it might be placed, when wanted, on the Communion Table from which the ceremony might be performed. The price is fourteen shillings; and it is to be had at Sharper's, Pall Mall East, London.' Such cheese-paring our clergyman would leave to the extreme Protestants who thought ostentation, stained glass, frontals, lecterns and banners smacked of Popery, and who thought with Dean Close of Cheltenham that 'the Restoration of Churches is the Restoration of Popery'. This explains why, to this day, unrestored churches with box-pews are generally Evangelical and locked. But the Evangelical did not wholly reject Gothic. Ullenhall (Warwicks) and Itchen Stoke (Hants) are Victorian Gothic churches designed to have the Table well away from the East wall and the lectern and pulpit dominant. Ullenhall retains its Protestant arrangement, and this arrangement was originally, we must remember, the 'High Church' of the 17th and 18th centuries. The Early English style was regarded as plain and primitive. Very few churches were built in a classic style between 1840 and 1900. The choice before young vicar is no longer Gothic or Classic, but what sort of Gothic?

Architects were turning their attention to churches. And the younger men were all for Gothic. Most architects were God-fearing folk of the new middle class. They felt privileged to build churches to the glory of God. Many of them were instructed in theology; they subscribed to *The Ecclesiologist* and to various learned antiquarian publications. They delighted to discuss the merits of Norman, and Decorated, Early English and Perpendicular, or Early, Middle and Late Pointed, according to which terminology they favoured. In the early 'forties they were still following Pugin. Pugin's chief Anglican equivalents were Benjamin Ferrey, Carpenter and Gilbert Scott. These men, and many others, were capable of making very good imitations of a medieval fabric. With the aid of the numerous books of measured drawings that were appearing, it was possible to erect almost exact copies of such famous monuments of the Middle Ages as the spire at Louth, the tracery of the Angel Choir at Lincoln, and the roof of Westminster Hall. The scale was different it is true, and architects had no compunction about mixing copies of what they considered the 'best' features of old churches in their new ones. They thought that a blend of the best everywhere would make something better still.

The earlier Gothic revival churches, that is to say those of late Georgian times, were in the late 14th-century style. One may see in some prim and spacious Georgian square, brick imitations of King's College Chapel with Bathstone dressings. But in the 1840s architects were attaching moral properties to Gothic styles. Pugin had started the idea and his successors surpassed him. Since Gothic was the perfect style, what was the perfect style of Gothic? I do not know who it was who started the theory that early Gothic is crude, middle is perfection, and late is debased. But – certainly from the middle of the 1840s, this theory was held by most of the rising young church architects. Promoters of new churches who could afford it, were advised to have something in the Middle Pointed or Decorated style. This is the reason why in mid-Victorian suburbs, while speculative builders were still erecting Italianate stucco mansions, in the last stuccoed gasp of the Georgian classic tradition – South Kensington and Pimlico in London are examples – the spire of Ketton or Louth soars above the chimney-pots, and a sudden break in the Palladian plaster terraces shews the irregular stone front, gabled porch and curvilinear tracery of a church in the Decorated style. Church architecture was setting the fashion which the builders followed, and decades later, even employing church architects (such as Ferrey at Bournemouth), they erected Gothic residences in the new winding avenues of housing estates for the upper middle classes. Most of the work of the late 'forties and early 'fifties was in this copying style. When an architect had a sense of proportion, there were often impressive results. Carpenter and his son and their partner Slater were always good. Their Lancing School Chapel must be regarded as one of the finest Gothic buildings of any period in England, and their London church of St. Mary Magdalen, Munster Square, so modest outside, is spacious and awe-inspiring within.

The most famous copyist was Gilbert Scott. He and his family have had a great influence on English architecture over the past century. Gilbert Scott was the son of a Buckinghamshire parson, the grandson of the Calvinist clergyman Thomas Scott, whose Commentary on the Bible greatly influenced Newman as a youth. There is no doubt of Scott's passionate affection for Gothic architecture. He pays a handsome tribute to Pugin's influence on his mind: 'Pugin's articles excited me almost to fury, and I suddenly found myself like a person awakened from a long, feverish dream, which had rendered him unconscious of what was going on about him.'

Our young clergyman would almost certainly have applied to Gilbert Scott for his new church. He would have received designs from Scott's office. They would have been a safe, correct, essay in the middle pointed style, with tower and spire or with bellcot only, according to the price. Scott himself, except when he first started in private practice, may not have had much to do with the design. He collected an enormous staff, and from his office emerged, it is said, over seven hundred and forty buildings between 1847 and 1878 when he died. When one considers that an architect in private practice today thinks himself busy if he has seven new buildings to do in a decade, it seems probable that Scott eventually became little more than an overseer of all but his most important work. His 'restorations' were numerous and usually disastrous.

Yet Scott, who was eventually knighted for his vast output, had a style of his own – a square abacus to his columns, plate tracery in the windows, much stone foliage mixed up with heads, and for east or west windows, three equal lancets with a round window above them. In five churches of his, St. Giles, Camberwell; St. George's, Doncaster; Leafield, Oxon; Bradfield, Berks, and St. Anne, Alderney, I can trace it clearly. He liked to build something big. He dispensed with a chancel screen. Instead of this, he often interposed between the congregation in the nave and the rich chancel, a tower or transept crossing which was either darker or lighter than the parts it separated. Add to this a sure sense of proportion and a workmanlike use of stone, and the dull mechanical details of his work are forgotten in the mystery and splendour of the interior effect. Scott realised some of Pugin's dreams for him. But he never did more. He was at heart a copyist and not a thinker in Gothic.

Church architecture by the 'fifties was very much an affair of personalities. The big London men and a few in the provinces had their individual styles. As Sir Charles Nicholson remarked in his comments on Henry Woodyer's beautiful building St. Michael's College, Tenbury (1856), which was designed as a church choir school: 'It was never, of course, intended that the College should be mistaken for anything other than a 19th-century building: for Gothic revival architects did not attempt such follies, though their enemies accused them of doing so.' What is true of St. Michael's College, Tenbury, is true also of most of the churches built in England after 1850. The chief of those architects who 'thought in Gothic' are listed below.

William Butterfield (1814–1900) was the most severe and interesting of them. He first startled the world in 1849 with his design for All Saints', Margaret Street, London, built on the cramped site of an 18th-century proprietary chapel where lights had been used on the altar since 1839, and a sung celebration of the Holy Communion introduced. All Saints' embodies architectural theories which Butterfield employed in most of his other churches throughout his long life. It is constructed of the material which builders in the district were accustomed to use, which in London at that time was brick. Since bricks do not lend themselves to the carving which is expected of a Gothic building, Butterfield varied his flat brick surfaces with bands of colour, both within and without. In those days the erroneous impression prevailed that Gothic decoration grew more elaborate the higher it was on a building. The patterns of bricks in Butterfield's buildings grew, therefore, more diversified and frequent towards the tops of walls, towers and steeples. But their arrangement is not usually capricious as it is in the work of some of the rather comic church architects who copied him, like Bassett Keeling. Where walls supported a great weight, they were striped horizontally, where they were mere screen walls, diaper patterns of bricks were introduced. Inside his churches Butterfield delighted to use every coloured stone, marble and other material he could find for the money at his disposal. He was a severely practical man, and a planner and constructor first. His decoration was meant to emphasise his construction.

The plan of All Saints' is in the latest Tractarian manner of its time. The high altar is visible from every part of the church. Indeed to this day not even the delicate and marked style of Sir Ninian Comper's side altar in the north aisle takes one's eye from the chancel. Butterfield disapproved of side altars and never made provision for them in his churches. The chancel is the richest part of the building, and the chancel arch, higher than the arcades of the nave, gives it an effect of greater loftiness than it possesses. There is, of course, no screen. The other prominent feature of any Butterfield church is the font. That sentence in the Catechism on the number of Sacraments, 'Two only, as generally necessary to salvation, that is to say Baptism, and the Supper of the Lord', is almost spoken aloud by a Butterfield church; altar and font are the chief things we see. But when we look up at arches and roofs, we see Butterfield the builder with his delight in construction. His roofs are described by that fine writer Sir John Summerson as 'like huge, ingenious toys'. The phrase is as memorable as all Butterfield's roofs, of which the ingenuity and variety seem to have been the only sportiveness he permitted himself.

In person Butterfield was a silent, forbidding man who looked like Mr. Gladstone. He was an earnest Tractarian with a horror of everything outside the liturgy of the Book of Common Prayer. Except for one Nonconformist chapel in Bristol, designed when he was a youth, and unlike the rest of his work, he built only for Tractarians. He supplied no attractive drawings to tempt clients. He was a strong disciplinarian in his office, and on the building site, scaffolding and ladders had to be dusted before he ascended to see the work in progress. He was averse to all publicity and show, and had little to do with any other architects. People had to take Butterfield or leave him. And so must we. Yet no one who has an eye for plan, construction and that sense of proportion which is the essential of all good architecture, can see a Butterfield church without being compelled to admire it, even if he cannot like it.

George Edmund Street, R.A. (1824–81), is chiefly remembered now for the Law Courts in London. He was in Gilbert Scott's office before setting up on his own. Early in his career he received the patronage of such distinguished High Churchmen as Prynne, Butler of Wantage, and Bishop Wilberforce of Oxford. Street himself was a Tractarian, singing in the choir at Wantage and disapproving of ritual without doctrine. The churches he built in the late 'fifties and throughout the 'sixties, often with schools and parsonages alongside them, are like his character, straightforward and convinced. They are shorn of those 'picturesque' details beloved of the usual run of architects of the time. The plan of Street's buildings is immediately apparent from the exterior. Some of his village schools of local stone built early in his career in the Oxford Diocese are so simple and well-proportioned, and fit so naturally into the landscape, that they might be the sophisticated Cotswold work of such 1900 architects as Ernest Gimson and F. L. Griggs. Street's churches are built on the same principles as those of Butterfield, one altar only, and that visible from all parts of the church, a rich east end, and much westward light into the nave. Street had a sure sense of proportion, very much his own; his work, whether it is a lectern or a pulpit or a spire, is massive, and there is nothing mean about it nor over-decorated. This massive quality of his work made Street a bad restorer of old buildings, for he would boldly pull down a chancel and rebuild it in his own style. He was a great enthusiast for the arts and crafts. With his own hands he is said to have made the wooden staircase for West Challow Vicarage in Berkshire. His ironwork was drawn out in section as well as outline, and there were some caustic comments written by him in the margin of his copy of Gilbert Scott's *Personal and Professional Recollections* (in the R.I.B.A. Library) where Scott confesses to leaving the detail of his ironwork to Skidmore of Coventry, the manufacturer. Street was an able sketcher of architecture, and clearly a man who could fire his pupils with his own enthusiasm, even though he never allowed those pupils a free hand in design, doing everything down to the smallest details himself. Street's influence on English architecture is properly appreciated in H. S. Goodhart Rendel's *English Architecture Since the Regency*. It comes down to us through his pupils, among whom were Philip Webb and Norman Shaw, whose domestic architecture brought about the small house of today, William Morris, to whom the Arts and Crafts Movement owes so much, and J. D. Sedding, the church architect and craftsman.

The third of the great mid-Victorian church builders was John Loughborough Pearson (1817–97). His later buildings are of all Victorian churches those we like best today. He was, like Street and Butterfield, a Tractarian. Before designing a building he gave himself to prayer and receiving the Sacrament. He seems to have been a more 'advanced' churchman than his two comparable contemporaries, for in his later churches he made ample provision for side altars, and even for a tabernacle for the reservation of the Blessed Sacrament. Pearson was articled in Durham to Ignatius Bonomi, the son of an elegant 18th-century architect. His early work in Yorkshire is competent copying of the medieval, and just distinguishable from the work of Gilbert Scott. But somewhere about 1860 he paid a visit to France, and early French Gothic vaulting seems to have transformed him. He built St. Peter's, Vauxhall, London, in 1862. Like most of his later work it is a cruciform building with brick vaulted throughout and with a clerestory. St. Peter's seems to have been the pattern of which all his subsequent churches were slight variants. Sometimes he threw out side chapels, sometimes he made aisles under buttresses. The Pearson style was an Early English Gothic with deep mouldings and sharply-pointed arches; brick was usually employed for walls and vaulting, stone for ribs, columns, arches and window tracery. Pearson also took great trouble with skyline, and his spires, flèches and roofs form beautiful groups from any angle.

One more individualistic Gothic revivalist was William Burges (1827–81), who was as much a domestic architect and a furniture designer as an ecclesiastical man. He delighted in colour and quaintness, but being the son of an engineer, his work had a solidity of structure which saved it from ostentation. His east end of Waltham Abbey and his cathedral of St. Finbar, Cork, are his most beautiful church work, though Skelton and Studley Royal, both in Yorkshire, are overpowering in their rich colour and decoration, and very original in an early French Gothic manner.

Neither Butterfield, Street, Pearson nor Burges would have thought of copying old precedents. They had styles of their own which they had devised for themselves, continuing from the medieval Gothic but not copying it.

These big men had their imitators: Bassett Keeling who reproduced the wildest excesses of the polychromatic brick style and mixed it with cast-iron construction; S. S. Teulon who, in his youth, did the same thing; E. Buckton Lamb who invented a style of his own; Henry Woodyer who had a fanciful, spindly Gothic style which is original and marked; William White and Henry Clutton, both of whom produced churches, strong and modern for their times; Ewan Christian, the Evangelical architect, who could imitate the style of Pearson; or that best of the lesser men, James Brooks who built several 'big-boned' churches in East London in a plainer Pearson-esque manner. There was also the scholarly work in Italian Gothic of E. W. Godwin, and Sir Arthur Blomfield could turn out an impressive church in almost any style.

There is no doubt that until about 1870 the impetus of vigorous Victorian architecture went into church building. Churches took the lead in construction and in use of materials. They employed the artists, and many of the best pictures of the time had sacred subjects. The difficulties in which artists found themselves, torn between Anglo-Catholicism, Romanism and Ruskin's Protestantism, is described well in John Steegman's *Consort of Taste*.

After the 'seventies, Norman Shaw, himself a High Churchman, became the leading domestic architect. The younger architects turned their invention to house design and building small houses for people of moderate income. Bedford Park was laid out by Norman Shaw in 1878. It was a revolution – a cluster of picturesque houses for artistic suburbanites. And from this time onwards we have a series of artistic churches, less vulgar and vigorous than the work of the now ageing great men, but in their way distinguished: slender, tapering work, palely enriched within in Burne-Jonesian greens and browns. The Middle Pointed or Decorated style and variants of it were no longer thought the only correct styles. People began to admire what was 'late' and what was 'English', and the neglected glory of Perpendicular, long called 'debased', was revived, and even the Renaissance style was used. For as the Reverend B. F. L. Clarke says in his *Church Builders of the Nineteenth Century*, 'the question of Style was coming to be regarded as being of small importance'.

The last quarter of the 19th century was a time when the Tractarian movement firmly established itself. Of the eight Religious Communities for men of the Anglican Church, six were of the 1890s, and one, the 'Cowley Fathers' (Society of St. John the Evangelist), was founded in 1865. Of the forty-five Communities for women, the first two, the Society of the Holy and Undivided Trinity and the Society of the Most Holy Trinity, Ascot, were founded in 1845, and well over half the rest are of Victorian origin. There are now in the Church of England more religious Communities than there were in medieval England, and this does not include Communities in Scotland, Wales, Ireland, America, Asia, Africa and Australia.

This was a time when the church was concerning herself with social problems, and building many new churches in England as well as establishing dioceses abroad. Many, and often ugly, little churches were built of brick in brand new suburbs. Cathedral-like buildings, subscribed for by the pious from wealthy parishes, were built in the slums. At the back of *Crockford's Clerical Directory* there is an index of English parishes with the dates of their formation. If you look up an average industrial town with, say, ten churches, you will find that the majority will have been built during the last half of the 19th century. Oldest will be the parish church, probably medieval. Next there will be a late Georgian church built by the Commissioners. Then there will be three built between 1850 and 1870, three built between 1870 and 1900, and two since then, probably after the 1914 war and in new suburbs.

It is entertaining, and not completely safe, to generalise on the inner story of the Church and its building in Victorian and later times. In, let us say, 1850, the vicar of the parish church had become a little old for active work, and left much to his curates. His churchmanship took the form mainly of support for the Establishment and hostility to Dissent. The word 'Dissenters' applied to Nonconformists always had a faint note of contempt. Methodists and Baptists, were building chapels all over the rapidly growing town. Their religion of personal experience of salvation, of hymn-singing, ejaculations of praise; the promise of a golden heaven after death as a reward for a sad life down here in the crowded misery of back streets, disease and gnawing poverty; their weekday socials and clubs which welded the membership of the chapels in a Puritan bond of teetotalism, and non-gambling, non-smoking and well-doing: these had an appeal which today is largely dispersed into the manufactured day-dreams of the cinema and the less useful social life of the dance hall and sports club. Chapels were crowded, gas-lights flamed on popular preachers, and steamy windows resounded to the cries of 'Alleluia, Jesus saves!' A simple ceremony like total immersion or Breaking of Bread was something all the tired and poor could easily understand, after their long hours of misery in gloomy mills. Above all, the Nonconformists turned people's minds and hearts to Jesus as a personal Friend of all, especially the poor. Many a pale mechanic and many a drunkard's wife could remember the very hour of the very day on which, in that street or at that meeting, or by that building, conviction came of the truth of the Gospel, that Jesus was Christ. Then with what flaming heart he or she came to the chapel, and how fervently testified to the message of salvation and cast off the old life of sin.

Beside these simple and genuine experiences of the love of Christ, the old-established Church with its system of pew rents, and set prayers and carefully-guarded sacraments, must have seemed wicked mumbo-jumbo. No wonder the old Vicar was worried about the Dissenters. His parish was increasing by thousands as the factories boomed and the ships took our merchandise across the seas, but his parishioners were not coming to church in proportion. He had no objection therefore when the new Bishop, filled with the zeal for building which seems to have filled all Victorian bishops, decided to form two new parishes out of his own, the original parish of the little village which had become a town in less than a century. The usual method was adopted. Two clergymen were licensed to start the church life of the two new districts. These men were young; one was no doubt a Tractarian; the other was perhaps fired with the Christian Socialism of Charles Kingsley and F. D. Maurice. Neither was much concerned with the establishment of churches as bulwarks against Dissenters, but rather as houses of God among ignorant Pagans, where the Gospel might be heard, the Sacraments administered, want relieved, injustice righted and ignorance dispelled. First came the mission-room, a room licensed for services in the clergyman's lodging, then there was the school, at first a room for Sunday school only, and then came the mission church made of corrugated iron. Then there was an appeal for a church school and for a permanent church. For this church the once young clergyman, now worn after ten years' work, would apply to the Incorporated Church Building Society, and to the Church Building Fund of his own diocese; he would raise money among his poor parishioners, he would give his own money (this was a time when priests were frequently men of means), and pay his own stipend as well. The site for the church would be given by a local landowner, and who knows but that some rich manufacturer whose works were in the parish would subscribe. Whatever their Churchmanship, the new parishes formed in the 'fifties generally had their own church within twenty years.

All this while the Commissioners' Church in the town, that Greek Revival building among the genteel squares where still lived the doctors, attorneys and merchants, had an Evangelical congregation and disapproved of the old 'high and dry' vicar of the parish church. The congregation and incumbent disapproved still more of the goings on of the Tractarian priest in charge of one of the two new districts. He lit two candles on the Table which he called an 'altar', at the service of the Lord's Supper he stood with his back to the congregation instead of at the north end of the Table, he wore a coloured stole over his surplice instead of a black scarf, and he did not preach in a black gown. He was worse than the Pope of Rome or almost as bad. The ignorant artisans were being turned into Roman Catholics. The pure Gospel of the Reformation must be brought to them. So a rival church was built in the Tractarian parish, financed by the Evangelical church people of the town, and from outside by many loyal Britons who throughout England, like Queen Victoria herself, were deploring the Romish tendency in the Established Church.

Many years have passed since this controversy, and the rival Evangelical fane probably has now a clergyman who always wears a surplice and sometimes a coloured stole, who has lights on the altar and faces east to celebrate Holy Communion, while the priest and congregation of the neighbouring Tractarian church, who now have incense, reservation of the Blessed Sacrament, daily mass, confessions and a High Mass on Sundays, still regard him as 'low church'.

If one may generalise about the ecclesiastical works of the last half of the century, when so many new churches were built, so many new dioceses established at home and abroad, one can say this. From the 'forties to the middle 'sixties, the majority of the new churches were built as missions to the poor in towns; from the middle 'sixties until the end of the century, and increasingly since then, most new churches have been built in the suburbs. This is not to say that the poor became neglected. Rich manufacturers, settled down as squires in country near Birmingham, Manchester, Liverpool, London, the Potteries and the East Riding, also often rebuilt their country parish church as did those established landowners who were pious and still wealthy. Hence the many rebuilt churches in the Home Counties, Cheshire, Shropshire, Warwickshire and Worcestershire. The 'Lux Mundi' group of the 'nineties, the Christian Socialism of such men as Father Adderley, Canon Scott Holland and Bishop Gore whose theology emphasised the Incarnation, laid great stress on the idea that the Catholic faith must play a part in the everyday life of factory and shop and not be a matter of Sunday worship only. Thus we find many slum Tractarian parishes building new mission churches on their smoky, overcrowded outskirts, churches with the names of black letter saints in the Calendar who always seem to be 'high': St. Anselm, St. Cyprian, St. Erkenwald, St. Mary Magdalen.

We like to think that the reason for the missions to the suburbs from the middle 'sixties onwards was that there were fewer poor. There may be some truth in this, but the reason lies more in the great growth of the middle classes – clerks, rich wholesalers and retailers, the Pooters, those dear, solid bits of English backbone. Few of them were more than one generation from a country village, and the churchgoing habit was ingrained in them from youth. They are the reason for the tall

Perpendicular walls of St. Philip's Church, in red brick with stone dressings, rising above the oak paling and evergreens where Victoria Drive intersects Tollemache Avenue. The Tollemaches, deriving an unexpected income in house rents from what had been a sandy warren, gave the site; the merchants in the detached houses at the richer end of Victoria Drive gave the woodwork; the rich brewer whose family have by now been absorbed into the country squirearchy gave the stained glass; and either George Gilbert Scott junior, John Olrid Scott, G. F. Bodley, J. D. Sedding, Norman Shaw, or, if it is in the North Country, Austin and Paley, designed the church. These architects were the young men who emerged from the enormous office of Sir Gilbert Scott, or the gay craftsman's studio of Street. They carried the faith of their masters with them. They were generally Tractarians, of a more advanced sort than their masters. They were musical and artistic. They knew such men as Burne Jones and Rossetti, and, much as they abhorred his atheism, they admired the decorative work of Street's pupil William Morris.

I think that the well-spring of this later church architecture is the work of George Gilbert Scott junior, who was a close friend of G. F. Bodley. This talented man was a scholar who wrote that learned and interesting *History of English Church Architecture until the Reformation*. He was not only a medievalist. He was one of the first Victorians to appreciate again the work of the Renaissance. The few churches he built are a foretaste of the work of Bodley and his followers. In 1877 he dared to build St. Agnes, Kennington, London, in the despised Perpendicular style. What is more, he used brick walls, put a screen and rood across the chancel arch, and had a chancel under the same roof as the nave. He designed side chapels for daily services, he had no capitals to the piers in the nave arcades, and he filled the windows with glass by an unknown young artist called Kempe.*

But we can see other churches influenced by the Neo-Perpendicular movement, and many of these are very fine buildings, no more imitations of medieval than were the works of the older Victorians. They are, however, less Victorian than the daring experiments of the 'fifties and 'sixties, and they seem, like the small houses designed by Norman Shaw, to come into our time or at any rate into the 1920s. Because they are near us, we do not appreciate their originality. In our desire to see a new style emerge from new materials, we notice only that the mouldings and fittings are copies of medieval Gothic. We do not realise that the proportions, plan and liturgical arrangement are nothing like our old churches.

See in your mind's eye a church built in the neo-Perpendicular style by G. G. Scott junior, Bodley, W. H. Bidlake of Birmingham, Edgar Wood, Sir Ninian Comper, W. D. Caroe, Sir Charles Nicholson, Temple Moore, J. D. Sedding, Edmund Sedding, Charles Spooner, E. P. Warren, Walter Tapper, Niven and Wigglesworth, Austin and

* This church was destroyed by the Southwark Diocese after war damage.

Paley, to name a few of these later Victorian architects. If you cannot see it, I will try to re-create such a church, and you will remember it in some newish suburb of a provincial town where you stayed with an aunt, or on a holiday in the outskirts of a south-coast watering place, and you can read of it in Compton Mackenzie's *Sinister Street*. 'Ting-ting' the single bell calls to Sung Eucharist, because the tower, designed for a full peal of bells, was never completed. Rather gaunt without it, the church rises above the privet and forsythia and prunus of its little garden, for there is no churchyard to these churches; we have reached the era of municipal cemeteries, and it is in their marble acres that the dead of this new parish are to be found. Inside the church, the tall nave is filled with chairs, and the narrow aisles are not used on a Sunday, as they give a view only of side altars where the weekday Celebrations and the very early Sunday masses are said. The floor is of oak blocks, the walls are cream and clean, the woodwork of the thick Devonshire style chancel screen, carved by Harry Hems of Exeter, is unstained. In more recent times a coloured statue of Our Lady under a gilded canopy is seen against one of the eastern-most pillars of the nave. Through the screen we glimpse a huge reredos painted green and red and gold, with folding doors. The high altar has a purple frontal, because just now it is Lent. The floor of the sanctuary is paved with black-and-white marble. Riddel posts with gilt angels on them – the famous 'English altar' introduced by Sir Ninian Comper in the 'eighties – hold curtains round the north, south and east of the side altars. The windows are filled with greenish glass in which are patches of dark blue, red and gold. These are the work of Kempe, and they allow more light into the church than earlier Victorian windows. The chief beauty of the church is its proportion. These architects favoured two kinds of proportion when they were building in the Gothic style – almost all of them designed Byzantine and classic churches as well – and they were either height and narrowness, or breadth and length. Their churches either soar or spread.

The Sung Eucharist is probably from the Prayer Book and with a crowd of acolytes at the altar. Blue incense rises to the golden reredos and the green Kempe window. The English Hymnal is used, and plainsong or more probably, Eyre in E♭ or Tours in C. Candlelights twinkle in the mist. The purple Lenten chasuble of the priest is worn over amice, alb, stole and maniple, and there is discussion of these things after the service and before among servers and the initiated. We are in a world which feels itself in touch with the Middle Ages and with today. This is English Catholicism. There is much talk of Percy Dearmer, correct furnishings and vestments, the Prayer Book and how far one is justified in departing from it. After church the acolytes in their Sunday suits hang round the porch, and the young curates too, and there is a good deal of backslapping and chaff. For months the Mothers' Union and the women's guilds of the church have been working on banners and a frontal to be ready for Easter. From these suburban parishes much of the Church life of modern England has sprung. They have trained their people in faith and the liturgy, they have produced many of the overseas missionaries and parish priests of today.

We are in modern times, out of the older and rich suburbs with their garden city atmosphere of guild craftsmen and Sarum Use, and into the big building estates. These large areas of semi-detached houses, built by private speculators or councils, have been eating up our agricultural land since 1920. They have been brought about by the change in transport from steam to motor-bus and electric train. People are moving out of the crowded early Victorian industrial lanes and terraces, into little houses of their own, each with its little patch of garden at the back and front, each isolated from its neighbour by social convention, in districts where miles of pavement enlivened by the squeak of perambulators lead to a far-off bus route and parade of chain stores, and a distant vita-glass school, used as a Community Centre in the evenings. To these places, often lonely for all the people in them, is the new mission Church.

Just as there is today no definite modern style in England, except in what is impermanent – exhibition buildings, prefabs, holiday camps and the like, so there is no definite modern church style. In the period between the two wars church architects were too often concerned with style, and they built places of worship which vied with the local Odeon or with by-pass modern factories in trying to be 'contemporary'. They now look dated, and will, I fear, never look beautiful. But the purpose of the church remains the same as it was at the beginning of this book, to be a place where the Faith is taught and the Sacraments are administered.

Bedfordshire

INTRODUCTION

THE NORTH-BOUND train traveller from St. Pancras retains a poor impression of Bedfordshire, the verdict generally being one of flat Midland scenery, at its most unrelieved; this is as unfair as it is uninformed. However, it must be admitted at once that the central clay vale is a wilderness, raped for brick-making, and with a similar fate awaiting still virgin land. Otherwise the county, for its limited area, is varied to a degree that is unique. In the north the Ouse winds through a landscape of gracious tranquillity, a summer country of stone villages and broad water meadows which rises in the north east to a continuation of Walpole's 'dumpling hills' of Northamptonshire. This is often surprisingly lonely country and though the woods are now few and far between, the ghost of the old 'Bruneswald' forest still haunts the land.

In the centre of the county lies the Greensand ridge, a corridor of fifteen miles which Hoskins in his *Midland England* considers as 'unsurpassed in sanctity and peculiar purity'; it broadens in the west to the ducal country of Woburn, scenically magnificent with pinewoods and open heaths. In the east, being in part overlaid by clay and dissected by the River Ivel, the scenery is even more varied and the several estate villages must surely be the *genius loci* of the 'cottage orné', in particular Old Warden which retains a delightful Victorian picture-book quality almost unimpaired.

Beyond the Greensand the Gault clay valley is a prelude to the chalk hills, and, save around Toddington where a considerable elevation is reached, is subdued to them, it is largely unspoiled country, much of it formerly marsh of which Flitwick Moor remains as a fragment. There are one or two chalk outliers in the valley of which Shillington church hill is the most renowned, and Billington the most beautiful.

The chalk reaches its greatest development at Dunstable, but its greatest beauty in the folded coombes and open windswept downs around Barton. At Totternhoe Knolls, a promontory of the lower chalk overlooking the vast Aylesbury Vale and the line of the Chilterns to the west, lies the site of the old quarries that gave to this area a building stone of poor external weathering quality, but one which served as inspiration for a local school of 13th-century carving, little known, but of high artistic merit.

Luton forms an industrial and suburban area 'as unexpected as it is unprepossessing', and with the dreadful tentacle that links it to Dunstable has straddled a large area of the foothills to the Downs. Much of the surrounding countryside is losing the battle against Suburbia, and unforgivable crimes have been committed in the hills, the worst perhaps the cutting of the skyline in the new chalk quarry at Totternhoe. In spite of all this, however, much charming country remains, particularly around Studham and Kensworth where at 700 feet the chalk attains its highest elevation in the county.

The varied geology of Bedfordshire is echoed in the variety of its churches; in the north of the county the influence of the Northamptonshire masons appears in the number of stone spires, fine ashlar masonry, and the use of the ferruginous brown stone which has been the scenic ruin of the iron mining districts of the neighbour county. Wymington is the finest example, but Swineshead, Podington, Keysoe, Colmworth and Pertenhall have churches of very great merit. Two of the grandest buildings in the county, Felmersham church of the 13th century, and Odell of the 15th, lie in this area. The sandstone country has contributed a building stone which gives great character to the churches of the district, Tingrith, Flitton and Northill are the most perfect examples, and at Husborne Crawley church the stonework in the tower is from the strata that gave the hills their name, being all shades of deep green, from a brilliant malachite to an almost navy blue. The churches of the south of the county are sometimes not very convincing from the outside since the Totternhoe stone has often weathered so badly that they have been encased in 19th-century cement plaster with frightful aesthetic results. Flint used in chequerboard pattern with clunch is a feature here and there, and a very attractive one. The showplaces of the area are Dunstable priory, and the churches of Leighton Buzzard, Eaton Bray and St. Mary's, Luton.

Bedfordshire has lain far enough from London to escape the overbuilding of, for example, Hertfordshire, and in consequence Victorian church building is limited to Luton and one or two examples connected with the big estates, of which Clutton's magnificent St. Mary's Woburn, is outstanding. Butterfield did a little work at Milton Ernest church, doubtless while engaged on his work at the Hall. Scott gave Turvey church a chancel which it would be a euphemism to call a vigorous example of his mature style; more suitable to some rich inner London suburb than a village church, it is saved by impeccable craftsmanship, and a Colleyweston roof. Scott also worked at Eversholt in 1864 but on a more limited scale. There is one building that must be seen by those who like their Victorian architecture 'neat', and that is the Bury Park Congregational church of 1895, an early example of *art nouveau Gothic* which is one of Luton's many architectural surprises; it is difficult to imagine it ever having been on paper! There is one interesting 20th-century church, St. Andrew's, Blenheim Crescent, Luton, a fine work by Sir Giles Gilbert Scott in his Cambridge University library manner, red brick and pantile roofs.

There has been a certain amount of ill-considered church restoration in the county, for example certain palpable falsities at Felmersham, referred to in the lists, but in the main, save for the barbarous rebuilding of Cardington, the county has been well served by its church restorers. Professor Richardson's rebuilding of Eaton Socon after the fire must rank as an achievement of a very high order, and the same may be said of his restorations at Streatley and elsewhere. **B.W.**

SELECTED LIST OF CHURCHES

by Bernard West, A.R.I.B.A.

AMPTHILL (*St. Andrew*)
Close-like setting; small; 14th-cent. arcades and chancel arch; Ashburnham pew by Hawkesmoor.

BARTON-LE-CLEY (*St. Nicholas*)
Oasis in housing estate under chalk hills; 15th and 17th cent. pews.

BEDFORD (*St. Mary*)
Central tower 12th cent.; plaster and whitewash interior of simple Protestant charm.

***(St. Paul*)
This, the largest church in Bedford, is in its final form mainly a work of the 19th and early 20th centuries, but its magnificent silhouette and striking scale justifies the process. The S. aisle with its porch is medieval, the former, a fine two-storied structure of the 15th century. It is from this side that one first appreciates that the building is a 'hall church', its clerestory windows being directly over those of the aisles. The N. aisle is in part a reconstruction of the old N. wall, and the N. arcade is a copy of the S.

The tower and spire are modern, a somewhat enriched reconstruction of an original 14th-century feature. The modern W. door a slightly anachronistic combination of 14th and 15th century details, is very fine in effect. F. C. Eden did much to improve the interior, and the chancel is now a model of rubrical correctness.

BIGGLESWADE (*St. Andrew*)
Porch; 18th-cent. tower.

BLUNHAM (*St. Edmund*)
Massive yet delicate sandstone and limestone tower in thatch and whitewash village.

BROMHAM (*St. Owen*)
Parkland setting; 17th cent.; alabaster tomb; triple brass in chancel.

CARLTON (*St. Mary the Virgin*)
Delightful small chancel screen 15th cent.; pews.

CHALGRAVE *(All Saints*)
Isolated site on plateau overlooking the Chiltern hills. A wonderful unspoiled interior, no doubt due to its poverty. The 13th-century carving of nave arcade capitals is very fine and belongs to the Totternhoe stone group mentioned later. There are 15th-century traceried bench ends in the old pewing. The tower has been reduced in height consequent on the failure of the Totternhoe stone as at Eaton Bray. Wall paintings.

CLAPHAM (*St. Thomas of Canterbury*)
Enormous Saxon 'look-out' tower.

COCKAYNE HATLEY (*St. John*)
Carved stalls, 1689, from French abbey; continental panelling to chancel; pulpit, 1559, from Antwerp.

COLMWORTH (*St. Denis*)
Prominent 15th-cent. building; spire; fine proportions.

COPLE (*All Saints*)
Attractive village; 15th-cent. screen; 16th-cent. pews and chapels.

DEAN *(All Saints*)
In the very north of the county, the village is scattered but unspoiled and embowered in trees. The church is perfect, at the time of the writing of the Victoria County Histories it was on the way to becoming derelict, but survived to a time when conservation was preferred to restoration, so that a perfect country interior remains intact. The roofs are all 15th century and wonderful specimens of their time, they belong to the remodelling of the church in the 15th century when only the 13th-century chancel arch, and the 14th-century tower and spire were retained. All the pewing is old, and fine screens remain at the W. end of both chapels, and also across the chancel arch.

DUNSTABLE PRIORY *(St. Peter*)
This truncated fragment of a once great church still has a grandeur, particularly in its fine Norman nave of 1150 which makes

the disappearance of the eastern parts a tragedy. The W. front is a magnificent makeshift, Norman and Early English in combination, of which the most lovely feature is the N.W. door, a sumptuous 13th-century creation loaded with ornament. The whole front has been most conservatively restored, originally by Bodley in 1900, and later by Professor Richardson. Perhaps the most scholarly thing in the whole church is the recreation of the Norman vaulting of the S. aisle, a restoration based upon the original survival of three bays at the E. end, as shown in plan in Worthington G. Smith's *Dunstable*. How much of the original material has been re-used it is hard to tell, but the general effect greatly enhances the monastic character of the building.

EATON BRAY *(St. Mary the Virgin)*
Externally a complete 15th-century reconstruction and a simple modern W. tower effectively conceal an interior, the core of the original 13th-century building which has nave arcades of absolute and quite unexpected magnificence. That on the N. is the richer, with deep mouldings and conventional leaf-carving on the capitals, which is a *tour de force* of craftsmanship. On the S. arcade the decoration is simpler and the mouldings more plain, but the corbels at each end carrying the arch abutment are wonderfully detailed. The font is of the 13th century, a large bowl with four columns at the corners, rich, with more foliage carving, and of very satisfying design.

The E. window of the S. aisle is well detailed, with a niche set into the lower half of the centre light, and brackets at the sides; it must have looked delightful with the original sculptured figures, for which the two present specimens, typical products of the ecclesiastical art workshops, are a poor substitute. Thomas of Leighton was responsible for the 13th-century ironwork of the S. door, similar in design to his door at Turvey.

The village may well have been the centre of the Totternhoe stone school of carving, though it is perhaps more than possible that the roughing out of the stone was done to order at the quarry face, and carved *in situ* by itinerant masons travelling to and working on the various church sites.

EATON SOCON *(St. Mary the Virgin)*
Almost completely destroyed by fire in 1930, this church was formerly a 15th-century enlargement and completion of a 14th-century building famed for its 'poppy-headed' pew ends. The reconstruction by Professor Richardson is of an excellence that compensates for the loss; local craftsmen were employed, and during the rebuilding the surroundings resembled a medieval mason's yard. Since the fire swept from the east the chancel suffered least, and, although it was gutted, its delicate 15th-century windows were capable of repair.

ELSTOW *(St. Mary & St. Helen)*
Another church of monastic foundation, this truncated but magnificent remnant of an originally cruciform church, is the central feature of one of the most attractive villages in the county. Lapped on the north by the suburban tide of Bedford, it has kept its character remarkably unspoiled. The W. end of the church is one of those ghost W. fronts, in much the same way as some of the Italian examples, e.g. San Lorenzo, Florence; something great that might have been. Begun as a 13th-century composition, probably along similar lines to Felmersham, it was never finished, but what remains after centuries of decay has been sensitively restored by Professor Richardson. Two coeval 13th-century bays remain at the W. end inside, the rest being fine and massive Norman work, though regrettably 'scraped' in the last century. A small vaulted room now used as a vestry is of the 13th century and is doubtless of monastic origin. The ex-Norman N. door is a prize example of insensitive reconstruction, reminding one of a similar piece of machine-made vulgarity at the Round Church in Cambridge.

A detached belltower, witness once to the religious doubts of a young 17th-century tinker's son who has made the village world-renowned, completes a noble composition.

EVERSHOLT *(St. John Baptist)*
Wooded setting; 14th–15th cent.; Scott restorations.

EYWORTH *(All Saints)*
Spire; 17th-cent. monuments.

FARNDISH *(St. Michael & All Angels)*
Tiny, of Northants type; 12th cent., except tower.

FELMERSHAM *(St Mary the Virgin)*
Begun in 1220 and finished in 20 years, this is the finest 'Early English' church in the county. The W. front is a noble arcaded

composition on a superb site overlooking the river, and the raising of the nave walls in the 15th century to give a flat pitched roof and clerestory has, with a tower in place of an intended spire, created a fine foursquare and massive composition. There is some supremely competent but quite inadmissible restoration in the chancel, carried out by J. Brandon in 1850 where he has reinstated lancet windows to match those existing. (What was it in 'Early English' which drove the Victorians to such zealous falsification, and how did a style so 'coltish' and youthful find a response in a period the churchmanship of which was so alien to that of the 13th century?) The interior is wonderful, particularly the great clustered piers of the crossing contrasting with the delicacy of an excellent 15th-century screen.

In recent years a particularly nasty reredos has been removed, and also much inadequate stained glass; the replacement of the latter by delicate greenish glass has effected a remarkable improvement on the interior.

FLITTON (*St. John Baptist*)
Mainly 15th cent.; rich in 17th-cent. and later monuments; De Grey mausoleum.

GRAVENHURST, LOWER: *see Lower Gravenhurst.*

HARLINGTON (*St. Mary the Virgin*)
Wide view from churchyard; charming interior with 14th-cent. arcades.

HENLOW (*Our Lady*)
Mainly 15th cent.; massive tower.

HOUGHTON CONQUEST (*All Saints*)
Sandstone and ashlar 14th cent. onwards; stalls, glass, wall-paintings 15th cent.

HULCOTE (*St. Nicholas*) GS
Late 16th cent.

HUSBORNE CRAWLEY (*St. Mary*)
Tower built of rare green sandstone; beside a farm in wooded, hilly setting.

KEMPSTON (*All Saints*)
Riverside setting; 12th-cent. tower and chancel arch.

KEYSOE (*St. Mary the Virgin*)
Prominent spire; 14th and 15th cent. roofs; 14th- cent. font.

LANGFORD (*St. Andrew*)
Unusually perfect example of 14th-cent. rebuilding.

LEIGHTON BUZZARD *(All Saints)*
Set in a quiet corner of a very attractive little market town, this building is considered the finest parish church in the county. Begun in the 13th century, and with a gigantic spire completing a cruciform composition, the church reached its final form in the 15th century, with the raising of the walls and the construction of magnificent timber roofs of typical flat pitch.

A complete collegiate chancel, its seating and screens intact, is the great treasure of All Saints; dating from the late 15th century, it has all the excellence of the period. Thomas of Leighton, creator of the delicate grille to the tomb of Eleanor of Castille in Westminster Abbey, is represented in his native town by the ironwork on the W. door, where his elaboration of the hinges is paralleled by his very similar work at Eaton Bray and Turvey.

The Kempe windows of All Saints form a unique range in which the style of a master of his craft can be assessed at the peak of his powers. One of the most fascinating features of the interior are the 'graffiti' on piers and walls, all medieval; the most interesting is a three-light geometrical window on a pier in the S. chapel.

The churchyard is worthy of all this architectural beauty, wonderfully kept; its pathway from the town side is a delight to walk on, a combination of a central brick strip with sets at the sides, laid in a sinuous curve to the N. porch.

LOWER GRAVENHURST (*Our Lady*)
14th cent., except tower; unspoiled interior with screen and benches.

LUTON *(St. Mary)*
Overshadowed by cooling towers and hemmed in by mean industrial buildings, this magnificent church by sheer architectural merit resists the desolation of its setting. Begun in the 13th century, enlarged in the 14th, it reached its present form in the 15th century when Lord Wenlock built his sumptuous chapel, with its wonderful open arches over the Wenlock tombs.

The octagonal 14th-century baptistry is a work of great richness and confident craftsmanship. The W. tower is an example of the local chequer-board patterning of flint combined with clunch, the latter, in part, replaced by harder limestone in modern times. Street's work in the chancel is of a dark richness, but the refacing of the E. end externally is of a peculiar heartlessness.

MARSTON MORETAINE *(St. Mary the Virgin)

In the 'wasteland' of the brickfields and with a 'prefab' colony to set it off, this magnificent building was begun, *c.* 1340, but practically rebuilt in 1445, in the typical and slightly 'pursey' style of the time. A legacy of what Harvey calls 'the rich harvest of the 1440s'. The nave is very grand inside and reminds one of some of the 15th-century interiors of the Marshland churches, bold and confident detailing, and rather bald today without the full richness of stained glass and screening. Interesting screen paintings. The detached bell tower, with diagonal buttresses and a stairway in the centre of the wall, is a fine massive building, and makes the whole composition very reminiscent of neighbouring Elstow.

MILTON ERNEST (All Saints)

15th-cent. nave roof; rich, dark Butterfield embellishments.

NORTHILL (St. Mary the Virgin)

Attractive blend of freestone and limestone; 14th-cent. stalls; 17th-cent. glass.

ODELL *(All Saints)

Set on an eminence in one of the best stone villages in the county, this is an excellent example of a unified 15th-century church built all at one time. The W. tower of Northamptonshire type is grand and massive, and the gentle batter up to a pinnacled parapet relieves what might otherwise be an overpowering bulk. The interior is lovely with tall arcades, an original rood screen, and very satisfying diamond-pattern flooring in nave and aisles. There is one particular remnant of stained glass, a group of seraphs in the E. window of the S. aisle, that is of a rare and naïve beauty.

OLD WARDEN (St. Leonard)

Magnificent woodwork; monuments; 18th cent.

PAVENHAM *(St. Peter)

On the hillside above one of the loveliest of the riverside villages, Pavenham church is like Old Warden, full of carved panelling and rich woodwork, most of it installed in the 19th century by Thomas Abbott Green of Pavenham Bury, it is actually of Jacobean date in the main and consists of everything from Marquetry to High Relief. The fabric of the church is also good in itself, there are in particular some excellent examples of 14th-century canopied work. The nave roof has only just (1956) been completed, of good simple construction it is fully in harmony with the rest of the church.

PERTENHALL (St. Peter)

Secluded among trees; 1790 Gothic chancel; some box pews; 15th-cent. screen.

PODINGTON (St. Mary the Virgin)

13th cent., with 14th-cent. leaning spire; stone Nene valley village.

RISELEY (All Saints)

Thatch and half-timber village; tower, roofs and seating of 15th cent.

SHARNBROOK (St. Peter)

Noble spire and tower; sensitive modern restoration.

SHELTON (St. Mary the Virgin)

Remote and rustic; old pews, screen and clear glass. (*See Plate 25*)

SHILLINGTON *(All Saints)

A clerestoried hall, hardly interrupted in its continuity from W. to E. by a chancel arch which is both high and wide, this building is mainly a work of 1300, only slightly altered subsequently. It has a wonderful hill-top site, typical of many similar church-crowned hills along the line of the Chilterns, and is rather too long to fit on to the top comfortably, a factor which doubtless caused the failure of the tower footings in 1701. The present red brick erection is utterly unworthy of the church.

The rood screen inside forms the only actual division from W. to E., and save for the loss of its loft is perfect. The E. window of the 15th century is the rather mean successor to what must have been a wonderful one of the 'Geometrical' period, the outline and jambs of which are visible internally. There is a fine vaulted crypt under the chancel, built in part into the slope of the hill.

STEVINGTON (St. Mary the Virgin)

On a terrace above the Ouse; pre-Conquest tower and windows; 14th-cent. additions.

STREATLEY (St. Margaret)

Mainly 15th cent.; well restored by Prof. A. E. Richardson.

THURLEIGH (St. Peter)

By a castle motte; 12th-cent. tower; 15th-cent. chancel windows.

TINGRITH (*St. Nicholas*)
15th-cent. brown sandstone walls with white light freestone tracery; setting.

TODDINGTON (*St George*)
Grand cruciform 13th–15th cent.; suited to former prosperity of this spacious hill-top town of chestnut-coloured ironstone; Totternhoe stone.

TOTTERNHOE *(St. Giles)*
This is one church built from the quarries in the village, which has a really fine exterior. It may well be that some more careful selection was made of the stone since the source was so near. In the gable of the nave there is 'flint-flushwork' decoration belonging to a local Chiltern tradition quite unconnected with that of East Anglia, it is a piece of richness in just the right place. The building was begun in the 14th century and brought to completion in the 16th century, with the creation of the pinnacled skyline which gives such a satisfactory silhouette.

TURVEY (*All Saints*)
Victorian-Jacobean Ouse valley village; pre-Conquest church with 14th–15th cent. additions sumptuously 'improved' by Sir Gilbert Scott; late 13th-cent. wall-painting.

WARDEN, OLD: *see Old Warden.*

WILLINGTON (*St. Lawrence*)
Grand early 16th-cent. N. chapel; part of manorial group.

WOBURN *(St. Mary)*
In 1865 the old church of St. Mary was pulled down and replaced by the present mortuary chapel. The new church was erected in Park Street between 1865 and 1868 by William, eighth Duke of Bedford, to the designs of Henry Clutton, Bath stone being used throughout. It is an absolutely magnificent building and must have been even finer with its spire which, having shown signs of insecurity in 1890 was pulled down and the battlements and turret heightened. The interior is vaulted in stone throughout, and the echoes of the 'Ile de France' are strong, though in some way sublimated at the E. end. The reredos, choir stalls and pulpit are later additions.

WYMINGTON *(St. Lawrence)*
Begun in 1350 by John Curteys, who, with his wife, is buried in the chancel, this church must be an example of work carried out by masons based on jobs in the neighbouring county of Northamptonshire, but working here on a slightly tighter budget. All the Nene Valley features are to be seen, though delightfully out of scale, particularly in the tower and spire which are lavishly ornamented. One can see in the belfry windows where local men have worked under supervision, but have not quite 'pulled off' the sophistication of the great churches of the 'boot and shoe' towns over the hill. The interior is rich and complex, with a fine nave roof; in fact, with the remains of a suitably horrific 'Doom', old pewing and some colour still on capitals and arches, the building forms the county's best example of the luxuriant spirit of the 14th century, and a late one considering the date. Perhaps the area was spared the worst ravages of the plague.

YELDEN (*St. Mary the Virgin*)
14th cent.; 1629 Communion table.

Berkshire

BERKSHIRE HAS four chief types of scenery. In the east of the county on the London side is much wild heath and pinewood, the sort of country which, almost uninhabited until the nineteenth century, now grows public institutions like schools, prisons and barracks, and small modern villas along main roads and by electric railways. The Thames forms the northern border, and here there is orchard land extending several miles south until the Downs are reached. The south-west and west of the county are mostly chalk downs, and the scenery is the same as the Wiltshire downland into which it merges. The older houses and farm buildings of these districts are timber, brick and cob, and generally thatched or red-tiled. The towns, except for Faringdon, are all built of brick and are all, except for Reading, comparatively small. The far north-west corner of the county is limestone, and Faringdon, and such villages as Wytham, Coleshill, the Coxwells and Buckland are like Cotswold places with houses and churches built of golden grey stone.

Until the end of last century when transport from London turned half of the county into a semi-suburb, Berkshire was thinly populated. There the churches were cottage-like with wooden belfries, thatched barns, farms and houses of downland hamlets: a few small flint towers arose from pleasant red-brick towns beside the Thames and Kennet, and there still are a great many commons and heath, such as are so beautifully described by Miss Mitford in *Our Village*, and in the far north-west, already mentioned, is the limestone district which looks like the Cotswolds. The brick-work in Berkshire was never so impressive as that of Kent and Sussex, nor is its limestone area comparable for beauty with Oxfordshire and Gloucestershire, except for the 13th-century tithe barn at Great Coxwell, one of the great medieval monuments of England. The eastern and London half of the county was transformed first by railways, and again by buses, bringing more monied people from London who have settled down in detached residences wherever the train-service is convenient. These people built themselves new churches, and re-built old ones.

Berkshire is not a great county for ancient churches. The only grand example is St. George's Chapel at Windsor (Perpendicular). Avington and Padworth have complete and small Norman churches. The best old churches will be found not in the Kennet valley where these two are, but along the Northern slopes of the Downs to which stone for building could be brought fairly easily by river and then by trackway. The few big medieval churches of Berkshire, with the exception of Lamborn and Newbury, are in the northern half of the county – Blewbury, East Hagbourne, Wantage, Sparsholt, Uffington, Childrey, Cholsey, North Moreton, Stanford-in-the-Vale, Faringdon, Abingdon, Sutton Courtenay, Cumnor, Shottesbrooke and Warfield. The churches on the downs and commons were nearly all small cottage-like buildings. One may see aquatints of some of them in *Views of Reading Abbey and the Principal Churches Connected Therewith* (1805), and in Buckler's drawings in the British Museum. They had flint and rubble walls, roughcast outside (the flint Norman towers of West Shefford and Welford were built circular like many church towers in East Anglia, because of the lack of stone for the corners); the roofs were of tiles with dormer windows, and there was usually a wooden belfry at the west end, and a 17th or 18th century porch in brick. Such buildings must have seemed very unecclesiastical to rich and pious landowners long or newly settled in Berkshire, which by the 19th century had become a 'home county' influenced by the prosperity of the Metropolis. So they were pulled down or else vigorously restored, stripped of their external and internal plaster and retaining perhaps only an arcade or window of the original building. Some churches of this small cottage type survive, as at Avington, Ashampstead, Catmore, East Shefford (Old church), Padworth, Wasing and Wootton.

The great Victorian architects left their mark on Berkshire. But because the county was not much industrialized until the present century, there is less Victorian building than in Middlesex, Surrey or Kent. G. E. Street (1824–81), who lived at Wantage at the beginning of his successful career, designed many charming church schools and vicarages in that district and a bold new church and adjoining buildings at Boyne Hill, Maidenhead. Butterfield beautifully and conservatively restored Shottesbrooke and published a monograph about it. The best work of Victorian architects, together with that of the 18th and present centuries, is noted in the lists below. On the whole Berkshire has not been well served by those who rebuilt its churches. They had more money at their disposal than sensibility. But at least they built churches.

J.B.

SELECTED LIST OF CHURCHES

by John Betjeman

ABINGDON *(St. Helen)*
Set among 17th and 18th century brick almshouses by the Thames. A large town church with a spire and five parallel aisles so that it is broader than it is long. There are decidedly graceful arcades and the whole building is mostly 14th, 15th, 16th century Perpendicular. Painted roof of late 14th century. Font cover and pulpit 17th century; Hawkins monument (1780) by

John Hickey. Late Georgian stained and enamelled glass window in N.W. corner; reredos G. F. Bodley, 1897.

(*St. Michael*) GR
Gilbert Scott, 1867.

ALDERMASTON (*St. Mary*)
Glass 13th–15th cent.

ALDWORTH (*St. Mary*)
Huge stone effigies, supposedly 14th cent.

ASCOT (*All Saints*) GR
T. H. Rushforth, 1864.

ASCOT, SOUTH: *see South Ascot.*

ASHAMPSTEAD (*St. Clement Romanus*)
Wall paintings.

AVINGTON *(St. Mark & St. Luke)*
Almost alone among trees at the end of a lane and beside the River Kennet: towerless, aisleless and mostly Norman; dark, mysterious and ancient-looking inside with rich Norman carving.

BAULKING (*St. Nicholas*)
Small, rustic; mainly 13th cent.; good nave roof and Jacobean pulpit.

BEARWOOD (*St. Catherine*) GR
1846; glass.

BEEDON (*St. Nicholas*)
Setting; charming early 13th cent. with triple lancets at E. end; old roof to nave.

BESSELSLEIGH *(St. Lawrence)*
Set in elm-shaded park, Cotswold-style and small. Only church in county to retain all its box pews and original seating and ritual arrangements.

BISHAM (*All Saints*)
Setting; tower 12th cent.; Hoby monuments early 17th cent.

BLEWBURY *(St. Michael & All Angels)*
A picturesque village of brick and cob and thatch among willows and orchards at foot of Downs; the large cruciform church in various medieval styles is, for Berkshire, large, spacious, light and impressive with pre-Perpendicular work predominating.

BRADFIELD *(St. Andrew)*
Brick and timber village and public school in a high, gravelly district. Church almost wholly rebuilt by Gilbert Scott, 1847, and turned into something which, inside, is long drawn, mysterious and vast in his transitional style called 'square abacus'.

BRIGHTWALTON (*All Saints*) GR
G. E. Street, 1863; Ford Madox Brown glass over font.

BUCKLEBURY (*St. Mary*)
Village; 15th cent. with early 18th cent. interior.

CATMORE (*St. Margaret*)
Setting; 12th cent.; early 17th cent. roof.

CHALLOW, WEST: *see West Challow.*

CHARNEY BASSETT (*St. Peter*)
Village; 12th cent., refashioned in late 15th cent.

CHOLSEY (*St. Mary*)
Setting; cruciform with central tower; 12th cent. with 13th–14th cent. additions.

COLESHILL (*All Saints*)
Setting; 12th–13th cent. fabric with 15th cent. tower; refashioned in 18th cent. and restored by Street.

COMPTON BEAUCHAMP *(St. Swithin)*
Small medieval church built of chalk, hidden among elms at the foot of the Downs and beside a moated manor house, a beautiful situation. Churchyard has painted tombstones. Uplifting white interior decorated with gilded altar, classic font cover, gilded monuments, rich rood and other furnishings, mostly by Martin Travers (20th century).

CUMNOR (*St. Michael*)
12th cent. and later.

DEDWORTH (*All Saints*) GR
G. F. Bodley, 1881; glass by Burne Jones and William Morris.

EAST HAGBOURNE *(St. Andrew)*
Picturesque village of cob and timber framing and thatch. Spacious church mostly 14th and 15th century. Porch in churchyard with many fine 18th-century tombs. Old porch survives. Interior light and full of texture, old wooden roofs, some 14th-century glass, remains of screen (15th century). Big Royal Arms of George III.

EASTHAMPSTEAD (*St. Michael & All Angels, & St. Mary Magdalene*) GR
1866; 5 Burne Jones windows.

EAST HANNEY (*St. James the Less*) GR
G. E. Street, 1856; village.

EAST SHEFFORD *(*Holy Innocents*)
Small, almost derelict church in Lambourne valley, with plastered walls and old tiles and clear glass. Like what average Berkshire church was before Victorian restoration and rebuilding.

FARINGDON *(*All Saints*)
Large, cruciform town church, backed by trees of Faringdon House, and looking down towards market place of this limestone county town. Interior over-pewed, but is mostly 12th and 13th century. Early English, and has many vistas. Stiff-leaved foliage Early English carving on capitals; 17th and 18th century monuments to Unton and Pye families.

FAWLEY (*St. Mary the Virgin*) GR
G. E. Street, 1865–6.

FINCHAMPSTEAD (*St. James*)
Various dates and brick 17th-cent. tower.
Hagbourne, East: *see East Hagbourne.*

HAMPSTEAD MARSHALL *(*St. Mary*)
Adjunct of vanished country house, whose large brick-walled garden and sculptured piers remain. Little rustic and medieval church, mostly Jacobean and Georgian inside with some old high pews, three-decker pulpit and brick floors.

HANNEY, EAST: *see East Hanney.*

HENDRED, WEST: *see West Hendred.*

HINKSEY, NEW: *see New Hinksey.*

HUNGERFORD (*St. Lawrence*) GR
J. Pinch, 1814–16 ext; setting.

HURLEY (*St. Mary the Virgin*)
Setting.

HURST *(*St. Nicholas*)
Set among trees and old brick and timber cottages, the brick having the dark richness of old Middlesex bricks. Brick tower 1612, church Norman and later. Interior full of 17th-century woodwork, and many grand 17th and 18th century monuments.

KINGSTON BAGPUIZE (*St. John the Baptist*) CL
J. Fidel, 1800.

KINGSTON LISLE (*St. John the Baptist*)
Village; 12th cent., refashioned in 14th cent. and later; late 14th cent. wall painting.

LAMBORN *(*St. Michael & All Angels*)
Small downland town of racing stables. Grand cruciform medieval church of various dates starting with late Norman,

to which are added 15th and 16th century chapels, the 16th-century work being much more than village masonry. In an arch of the S. transept lively carving of hounds coursing a hare. 16th-century tombs and brasses and remains of glass. The whole interior very white, and exterior recently pleasantly replastered.

LECKHAMPSTEAD (*St. James the Apostle*) GR
S.S. Teulon, 1859.

LONG WITTENHAM (*St. Mary the Virgin*)
Village; mainly 13th and 14th cent. with earlier and later details; much 17th-cent. woodwork, some from Exeter College, Oxford.

MAIDENHEAD *(*All Saints, Boyne Hill*)
A Tractarian group, vicarage, school, church buildings, church, separate tower and spire (1865), all by G. E. Street, 1854–8, in local red brick. The buildings look well from all directions in the amply laid-out rich Victorian suburb where they stand. Interior of church vast, violently coloured, richly dark with, as in all Street buildings, careful detail in ironwork, wood and coloured decoration.

MORETON, NORTH: *see North Moreton.*

NEWBURY (*St. George, Wash Common*) CL
F. C. Eden; modern.

(*St. Nicholas*)
Late town Perp., much restored.

NEW HINKSEY (*St. John the Evangelist*) GR
Sir Ninian Comper, 1899; unfinished.

NORTH MORETON *(*All Saints*)
Attractive brick and cob and timber village among elms. Fair-sized village church, late 13th century; superb 14th-century chantry chapel of Stapleton family, with geometrical tracery, spirited carving outside, and its E. window of five lights filled with 14th-century glass, showing the Passion and incidents in the life of Our Lady, St. Peter, St. Paul and St. Nicholas. Remains of 14th-century glass in other windows.

PADWORTH *(*St. John the Baptist*)
A large plain 18th-century house, with this aisleless Norman (12th century) church beside it. Exterior still plastered, and with charming limewash on the tracery to the

five Perpendicular windows. The interior is impressive and seems vaster than Avington, with which it compares for Norman perfection. Semi-domed apse, Norman chancel arch and north and south doors; remains of wall painting, 18th-century monuments.

PUSEY (*All Saints*) CL
18th and early 19th cent.

RADLEY *(St. James)*
Oxfordshire style limestone, with fine 18th-century headstones in churchyard. Dark, and interior filled with 16th and 17th century armorial glass, well repaired and added to by Thomas Willemant, 1840. 17th-century stalls in chancel and other old woodwork elsewhere.

READING (*Christ Church*) GR
H. Woodyer, 1862–74.

(*St. Giles*)
Mostly Victorian.

(*St. Lawrence*)
Mostly 15th cent.

(*St. Stephen*) GR
W. White, 1865.

SHEFFORD, EAST: *see East Shefford.*

SHELLINGFORD *(St. Faith)*
Aisleless, stone-spired limestone church beside remains of an old house. Interior rendered impressive by good modern restoration by Frederick Etchells. Low, new box pews, plastered walls, tall Norman chancel arch, wide, light chancel with fine 17th and 18th century monuments; fragments of 15th-century glass re-set in E. window.

SHOTTESBROOKE *(St. John the Baptist)*
A park-surrounded church in flat country near Maidenhead. Externally and internally a singularly complete cruciform 14th-century design with central tower and lofty, elegant spire. Deeply moulded curvilinear window tracery. The church is clearly the work of one man, and he an architect with a sense of proportion. The white interior is tall and light and full of delicately carved 14th-century details, particularly Founder's tomb (hard white chalk) in south transept, and sedilia in chancel. Brasses and pieces of 14th-century glass. This complete church is just the sort of thing the more medievalist Victorians tried to copy and could not quite manage. The Victorian restoration by W. Butterfield, 1844, has done little harm. (*See Plate 38*)

SHRIVENHAM (*St. Andrew*)
17th-cent. rebuilding around a 14th-cent. central tower.

SOUTH ASCOT (*All Saints*) GR
J. L. Pearson, 1896–7.

SPARSHOLT *(Holy Rood & St. Mary the Virgin)*
Cob and thatched village among elms at foot of N. Downs. Spired church has plastered exterior and several stately Decorated 14th-century traceried windows. Interior spacious and countrified with ancient wooden nave roof, stone floors, and in south transept three carved wooden effigies of 14th century, one of a woman being singularly beautiful. Hard chalk sedilia in chancel and Easter Sepulchre (14th century). Fragments of medieval glass; chancel unfortunately stripped of plaster has unlovely east window.

STANFORD-IN-THE-VALE (*St. Denys*)
Village; mainly 13th and 14th cent.

STOCKCROSS (*St. John the Evangelist*) GR
1839 and J. N. Comper.

STRATFIELD MORTIMER (*St. Mary the Virgin*) GR
R. Armstrong, 1869.

SUNNINGWELL (*St. Leonard*)
Octagonal porch, 1562.

SUTTON COURTENAY *(All Saints)*
A show Thames-side village with wide tree-lined street of old houses of various dates. Large church for Berkshire, of various dates, too, from 12th century onwards. 15th-century woodwork, remains of glass, old floors, some box pews. Nothing is outstanding, but the general effect outside and within is of gradual growth through the centuries, and full of gentle texture and colours.

THEALE (*Holy Trinity*) GR
E. Carbett, 1822; in manner of Salisbury Cathedral.

TIDMARSH (*St. Lawrence*)
13th-cent. apse.

TUBNEY (*St. Laurence*) GR
A. W. Pugin.

UFFINGTON *(Assumption of St. Mary the Virgin)*
Large cruciform stone and pebble-dashed church, almost wholly Early English (13th century), at a corner of chalk and thatched

vale village among willows and elms. 17th-century school-house nearby. Church quite cathedral-like outside, though spire fell in 18th century. Stone porches, transeptal chapels. Interior rather bare after restoration by G. E. Street, 1850. Clear glass. 17th-century monument.

WALLINGFORD (*St. Leonard*)
Norman, and Victorian Norman.

(*St. Peter*) CL
Spire Sir Robert Taylor, 1763.

WALTHAM (*St. Lawrence*)
Lych gate N. Hannen, 1907.

WANTAGE (*St. Peter & St. Paul*)
Large cruciform; 13th cent. with Perp. additions.

WARFIELD *(St. Michael & All Angels)*
Large and fine for Berkshire, mostly 14th century. Decorated. Light, spacious and stately chancel, E. window with beautiful tracery and much carved chalk. Remains of 14th-century glass, 15th-century wooden screen and loft in north aisle, also graceful 19th-century stone screen by Street, who restored the whole church most carefully.

WASING (*St. Nicholas*) CL
Setting; 18th cent.

WELFORD (*St. Thomas*) GR
T. Talbot Bury; 12th-cent. round tower; setting.

WEST CHALLOW (*St. Lawrence*)
Village; rustic church.

WEST HENDRED *(Holy Trinity)*
Not such a show village as its neighbour, East Hendred, but stream-side church, mostly 15th-century Perpendicular. Pleasant plastered exterior and lead roofs. Interior not a disappointment; pieces of old glass: 17th-century woodwork, stone floors. Rustic attraction preserved by gentle restoration by Philip Johnson, 1929.

WICKHAM *(St. Swithin)*
Brick and thatch village, with church on hill above it. 11th-century tower to which is added a church rebuilt in expensive knapped flint with stone dressings, Benjamin Ferrey, 1854-9. The sumptuous interior is a mid-Victorian extravaganza. Life-size elephants' heads in papier mâché in N. aisle roof, papier mâché angels in nave roof, windows of mid-Victorian purple and red stained glass. Only inharmonious note is later E. window. Carving everywhere.

WITTENHAM, LONG: *see Long Wittenham.*

WOKINGHAM (*St. Paul*) GR
H. Woodyer.

WOOTTON (*St. Peter*)
Simple village interior; Comper fittings.

Bristol

INTRODUCTION

AMONG ALL our provincial cities Bristol has few rivals in the matter of old parish churches; some of its best are buildings which once served villages now engulfed in the city's suburbs or outer 'neighbourhoods'. York and Norwich may both beat Bristol in the actual numbers of their parish churches which have outlasted both the Reformation and later, more insidious, nibblings by demolition gangs, bombs, and the amalgamators of livings. But Bristol's surviving medieval churches and church ruins make up a group whose sheer architectural quality is hard to beat, and after them come several which are good Georgian, and a few worth mentioning among the myriads of the Victorian host. Too many Bristol churches, alas, have themselves fallen victims to bombs and deliberate demolition; the latter process has been going on at intervals ever since St. Lawrence's was pulled down about 1580. Bristol has been too zealous a 'beautifier' for any parish church interior to be left untouched by the inroads of church furnishers of various dates. So one finds many Bristol churches whose contents include good monuments, ironwork, or other curios, but not one which can show a complete 'period' interior, whether medieval, 17th-century in the manner of Staunton Harold, or even Georgian. To see exactly how Bristol's churches looked inside in the days of high pews and parson and clerk, one must go to the City Art Gallery and look through the unique collection of Braikenridge drawings and water-colours – a perfect record, nearly 1,500 drawings strong – of how Bristol appeared at the tail end of her great Georgian phase.   B.L.

SELECTED LIST OF CHURCHES

by Bryan Little

CITY *(All Saints)*
A very old foundation and a truly lovely English town church. Half the nave is late Norman, the rest particularly graceful Perpendicular with the mullions of some windows continued down the wall. The simple N. tower is early Georgian, with a delightful Corinthian cupola of 1807. The church is full of monuments to commercial families, the best being to the Colstons. One Colston mural, set up soon after 1701, is a brilliant little baroque work, probably

by some such London sculptor as Richard
Crutcher. The one to Bristol's famous
philanthropist Edward Colston is an Ionic
composition by Gibbs, erected in 1729 by
the local mason Daniel Sidnell. The magnificent reclining figure is by Rysbrack and is
worth coming a long way to see.

*(Christ Church)

Another church of very old foundation, but
rebuilt 1786–90, the architect being the
Bristolian William Paty. 17th-century clock
jacks, etc. from the older church. An admirable late Georgian building, with a
lyrically lovely interior whose pillars and
saucer domes derive from Gibbs at St.
Martin-in-the-Fields. The tower and spire
a cross between Gibbs and Gothic. A
notably good Adam Communion table,
and some bad Victorian Renaissance
alterations.

*(St. John's)

A lovely little unaisled church, early
Perpendicular above a vaulted crypt. The
tower and spire are specially picturesque
as they have one of the city's gates immediately below. A fine civilian effigy commemorates Walter Frampton (1388), and
the church is full of good things of various
dates. The gallery, font, and other fittings
are of the 17th century, and the Holy Table,
Elizabethan or early Stuart, is perhaps
England's finest of its kind. A church of
great character, not much Victorianised.

*(The Lord Mayor's Chapel)

This, in the Middle Ages, was the chapel of
St. Mark's Hospital and has never been a
parish church. At the Dissolution it passed
into civic hands and is the only church in
England owned by a Corporation. Some of
the building is of the 13th century, there
are interesting 'Decorated' portions, the
Perpendicular tower is of 1487, and the
early 16th-century architecture, including
the delightful little fan-vaulted Poyntz
chantry with Spanish floor tiles, is really
brilliant late Perpendicular. This chapel is
one of the most important sepulchral
churches in England. Many tombs are of
civic magnates, but they include a Bishop
of Llandaff and the mail-clad effigies of the
Berkeley founders. Generally speaking a
complete church-trotter's paradise and
beautifully kept out of the Bristol rates.
Hatchments, Baroque ironwork by William
Edney, Charles II's arms, and a specially
magnificent collection of glass, some of it
always in St. Mark's, the rest foreign from

the Bagot collection and that of William
Beckford of Fonthill. For its size one of
the *very best* churches in England. Shut
Fridays and all August.

*(St. Mary Redcliffe)

The most splendid church in England which
has always been parochial. Its main distinction is its abbey-like size and plan, with
doubly aisled transepts, ambulatory, and
E. Lady Chapel. One must spend hours
admiring it, not overlooking the important
work of about 1200 and the glorious
hexagonal N. porch of the early 14th century with the poet Chatterton's muniment
room above it. Otherwise mostly early
Perpendicular with stone vaults and hundreds of bosses. Good medieval tombs,
some brasses, but the Renaissance monuments disappointing. A brass eagle lectern
of 1638 and a fine Baroque iron screen by
Edney. Three fonts, one medieval, one
Georgian, one Victorian. Quite good
Victorian furniture, and a stone to THE
CHURCH CAT, 1912–27, in the churchyard.
(See Plate 31)

(St. Nicholas)

Late 14th or 15th cent. crypt; ironwork;
monuments; 18th-cent. Gothick steeple.

*(St. Stephen's)

One merchant's tomb of the late 14th
century, otherwise all Perpendicular of
about 1475, a fine, clerestoried hall church
with lofty arcades and no chancel arch.
The elaborate tower, with its coronal of
pierced pinnacles, was probably by a
designer of the group which worked on
Gloucester Cathedral; we know that Benet
the Freemason did the charming fan-
vaulted porch. This church has good monuments, and in pre-Victorian days had superb
early Georgian mahogany furniture.

*(Temple)

Leaning tower of Perpendicular date
unique in England. Ruins being repaired
and preserved by Ministry of Works.

BISHOPSWORTH *(St. Peter)

Entertaining early Victorian Norman by
local designer S. C. Fripp.

HENBURY *(St. Mary the Virgin)

Another village church whose tall arcades
are good Early English. Much restoration
and rebuilding by Street and some very
queer Victorian grisaille glass. An unusual
wealth of mural monuments, of the
Baroque and later schools, to 18th-century

D

business men who had country residences at Henbury. Best of all are the twin gravestones to Scipio Africanus, negro boy servant to the Earl of Suffolk, who died in 1720.

HORFIELD *(St. Gregory's)
Good neo-Byzantine of the 1930s by A. R. Gough. Martin Travers furnishings, and an attractive interior with its soft tones of brick and plaster.

KINGSDOWN *(St. Matthew's)
By Thomas Rickman, and built in 1833–5. A good, stiff piece of pre-Tractarian Perpendicular. Inside, it has a more recent reredos, but otherwise a remarkable unaltered composition of arcades and three galleries, an organ case in correct early Revival Gothic, and the arms of William IV.

REDLAND *(no dedication)
Once a chapel in Westbury parish. A delightful classical building, with western cupola and Ionic façade. Built in 1740–3, being possibly designed by Richard Strahan and certainly finished by William Halfpenny. Fine Georgian woodwork inside, and some busts by Rysbrack. Victorian pews, but the general feeling still Georgian. On no account miss this one.

STAPLETON *(Holy Trinity)
Another replacement of an older building, and dating from 1856–7. Victorian Decorated in the manner of Pugin, the architect being J. Norton, a pupil of Benjamin Ferrey who himself studied under Pugin. An opulent composition and Bristol's best Victorian church, a mixture of carved stone and polished marble, with a really fine crocketted spire in the manner of the East Midlands. A Norman font, also a good set of Georgian murals to local residents.

WESTBURY-ON-TRYM *(Holy Trinity)
The best of Bristol's outlying churches, once partly collegiate, partly parochial. Much of it is of the 13th century, including the 'collegiate' sedilia in the S. aisle. The chancel, once the college choir, has graceful 15th-century architecture and the rarity of a Perpendicular apse (but cf. the bombed Coventry Cathedral). The tower is of the delicate beauty evolved by late 15th-century local designers who made one pinnacle rise like a needle above the rest. A Victorian tomb of Bishop Carpenter of Worcester (d. 1476), also many Georgian monuments to wealthy Bristolians who came to live in what was then a country parish.

Buckinghamshire

INTRODUCTION

BUCKINGHAMSHIRE IS a somewhat curious county as regards its church architecture. It has never had a cathedral or any major monastic church. There are few large town churches to compare with those in many other counties, Aylesbury, High Wycombe, Chesham and Amersham being about the largest. There are few outstanding churches of major architectural note. But what the county lacks in this respect is more than made up in variety, and in very numerous points of individual interest.

There is no 'Buckinghamshire type' of church, spire, tower or window, and in this county the architecture follows, in most instructive and interesting fashion, the geological formations of the land. The churches in the extreme south, in, or bordering the Thames Valley have an enormous variety of materials where stone is absent – brick, in such places as Dorney, Langley Marish, Fulmer, Hitcham, Penn and elsewhere. The earliest brickwork in the county, though it does not appear in the Chapel, is at Eton College, 1442. Then in the Chiltern belt there is, as one would of course expect, extensive use of clunch, chalk rubble and flint, with the use of stone only for the dressings. The Vale of Aylesbury, again a stoneless area, provides more brick, as in the ruined church of Stoke Mandeville and a further variety of materials; while the north of the county penetrating into the limestone belt produces good stone building in many of its churches comparable with that in the neighbouring counties of Northamptonshire and Oxfordshire.

The only 'groups' which can be identified in Buckinghamshire are those of stone carvers. At Ivinghoe there is a very fine set of mid or late 13th-century carved capitals in the nave which came obviously from the same mason's workshop as Pitstone, Eaton Bray, Flamstead, Chalgrave and several other churches in the neighbourhood. Masons' marks also relate work at Eton College, North Marston and Hillsden with a group of travelling masons.

Then there is the series of Aylesbury fonts – a fine late 12th-century group taking its type-name from the font in Aylesbury church. Others may be seen at Bledlow, Buckland, Chenies, Great Kimble, Great Missenden, Little Missenden, Wing, Pitstone and Weston Turville, with some in Bedfordshire and Northamptonshire, besides several more obviously deriving from the same source.

The monuments at Chenies, Wing, Quainton and Amersham are equal to anything elsewhere; and the Kederminster Library at Langley Marish is an unique treasure.

E.C.R.

SELECTED LIST OF CHURCHES

by E. Clive Rouse, F.S.A.

AMERSHAM (*St. Mary*)
Town church; 14th–15th cent.; much Victorianised; many important monuments; Drake chapel.

ASTWOOD (*St. Peter*)
Medieval; restored; setting.

AYLESBURY *(St. Mary)*
A large and handsome cruciform town church, with interesting outline to its lead spirelet, and an intriguing plan full of surprises, with side chapels in unusual places. It stands in a backwater of the town amidst a somewhat neglected churchyard approached by the charming Church Street and accompanied by many Georgian houses. Its character is a good deal spoilt by over-heavy Victorian restoration: but it is substantially 13th century. On the 17th-century Lee monument from Quarrendon a fresh red flower will be found constantly placed. The font, c. 1180, is the type specimen of a group in this and surrounding counties.

BEACONSFIELD (*St. Mary*)
Medieval; heavily but well restored; monuments; setting. Comper glass.

BIDDLESDEN *(St. Margaret)*
Remote, on the Northamptonshire border. The little box-like church was once the private house chapel, attached to the stable block, and is of the same date as the house, Biddlesden Park, 1730, which occupies the site of a Cistercian Abbey. 18th-century fittings, and clear glass, but undistinguished, its charm consisting of its private, park-like situation and pleasant texture.

BIERTON *(St. James)*
A really good architectural composition, with lofty 14th-century arcades and central tower on clustered piers. The walls retain much old plaster and whitewash, with glimpses of paintings peeping through here and there; and the floor is a pleasant mixture of square red tiles or bricks and stone. There are several good details and fittings including the Bosse monuments by William Stanton.

BLEDLOW *(Holy Trinity)*
Splendidly placed on the lower Chiltern slopes, on the brink of the Lyde – a chalk coombe or gully – overlooking the Vale of Aylesbury. The church contains many things worth while – nave arcades with carved capitals of about 1200: an Aylesbury font: fragments of wall painting including an amusing Adam and Eve; and a splendid S. doorway and porch, 13th–14th century, with traces of original colouring. The whole plan is very irregular, and the inclusion of the tower within the aisles lends interest and importance to the interior at the W. end.

BLETCHLEY (*St. Mary*)
Mainly 15th cent. with some earlier features; altar tomb 1430.

BOVENEY *(St. Mary Magdalene)*
For long neglected and semi-derelict, this little aisleless chapel with its western bell turret stands remote and embowered in elms on the Thames bank above Windsor, and is now more cared for. It has little architectural merit, but is a place where exciting things might well be found, and owes everything to its situation.

BRADWELL, OLD: *see Old Bradwell.*

BROUGHTON (*St. Lawrence*)
Medieval; restored; wall paintings.

BUCKINGHAM (*St. Peter & St. Paul*) GR
Twice rebuilt: 1777 and Sir G. Scott, 1862; well paced on site of castle.

BUCKLAND (*All Saints*)
Medieval; pleasantly whitewashed; setting.

CALVERTON (*All Saints*) GR
Instructive Victorian Gothic with complete contemporary fittings.

CASTLETHORPE (*St. Simon & St. Jude*)
Medieval, of remarkable plan; 18th-cent. tower; monuments.

CHALFONT ST. GILES (*St. Giles*)
Interesting development of plan throughout Middle Ages; wall paintings.

CHALFONT ST. PETER (*All Saints*) GR
Temple Moore, 1912.

CHEARSLEY *(St. Nicholas)*
A charming place, the Church lying at the
foot of a steep lane below the village which
overlooks the Valley of the Thame and its
rich water-meadows not far from Notley
Abbey. The medieval building (like
Nether Winchendon nearby) has mercifully
escaped serious recent restorations and has
a gallery and old pews, with good 18th-
century monuments. The step down into
the chancel is unusual, and the whole place
has a pleasant, mellow, uneven quality.
What one sees of the structure is mostly
15th century, but the font is two hundred
years earlier.

CHENIES *(St. Michael)*
This Church must be included here; for
while it is in the main architecturally
unimportant and somewhat spoiled by
modernisation, it stands most delightfully
among the trees above the Chess Valley
hard by the mellow brick manor house of
the Cheyneys and Russells and the 'model'
cottages of the village. But its principal
feature is the fabulous series of monuments
to the Russells, Dukes of Bedford, and their
connexions, in the N. chapel. The late Mrs.
Esdaile described these as 'one of the finest
collections of tombs in England', ranging
from the 14th to the 20th centuries.

CHESHAM *(St. Mary)*
Over restored; medieval town church;
setting.

CHETWODE *(St. Mary & St. Nicholas)*
This is a remote and exciting place to
reward the persistent voyager who may
have approached it by way of the 'gated
road route'! It is the choir or chancel of
a small Augustinian priory, and became
parochial as long ago as 1480 when the then
parish church was ruinous and the monks
hopelessly impoverished. It has the best
13th-century work in Bucks; and though
some of it is re-set and restored, the range
of dog-toothed and deeply-cut sedilia, the
great five-lancet E. window, and the triple-
lancet on the S. with 13th and 14th century
glass would be notable anywhere. The 14th-
century N. chapel has become the manor
pew with fireplace: and there are hatchments and other good things.

CHICHELEY *(St. Lawrence)*
Here is one of those splendid mixtures of
dates and styles, from medieval to Comper,

that make so many English village churches
the delightful places they are. The church
stands near the Hall and has a Decorated
nave and N. aisle, a 15th-century central
tower not unlike Sherrington, and a classical chancel with delicate detail dated 1708
and clearly by the same hand as the house –
so far unattributed. The central space was
dealt with by Comper in 1907 and is
effective. There are good Renaissance
monuments to Caves and Chesters; box
pews and a nicely antiquated air.

CHILTON *(St. Mary)*
12th–16th cent.

CLIFTON REYNES *(St. Mary the Virgin)*
Awkwardly placed (from the tourist's
point of view) on the S. side of the
Ouse away from Olney, and thus happily
secluded. The church is of great interest,
and by the odd proportions of its tall nave
suggests a Saxon origin, though most of
what we see is 13th, 14th and 15th centuries.
The principal features are the font with
figures of Saints (14th century) and the
series of medieval monuments to the
Reynes family, including the great rarity
of two pairs of wooden effigies – Ralph and
Amabel de Reynes, *c.* 1320–30, and an
unidentified couple, *c.* 1300–10. The
church has suffered the disaster of the
removal of its interior ancient plaster by
some ignorant and misguided Victorian
enthusiast 'to show the beautiful stonework'
– rough rubble that was never meant to be
seen.

CRAWLEY, NORTH: *see North Crawley.*

CRENDON, LONG: *see Long Crendon.*

DINTON *(St. Peter & St. Paul)*
Norman door with inscribed lintel; next to
gabled manor house.

DORNEY *(St. James)*
Dreams away in a backwater beside the
splendid timbered house of Dorney Court.
Tudor brick tower and bits of every period
of architecture before and since, from
Norman times to a 19th-century window
of King Charles the Martyr, all on an
intimate and miniature scale. Note
especially 12th-century font; W. gallery
1634; S. porch 1663; 15th-century stalls
and base of screen brought from elsewhere;
17th-century communion rails and other
woodwork; and the fine Gerrard monument, 1607, by Nicholas Johnson in the
little N. chapel.

DRAYTON BEAUCHAMP *(St. Mary)*
Setting; monument; glass.

DUNTON **(St. Martin)*
A church with hardly any village, small and pleasantly unrestored. Box pews, W. gallery with texts and Rectors' and Church-wardens' names, 18th century, painted on the front. Whitewashed walls and ceiling with a hint of medieval timbers above. Many Bucks. churches must have been like this a century or more ago.

EDLESBOROUGH **(St. Mary the Virgin)*
Not to be confused with Ellesborough somewhat similarly placed below the Chiltern scarp. In this case the great mound on which it stands, isolated and exposed to all the winds that blow across the vale, is probably artificial. Horribly maltreated in the last century (plaster stripping inside, cement rendering out) but contains the most wonderful things – complete screen, stalls, pulpit and tester, and roofs of the 15th century; transverse arches in the aisles, and a series of exceptionally interesting brasses, as well as a complicated succession of building periods that form one of the best medieval test papers I know.

ELLESBOROUGH *(St. Peter & St. Paul)*
Setting; monument; Comper reredos.

FENNY STRATFORD *(St. Martin)* CL
1726; Browne Willis with Victorian additions; curiosity.

FINGEST *(St. Bartholomew)*
Norman tower; setting.

GAYHURST **(St. Peter)*
Has of late years come into its own with the revived interest in, and appreciation of 18th century classical work. It was a complete rebuilding in 1728 of a medieval church in the grounds of the great Elizabethan house near by – designer unknown. The tower has urns at the corners, and a charming, airy little cupola in the centre. The sides of the nave are unusual with a central pediment, pilaster and doorway. The interior is practically unaltered, with good plaster work, pews, pulpit and panelling, and the splendid monument to Speaker Wright and his brother by Roubilliac (his first English commission). *(See Plate 47)*

GERRARDS CROSS *(St. James)*
Sir W. Tite, 1859; Italian Byzantine; curiosity.

GREAT HAMPDEN *(St. Mary Magdalene)*
Medieval; font; monuments; setting.

GREAT LINFORD **(St. Andrew)*
A happy blend of 18th century and Deco-rated Gothic, pleasantly seated in company with stone almshouse and village school range, in a formal, tree-planted vista near the canal. There are box pews and good altar rails, and a monument to Sir W. Pritchard, the builder of the almshouses, as well as earlier brasses and a two-storey medieval porch, *c.* 1320.

HADDENHAM **(St. Mary the Virgin)*
A good 13th century and later church lying at the extreme end of one of the most remarkable and complicated villages in Bucks., where many of the houses and walls are largely composed of wichert – a hard, compressed chalk marl. The W. tower over-looking the green, is a good composition of the Early English period; and inside the spacious church, work of this date as well as of many other periods is found. Note 15th-century glass in N. transept window. A flat plaster ceiling of early 19th century date tantalisingly hides a 14th-century timber roof. Another good mixture.

HAMBLEDEN **(St. Mary the Virgin)*
The church, though much Victorianised and unexciting architecturally, sits pleasantly in the centre of the village, in one of the most attractive Chiltern valleys leading up from the Thames. The nave is unusual in its width and length without aisles. The fittings are the most interesting things – Norman font; Decorated sedilia and piscina; curious chest in the vestry; and the lovely Doyley monument (perhaps by Epiphanius Evesham) in the N. transept. The octagonal corner buttresses of the tower are in a local tradition commenced probably at Henley, and seen at Remenham, High Wycombe and elsewhere.

HAMPDEN, GREAT: *see Great Hampden.*

HAMPDEN, LITTLE: *see Little Hampden.*

HANSLOPE *(St. James the Great)*
12th-cent. chancel; spire.

HARTWELL *(St. Mary the Virgin)* GR
Henry Keene, 1753; Gothick; now ruinous.

HAVERSHAM *(St. Mary)*
Medieval; well restored; tomb.

HEDGERLEY **(St. Mary the Virgin)*
The best modern Gothic church in the county – by Benjamin Ferrey about 1860. It is built of the local flint, with a little stone and conglomerate, and stands high on a

grassy slope surrounded by trees watching over the village tucked in the valley bottom below. It is the third church on the site, and has some oddments from the older buildings – a medieval font with Jacobean cover; an old painting of the Commandments; some brasses; and a reputed piece of Charles I's cloak.

HIGH WYCOMBE (All Saints)
Large town church; 13th cent. outside, 15th cent. inside; late tower; vast Scheemakers' monument to Earl of Shelburne.

HILLESDEN *(All Saints)
This is another of Buckinghamshire's lovely and lonely places. The church is almost entirely of the 15th century and of a quality encountered hardly anywhere else in the county. It has much in common with the chancel at North Marston (q.v.). There are contemporary roofs, seats, screen and glass (legend of St. Nicholas) and a Te Deum frieze of alternate instrument-playing and scroll-bearing angels in the chancel. Note also good monuments: and the lovely canopy over the stair turret attached to the two-storey vestry and sacristy, once communicating with the great house of the Dentons, destroyed in the Civil War, whose site is marked by a grassy terrace. This is the church that inspired Sir Gilbert Scott with his gothic passion – his father was a clergyman at Gawcott near by.

HITCHAM *(St. Mary)
Dangerously near Slough and the Bath Road, but sufficiently withdrawn to retain some character. The small church is an admirable mixture of materials and styles that give it texture and interest – 16th-century brick tower; flint; chalk and plaster nave; Norman chancel arch; and one of those spacious rebuildings of chancels, c. 1330–40 that seem to abound. The chancel windows retain much of their original glass depicting the Nine Orders of Angels and the Four Evangelists. Good monuments and brasses; the whole set among trees in a well-kept churchyard surrounded by ancient tawny brick walls.

HORWOOD, LITTLE: see Little Horwood.

IBSTONE (St. Nicholas)
Primitive; setting; mainly 12th and 13th cent.

ICKFORD (St. Nicholas)
13th cent.; glass; interior suitable refitted by Vernon Staley who was Vicar here.

IVINGHOE (St. Mary the Virgin)
13th–15th cent.; cruciform; finely carved capitals; rood ceilure.

LANGLEY MARISH *(St. Mary)
Packed with interest: sandwiched between two lovely groups of brick and plaster almshouses – the old on the S. built by Sir John Kederminster in 1617, the new on the N. by Sir Henry Seymour about 1670. Unlovely pre-fabs. just beyond, and the tentacles of Slough already gripping. Brick 17th-century tower; remains of nave arcade, c. 1200 replaced by a timber one dated 1630: another spacious and rich 14th-century chancel: but above all, the Kederminster and Seymour transept, pew and library all of the first half of the 17th century and largely unaltered, with books on their shelves, painted panelling and grille, and heraldic overmantel over the fireplace. Hatchments, glass, carved Royal Arms, monuments, and everything a church should have.

LATHBURY *(All Saints)
Another dead-end place down by the Ouse just outside Newport Pagnell hard by a rather dispiriting house more or less wrecked by the army in the War. The church is dark and mysterious with fragments of painting and robust carvings from its Norman past. Pleasantly battlemented without and having a good stone texture.

LAVENDON (St. Michael)
11th-cent. tower.

LECKHAMPSTEAD (St. Mary the Virgin)
Remote; setting; paintings; effigy.

LILLINGSTONE DAYRELL AND LOVELL *(St. Nicholas, and Assumption of the Blessed Virgin Mary)
A pair of remote hamlets on the Oxfordshire border not far from Stowe, each with a church of some character. Lillingstone Dayrell has early features in its chancel and tower arches (11th century) and the handsome Renaissance Dayrell tomb standing in the middle of the chancel. Lillingstone Lovell (formerly in Oxfordshire) has had its rural effect of Decorated structure and 17th and 18th century fittings (pulpit, rails, pews, hatchments, etc.) somewhat spoiled by the senseless removal of the plaster from the interior walls. Nevertheless one of the least altered small churches in the county.

LINFORD, GREAT: see Great Linford.

LITTLE HAMPDEN *(dedication un-known)*
Humble and withdrawn among a few cottages and scattered farms. Its simple interior with wall paintings of 13th to 15th century date (including the earliest St. Christopher in England) leaves a great impression of the medieval hamlet church. The timbered, two-storey N. porch is unique in Bucks.

LITTLE HORWOOD *(St. Nicholas)*
Paintings.

LITTLE KIMBLE *(All Saints)*
Small and undistinguished externally, with little western bell turret standing amidst beeches and greenery on the edge of Chequers park. Inside are to be found, artistically, the best wall paintings in Bucks, including St. Christopher, St. James major, St. George (a notable standing figure), St. Lawrence, St. Francis preaching to the birds (only two in England), St. Clare, St. Bernard, and assorted ecclesiastics, plus part of a Doom, and a life of St. Margaret and St. Catherine, all early 14th century. There is also a square of Chertsey tiles under a mat in the chancel, with enchanting scenes from the life of King Mark of Cornwall and other Arthurian romances.

LITTLE MARLOW *(St. John Baptist)*
Another good Thames-side village at a dead end and consequently almost unspoiled. The church has the unusual feature of a triple-gabled E. elevation reminiscent of Devon or Cornish churches; and has a light, lime-washed interior. The chancel shows good 13th-century detail; and the S. aisle and chapel were 'beautified' by Sir Nicholas Ledewich, so the inscription on his tomb tells us, about 1430. There are relics of glass of this date. The whole, with 17th-century manor house, 18th-century rectory, and brick and timber cottages among elms makes an admirable group.

LITTLE MISSENDEN *(St. John Baptist)*
Principally renowned for its series of wall paintings discovered in the 1930s – St. Christopher, St. Catherine, Crucifixion, 14th century; and numerous fragments from the 12th to the 18th century. A primitive, whitewashed interior with interesting architectural features and development of the plan. There is an interesting series of modern stained glass windows. It stands hard by the Manor House and a number of pleasant houses in the village.

LONG CRENDON *(St. Mary)*
Medieval; cruciform; well placed in attractive village.

LUDGERSHALL *(St. Mary)*
Carved capitals.

MAIDS MORETON *(St. Edmund)*
15th cent.

Marlow, Little: *see Little Marlow.*

Marston, North: *see North Marston.*

MILTON KEYNES *(All Saints)*
Text book 14th cent.

Missenden, Little: *see Little Missenden.*

MONKS RISBOROUGH *(St. Dunstan)*
The general effect of this church is especially pleasing from the exterior, as it stands in a good churchyard with high hedges and trees and the Rectory hard by. The main part of the structure is 15th century: but inside there are good things to see of several dates such as the font (12th century), tower arch and brass (14th century), fragment of painted screen and remains of old glass.

NASH *(St. Michael & All Angels)* GR Street, 1851.

NETHER WINCHENDON *(St. Nicholas)*
One of the most attractive church interiors in the county and entirely unspoiled, in a rural village setting, at the foot of a steep hill. The structure is medieval, but the atmosphere is of the 18th century, with gallery, and high pews, hatchments, sentences, and a Jacobean pulpit. Notice an unusual modern memorial to Colonel Barnard in miniature medieval manner, but not wholly successful in effect.

NEWTON BLOSSOMVILLE *(St. Nicholas)*
The Ouse flows past the churchyard and gives the place a pleasant and unusual setting. Parts of the fabric are very early (late 11th century), but the general impression of the interior is of simple countrified work of the 18th century, with pulpit and gallery, plus a little medieval glass.

NORTH CRAWLEY *(St. Firmin)*
This is another village in the remote north corner of the county with an important medieval church, restored in the 18th century. The rebuilding of the chancel in the 13th century is recorded by a rare carved inscription outside the E. window. The nave has a S. arcade of 13th century

date with good carved capitals, and 14th-century N. arcade. The 15th-century screen is the only painted one to remain complete in the county: the figures on the panels are those of Prophets, Kings and Saints. There are box pews, and a brass to the son of a Dutch bookseller in Oxford, 1589.

NORTH MARSTON *(St. Mary)*
The church associated with John Schorne, Rector in the late 13th and early 14th century, who performed miraculous cures of the gout and became venerated as a Saint. The S. aisle contains the original (14th century) remains of his elaborate shrine, and the nave has good medieval work of various dates. Windsor filched the Saint's relics and, probably as a sop to the disgruntled parishioners, built the superb chancel and two-storey vestry and sacristy in the late 15th century. The whole restored at Queen Victoria's expense in memory of John Camden Neild in 1852. Wall paintings await uncovering here.

OLD BRADWELL *(St. Lawrence)*
Considerable 13th–14th cent. remains; rare inscriptions on chancel arch; two of the earliest bells in county.

OLNEY *(St. Peter & St. Paul)*
14th-cent. spire; scraped.

PADBURY *(St. Mary the Virgin)*
14th–15th cent.; restored; paintings awaiting uncovering.

PENN *(Holy Trinity)*
Somewhat beset by week-end hikers: but the splendid views from the churchyard or tower are ample justification. The church, of wonderfully varied textures and materials, with two great porches, has a medieval structure, the roof of about 1400 being one of the finest in the county. But it was much altered by the Penns and Curzons in the 18th century, which is the date of the chancel and its fittings, and many of its monuments. The great treasure is the painting of the Doom or Last Judgement, on oak boards found in the roof in 1938. The series of brasses is good for costume; and the curious may like to lift the mat in the centre aisle to see the tombstone of a descendant of William Penn, described as 'proprietor of Pennsylvania'. Recently whitewashed inside with most pleasing effect.

PENN STREET *(Holy Trinity)* GR
Benjamin Ferrey 1849; good Victorian cruciform.

PITSTONE *(St. Mary)*
This small church lying in chalk fields below the Chilterns has a most satisfactory interior, with work of many dates and textures – 13th-century capitals like Ivinghoe, 15th-century nave arcades, 12th-century font – the whole dominated by a fine Jacobean pulpit and tester beneath 18th-century 'sentences' over the chancel arch probably concealing a medieval Doom.

PRINCES RISBOROUGH *(St. Mary)*
Heavily-restored 13th–14th cent.; modern spire.

QUAINTON *(Holy Cross & St. Mary)*
A church deplorably mauled in 19th-century restorations, with hideous tiles and awful roof, but standing beautifully next the Winwood Almshouses (1687) in one of Buckinghamshire's best villages, and containing the finest set of Renaissance sculpture in the county. Note especially the following monuments: in the tower, S., to Fleetwood Dormer and others, by Marshall and Grinling Gibbons; N., to Robert Dormer and his son, a most moving masterpiece by Roubilliac; N. aisle, to Susannah Dormer and her husband with busts by William Stanton; to Sir Richard Pigott, by Giacomo Leoni and Rysbrack; S. aisle, to Richard Winwood and his wife, 1689 by Thomas Stayner. There is also a monument to Richard Brett, one of the translators of the Authorized Version of the Bible; and a modern tablet to Dr. George Lipscomb, the historian of Bucks., born in the village, who died in poverty in London in 1846.

RADNAGE *(St. Mary)*
A scattered village of several 'end-ships', one of which is clustered round the church and rectory, perched on the wooded slopes of the tumbled ground behind the Chiltern scarp below Bledlow Ridge. A simple village interior with all its original plaster, covered with a medley of medieval paintings and post-Reformation texts. Much of the structure is of about 1200 with aisleless nave and chancel and a plain tower between. The exterior, of partly plastered chalk and flint with brick repairs, fits perfectly into the landscape.

RAVENSTONE *(All Saints)*
13th, 15th cent. and Georgian.

RISBOROUGH, PRINCES: *see Princes Risborough.*

SHALSTONE (*St. Edward the Confessor*) GR
1820 and Sir G. Scott, 1862.

SHENLEY (*St. Mary*)
Medieval; heavily Victorianised; monuments; Royal Arms.

SHERINGTON (*St. Laud*)
Medieval; axial tower.

STANTONBURY (*St. Peter*)
Old church in the wilds; ruinous.

STEWKLEY *(*St. Michael & All Angels*)
A very fine Norman church, comparable with Iffley, Oxon. The W. front particularly rich Norman. Inside, a restoration by Street took away something of the texture, but enhanced the lofty scale, culminating in a distant dark chancel.

STOKE POGES *(*St. Giles*)
A good church in a medley of styles somewhat overweighted by the Gray's Elegy association and the 'bicycle window' which thousands of tourists come to gape at year by year. The main points of interest are the 14th-century timbered and traceried porch, the limewashed walls of the oddly-placed 13th-century tower; and the renovated Hastings chapel in which one rather regrets the disappearance of a good gallery. The fine panels of 17th and 18th century glass have been placed here.

STONY STRATFORD (*St. Giles*) GR
Hiorn, 1776; fancy Gothick.

STOWE *(*The Assumption of the Blessed Virgin Mary*)
A humble little medieval church in the grounds of the palatial mansion (now a school) and somewhat overshadowed by it. The august owners in the 18th century fortunately did not see fit to spend any money on the parish church, all being lavished on the private chapel in the house with its cedar fittings, and now transferred to a new building by Sir Robert Lorimer, and all further glorified. The little church is all the more worth visiting. It has an interesting medieval statue, and some good 17th-century monuments, but is notable for its general atmosphere and setting more than anything.

STRATFORD, STONY: *see Stony Stratford.*

TATTENHOE *(*St. Giles*)
Tiny, remote, with not a road to it, and altogether fascinating. The building is set in the midst of the moats, banks, ditches and other evidences of a deserted village, only a farm and a cottage or two surviving. The place is a mass of primroses, violets and bluebells in the spring; and almost unapproachable in winter. There is a simple interior with box pews and an amusing 13th–18th-century composite font. Much of the materials are said to have come from the destroyed priory of Snelshall nearby. One of the few remaining places where one may still savour the authentic aroma of the past – stale paraffin and mouldy hassocks.

TERRIERS (*St. Francis*) GR
Good modern; Sir Giles G. Scott.

THORNTON *(*St. Michael*)
The church, shorn of its chancel in the late 18th century, stands opposite the front door of the big house, now Thornton College. It is mostly 15th century in date, but has been amusingly refurnished in the 18th–19th centuries with black-and-white diamond paving and box pews facing inwards, college chapel-fashion. The great feature of the church is the Ingylton tomb (1472) with its fine brass, recovered in recent years from a grotto in the park.

TWYFORD *(*Assumption of the Blessed Virgin Mary*)
A church of exceptional interest for its details and fittings, though not giving the impression of an architectural composition as an entity. The Norman doorway is notable, and inside there are good 13th-century arcades, with a good deal of 15th-century wood-work – roof, pews, and screen with some painting. There are several good monuments, both medieval and later. Note especially the chain armour Knight, and mutilated priest: Viscount Wenman, 1640; Thomas Gifford, 1550, and a brass to John Everden, rector, 1413.

UPTON (*St. Lawrence*)
12th and 19th cent.; with Stewkley has the only other vaulted chancel in Bucks.

WATER STRATFORD (*St. Giles*)
Norman doors and tympana re-set.

WAVENDON *(*St. Mary the Virgin*)
A study in one of the more successful Victorianisations of a medieval church, largely by Butterfield in 1849. There is a varied collection of Victorian glass for those who like it. A more venerable relic is the fine 17th-century pulpit brought out of London. And the whole place stands pleasantly on the Bedfordshire border.

WESTCOTT *(St. Mary)
A simple Victorian chapel of ease, by G. E. Street. The interior is made effective entirely by proportion, for there is no mechanical carving, mouldings and capitals are strong and simple, and there is thought everywhere.

WESTON TURVILLE *(St. Mary the Virgin)
The village is one of those peculiarly Buckinghamshire types composed of several separate huddles of buildings or 'end-ships', grouped round manor, church, mill or green, and only thinly strung together by other cottages. The church is at the end of a lane near the 18th-century manor house in whose grounds is the motte of a Norman castle. The building is of many styles and of an attractive irregularity with things in it to please everyone – 12th-century 'Aylesbury' font, 13th-century arcades, 14th-century chancel with good window tracery, 15th-century tower, fragments of old glass (a tantalizing medley, this), 16th-century pulpit, etc.

WESTON UNDERWOOD (St. Laurence)
Medieval; heavily restored; remains of original glass.

WHITCHURCH *(St. John the Evangelist)
Set back from the village in which are many good houses and cottages and a Norman earthwork castle. It explains its name, when its tall white, weathered limestone tower is seen gleaming against the clouds or elmy background from a neighbouring hill. Inside, it is spacious and surprisingly little tampered with. There are scraps of wall painting and glass, and like Bledlow the tower arches are all inside the W. end.

WILLEN *(St. Mary Magdalene)
Like a city church transported to the remote countryside, with dramatic effect – brick, stone, classical pilasters, urns, high pews, pedestal font and all the rest. It is to the designs of Robert Hooke, and built in the 1670s through the munificence of Dr.

Busby, the famous headmaster of Westminster School. There are two little rooms flanking the tower – one a vestry and one to house a library presented by Busby in 1698 and augmented in the 18th century. Both are now derelict and used for coke, oil lamps, superannuated hassocks and mouldy hymn books, and the library was burnt when the Rectory was destroyed by fire some years ago.

WINCHENDON, NETHER: *see Nether Winchendon.*

WING *(All Saints)
The most important Saxon church in the county, but containing much of interest of later date, particularly the fine roofs and screen and porch, and the splendid series of Dormer monuments. The approach is somewhat spoiled by the erection of poorly designed council houses on the green.

WINGRAVE (St. Peter & St. Paul)
Medieval.

WOOBURN (St. Paul) GR
Almost rebuilt mid-19th cent.; Comper screen.

WEST WYCOMBE *(St. Lawrence)
Dramatically placed inside an Iron Age earthwork with the flint Dashwood Mausoleum on a yew-covered promontory of the Chilterns high above the model village. The chancel and base of the tower are medieval; but the tower top with its golden ball that opens to admit half a dozen people, and the nave are pure 18th-century fantasy inspired by Sir Francis Dashwood. The plasterwork and ceiling paintings are admirable: but the fittings – font, desk-pulpit, etc., are more curious than beautiful. (*See Plate 50*)

WEST WYCOMBE (St. Mary & St. George)
Wellesley and Wills; modern Italianate.

WYCOMBE, HIGH: *see High Wycombe.*

WYCOMBE, WEST: *see West Wycombe.*

Cambridgeshire

INTRODUCTION

PERHAPS BECAUSE Cambridge University and Ely Cathedral are so out-standingly beautiful, people underrate the county which contains them. Cambridgeshire scenery is nowhere obvious or dramatic – the famed Gog Magog Hills, south of Cambridge do not reach three hundred feet. In the south, the county is rolling and chalky, giving surprisingly fine and wide views. In the north it is fens, where the eye sees mostly sky. As Miss Olive Cook writes of it 'It would not be possible to find elsewhere so unexpected a contrast between the chalk uplands with their carpets of delicate grasses and rare flowers, wild yet amiable, and the expanse of the Fens, dyked, drained and filled, yet still boundless, awe-inspiring and alien'. Such unassuming country as this is more easily wounded than most by modern vertical intrusions like factory chimneys, pylons, poles and aeroplane hangars and the geometric cubes of 1930 functionalism. But the towers and spires of the 14th century, the great time of church building here, show the sense of skyline peculiar to the Middle Ages and still dominate much of the landscape.

Cambridge is not a unity. In the south it is like its neighbours, Essex, Suffolk and Herts. Steep roofed cottages are reed thatched and their walls colour-washed. Parish boundaries are long strips, parallel to the Anglo-Saxon Devil's Dyke and so designed as to make best use of a variety of resources on every strip. In this rolling scenery are country houses in well-wooded parks and the thatched villages, which are seen best in sunlight when their colour washes are shown up, cluster round flint churches whose mouldings and carvings internally are of hard chalk. In the west of the county a coarse rubble is used for the churches.

Until 1836 the northern part of the county, the Isle of Ely, was separate from Cambridgeshire, and has even now its own administration. Until the 17th century, when the Fens were drained on a grand scale, the Isle was mostly shallow water with monastic settlements and churches on raised banks and islands. The greatest of these is the Benedictine Abbey of Ely itself. Whittlesey, Sutton, Thorney, Swaffham Prior, Wisbech and St. Wendreda's March are other examples of island or peninsular medieval churches which rose over the shallow water like ships made of limestone from Lincolnshire and Northants. Beside them, the houses and churches of modern Fen settlements seem mean and unimportant.

In 1839 two Cambridge undergraduates, J. M. Neale and Benjamin Webb, formed the Camden Society for the restoration of old churches on what were thought 'correct' principles – the abolition of box pews, the removal of plaster and whitewash, the adornment of the sanctuary with stained glass and colour and the promotion of 13th-14th century Gothic (Middle pointed or Decorated) above every other style. Yet Cambridgeshire remained Low Church with a good deal of Perpendicular Tudor cement affixed to crumbling fabrics. The Camden movement was not without its effect on local churches, though its influence spread later all over England. The Cambridgeshire churches, for this and other reasons, were subject to more than usually vigorous Victorian re-tooling and refurbishing.   J.B.

SELECTED LIST OF CHURCHES

by Peter Eden, F.S.A.

ABINGTON, LITTLE: *see Little Abington.*

BABRAHAM *(St. Peter)*
A rural spot with a big house in the Tudor manner (1832). The church is unobtrusively but picturesquely sited behind the domestic offices, and has an impressive plain tower which has been claimed as pre-Conquest, but is more probably 13th century. The Bennet monument in the S. aisle (second half of 17th century) is highly individual, and attractive.

BALSHAM *(Holy Trinity)*
Dignified, somewhat austere nave, dating from the rectorship of John of Sleford (d. 1401); the richly-carved stalls were also commissioned by him. His brass and that of John Blodwell (d. 1462) are in the chancel. Late medieval rood-screen with loft. Lofty font cover by F. E. Howard. The perverted may derive pleasure from the large brick and flint rectory (Swiss Cottage x Perp.) built in the 1840s, which adjoins the church to the east.

BARRINGTON *(All Saints)*
Village setting with large green; 14th–15th cent.; 15th-cent. seating.

BARTLOW *(St. Mary)*
Round tower; wall painting 15th cent.

BASSINGBOURNE *(St. Peter & St. Paul)*
14th-cent. chancel.

BOROUGH GREEN *(St. Augustine)*
The fragment of a 16th-century mansion lies to the N.E. of the church, from which it is hidden by the churchyard elms. Patching and altering have given the walls an agreeable colour and texture, especially the much-gabled and buttressed S. aisle; and there is a pair of urns quaintly placed on the top of the responds of the decapitated chancel arch. Fine monumental effigies (15th century) of the de Burghs and Ingoldesthorpes.

BOTTISHAM *(Holy Trinity)*
Perhaps the best in the county. Early 14th century, with indent for what must have been the very sumptuous brass of Elias de Bekyngham, one of Edward I's judges, renowned in story for his integrity. Stone chancel screen and wooden parcloses (re-set). Monuments including one by Bacon to the Jenyns and Allington families.

BOURN *(St. Helen & St. Mary)*
Good Transitional; Comper reredos.

BURWELL *(St. Mary the Blessed Virgin)*
The best approach is from Cambridge through the Swaffhams, and the right light a sunny evening in August. You look over and across a mile of stooked corn and the Devil's Dyke to the noble tower and, left of it, the windmill. If you are lucky the windmill will be working. Church good Perpendicular (the nave was roofed in 1464) save for the tower, the lower stages of which are 12th century.

CAMBRIDGE *(All Saints)*
Rebuilt by Bodley in 1863–4 on a new site in Jesus Lane; meritorious.

(*Great St. Andrew's*)
Monument to Captain Cook; perhaps the most interesting of Cambridge's three Tudoresque churches by Ambrose Poynter; built in the late thirties and early forties of the last century amid fierce controversy; some original glass and other fittings.

(*Great St. Mary's*)
Worth a visit.

(*Holy Sepulchre*)
Extensively restored by Salvin in 1841, when some 'ecclesiological' fittings were introduced.

(*St. Benet's*)
10th-cent. tower.

(*St. Edward's*)
Slender nave arcades of *c.* 1400.

(*St. Mary the Less*)
Aisleless spacious 14th-cent. hall.

*(*St. Michael's*)
14th-century collegiate plan.

CARLTON (*St. Peter*)
Pleasant setting; mainly 14th–15th cent.

CHERRY HINTON (*St. Andrew*)
Fine E.E. chancel.

CHIPPENHAM (*St. Margaret*)
Village (planned); 14th–15th cent.; seating and wall paintings.

CONINGTON *(*St. Mary*)
Nave rebuilt in 1737 with, inside, a series of arched recesses between the windows framing 17th and 18th century wall monuments (several of merit, one signed 'G. Gibbons fecit').

CROYDON (*All Saints*)
Setting; charming interior.

DULLINGHAM (*St. Mary the Virgin*)
Village.

ELSWORTH (*Holy Trinity*)
Good Dec.; pulpit, seating and stalls 15th cent.

ELTISLEY (*St. Pandiana & St. John Baptist*)
Spiritually in Hunts; church with good small spire alongside village green.

ELY (*St. Mary*)
Trans.

FORDHAM (*St. Peter & St. Mary Magdalene*)
Chapel over N. porch.

GAMLINGAY (*St. Mary the Virgin*)
Decayed market town with characteristic church.

GRANTCHESTER (*St. Andrew & St. Mary*)
Meadowy, self-conscious village; Dec. chancel.

GUILDEN MORDEN (*St. Mary*)
Screen.

GUYHIRNE *(*St. Mary Magdalene*)
The small church by Sir G. Gilbert Scott, erected in 1878 in gault brick with stone dressings, is a commendable effort, making allowance for limited resources. The old chapel of ease 1660 has dove-grey pews, narrow pens, and untouched Puritan simplicity.

HARLTON *(*Assumption of the Blessed Virgin Mary*)
The church and adjoining Manor Farm make a pleasant group. Much Roman cement on the outside over decaying clunch. The interior is a stately example of Decorated-Perpendicular transition. The Fryer monument (mid 17th century) in the S. aisle is above the average of its genre.

HASLINGFIELD (*All Saints*)
Tower.

HAUXTON (*St. Edmund*)
Wall-painting of St. Thomas à Becket.

HILDERSHAM *(*Holy Trinity*)
Wickedly over-restored, but worth a visit for all that, if only to savour the effect of its attractive and characteristic 13th-century plan. A pair of life-size wooden effigies, *c.* 1300, brasses, glass. The building stands well and the churchyard is effectively planted with some unusual trees and shrubs.

HORSEHEATH (*All Saints*)
Setting; brasses and monuments.

ICKLETON (*St. Mary Magdalene*)
Village street; Romanesque nave arcades.

ISLEHAM *(*St. Andrew*)
Spacious, cruciform; Decorated save for poor modern W. tower. The nave was elaborately panelled and a splendid clerestory and roof of unusual design added (affinities with Mildenhall and Soham) by the mercantile family of Peyton, *temp.* Henry VII. Good brasses; fine 17th-century communion rails. To the W. across the road is a small Norman monastic

church, with apse. Isleham Hall, now tenements, is worth a detour for those with a taste for picturesque decay.

KENNET (*St. Nicholas*)
Bosky setting; 13th–15th cent.; good details.

KIRTLING *(All Saints)*
Once had a Tudor mansion built by the first Lord North, all gone save for the gate tower, but the moated site is impressive. The church has several good monuments to the North family in the 16th-century brick-built family chapel. Norman and Early English features.

LANDWADE *(St Nicholas)*
A pocket parish of a hundred acres or so has a delightfully situated church built by Walter and Joan Cotton in the first half of the 15th century and later extended. A number of attractive medieval fittings, and monuments to the Cottons of Landwade. The place takes a little finding but should not be missed. Masses of daffodils in spring.

LEVERINGTON *(St. Leonard)*
Spacious nave, rather marred by ugly wooden strainer arches. The draw here is the glass, especially the Jesse Tree window at the E. end of the N. aisle (15th century restored).

LINTON (*St. Mary the Virgin*)
Small market town with some interesting houses; an archaeologist's church, very enigmatic.

LITTLE ABINGTON (*St. Mary the Virgin*)
11th-cent. work.

LOLWORTH (*All Saints*)
Setting. Wall painting.

LONGSTOWE (*St. Mary*)
Bovey monument.

MADINGLEY *(St. Mary Magdalene)*
Placed in an idyllic park setting above a little lake margined with bamboos near a fine house with noble cedars. There is a fair mixed bag of fittings including a 14th-century bell now standing in the aisle.

MARCH (*St. Wendreda*)
Hammer-beam roof with host of angels. (*See Plate 34*)

OVER (*St. Mary the Virgin*)
Good Dec.; screen and font with cover 15th cent.

SHEPRETH (*All Saints*)
Setting; Norman doorway and chancel arch.

SNAILWELL *(St. Peter)*
The River Snail rises here (hence the name) among a complex of wooded moats, and meandering past Fordham runs ultimately into Soham Lode. The church which is reached by a cul-de-sac from the village street has a 12th-century round tower.

SOHAM (*St. Andrew*)
Fine Transitional and later; tower.

SUTTON *(St. Andrew)*
The tower with its odd two-stage octagonal lantern stands up splendidly above the fen. The whole was rebuilt *c*. 1370, perhaps by Bishop Barnet of Ely. The window tracery is notable.

SWAFFHAM BULBECK (*St. Mary*)
Bench ends; chest.

SWAFFHAM PRIOR *(St. Mary, St. Cyriac)*
Two churches here in one churchyard standing on a little hillock above the village street. Both are partly ruinous, and both have good towers – St. Mary's 12th century, formerly crowned by a stone spire; St. Cyriac's with a fine late medieval octagonal upper stage; box pews and a little gallery adorn its ruinous interior.

THORNEY *(St. Mary & St. Botolph)*
Has 'atmosphere', ascribable in part to fine trees growing in and around the little town. The church is a fragment of the Romanesque abbey, with an E. end added by Blore, 1840–1, including an effective window copied from glass in Canterbury Cathedral.

THRIPLOW (*St. George*)
Well-placed on a little hill; central tower.

TRUMPINGTON *(St. Mary & St. Nicholas)*
Highly elegant 14th-century cruciform, though rather over-restored, with the famous brass of Sir Roger de Trumpington (d. 1289). John and Aleyn may well have passed this way as they fled back to Cambridge after their successful skirmish with Chaucer's miller, and doubtless breathed a thankful prayer.

WESTLEY WATERLESS *(St. Mary the Less)*
Stands high on the chalk and has some of the deepest wells in the county. The neat

little church has lost its small round tower. It is in an original if somewhat finicky Decorated idiom. Another good brass, to Sir John and Lady de Creke (early 14th century).

WHITTLESEY *(St. Mary the Virgin)*
Has the best tower and spire in the county. The spire can be seen for miles around, though rather dwarfed by the forest of chimneys to the left as you approach by road from the S. There is a representative selection of sub-modern stained glass. Monument to General Sir Harry Smith (d. 1860) by G. G. Adams of London, in the Westminster Abbey tradition. Another in the chancel to Elizabeth Kentish (d. 1792) was designed at Rome by her sorrowing husband Richard Kentish.

WICKEN *(St. Lawrence)*
Cromwell associations; brasses.

WILLINGHAM *(St. Mary & All Saints)*
14th-cent. Treasury; roof and wall paintings 15th cent.

WIMPOLE *(St. Andrew)*
A church in the squire's backyard, 14th century in origin but almost entirely rebuilt by Flitcroft in 1749. Fine heraldic glass in a window in the N. chapel. Remarkable series of monuments by Scheemakers, Banks, Bacon, Flaxman, Westmacott and others.

WISBECH *(St. Peter & St. Paul)*
With once prosperous 18th-century and later houses on the 'brinks' fronting the River Nene, can look quite Canaletto under favourable conditions. St. Peter and St. Paul is a typical town church with four-aisled nave, rather dark and on the dusty side. Wall monument by Nollekens; reredos (1885) designed by Basset-Smith and executed by Salviati. Free-standing bell-tower to the N. The Octagon Church by Swansborough erected in 1827–9 was pulled down in 1952, which was a pity. (*See Plate 54*)

WISBECH ST. MARY *(St. Mary)*
In origin 12 cent., but now mainly Perp. with rebuilt chancel. There are interesting fittings of various periods and largely of foreign provenance.

Cheshire

INTRODUCTION

BIRKENHEAD IS more often gone through than visited, and this slight upon a city which is classic ground for the study of town planning is a slight also often put upon the county of which it is, by a few hundreds, the largest town. Cheshire is crossed by many whose eyes are on a target beyond. It is on the way to Wales, on the route north and south, on the path of the Irish Mail; and Cheshire does little to arrest the unseeing eye. It is flat except at the edges, and the roads are so good and the corners so hideously made safe, that the visitor is almost hustled through it. To those, however, who treat Cheshire as an end rather than as a means, the county is surprisingly rewarding. True, the northern horns of the Cheshire crescent have had applied to them the pancake make-up of commuters' housing, but, in the western horn, there is Chester itself, and, in the eastern, country which is wild and weird however near to Manchester it be.

Elsewhere the county has an almost regular pattern. The background is always richly pastoral, but, along the northern boundary formed by the Mersey and the Ship Canal, there is sporadic industry, and, from north to south down the centre, chemical works have followed the line of the three salt towns, Northwich, Middlewich and Nantwich. The smaller elements in the pattern are more ancient, and stem from Welsh as well as English settlement: there are few villages, and many scattered farms and hamlets. The typical medieval parish church, especially in the south and east of the county, served a vast area, often as much as thirty square miles in extent. Malpas, Great Budworth, Bunbury, Acton and Astbury are churches of this kind. It is not surprising, therefore, that there should be so many interesting private chapels and former chapels of ease, nor that some of the ancient parochial churches of the county should be of such splendour.

It is not only, however, for size or interest that some Cheshire churches are remarkable. A great many of them are cleverly sited, using slight eminences to dominate their surroundings, and most of them are built of red sandstone, a stone never much used for houses. The typical 15th-century Cheshire church must have looked fine when its mouldings were sharp and the houses beneath it half-timbered. Now the detail is frayed or replaced, the surrounding black and white is yearly giving way to modern uniformity, and it is to the untypical church that one is attracted, to Astbury, built of millstone grit, to the brick churches of Cholmondeley and Tushingham, to the Peovors, to curious Baddiley and freakish Birtles. Here, perhaps, in these untypical Cheshire churches, the county now is typified, a county that only reveals itself to him who leaves the fast through roads, and then rewards him handsomely.

R.W.

SELECTED LIST OF CHURCHES

by Robert Wakeford

ACTON *(St. Mary)
This great church dwarfs its tiny main-road village. Mostly of the 13th and 14th centuries. Stone seats round the inner walls; a canopied wall-tomb of the early 15th century; some fine 17th-century effigies. The low screen and other chancel furnishings are probably of the late 17th century, although they look earlier. The tower is an interesting specimen of 18th-century Gothic, preserving perhaps a memory of the older tower.

ALDERLEY (St. Mary, formerly St. Lawrence)
Manorial balcony; setting.

ASTBURY *(St. Mary)
The size and battlements of the church make the sloping village green look a glacis and the lych-gate, a barbican. Outside details are sharp and well-preserved because the building stone is millstone grit, rare in Cheshire. The detached spire is mid-14th century, but looks earlier. Inside, proportions and furniture are both distinguished. 15th-century stalls, screen, wooden eagle-lectern and magnificent roofs with pendants; 17th-century altar rails, Royal Arms and nicely-mechanical font cover; box-pews. Notable also for the light hand used by Sir Gilbert Scott in the restoration of 1862.

BADDILEY *(St Michael)
By farm lanes in flat country, not easy to find and not easy to interpret. Small aisleless nave and chancel of half-timbering, largely replaced by brick in 1811; Gothick windows. The tympanum is one of the most interesting in England; its structure is pre-Reformation; its painted Creed, Commandments, Lord's Prayer and Coats of Arms are dated 1663. This great tympanum, some 20 feet square, is supported on an eight-foot screen, and divides the low chancel from the nave with claustrophobic thoroughness. Box-pews and a pretty pulpit.

BARNSTON (Christ Church) GR
G. E. Street, 1871.

BARTHOMLEY (St. Bertoline)
Setting; monuments.

BIRTLES *(St. Catherine)
A freak church of 1840 brick in a wooded and park-land setting. Seats for about 120. The inside is all self-confident vitality. Frescoes by the founder's son, a Crimean colonel, after designs from All Saints, Margaret Street. Continental glass, mainly Swiss 1570–1640, lots of Renaissance Dutch and Flemish oak, including a manorial pew. A great organ built by the colonel himself. Candelabra copied from Milan cathedral.

BOUGHTON (St. Paul) GR
J. Douglas, 1876.

BOWDON (St. Mary the Virgin) GR
A re-building of 1856–60; older monuments.

BRERETON (St. Oswald)
Setting; Cheshire Perp.; roofs.

BRIGHTON, NEW: see New Brighton.

BUDWORTH, GREAT: see Great Budworth.

BUDWORTH, LITTLE: see Little Budworth.

BUNBURY *(St. Boniface)
A large well-sited 14th-century collegiate church, with nave arcades and wide aisle-windows of about a hundred years later. Four of the original doors have survived, and there are also 16th-century oak doors with lattice panels in the stone screen of the chantry chapel. Important early alabaster effigy of the founder of the college; other effigies and a fine early 17th-century tomb; many interesting fittings. This

church is notable for its colourful and successful restoration after severe bomb-damage, and for its scholarly documentation in 'The Bunbury Papers', issued periodically since the war.

BURTON (*St. Nicholas*) CL
1721; setting; altar rails late 17th century.

CAPESTHORNE *(Holy Trinity)*
The chapel of a great house. Both were built in 1722, but the house has since been re-modelled. The drive to house and chapel sweeps through a park with views over woods and lake. The chapel itself, of brick with stone facings, is rectangular with a shallow apse. Inside, it is somewhat dark with injudicious Victorian glass and a mosaic reredos of 1886-8, but the pews face each other college-fashion and there is a raised manorial pew at the west end. Original rails and good font. This chapel may be the earliest surviving work of John Wood of Bath.

CHADKIRK (*St. Chad*) CL
1747 *et al.*; setting.

CHEADLE (*St. Mary*)
Tombs; screen.

CHESTER (*St. John the Baptist*)
Norman.

(Chapel of St. Mary de Castro)
Late 12th-cent. chapel in early 19th-cent. castle.

CHOLMONDELEY *(St Nicholas)*
The private chapel of Cholmondeley Castle, sited, rather squatly, on a plateau in the park. The church is cruciform, of brick and stone. Vanbrugh is popularly reputed to have built the nave and the walls that encase an older chancel, but this work was in fact contracted for by one Thomas Fetherston. The transepts were added in 1829. Chancel roof medieval; rails, screen and other chancel furniture, of about 1552. The Cholmondeley pew is called the State Gallery; its cushions were made from robes used at the coronation of William IV.

CHRISTLETON (*St. James*) GR
W. Butterfield, 1876-7.

CHURCH MINSHULL (*St. Bartholomew*) CL
1702; setting.

CONGLETON *(St. Peter)*
An unspoilt town church of 1742. Plain outside and most pleasing within. Galleries on three sides, supported on piers with columns above. Fine box-pews throughout; those in the galleries are steeply tiered. William III arms; a particularly good brass candelabrum of 1748; interesting 18th-century glass. Font and altar rails are original. The pulpit, alone in Cheshire, is centrally placed in front of the altar.

DISLEY (*St. Mary the Virgin*)
Roof; glass; setting.

DUNHAM MASSEY CHAPEL, CL
Late 17th cent.; intact.

ECCLESTON (*St. Mary the Blessed Virgin*) GR
G. F. Bodley, 1899; setting.

FARNDON (*St. Chad*)
Setting; 17th-cent. window to Cheshire Royalists.

GAWSWORTH (*St. James*)
Setting; tombs; roof.

GRAPPENHALL (*St. Wilfrid*)
14th-cent. glass.

GREAT BUDWORTH *(St. Mary & All Saints)*
An imposing village church standing on a hill. 14th and 15th century structure, of good proportions and very light inside. Some medieval stalls which may be early 14th century. Many monuments. The most impressive feature of the church is the 16th-century roof and the delicate stone shafts which support it.

HARTHILL *(All Saints)*
Harthill is within a few miles both of Burwardsley and of Hargrave. All three have early 17th-century churches. This suggests a vigorous church life preceding the equally vigorous Puritanism in the area. Of the three, Harthill is the most pleasantly sited, high up on the Broxton hills, and, alone of the three, has a screen and also some other original fittings which survived a drastic restoration in 1862.

HOLMES CHAPEL (*St. Luke*) CL
Classic walls to medieval wood-frame.

KNUTSFORD (*St. John the Baptist*) CL
1744.

LITTLE BUDWORTH (*St. Peter*) CL
1800; setting; font 17th cent.; pulpit 18th cent.

LITTLE MEOLS, WEST KIRBY (*St. Andrew*) GR
Douglas and Fordham, 1889-1907.

LOW MARPLE (*St. Martin*) GR
J. D. Sedding 1870; N. aisle H. Wilson
1906.

LOWER PEOVER *(St. Oswald)*
Tidied up, but still a fine example of a
church built of timber, with a massive
stone tower. The furniture is very good
indeed: box-pews, some with the lower
halves of the doors fixed to retain the
rushes, Jacobean rails, altar and screen.
This church still looks as must once have
looked many Cheshire churches. The effect
inside is of dark oak and whitewash. Rural
setting. A cobbled lane to church, inn and
school. The old schoolroom is dated 1710
and is still in use.

LOWER WHITLEY (*dedication unknown*)
CL
Roof.

MACCLESFIELD (*Christ Church*) CL
1755; Gothick windows and box-pews.

(St. Michael)
Tombs.

MALPAS *(St. Oswald)*
A large handsome church, mainly late 15th
century, built on the highest point in the
village. Spacious, light and well-proportioned. Two family chapels and a number
of tombs, most of them of the 16th century.
Good screen-work and a few old stalls.
Recent sympathetic improvements have
added to the beauties of this fine church.
The vestry has been attributed to Vanbrugh
and so have the remarkably beautiful
churchyard gates.

MARBURY (*St. Michael*)
Setting; medieval pulpit; mainly 15th cent.

MARPLE (*All Saints*) CL
1808.

MARPLE, LOW: *see Low Marple.*

MARTON (*St. James*)
Black and white; recently discovered 14th
cent. Doom.

MEOLS, LITTLE, WEST KIRBY: *see Little
Meols.*

MOBBERLEY *(St. Wilfred)*
The design is a typical late medieval one
for east Cheshire, aisle walls with small
three-light square-headed windows, no
battlements, but deep eaves. There is a
magnificent rood-screen of 1500 and a
good roof. Some ancient glass and some

interesting wall-paintings. The tower screen
is 1683.

MOTTRAM-IN-LONGDENDALE (*St.
Michael*)
Setting; late 15th cent.

NANTWICH *(St. Mary)*
A large town church built, like the majority
of Cheshire churches, of local soft red
sandstone which weathers badly and
blackens quickly. Despite extensive rebuilding in 1885, the exterior is impressive,
and the chancel very fine, both outside and
in. There are twenty magnificently canopied
choir-stalls dating from the late 14th century.

NETHER TABLEY (*St. Peter*) CL
Late 17th cent.; most fittings intact.

NEW BRIGHTON (*St. James*) GR
Sir Gilbert Scott, 1854.

OLD RODE (*All Saints*) GR
Sir Gilbert Scott, 1864.

OVER PEOVER *(St. Lawrence)*
In a park, near splendid 17th-century
stables and backed by the Tudor bit of a
house of many periods. The main body of
the church is brick of 1811 by William
Turner of Whitchurch. A pleasant Georgian
pitch to the roof. The tower is 1739. At the
re-building, two earlier chapels were
retained, each with fine monuments,
medieval and 17th century. Note 1650
roof of N. chapel. The church possesses
interesting medieval glass and some 17th-
century heraldic glass.

PEOVER, LOWER: *see Lower Peover.*

PLEMSTALL (*St. Peter*)
Setting and unusual wood-work.

POTT SHRIGLEY (*St. Christopher*)
Setting; medieval bells; monuments;
furniture.

PRESTBURY (*St. Peter*)
Village; 18th-cent. murals; detached 12th-
cent. chapel.

REDDISH, STOCKPORT (*St. Elizabeth*)
GR
A. Waterhouse, 1883.

RODE, OLD: *see Old Rode.*

ROSTHERNE (*St. Mary*)
Setting; 1640 lych-gate; memorials.

RUNCORN (*Christ Church, Weston Point*)
GR
1841; built by the Weaver Navigation
Company for their workmen.

SALTERSFORD, JENKIN CHAPEL
*(St. John the Evangelist)
This remote mountain chapel looks like a converted farm-house with a low tower added. The roof is of heavy Kerridge slabs; the windows are square, sash and domestic; there is a chimney stack half-way along the S. wall. It was in fact built as a chapel in 1733 (tower 1754–5) and its furniture and fittings are intact.

SANDIWAY (St. John) GR
J. Douglas, 1902.

SHOCKLACH (St. Edith) Small; rustic.

SHOTWICK *(St. Michael)
By-passed and secluded hamlet without shop or inn, once washed by the Dee. The village and church were strategically important, and the tower is fortress-like. The interior is interesting: twin naves separated by a low arcade. Perhaps originally planned, like many similar churches the other side of the Welsh border, to provide a chapel to Our Lady as big as the church itself; since the Reformation, one nave has been used for the offices and the other for the sacrament. Box-pews, three-decker pulpit and notable canopied seat for the churchwardens. Two fine quatrefoil lights of 14th-century glass portraying the Annunciation.

STOCKPORT (St. George) GR
Austin and Paley, 1893–7; large and magnificent.

(St. Mary)
Medieval bits overshadowed by 1812–14 Gothick.

(St. Peter) CL
1768.

TABLEY, NETHER: see Nether Tabley.

TARPORLEY (St. Helen)
Monuments.

TARVIN (St. Andrew)
14th-cent. screen and roof.

THURSTASTON (St. Bartholomew) GR
J. L. Pearson, 1885.

TUSHINGHAM (St. Chad)
Made redundant by a new church, St. Chad's is now only used for an occasional funeral. 1689–91, small, simple and rectangular. Royal Arms above the two round-headed E. windows; plain square quarries in the N. and S. windows. The font, like so much else in this charming church, is of oak. It has a removable pewter bowl. There is also a rare pewter collecting shovel of 1678.

WALLASEY (St. John) CL
1833.

WARBURTON *(St. Werburgh)
The old church is small and secluded and of great interest. The building is of timber, with some walls replaced with stone-work in 1645, and some with brick in 1711, the date also of the brick tower. The roof is of Kerridge slabs. Inside, the constructional timbers divide off the aisles. Screen, pulpit, altar and rails are Jacobean; the box-pews are 1813 but look earlier.

(St. Werburgh) GR
J. Douglas, 1883.

WEAVERHAM (St. Mary the Virgin)
Village; pews and other furniture.

WITTON, NORTHWICH (St. Helen)
Large and late Perp.; apse and roof.

WOODCHURCH (Holy Cross)
Box-pews.

WOODHEY *(private chapel)
The house has gone, but there are some traces of a garden terrace and a great barn to the fine farm. The site is flat and lonely. Chapel of about 1700, with portico which may be a hundred years earlier. This portico is of great interest with its three arches on fluted pillars and a parapet carved with strap-work. The chapel has round-headed windows of plain glass; it is tiny, but with separate entrances to the ground-floor and to the manorial pew above, with its two fire-places. Panelled walls, black and white marble floor, no altar, but a notable pulpit. The pews are set college-fashion.

WRENBURY *(St. Margaret)
An early 16th-century church overlooking a village green. Tower, nave and aisles are conspicuously battlemented. The interior is pleasing, and must have been very fine indeed before the renovations of the 1920s and 1930s. The pink masonry looks, however, less scraped than is usual when the plaster is removed, and the box-pews, though lowered, are of a good colour. There are crests on pew doors, hatchments, some signed monuments and a western gallery.

Cornwall

INTRODUCTION

CORNWALL IS a Duchy. It is separated from England by the picturesque Tamar Valley, and has more sea coast than anywhere else in Britain.

The prevailing building materials are slate and granite. The granite bursts up through the slate and forms Bodmin Moor, which is mostly desolate, except for pre-historic remains and the beehive cells of Celtic Christians. A district half granite and half great white pyramids of decomposed granite, known as China clay, is near St. Austell. Moorland covers the far western granite promontory between St. Ives and Lands End. The Scilly Isles, where the churches are small, simple and comparatively new, are the nearly submerged tops of granite hills, between which and Lands End was the lost territory of Lyonesse. The rest of the county is slate, varying from bluish silver to deep green. The little-visited peninsular of the Lizard is made of coloured rocks called Serpentine. Tin mines have brought 19th-century industrial scenery, with its chapel and streets, to the districts round Camborne and Redruth. Visitors of our own generation have pocked the tremendous coast with bungalows but they have also preserved the humble slate grey fishing ports because of their picturesque qualities. The two most attractive towns in Cornwall are Launceston, a border fortress to which have been added Georgian houses, and Truro, where Pearson's noble Victorian Cathedral rises in the French manner out of the old houses and shops. Truro has its Georgian streets and so have Helston, Penzance and Falmouth. Calstock is the least known and most uninterruptedly Cornish town. The Duchy becomes its native self in winter, and that is the time to see it.

Inland Cornwall is mercifully considered dull. The wooded valleys like those of the Allen, Camel, Inny, Fowey and Lynher, with their steep slopes of thin Cornish elms, carpeted underneath with spring anemones, their slate-hung houses, whose gardens in summer are bright with hydrangea, veronica and fuchsia, are remotest and loveliest Cornwall. The coast is awe-inspiring. Rocks fall sheer into the peacock blue Atlantic and English Channel and rock pools are full of many-coloured seaweeds and marine life.

Before Southern England was Christian, Cornwall had been visited by Celtic missionaries from Wales and Ireland. Their names survive as those of Saints, though little is known about many of them. The Cornish are the same sort of Celts as the Welsh and Bretons, but the Celtic field system makes the Duchy look different from England. The Celtic Saints were hermits who lived in beehive cells and are said to have recited the Psalms waist-deep in cold streams. The crosses of their age survive and so does the siting of their churches, for the parochial system came late to Cornwall and the church on the site of a Celtic hermit's cell is often remote from the chief village in the parish, and it is in the larger villages that one finds the chapels of Methodism, which has made as deep an impression on Cornwall as it has on Wales.

The old Cornish churches are rugged and windswept and their charm is in their storm-resisting construction and their lichen crusted texture. Mr. Attlee thinks that the rather unenterprising nature of Cornish churches, which were nearly all rebuilt or added to on the same pattern in the 15th century, was for two main reasons. (1) The local stone was hard to work. Cornwall is deficient in lime and so the mason used mud and walls had therefore to be kept low. Roofs had to be barrel-vaulted so as to distribute their weight evenly along the walls. This sort of roof suited a boat-building people and their tools – the adze and spokeshave. Hence Cornishmen never reached realization of wall and window, voids and solids, as a composition. They stuck at the stage of regarding them as an aggregate of lumps with holes left in it, as did their Celtic forebears. (2) Most Cornishmen made their living from the sea, so they saw no pattern in town and village, as for instance did the sheep and wool masters who lived off the surface of the land. So the true village church can only be found far inland, as at Altarnun, Blisland, St. Neots and Bodmin.

J.B.

SELECTED LIST OF CHURCHES

by T. S. Attlee, F.R.I.B.A. and John Betjeman

ADVENT (*St. Athwenna*)
Lonely moorland situation; poor inside.

ALTARNUN *(St. Nonna)*
Large 15th-century church with lofty tower; fine display of 16th-century bench ends. Norman font of local type. Communion rails extending across chancel and aisles, 17th century. Noble rood screen. Early 17th-century panels on E. wall, one depicting the Holy Communion and the other the Crucifixion.

BLISLAND *(St. Protus & St. Hyacinth)*
The village of old granite and slate houses has a green with ash trees on it. The church, with a fifteenth-century tower made of enormous blocks of local moorland granite, looks out over a steep wooded valley. It has two transepts, a south aisle and two chancel chapels. The old carved wagon roofs remain throughout, and nave floor is of slate, the walls are white, a few old carved bench-ends survive; otherwise there are chairs. The Georgian-style wine-glass pulpit is by F. C. Eden (early 20th century) as is virtually all the amazingly rich screen and loft which extends the whole width of the church, a blaze of red and gold and green and white, with a rood over its centre. This screen gives to this weather-beaten village building, with its 15th-century S. arcade of granite sloping this way and that, an unforgettable sense of joy and mystery. Through the delicate tracery of the screen may be glimpsed splendid altars and harmonious windows by F. C. Eden. As a restoration and even improvement on a medieval church, this holy and peaceful place on the edge of Bodmin moor can hardly be bettered in the kingdom. (*See Plate 30*)

BODMIN *(St. Petrock)*
The largest parish church in Cornwall. Though much furbished up in Victorian times, it retains its old wagon roofs and a grand Norman font of local type. Mainly late medieval. Note the splendid table tomb in Catacleuse stone of Thomas Vyvyan (1533), Prior of Bodmin and titular Bishop of Megara, a delightful blend of Gothic and Renaissance decoration.

CALSTOCK *(St. Andrew)*
Included mainly because of its situation high above the Tamar valley.

CHACEWATER *(St. Paul)*
A church was built in 1828, repaired in 1866, greatly damaged by lightning in that same year, entirely rebuilt (except the tower) by Edmund Sedding in 1892. Lofty interior with arcade of granite and Polyphant stone. The village street, composed of inns and little shops, the sort that have a small-paned window and a latched door with bobbing bell, lies along the main Truro-Redruth road. The church is a few yards south of the road on a steep knoll. The tower, a gaunt shaft, bare of windows except in the uppermost of four lightly indicated stages, is impressive. Inside, the church is remarkable for the colour of the unplastered walls of local stone, buff, grey, yellow and brown setting off effectively the shallow-sea-water green of the octagonal shafts of Polyphant stone and granite arches. The nave has a wagon roof 43 feet high, the aisles lean-to roofs. An arched recess in the E. wall provides a bent eyebrow to the five-light E. window whose bright stained glass comes from St. Mary's, Truro. There are lancets in the clerestory and square-headed windows in the aisle walls which have shallow recesses inside and corresponding projections without. A satisfying sense that Sedding here knew what effect he wanted to get; and got it.

CRANTOCK *(St. Carantoc)*
Originally a Norman cruciform church with central tower; after fall of tower another erected at W. end; chancel rebuilt when college was established *c.* 1236; further reconstruction in 14th and 15th cent.; restored on conservative lines by Edmund Sedding in 1899–1902; much restored rood screen, Norman font; devotional atmosphere.

CREED *(St. Crida)*
Exceptionally graceful arcade; mats and chairs instead of pews allow its full effect; fine range of windows to S. aisle.

FALMOUTH *(King Charles)*
A 17th-cent. oddity with its diffident little oblong tower and two tiers of broken-backed aisle windows (Gothic, more or less) which have no sympathy with the Classic features inside which garnish the three dark tunnels composing the church.

FALMOUTH *(All Saints)* GR
By John Sedding; almost a triumph; the spacious nave, lofty with passage aisles and rich adorned E. end; but the W. end an anti-climax, plain wall with openings in it 'Chill as a dull face frowning on a song'.

FOWEY *(St. Fimbar)*
Groups well with Place, a late medieval mansion enlarged in an imposing manner in the 19th cent.; mainly 14th cent., has a clerestory rare in Cornwall; a Norman font, Jacobean pulpit and 17th-cent. Rashleigh monuments.

GOLANT *(St. Sampson)*
Wonderful situation on height above Fowey River; snug little 15th-century church; trim, stiff box pews, extremely uncomfortable, recall the fidgets of Gus and Flora in *Ravenshoe.* Three-sided altar rails; fragments of 16th-cent. glass.

GUNWALLOE *(St. Winwalloe)*
Romantically sited all alone near the sea, with a detached tower built into the rock; 14th and 15th centuries and typical of the area. Remains of screen with figure painting and attractive tracery.

HELSTON *(St. Michael)*
A pleasant market town with much late Georgian building. Church rebuilt in 1762 by Bland of Truro in Classical manner; one of the few Georgian churches in Cornwall. Exterior very effective with good tower; interior rather dull owing to Victorian meddling; chancel has handsome moulded plaster ceiling.

KILKHAMPTON *(St. James)*
A large church in the village centre. Mostly rebuilt in 16th century, but retaining an elaborate Norman doorway. Lofty arcades of seven bays with tall granite monolithic columns; rich wagon roofs and the largest collection of carved bench ends in Cornwall; organ from Westminster Abbey on which Purcell played; Grenville monuments.

LANDULPH (*St. Leonard*)
Sylvan setting on Tamar between two in-lets; Rood screen; bench-ends, manorial pew and monument of Theodore Palaeologus.

LANEAST *(St. Michael or St. Sidwell)*
13th-century cruciform; fabric enlarged and refashioned in 15th century. Set in a secluded nook not far from the Polyphant quarry, it exhibits the standard Cornish arrangement at its best; four centred arches of arcade, wagon roof; it has good early 16th-century pulpit; bench-ends, mutilated, and screen. Remains of painted glass. It is hard to say why this little church is more delightful than its fellows of the same pattern. The same recipe produces the light omelette and the leathery. Laneast should be visited first of Cornish churches as it gets one's eye in for the general run of them. In spring the surrounding church-yard is a mass of wild daffodils.

LANLIVERY (*St. Brevita*)
Stands high with a lofty granite tower over-looking the Fowey valley as it widens towards the estuary; in spite of considerable renewal, one of the great churches of Cornwall; as usual, a cruciform fabric was re-fashioned in the 15th cent. when an aisle replaced the S. transept; granite ashlar masonry, aisle, roof and ringers' rhyme board in tower.

LANREATH (*St. Marnack*)
Stands in the village; Norman cruciform, refashioned in 15th cent. and well restored by Bodley in 1887. Norman font, 17th-cent. cover, late medieval screen with figure painting, 17th-cent. seating; monument to Grylls family.

LANTEGLOS-BY-FOWEY *(St. Willow)*
Difficult of access, both the ferry across the Fowey River and the narrow, winding and precipitous lanes from Lostwithiel. A 14th-century church, refashioned in 15th century. Font, 13th century; early 16th-century bench-ends, and altar tomb with brass, 15th century. Remarkable for the very effective arrangement at the W. and where the N. and S. aisles are pro-longed to embrace the tower, to which they give arched access. Edmund Sedding gives a graphic description of the condition of the church before he undertook its restora-tion; and it remains an outstanding exam-ple of careful and conservative repair – the decaying roof with decay arrested, the leaning walls stabilised in the act. The panelling from family pews, removed from the E. end of the church and erected at the W., is interesting and unusual.

LAUNCELLS *(St. Andrew)*
In a wooded valley. The only Cornish church wholly undisturbed by Victorian 'restoration'. Outside it is like other churches in the district, but the interior comes as a welcome surprise; old plaster on the walls, ancient roofs intact; the finest bench-ends in Cornwall; box pews, pulpit, three-sided altar rails, reredos and organ case; granite and Polyphant arcades; Norman font with 17th-century cover.

LAUNCESTON *(St. Mary Magdalene)*
Erected by Sir Henry Trecarrel, in early 16th century; the tower is older. Chiefly remarkable for a profusion of panelled ornament on its exterior. Painstaking work in inappropriate material. Granite with its coarse and conglomerate structure does not allow precision in delineation. A recumbent figure of St. Mary Magdalene in a niche under the E. window will be seen to be covered with pebbles thrown up by the local people. The present Vicar says that the old custom is to stand with your back to the figure and try to throw a stone so that it will land on the back of the recum-bent figure. This is supposed to bring you good luck for the rest of the week. Scraped interior has early 16th-century pulpit; 17th and 18th century monuments, carved with Royal Arms; organ case early 18th century.

LINKINHORNE *(St. Melor)*
The noble granite 16th-century tower is the second highest in Cornwall. A spacious church in remote, unspoiled village, with wagon roofs, that of nave with some original colour; large wall painting of the Works of Mercy; mural monuments of 1688 and 1735; memorial slate slabs of local type; Holy well in late medieval structure in field nearby.

LISKEARD (*St. Martin*)
Large and notable for its three lofty pro-jections (?chapels) in N. aisle; tower 1899 and most effective; pulpit 17th cent.

LITTLE PETHERICK (*St. Petrock*)
In a wooded valley; rebuilt by William White, 1858. Interior refitted by Comper, 1908, with the result that it is now one of the more attractive churches in the Duchy. Vestments and ornaments of Continental origin.

LOSTWITHIEL *(St. Bartholomew)*
Both the tower and the body of the church are different in character from the usual Cornish type. The tower and spire make a most satisfying composition, viewed from the S.W. Short, stout buttresses to the lowest stage, narrow lancets in the next, little louvred openings just below the transition by bold set-offs from the square to the octagon, and at junction of tower and spire eight traceried, gabled, unglazed window-like features which carry successfully the vertical lines of the tower into the pyramid of the spire. Inside the church the arcade on piers without capitals lacks emphasis, and the little irregularly spaced clerestory windows are insignificant. But the great five-light E. window is fine. (Corfield considers the church French both in style and in stone employed.) Font, 14th century.

MADRON *(St. Madern)*
The mother church of Penzance, which looks at its best in hydrangea time when it stands amid a blaze of colour looking towards St. Michael's Mount. Though now mainly late medieval, its core is far older; on the whole it has fared better than many of its neighbours and the interior is quite atmospheric. Wagon roofs, a rood screen richly carved with 16th-cent. base and modern upper part; carved bench-ends, a coloured alabaster panel from a reredos, early 17th-cent. brass, and 18th-cent. altar rails.

MICHAELSTOW *(St. Michael)*
Unspoiled embowered village on hill-slope; church in trees; pleasant village-like interior, though much 'restored'.

MINSTER *(St. Merteriana)*
Far from houses, approached by paths, at head of steep wooded valley near the sea.

MORWENSTOW *(St. Morwenna)*
In steep valley high above the sea. Hawker, the poet, was Vicar here a century ago. Norman N. arcade, S. doorway and font; two E. bays on N. 13th cent., arcade 15th cent., and 16th cent., the earlier part in Polyphant and the later in granite; 10th-cent. seating; mural monuments; scraped walls.

MORVAL *(St. Wenna)*
Setting remote, and comparatively unrestored.

MULLION *(St. Melan)*
Set on a windy hill above the cove, long and low in the Cornish manner and mainly late medieval. The inside was restored and adorned by F. C. Eden who designed the screen and loft, S. aisle, glass, and altars. Wagon roofs and many old bench-ends.

MYLOR *(St. Mylor)*
Delightfully set just above a creek. Norman in origin and refashioned later, it was rather drastically 'restored' by Victorians; 16th-cent. carved screen and pulpit.

NEWQUAY *(St. Michael)* GR
Spacious modern church in Cornish medieval manner by Sir Ninian Comper.

NORTH HILL *(St. Torney)*
Old village, unspoiled. Grand 15th-cent. church, granite tower. Spacious interior with 16th and 17th-cent. tombs.

PAR *(St. Mary)*
G. E. Street's first church and among his most successful, 1848; E.E. with a steeple obviously inspired by Lostwithiel, which early called forth Street's admiration.

POUGHILL *(St. Olaf)*
A typical 15th-cent. Cornish church; bench-ends; Royal Arms of Charles II and two striking wall paintings of St. Christopher.

PROBUS *(St. Probus & St. Gren)*
A magnificent early 16th-century tower well placed at the head of the village street. The tallest in the Duchy; Somerset rather than Cornish in character. Emphatically moulded at the base, its soaring lines have a firm foundation. Lavishly ornamented on granite, there is enough plain surface to escape any impression of over-elaboration. Inside, the church, though without clerestory, is more lofty than most. The arcades between nave and aisles are composed of slender and graceful piers delicately moulded between the shafts and crowned with chaplet capitals. The pews should be unfastened from their ancles. The three great E. windows are impressive, and, on turning to the W., one is delighted by the lofty arch into the tower and the vision of the tall window through it. Early 16th-century brass and mural monument to Thomas Hawkins, 1766.

ST. AUSTELL *(St. Austolus)*
The inside is scraped and towny, but the 15th-cent. tower is one of the best in

Cornwall with 15th-cent. carvings of Cornish saints in its niches.

ST. BLAZEY (*St. Blaise*)

Restored and added to by G. Gilbert Scott, well done; plaster unfortunately removed; excellent windows.

ST. BURYAN (*St. Borian*)

Its lofty tower rising above the village square is a landmark; the church is mainly 15th cent. reconstruction; rood screen with carved rood beam above and traces of colour; 15th-cent. font.

ST. CLEMENT *(NR. TRURO)

Whitewashed cottages with bushes of mauve and pink hydrangeas form two sides of a little forecourt and hold in the angle a slate-hung lych-gate. On the walls of the lych-gate, inside, are fixed slate headstones, and in the churchyard are many others, all worth scrutiny. Their lettering is free and sinewy diversified with endearing errors in spelling and spacing. Most have ornament, fanciful and cut with precision. Inscriptions show originality in sentiment and rhyme. The church was reconstructed (except the tower) in 1865; and it was very well done. The roofs of nave and aisle are carried on 32 arch-braced principals four feet apart. The E. part of the nave roof is top-lighted by a course of glass instead of slate each side of the ridge; an unusual expedient. The glazing of the windows is all of the same character – clear glass leaded in elaborate geometrical patterns with borders and lozenges of emerald green, hot red, midsummer-sky blue, gold and violet. While a single window may strike one as garish, the sparkle and shimmer of the whole series taken together is extremely pleasing. The device of the Foul Anchor which the Admiralty shares as an emblem with St. Clement, appears more than once in windows and walls, appropriate to two admirals and a naval lieutenant commemorated in the church.

ST. ENDELLION *(St. Endelienta)

Stands almost alone on a hill top and a long way from its nearest village, Trelights, and its nearest town, Port Isaac. One steps down from the lichened granite exterior into a light and airy building with two aisles, slate floors, grey walls and light oak benches of a modern and impressively simple design. There are three single altars, that in the S. aisle being a 15th-century able tomb of blackish-blue cataclewset stone and possibly the shrine of St. Endelienta. The font is Norman. The glass is unstained; the old roofs survive. Indeed, the church gives the impression that it goes on praying day and night whether there are people in it or not. St. Endelienta's touching hymn by Nicholas Roscarrock, *c*. 1550, is pasted into the hymn books. In the tower is a Georgian Ringers' rhyme on a painted board. It is a prebendal church which somehow escaped all reformations. The low slate houses for the prebends survive round the church.

ST. ENODOC (*St. Enodoc*)

Among grassy hillocks on the golf course; small crooked spire, 13th cent.; restored interior, dark and ancient.

ST. GERMANS (*St. Germanus*)

Differs from other churches in Cornwall since it is of monastic origin and was attached to an Augustinian Priory founded in the 12th cent.; earlier St. Germans was the seat of the Bishops of the S.W. before Crediton and Exeter. It consists of the nave and S. aisle, of what must have been an imposing structure. The W. front has a magnificent Norman doorway and is flanked by two dissimilar towers. Interior horribly scraped and refurbished by St. Aubyn, 1887–94, and interesting rather for its architecture than its contents. Monument to Edward Eliot, 1722.

ST. JUST-IN-ROSELAND (*St. Just*)

Remarkable for setting, where you look down from steep churchyard paths over the church to the still water of a tiny creek. 15th cent., but heavily restored.

ST. KEVERNE (*St. Keveran*)

Dominates the village square, up a flight of steps through a lych gate to good tower and spire; spacious 15th cent. interior with wall painting and bench-ends.

ST. KEW (*St. Kewa*)

A stately church in a wooded valley with inn and Georgian rectory nearby. 15th-cent. interior vilely scraped; the screen incorporates a little old work; wagon roofs; much 15th-cent. painted glass, Elizabethan pulpit, bench ends and Royal Arms, 1661, in coloured plaster.

ST. MARTIN-BY-LOOE (*St Martin*)

The parish church of East Looe, but right away in a narrow valley. The nucleus, as so often in Cornwall, is a cruciform. Norman fabric refashioned in 15th cent.

Wagon roofs; modern rood screen; 17th-cent. parclose, Norman font and 16th and 17th cent. monuments.

ST. MICHAEL PENKEVIL (*St. Michael*)

A feudal village in a bosky setting at the entrance to Tregothnan, Wilkins's vast early 19th-cent. mansion. The church, faithfully reconstructed by Street (1862) must have been and still is to a great extent one of the most impressive in Cornwall; late 13th and early 14th cent. in character, and of aisleless cruciform plan, the proportions and details are alike impressive. A small college was established in 1319 but much of the detail looks earlier, though this may be due to time lag. Boscawen monuments, 17th–19th cent., and late 15th-cent. brass.

ST. MINVER

Attractive wooded church-town. Spired church; bench-ends; rich Victorian E. window by O'Connor.

ST. NEOT *(St. Neot)*

A slate and granite village in a wooded valley below Bodmin Moor and dominated by the church with handsome Decorated tower and buttressed 16th-century double-aisled exterior. This is the Fairford of the west and has 15 windows of medieval glass sensitively renewed by W. Hedgeland in 1829; the most interesting show the lives of St. Neot and St. George. There are a rood screen and old roofs. The walls are scraped.

ST. WINNOW (*St. Wynnocus*)

In a lovely situation on Fowey River, which laps the churchyard wall. There are woods in tiers across the wide river, an old stone boathouse and a farm, once the rectory, by the church. There is a fine early 16th-cent. rood-screen, well restored by Edmund Sedding, 1907, and a splendid E.

window to the S. aisle filled with 15th and 16th cent. glass whose wealth of imagery may well occupy the wandering attention of the congregation. The old stained glass, the Crucifixion, in the E. window of the chancel is to be noted, also the shape of the arches of the arcade – slightly stilted.

SANCREED (*St. Crida*)

Snuggles down behind a fine churchyard wall of dressed granite topped with flowering shrubs which sweeps round the curve of the road where a few solid and dignified buildings – school, schoolmaster's house, vicarage and another – make a group in a lonely landscape. The church has the usual Cornish arrangement, but low and small in scale. That seems appropriate in a situation where one is conscious of the narrow, wind-and-rain-swept peninsula which finishes in a mile or two at Land's End.

TINTAGEL (*St. Materiana*)

All alone on the open cliffs above the Atlantic. A large Norman cruciform church refashioned in 13th cent. and later, but retaining its original plan. Scraped interior contains late 15th-cent. rood screen, Norman font, and ancient stone altar in the vestry.

TRESILLIAN (*Holy Trinity*) GR

Tiny church showing Street at his best, and sympathetically enlarged in 1904; smiling quirk to foliation of little windows three bells astride nave gable, chimney sensibly perched on gable of aisle.

TRURO (*St. Paul*)

1848; traditional Cornish Perp. with granite arcades; chancel and tower by J. D. Sedding, 1882–9; excellent modern rood screen and old stone pulpit of unknown provenance.

Cumberland

INTRODUCTION

THE ESTABLISHMENT of Henry the First held when the testing time came. Barons to fight. Bishops to pray. In Durham, where they do things differently, one man did both and was Prince as well. That glance across the county boundary is justified, because where Cumberland sweeps up to Alston, the highest of England's country towns is already proclaiming affinities with Durham. Henry divided Carliol from Westmarieland. In 1157 it became finally a part of England. Its history since has been that of its great border town, Carlisle.

The buildings reflect the stones beneath them, the old slates of Skiddaw, Old Red Sandstone and, as at Dacre, limestone, and the New Red Sandstone of the south-west coast from Silecroft to Whitehaven. The Abbey of Holme Cultram is built of this sandstone in its northern stretch from Marypoint to Wigton. From Carlisle it runs down the east of the Eden Valley to Westmorland's Appleby and Kirkby Stephen. The Roman wall provided a special quarry, making possible for example, the great achievements of the county at Lanercost Priory, beautiful in the early English style, and in some unearthly mode of its own, and for another the Norman portions of Carlisle cathedral, the rest of which is New Red Sandstone. With the exception of the cathedral choir, Brigham church near Cockermouth, is the only good example of decorated architecture. Greystoke church is a good example of perpendicular.

The coastal plain is really a further extension northwards of the Red Sandstone of Cheshire.

The Cumbrian coastline sweeps round from Carlyle's 'grand old Solway Firth . . . with everlasting roar of the loud winds, and the going and coming of the great atlantic brine . . . doomed to a course of transcendent monotony, the very image as of a grey objectless eternity . . . ' (wheer's Lincoln's Tennyson noo?) . . . to just beyond Black Combe, that most southern out-thrust of Skiddaw slate, the oldest of the rocks, whose outline, like that of some heraldic couchant animal, dominates the view from the sitting-rooms of Morecambe, from ships at sea, from Scotland and from the Isle of Man.

The coast is alternately wild and industrial, old-fashioned and startlingly contemporary. A century ago Whitehaven had already outlived the fame and prosperity which followed the inventions of the 18th-century engineers – coal-mining beneath the sea, steam pump and steam engine, coal, gas and railways. Science is seen here not only in the unusual role of the old

125

fashioned. It is out-dated almost daily. The promising, ever-renewed output of the many schools hereabouts may turn a speculative eye on the architecture of the plutonium factory at Sellafield, and adjoining it at Calder Hall, Britain's first atomic power station. Their parents may turn, for escape, to the equally numerous golf courses, or to pray among the lovely ruins of Calder Abbey when the setting sun turns its red stone arches to gold.   F.S.

SELECTED LIST OF CHURCHES

by Frank Singleton

ARMATHWAITE *(Chapel of Christ & St. Mary)*
Stands on a hillock, 12th-century Ermitethwaite, Hermit's Field, in fine scenery by the River Eden. The original chapelry fell into a ruinous state and was used as a cattle-shed until rebuilt before 1688 by Richard Skelton of nearby Armathwaite Castle. Today it is a plain stone edifice consisting of chancel, nave, with wooden roof, small western turret containing one bell, and something about it still of the manger and the cattle in the straw that makes one think of it as a true church of the Nativity. Alternatively, how it would have made a 19th-century restorer itch to be at it.

ASPATRIA *(St. Kentigern)*
Setting; 12th-cent. doorway and tower arch; Norman font; well-restored 1848; monuments.

BECKERMET *(St. John the Baptist)*
Rebuilt 1810 and 1878 in a striking situation high above the confluence of two becks. This is a most successful example of a small Victorian Church. Red sandstone and pitch pine do not tone happily but the interior is pleasing and access to vestry, porch, and bell and clock tower well and conveniently designed. Neat and simple with a collection of ancient stones in the porch and on the window-sills, some gravestones, crosses, big fragments going back 1000 years. Nearby 13th-century St. Bridgets, now a mortuary chapel, has two shafts of Norman crosses in churchyard.

BEWCASTLE *(St. Cuthbert)*
Bewcastle Cross (7th or 8th cent.) in churchyard, its single glory.

BOLTON *(All Saints)*
Originally Norman; rebuilt late 14th or early 15th cent; stone-vaulted roof to nave.

BRIGHAM *(St. Bridget)*
Early Norman, rebuilt early 15th cent.; crowned with cabled or saddle-backed roof by Butterfield in 19th-cent. restoration.

BURGH-BY-SANDS *(St. Michael)*
Late Norman; built largely of stone from the Roman wall and strongly defensive against the Scot.

CALDBECK *(St. Kentigern)*
Large; mostly 1512 and well restored; Gravestone of John Peel.

CAMERTON *(St. Peter)*
Ancient and plain little church with neat pews and bobbin-ends; effigy of Black Tom Curwen, 1510.

CASTLE SOWERBY *(St. Kentigern)*
Medieval and 17th century. The structure of Norman origin has been extended to a long attractive nave with five Tudor arches to the aisle which inclined to the S. so that the church narrows from E. to W. Panelled pulpit and low screen and charming chancel roof.

CROSSCANONBY *(St. John the Evangelist)*
Medieval, incorporating Roman stones. Other stones which were memorials before the Normans came include a hogback gravestone carved like a little house of the dead. Carved gallery 1730 and older carving in pews. Carefully restored in 1880 by C. J. Ferguson, F.S.A. of Carlisle.

CROSTHWAITE *(St. Kentigern)*
The present church was built on an ancient site in its present form probably in the first year of Mary 1553 though it includes 14th-century arches. In 1915 were discovered twelve consecration crosses outside and nine inside, memorials of the consecration of the restored Tudor church. This

is the only church with such a set. The 14th-century font is finely carved. There are 15th-century effigies and many curiosities such as a pre-Reformation candlestick, an 18th-century pitch-pipe and conductor's baton, old rhymes warning bell-ringers not to swear, or ring in spurs or a hat. In 1844 the church was restored as part of the memorial to Southey by Gilbert Scott.

CUMWHITTON (*St. Mary*)
Arcade 12th cent.; font 1662.

DACRE (*St. Andrew*)
13th-cent. chancel with lancet windows; 17th-cent. altar rails; effigy 13th cent.; cross shafts 10th cent.

DEARHAM (*unnamed*)
12th and 13th cent.; Norman and 13th cent.; Saxon crosses.

EDENHALL (*St. Cuthbert*)
Medieval with quaint tower and comical little spire; brass 15th cent.; mural monuments 17th and 18th cent.

GOSFORTH (*St. Mary*)
Saxon Cross.

GREYSTOKE *(St. Andrew)*
Anciently (1382) made collegiate. Much restored but still the great church of the great house nearby, the ministering village at the gates. The church is vast and gracious. The chancel arch is transitional, most of the rest 15th century. Tower and chancel were rebuilt last century. The 20 canon stalls have interesting misericords, and in the E. window of the chancel is a collection of fine old glass.

HESKET-IN-THE-FOREST (*St. Mary*)
Built 1530; black and white roof.

HOLME CULTRAM, ABBEY TOWN
(*St. Mary*)
Fragment of great Cistercian abbey that flourished here; blind effect of filling up of the noble 13th-cent. arches of the nave to make the outer walls.

IRTHINGTON (*St. Kentigern*)
Arcades and chancel arch 12th cent.

ISEL *(St. Michael)*
Chiefly Norman. One 15th-century window has three sundials on it, to mark the monastic hours, for up to the Reformation, this living was in the gift of Hexham abbey. Two pre-Norman stones, one part of 10th-century cross and the other having rare three-armed symbol called the tirskele, one

of the earliest devices found on Christian monuments. This is a perfect English harmony of man and nature – a setting for Jane Austen. The old church stands on the banks of the Derwent. There is an ancient bridge of three arches rebuilt in 1812. The Hall, with its embattled pele tower and rows of square-mullioned windows, looks down from its eminence which is washed by the Blumer beck, a tributary of the Derwent. The tree-hung stream near the church flows past the lawns of the delightful old vicarage. All around stretches a lost landscape of pasture and river. *O fortunatos nimium . . . !*

KIRKANDREWS-ON-ESK *(St. Andrew)*
A church in a fine setting. Rebuilt 1776 in the local red sandstone by the Rev. Robert Graham of Netherby Hall, still the home of the Grahams, on which, amid its trees and meadows, the church looks from across the River Esk. The interior was restored in 1893 by Temple Moore, when chancel screen and new organ were provided.

KIRKOSWALD *(St. Oswald)*
Like all churches dedicated to St. Oswald this one is associated with a spring, but it is almost certainly the only one in which a pure spring of water issues from the conical hill at the foot of which the church stands, flows under the length of the nave and issues as a drinking well outside the W. wall. The church tower, oddly, stands at the top of the hill 200 yards away. The church has interesting 12th, 13th and 14th century remains. The little old sandstone town with its trees and moated castle and house (now museum) with tower is one of the most charming in the county.

LANERCOST *(Priory of St. Mary Magdalene)*
Beautifully situated in the richly-wooded valley of the River Irthing. An ancient gate-house gives entrance. Much of the priory was built from stones from the Roman wall. The differing shades of red sandstone and white seen in the ruins outside have been uniformly bleached in the W. arms of the priory which now serve as the parish church. This portion consists of the nave and N. aisle, restored and fitted in the last century. One bell, cast by Park and Chapman in 1773, hangs in a cot on the W. face of the tower. The priory was founded about 1169 by Robert de Vallibus (de Vaux). The tablet at the W. end giving 1116

is erroneous. Edward I, Queen Eleanor, Robert Bruce, David King of Scotland, cross and re-cross its history in the 14th century. The earliest portions, such as the base course on the S. of nave and transept are transitional, the remainder elegant Early English. Beautiful clerestory, and W. front with bold recessed doorway with arcading, and over this seven tall lancets, three pierced as windows, and in a niche an effigy of St. Mary Magdalene and kneeling monk. Behind the church are many interesting and beautiful memorials and tombs, especially Dacre of battle of Flodden fame in S. chapel. Inside there are Burne Jones lancets in rich colours and monuments by Boehm. A grey woollen curtain behind the W. door has recently been worked, most effectively, with the brightly-coloured coats of arms of the relevant Dacres, Broughams, Carlisles, Vaux, etc. A staircase in the N.W. leads up into the old monastic building known as the Dacre Hall which looks down on the cloisters outside whence the steps lead to the 102-foot long undercroft, with its beautiful vaulted roof, 13th-century pillars, and interesting Roman fragments. The E. end of the present church, built after the priory was dismantled, has a little 16th-century glass, but is mostly clear. To watch through this window sun and shadow dramatizing the soaring ruins of the transepts, tower and roofless choir outside, the walls still rising to their full height and carrying high up on one of them a Roman altar to Jupiter, one of the few in an English church, is to know life and death in the same moment.

LONGTOWN (*St. Michael*) GS
Built 1609 in Gothic style; monuments.

MATTERDALE (*no dedication*) GS
Built 1685; restored 1856; setting; panelled woodwork; canopied pulpit.

MELMERBY (*St. John the Baptist*)
Above the solid oak table altar, E. window low-silled plain glass in which the lovely fells are framed.

MILLOM *(*Holy Trinity*)
Ancient church shelters against 13th-century castle mostly rebuilt 1322. Church has tall N. doorway which like piers in the nave is Norman and a fine little N. Lancet and simple piscina probably also Norman. Chancel mainly 15th century. 14th-century windows, with five light eastern window especially fine, charming oval at the W.

called the fish window. One blocked window can be seen outside. Nave has fine black-and-white roof into which the organ in the old gallery seems to merge. Notice also splendid old roof in S. aisle, modern screen with massive twisted pillars.

MORESBY (*St. Bridget*) GR
1823.

MUNCASTER (*St. Michael*)
Embattled church in park of Muncaster Castle; Pennington monuments; Saxon and Viking stones in churchyard.

MUNGRISDALE *(*St Kentigern*)
Rebuilt 1756. This is one of the smallest churches in the district. The box pews have been made into ordinary wooden ones. Through the clear windows that break the plain white walls are charming views. A panelled double-decker pulpit.

NEWTON ARLOSH (*St. John the Evangelist*)
Small fortified 14th-cent. church; aisle Victorian.

OVER DENTON *(*no dedication*)
A small pre-Conquest church built by Saxons with stone from the Roman Wall. Although new windows were put in during restorations in 1881 it retains a small Saxon window with wooden lintel. The chancel 12 feet by 11 feet retains the original Roman chancel arch which the Saxons brought across the fields to incorporate in their church as did the Saxons at Corbridge across the border. These are the only Roman arches known in any of our churches. The nave is 27 feet by 16 feet. This is a most interesting example of the earliest type of church in the country.

PENRITH *(*St. Andrew*) GL
13th century in origin but rebuilt in classic style in 1720 except the tower which consequently stands with idiosyncratic massiveness twenty square feet of red sandstone out to base, walls six feet thick, probably Norman, crowned with 13-century work, belfry, and much 15th-century rebuilding. Restored by A. E. Richardson, 1945.

PLUMBLAND (*St. Cuthbert*)
Setting; hogback stone under yew; Norman chancel arch and door under tower, but rebuilt 19th cent.

RAUGHTON HEAD (*no dedication*) CL
18th cent.; three times re-fashioned since built; Rose Castle in park, home of Bishops of Carlisle.

1. Celtic Christianity. Cornish cross on Bodmin Moor in the parish of St. Cleer

2. *Saxon architecture. The crypt at Repton, Derbyshire. 10th century*

3. Saxon carving. Crucifixion. Daglingworth, Gloucestershire

4. Scandinavian Romanesque. Late 12th century carving at Kilpeck, Herefordshire

5. *Southrop, Gloucestershire. Norman font; representation of the virtue Patience triumphing over the vice Anger*

6. Late rich Norman. The West front of Iffley, Oxon. 1170

7. *Norman carving. South door of St. Nicholas, Barfrestone, Kent*

8. *The lonely Norman church of Tixover in the Welland Marshes, Rutland*

9. London Norman. St Bartholomew, Smithfield. 12th century

10. *Morston church, Norfolk. 15th century font and screen*

11. Early English. St. Hilda, Hartlepool, Co. Durham. Late 12th century

12. *Built by the masons of Westminster Abbey. Stone, Kent. 13th century*

13. The Baptistry. 15th century heraldic font, Herne, Kent

14. The 14th century Percy Tomb. Beverley Minster, East Riding, Yorkshire

15. East Anglia. South chancel, St. Mary, South Creake, Norfolk,
15th century

16. Decorated. East end of Dorchester Abbey, Oxon. 14th Century

17. Plain and fancy. Geddington steeple, late 13th century, and the Eleanor cross. Northamptonshire

18. An Essex bell-tower. Blackmore. 15th century

19. A nave without a chancel. Fotheringay, Northamptonshire. 15th century

20. *Mutford church, Suffolk. 11th century tower with 15th century belfry*

21. Huish Episcopi, Somerset. 15th century tower

22. The loftiest tower in England. Boston, Lincolnshire.
Late 14th century

23. Batcombe, Somerset. Stately West Country Perpendicular

24. Pleasing decay. A Norman blocked doorway. An original plaster external wall at Tugford, Shropshire. The window has Georgian leaded clear glass

25. A simple village church. Shelton, Bedfordshire. Mainly 15th century

26. Whitcombe, Dorset. 13th century church associated with William Barnes

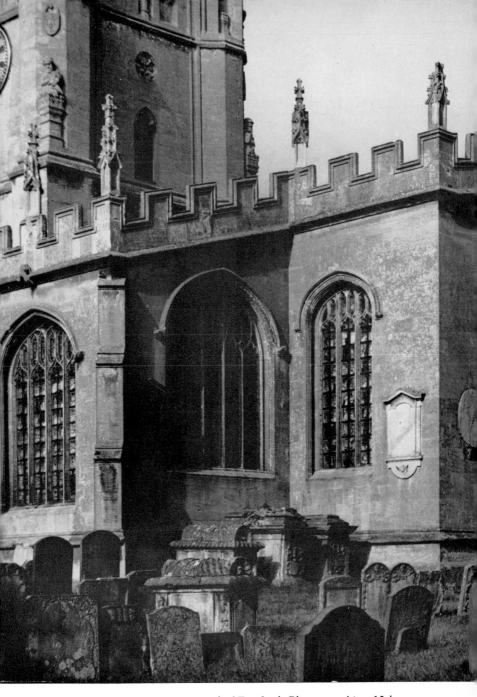

27. A great wool church. The East end of Fairford, Gloucestershire. 15th century

28. Our Lady holding crowned Child. Isle Abbots, Somerset.
15th century

29. A remote Suffolk interior. Badley. 15th century. Mediaeval and later pews and benches. Stone floors

*30. A Cornish church restored. Blisland. 15th century. The screen
and pulpit by F. C. Eden, early 20th century*

31. *Civic splendour. The 15th century nave of St Mary Redcliffe, Bristol*

32. Village wood carving. The 15th century screen in the unrestored church of Inglesham, Wiltshire

ST. BEES (*St. Mary & St. Bega*)

The parish church is the part of the conventual church of the old priory that was retained after the dissolution of the monasteries, a cruciform structure of red sandstone with a quire of six bays, transepts, central tower, 1200, and clerestoried nave of six bays, 1250. Although much restored, indeed cobbled together in some ways, the church is unassailably imposing. The Norman doorway is magnificent, almost unequalled with four rich chevron mouldings, beak-heads of man and serpents and a ram. The modern roof to the nave is impressive and the metalwork screen in the noble chancel arch ought to be, yet somehow disappoints. There are two rose windows and many lancets, the eight most beautiful, seen from outside, being in the chancel. Inside you discover that some are in that part of the original chancel of which the greater part is cut off by a carved but windowless wall. The tower was heightened during Butterfield's restoration in 1858. There are many ancient stones of great interest, outstanding being a lintel stone probably dating from the 8th century in the wall between the church and the vicarage. Probably a relic of the original nunnery of St. Bega, it depicts St. Michael and the dragon.

TORPENHOW *(St. Michael)*

Norman in origin, door, arches and chancel arch (with faces and little men on capitals) and font still preserved. The ceiling of the nave was erected about 1680 'a fair canopy of painted fir' with conventional flowers and gilding. No restoration has spoilt this church which has superb views of Solway, Scotland, Lake District hills and Pennines.

ULPHA *(St. John)*

Lovely old church more or less as Wordsworth knew it, with fragments of 18th-century decoration and old timbers in black-and-white roof. It is built of local stone in a beautiful spot on the River Duddon. See Wordsworth's sonnets on the subject especially the one beginning 'The Kirk of Ulpha to the pilgrim's eye'.

WABERTHWAITE *(St. John the Baptist)*

Some 15th-century windows, Norman font, 300-years old pulpit and Saxon crosses. There is a beautiful view of Lake mountains and Scafell from the churchyard, which thrusts out into the very sands of the Esk estuary – the strangest, most remote little church.

WARWICK (*St. Leonard*)

Apse and tower arch 12th cent.

WASDALE, NETHER *(dedication unknown)*

A diminutive white church in a beautiful setting with a village green and maypole. Oak panelling from York Minster. 14th-century cherubs round roof. Elizabethan silver chalice. Chancel, nave and modern aisle. Neither this structure, a chapel of St. Bees, nor the quaint tiny church at Wasdale Head, the other end of the lake, is, as is sometimes claimed 'the smallest in England'. Wasdale Head where many distinguished climbers are buried is a chapel of Eskdale to which for centuries funerals had to trek over Burnmoor.

WHICHAM (*St. Mary*)

Setting; medieval with massive font.

WHITEHAVEN (*Holy Trinity*) CL

18th cent.

(*St. James*) CL

18th cent.; has a beautiful altar piece of a painting of the Transfiguration by Correggio's pupil Procaccini.

WIGTON (*St. Mary*) CL

Built in 1788; interior is a triumph of paint, a study in grey and gold and strawberry pink; 18th-cent. elegance extends to modern striped pink in the lady chapel; excellent taste in ornaments and flowers.

WORKINGTON *(St. John)*

The parish church is St. Michael's. St. John's is an ecclesiastical parish founded in 1835. The church in Washington Street built in 1823 by the Commissioners for Building Churches is a plain rectangular edifice in the Italian style. It has an enormous portico supported by massive pillars of the Doric order so that it looks rather like Euston station. It has a turret with a cupola. The interior with its fittings by Comper, contains perhaps the most remarkable venture of the movement to make the interior of churches more comely. This one, painted, but rather barn like, is dominated by the 20-feet high coloured canopy whose flat top is sustained over the altar by four gleaming round gold pillars. Hanging at the back is an elaborate star-like medallion with a figure of St. John against rich red altar drapery.

E

Derbyshire

INTRODUCTION

DERBYSHIRE IS a microcosm of England except that it has no sea. In the south it has pastoral country which merges into Leicestershire across the Trent, and here the older cottages and farms are of a dark red brick and the churches are of pale limestone. In the northern half of the county, stone never seems far below the surface, and stone of such variety of colour and quality as is found nowhere else in England – the silvery white stone of the Peak district where the drystone walls seem to take up more room than the grass in the little fields, and where the windswept farms are of a blue grey limestone with mullions and transoms of a darker stone: limestones and ironstones of pale yellow, orange and brown: great rock formations suddenly intruding into landscaped gardens as at Chatsworth: stone which the Saxons delighted to carve into crosses, and of which they built their churches, the crypt at Repton being the most perfect survival: stone which the Normans used for churches as at Steetley and Melbourne. With this stone goes the remarkable scenery of the Peaks and Dales and of the moors of Derbyshire which produce a wild natural landscape big enough to absorb the coach and car-loads of pale mechanics from Leeds, Sheffield and Manchester, whose natural playground it is. Derbyshire has been mined for lead and alabaster and blue john and coal, and quarried for monumental stone as at Hopton Wood. Derbyshire has also its industrial districts – the earliest are Georgian and associated with the spinning mills of Crompton and Belper and the names of Arkwright and Strutt. On the eastern borders are coal districts, sooty, wire-strung and upheaved with excavations, and pitted with those sudden semi-towns one finds in neighbouring Notts. It has railway works at Derby, iron and steel at Staveley; it has the Rolls Royce Factory, and aeroplane and celanese factories.

After its wonderful natural scenery and its less wonderful industrial districts, Derbyshire is chiefly a place of great houses – Chatsworth a palace, 'Hardwick Hall more glass than wall', and Bolsover, all associated with the Cavendishes: Haddon Hall, ancient and intimate, which belonged to the Vernons: Kedleston and Melbourne in the south. And here and there on hillslopes are the Gothic Revival castles and abbeys of the Georgian and later industrialists, mostly now converted into institutions. In the north, too, it is a county of wells, dressed with pictures made of flowers at Whitsun and summer festivals. There are mineral springs and the hydros that go with them, the boarding houses, conferences, conventions, kiosks, souvenirs and car parks of holiday makers.

Churches are lower on the list of the county's attractions than scenery and houses. Those least spoiled by Victorian 'restoration' are private chapels – that at Haddon with its wall paintings, monuments and old woodwork and glass, like an untouched country church, and that at Chatsworth, sumptuous Renaissance of 1694 with marble and wood carving and a painted ceiling by Verrio. The parish churches, besides the Saxon and Norman work mentioned, are mostly small and severely restored, because there was plenty of money here in Victorian times and the churches were generally stripped of their plaster and had their windows filled with greenish-tinted glass. The large churches are Ashbourne (13th-century), Tideswell, Hathersage, Chesterfield, Bakewell, Norbury and Sandiacre, all with grand 14th-century features. 15th-century architecture, 'Perp', so common in the rest of England, is rare here and the tower of Derby All Saints is its noblest expression. The 18th century produced much good wrought iron work, particularly that of Robert Bakewell and Gibbs' design for All Saints Church (1723–6), now the cathedral, is the most distinguished classic church in the county.

J.B.

SELECTED LIST OF CHURCHES

by Marion Adnams

ALFRETON (*St. Martin*)
Medieval; one exquisite monument.

ALVASTON (*St. Michael & All Angels*)
1856; wrought iron reredos (Robert Bakewell).

ASHBOURNE *(St. Oswald)*
A graceful church, with breath-taking tower and spire. An attractive setting – you enter the churchyard through wrought-iron gates from Church Street, with its 16th-century Grammar School, 17th-century almshouses and 18th-century houses. The chancel is Early English; other parts are Decorated, and there are great Perpendicular windows. The whole building has a curious irregularity, but ever-changing vistas. Plenty of monuments, most in the N. transept, including the famous little girl, Penelope Boothby (1781). (*See Plate 52a*)

ASHFORD-IN-THE-WATER (*Holy Trinity*)
Setting; 1870; Norman remains; 'maidens' garlands'.

ASHOVER *(All Saints)*
Beautifully placed among trees by the roadside; by the churchyard, the Crispin Inn of 1416, when Thomas Babington of Dethick returned after Agincourt. The church mainly of the 14th and 15th centuries; the spire and rood screen given by the Babingtons. There are good alabaster tombs and brasses, and a lovely Norman lead font with figures in an arcade.

ASTON-ON-TRENT (*All Saints*)
Medieval; interesting fabric.

AULT HUCKNALL (*St. John the Baptist*)
Setting; mainly Norman embattled church; crossing tower.

BAKEWELL (*All Saints*)
Medieval, above the town; Vernon monuments; tombstones.

BARLBOROUGH (*St. James*)
Norman; village setting; near Hall.

BARLOW (*St. Lawrence*)
Norman and Victorian; 'well dressings'.

BELPER (*St. Peter*) GR
Harbershon, 1824; pleasant interior.

BOLSOVER (*St. Mary*)
Medieval tower; Portland chapel (Elizabethan).

BONSALL *(*St. James*)
Perched on a hill, embattled and pinky-grey – the spire a flight of fancy. Inside, tall quatrefoil or octagonal piers, 13th century, with pointed arches, the stone silvery; the walls cream-plastered. Texture and soft colour everywhere. A steep stone village, with a splendid cross.

BRAILSFORD (*All Saints*)
Rural setting; medieval.

BRAMPTON (*St. Peter & St. Paul*)
13th-cent. monument.

BRASSINGTON (*St. James*)
Norman.

BREADSALL (*All Saints*)
13th and 14th cent.; best steeple in county.

BUXTON (*St. John the Baptist*) CL
Sir Jeffry Wyatville, 1811.

CARSINGTON (*St. Margaret*)
Re-edified, 1648 – but still Gothic.

CASTLETON (*St. Edmund*)
Setting; plastered; 17th-cent. box-pews.

CHADDESDEN (*St. Mary*)
Specious Dec. chancel.

CHAPEL-EN-LE-FRITH (*St. Thomas à Becket*)
14th cent.; entirely Classicised without (1733).

CHESTERFIELD *(*St. Mary & All Saints*)
The church of the crooked spire. The interior large, cool and elegant; 14th-century nave of six bays, with tall, graceful columns, appears almost sophisticated after the Norman homespun of many Derbyshire churches. The transepts and crossing are 13th century, the chancel 14th. A complicated and beautiful E. end, with High Altar and four richly adorned chapels, one with polygonal apse. In the Lady Chapel, alabaster tombs of the Foljambes – strange and fascinating and of delicate workmanship. Rich furnishings everywhere – medieval screens. Jacobean pulpit, exquisite 18th-century candelabra of wrought iron. Recent stained glass by Sir Ninian Comper and Christopher Webb.

CHURCH BROUGHTON (*St. Michael & All Angels*)
14th cent.; unspoilt.

COTON-IN-THE-ELMS (*St. Mary the Virgin*) GR
Stevens, 1844–6.

CRICH (*St. Mary*)
Medieval; stone lectern in chancel N. wall; monuments.

CUBLEY (*St. Andrew*)
Medieval; fine Perp. tower.

DALE ABBEY *(*All Saints*)
Romantic setting in a secluded valley, with ruined arch of Dale Abbey (12th century). Tiny church (26 ft. by 25 ft.) and farmhouse under one roof. Furnishings follow usual 17th-century plan – 'cupboard' altar, with pulpit (1634) and reading desk behind; box-pews all round. 15th-century mural – *The Visitation*. Hermitage close by.

DARLEY DALE (*St. Helen*)
Medieval cruciform; giant yew tree.

DENBY (*St. Mary the Virgin*)
Medieval; interesting S. porch.

DERBY *(*St. Alkmund*)
Handsome town church by Stevens (1846). Neo-Decorated style – clustered columns and flowing tracery – tasteful if rather cold. The best part is outside – a pretty square churchyard with weeping ash-trees, iron railings, and decayed Georgian houses on three sides.

*(*All Saints*)
An impressive Perpendicular tower (1525) tall and powerful, dominating the town. The body of the church Classical (James Gibbs, 1725); an interior of quality – wide and light. Exquisite wrought-iron screen by Robert Bakewell (d. 1752). The altar, gilded reredos, and tester (Sir Ninian Comper) added in 1927 when the church was raised to Cathedral status. Interesting tombs, including an ostentatious monument to Bess of Hardwick. Spectacular display of 17th and 18th century plate. St. Mary's Chapel.
14th-century bridge chapel. Now stands alongside the new 18th-century bridge. Picturesque view from the opposite river bank.

(*St. Andrew*) GR
Sir George Gilbert Scott, 1866.

(*St. Luke*) GR
Very impressive; 1871.

DETHICK *(*St. John the Baptist*)
Fine position on a hill. Remarkable W. tower built by Sir Anthony Babington (1539) – it has eight pinnacles, a curious stair turret at one corner, and Babington

Coats-of-Arms. The Manor house has gone but a 16th-century tithe barn still stands.

DOVERIDGE (*St. Cuthbert*)
13th-cent. chancel; setting.

DRONFIELD (*St. John Baptist*)
Huge Dec. chancel.

ECKINGTON *(*St. Peter & St. Paul*)
Massive 13th-century tower with round arched W. doorway, lancet windows, and low, thickset 14th-century spire. Inside, too, history in stone. The E. bays of the nave arcades late 12th century, the rest 13th; the N. aisle 14th and 15th; S. aisle and S. porch 18th; the chancel Classical also – but turned Gothic again in the 19th.

EDENSOR (*St. Peter*) GR
Sir George Gilbert Scott, 1867; pretty village in Chatsworth Park.

EGGINGTON (*St. Wilfrid*)
Pretty village church; 13th cent.

ELVASTON (*St. Bartholomew*)
Medieval and 19th cent. Bodley; unusual 13th cent. W. tower; fantastic 'Gothick' castle.

ETWALL (*St. Helen*)
Village; Norman and later; brasses.

EYAM (*St. Lawrence*)
Medieval church and village.

FOREMARK *(*St. Saviour*)
Built by Sir Francis Burdett (1662) in his park at Foremark Hall, Gothic without (except for window spacing and some strapwork) but completely Renaissance within. Most of the original furnishings: Jacobean screen, triple-decker pulpit; box-pews; communion rail of wrought iron probably by Robert Bakewell.

GLOSSOP (*All Saints*) GR
Mainly 19th and 20th cent.; Hadfield.

HALLAM, WEST: *see West Hallam.*

HARTINGTON (*St. Giles*)
Setting; mainly 13th cent.

HATHERSAGE (*St. Michael*)
Setting; medieval; restored Butterfield, 1852.

HOGNASTON (*St. Bartholomew*)
Queer Norman doorway.

HOLLOWAY (*Christ Church*) GR
P. H. Currey, 1903; setting.

HOPE (*St. Peter*)
Medieval and 19th cent.; sombre setting.

HORSLEY (*St. Clement*)
14th cent.; setting; view over valley.

HULLAND (*Christ Church*) GR
Mason, 1851; Pure Victorian; gallery; box-pews; whitewash.

ILKESTON (*St. Mary the Virgin*)
Enlarged, 1907; early 14th cent. stone screen.

KEDLESTON (*All Saints*)
Setting, by the Hall; medieval.

KIRK LANGLEY (*St. Michael*)
Medieval; village setting.

LONGFORD (*St. Chad*)
Setting, by the Hall; interesting alabaster effigies.

LONGSTONE (*St. Giles*)
Medieval; Perp. woodwork.

LOSCOE *(*St. Luke*)
A brick church of 1937. Tall lancet windows and cream plastered walls – light, simple and lucid. Furnishings designed by the architect (Bernard Widdows, 1937) and therefore pleasantly harmonious.

MACKWORTH (*All Saints*)
Medieval and 19th cent. Two-storied porch; 'Squint' from parvise into church.

MAPLETON (*St. Mary*) CL
Small; 18th cent.

MARSTON-ON-DOVE (*St. Mary*)
13th and 14th cent.; wide and light; 18th-cent. organ.

MELBOURNE *(*St. Michael & St. Mary*)
A singularly ambitious cruciform Norman church (*c.* 1130) with twin W. towers and crossing tower, stone-vaulted narthex, and (originally) circular apses to chancel and aisles. Why was it built in this small market town? An austere and noble interior, fortunately little changed. Nave of six bays, with tall, heavy circular piers, stilted arches and much zig-zag. Above, triforium with arches in groups of three, clerestory behind, and a processional way all round. The rood now restored. The Hall, with enchanting wrought iron arbour by Bakewell, and the 'Pool' close by.

MONYASH (*St. Leonard*)
Medieval; moorland setting.

MORLEY *(*St. Matthew*)
Spired country church among lawns and trees, with attractive 18th-century rectory, apart from the village. Inside, a golden

light and much texture. S. nave arcade Norman; the rest 14th and 15th centuries. Glass from Dale Abbey. Fascinating brasses, monuments and incised slabs telling 500 years of family history. Katherine Babington (d. 1543) is the best. Sensitive representation of St. Christopher on brass of John and Cecily Stathum (1453) 'which yaf to ys. churche iii belles'.

MUGGINGTON (*All Saints*)
Setting; 13th and 14th cent.; brasses.

NORBURY *(St. Mary & St. Barloke)*
Quiet leafy setting on Derbyshire bank of the Dove. The church, otherwise small, has a splendid 14th-century chancel – spacious and wide, the windows fine and tall, with much of the original glass – patterns and heraldry in grisaille and soft colours. Altar tombs of the Fitzherberts, with good effigies and enchanting figures of 'weepers'. A curious little 'bedesman' sits under Sir Ralph's foot. An interesting palimpsest brass, and two Saxon cross shafts with interlaced pattern.

NORTH WINGFIELD (*St. Laurence*)
Good Perp. tower.

OSMASTON (*St. Martin*) GR
Stevens, 1845; setting.

PINXTON (*St. Helen*) CL
1750; tower 13th cent.; N. aisle 1939.

RADBURNE *(St. Andrew)*
In Radburne Park; a fine old yew tree in the churchyard. Small, mainly of the 13th and 14th centuries. The zig-zagged sedilia have a bishop's crozier marked on the shaft; there is a 'crusader's stone' in the N. wall. Proud display of Pole monuments and hatchments. Carved wood from Dale Abbey.

REPTON *(St. Wystan)*
Church with graceful spire, old Priory arch leading to the School, pleasant country town with market cross – a satisfying group. The church has all types of architecture from the 10th century to the 15th, but the most exciting part is the Saxon chancel and little crypt beneath. Winding stairways lead to it; it has a rough stone vault and four pillars wreathed with spiral bands. (*See Plate 2*)

RISLEY (*All Saints*) CL
Built 1593; consecrated 1632; Gothic changing to Renaissance; setting; charming group of 18th-cent. buildings.

ROSLISTON (*St. Mary the Virgin*) GR
Hideous and interesting; medieval tower.

SANDIACRE *(St. Giles)*
Set on a hill, with the mines all round. An almost fantastic silhouette – high Norman nave, and still higher Decorated chancel, with tall, pinnacle-topped buttresses. Inside, the same contrast; the nave dim, with simple Norman windows, the chancel lofty and spacious, with star and leaf shapes in the tracery, and richly ornamented sedilia. The chancel arch Norman, with much carving, the S. porch also.

SAWLEY (*All Saints*)
13th, 14th and 15th cent.; stone screen behind altar; brasses; pulpit with tester Jacobean screen 15th cent.

STANTON-BY-BRIDGE (*St. Michael*)
Norman and 13th-cent. Saxon remains.

STAPENHILL (*St. Peter*) GR
Evans and Jolly, 1880; tall Perp. tower; setting.

STEETLEY *(All Saints)*
Stands alone in the fields, a small Norman chapel consisting of nave, chancel and apse. Built about 1160 but desecrated during the Commonwealth. Restored (J. L. Pearson) and reconsecrated, 1882. In spite of Victorian renewals, an astonishingly complete picture of a Norman building, with vaulted apse, lavishly decorated nave and chancel arches; capitals scalloped, or with leaves or animals or people (Adam and Eve; St. George and the Dragon).

STONEY MIDDLETON (*St. Martin*) CL
Setting; Peak village; small octagonal Perp. tower (1759).

SWARKESTONE (*St. James*)
Over restored; alabaster monuments.

TADDINGTON (*St. Michael*)
14th cent.; dale setting; impressive chancel.

TIBSHELF (*St. John the Baptist*) GR
Bodley, 1888; medieval tower.

TICKNALL (*St. George*) GR
Stevens, 1842.

TIDESWELL *(St. John the Baptist)*
'The Cathedral of the Peak', sheltered in hollow on the bleak moors – a church of the 14th century, inspiring and grand. A fine chancel (like Ashbourne, Norbury and Sandiacre); flowing tracery in the windows and a stone screen behind the altar, with canopied niches recently filled

with coloured figures by the Warham
Guild. A Perpendicular tower of character,
with immense turrets and pinnacles; a
great arch to the nave and a great panelled
W. window. Interesting tombs and brasses.
A long tradition of wood-carving in the
town. In the church both medieval and
modern work (Advent Hunstone).

TISSINGTON *(St. Mary)
Jacobean Manor House, grey stone
cottages, a triangular green, and five wells
('dressed' with flower mosaics on Ascension Day) form a perfect village setting.
The church, with a sturdy Norman tower,
stands on a bank in the midst. Inside, too
much 'restoration' (1859). An entertaining
Fitzherbert monument (1643) with ladies
in pretty Jacobean dresses; a two decker
pulpit and a Norman font with incised
creatures.

TRUSLEY *(All Saints)
A small brick church (1713) with stone
edged windows and an elegant pedimented
doorway. The interior is delightfully 'all-
of-a-piece' – communion rails, three-
decker pulpit, box-pews and font, all contemporary. Pretty little churchyard adjoins
the Hall.

WALTON-ON-TRENT (St. Laurence)
Riverside village setting; Norman arcade;
13th-cent. chancel.

WEST HALLAM (St. Wilfrid)
14th cent.; Perp. tower.

WESTON-ON-TRENT *(St. Mary)
Alone among trees by the river; small and
mostly 13th century. The nave and aisles
wide, not long, with very tall slim pillars,
unexpectedly dignified and impressive. A
Jacobean pulpit, and fragments of a monument in the gruesome taste of the early
17th century – a skeleton with hour-glass,
pick and shovel. 18th-century timber-
framed porch.

WHITWELL *(St. Laurence)
Pleasantly placed in a once pretty village –
now surrounded by collieries. The core of
the church is Norman – W. tower, S.
doorway, nave and clerestory. The chancel
arch round, but with keeled shafts, preparing one for the Decorated chancel with
rich sedilia; the transepts are Decorated
too. The stone is warmly golden and the

church is full of colour and texture –
fortunately unspoilt by too much 'tidying-
up'.

WILNE *(St. Chad)
In the meadows by the Derwent, the well of
St. Chad near by, 14th and 15th century
work (restored after the fire of 1917).
Nave and aisles are spacious and light
(wide 3-light lancet windows and clear
glass), in contrast to the 17th-century
Willoughby chapel which takes sombre
colour from the original Flemish glass.
Alabaster monument of 1622 – bad but
amusing. Good slate headstones 17th and
early 18th centuries in the churchyard.

WINGERWORTH (All Saints)
Norman; 13th cent. and Perp. rood loft.

WINGFIELD, NORTH: see North Wingfield.

WINSTER (St. John the Baptist) GR
1842 and Barker, 1883; curious but
imaginative treatment.

WIRKSWORTH *(St. Mary)
A grey market town with steep, winding
streets, set among bleak hills. A large,
cruciform church, dating from the 13th
century, much added to and restored (Sir
George G. Scott, 1876). The interior is
impressive, with lovely vistas. Exceptionally
interesting sculptured 9th-century coffin lid
with scenes from the gospels. Two fonts,
one Norman, one 17th century. Brasses
and good monuments. Charming bits of
medieval sculpture – Adam and Eve, David
and Bathsheba; a miner with his pick and
kibble.

YOULGREAVE *(All Saints)
A massive, stately Perpendicular tower
stands foursquare to the winds of the Peak.
The church, too, is battlemented without;
but inside is a wide Norman nave, the S.
arcade particularly impressive, and fine
Norman carving. The font (c. 1200) has a
separate holy water stoup supported by a
salamander. Two delightful alabaster
monuments; a miniature tomb-chest to
Sir Thomas Cokayne (d. 1488) with effigy
only 3½ ft. long, the workmanship perfect;
and a panel, of great charm, to Robert
Gylbert (d. 1492), who stands with his
wife and seventeen children, the Virgin and
Child in their midst. E. window by Burne
Jones.

Devon

INTRODUCTION

THE POPULAR idea of this large south-western county is not far from the right one. The steeply banked lane stuffed with fern and foxglove and honeysuckle, winds down through oaks which interlace their lichened branches to an old stone bridge over a stream which babbles against boulders. Soon we come to the barton or farm, pink-washed and snug, cob-walled and thickly thatched among its steep little fields of red earth. On the hill slope higher up is the village. Here are thatched walls too and cob cottages with rounded corners and bulging hearths and hollyhocks and fuchsias in the garden. Out of the sycamores near the hill top peep the tall pinnacles of a thin church tower. Inside the church, low 15th-century arcades of clustered columns support a barrel-shaped wooden roof whose timbers are carved. And right across the east end, for we do not expect to see a chancel arch in Devon, will be a wooden screen with carved base and painted Saints on its panels, and through the wooden tracery above the panels we can see the altar. Above the tracery is a beam carved with grapes and vine leaves from which wooden vaults over-arch to support a loft which has painted panels. Above this once stood the rood, looking down the chancel into the nave. And out into the scented warmth of the churchyard we will go back to the village for Devonshire tea, with strawberries and cream, where people will call us 'my dear' and rustics will be waiting on the cobbles outside the village inn to drink cider at opening time.

Such places may indeed be found inland in south Devon. This part of the county has luscious vegetation, flowers seem bigger and brighter than in the rest of England and the sheltered estuaries on the south coast are almost tropical. But the uplands of west Devon are bare and flattened, to quote Sir John Fortescue, 'between the hammer of west wind and the anvil of the yellow clay'. Even here the stony valley villages have the sheltered look of the south.

But there are other sorts of Devon scenery, Exmoor with its smooth moorlands, Dartmoor with its sharp outcrops of granite, Lynton and Lynmouth with their Alpine steeps, south coast seaside towns like Sidmouth, Teignmouth, Dawlish and Torquay, where stucco Georgian terraces and Gothick cottages ornés look through boughs of ilex to the Channel. In the three towns now called Plymouth–Devonport, of marble pavements and Greek Revival public buildings, slate-hung Stonehouse, with its Royal William victualling yard, and Plymouth itself, old at the sea, pseudo-simple in its arid new centre – one can find maritime Georgian at its best and at Tiverton there is fine architectural evidence of a long prosperous agricultural market town.

Nearly all the old churches of Devon were rebuilt or enlarged in the 15th century. The inspiration behind Exeter Cathedral, with its square Norman towers and beautiful nave and choir rebuilt in the late 13th and early 14th centuries, and behind that miniature Cathedral, the Collegiate church of Ottery St. Mary, did not survive into the 15th century prosperity of country parishes, for it was monastic in origin. The Devon 15th-century churches have the low West Country proportions of Exeter Cathedral and Ottery, but they are much of a pattern. The towers, though often graceful, have less variety than those of Somerset. Devonians seem to have been primarily carvers of wood and stone and only secondarily architects. Almost every old church has remains of wooden screens or pulpits or benches. Painting seems to have interested them less than carving and screen painting is not as impressive as that of East Anglia. The county was conservative and Catholic, and in 1549 the Prayer Book Rebellion, a gallant attempt to reinstate the old religion after the Reformation, started in Devon. Love of the old ways probably accounts for the survival of screens in so many churches and even the building of them so late as the 18th century as at Cruwys Morchard. But it does not account for the disappearance of almost all old stained glass in the county. In the 19th century Devon was High Church under the autocratic reign of the great Bishop Philpotts, 'Henry of Exeter'. It is not surprising, therefore, to find work of the London Tractarian architects, Street and Butterfield and the talented local church architect, F. Hayward, building new churches and making good use of the various marbles available in the county. Plymouth remained what it had long been, Puritan and iconoclastic. Devon is different from the rest of Britain. It is brighter coloured, more West Country than Somerset, where one still feels the pull of Bristol, and less Celtic than sea-swept Cornwall. Exeter is not only its county and cathedral town – vilely developed of recent years on its outskirts – but it is the capital of a country, the country of Devon, and the mother city of the ancient Celtic kingdom of Dumnonia.

J.B.

SELECTED LIST OF CHURCHES
by W. G. Hoskins

ASHBURTON (*St. Andrew*)
Town church; mainly 15th cent.; handsome granite tower.

ASHCOMBE *(St. Nectan)*
At head of the long combe of Dawlish Water. Originally a small cruciform 13th-century church: see tower, S. transept, and chancel. In 15th century the Kirkhams enlarged the N. transept into an aisle. The renovation of 1824–5 removed much of its medieval character, including the rood screen, though the carved 15th-century bench-ends remain. It is now light, charming, and Gothick, with delicate plaster

panelling and colouring everywhere. The adjacent vicarage is of the same happy period.

ASHTON *(St. John the Baptist)
A singularly attractive church in every way: worth going fifty miles to see. Lies on the luxuriant W. slopes of Haldon where they cascade down to the Teign valley. Entirely rebuilt and refurnished between about 1400 and 1485, Ashton is the 'typical' Devonshire church at its best. The plastered walls and white Beer-stone arcade set off the rich colouring of the medieval screens, glass, and wall-paintings; and the lavish carved woodwork so characteristic of Devon churches is here in abundance. The 15th-century rood-screen and parclose screens have some of the best figure-paintings in Devon, especially those on the N. parclose screen and at back of aisle screen. Carved bench-ends, heraldic glass, and wall-painting all of same period. Elizabethan pulpit with canopy, 17th-century altar rails, wooden monument to Sir George Chudleigh (1657), who lived at the adjacent Place. Note also original 15th-century S. door, and wagon roofs. Groined canopy of rood-screen added in 1908.

ATHERINGTON *(St. Mary)
Not exciting structurally: mostly plain Devon Perpendicular over-restored by Pearson, 1884. Notable however for its screens, original wagon roofs, and fine series of 15th-century carved and crocketed bench-ends. The N. aisle screen retains its rich original rood-loft (the only one left in Devon), the work of two Chittlehampton carvers c. 1540. Chancel section of screen replaced about 1800 by poorer and earlier type from Umberleigh chapel near by. Medieval effigies, some medieval glass in N. chancel aisle.

AXMOUTH *(St. Michael)* Village and river setting; church of all periods: mainly 12th and 15th cent.

BERE FERRERS *(St. Andrew)
Mostly rebuilt about 1300–35 and unusual (for Devon) in retaining so much 14th-century work. Note the early 14th-century glass in E. window. Vigorous Norman font of local Hurdwick stone, early 16th-century benches with carved ends, medieval tombs of the Ferrers (who built the church and lived in the medieval house near by). Handsome table-tomb in N. transept to Lord Willoughby de Broke, 1522. Lovely estuary of Tavy should be seen here.

BERRY POMEROY *(St. Mary)
Setting; late 15th cent.

BICKINGTON, HIGH: *see High Bickington*

BLACKAWTON *(St. Michael)
Font; screen; 14th and 15th cent.

BOVEY, NORTH: *see North Bovey.*

BRANSCOMBE *(St. Winifred)
A delightful church from beginning to end. Sited in a combe about a mile back from the sea, in a parish with no village but interesting houses scattered everywhere. Important for the antiquary as it shows a process of continuous development from 11th century to the 16th, though the dominant features are the crossing tower (mostly Norman), the 13th-century work in transepts and nave, and 14th-century chancel. Woodwork all worth study, especially Elizabethan W. gallery, altar rails enclosing the altar on four sides, excellent three-decker pulpit (rare in Devon), box-pews in N. transept. Monuments to Wadhams and other local gentry. The Wadhams lived up at Edge Barton, which is worth seeing.

BRATTON CLOVELLY *(St. Mary the Virgin)
14th-cent. nave arcades of beautiful Polyphant stone.

BRAUNTON *(St. Brannoc)
Set in the largest village in Devon, now over-run by suburban building but many 16th and 17th century houses in the native tradition remain. A large barn-like church, not very prepossessing but well worth visiting. The Celtic missionary-saint Brannoc (who came across from S. Wales) founded a minster here in the 6th century and is almost certainly buried under the high altar. Present church mostly 13th century, but much later detail. Note the Norman S. tower, with lead-covered broach spire. Remarkably wide nave covered by fine roof enriched with bosses, c. 1500. Splendid collection of carved 16th-century bench-ends. Much Jacobean woodwork (pulpit, reading-desk, gallery). Many 16th–18th century mural monuments to local families. Parish was always large, fertile, and full of gentry and good houses.

BRENT, SOUTH: *see South Brent.*

BRENTOR *(*St. Michael*)
A wonderful site, perched on the very
summit of an extinct volcanic cone, 1,100
feet above the sea. Great masses of volcanic
ash all the way up, and views over half of
Devon and Cornwall. First church planted
here about 1140, but an ancient religious
site long before that. Mainly 13th century,
plain and primitive.

BRIDFORD *(*St. Thomas à Becket*)
A granite Perpendicular church set in a
granite village, with Dartmoor in view to
W. Some late medieval glass, carved stalls
and bench-ends, wagon roofs, and other
medieval woodwork. Best of all the splendid rood-screen, made about 1530, which
retains much of its soft ancient colouring.

BROAD CLYST (*St. John the Baptist*)
Tower; monuments; early 15th and 16th
cent.

BRUSHFORD (*St. Mary the Virgin*)
Rustic setting; screen; original medieval
bells.

BUCKERELL (*St. Mary & St Giles*)
Medieval, but Georgian air.

BUCKLAND-IN-THE-MOOR (*St. Peter*)
Screen; paintings; mostly 15th-cent.
granite.

BUCKLAND MONACHORUM (*St.
Andrew*)
Handsome, 15th to early 16th cent.

BURLESCOMBE (*St. Mary*)
Arcades; monuments; wagon-roofs; Beer-
stone arcades.

BURRINGTON (*Holy Trinity*)
Early 16th-cent. screen; carved roof.

CADELEIGH (*St. Bartholomew*)
Scenery; pleasant 15th cent.

CHAGFORD (*St. Michael*)
Granite, moorland town; fine 15th-cent.
granite church.

CHERITON BISHOP (*St. Mary*)
Setting; mainly 15th cent.; fittings.

CHITTLEHAMPTON *(*St. Urith or
Hieritha*)
Dedicated to local Celtic saint murdered by
pagan villagers about the year 700. Her
holy well lies at E. end of village, and she
is buried in the church (probably under
passage leading to vestry). Large, late
Perpendicular church with noble W. tower
of Somerset type. Medieval stone pulpit.
17th-century monuments.

CHRISTOW (*St. Christina*)
Granite tower; woodwork.

CHULMLEIGH (*St. Mary Magdalene*)
Spacious; roofs; screen; Collegiate church
mainly 15th cent.

CLOVELLY (*All Saints*)
Cary memorials; modern glass.

CLYST, BROAD: *see Broad Clyst.*

COLDRIDGE *(*St. Mary*)
Church and village on summit of high
ridge, with views across to Dartmoor.
Some Norman work, but mostly late 15th
to early 16th century. Highly interesting
contents include medieval screens (flamboyant work in parclose screen as at Colebrooke); fine medieval carved pulpit; late
medieval bench-ends, tiles, glass, wagon-
roofs with carved bosses. Table tomb of
Sir John Evans, who gave many of the
fittings in 1511–12.

COLEBROOKE *(*St. Andrew*)
Stands boldly by itself. A 14th-century
church, enlarged in the 15th. Good W.
tower. Unusual carved bench-ends (late
15th century) and good screens of same
date.

COLYTON (*St. Andrew*)
Handsome; tombs and monuments; unusually late medieval building.

CORNWORTHY *(*St. Peter*)
15th-century church in a Dartside village.
Norman font and much restored medieval
screen, but essentially a late 18th-century
interior, with box-pews, canopied pulpit,
altar-piece, clear glass and altered window
tracery – most of it done in 1788. Delightful
repose everywhere, quite unharmed by
Victorian meddlers.

CREDITON *(*Holy Cross*)
A splendid collegiate church in a sleepy
little town, successor to a Saxon minster
and cathedral. Red sandstone, noble
central tower. Began as a 12th-century
cruciform church, remodelled in late 14th
to early 15th. Very beautiful clerestory,
unusual even in good Devon churches.
Muniment chest, *c.* 1420. Three notable
monuments (Sir John Sully 1387, Sir
William Periam 1604, John Tuckfield 1630).
Unfortunate memorial by Caroë above the
chancel arch to Sir Redvers Buller, who
was vastly admired by Devonians if not by
the outside world.

CRUWYS MORCHARD *(*Holy Cross*)
Highly 'atmospherick', for it stands beside the ancient house of the Cruwys family who have lived there since the 12th century. No other house near. Mostly 14th century and early 16th, but interior is quite Georgian in feeling, all done after the great fire of 1689. Plastered walls, remarkable Georgian chancel and parclose screens. Chancel fittings show continuity of traditional forms. Cut-down box-pews all very decent and orderly.

CULLOMPTON *(*St. Andrew*)
Another splendid town church, but unlike Crediton in being all of one style – Perpendicular, 15th and 16th century. The fine red tower – one of the things one looks for from the Western Region expresses dashing down to Exeter – was finished in 1549. The second S. aisle built by a rich cloth merchant 1526: rich fan-traceried roof and exterior carvings of ships, sheep-shears, and so forth. The gorgeously coloured roof runs unbroken throughout the entire length of the church; the splendid coloured roodscreen runs across its entire width. Cullompton brings home to one the lavish colour of a medieval church against the white background of the Beer-stone arcades. Jacobean W. gallery: remarkable, gruesome Golgotha in Lane's Aisle.

DARTINGTON (*St. Mary*) GR
Pearson, 1878–80; on a new site, but following the exact dimensions and plans of the old church.

DARTMOUTH *(*St. Petrock*)
A splendid site at the very mouth of the Dart: highly effective grouping with the castle and the wooded cliffs. An ancient Christian site, but the present church entirely rebuilt in Gothic style 1641–2, with much woodwork of that period and fine brasses to Dartmouth merchants.

(*St. Saviour*)
Medieval screens; pulpit; brasses; 17th-cent. woodwork.

DODDISCOMBSLEIGH (*St. Michael*)
Best medieval glass in Devon (N. aisle) outside Exeter Cathedral.

DOWLAND (*St. Peter*)
Rustic; timber arcade; 15th cent.

DREWSTEIGNTON (*Holy Trinity*)
Moorland type; late medieval granite; granite church house near by (1546).

DUNCHIDEOCK (*St. Michael*)
Medieval woodwork; scenery.

EAST BUDLEIGH (*All Saints*)
Bench-ends; 15th-cent. red sandstone.

EGGESFORD (*All Saints*)
Setting in former park; monuments.

EXETER (*St. David*) GR
Caroë's best church, 1897.

(*St. Martin*)
Fittings; characteristic little city church, 15th cent.

*(*St. Mary Arches*)
The city churches in Exeter are small and generally poor: more picturesque as an element in the street scene, with their rough red sandstone towers against a windy blue-and-white sky. St. Mary Arches is worth seeing, however, as the completest Norman church in Devon: beautifully light and airy after its restoration from the bombing of 1942. 18th-century altar arrangements. Memorials to Exeter worthies, 16th to 18th centuries.

(*St. Mary Steps*)
Medieval city church; font.

(*St. Michael*) GR
Victorian, on a fine site.

(*St. Thomas*)
Fittings.

GITTISHAM *(*unknown dedication*)
In deepest E. Devon: luxuriant colouring everywhere. Cob and thatch village. The usual Perpendicular village church, but atmosphere is 18th century: box-pews, ceiled roofs, hatchments, gallery. Several pleasant mural monuments, 16th to 18th century.

HACCOMBE *(*St. Blaize*)
In the park of the Carews. Notable for its fine collection of medieval effigies and brasses, 13th to 17th century, of various lords of Haccombe. Some 14th-century glass. Stone screen, pulpit, and reredos by Kendall of Exeter, 1821–2.

HALBERTON (*St. Andrew*)
Medieval screens and pulpit; early 14th and 15th cent.

HARBERTON *(*St. Andrew*)
A large unspoilt village in a fertile landscape, and a splendid 14th–15th century church, with a handsome tower. Fine late

medieval rood-screen: vaulting and cornices especially rich. Paintings in lower panels of screen are said to be portraits of young ladies of the congregation in 1870. Pulpit 15th century, one of the best in Devon, figures in panels 17th century. Font Norman and unusually beautiful with almost pure Byzantine ornament.

HARFORD (St. Petrock)
Moorland type; roofs; setting; 15th cent.

HARTLAND *(St. Nectan)
Not in the old borough but two miles W. at Stoke, overlooking the open, restless Atlantic: the tower (123 ft.) built as a landmark for mariners. Large 14th-century church with late 15th-century embellishments. Splendid Norman font, carved bench-ends (1530), wagon-roofs (partly unceiled, partly ceiled and coloured), priest's chamber in which Parson Hawker wrote *The Cell by the Sea*, numerous modest little monuments and floor-slabs to local gentry, in whom the parish abounded for centuries. Magnificent rood-screen (late 15th century) extending entire width of church: note the rich cornices especially. An impressive church altogether, in a wild, enchanting landscape.

HEANTON PUNCHARDON (St. Augustine)
Setting; late medieval, plastered interior; views from churchyard.

HIGH BICKINGTON *(St. Mary)
A hill-top church, like so many in N. Devon. 12th-century building, altered and enlarged in early 14th and early 16th. Original wagon-roofs of nave, chancel, N. aisle, and magnificent series of about seventy carved bench-ends of two distinct types, late Gothic (c. 1500) and Renaissance (c. 1530).

HITTISLEIGH *(St. Andrew)
An ordinary little Devonshire country church in lonely country bordering Dartmoor, but restored late and lovingly. Nave and chancel 14th century, granite aisle 15th century. Plastered cream-washed walls, ceiled roofs (some carved bosses), usual floor-slabs to Tudor and Stuart yeomen and small gentry of the parish: an endearing little church.

HOLCOMBE BURNELL (St. John the Baptist)
Setting; essentially late 15th cent.

HONEYCHURCH *(St. Mary)
Even more remote than usual in Devon, far from any village and as delightful as its name. A simple Norman building, done up in the 15th century and given three new bells (still here), new benches (still here), and a little tower. Elizabethan pulpit. Norman font with Jacobean cover. The blackest-hearted pagan would smile at Honeychurch as he pushed open the door and saw this touching little interior.

HORWOOD *(St. Michael)
Delightful little church up in the hills: again no village. All about 1500, decently kept. Pollard Aisle (medieval squires) has alabaster effigy of lady, mid-15th century. 16th-century bench-ends. 17th-century altar rails. Some medieval glass and tiles. Numerous floor-slabs and memorials to centuries of squires. Nothing at Horwood is outstanding, but all is in rustic harmony.

IPPLEPEN (St. Andrew)
Medieval screens; pulpit; late medieval windows.

KENN (St. Andrew)
Setting; screen; bench-ends; 14th and 15th cent.

KENTISBEARE *(St. Mary)
Good Perpendicular throughout in a luxuriant countryside: beautiful checkered tower (red sandstone and white Beer stone). Fine rood-screen, early 16th century; W. gallery, 1632; carved woolpacks and ship on arcade. Tombs.

KENTON *(All Saints)
Fine late 14th-century church in large, rich village. Red sandstone country everywhere. Church built of it; the fully-aisled Devonshire plan at its best. Handsome tower and S. porch. Beer stone arcade with carved capitals. Massive and stately rood-screen, ancient colour and good series of figure-paintings. Medieval pulpit, restored by Read of Exeter. Reredos by Kempe. Monuments. (See Plate 35)

LANDKEY (St. Paul)
Setting; monuments, etc.; 15th cent.

LAPFORD (St. Thomas of Canterbury)
Screen; bench-ends; wagon-roofs; 15th cent.

LEW, NORTH: see North Lew.

LEW TRENCHARD (St. Peter)
Woodwork; over-restored 15th cent.

MARYSTOW (*St. Mary the Virgin*)
Setting; font; monument; 12th–16th cent.

MOLLAND *(St. Mary)*
On the Exmoor foothills. An unremarkable 15th-century church outside: inside a peaceful Georgian oasis in the desert of the 20th century. Plastered and whitewashed. Three-decker pulpit, box-pews, ceiled roofs. Chancel shut off by rustic 18th-century 'screen', with plastered tympanum above. Good mural monuments – like pictures on the wall – to the Courtenays (17th and 18th centuries), who lived at West Molland.

MOLTON, NORTH: *see North Molton.*

MONKLEIGH (*St. George*)
Setting; screens; bench-ends; early 15th cent.

MORCHARD BISHOP (*St. Mary*)
Medieval; 18th cent.

MORTEHOE *(St Mary)*
Largely escaped the 'restorer', a dark cruciform church of older period than usual in Devon. Some Norman; mostly early 14th century; some early 16th. Carved bench-ends, early 16th century. Long, open wagon-roof of nave, 15th century. Table-tomb of rector William de Tracey (1322). At harvest festival, fisherman's nets are hung here. Spectacular coastal scenery near by, formed by the deadly Morte Slates.

NEWTON ST. CYRES *(St. Julitta & St. Cyriac)*
On a bold site above an unusually attractive village of cob and thatch. Early 15th-century church in local volcanic stone. Beer stone arcade. 18th-century canopied pulpit, but the box-pews (shown in Stabb's photograph 1911) were replaced in 1914–21 at the otherwise inoffensive restoration. Striking monuments to Northcotes, especially that of John Northcote (1632).

NORTH BOVEY (*St. John the Baptist*)
15th-century granite.

NORTH LEW (*St. Thomas of Canterbury*)
Roofs; screen; bench-ends; late medieval.

NORTH MOLTON (*All Saints*)
Decayed town setting; medieval and later woodwork.

NYMET ROWLAND (*St. Bartholomew*)
Rustic; remote; mostly 15th cent., including remarkable oak nave arcade.

OGWELL, WEST: *see West Ogwell.*

OTTERY ST. MARY *(St. Mary)*
Another grand town church, of even higher rank than Crediton and Cullompton. Rather squat exterior, like Exeter Cathedral on which it was closely modelled by the munificent Bishop Grandisson. He reconstructed (1338–42) a large 13th-century church, to which was added the Dorset Aisle about 1520 with beautiful fan-vaulted roof. Impressive interior with much detail for study, e.g. roof bosses. Of the 14th century are the clock (S. transept), the excellent canopied tombs of Otho Grandisson and wife, choir stalls, altar screen, sedilia, minstrels' gallery, and gilded wooden eagle given by Bishop Grandisson. Good 18th-century pulpit. Thorough restoration by Butterfield (1850) did less harm than might be expected. His font is dreadful. Various monuments 16th to 19th centuries. Colour and light everywhere.

PARRACOMBE *(St. Petrock)*
The old church is up on the moorside, well away from the village, saved from destruction when the new Victorian church (1878) was built in a more convenient place. Most North Devon churches were terribly 'restored' in these years, but Parracombe was spared all this because of the new church and is a completely unspoiled, unrestored Georgian interior: everything is irregular and just as it was 200 years ago – box-pews, screen with tympanum above, hat-pegs, text-boards, mural tablets to local yeomen. Whitewashed walls and ceilings. Some 16th-century benches. Chancel is Early English, the rest a plain Perpendicular.

PLYMOUTH (*St. Catherine*) CL
Foulston, 1823; last building of Foulston's fine civic centre for Plymouth (1811 onwards).

PLYMPTON ST. MARY (*St. Mary the Virgin*)
Setting; tower; monuments; early 14th and 15th cent.

PLYMTREE (*St. John Baptist*)
Medieval screen; bench-ends; 14th and 15th cent.

PLUTFORD, WEST: *see West Putford.*

ST. MARYCHURCH *(St. Mary)*
Rebuilt 1852–61 by S. W. Hugall; tower 1871, wrecked by enemy action in 1943; subsequent reconstruction has converted a dull Victorian building into a beautiful and

stately church. Light walls with pleasing pastel colours, much clear glass, attractive fittings and plenty of open spaces. Amidst all the vicissitudes of the church's history the early 12th-century font has survived with its notable sculpture intact.

SALCOMBE REGIS (*St. Peter*)
Setting; 12th–15th cent.; medieval oak lectern.

SAMPFORD COURTENAY *(St. Andrew)*
Silvery granite, mostly early 16th century, with elegant lichened tower. Interior spacious and light: much clear glass which suits a granite interior. Good arcades: part of S. arcade is very beautiful dove-grey Polyphant stone from E. Cornwall. Screen. Norman font. Carved bosses and wallplates in roofs. A cheerful whitewashed cob and thatch village. Prayer Book Rebellion of 1549 began and ended here.

SHUTE (*St. Michael*)
Setting; 13th to 15th cent.; Pole monuments.

SIDBURY (*St Peter & St. Giles*)
Setting; structure; Saxon crypt; Norman and medieval work above.

SOUTH BRENT (*St. Petrock*)
Setting; front; essentially a Norman cruciform church.

SOUTH TAWTON (*St. Andrew*)
Moorland type; handsome late medieval church; tower.

STOWFORD (*St. John*)
Setting; medieval roofs; Victorian woodwork.

SUTCOMBE *(St. Andrew)*
Dullish village in a remote, unvisited part of Devon, but an excellent granite church. Some Norman, but mostly late 15th to early 16th century. Large collection of carved bench-ends (early 16th century), pulpit of same date, and many late medieval floor-tiles of Barnstaple manufacture. Restored rood-screen. Some medieval glass. Solid Devon granite and oak the predominant feeling.

SWIMBRIDGE *(St. James)*
Has one of the three medieval spires in N. Devon. Tower and spire 14th century; rest is 15th. Furnishings unusually rich and interesting. Medieval stone pulpit (*c.* 1490) with some original colour. Splendid 15th-century rood-screen, well restored by

Pearson. Font cover a remarkable piece of Renaissance work. Some bench-ends. Wagon-roofs.

TAVISTOCK (*St. Eustace*)
Large 15th-cent. town church; monuments; modern glass.

TAWSTOCK *(St. Peter)*
A fine cruciform church, nearly all early 14th century (and therefore unusual in Devon) in the former park of the earls of Bath. Good Georgian rectory some way off. Those who like church monuments will reserve fifty miles to Tawstock: a splendid collection, mainly of the earls and countesses of Bath, their connexions, and their household officers. In N. transept: ceiling of Italian plaster-work, medieval glass, beautiful 16th-century gallery, manorial pew of the earls of Bath (Renaissance work), carved bench-ends, monuments. In S. transept: similar ceiling, monuments. In S. chancel aisle: fine open roof (*c.* 1540), Burman's figure of Rachel, Countess of Bath (1680), and tomb of Lady Fitzwarren (1589), with most beautiful effigy.

TAWTON, SOUTH: *see South Tawton.*

TETCOTT (*Holy Cross*)
Rustic; Arscott associations; 13th and 16th cent.

THROWLEIGH (*St. Mary the Virgin*)
Setting, moorland type; Anglo-Catholic atmosphere; late medieval.

TIVERTON (*St. Peter*)
Handsome exterior; Greenway aisle, 15th cent.; over-restored.

(St. George) CL
The best Georgian church in Devon. 1714–30.

TORBRYAN *(Holy Trinity)*
Imposing Perpendicular outside but no suspicion of what bursts upon the eye on pushing open the door: the most completely characteristic Devon interior in plan, fittings, colour, and atmosphere. First impression is of uninterrupted light – large windows of clear glass, whitened walls and ceilings, white Beer stone arcades. Then against this background the vivid colouring of rood-screen, pulpit, and altar, nearly all 15th century, though the altar is actually made up from the original pulpit. 18th-century box-pews encase earlier benches, and have brass candle-holders: all very charming. Evensong in winter at Torbryan

must be an experience. The four original medieval bells remain.

TORQUAY (*All Saints, Babbacombe*) GR
Butterfield, 1868–74; chancel.

(*St. John*) GR
Street 1861–71; Morris glass.

TOTNES (*St. Mary*)
Handsome 15th-cent. town church; medieval stone screen and pulpit; arcades; Caroline pews.

UPTON HELLIONS *(*St. Mary*)
Unsophisticated country church in deep country, though not far from Exeter. Plastered and whitewashed interior (always a good start for a country church). Essentially Norman disguised by some Perpendicular (like Honeychurch). 15th-century wagon-roofs, some carved benches of same date. Georgian pulpit. Country-made monument to a Caroline squire and his wife.

UPTON PYNE (*Church of Our Lady*)
Setting; tower; mainly 14th and 15th cent.

WEST OGWELL *(*dedication unknown*)
Delightful little church in a park. Unaltered early 14th-century cruciform building, with a late Georgian interior. Plastered and whitened walls, clear glass, box-pews, altar rails. Jacobean pulpit. All very appealing.

WEST PUTFORD *(*St. Stephen*)
In a very remote part of Devon, the deep country of the upper Torridge valley. Cruciform church of early 14th century. W. tower added about 1500. Norman font. Chancel floored with medieval tiles. Mural tablets to local families of the Georgian age. Plastered and whitened walls. Escaped the Victorian restorer.

WIDECOMBE-IN-THE-MOOR *(*St. Pancras*)
A fine granite church well into the Moor, but the village has been terribly commercialised. Best seen in winter against the austere lines of the moorland above. The church remains unspoilt by all this vulgarity. Essentially early 14th-century cruciform; the original transepts enlarged into aisles in late 15th century or early 16th. This was a common development in the larger Devon churches, which are not as purely Perpendicular as they seem. Widecombe has a noble tower – granite at its most graceful – said (and probably rightly) to have been built at cost of prosperous tinners. Remains of rood-screen with thirty-two figure-paintings. Rustic verses on the great disaster of 1638. Church House, near by, built about 1500 and one of the best of its kind in Devon.

YEALMPTON (*St. Bartholomew*) GR
Rebuilt in 1850 by Butterfield, who spared the tower which was unfortunately reconstructed in 1915. The interior is most effective, being well proportioned and restrained with free use of local stone and marbles.

Dorset

THIS IS a county of small churches and enormous scenery. Its long extent of shadowy coast, so varied and dramatic, is in most places too steep or too strange – one thinks of the sixteen miles of pebbles called the Chesil Beach from Portland to Bridport – to admit many colonies of hideous holiday bungalows. Only at three places, Poole with its satellites, Weymouth still with remains of Georgian dignity, and Swanage is there very much 'development'. This beautiful little county divides itself into three kinds of scenery, for long described as Felix, Petraea and Deserta, and the ghost of that immortal fatalist, Thomas Hardy, haunts all three. More recently the Central Electricity Board and the Army and other Government departments have done their best to lay his ghost and kill the remoteness.

Felix is the clay vales of the west and north-west, with Beaminster, Bridport and Sherborne as their chief towns, all in rich farming country abounding in oaks and elms, a land of rivers and stone manor houses and butter pastures and, in the Blackmore Vale, of hunting people.

Petraea is the chalk downs and rocky formations of Purbeck and Portland. The chalk comes in from Wiltshire and crosses the county diagonally from north-west to Lyme Regis in the south-west. The hills are higher and steeper than those of Wiltshire and topped by a marvellous series of earthworks, including Maiden Castle, with its two miles of ramparts, one of the biggest pre-historic earthworks in the world. From the chalk heights you may often see the English Channel on one side and the azure blue of the rich vales inland. The red brick 18th-century town of Blandford and the white limestone county town of Dorchester are in the chalk. The Isle of Purbeck, with Wareham at its gate and Swanage on its coast and Corfe Castle in the middle, is a hilly diversity of geological formations which makes the crumbling cliffs, with their boulder-strewn shores, strange indeed. Purbeck marble, such as supplied columns for Westminster Abbey, the Temple Church, London, Salisbury Cathedral and many a medieval font and effigy, may be seen at Durlston Head near Swanage. The loveliest part of the island of Purbeck is cut off by the military. The Isle of Portland, with its own tall fairhaired people a separate race from the mainland, is a block of limestone nearly four miles long and with hardly any trees. Hence was quarried the white stone Wren used for St. Paul's Cathedral, for Greenwich Hospital and many of his churches. It is quarried today.

145

Deserta is south-east Dorset behind the isle of Purbeck, 'a thousand furlongs once of sea, now of barren ground, ling, heath, furze, anything'. Hardy's Egdon Heath is part of it, so is that inland sea with the town of Poole on its shore and looking over to wooded Brownsea Island.

In all this variety of material, it is not surprising to find much beauty of many coloured building stones varying from the deep gold of Sherborne to the silver-white of Portland and the lavender of Milton Abbey, in churches, manor houses and cottages. And even in the centre of the county, where flint was most easily available, the church builders varied their outer walls with bands of limestone. Brick was not used till the 18th century.

Most of the Dorset churches are mainly Perpendicular, few have clerestories and many have squat and sturdy towers with a prominent stair turret carried up to or above the battlements and pinnacles. The only grand monastic buildings still used as churches are those of Wimborne, Sherborne and Milton Abbas.

Victorian architects seem to have been fascinated by the local stones and fortunately used them both for their 'restorations' and in new churches.

J.B.

SELECTED LIST OF CHURCHES

by E. T. Long, F.S.A.

ABBOTSBURY *(St. Nicholas)*
Adjoining the scattered remains of the former Benedictine Abbey in a large and picturesque village. The fabric is mainly 15th century. The chancel was classicised in 18th century and has retained its plastered barrel ceiling and handsome altar piece. Note 15th-century painted glass with upper portion of figure of the Blessed Virgin from a Crucifixion scene, stone effigy of Abbot in porch and Jacobean canopied pulpit.

AFFPUDDLE *(St. Laurence)*
A picturesque thatched village in the Piddle Valley below the great heath. The church and the former parsonage with its spreading lawns form a charming picture on the river bank. A 13th-century fabric enlarged with aisle and comely tower in 15th century. Note the Norman font, S. doorway, and the fine array of mid-sixteenth century woodwork seating and pulpit dated 1548 'the tyme of Thomas Lyllynton vicar of thys church'. Interior well restored in recent years.

BERE REGIS *(St. John Baptist)*
The village is large but not particularly distinguished. The church is a fine fabric of 12th-century origin refashioned and enlarged in the three succeeding centuries. The tower exhibits the stone and flint chequer work characteristic of the district. The elaborate timber roof of the nave is said to have been given by Cardinal Morton who was born near-by at Milborne Syleham. Note the arcades, some mid-16th-century seating and interesting Purbeck marble monuments of local type. The interior was not improved by Street's restoration.

BLANDFORD *(St. Peter & St. Paul)*
A devastating fire destroyed the church and town in 1731 and the whole place was rebuilt in a pleasing manner by the Bastards, a local family of builder architects. John was responsible for the church (1731–9), a fine specimen of Georgian design in ashlar. The interior has largely escaped Victorian interference and retains its galleries, font, pulpit, box-pews and

mayoral seat. In 1893 the apsidal sanctuary was cleverly moved out on rollers to newly prepared foundations and a chancel inserted; the new work is in complete harmony with the rest.

BRADFORD ABBAS *(St. Mary)
With its embattled parapets, pinnacled tower and large Perpendicular windows the church is characteristically North Dorset. The interior has been scraped, to the loss of much atmosphere. Note the handsome panelled roofs, stone rood-screen, late 15th-century bench-ends and 17th-century pulpit. Some original figures in the tower niches.

BRANKSOME *(St. Aldhelm)
Set among pine woods near the county boundary. A typical Bodley church not of local type but eminently satisfying. Ashlar masonry and Decorated in style with fine arcades and panelled roofs. A tower with spire was planned but has not been carried out. Good font and cover and decent woodwork.

BUCKLAND NEWTON (Holy Rood)
13th and 15th cent; seating early 16th cent.

BURTON BRADSTOCK (St. Mary)
14th, 15th, 16th, late 19th cents.; cruciform with central tower.

CATTISTOCK *(St. Peter & St. Paul)
A pleasant village in the upper valley of the Frome with an attractive group of cottages near the church. The church was mostly rebuilt by Sir Gilbert Scott but its claim to fame is due to the work done in 1874 by his far more able elder son and namesake. This consists of the tower, porch, N. aisle, and vestry. The tower is superb in the best local manner and obviously influenced by that of Charminster. Excellent, too, is the N. arcade, the open porch with its wooden vault and a stone screen.

CAUNDLE STOURTON (? St. Peter)
14th and 15th cent.; font and cover 18th cent.; monument 15th cent.; chancel refitted by W. H. Randoll Blacking.

CERNE ABBAS *(St. Mary)
The handsome 15th-century tower dominates this delightful little mid-Dorset town, once the seat of an important Benedictine Abbey of which there are still some scattered remains. The fabric is of late 13th-century origin, but was largely rebuilt in 15th century and early 16th

century, and partially reconstructed in 17th century. Note the stone screen, the 14th century wall paintings in the chancel, the 17th-century pulpit with tester and the great E. window which probably came from the Abbey and has been cut down to fit its present position. Church Street is mostly composed of late medieval houses with the Abbey House at the far end.

CHALBURY *(dedication unknown)
A charming little hamlet church set in typical East Dorset scenery. Plastered walls and timber bellcote. The fabric is of 13th-century origin with 14th-century E. window. The interior was refitted in 18th century and has escaped 'restoration'. Note the box-pews, three-decker pulpit, W. gallery and clear glass. In place of chancel arch is triple opening supported on slender wooden columns.

CHARLTON MARSHALL *(St. Mary)
With the exception of the late medieval tower the church was rebuilt in 1715, probably by one of the Bastards of Blandford. The plan and elevations are medieval in manner with chequered flint and ashlar walling but the details are entirely Classical. The interior retains much of its Georgian atmosphere with clear glass, altar rails and fine canopied pulpit.

CHARMINSTER *(St. Mary)
An aisled 12th-century church which was virtually rebuilt early in 16th century with a fine tower of Ham stone which obviously influenced G. G. Scott, Jr., when he designed that of Cattistock; the long paired belfry windows are particularly effective. The diminutive chancel is early 19th century and quite attractive. Note 12th-century arcades and chancel arch, remains of wall paintings and 16th-century Purbeck marble monuments.

COMPTON VALENCE (St. Thomas of Canterbury) GR
Tower 15th cent.; rest rebuilt by Ferrey 1838 with vaulted apsidal chancel.

CRANBORNE *(St. Mary & St. Bartholomew)
A large church for Dorset of 12th-century origin as shown by the fine N. doorway but now mostly 13th century and 15th century. The chancel was unfortunately rebuilt in 19th century and is dull. Massive 15th-century tower. It is rare to find 13th-century arcades in Dorset. Note within

14th-century wall paintings over S. arcade and early 15th-century pulpit.

FLEET (*Holy Trinity*) GR
1827 by Stickland; apsidal sanctuary, nave and W. tower; Gothick.

HAZELBURY BRYAN *(*St. Mary & St. James*)
A good example of a Dorset village church in a typical Blackmoor Vale setting. Mainly 15th century with embattled parapets and sturdy W. tower. Nave and aisles have 15th-century roofs. Note 13th-century font with 18th-century cover, canopied pulpit and remains of 15th-century painted glass. Interior well restored by Sir Charles Nicholson.

HILTON *(*All Saints*)
Another typical Dorset country church picturesquely situated above the thatched roofs of the village in the heart of the Downs. As generally in these parts mainly late Gothic and incorporating in the N. aisle a fine range of 15th-century windows from the destroyed cloisters of Milton Abbey. The fan vault of the porch probably comes from the same source. In the tower are twelve tall panels with figure paintings of the Apostles which also came from Milton Abbey; the work is of high quality and early 16th century date.

HORTON (*St. Wolfrida*)
Mostly rebuilt in 18th cent.; effigies early 14th cent.; Georgian fittings.

IBBERTON (*St. Eustace*)
Mainly 15th cent.; finely situated and attractive within and without; some painted glass, 15th cent. and later.

IWERNE MINSTER (*St. Mary*)
12th–15th cent.; old stone spire; S. chapel by Pearson.

KINGSTON *(*St. James*)
One of Street's latest and certainly one of his best churches. Though more suggestive of the Ile de France than Purbeck it is built of local materials and the lofty central tower is among the most successful of the Victorian era. The apsidal chancel is vaulted. The fittings though typical of Street are less successful than the fabric, except for much beautiful ironwork. The former parsonage, a most pleasing structure, is also by Street.

LODERS (*St. Mary Magdalene*)
Charming inside and out; 12th, 13th, 14th, 15th cent.; font early 13th cent.; painted glass and sculpture 15th cent.

LYME REGIS *(*St. Michael*)
An attractive little seaside resort on the borders of Devon with many late 18th-century and early 19th-century houses and a few earlier survivals. The church has an interesting architectural history. Originally a 12th-century tripartite structure with axial tower. Transepts were added c. 1200 and later in the 13th century aisles to the nave. Early in 16th century a new church was erected to the E. of the tower and the transepts, aisles and old chancel removed. Early in 19th century the Norman nave was shortened. The later church is typically Devonian with continuous nave and chancel and aisles. Note the Tudor arcades, the canopied pulpit, W. gallery and lectern, all 17th century, and early 16th century tapestry panel.

LYTCHETT MATRAVERS (*St. Mary*)
13th cent. in origin, but mostly c. 1500; brasses, font and painted glass; 'atmospherick'.

MAIDEN NEWTON (*St. Mary*)
12th-cent. fabric; refashioned and enlarged in 15th cent.; axial tower and 12th-cent. detail.

MARNHULL (*St. Gregory*)
12th cent. in origin; refashioned and enlarged in 15th cent. and 19th cent.; tower and monument 15th cent.

MILTON ABBEY *(*St. Mary, St. Michael, St. Sampson & St. Branwaleder*)
The most impressive church in Dorset; set in the heart of the hills beside the great 18th-century house which incorporates remains of the monastic buildings. The little town which clustered on its southern flank was swept away in the second half of the 18th century and the inhabitants transferred to a delightful model village nearly a mile away, a new church being erected among the thatched cottages. The abbey church consists of quire, central tower, and transepts; the eastern Lady Chapel was destroyed after the suppression and the nave probably never built. Begun on an enlarged scale after a fire in 1309 it is mainly 14th-century work of great refinement with 15th-century detail in the tower and N. transept. The interior retains more of its medieval atmosphere than most large

churches in spite of Wyatt's destructive activities at the end of the 18th century and and Sir Gilbert Scott's encaustic tiles. Note the 14th-century pulpitum and sedilia, 15th-century reredos and pyx canopy, portions of the stalls incorporated in modern work, 16th-century monument to Sir John Tregonwell and the striking marble memorial with reclining effigies to Lord and Lady Milton (1775) in the N. transept which was decorated in pastel shades as a setting for it, and this decoration though faded still remains to delight us. The Benedictine Monastery of which this was the church was founded by King Edgar in 964 in place of a college of secular canons who were established here by Athelstan in 933.

MORETON (*St. Nicholas*) GR
Amusing 1777 Gothick 'restored' by Victorians.

PIDDLETRENTHIDE (*All Saints*)
15th-cent. fabric; tower.

PORTESHAM (*St. Peter*)
Typical Dorset church mostly 15th cent.; tower; arcades with panelled arches.

PORTLAND *(St. George)*
Situated in a bleak position on the W. side of the 'island'. A cruciform fabric with central drumless dome and W. tower with cupola; erected in 1777 to the designs of a Mr. Gilbert with fine ashlar faced exterior. The interior is quite unaltered with box-pews, galleries and twin pulpits. A most satisfying church.

PUDDLETOWN *(St. Mary)*
A large village with some good groups of rural architecture and a fine early 18th-century parsonage in the Blandford manner. The church has one of the most 'atmospherick' interiors in Dorset. Mainly late medieval with an earlier core. Fine panelled roof to nave. Note the beaker-shaped font, probably 11th century, box-pews, canopied pulpit and gallery, all 17th century, fine array of 15th century and 16th century brasses and monuments and Comper glass in S. chapel.

SHAFTESBURY (*St. Peter*)
15th-cent. fabric with elaborate parapet to N. aisle; not 'restored'.

SHERBORNE *(St. Mary)*
Formerly the church of a Benedictine Abbey which became parochial after the dissolution. The large cruciform fabric is externally mostly 15th century, but it is actually a Norman church transformed with slight remains of Saxon work at the W. end. The old portion of the Lady Chapel and Bishop Roger's Chapel are 13th century. The fan vaults of the nave and quire are among the finest in existence. The interior was vigorously restored and decorated by Carpenter and Slater in the middle of the 19th century and the nave and transepts are crowded with seating. In the S. transept is the imposing monument of the Earl of Bristol (1698) and his two wives. The mainly modern stalls possess an interesting series of 15th-century misericords. Note the 15th-century painted glass in the Leweston Chapel, the 12th and 13th century abbatial effigies, the Elizabethan Horsey and Leweston monuments, and some 18th-century mural tablets. Considerable remains of the monastic buildings are incorporated in the school to the N. of the church. The town pleasantly sited on a slope above the Yeo, has many attractive houses of various dates and styles.

SHILLINGSTONE *(Holy Rood)*
A large village in the Stour Valley with many picturesque cottages and a restored cross. The church stands somewhat away from the main part of the village and is of 12th-century origin. There was the usual refashioning in the 15th century and restoration and enlargement by Bodley who added the N. aisle. Note the good modern roofs and pleasant Bodley fittings, several 12th-century windows, 12th-century font and 17th-century pulpit. The banded flint and ashlar masonry is a local feature. A worshipful church.

STAFFORD WEST: *see West Stafford.*

STUDLAND *(St. Nicholas)*
The most complete Norman church in Dorset. Tripartite plan with low axial tower and vaulted tower and chancel. Much good 12th-century detail. Chalice shaped font 12th century and mutilated 18th-century pulpit. Other fittings 19th century and poor. Interior has been scraped. E. window 13th century.

SYDLING ST. NICHOLAS
    (*St. Nicholas*)
15th cent. with 18th-cent. chancel and tower screen.

TARRANT CRAWFORD (*St. Mary*)

Mostly 14th cent.; pleasant setting, with adjacent house and medieval barn; 14th-cent. wall paintings.

TRENT *(St. Andrew)*

The village, formerly in Somerset, abounds in good architecture, medieval, Tudor and later with plenty of well-established trees as a background. The church is interesting architecturally and is full of excellent fittings. The lateral tower is crowned by one of the three ancient stone spires of Dorset. A 13th-century fabric enlarged and refashioned in 14th and 15th century. Chancel good Somerset Perpendicular. Much restoration and refitting *c.* 1840 in a pre-Victorian manner. Fine rood-screen with vaulting intact. Pulpit of continental origin. E. window contains interesting old painted glass, mostly 16th and 17th century foreign work. Fine array of early 16th-century carved bench-ends.

WAREHAM *(St. Martin)*

Well situated at the N. end of the town. A small Pre-Conquest church enlarged and refashioned in 13th century. After a long period of neglect it was well restored by W. H. Randoll Blacking before the war. Note remains of 12th-century wall paintings in chancel and fine monument to Lawrence of Arabia by Eric Kennington.

WEST STAFFORD (*St. Andrew*)

Late medieval fabric refitted *c.* 1640.

WHITCHURCH CANONICORUM *(St. Candida & Holy Cross)*

A large church in the heart of Marshwood Vale approached only by lanes. Mainly late 12th and 13th century with some good detail, especially in the arcades. Fine 15th-century W. tower. The church is probably unique in this country in that it retains the relics of its patroness in a 13th-century shrine. Note late 12th-century font, early 17th-century pulpit, fragments of 15th-century painted glass and some 16th and 17th century monuments.

WHITCOMBE *(dedication unknown)*

By the roadside with an old farm and thatched cottages to keep it company. Nave 12th century, chancel 13th century, tower and windows late medieval. Interior less spoilt than many in Dorset. Note Saxon cross shaft, 13th-century font and 15th-century wall painting of St. Christopher. William Barnes, Dorset poet, held this church with Came and here he preached his first and last sermons. (*See Plate 26*)

WIMBORNE MINSTER *(St. Cuthberga)*

Set in the heart of a small market town with many pleasant Georgian houses. Formerly a collegiate church and the only instance of a two-towered fabric in Dorset. Cruciform plan. The central tower and parts of the arcade are 12th century. The rest 13th 14th, and 15th century. Drastically restored as a result of which much good Jacobean woodwork and other fittings were destroyed. Good foreign painted glass in E. window. Remains of Jacobean screen and stalls. Interesting medieval and later monuments. Notable clock of 14th-century origin.

WIMBORNE ST. GILES *(St. Giles)*

A small village in the undulating country between Cranborne and Wimborne. The church, well placed on the E. side of a green flanked by a row of almshouses on the N. was completely rebuilt in excellent Georgian in 1732. Interior Gothicised by Bodley in 1887. A fortunate fire in 1908 necessitated reconstruction superbly carried out by Sir Ninian Comper. The interior is a treasure house of Comper work, screens, pulpit, seating, altars and glass. Some fine 17th-century monuments well restored after the fire.

WINTERBORNE STEEPLETON (*St. Michael*)

12th-cent fabric refashioned in 14th and 15th cents.; tower with stone spire; Saxon sculpture.

WINTERBORNE TOMSON *(St. Andrew)*

A small 12th-century hamlet church pleasantly placed in the Winterborne Valley hard by the old manor house. Apsidal E. end and plastered wagon roof. Refashioned early in 18th century and well restored after long disuse in memory of Thomas Hardy. Complete set of early Georgian fittings. The W. gallery is formed from the medieval rood loft.

WORTH MATRAVERS *(St. Nicholas)*

A stone village in the austere Purbeck manner with modern cottages in keeping. The church is next to Studland the most complete Norman fabric in Dorset. Here the tower is at the W. end and not axial like Studland. The chancel was altered in the 13th century and has a fine 14th-century E. window. Note the external corbel tables, inner S. doorway and chancel arch all good Norman. The interior was rather drastically restored in 19th century.

WYKE REGIS (*All Saints*)
Rebuilt early in 15th cent. in spacious manner; tower.

YETMINSTER *(*St. Andrew*)
A large village on high ground which in spite of some modern development is attractive with mullioned windows and thatch and stone slate roofing. A good type of Dorset village church. Chancel late 13th century. Rest rebuilt in 15th century with embattled parapets and good roofs retaining much original colour decoration. Some early 16th-century seating and a good brass of 1531. The churchyard is rich in table tombs and headstones of late 17th and 18th century.

County Durham

INTRODUCTION

D URHAM IS a grey, gaunt, curiously withdrawn county. To strangers it means little except a succession of pit-heaps along the Great North Road or a heart-stirring view of Durham Cathedral glimpsed from the railway train. You must live in County Durham, grow to love the gauntness and the greyness, before you can properly appreciate its highly individual beauty, a beauty of contrast and paradox, to be found where rows of workmen's cottages sprawl across the heather of the open fells, or where a Saxon church stands neighbour to a coke-oven.

Durham people do not wear their hearts on their sleeve, and Durham county conceals its treasures from the casual passer-by. How many of the tourists who visit the Yorkshire Dales and the Roman Wall know anything of the barren and beautiful land that lies between, the high fells of Weardale and upper Teesdale, where the Romans mined for lead and the Prince-Bishops hunted the red deer, and where today, if you know the country well enough, you may come upon blue pools of gentians spilled in the hollows of the hills? Eastwards, too, where the grim ship-building towns edge the cliffs between the mouths of Tyne and Tees, unexpected rewards await the discerning explorer, the foundations of a Roman fort lying exposed to view between the rows of little red-brick houses, a railway-station in the high Grecian style standing elegant and aloof amidst the worst of slums, a wooded valley, one of those steep, secretive denes so characteristic of the Durham countryside, winding its way down to the coal-blackened sea. Coal and the sea – these two are the kings of County Durham. But it would be a mistake to picture the county as a solid industrial area like South Lancashire; the Durham pitman is a villager with the open country at his door and the ship-yard worker has fine stretches of sandy beach for playground. Country and town live side by side in odd but not unhappy contrast.

This element of contrast, so characteristic of Durham, gives a peculiar charm to her medieval churches. One of these ancient and seemingly indestructible buildings is often to be found standing overshadowed by pitheaps in a derelict mining village or isolated in the middle of a slum clearance area, and the bizarre contrast between church and setting can be strangely moving. Especially is this so in the case of those Saxon churches which are the particular glory of County Durham. The churches of Jarrow, Monkwearmouth and Escombe are all situated among the worst refuse of industrialism, yet the decay and squalor of their surroundings lends to the churches themselves a certain desolate romance.

In Durham the pre-Conquest period is of the first importance. In any medieval church it is the rule rather than the exception to find Saxon work still in existence and it is always worth while to enquire for Saxon crosses and carved stones. By contrast Norman work is rare and seldom of the first class. (Kirk Merrington, the most complete Norman church in the county, was deliberately destroyed during the 19th century.) With the exception of Pittington there is no church worth a visit for the sake of the Norman work alone and the great Norman cathedral in Durham seems to have provoked few imitators.

From the Conquest until the Reformation Durham remained a poor and isolated area so that it is not surprising to find that St. Hilda's, Hartlepool, St. Cuthbert's, Darlington, and the parish churches of Staindrop, Chester-le-Street and Houghton-le-Spring are the only large medieval churches that can stand comparison with those of the wealthier South.

The most notable post-Reformation development was the appearance of a school of wood-carving peculiar to County Durham. The carvers worked in a gothic rather than a classical tradition, a fact partly accounted for by the northern 'time-lag', which allowed artistic styles to continue to flourish here long after they had fallen out of fashion in the more sophisticated South. The chief patron of these wood-carvers was Bishop Cosin and when he gave orders for the construction of new stalls for the Cathedral he decided to reproduce as nearly as possible the design of the medieval ones destroyed during the Commonwealth. 'Cosin' woodwork is to be found in many churches throughout the county, much of it clearly influenced by the design of these stalls.

Of classical churches the most notable are Sunderland, Stockton, and the unspoilt Gibside Chapel, which is not strictly speaking a parish church at all. Following the Industrial Revolution came an outburst of church-building, but the results are disappointing in the extreme. Architects of the Victorian Gothic school did their best work under the influence of the Oxford Movement and often at the behest of a pious squire whose hobby was ecclesiology. Neither of these factors was powerful in County Durham, where the typical pit-village church is a bare, barn-like structure usually designed by one of the local architects, the best of these being Hodgson Fowler.

The poverty of the Victorian churches has at least the negative virtue of plainness, and where the proportions of the building are good an imaginative scheme of re-decoration can work an astonishing transformation. Unhappily such transformations are rare. Durham remains a comparatively poor county remote from contemporary artistic influence, and, with a few notable exceptions, the 20th-century work is as indistinguished as the 19th. But even modern Durham has her pleasant surprises. The date is 1907, the parish a seaside suburb of Sunderland, neither the time nor the place likely to produce a near-masterpiece, yet in the church of St. Andrew at Roker, County Durham, has a 20th-century building that may reasonably lay claim to greatness.

G.B.

SELECTED LIST OF CHURCHES

by Georgina Battiscombe

AYCLIFFE (*St. Andrew*)
Saxon foundation; present church mostly 12th and 13th cent.; carved Saxon stones.

BARNARD CASTLE (*St. Mary the Virgin*)
Norman and later.

BILLINGHAM *(St. Cuthbert)*
Remarkable example of successful combination of ancient and modern, symbolic of transformation of ancient village of Billingham into large industrial town. Saxon tower, high, black, narrow Saxon nave, altered in 12th century, leading up to wide, light chancel vaguely Perpendicular in style, completed in 1939 (architect, G. E. Charlewood). Windows by Marion Grant. Sudden emergence from darkness and constriction into light and space very dramatic and satisfying.

BISHOP AUCKLAND (*St. Andrew*)
Chiefly late 13th cent.; good tower and porch; Saxon cross; carved wooden effigy.

(St. Helen)
Small medieval church mostly 12th and 13th century.

BISHOPWEARMOUTH (*The Good Shepherd*)
1937; architect Cachemaille Day; church and hall successfully combined.

(*St. Mary Magdalene*)
Modern basilica; architect G. E. Charlewood.

(*St. Michael*) GR
Successful modern Gothic (1933–5) by W. D. Caroë; tower 18th cent.

BOLDON, WEST: *see West Boldon.*

BRANCEPETH *(St. Brandon)*
Prettily situated in park, a few hundred yards away from prodigious Victorian block of Brancepeth Castle. Church of many dates, from 12th to 17th century, and particularly noteworthy for magnificent woodwork given by John Cosin, Rector here from 1626 and later Bishop of Durham. The craftsman Robert Barker, the style a curious combination of classical convention with deliberate imitation of medieval Gothic carving. Magnificent chancel screen, pews, pulpit, ceiling, choir-stalls, font-cover, and admirable small details such as carved wood 'lining' to arch in choir, and carved plaques bearing texts. Over chancel arch two fragments of medieval rood-screens. Carved wooden effigy. Fine Flemish carved chest. Royal arms of James I. Jacobean N. porch.

CASTLE EDEN (*St. James*) GR
Pretty setting; early Gothic Revival church (1764–1800).

CHESTER-LE-STREET *(St. Mary & St. Cuthbert)*
Early medieval church of various periods. Curious tower with octagonal storey and on top of this one of the few good spires in County Durham. At N.W. end of church an Anchorite's cell with squint window. In N. aisle a long line of effigies of the Lumley family, placed here by John, Lord Lumley during reign of Elizabeth I. Two are medieval brought from graveyard of Durham Cathedral, the others, Elizabethan, deliberately archaic in style, representing ancestors going back to time of Edward the Confessor.

CRAGHEAD (*St. Thomas*)
Plain barn of a church (1912), recently redecorated and refitted by Stephen Dykes-Bower; excellent example of what could be done to improve the average pit-village church.

DARLINGTON *(St. Cuthbert)*
An important Early English church with transepts, very large and fine, but curiously uninspiring. Today its size and grandeur are hopelessly dwarfed by the proximity of two enormous cooling towers. One of the few Durham churches which has lost rather than gained by contact and contrast with industrialism. Medieval stalls with good misericords, 'Cosin' Gothic font-cover, curious chancel arch with stone

rood-loft or 'pulpitum' now carrying the organ.

DURHAM (*St. Giles*)
12th to 13th cent.; some Norman work; wooden effigy.

(*St. Margaret's*)
Medieval church of many dates; some Norman work.

*(*St. Mary-le-Bow*)
Church re-built in 1685, tower added 18 years later, but whole effect medieval in style. Charming woodwork, of 18th century, but appearing to be earlier. The whole church a curious example of Northern 'time-lag'.

(*St. Mary the Less*)
Small Norman church almost entirely rebuilt in 19th century. 13th-century sculpture in chancel.

(*St. Oswald's*)
Medieval church of many dates; Ford Madox Brown window.

EASINGTON (*St. Mary the Virgin*)
Mostly E.E.; 'Cosin' woodwork.

EGGLESCLIFFE (*St. John the Baptist*)
Mostly 15th-cent. Perp.; fine setting above River Tees; 'Cosin' woodwork; *Eikon Basilike* and other chained books.

ESCOMBE *(*dedication unknown*)
Tiny, blackened Saxon church situated at the bottom of a steep hill in a derelict, hopelessly decayed pit-village. Very bare, very simple, almost untouched since Saxon times except for the insertion of windows. Inscribed stone from Roman fort at Binchester built into N. wall. Curious sundial above porch. After Durham Cathedral the most impressive ecclesiastical building in the county.

GAINFORD (*St. Mary*)
Pretty setting; church mostly 13th cent.; carved stones, mostly Saxon.

GATESHEAD (*Holy Trinity*) GR
S. aisle E.E., originally St. Edmund's chapel, remainder 19th cent.

St. Mary)
14th-cent. church, remodelled 18th cent.

GIBSIDE CHAPEL *(*no dedication*)
Strictly speaking, not a parish church, but now used for public worship and too remarkable to be omitted. Situated in the neglected wilderness which was once the grounds of Gibside House, now in ruins. Built in 1760 (architect James Paine) and originally intended as a mausoleum for the Bowes family. Fitted up as a chapel in 1812, remaining unchanged since that date. Under central dome altar draped table-wise with blue velvet cloth and surrounded by circular rail. Behind altar, fine three-decker pulpit. Box-pews of excellent workmanship. Perfect example of pre-Tractarian arrangement, and remarkable for the admirable quality both of design and material.

HART (*St. Mary Magdalene*)
Pretty setting; village church of many dates from Saxon onwards; Saxon baluster shafts and carved stones; 15th-cent. sculpture.

HARTLEPOOL *(*St. Hilda*)
Magnificent Early English church situated near sea and docks in remarkably squalid neighbourhood. Particularly fine tower with enormous buttresses. Chancel a restoration (1931) by W. D. Caroe. Fittings and ornaments of unusually high standard for Durham. Pleasant if indistinguished, 19th and 20th century glass. (*See Plate 11*)

HARTLEPOOL, WEST: *see West Hartlepool.*

HAUGHTON-LE-SKERNE *(*St. Andrew*)
Situated in a pretty village (now a suburb of Darlington), at the end of a street of handsome 18th-century red-brick houses. Medieval church of various dates. Some Norman work, including chancel arch, which has curious later arch cut through the wall above it. Interior beautifully furnished with 'Cosin' woodwork, box-pews, font-cover, pulpit and reading desk identical in design one with the other, the whole interior a very pleasant example of an ancient church adorned and furnished in post-Reformation manner. Interesting Saxon and medieval carved stones.

HEIGHINGTON (*St. Michael & All Angels*)
Village church, mostly Norman; pulpit and stalls early 16th cent.

HOUGHTON-LE-SPRING (*St. Michael*)
Fine large church with transepts, work of various dates; mainly 15th cent. with later windows; tomb of Bernard Gilpin (d. 1583) 'the Apostle of the North',

HUNSTANWORTH (*St. James*)
Church, vicarage, schools, and entire village designed by Teulon, 1863.

JARROW *(St. Paul)*
The actual church where Bede worshipped, now engulfed in industrial squalor yet preserving a curious flavour of romance as it looks out over the mudflats to the ships passing up and down the River Tyne. Originally two churches, joined into one in the late 11th century by the addition of a crossing tower. Above chancel arch, the dedication stone of original Saxon basilica (destroyed in the 18th century) dated 685. Smaller Saxon church now forms chancel. Undistinguished 19th-century nave by Gilbert Scott. Good carved stones and medieval chair in chancel. Saxon carved stones in N. porch. Ruins of monastery S. of church.

KELLOE (*St. Helens*)
Mostly 12th to 13th cent.; some Norman work; early medieval carved cross.

LANCHESTER *(All Saints)*
Large village church of many dates. In the porch a Roman altar. Monolithic columns of N. nave presumably from Lanchester Roman station. Norman chancel arch leading to raised choir and sanctuary. Curious arches in N. and S. walls of chancel. Good carving above vestry door also carved head corbels in sanctuary. General effect of church high light and spacious, much helped by well-designed and well-spaced modern pews.

MONKWEARMOUTH *(St. Peter with St. Cuthbert)*
Like St. Paul's, Jarrow, the church of a Saxon monastery situated at the mouth of a river, and, like Jarrow, in the middle of an industrial slum area. Originally built by Benedict Biscop (674). Of his church only the W. wall and the tower remain and the tower has been altered and heightened many times between the 7th and 11th centuries. In the porch under the tower Saxon baluster shafts still in original position also carved stones (much decayed). Inside the church an exceptionally fine collection of Saxon carved stones.

NORTON (*St. Mary the Virgin*)
Pretty group of church, village and churchyard standing beside village green more reminiscent of Southern England than of the suburbs of Stockton; cruciform church of various dates with Saxon crossing tower; furnishings good and some fine windows by Kempe and Tower.

(St. Michael & All Angels) GR
Built 1912–13, architect, Temple Moore. Successful design for inexpensive church.

PITTINGTON *(St. Lawrence)*
Set in a rural oasis between two pit-villages. Chiefly remarkable for Norman work. Strange and exuberant late Norman carved pillars forming N. arcade of nave. Open Saxon or early Norman window-slits above nave arches. Fragments of wall-painting. Jacobean font-cover. Tiny tombstone, 13th-century, carved with two little swords, commemorating twin baby boys.

REDMARSHALL (*St. Cuthbert*)
Much Norman work, including chancel arch; box-pews.

ROKER *(St. Andrew)*
Built in 1906–7, a massive and original design by E. S. Prior, carried out in local stone. Fittings and ornaments in style of Arts and Crafts movement. Burne-Jones tapestry woven by firm of William Morris. Morris carpet. Altar ornaments, processional cross, choir-stalls, pulpit and lectern by E. W. Gimson, tablets by Eric Gill, most of the glass by H. A. Payne. A bold and imaginative experiment which has triumphantly succeeded. (*See Plates 62 and 63*)

RYTON (*Holy Cross*)
Pretty setting; church chiefly E.E.; 19th-cent. furnishings of some taste; painted windows (Flemish?) and wood carvings (German?), presumably brought from abroad by rich benefactor.

SEAHAM *(St. Mary the Virgin)*
Romantic and desolate setting near the edge of the sea cliffs. Cooling towers and coke ovens overlook gaunt and tiny church surrounded by trees bent and stunted by easterly gales. Very plain and well-kept, in date Saxon or early Norman, with Roman stones built into walls. Double piscina with mysterious design of priest's hand raised in blessing incised within its arch. Pleasant windows by Kempe. Parish register contains entry of Byron's marriage to Arabella Milbanke, which took place in drawing-room of neighbouring Seaham Hall.

SEDGEFIELD *(St. Edmund)*
Medieval church of many periods. Fine tower. Interior contains good 'Cosin' woodwork almost certainly by Robert Barker (*see* Brancepeth), of a style more classical than Brancepeth, with the exception of chancel screen which is clearly reminiscent of 14th-century Neville Screen in Durham Cathedral. Particularly good epitaph on tablet on N. wall of chancel, date 1708. Good 13th-century carved capitals in nave. Organ case and font *c.* 1708.

SOUTH SHIELDS *(St. Hilda)*
Early 19th cent.; pleasant 'pre-ecclesiological' church of no particular style.

STAINDROP *(St. Mary)*
Prettily situated in large village beside Raby park. A church which has been enriched and cared for during many centuries by the various lords of Raby Castle. Architecturally of many dates. Spacious wide nave built out to include 13th-century transepts. Curious Saxon window above nave arcading. Pre-Reformation stalls and chancel screen. Two-storied priest's dwelling (now vestry). Especially interesting tombs and effigies, including alabaster one of Ralph Neville, Earl of Westmorland, died 1425 and carved wooden tomb-chest of Henry Neville, Earl of Westmorland, died 1564. Good 18th-century monuments, including two by Nollekens, with some pleasing epitaphs.

STANHOPE *(St. Thomas)*
Typical solid, plain North Country medieval church, mostly Norman and E.E.

STOCKTON *(properly speaking no dedication but usually known as St. Thomas after ancient chapel on same site)*
Spacious and stately classical church. Records prove that Wren had some hand in the design. Chancel and side-chapel modern additions. Imposing pulpit which once formed part of three-decker. 18th-century altar with rails carved from wood of Captain Cook's ship *Endeavour*. Other woodwork and fittings mostly modern, including good pews with carved ends.

SUNDERLAND *(Holy Trinity)*
Parish church of Sunderland built in 1719 and situated in the oldest part of the town amongst the rubble of slum-clearance and derelict 18th-century houses once lived in by rich merchants and ship-builders. Pleasant red-brick and stone exterior with good tower. Interior rather disappointing. W. screen with Coats of Arms and seats for churchwardens and overseers. Good font contemporary with church, cover richly ornamented with carved and gilded cherubs. Curious curved altar rails.

(St. John the Evangelist)
Built 1769, much altered.

TOW LAW *(St. Philip & St. James)*
Church built 1869; worth a visit for the sake of chancel screen, an excellent piece of 19th-cent. 'folk-art'; fir-cones, acorns, etc., are glued to wood frame; reputedly made by local vicar.

WEST BOLDON *(St. Nicholas)*
Mostly 13th cent.; good spire.

WEST HARTLEPOOL *(Christ Church)*
Built 1854, architect E. B. Lamb; a collector's piece for the connoisseur of odd and ugly churches.

WEST RAINTON *(St. Mary)*
Built 1864, architect E. Robson; imposing exterior and position; details poor.

WINSTON *(St. Andrew)*
13th cent.; rebuilt in 19th cent.; fragment of Saxon carved stone.

Essex

INTRODUCTION

Essex is a large square with two sides water. It is a stronger contrast of beauty and ugliness than any southern English county. Most of what was built east of London in this and the last century was a little bit cheaper and a little bit shoddier than that built in other directions. Southend is a cheaper Brighton, Clacton a cheaper Worthing and Dovercourt a cheaper Bournemouth. Over a million Londoners live in Essex. Leyton, Canning Town, Silvertown, Barking, Ilford and West and East Ham are all in the county. Only the Norman parish church of East Ham and the scant abbey remains of Barking and Leyton parish church tell us that these were once country places. Our own age has added the planned and sad dormitories of Becontree and Harold Hill. Along the Thames bank factories and power stations can be seen for miles over the mud flats and the hills of Kent on the opposite bank look countrified by comparison.

But Essex is a large county and the ugliness is only a part of it. The county has the deepest and least disturbed country within reach of London. Between the Stour, Blackwater, Crouch and Thames Estuaries is flat agricultural scenery with its own old red brick towns with weather-boarded side streets like Rochford, Maldon and Georgian Harwich, the first named the headquarters of the Essex puritan sect, The Peculiar People. Colchester is, as Dr. Pevsner says in *Essex* (Buildings of England Series), more impressive than any town in England for 'the continuity of its architectural interest. It began before the time of the Romans and lasted through to the 18th century'. The flat part of Essex has not the man-made look of the fens. It is wild and salty and its quality is well described in Baring-Gould's novel of Mersea, *Mehalah*. It is part of that great plain which stretches across to Holland and Central Europe. Most of inland Essex, east and north of Epping Forest, is undulating and extremely pretty in the pale gentle way suited to English water-colours. Narrow lanes wind like streams through willowy meadows past weather-boarded mills and unfenced bean and corn fields. From elms and oaks on hilltops peep the flinty church towers, and some of the churches up here are as magnificent as those in neighbouring Suffolk – Coggeshall, Thaxted and Saffron Walden and Dedham are grand examples of the Perpendicular style. Thaxted, for the magnificence of its church and the varied textures of the old houses of its little town, is one of the most charming places in Britain.

Chiefly, Essex is a place of varied building materials. 'It would be an interesting study for an antiquary of leisure to trace the various sources of materials employed in Essex church-building, and the means by which they were brought to their destination.' (G. Worley, *Essex, A dictionary of the county*, 1915.) To build their churches, the East Saxons and the Normans used any material that came to hand, Roman tiles, split oak logs, as at Greensted, pudding stone taken from the beach deposits and flint. The 15th-century tower of South Weald was made of ragstone brought across from Kent on the opposite shore. But chiefly Essex is a country of brick which was made here as early as the 13th century. There are many brick church towers of unexampled beauty, red as a bonfire; there are brick arcades and brick porches and brick window tracery. And when they left off building churches in this beautiful red brick, moulded into shapes and patterned with blue sanded-headers, the Essex people continued it in houses until the past century.

Essex looks its best in sunlight when the many materials of its rustic villages, the brick manor houses, the timbered 'halls' and the cob and thatched churches, the weather-boarded late-Georgian cottages, the oaks and elms and flints recall Constable. The delightful little town of Dedham and one half of the Stour Valley, be it remembered, are in Essex, and were as much an inspiration to Constable as neighbouring Suffolk, where he was born, and to which Essex is often so wrongly regarded as a poorer sister. It may be poorer in church architecture, but what it lacks in architecture it makes up for in the delicacy and variety of its textures.

J.B.

SELECTED LIST OF CHURCHES

by Laurence King, F.R.I.B.A.

ASHDOWN (*All Saints*)
Setting; medieval.

AVELEY (*St. Michael*)
Medieval.

BADDOW, LITTLE: see *Little Baddow*.

BARDFIELD, GREAT: see *Great Bardfield*.

BARKING (*St. Margaret*)
Medieval.

BEECH, HIGH: see *High Beech*.

BELCHAMP ST. PAUL (*St. Andrew*)
Medieval stalls.

BENFLEET, SOUTH: see *South Benfleet*.

BERDEN (*St. Nicholas*)
Setting; medieval.

BLACKMORE *(St. Laurence)*
In an attractive little village and close to a fine house known as 'Jericho' stands the Norman church which was once a small priory of Augustinian Canons. Very impressive 15th-century timber bell-tower of intricate and elaborate construction; externally three diminishing stages terminated by a broach spire. (*See Plate 18*)

BLACK NOTLEY (*St. Peter & St. Paul*)
Setting; typical Essex church with shingled broach spire.

BOCKING (*St. Mary the Virgin*)
Impressive chancel restored by Micklethwaite, 1913.

BOREHAM (*St. Andrew*)
Norman central tower; monument.

BRADWELL-JUXTA-MARE *(*St. Peter-ad-Murum*)
Approached by a cart track through fields, and situated on the sea wall at the mouth of the Blackwater. One of the oldest churches in the country having been built by St. Cedd about the year 654. Its materials were mostly taken from the ancient Roman fort of Othona on the gateway of which the church is said to stand. The 7th-century nave remains.

BRENTWOOD *(*St. George*)* GR
Erected in 1934, though unhappily not completed, this brick church is characteristic of the so-called modern movement of that time. Free standing stone altar in large apsidal sanctuary. Unique feature for Essex – an outside pulpit.

*(*St. Thomas the Martyr of Canterbury*)
A large church the work of E. C. Lee, pupil of William Burges, erected in 1883. Though somewhat uninspiring internally, adhering too slavishly to 13th-century detail, the outside is good. Notable feature is the very magnificent tower and spire rising to a great height and forming a prominent landmark.

BRIGHTLINGSEA *(*All Saints*)
An attractive little town of old buildings on the Colne estuary has as its parish church, situated on a hill about a mile inland, a building with a glorious late 15th-century tower of some considerable height, one of the finest in the county. There are many niches in the church, some of which have fragmentary medieval painting. Several ancient brasses.

BROMLEY, GREAT: *see Great Bromley.*

BURNHAM-ON-CROUCH *(*St Mary*)
Setting; principally 14th and 15th cent.

BURSTEAD, GREAT: *see Great Burstead.*

BUTTSBURY *(*St. Mary*)
Setting; 14th cent.; 18th-cent. chancel.

CANFIELD, GREAT: *see Great Canfield.*

CASTLE HEDINGHAM *(*St. Nicholas*)
A large Norman church standing in the middle of the village and close to the famous castle of the De Veres. Three of the 12th-century doorways still have their original wooden doors. There is a fine hammer-beam roof to the nave of early 16th century date. An elaborate 14th-century rood-screen separates the nave from the chancel,

on the S. side of which are some 15th-century stalls with misericords. An altar tomb in the chancel to John, Earl of Oxford, 1539 has low relief figures. The 17th-century brick tower incorporates a stone inscribed 'Robert Archer the master builder of this stepell 1616'.

CHELMSFORD *(*St. Mary the Virgin*)
Now the Cathedral, but nevertheless remaining a late medieval parish church in spite of the changes effected in 1926 by the lengthening of the chancel. Principally 15th century with many changes in the 18th and 19th centuries. Attractive 'Gothick' plastered ceiling. Archway between chancel and N. chapel is most unusual in form being semi-circular divided into two pointed arches. Sanctuary greatly cluttered up with chairs and prayer desks. Unhappy arrangement of double choir of canons and surpliced singers separated from each other by heavy 17th-century communion rails cutting the chancel into two equal parts. Very fine S. porch and W. tower showing East Anglian knapped flint work within traceried panels. Charming mid 18th-century spire to tower.

CHICKNEY *(*St. Mary the Virgin*)
A pre-Conquest church set in an isolated position. It has a most irregular shaped plan, a pre-reformation altar stone set up in its former position and a very beautifully carved 15th-century font. There is a double-light squint on the N. side of the chancel arch.

CHIGNAL SMEALEY *(*St. Nicholas*)
Brickwork; early 16th cent.

CHIGWELL ROW *(*All Saints*)* GR
J. P. Seddon, 1867.

CHRISHALL *(*Holy Trinity*)
Large 14th-cent. church; brasses.

CLACTON *(*St. James*)
The work of Temple Moore. An uncompleted church of no special merit externally. The interior, though severe, is most refreshing. The chancel stands high up above the nave, and each side is treated entirely differently. The walls have been whitened, and there has recently been undertaken a new decoration of the high altar which is quite pleasing.

CLAVERING *(*St. Mary & St. Clement*)
Setting; principally 15th cent.

COLCHESTER *(Holy Trinity)*
Particularly noted for the Saxon tower with its W. doorway formed entirely of Roman brick with a triangular shaped head. The church plate includes a fine 15th-century mazer bowl in maple wood with silver gilt rim inscribed in Latin.

(St. James the Greater)
Perp. work.

COPFORD *(St. Michael & All Angels)*
Remotely situated and somewhat difficult to find since it lies some way from the main road this church must not be missed. The nave and chancel were originally vaulted, a rarity in the English parish church, and still more rare was this vaulting which was continuous and not cross ribbed. The fame of this church lies in the remains of wall paintings over the whole of the original building. They date from the middle of the 12th century though considerably restored since their discovery in 1865. In the half-domed vault over the apse is a fine painting of Our Lord in Majesty.

CORRINGHAM *(St. Mary)*
The storage of motor spirit has industrialised this parish, but its village atmosphere is still preserved in the group of buildings consisting of the Saxon church, some old cottages and the 15th-century inn. Though dating from pre-Conquest days the greater part of the church is 14th century. There is a good screen of that date. The church is well cared for, and there are some furnishings by Martin Travers.

DANBURY *(St. John the Baptist)*
Setting; early monuments.

DEBDEN *(St. Mary & All Saints)*
Chancel rebuilt in the 18th cent. in the Gothic manner – very attractive.

DEDHAM *(St. Mary the Virgin)*
Attractive town; large Perp. church.

DUNMOW, GREAT: *see Great Dunmow.*

DUNMOW, LITTLE: *see Little Dunmow.*

EASTER, HIGH: *see High Easter.*

EAST HAM *(St. Mary Magdalene)*
A complete 12th-century building situated close to the docks of East London. There is interlacing arcading along the wall of the chancel. Taking up a considerable area of the Norman apse in an inappropriate position is a fine monument to Edward Nevill, Earl of Westmorland, and his wife. An elegant marble font dated 1639 'the Gift of Sir Richard Heigham Knight'. A bell in the tower is inscribed *Dulcis Sisto Melis Vocor Campana Gabrielis.* Remains of wall paintings.

EAST HORNDON *(All Saints)*
Standing in an isolated position on the top of a hill this all-brick church is particularly worth seeing. It has a cruciform plan with the unique feature of an upper room to each transept forming small galleries. The Tyrell family have long been associated with this church. There is an early 16th-century Tyrell chantry. The fittings include a beautifully incised stone slab dated 1422 bearing a portrait of one of the family.

ELMSTEAD *(St. Ann & St. Laurence)*
Oak effigy of a cross-legged knight.

ELSENHAM *(St. Mary the Virgin)*
Setting; mainly Norman.

EPPING *(St. John the Baptist)*
Alongside an attractive wide High Street stands this very dignified church built in 1889 by Bodley and Garner. The tower was erected by Bodley in 1908. A striking example of the Gothic Revival. Good internal furnishings by Bodley. Windows by Kempe.

FAIRSTEAD *(St. Mary the Virgin)*
Wall paintings.

FEERING *(All Saints)*
Setting; mostly 15th cent.

FINCHINGFIELD *(St. John the Baptist)*
The parish church has one of the loveliest settings standing on a hill. The massive Norman tower with its quaint 18th-century cupola dominates one of the most attractive villages in the whole country. The church does not entirely come up to the standard of its setting. The W. door into the tower, with its three orders of columns and chevron ornament in a semi-circular arched head, is a good example of Norman work. The rest of the church mostly 14th century. Two fine screens of which the rood-screen (early 15th century) is perhaps the best in Essex. In S. chapel tomb of John Burners and his wife 1523, consisting of tomb chest with brass figures on Purbeck marble slab. Late 17th-century Stuart Royal Arms. Curious scratched diagram on window ledge of S. aisle of 'Nine Men's Morris'.

F

FOBBING (*St. Michael*)
Setting; mainly 14th and 15th cent.; typical Essex S. porch.

FYFIELD (*St. Nicholas*)
14th-cent. chancel.

GALLEYWOOD *(*St. Michael & All Angels*) GR
The work of St. Aubyn, who was also architect to Widford Church near Chelmsford, this church was erected in 1873. It is quite a good example of the Gothic Revival and has a tall spire which forms a noted landmark.

GESTINGTHORPE (*St. Mary the Virgin*)
Fine brick tower.

GOSFIELD (*St. Katherine*)
Setting; quaint theatre box-type of squire's pew.

GREAT BARDFIELD *(*St. Mary the Virgin*)
The church looks down on one of the most attractive little towns in Essex, full of beautiful old houses. The church, mostly of 14th century date, is remarkable for the stone rood-screen of excellent craftsmanship filling the whole of the chancel arch. The influence of the Catholic Revival is strongly maintained. Two chapels have recently been restored with simple stone altars and good furnishings.

GREAT BROMLEY *(*St. George*)
A church of considerable architectural interest mostly of 15th century date. Magnificent tower and S. porch. Glorious double hammer-beam roof to the nave. Very fine brass of priest in Mass vestments.

GREAT BURSTEAD (*St. Mary Magdalene*)
Medieval; 15th-cent. benches.

GREAT CANFIELD (*St. Mary*)
Setting; 13th-cent. mural.

GREAT DUNMOW (*St. Mary the Virgin*)
Setting; principally 14th and 15th cent.

GREAT LEIGHS (*St. Mary*)
Norman round tower.

GREAT SAMPFORD *(*St. Michael*)
Pleasantly situated by some old cottages, the church was almost entirely rebuilt in the 14th century by the Knights Hospitaller, whose stone seats remain below a continuous arcading running along both sides of the chancel. Fine tomb recess in S. chapel. Six consecration crosses still remain. A

15th-century bowl font stands on a 14th-century stem. Late 16th-century cupboard.

GREAT TEY *(*St. Barnabas*)
Magnificent Norman tower at crossing of nave and chancel.

GREAT WARLEY *(*St. Mary the Virgin*)
An excellent example of L'Art Nouveau period, this church was built in 1904 by Harrison Townsend. The internal furnishings are mostly by Sir William Reynolds Stevens. A unique church typical of the Arts and Crafts Movement.

GREAT YELDHAM (*St. Andrew*)
Medieval; E. porch, 14th cent.; unusual feature of two storeys and an attic.

GREENSTED-JUXTA-ONGAR (*St. Andrew*)
The only surviving example of a timber Saxon church. The walls of the nave consist of split oak logs. The chancel is early 16th century. The church was drastically 'restored' in the 19th century. Within these walls the body of St. Edmund rested on its way back to Bury St. Edmunds. A well-wooded setting surrounds this famous church.

HADSTOCK *(*St. Botolph*)
This is most likely to be the minster erected by Canute in 1020 to commemorate the victory at the battle of Assendun over Edmund Ironside. (Ashdon the neighbouring parish is said to be the scene of the battle.) A remarkable Saxon cruciform church approached by a S. door which must be one of the oldest in the country, being contemporary with the building.

HALSTEAD *(*St. Andrew*) GR
This church, principally of 14th century date though much 'restored' in the 19th century, has monuments consisting of tomb chests with effigies belonging to the Bourchier family. One dated 1400 has richly carved canopy above. Well designed W. tower of 1850 of typical East Anglian pattern.

*(*Holy Trinity*)
An early example of the work of George Gilbert Scott in the 13th-century manner. In the S.W. corner stands the tower with tall stone broach spire.

HAM, EAST: *see East Ham.*

HATFIELD BROAD OAK *(*St. Mary the Virgin*)
Lying south of the Hatfield Forest and

dominating a village of attractive old houses, this church formed the nave of the priory founded by Aubrey de Vere about 1135. Good 14th and 15th century work with a fine tower. Very notable sculptured monument to Robert de Vere, 1221. The reredos, panelling and Communion rails are excellent examples of early 18th-century work probably by John Woodward, pupil of Grinling Gibbons. A library has been built on to the church to house some 300 books given in 1680, among them is an Aldine Aristotle 1498.

HIGH BEECH (*Holy Innocents*) GR
Sir Arthur Blomfield, 1873.

HIGH EASTER (*St. Mary the Virgin*)
Setting; dating from Norman times; 15th-cent. tower.

HOCKLEY (*St. Peter*)
Setting; tower.

HORNDON, EAST: *see East Horndon.*

HUTTON (*All Saints*) GR
Rebuilt by Street, 1873.

ILFORD (*St. Barnabas*) GR
Early Comper

INGATESTONE *(St. Mary the Virgin & St. Edmund)*
Here is seen the finest of the many brick towers of Essex – an excellent example of late 15th-century brickwork. A Norman church with additions in the 15th, 16th, and 17th centuries. Fine monuments to the Petre family including one to Sir William Petre, Secretary of State of Henry VIII.

INGRAVE (*St. Nicholas*) CL
One of the best 18th-cent. churches in Essex, 1735; red brick with good W. tower.

LAINDON (*St. Nicholas*)
Priest's house attached to church. Mainly 13th cent. with later windows.

LAMBOURNE (*St. Mary & All Saints*) CL
Remote Essex setting near London; a simple aisleless medieval church, sumptuously plastered in Georgian times.

LANGDON HILLS (*All Saints*)
Setting; dating from early 16th cent.

LANGFORD (*St. Giles*)
Unique W. apse; dating from Norman times.

LAWFORD *(St. Mary)*
Situated above the waters of the River Stour this church is noted for its remarkably rich 14th-century stone carving in the chancel. In the arch moulds of some of the windows are some amusing carved figures forming a chain and holding each other by the leg. Magnificent sedilia and piscina.

LAYER MARNEY (*St. Mary*)
Setting; monuments.

LEIGHS, GREAT: *see Great Leighs.*

LINDSELL (*St. Mary the Virgin*)
Rustic setting; 12th-cent. chancel arch.

LITTLE BADDOW (*St. Mary the Virgin*)
St. Christopher painting.

LITTLEBURY *(Holy Trinity)*
Much restoration; early 16th-century font case.

LITTLE DUNMOW *(St. Mary the Virgin)*
A place well known for its flitch of bacon awarded to the man and woman who had not repented of their marriage for a year and a day. The church is all that remains of an Augustinian Priory of which it formed a chapel on the S. side of the choir, and from which it was separated by a beautifully proportioned arcade which remains. Some excellent 14th-century stone carving mostly of animals and flowers can be seen in panels along the S. wall. The 'Dunmow Flitch Chair' in the sanctuary is made up from a 13th-century stall. Two fine 15th-century altar tombs with alabaster effigies. The pulpit includes seven ancient Flemish traceried panels.

LITTLE MAPLESTEAD *(St. John the Baptist)*
Built by the Knights Hospitaller about the year 1340, it is one of the five 'round churches' in England and the only one in Essex. The hexagonal nave is separated from the circular aisle by a well-proportioned 14th-century arcade very much restored in 1850. On the E. side of the circular plan projects the chancel.

LITTLE SAMPFORD (*St. Mary the Virgin*)
Setting; monuments.

LITTLE WARLEY (*St. Peter*)
Box-pews.

MALDON *(All Saints)*
In the midst of an attractive little hill town above the Blackwater, this church dating from the 13th century has an unusually shaped tower in the form of a triangle.

The 14th-century stone arcading along the inside of the S. wall is very rich in its decoration. The church has been much altered in the 18th and 19th centuries.

MANUDEN (*St. Mary*)
Village; church mostly rebuilt, 19th cent.; early 15th-cent. screen.

MAPLESTEAD, LITTLE: *see Little Maplestead.*

MARGARETTING (*St. Margaret*)
Jesse window 15th cent.

MISTLEY (*St. Mary*)
Only the towers by Robert Adam remain.

NEWPORT *(The Assumption of Our Lady, now St. Mary the Virgin)*
The large parish church stands in a town of most attractive buildings lying along the Roman road to Cambridge. It demonstrates a continuous growth from the 13th to the 16th centuries. Of its furnishings, the most important is a 13th-century portable altar in the form of a chest, the lid of which when opened becomes a reredos with early paintings of the Crucifixion, Our Lady, St. John, St. Peter and St. Paul. Good pre-Reformation lectern. Early 15th-century chancel screen. Fragments of old glass.

NORTH END BY FORD END
The Black Chapel (dedication unknown)
Furnishings; box-pews.

NOTLEY, BLACK: *see Black Notley.*

PENTLOW (*St. Gregory formerly St. George*)
Round tower.

RADWINTER (*St. Mary the Virgin*)
Mostly Victorian; S. porch, 14th cent.

RAINHAM *(St. Helen & St. Giles)*
An entire Norman church with nave, N. and S. aisles, chancel and tower all dating from about 1170. The massive nave piers with attached shafts and scalloped capitals are very impressive. On the wall of the rood-loft staircase is a large scratched 16th-century drawing of a two-masted ship.

RAYLEIGH (*Holy Trinity*)
Setting; mostly 15th cent.

RIVENHALL *(St. Mary & All Saints)*
This church was almost entirely rebuilt in 1838. It possesses, however, the finest medieval stained glass in the county. In 1840 the then Rector brought over from France some 12th-century glass said to have come from the church of St. Martin at Chenu in Sarthe and fitted it into the E. window. A visit to the church should not be missed.

RUNWELL (*St. Mary*)
Medieval; timber porches; 15th-cent poor box.

ST. OSYTH *(St. Peter & St. Paul)*
Delightfully situated close to the old Abbey, the gateway of which is a noted monument. Though the church dates from the early 12th century its most remarkable architectural feature is the fine 16th-century brick arcades separating nave from aisles. The furnishings include some very fine alabaster monuments to the Darcy family. There are also some early 19th-century 'sheep fold' Communion rails in a horse-shoe plan.

SAFFRON WALDEN *(St. Mary the Virgin)*
Perhaps the largest and finest church in the county. Designed in the grand East Anglian manner, it is almost foreign to Essex. It was rebuilt in the late 15th and early 16th centuries and consists of a nave and chancel with N. and S. aisles and N. and S. chapels. There are N. and S. porches and a W. tower to which was added a spire in 1831. The stately and impressive arcades to the nave deserve special attention as exhibiting a very high standard of stone mason's craftsmanship. There is a great architectural link between this church and King's College, Cambridge, not many miles away. The furnishings are not of the same standard as the fabric. There are far too many pews in the church and other 19th-century 'embellishments'. The hand of the church 'restorer' has done much to destroy the medieval atmosphere of this building.

SAMPFORD, GREAT: *see Great Sampford.*

SAMPFORD, LITTLE: *see Little Sampford.*

SANDON (*St. Andrew*)
Early 16th cent.; brick tower.

SHENFIELD *(St. Mary the Virgin)*
Built in the 15th century but drastically 'restored' in Victorian times, and much of the 'atmosphere' of an old parish church has gone. It possesses one great feature, a timber arcade separating the nave from the aisle in which the piers, fashioned like stone columns with attached shafts, are each

hewn out of an oak tree. The tower has a pleasantly shaped shingled broach spire.

SOUTH BENFLEET (*St. Mary the Virgin*)
Timber porch fabric on S. in 1906; new chancel added by Eden in 1932; charming ensemble.

SOUTHCHURCH (*Holy Trinity*)
Small Norman church to which Comper added.

SOUTHEND *(St. Erkenwald)*
A tall yellow brick church designed with great feeling for ecclesiastical architecture by Sir Walter Tapper in 1905.

STANFORD-LE-HOPE (*St. Margaret*)
Medieval; 19th-cent. tower.

STEBBING *(St. Mary the Virgin)*
At the south end of a typical Essex village of attractive old buildings stands the church of mainly 14th-century date. Light and spacious. Graceful arcades. A fine stone chancel screen filling the whole chancel opening. Good timber roofs especially over chancel. Richly carved sedilia and piscina. A rare feature in the chancel is the pulley block for drawing the Lenten veil.

STEEPLE BUMPSTEAD (*St. Mary the Virgin*)
Dating from late 11th cent.; refashioned 14th–16th cent.; aisle roof (early 16th cent.).

STIFFORD (*St. Mary*)
Medieval brasses.

STOCK (*All Saints*)
Pleasant village; typical Essex belfry and spire; much modern restoration.

STONDON MASSEY (*St. Peter & St. Paul*)
Setting; Norman church with 19th-cent. additions.

STRETHALL *(St. Mary the Virgin)*
A small late Saxon church in a very beautiful setting. One of the most rural parishes in the county with probably the smallest population. The nave is separated from the chancel by a finely proportioned and decorated archway of the time of Edward the Confessor. A church with a very definite 'atmosphere'.

TAKELEY (*Holy Trinity*)
Font-cover late 15th cent.

TEY, GREAT: *see Great Tey.*

THAXTED *(St. John the Baptist, St. Mary the Virgin & St. Laurence)*
Standing high up above a town of attractive old houses is one of the grandest churches in the county. Approaching the town from the S.E. is an unforgettable sight as the houses converge towards the old Moot Hall, above the roof of which on high ground, dominating the picture, is seen this magnificent parish church. Principally of 14th, 15th, and early 16th-century dates it consists of a narrow nave with much wider aisles, a crossing with N. and S. transepts, a spacious chancel with N. and S. chapels, N. and S. porches each with a parvise room above, and a W. tower with spire. The interior is very light. There are good fragments of old stained glass remaining and there are two windows by Kempe. The absence of customary pews gives a great feeling of spaciousness. Good craftsmanship can be seen in the roofs. Font completely hidden by font case and cover of late 15th-century date. Very fine carved pulpit 17th century. 18th-century Communion rails.

THEYDON MOUNT (*St. Michael*)
Early post-Reformation; mixture of Gothic and Classic; monuments.

TILTY *(St. Mary the Virgin)*
Formerly the chapel by the gate of the neighbouring Cistercian Abbey. A 13th-century nave with regularly spaced lancet windows leads into a very large 14th-century chancel which may well be described as a work of great architectural beauty. The E. window has some of the loveliest tracery in the whole country. The N. window displays similar good craftsmanship. Very fine sedilia and piscina. The belfry is surmounted by a charming 18th-century cupola. Some good brasses in the chancel.

TOLLESHUNT D'ARCY (*St. Nicholas*)
15th cent.; brasses and monuments.

UPSHIRE (*St. Thomas*)
A good rustic church in Temple Moore style by Freeman and Ogilvy, 1902.

WALTHAM ABBEY *(Holy Cross & St. Laurence)*
Only the nave, aisles, and S. chapel remain of what must once have been a most imposing monastic establishment. The tower was added after the Dissolution. The splendid Norman nave is comparable with the nave of Durham Cathedral, and

has spiral and zig-zag ornament on the pillars. Unhappily the church is spoilt by far too many Victorian pews. Much 19th-century restoration undertaken by William Burges. The painted ceiling is the early work of Sir Edward Poynter. Very excellent E. window by Burne Jones. Lady Chapel (14th century) has fragmentary painting of the Last Judgement. Many fine monuments in the church. Ancient stocks, whipping post and pillory can be seen. Queen Eleanor's body rested here on the way to Westminster Abbey.

WANSTEAD *(St. Mary the Virgin)
The best example surviving in Essex of an 18th-century church. Entirely rebuilt in 1790 by Thomas Hardwick. Tuscan porch. Well designed bell-turret. Use of Corinthian Order internally. Charming pulpit with sounding board supported by slender palm tree columns. Box-pews. The principal glory of this church is the magnificent monument to Sir Josiah Child 1699, perhaps the finest in the county. Sir Josiah is shown in Roman costume but wearing a full bottom wig.

WENDENS AMBO *(St. Mary the Virgin)
Dating from the end of the 11th century this delightful little country church has a most attractive setting and is approached by a lane bordered with typical Essex

thatched cottages. The furnishings of the church include a 15th-century pulpit and carved seating.

WESTCLIFF-ON-SEA *(St. Albans)
A good example of the work of Sir Charles Nicholson erected 1895–1908. It possesses the ancient font from the Church of St. Mary-le-Bow by Sir Christopher Wren. A pity this font cannot find its rightful home once more in Wren's masterpiece, to which it was presented in the 18th century by Sir Francis Dashwood. It is singularly out of place in its present setting.

WETHERSFIELD (St. Mary Magdalene)
Village; dating from pre-Conquest times; effigies in chancel.

WILLINGALE DOE (St. Christopher) and WILLINGALE SPAIN (St. Andrew & All Saints)
Two medieval churches in one churchyard.

WIMBUSH (All Saints)
Setting; screen work; elegant 14th-cent. brass.

WOODHAM WALTER (St. Michael)
Gothic survival, 1563–4.

WRITTLE (All Saints)
Village green; largely rebuilt, 19th cent.; monuments including one by Nicholas Stone.

YELDHAM, GREAT: see Great Yeldham.

Gloucestershire

INTRODUCTION

GLOUCESTERSHIRE IS richer than any county in variety of colour and outline. Indeed rich is the adjective which best suits it. Its great port of Bristol was formed into a separate county in 1425. The Severn and Avon brought vessels to Gloucestershire from Spain and later from America. The wool trade in the late middle ages brought prosperity to the limestone Cotswold Hills and many fine Perpendicular churches rose in the little wool towns of which that at Northleach is an impressive example. Before the Normans had built the great naves of Gloucester Cathedral and Tewkesbury Abbey with their cylindrical columns and many a country church has a Norman arch or window or tympanum. The Black Death hardly touched the county, so that the building tradition was continuous and nowhere are there such fine farm buildings, enormous barns and stone-built manor houses as in Gloucestershire, the medieval tradition continuing in the construction of tithe barns, dovecotes and outbuildings, until early in the 18th century.

In the 16th and 17th centuries there was what Anthony West has called a waterpower industrial revolution, when the rapid streams of the Stroud valley were used to turn mills employed to make cloth. These old mills, stone built equivalents of the card mills of the north of England, survive in the deep Stroud valley and are still, some of them, used as factories. At this time in the western half of the county and near Bristol, there was an iron industry. Later came the coalfields to the oak woods of the Forest of Dean.

The greatest richness of the county is in its stone and scenery. As you enter Gloucestershire from the east you continue with the limestone scenery of Oxfordshire and North Berks and North Wilts. This is a warm yellowish-grey which breeds a delicate patina of lichens. In the little piece of Gloucestershire north of Moreton-in-Marsh, the limestone takes on a golden tinge as though bathed in perpetual late sunlight. Farther west and north of Bristol, the stone is a cold grey and houses have red tiles in the Somerset manner. The most spectacular scenery of all is in the middle of the county by the Stroud valley and Minchinhampton Common and Amberley. Here the stone is silver-white, and at Painswick it is almost as white as Portland stone, but with a warmth in it which Portland lacks. The central tower of Gloucester Cathedral is built of Painswick stone. As may be expected in this part of the country where stone is so plentiful and where it has been worked for centuries, the workmanship is of high quality. Stone tiled roofs have graded tiles, large at the eaves and small at the ridges; stone is used for mullions and transoms of windows as easily as if it were timber, moulded stone arches are used for doorways, nobly carved tombstones in a local baroque style diversify country churchyards and everywhere you descend from barren heights, which once tinkled with sheep bells, to enclosed valleys shaded by beech and elm where the stone villages cluster, and at the western heights of this stone kingdom you may look over miles of the Severn valley below you to the blue mountains of Wales and the gigantic outline of the Malvern Hills.

The Severn Vale and the Vale of Berkeley (in the second the famous double-Gloucester cheeses were made), is a complete contrast with the eastern stone area. The Severn winds through muddy flatness, willows abound and orchards and pastoral scenery. Stone, used here for churches and barns and raised causeways above flood-level, could easily be carried up the Severn. But humbler buildings were timber framed and many old cottages survive among drabber brick cottages of the last century. The least visited part of the county, is the north-west, which has the Georgian red brick town of Newent as its capital. Here on the Herefordshire border are oakwoods and wild daffodils and steep hills and forgotten farms down steep-banked lanes and red earth and pink sandstone. The land between the muddy flatness of the Severn and the steep wooded splendour of the Wye Valley is occupied by the Forest of Dean. Mitcheldean on the north might be a small Welsh town with its high narrow streets and weatherworn appearance. The Forest itself is among high hills and has a rather unpleasantly large quota of conifers, but once you leave these you find oak woods and brown streams and grass-grown mineral lines leading to ruined industries, and then suddenly and unaccountably a coal-tip and a mine and a hideous township of miners' red-brick cottages. One might be in Durham. The churches are mostly poor late Georgian and Victorian buildings architecturally, which have the used and highly polished interiors of industrial churches. Forest of Dean stone is a pink sandstone which does not weather well.

One exotic in the county of Gloucestershire is the late-Georgian spa of Cheltenham set in flat land at the foot of the Cotswolds. It is a stucco and limestone town of ample tree-shaded squares and crescents and streets, a town of gardens and sunlight, where the stately houses are adorned with most delicate and inventive ironwork verandahs and porches designed to give lightness to the Classic severity of their architecture. Cheltenham is, as it were, St. John's Wood and Regent's Park set down over square miles of Gloucester meadowland.

With such richness of natural and man-made beauty, it is not surprising that Gloucestershire has attracted artists and art-workers. Chipping Campden and Painswick, Sapperton and Cirencester have, for half a century and more, been the homes of artists and handicraftsmen, stained-glass artists, potters, weavers and cabinet makers – such famous men as Ernest Gimson, Peter Waals, the Barnsleys and Christoper Whall, F. L. Griggs and C. R. Ashbee. Their love of the native crafts of the county, though it may have unwittingly inspired much arty craftiness of the aubritia and staddlestone variety, has saved Gloucestershire from much vandalism. And Council Houses in the Cotswolds even today pay much more attention to local materials and scale than is usual, and every town in the county is not ruined yet by concrete lamp standards. The beauty of the county has tamed even the borough surveyors, engineers and park superintendents.

J.B.

SELECTED LIST OF CHURCHES

by David Verey, F.S.A.

ALDERLEY (*St. Kenelm*) GR
1802; pretty; early Gothic revival.

ALDSWORTH (*St. Bartholomew*)
Dec. aisle; 12th-cent. N. door; setting.

ALMONDSBURY *(*St. Mary the Virgin*)
Random coursed dark grey rubble church with unusual lead-covered brooch spire, almost hidden under the escarpment which takes the main Gloucester-Bristol road. The church is cruciform with central tower, the nave rebuilt in 1834. The chancel is very pure Early English. In the S. transept there is a fine Renaissance tomb but the lovely marble pyramid which used to be there has been recently removed and destroyed.

AMPNEY CRUCIS (*Holy Rood*)
14th-cent. churchyard cross.

AMPNEY ST. MARY (*St. Mary*)
Wall paintings in a Norman church.

ARLINGHAM (*St. Mary the Virgin*)
14th-cent. glass; Dec. chancel.

ASHCHURCH (*St. Nicholas*)
15th-cent. rood-screen.

ASHLEWORTH (*St. Andrew & St. Bartholomew*)
Setting next tithe barn and court house; 14th-cent. spire.

ASTON BLANK (*St. Andrew*)
Norman tympanum. No E. window, but remains of a stone reredos.

ASTON-SUB-EDGE (*St. Andrew*) GR
18th-cent. Gothic revival.

AVENING (*Holy Cross*)
Norman; Cruciform with central tower.

BADGEWORTH (*Holy Trinity*)
Dec. ball-flower windows.

BAGENDON (*St. Margaret*)
Norman arcade.

BARNSLEY *(*St. Mary the Virgin*)
Set high in the middle of an entirely stone-built village; pretty tower built about 1600, Norman corbel-table with grotesque heads. Severe re-modelling 1848. The W. window is late Perpendicular with good tracery and notable Victorian glass. Carved small marble monument (1691).

BARRINGTON, GREAT: *see Great Barrington.*

BARRINGTON, LITTLE: *see Little Barrington.*

BAUNTON (*St. Mary Magdalene*)
14th-cent. wall-painting of St. Christopher in small church of Norman origin.

BERKELEY (*St. Mary the Virgin*)
Setting; fine E.E. nave and W. front.

BEVERSTON *(*St. Mary*)
Approached by a muddy farm track near the picturesque ruins of the castle, a Norman church most carefully kept. The S. arcade dates from *c.* 1200; it is tall, of three bays with carved circular caps. A beautiful restored 15th-century rood-screen, a painted chantry chapel, large decorated windows with clear glass, lime-washed walls, blacksmith-made electric light pendants, and ancient roof combine to make this a very special church.

BIBURY *(*St. Mary*)
Here is the River Coln, dividing into dozens of streams and canals across the fish hatcheries, united and rapid past the Swan Hotel, broad and calm by Bibury Court. The church's late 15th-century embattled tower stands above the steep-pitched, grey, stone roofs of this as yet unspoiled village, with a wooded bank

rising sheer the other side of the river. A more charming churchyard could not be imagined – no modern graves and not much clearing away, but carefully mown lawn around the carved altar tombs of the wool staplers with their rococo motifs now made more beautiful than ever by the rich patina of black stains and yellow and orange lichens. Inside what was once a great Saxon church all is clean and lime-washed white, the colour and bric-à-brac of Sir Gilbert Scott's restoration now swept away.

BISHOPS CLEEVE *(St. Michael & All Angels)

Magnificent late 12th-century church sympathetically restored, specially in that the beautiful 17th-century gallery was preserved. The Norman W. front is striking with turrets and a rich doorway, as is also the S. porch. The chancel is Decorated and has a fine window with ball-flower mouldings. The tower was rebuilt in 1700. There is an excellent monument of 1639.

BISLEY (All Saints)
Setting; restored, 14th cent.

BLEDINGTON *(St. Leonard)
Set in an attractive village with a large square green with some excellent houses, the church is mainly Perpendicular with an aisle-less clerestory, beautifully sculptured and windows containing brilliant 15th-century glass. There is a tiny chantry chapel, a Transitional Norman S. arcade, Norman bellcote and Early English E. window. The whole is lime-washed inside and very light and unspoiled, having been restored by F. E. Howard who designed the sanctuary.

BLOCKLEY (St. Peter & St. Paul)
18th-cent. Gothic survival tower; Rysbrack monument.

BOURTON-ON-THE-HILL (St. Lawrence)
Norman S. arcade; setting.

BOXWELL (St. Mary)
Small E.E. church with bellcote; setting.

BRIMPSFIELD (St. Michael)
17th and 18th cent. churchyard altar tombs; church Norman in origin; setting.

BROCKWORTH (St. George)
Norman central tower; spire rebuilt, 19th cent.

BUCKLAND *(St. Michael)
Set in a shallow fold of the N. Cotswolds, a little gold and grey church, chiefly Perpendicular, it has, although the walls are scraped, almost completely escaped the hands of the restorers and is full of treasures. The nave arcades are late 13th century and the clerestory is perpendicular. This church's outstanding features inside are the 17th-century oak panelling complete with tester heads in the S. aisle and hat pegs in the gallery. The glass in the E. window is 15th century and depicts three of the Seven Sacraments. There is a rare silver-mounted wooden bowl (16th century) kept in the S. aisle which is tiled with 15th-century tiles. There is a 15th-century pall kept in the N. aisle finely embroidered. The Rectory has a 15th-century hall still open to the roof with contemporary coloured glass in situ.

BUSSAGE (St. Michael & All Angels) GR
Built 1844 by twenty scholars of Oxford.

CAINSCROSS (St. Matthew) GR
1837; late 19th-cent. alterations.

CHACELY (St. John the Baptist)
Norman.

CHEDWORTH *(St. Andrew)
The church is situated with the village straggling below it on two hilly slopes, and at some distance from the famous Roman Villa. Another wool church, one thinks as one walks up the stone cobbles to the S. porch, admiring all the time the fine range of five Perpendicular windows in the tall nave. Inside one sees that it is all a façade on one side, for on the N. there is a fairly low Norman arcade and an aisle. In spite of this curious lack of balance the church has considerable dignity. The pulpit is a really fine one, 15th century, carved stone and shaped like a wine glass. The font is a Norman tub with interlacing arcades. The electric lighting is most unfortunate, huge arc lamps on the medieval roof.

CHELTENHAM (Christ Church) GR
1840 by R. W. and C. Jearrad.

(Holy Trinity) GR
1820–2; Gothic, by G. A. Underwood.

(St. James) GR
Begun 1829–30 by Edward Jenkins, finished by J. B. Papworth.

*(St. Paul's) CL
This church cost £6,500 when it was built in 1831 and a more successful cheap church

could not have been built. One cannot do better than quote the contemporary *Stranger's Guide*. 'With a spirit as honourable as it is rare, Mr Pitt engaged J. Forbes, Esq., an architect of Cheltenham, to furnish the designs and to superintend the erection of the building. This gentleman taking the architecture of the celebrated Temple of Ilissus as his model, with great skill and ability' . . . etc. It had been felt that every facility was 'afforded to the wealthy and the affluent, of hearing proclaimed those glad tidings of salvation, but comparatively little care had hitherto been manifested to provide for the Spiritual instruction of the poor and the portionless.' A plot of ground was given by Pitt in the poorer quarter of Cheltenham where the builders and artificers of the grander buildings had housed themselves, and here Forbes built a pure classic church with a great Ionic portico.

(*St. Peter*)
1840–9 by S. W. Dawkes in Romanesque style.

(*St. Stephen*) GR
Careful and elaborate copying of richest Dec. detail.

CHIPPING CAMPDEN *(St. James)*
Set at the end of this unspoiled little town, a great golden Perpendicular 'wool' church with a magnificent tower. Inside, the tall nave arcades have concave chamfers on the columns and very pretty capitals in consequence. Clerestory and well-proportioned window over chancel arch. Brasses to the wool staplers. The great monument to Lord and Lady Noel (1664) is, according to Gunnis, the finest work of Joshua Marshall, one of the greatest statuaries of the 17th century. Macabre swathed figures in grave clothes are revealed by the open doors of the tomb. Embroidered frontal and dorsal, late 15th century.

CHIPPING SODBURY *(St. John the Baptist)*
15th cent.

CHURCH ICOMB (*St. Mary*)
Effigy of Agincourt soldier; mainly E.E. church.

CIRENCESTER *(St. John the Baptist)*
The largest and most splendid of the Cotswold 'wool' churches, it is also perhaps one of the most beautiful Perpendicular churches in all England. The nave and aisles have parapets with ornamental embattlements, completely open with tracery and punctuated by tall crocketed pinnacles, which make an exciting skyline as at Gloucester Cathedral. The three-storey porch is also the Town Hall. It has three two-storey oriel windows and is completely covered in Perpendicular tracery and empty niches, and is at present a gleaming white having been recently limewashed for preservation. Inside, one is immediately struck by the enormous height of the clerestoried nave of six bays, and the characteristic window over the chancel arch. Other features to notice are the 'wineglass' pulpit, of *c.* 1450, painted and gilded, one of the few pre-Reformation pulpits left in Gloucestershire, late 16th-century German brass candelabra, the roof of the Trinity Chapel 1430, the Lady Chapel monuments, St. Katharine's Chapel fan vaulting, the lime-washed chancel, and the 15th-century glass in the E. window.

COALPIT HEATH *(St. Saviour)*
W. Butterfield 1845. Lych-gate, vicarage and church all a well-proportioned group in fine materials.

COBERLEY (*St. Giles*)
Medieval effigies; mostly rebuilt, 19th cent.

COLN ROGERS (*St. Andrew*)
Saxon and later, but over-restored; stone pulpit, 15th cent.

COLN ST. DENYS *(St. James the Great)*
Prettily situated in the Coln Valley near the Fosse Way, the church is both picturesque and interesting, for it retains its original Norman ground plan and its central Norman tower. The belfry on top of the tower is a 15th-century addition. The Norman tower is massive, as wide as the church and heavily buttressed. E. and W. windows are Perpendicular insertions. Electric floodlighting from the roof is deplorable though there is a nice brass candelabrum under the tower.

COMPTON ABDALE (*St. Oswald*)
Setting; good Perp. tower.

DAGLINGWORTH *(Holy Rood)*
A Cotswold Saxon church with distinctive features *in situ* such as the long and short quoins in the S. wall of the nave and the porch with its sundial. The tower is a 15th-century addition, decorated with grey lichens. Inside all is lime-washed white, and now set on walls of nave and aisle are three beautiful very early sculptures found in the

ruins of the priory here; a crucifixion, a majesty and St. Peter. There are also some nice baroque wall tablets of black and grey coloured marbles. The Victorian E. window now has clear glass except for the central figures, and the effect of light seen through the low chancel arch is very beautiful. (*See Plate 3*)

DAYLESFORD (*St. Peter*) GR
J. L. Pearson, 1860: dark and Dec.; Warren Hastings' tomb in churchyard.

DEERHURST *(St. Mary)*
In pleasant, sleepy, riverside country there is a Saxon church dating perhaps from as early as the 7th century. It has an apsidal E. end. The tall thin tower, Saxon in the lower part and medieval above, is very striking as one approaches across the large churchyard. There is a double triangular-headed window in the E. wall of the tower opening into the nave. The font is said to be the best preserved Saxon font in existence. The chancel keeps communion seating on all four sides of the altar according to 17th-century practice.

DIDBROOK (*St. George*)
Setting; Perp.

DIDMARTON (*St. Lawrence*)
E.E. with 18th-cent. furniture.

DODINGTON (*St. Mary*) CL
Early 19th cent. by James Wyatt; interior gutted.

DOWDESWELL (*St. Michael*)
Setting; tower; monuments.

DOWN AMPNEY *(All Saints)*
The church stands close to the Manor forming a pretty group with its Tudor Gatehouse, rather alone in flat Upper Thames country. The churchyard is enclosed by tall yew hedges. The Early English tower has a spire with a gilded weather-cock. From the outside it looks as if the 1897 restoration had gone too far; but inside there is still a great deal to surprise and delight one – the charming 13th-century arcades – the chapels in the transepts (for the church is cruciform), that in the N. where the Sacrament is reserved has a beautifully carved and painted Jacobean screen and tomb of Sir Anthony Hungerford, that in the S. has a Gothic screen, 14th-century recumbent effigies, and a copy of Giorgione's *Madonna and Child* over the altar. There is a modern rood-screen and

loft, separating the over-restored but dignified chancel from the nave which is paved with decent stone flags. The walls are plastered and the electric light pendants are good.

DUMBLETON (*St. Peter*)
Setting; Norman; monuments.

DUNTISBOURNE ABBOTS (*St. Peter*)
Setting; Norman and E.E.

DUNTISBOURNE ROUS *(St. Michael)*
On the steep bank of the brook, an enchanting place, stands a small Saxon church. The saddle-back tower, nave roof and chancel step down the hill, but even so, the chancel added by the Normans is so high at the E. end that there is room for a crypt below, which is now approached down fern-covered steps in the churchyard. The crypt has a narrow unglazed Norman slit window, while those in the chancel are little bigger. Inside it is unspoiled by antiquarianism, with 17th-century panelled box-pews in the nave, and misericords in the choir.

DURSLEY (*St. James the Great*)
18th-cent. Gothic survival tower.

DYMOCK (*St. Mary the Virgin*)
Norman and subsequent work.

DYRHAM (*St. Peter*)
Set in a combe on the Cotswold edge near Bath, a great house architected by Talman in 1698 in grounds laid out by Le Nôtre and an adjacent church, which gives the impression of being Perpendicular though the N. arcade inside is Transitional Norman. It is beautifully light with clear glass; contains a Jacobean pulpit with tester, and the magnificent tomb of Sir George Wynter 1581.

EASTLEACH
Is a village with two Norman churches either side of a clear brook in one of the most charming spots in the county. The flat stone bridge which spans the stream is known as Keble's bridge from the saintly poet who was incumbent here.

(*St. Andrew*)
Situated on the N. bank of the stream, it has a saddle-back tower, a richly-carved Norman S. doorway, a nave and broad chancel with three lancets at the E., all plain, simple and beautiful.

(*St. Michael & St. Martin*)
The tower is rather squat with a hipped

roof, the walls are faced in rough cast; inside are some nice old pews but it is a bit dank and there are a lot of oil lamps; a rather forlorn sister, in fact.

EBRINGTON (*St. Eadburgha*)
Norman work; pulpit; 15th-cent. effigy.

EDGEWORTH (*St. Mary*)
Setting; Norman.

ELKSTONE *(*St. John the Evangelist*)
In the high Cotswolds, one of the most famous Norman churches in the county. There is a tall Perpendicular tower at the W., the original Norman tower having collapsed. This is built of huge freestone blocks which contrast with the rubble walls of the Norman nave. The S. doorway is richly carved with Christ in Majesty in the tympanum. Inside there are two arches which formerly supported the central tower and which effectively divide the exquisite little sanctuary from the tall body of the church. A tangle of laurels, fir trees and golden yews, holly and cypress trees separate the Georgian rectory from the church-yard.

ELMORE (*St. John the Baptist*)
18th-cent. mausoleum.

FAIRFORD *(*St. Mary the Virgin*)
A complete and perfect Perpendicular church. Chancel, aisles, porch and cleres-toried nave have continuous embattled parapets with pinnacles; the smooth free-stone is warm and mellow. The parapet of the central tower is pierced with quatrefoils and has pairs of pinnacles at the corners. It is perhaps smaller than the other great Perpendicular wool churches in the county but it is unique in that it contains the best 15th–16th century glass in England, in sufficient quantity to be judged apart from its antiquarian interest, and it is exceedingly beautiful. (*See Plate 27*)

FORTHAMPTON (*St. Mary the Virgin*)
Setting; 14th cent. and later.

GLOUCESTER (*St. Nicholas*)
Tower; general medieval details.

(*St. John*)
1734; classical.

(*St. Mary-de-Crypt*)
12th-cent.; cruciform plan; monuments.

GREAT BADMINTON *(*St. Michael & All Angels*)
An 18th-century classical church attached to the great house of the Duke of Beaufort, and approached through the garden. Inside it is plastered with marble monuments to the Beaufort family including a very grand one of the first Duke in full Garter robes and beauty queens pretending to be Fates. The box-pews and specially the pulpit with its tester are admirable. There are por-traits of the Gospel writers by Guido Reni, brass candelabra fitted for electric light, and the atmosphere of a large private chapel rather than of a parish church.

GREAT BARRINGTON *(*St. Mary the Virgin*)
Norman, Early English, and Perpendicular; Nollekens monument.

GREAT WASHBOURNE *(*St. Mary*)
A small hamlet near Alderton hill on the Worcestershire border, has a tiny Norman church which retains its 18th-century box-pews, reading desk and pulpit. The font is placed directly between the small chancel arch and the altar. Over the S. door is a tympanum carved with Maltese crosses.

HAILES *(*dedication unknown*)
The little church near the Abbey ruins is one of the most unspoilt in the county. Cement-rendered on the outside it perhaps does not look very interesting but inside everything is old, the Elizabethan benches, the 17th-century pulpit and tester, the 15th-century tiles, glass, and screen, and the 14th-century wall-paintings. It has its own specially rewarding atmosphere.

HARDWICKE (*St. Nicholas*)
E.E. work; altar tombs.

HARNHILL (*St. Michael*)
Setting; E.E. and Dec.

HAWKESBURY (*St. Mary*)
Setting; all periods.

HEWELSFIELD (*St. Mary Magdalene*)
Norman.

HIGHNAM *(*Holy Innocents*) GR
The church was built by Thomas Gambier Parry in 1850 of a grey-green limestone in Decorated style. The spire is covered in ball-flower and has crocketed pinnacles. Inside it is pleasantly dark with painted walls by Gambier Parry to simulate drapery. There is a continuous frieze of Biblical characters all with golden haloes. The chancel arch is tall and elegant with painted mouldings, and the chancel is brilliant with shining tiles, painted organ

and walls with texts, vines, and symbols of the Passion. Set in the middle of Mr. Gambier Parry's park.

HILL (*St. Michael*)
Bellcote; pulpit; benches, all ancient.

HUNTLEY (*St. John the Baptist*) GR
S.S. Teulon, 1863.

IRON ACTON *(*St. James the Less*)
Handsome mainly Perpendicular church with Saxon remains; and in the churchyard a uniquely beautiful 15th-century Memorial Cross, mutilated and lichen-covered. Inside the church there is much to excite one's admiration; whitened walls, some ancient glass, Laudian altar rails, brass candelabrum, Jacobean pulpit and canopy, medieval effigies of the Poyntz family and in the chancel and sanctuary, 19th-century mosaic floors like those in the early Christian churches of Rome. The modern reredos and side chapel screen are full of colour and joy, designed by F. C. Eden.

KEMPLEY *(*St. Edward The Confessor & St. Mary*)
Randell Wells built a church here in 1903. Stone-built with thatched roof. A fine design with a large reticulated W. window, heavy rood, and beautiful contemporary fittings and sculpture. Besides this there is the old church of St. Mary isolated with its Vicarage on the Herefordshire border. It has an early Norman nave and chancel with rubble barrel vault, and the most important Romanesque frescoes in England, unfortunately treated with shellac in the past; but now restored to their pristine beauty.

KEMPSFORD *(*St. Mary the Virgin*)
On the upper Thames here is a very fine tower built by John of Gaunt, the lower stage has large Perpendicular N. and S. windows, there are three stages and the parapet has trefoil-headed openings and crocketed pinnacles all with weather-vanes. The grey stone is covered in a whitish kind of lichen. The nave has an ashlar clerestory. Entering the S. doorway which is Norman, the church seems dark, though lofty, chiefly because of the large amount of Victorian stained glass (some of it very good, by Kempe), and tesselated tiles. The vaulting under the central tower has painted heraldic shields. The chancel aisle was added by Street in 1858. On the walls of the nave are framed Puritan texts. This is the only English church where an Irish peer is buried in the organ.

LECHLADE (*St. Lawrence*)
Setting; Perp.

LECKHAMPTON (*St. Peter & St. Paul*)
Early 14th-cent. tower and spire.

LEONARD STANLEY *(*St. Leonard*)
Leonard Stanley is set under the escarpment of the Cotswold hills near Stroud. The large church is part of a Norman priory, cruciform in plan with a massive central tower. Perpendicular windows inserted on the N. of the nave and all have clear glass. Lime-washed walls. The crossing has splendid Norman arches with carved caps, and those in the chancel are specially good, one representing Our Lord with the woman who was a Sinner. The former cloisters are now in the farmyard of a very fine farmhouse.

LITTLE BARRINGTON (*St. Peter*)
Setting; Norman.

LONGBOROUGH (*St. James*)
All periods; monuments.

LOWER SWELL (*St. Mary*)
Norman S. aisle.

MINCHINHAMPTON (*Holy Trinity*)
Rood-screen by F. C. Eden; 14th-cent. S. transept, with vaulted roof and window.

MISERDEN (*St. Andrew*)
17th-cent. alabaster effigies.

MITCHELDEAN (*St. Michael & All Angels*)
Spire, all periods.

MORETON VALENCE (*St. Stephen*)
Norman tympanum.

NAUNTON (*St. Andrew*)
Setting; chiefly 16th cent.

NEWENT (*St. Mary*)
17th-cent. nave (Wren style).

NEWINGTON BAGPATH (*St. Bartholomew*)
Setting; E.E. origin.

NEWLAND (*All Saints*)
This great church in the Forest of Dean, sometimes called the Cathedral of the Forest, has most noble interior proportions. It was built during the 13th and 14th centuries and has later insertions, and was restored in 1862. The great width of the aisles gives a tremendous feeling of spaciousness. The heavy, handsome W. tower is finely pinnacled. There are some fair recumbent effigies in the church. Some

good houses and a row of almshouses form a close around the churchyard.

NEWNHAM (*St. Peter*)
Norman font.

NORTH CERNEY (*All Saints*)
In the Churn valley the church and its Rectory can be seen from the Cheltenham-Cirencester road. Chiefly Norman, with Early English upper stage to the saddle-back W. tower, and the larger windows Perpendicular. The church has been extensively refurbished inside by the late F. C. Eden and owes much to the taste of Mr. W. I. Croome, with the result that it is the most beautifully furnished and colourful little church in the county. The painted rood is modern though the Christ is Italian work of 1600. The great twenty-light brass candelabrum dates from Queen Anne, and there are other brass candelabra, though electric light has now been most discreetly installed. The fine modern reredos like the Lady Chapel screen and altar were designed by Mr. Eden.

NORTHLEACH *(St. Peter & St. Paul)*
Once an important centre of the wool trade, Northleach has one of the most beautiful of the Perpendicular 'wool' churches in the Cotswolds, and the S. porch has been called the most lovely in all England, with its tall pinnacles and statue-filled niches. The nave of five bays has columns with concave chamfers and a tall clerestory with a very broad window over the chancel arch. This was built by John Fortey who died in 1458 and has his brass in the central aisle of the nave.

NOTGROVE (*St. Bartholomew*)
Effigies of Dick Whittington's relations.

ODDINGTON *(St. Nicholas)*
St. Nicholas' church is away from the village surrounded by lovely trees, and for some years it was in disuse. However, it is a most beautiful church with nave, chancel, and S. aisle. All the windows have clear glass and those in S. aisle, reticulated tracery. There is a large Doom painting on the N. wall, a William IV arms over the chancel arch, and its Jacobean pulpit high on a single pillar is a beauty.

OLDBURY-ON-SEVERN (*St. Arild*)
Setting on tumulus; Perp. tower.

OZLEWORTH (*St. Nicholas*)
Norman polygonal tower.

PAINSWICK (*St. Mary the Virgin*)
Churchyard.

PARKEND (*St. Paul*) GR
1822; octagonal plan; reredos.

PAUNTLEY (*St. John the Evangelist*)
Norman.

QUENINGTON (*St. Swithin*)
Norman-carved tympana.

RENDCOMB *(St. Peter)*
A lovely late Perpendicular church built by the same John Tame who built Fairford, and set in a churchyard which has an embattled golden yew hedge close by Hardwicke's Italianate house, and some magnificent trees including a Cedar of Lebanon. The church is built of a golden grey freestone, a real work of art and all of one piece. Inside it consists of a nave and a S. aisle of almost equal breadth, and with contemporary roofs, divided by an arcade the columns of which have delightful concave chamfers. There is a 16th-century screen across both nave and aisle. There is much colourful old glass, and excellent early Victorian glass in the E. window. The Norman font is a noteworthy example carved with the twelve Apostles.

RUARDEAN (*St. John the Baptist*)
Norman tympanum.

ST. BRIAVELS (*St. Briavel*)
Setting; Norman cruciform church.

SAINTBURY (*St. Nicholas*)
Setting; 14th-cent. spire.

SAPPERTON (*St. Kenelm*)
Setting; monuments and fittings.

SELSLEY *(All Saints)* GR
Set in a spectacular position on the edge of the Cotswold escarpment. It is a copy of the church in Marling in Tirol (to please Sir William Marling) by Bodley, and decorated by Morris, Holman Hunt, and the Rossettis. The W. window is by Burne Jones.

SHERBORNE (*St. Mary Magdalene*) GR
Rebuilt 1850 except tower; monuments.

SHIPTON SOLLERS *(St. Mary)*
A dear little Norman church with all Perpendicular features, most sympathetically restored in 1929. The small nave is divided from the chancel by a low arch through which can be seen the colourful modern reredos and window. Glass by Geoffrey Webb. The roofs are barrel vaulted and the

electric light pendants are of wrought iron. It is closed in the winter.

SLIMBRIDGE (*St. John the Evangelist*)
Late 12th-cent. nave arcades.

SOUTHROP (*St. Peter*)
Norman nave and font; E.E. chancel. (*See Plate 5*)

STANDISH (*St. Nicholas*)
Early 14th cent.

STANTON *(*St. Michael & All Angels*)
A specially pretty village below the banks of the N. Cotswolds. The church has a Perpendicular S. aisle and porch, embattled, and of a beautiful brown and golden texture. The W. tower has a spire. Inside Sir Ninian Comper has designed the rood-screen, reredos, gallery and stained glass. There is also good medieval glass.

STOKE ORCHARD (*St. Peter*)
Wall-paintings.

STONE (*All Saints*)
Dec. tower and spire.

STOW-ON-THE-WOLD (*St. Edward*)
All periods.

SWELL, LOWER: *see Lower Swell.*

TEDDINGTON (*St. Nicholas*)
17th-cent. fittings.

TEMPLE GUITING (*St. Mary the Virgin*)
Norman, Perp. and Georgian.

TETBURY *(*St. Mary*)
Francis Hiorne's church finished in 1781 except the steeple, is one of the triumphs of the Gothic revival. Extremely effective from the outside, it has a very graceful interior with box-pews and gallery. The interior is, in fact, unspoiled, retaining its 18th-century furniture, including the magnificent candelabra which have recently been reinstated in their lacquered glory, and the Ten Commandments and picture, replaced behind the Holy Table. The thin tall columns like giant bamboos, give one a splendid feeling of period. It also has the unique and altogether, delightful arrangement whereby it is surrounded by an enclosed cloister. (*See Plate 55*)

TEWKESBURY *(*St. Mary the Virgin*)
The Abbey Church is in the flat meadows where the Avon joins the Severn, which once ran red with the blood of the Lancastrians. To the W. and E. of it there has grown up a fair medieval town, now busy and congested with the main Bristol-Birmingham road. It is one of the finest parish churches in Southern England and as big as a Cathedral. It has a grand Norman nave and tower, lovely choir with side chapels of the early 14th century, and superb vaulting to the nave and transept of 1349–59. There are a number of 14th-century monuments, and there is a great deal of delicate stone-work of that period which is worth seeing. The view of the Abbey from before the great W. end, where sometimes plays, such as *Everyman*, are performed, is quite unforgettable.

THORNBURY (*St. Mary the Virgin*)
Early 16th cent.; setting.

TODDINGTON *(*St. Andrew*) GR
Set in the park of Lord Sudeley's fantastic Gothic revival house, and built by G. E. Street, a good example of his work. In a lovely deep golden-coloured ashlar, with a tall broach spire, and rich Decorated style much whiter inside than out, it contains a forest of Purbeck marble columns and the 19th-century marble effigies of Lord and Lady Sudeley by Lough.

TODENHAM (*St. Thomas of Canterbury*)
Dec. tower with broad spire.

UPLANDS (*All Saints*) GR
Early 20th cent. by Temple Moore; striking development of Gothic manner.

UPPER CAM (*St. George*)
14th-cent. tower.

WASHBOURNE, GREAT: *see Great Washbourne.*

WESTBURY-ON-SEVERN (*St. Peter & St. Paul*)
Detached 13th-cent. tower and spire.

WHITTINGTON (*St. Bartholomew*)
13th and 14th cent. monuments.

WINCHCOMBE *(*St. Peter*)
Begun *c.* 1460 it is a smooth Perpendicular building, a typical 'wool' church of the Cotswolds. The embattled, pinnacled tower has the finest weather-cock in the county, richly gilt, and there is a particularly grotesque collection of gargoyles. The E. end has been rebuilt and there is no structural division between nave and chancel. There is a fine brass candelabrum of 1753, late 17th-century organ case, and a richly-painted Royal Arms of George III. The church is in the middle of this small town.

WINSON (*St. Michael*)
Setting; Norman.

WITCOMBE (*St. Mary the Virgin*)
Setting; Norman.

WITHINGTON *(*St. Michael*)
A good Cotswold church in an interesting village. The nave is almost entirely lit by the Perpendicular clerestory windows. There is a fine Perpendicular tower. The S. chapel which has a Decorated S. window, has been recently lime-washed and furnished; but the main body of the church is unfortunately scraped and the chancel rebuilt, and the artificial lighting is by floodlights in the roof. A rather splendid sculptured monument is signed by Edward Marshall and dated 1651.

WORMINGTON (*St. Catherine*)
Norman crucifix.

WOTTON-UNDER-EDGE (*St. Mary the Virgin*)
Dec., Perp. and 19th cent.; 18th-cent. organ.

YANWORTH (*St. Michael*)
Setting; Norman and Perp.

YATE (*St. Mary*)
The Perpendicular tower is a feature of the Bristol Vale, and is a singularly fine example nearly 100 feet high, built of coursed grey rubble with freestone quoins, buttresses and pinnacles.

Hampshire
and the Isle of Wight

INTRODUCTION

H AMPSHIRE FALLS naturally into four divisions. The main portion of the county consists of chalk downs, through which the swift-flowing Itchen, Test and Meon cut their way. All along these valleys the villages cluster thickly, sometimes not a mile apart, many of them boasting an ancient church, while on either side of the valleys the vast rolling uplands stretch away for miles. The churches in this region are chiefly built of the local flint, with wooden belfries supported internally upon great baulks of timber. Notable among them are the Saxon churches of Corhampton in the Meon valley and Headbourne Worthy in the Itchen valley.

The western part of the county, beyond Southampton Water, consists largely of the New Forest. Here Romsey Abbey and Christchurch Priory bear witness to one good result of the Norman invasion, though the area also includes such varying churches as the perfect Saxon example at Breamore, the Early English parish church of Beaulieu (once the refectory of the Monastery), the delightful 'unrestored' Minstead, with its box pews and galleries, and the 'copy-book' examples of the Gothic Revival at Bournemouth and Lyndhurst.

The third division of Hampshire, lying along the Sussex border, is characterized by the great steeply-wooded hills known as 'hangers'. Only here in the county is there any local stone, and Selborne is the most perfect ensemble of village and church lying under its Hanger, the whole district enshrining the memory of Gilbert White.

Finally, there is the border region of the north-east, an extension of the Surrey pine and heather country, now much bitten into by the vast military 'conurbation' of Aldershot and its jet-propelled 'overspill' of Farnborough, to use two horrible new words beloved of the planners. Crondall is the only noteworthy church in this district.

As regards its coast, Hampshire is not remarkable. For the most part it consists of broad tidal creeks, the only cliffs being those of Bournemouth.

In few counties are there such opportunities for the study of church architecture. The perfect E.E. lancets of Pamber Priory, near Basingstoke, the glorious Perpendicular nave of Winchester Cathedral, the 17th and 18th century red-brick churches of Wolverton and Avington, the modern church

178

of St. Francis of Assisi at Bournemouth; every age and style are represented. Hampshire, which possessed (at Silchester) the only Christian church so far discovered in Roman Britain, has continued to maintain and demonstrate the art of church building by succeeding generations throughout the Christian era.

R.L.P.J.

ISLE OF WIGHT

WHEREAS Hayling Island is a bit of Hampshire which has slipped into the sea, the Isle of Wight has a personality of its own, and this persists despite pylons, poles, wire, tarmac, caravans, flash shop fronts and shoddy bungalows, which have spread over so much of its 150 square miles. From east to west there stretches a high chalk ridge, from Culver Cliff to the Needles, as noble as the Sussex Downs and known as the 'back' of the Island. South of this and facing the open sea are very few old buildings and the modern Victorian towns of Ventnor, Shanklin and Sandown. Inland the chalk slopes gently to a lower range of hills and then slopes still more gradually until it reaches the low coast along the Solent. Newport is the ancient capital of the island and here the Medina River divides it into two. Cowes at its mouth, Yarmouth and Brading are the other old ports, and Newtown, once large for its date, has almost disappeared.

What strikes one about the island is the luxuriance of its vegetation after the comparative aridity of Hants. Myrtles, fuchsias and geraniums grow unprotected in the open air. In the under-cliff, beyond the back of the island, there is steamy tropic richness. And next one notices the variety of local building stone, differing in colour from village to village, almost as much as those amazing streaks to be seen on the cliffs when the afternoon sun strikes Alum Bay. This stone and the style of building shown in old churches and cottages has affinities more with Dorset than Hampshire and is best of all seen in West Wight, the most countrified part of the island.

The island became popular in the 18th century, though families like the Worsleys of Appledurcombe (now a baroque ruin), the Barringtons of Swainston, the Holmes's and Oglanders had lived here for many generations. But in the 18th century Garrick and his wife settled here, George Morland fled from his creditors and Wilkes set up house. In the next century came Keats and later Tennyson. First the more gentle and less 'horrid' scenery was preferred, so that most Georgian buildings are on the Solent side of the island. The Victorians favoured the open sea and not even the example of Queen Victoria at Osborne could tempt holidaymakers back to the tamer Solent coast. That was left to the yachtsmen who have created a nautical civilization of their own at Cowes, Ryde, Yarmouth and Bembridge.

The old churches of the island are humble stone buildings with a West Country look and their beauty is largely in their texture. The characteristic of their plan is aisles extending the full length of the chancel. Their prevailing style is 15th century. The Georgian churches are mostly in unsophisticated Gothic and have the look of proprietary chapels for Evangelical valetudinarians. The most distinguished 19th-century church is by Temple Moore at Lake (1892).

J.B.

SELECTED LIST OF HAMPSHIRE CHURCHES

by R. L. P. Jowitt

ABBOTS ANN (*St. Mary*) CL
Well-designed brick, 1716; virgins' garlands.

ANDOVER (*St. Mary the Virgin*) GR
Smirke, 1840; dignified E.E. interior inspired by Salisbury.

ASHMANSWORTH (*St. James*)
Small and rustic Norman; wall-paintings.

AVINGTON *(St. Mary)*
Well situated on the edge of the Park, this is the most perfect 18th-century church in the county. Of brick with massive tower and aisleless nave, it has retained its internal appearance completely unspoilt – reredos, two-decker pulpit with tester, and pews, including the squire's. In the gallery, with its Royal Arms, is a barrel-organ which still works. The church was built 1768–71 by Margaret, Marchioness of Carnarvon. Her tomb records: 'Amongst many other Acts of Piety, this Church was built from the ground by her Order and at her Expence, though it pleased God to remove her to a better World, a few Months before it was begun'.

BADDESLEY, NORTH: *see North Baddesley.*

BASING *(St. Mary)*
Large and handsome 15th and 16th century church of mellow red brick with stone dressings, adjoining pleasant old thatched cottages and the ruins of Basing House, destroyed during the Civil War after an epic defence by John Paulet, Marquis of Winchester, whose ancestors had built the church. Their heraldic key is to be found all over the building, notably on the beautiful exterior of the N. chapel. The good pinnacled tower is largely a post-Civil War reconstruction. The lovely statue of the Virgin and Child on the W. front fortunately escaped the Puritans,

being then hidden by ivy. The dignified interior is lime-washed and spacious and the chancel perfectly balanced by the four Paulet tombs.

BASINGSTOKE (*All Saints*)
Temple Moore (1915); impressive and beautiful; stands well.

***(St. Michael)* GR**
The parish church. Mainly 15th and early 16th century with N. chapel by Sir Charles Nicholson. The chancel has been restored by Randoll Blacking after damage by enemy action. Note 18th-century memorial to Thomas Warton and Royal Arms of Elizabeth, James I and William III.

BEAULIEU *(St. Bartholomew)*
The parish church was formerly the great refectory of the Abbey, in whose lovely precincts it is situated. The refectory lay N. and S., the N. end facing the cloister court. At the S. end is a huge buttress, which is the most prominent feature of the exterior of this wizened and beautiful old monastic building. The magnificent 13th-century reader's pulpit with its graceful arcaded approach in the thickness of the wall, and the wooden roof-bosses, some bearing the antelope of Henry IV, are the most notable interior features. In view of the total destruction of the once glorious Abbey Church, we are fortunate in being still able to enjoy this surviving relic of the great Cistercian house.

BOARHUNT (*St. Nicholas*)
Plain Saxon; lonely rural setting.

BOLDRE *(St. John)*
One of the most charmingly situated churches in the county, it stands upon a hill overlooking the wooded valley of the Lymington River, away from all habitations, on the edge of the New Forest. The

squat tower, with its stone base and upper stage of lovely old brickwork, stands on the S. side of the church. The long interior, though ancient and well cared for, has not quite the outstanding charm of the exterior. Its varying styles show the gradual growth of the building from a small Norman church to its present size.

BOSCOMBE (*St. Clement*) GR
J. D. Sedding, 1873–93; carefully detailed; both scholarly and original.

(*St. Mary*) GR
Airy seaside Perp.

BOURNEMOUTH (*St. Alban*) GR
Fellowes Prynne, 1909; individualistic late-Gothic-freely-treated.

(*St. Francis of Assisi*)
J. H. Gibbons, 1929; beautiful reproduction of early Romanesque.

(*St. Michael*) GR
Norman Shaw, 1876; impressive pinnacled tower by Oldrid Scott, 1901.

(*St. Peter*) GR
G. E. Street, 1855–79; lavishly decorated; Clayton and Bell glass.

(*St. Stephen*) GR
J. L. Pearson, 1881–1908; Bournemouth's most beautiful church; spire not yet built.

BRAMLEY *(St. James)*
The church has a brick tower dating from 1636, a dormer-windowed nave and a large brick S. chapel surmounted by two large weathervanes in the shape of Moors' heads, the crest of the Brocas family, who built it. The interior of the church is a delight; a handsome gallery of 1738, Norman nave with much medieval wall painting; 16th-century pews, rood-screen and old roof. The Brocas chapel contains a huge monument by Banks, Royal Arms and much old Flemish glass.

BRAMSHOTT *(St. Mary)*
Beautifully set in a very well kept churchyard with many old headstones and a great yew. The central tower with spire, transepts and chancel are medieval and of warm sandstone rubble; the nave is Gothic Revival of 1871. The interior is maintained with most loving care, and scraping of walls in the past is being gradually put right. Canadian Army occupation of neighbouring common is commemorated by dignified modern pulpit and priest's desk, as well as good glass by Martin Travers.

BREAMORE *(St. Mary)*
Important Saxon church charmingly situated on edge of park among noble cedars and close to mellow red-brick Elizabethan manor-house. N. transept has been destroyed, but over archway to S. transept is an Anglo-Saxon inscription meaning 'Here the Covenant becomes manifest to thee'. Much 'long-and-short' work and some double-splayed windows. Glory of the church must once have been the great stone rood (compare Headbourne Worthy) over S. door, which was protected by a later porch, but grievously mutilated at the Reformation. A painted background, added in the 15th century, has survived.

BROCKENHURST (*St. Peter*)
Delightfully set on a wooded knoll; Norman and 18th cent.

CHILCOMB (*St. Andrew with All Saints*)
Small late Saxon; lonely downland setting.

CHILWORTH (*St. Denys*) GR
1812; charming small 'neo-Gothic'.

CHRISTCHURCH *(Christchurch)*
The Priory Church became the Parish Church at the Dissolution of the Augustinian Priory, founded in 1150. It stands well on a tongue of land between Avon and Stour, its massive 16th-century tower dominating the scene. The best view of the church is from the Avon bridge, where it forms a background to the Norman ruins of the Castle, as fine a view of its kind as any in England. This magnificent church, one of the best known in the country, has a massive Norman nave and a quire rebuilt in the 15th century. Particularly notable are the great screen, with its Tree of Jesse, the Renaissance Salisbury Chantry, the misericord seats and perhaps most beautiful of all, the chequer-work Norman turret of the N. transept.

CORHAMPTON *(dedication unknown)*
Perfect little Saxon church dating from first half of 11th century, the only blemish being the debased brick-work E. end. To appreciate the church, it should be viewed from the N.W., where the Saxon work is well seen, the S. side being completely concealed by a gigantic old yew. Outside, Saxon sundial, pilaster strips and 'long-and-short' work are all very characteristic. Inside, the chancel arch, an old stone chair of Saxon date, as well as much wall-painting, are noteworthy.

COSHAM (*St. Philip*) GR
J. N. Comper, 1936; brick; interior extremely rich, colourful and impressive.

CRONDALL *(All Saints)*
The church stands in a well-kept church-yard and is approached by a lime avenue, one of the county's finest churches. Majestic 17th-century brick tower on N. side and Transition-Norman nave with huge buttresses. Internally, scarifying 'restoration' has done damage to walls, but nobility of architecture remains in spite of it. Beautifully vaulted roofs with an *Agnus Dei* boss in chancel and an early brass to a priest (Nicholas Caerwent, 1381) are noteworthy.

DEAN, PRIOR'S: *see Prior's Dean.*

DEANE (*All Saints*) GR
1818; 'neo-Gothic'; parkland setting.

DUMMER (*All Saints*)
Village setting; charming interior; rood ceiling, 15th cent.

DURLEY (*Holy Cross*)
Small; rustic; dormer windows; yew and old headstones.

EAST MEON *(All Saints)*
Strikingly beautiful church in commanding situation above village with green down for a background. Enriched Norman tower, crowned by lead spire, surmounts cruci-form church, the nave and transepts of which are still largely Norman. Magnificent font of Tournai marble, similar to that in Winchester Cathedral. Chancel rebuilt in late 15th century. Good E. window by Comper.

EAST TISTED (*St. James the Apostle*) GR
1846; village setting; contemporary cottages.

EAST WELLOW (*St. Margaret*)
Beautifully restored; much wall-painting; deeply rural setting.

ELLINGHAM *(St. Mary)*
Homely, rustic and largely unspoilt church in water-meadows of the Avon. W. end and S. porch of 18th-century brick, latter with remarkable painted sundial. Interior has 15th-century barrel-vaulted roof and screen, space above which has been filled in and painted with Commandments, Lord's Prayer, Creed and texts of Eliza-bethan date, Royal Arms of 1671, etc. Adjoining screen is a pew parclose with tester head. Altar rails, 18th century, and reredos attributed to Grinling Gibbons.

FAREHAM (*St. Peter & St. Paul*)
Everything from Saxon to Sir Charles Nicholson.

FARLEY CHAMBERLAYNE (*St. John*)
Norman; remote downland setting; old woodwork.

FAWLEY *(All Saints)*
Formerly rural parish at mouth of Southampton Water, but now contains the vast oil refinery. Norman W. door and chancel arch and lime-washed tower on S. side. Chancel severely damaged by bomb in 1940, but re-opened after excellent restoration and re-furnishing by Randoll Blacking in 1954. Good modern glass by Smith (successor to A. K. Nicholson). E. window survived bombing and contains very early Decorated tracery. Fine assem-blage of old headstones in churchyard.

FORDINGBRIDGE (*St. Mary the Virgin*)
Norman and Dec.; large and dignified; well restored by Ponting; handsome Georgian Royal Arms.

FROYLE *(Assumption of the Blessed Virgin Mary)*
Red-brick church, and grey stone gabled Manor House stand together at upper end of park. Nave has Royal Arms of George III and early Decorated chancel has good reticulated E. window, containing much ancient heraldic glass. Beauty of church somewhat marred by wilderness-like churchyard.

HALE (*St. Mary*) CL
Small classic gem by Archer, 1754; tombs; woodland setting.

HAMBLEDON (*St. Peter & St. Paul*)
Large and gradual growth around Saxon core. Well placed above village.

HARTLEY WESPALL (*St. Mary the Blessed Virgin*)
Remarkable timber-built church; *c.* 1340.

HARTLEY WINTNEY, OLD CHURCH (*St. John the Evangelist*)
Unrestored; well placed; used only occasionally. Queen Anne Royal Arms.

HAYLING, NORTH: *see North Hayling.*

HAYLING, SOUTH: *see South Hayling.*

HEADBOURNE WORTHY (*St. Swithin*)
Delightfully set; mutilated Saxon Rood.

HOOK (*St. John the Evangelist*)
Modern village church (1938) in red brick by Sir Edward Maufe.

HURSLEY (*All Saints*) GR
Rebuilt by Keble, 1848, except tower; contemporary glass.

HURSTBOURNE TARRANT (*St. Peter*)
Charming village setting among downs; timber tower.

IDSWORTH *(*St. Hubert*)
This small chapel stands remote in a downland valley and is crowned with a charming 18th-century bell-turret. Norman nave retains complete atmosphere of 18th century with box-pews, gallery, pulpit, Royal Arms, etc. Wall-painting, 14th century, in chancel illustrates legend of St. Hubert with much detail.

LONGPARISH (*St. Nicholas*)
'Copy-book' example of 1857 restoration.

LYMINGTON *(*St. Thomas the Apostle*)
The church with its cupola crowned tower stands very well at the top of High Street. Nave is Georgian with good galleries and chancel Early English. A plan to replace the galleries by dull and lifeless modern work would rob the church of its character and it is much to be hoped that it will not materialise. Coved plaster roof of 1910 replaced 15th-century one with bosses, now preserved in porch. Some of the walls have unfortunately been scraped.

MATTINGLEY (*dedication unknown*)
Brick and timber; 15th cent.

MEON, EAST: *see East Meon.*

MICHELDEVER (*St. Mary*) GR
Octagonal nave, 1806; Perp. tower, 1527.

MILFORD-ON-SEA *(*All Saints*)
Large church with rough-cast exterior in well-kept graveyard. The 13th-century W. tower with short lead spire has curious penthouses on either side with arched openings into tower. Original small Norman church of two bays remains, much broadened out eastwards by 13th-century cruciform church, distinguished by interesting windows, showing early forms of tracery. Notable chancel roof with extremely late bosses, 1640. A beautiful church, somewhat marred in places by scraping and cement rendering.

MINSTEAD *(*All Saints*)
Stands well upon a commanding knoll a short distance from this New Forest village. It is perhaps the most delightful of its kind anywhere existing and is completely 'unrestored'. The core of the building is

13th century, to which have been added a Georgian brick tower, S. transept and two squire's pews, complete with fireplaces, opening into church like boxes in a theatre. A three-decker pulpit, box-pews and double-tiered gallery, hat pegs and brick floors completes the ensemble. The primitive Norman font shows an *Agnus Dei.*

MOTTISFONT (*St. Andrew*)
Norman work; 15th-cent. glass.

NATELY SCURES (*St. Swithin*)
Tiny apsidal Norman; delightfully set next farmhouse.

NORTH BADDESLEY (*St. John the Baptist*)
Small, rustic and charming; 17th-cent. tower and fittings.

NORTH HAYLING (*St. Peter*)
A delightful little church; timber belfry.

NORTHINGTON *(*St. John the Evangelist*) GR
Set amid wooded rolling country, this extremely beautiful Gothic Revival church in 15th-century style by T. G. Jackson, was built by a former Lord Ashburton in 1889. It has a commanding pinnacled tower with pleasing band of flint and stone chequerwork below belfry windows and an apse. The interior marks a revival in craftsmanship, all details being of the best. The former church (built 1832, much beautified by Butterfield, 1864, and demolished 1889) replaced a Norman predecessor.

NORTH STONEHAM (*St. Nicholas*)
Perp.; Lord Hawke's monument, 1759; pleasant parkland setting.

ODIHAM *(*All Saints*)
A large parish church standing well at highest point of this small country town; on the S. side are extremely pleasing 17th-century almshouses, their ancient brickwork blending well with contemporary church tower. Exterior walls of body of church (14th century) wrongly scraped of old rough-cast in 1897. Interior spacious, with much good woodwork of 17th-century date (gallery with Royal Arms, pulpit, etc.). There is also a 13th-century font and numerous brasses.

PAMBER PRIORY CHURCH *(*dedication unknown*)
Formerly the property of an alien priory suppressed in 1417 and later granted to the

Queen's College at Oxford, the present owners. Of the former monastic church, the very beautiful and dignified Early English quire remains in use, together with the low, Norman, pyramid-capped central tower. Nave, transepts and conventual buildings have long since disappeared. Interior contains notable wooden cross-legged effigy, *c.* 1270, several Purbeck marble coffin-slabs, a 15th-century screen and pews of same date. Situation remote and rural; approached by an avenue.

PORTCHESTER *(St. Mary)*
The church is romantically situated in the S.E. corner of the old Roman fort of Portchester Castle. Originally the monastic church founded in 1133 by Henry I for Augustinian Canons; the monks removed to Southwick, near by, about 15 years later owing to their peace being disturbed by the presence of the soldiers. The church is very perfect Norman, cruciform with central tower, pyramid-capped, but the S. transept is missing. It connected with the conventual buildings, between church and Roman wall. The grim interior, drastically scraped, has a Norman font and Royal Arms of both Elizabeth I and Anne, the latter a very fine specimen.

PORTSMOUTH *(St. Thomas of Canterbury)*
Now the cathedral; nave and aisles by Sir Charles Nicholson, 1935; Jacobean tower and quire; medieval transepts and chancel, late 12th cent.

PRIOR'S DEAN *(dedication unknown)*
Rustic little building; Norman and E.E.; remotely situated amid lovely scenery.

ROMSEY *(St. Mary & St. Ethelfleda)*
The Abbey Church became the Parish Church at the Dissolution, when the townspeople purchased it for £100, it having formerly been the church of a nunnery founded by Edward the Elder, *c.* 907. When approached from the town, its impressive bulk and squat central tower with its curious bell-cage, looks well when seen above pleasant Georgian shops in foreground. This magnificent Norman church dates chiefly from the 12th century, except the W. end with its tall lancets. Apart from its architecture, it possesses many treasures – a painted reredos of early 16th-century date, a wonderfully impressive Saxon Rood, as well as a smaller Saxon carving of the Crucifixion. There is also a

beautiful Purbeck marble effigy of a lady of the 13th century and the St. Barbe monument by Thomas Stanton, 1660. A painted relief of the Virgin and Child by Martin Travers is noteworthy.

SELBORNE *(St. Mary)*
The church stands beautifully on a shelf above a wooded ravine. It is approached from the village square by a path through the graveyard passing beneath a gigantic old yew. Chiefly of Norman and Early English periods, the church is light, spacious, well cared-for and full of interest. But Gilbert White predominates; he is commemorated by an excellent window illustrating St. Francis and the birds. His humble grave, inscribed simply 'G. W. 1793', is in the churchyard.

SILCHESTER *(St. Mary)*
Apart from the church and the adjoining farmhouse, the Roman wall of the lost city of Calleva Atrebatum now encloses nothing but empty fields, the population having migrated. This charming little church which stands upon the city wall, though no longer as delightful as it must once have been when it contained box-pews and had dormer windows, yet remains full of charm and interest. The Jacobean pulpit, with domed canopy, the 15th-century screen and, beyond it, the Early English chancel with its original painted walls, make an unforgettable picture. An effigy of a 14th-century lady is of great beauty.

SOPLEY *(St. Michael & All Angels)*
Beautifully situated on knoll overlooking Avon valley; largely E.E.

SOUTH HAYLING *(St. Mary)*
Dignified E.E. Sussex type; modern glass.

SOUTH WANBOROUGH *(St. Andrew)*
Rood-screen; old glass; well-kept graveyard.

SOUTHAMPTON
(St. Alban's, Swaythling)
Imposing group of buildings; church, with central tower, and parish hall forming two sides of a square; nave still incomplete. Inter-war design by Cachemaille Day; E. window by Christopher Webb.

(Church of the Ascension, Bitterne)
A most impressive modern church, brick-built with stone dressings, designed by Sir Charles Nicholson and built during 1924–6. His brother, A. K. Nicholson, beautified

the church with a wonderful series of windows, worth coming far to see. They illustrate the story of the Christian Faith with particular reference to English Church history. The W. window showing the symbolic Ship of the Church is particularly impressive.

SOUTHWICK *(St. James)

Standing well at the meeting of the three village streets, this church is low-built and very rustic and contained until quite recently a marvellous collection of box-pews, but most unfortunately many of these have had to be destroyed owing to the ravages of the death-watch beetle. There still remain, however, the gallery, pulpit, altar-rails and handsome painted reredos, all of 17th-century date.

STOKE CHARITY *(St. Michael)

The place derives its name from the de la Charité family. The church now stands lonely in the middle of a field, but once the Manor House stood adjacent to it. This gem-like little church is a veritable treasure-house of beautiful things and in itself it is also of great beauty. The Hampton and Waller monuments and brasses have all been lovingly repaired and the paint-work correctly restored. *The Mass of St. Gregory*, a remarkable sculpture, concealed at the Reformation, was found last century. Much 15th-century glass remains.

STONEHAM, NORTH: *see North Stoneham.*

TADLEY *(St. Peter)

The church is very small and rustic and stands in complete isolation. Of 17th-century brick-work, it has dormer windows and a humble little tower. The interior contains good gallery, pulpit, seats and altar-table, all contemporary.

TICHBORNE *(St. Andrew)

High on a hill above the charming village below with its well-kept thatched cottages, the 17th-century brick tower is a prominent landmark. The church has a delightful atmosphere with its box-pews of various dates, Royal Arms of 1735, etc. The chancel is Saxon and the N. aisle railed off and belongs to the Roman Catholic family of the Tichbornes, whose monuments it contains.

TISTED, EAST: *see East Tisted.*

TUFTON *(St. Mary)

Charming little Norman church next to farm; wall-paintings.

WARBLINGTON *(St. Thomas of Canterbury)

Near the shores of Langstone Harbour with only a farm and the ruined Castle as neighbours, the rough little Saxon tower sits pleasantly above the ample mellow old roofs and gables of the church. There is a good timber N. porch of the 15th century. The interior is very long, narrowed where Early English arches support Saxon tower, now central, but formerly at W. end. There are two beautiful female medieval effigies, old tiles and a 13th-century vestry. The large graveyard has many finely carved headstones and two watchers' huts, dating from 'body snatching' days.

WARNBOROUGH, SOUTH: *see South Warnborough.*

WELLOW, EAST: *see East Wellow.*

WIELD *(St James)

Rustic and Norman; wall-paintings; Wallop monument, 1617.

WINCHESTER *(St. Cross)

This was the chapel of the Hospital founded by Henri de Blois, Bishop of Winchester, in 1133 and is now the parish church of the district. Situated in the lovely quadrangle of the Hospital, it is one of the county's noblest churches. Cruciform with central tower and vaulted throughout, it was built from E. to W. between 1160 and 1345. Thus enriched Norman at E. end gradually merges into Decorated at W. end. Much old painting on the walls, many old tiles, besides other treasures such as beautiful Renaissance woodwork and some good brasses.

*(St. John)

City's most interesting church; trans. Norman; old woodwork and wall-paintings.

WINCHFIELD *(St. Mary)

Lying remote and with a well-kept graveyard, the church is a small Norman gem. The broad tower, which has unfortunately been treated with ugly cement rendering, had formerly a brick top stage, but this was replaced by 1849 by present belfry stage and pyramid cap. The S. door and narrow chancel arch are both much enriched, the latter having roll mouldings extending under the soffit. The chancel is gloomy owing to bad Victorian glass; some windows original, others dating from 1849 replacing later medieval insertions. The Jacobean pulpit and some old oak seats are noteworthy.

WOLVERTON *(St Catherine)*
The church stands alone on a wooded hillside. With its heavy brick tower, it might have strayed out of the city of London. An elegant cruciform church in the Wren manner, it dates from 1717. Architecture and fittings together form a classical masterpiece. Unfortunately, Victorian tinkering caused mullions and absurd tracery to be inserted into windows and the gallery was stupidly destroyed, also the chancel gates. However, the pews, pulpit, reading-desk, reredos and wrought-iron altar-rails fortunately remain to us. The 15th-century roof timbers from an older church have been re-used.

YATELEY *(St. Peter)*
Originally Saxon, rebuilt and lengthened in Norman times, this church has an Early English chancel and a charming 15th-century brick and timber tower. It has a number of interesting features; a 15th-century timber porch with original figure of St. John, some good encaustic tiles, a number of brasses and traces of an anchorite's cell, but its greatest treasure is the priceless crystal cup, given in 1675 and preserved in its own special cupboard. This church is lovingly cared for and a delightful feature is the lighting by numerous brass candelabra. The graveyard is also beautifully maintained.

SELECTED LIST OF CHURCHES IN THE ISLE OF WIGHT

by R. L. P. Jowitt

ARRETON *(St. George)*
In the W. wall of this church which stands closely adjacent to the farm buildings of the neighbouring Manor House is incorporated the oldest piece of church architecture in the Island. This is the Saxon W. front of the first church to stand on this site. The heavily buttressed tower of 14th-century date conceals the original Saxon door behind it. The church was much enlarged during succeeding centuries, particularly beautiful being the Purbeck marble arches between chancel and S. chapel. Horse-box pews unfortunately disappeared in 1886, when what was described as 'a good restoration' took place.

BRADING *(St. Mary)*
The church stands well upon a ridge at one end of this small town. A striking feature is the tower (13th century). Standing upon arches, it was built thus so as to include a processional way round the church without the procession having to leave consecrated ground. Successive alterations have been made to the original Transition-Norman building, the last being the Oglander Chapel (15th century) containing a fine collection of monuments of that family, still resident at Nunwell in this parish. An older monument is an engraved slab of Purbeck marble to John Cherowin (1441), Constable of Portchester Castle.

CARISBROOKE *(St. Mary)*
What has been described as 'the most important ecclesiastical building in the Island' stands well at the top of the village street; its finest feature is the grand 15th-century tower, the Island's most beautiful example. Church formerly both monastic and parochial, but priory suppressed in 1414, when conventual buildings, northward of church, disappeared. The chancel was demolished in the 16th century, but the spacious Norman nave with its Early English S. aisle remains, the five Transition-Norman arches dividing them being particularly fine. There is a notable tomb with effigy to Lady Margaret Wadham (16th century) and a good Jacobean pulpit of 1658.

GODSHILL *(All Saints)*
On a fine hill-top site, the church tower rises nobly above old thatched cottages. The church itself is wholly Perpendicular work of the 15th century and contains much of interest. Best of all is wall-painting of Christ crucified on a budding tree, in the S. transept. Finest monument is to Sir John Leigh with effigies of himself and wife

(16th century). From them descended the Worsleys of Appledurcombe, whose many monuments, mostly 18th century, are in various parts of the church. A large painting of Daniel in the lions' den is a reputed Rubens.

LAKE (*The Good Shepherd*)
Temple Moore, 1892.

NEWCHURCH (*All Saints*)
Commanding site; Georgian pulpit; 18th-cent. tower.

NEWTOWN (*Holy Spirit*) GR
Revived E.E. (1835); excellent period piece.

RYDE (*St. James*) GR
Embattled 'Gothick' 1829.

(*All Saints*) GR
Majestic work by Gilbert Scott with tall spire, 1870.

SHALFLEET *(dedication unknown)*
The church has a large fortified tower like a Norman keep, with walls of enormous strength. Formerly crowned with an onion-shaped dome, which was removed last century. The N. door has a Norman tympanum, carved with a crude representation of what may be Daniel in the lions' den. The S. aisle has interesting arches and windows of the late 13th century. Chancel shows good early work of the 14th century. Pulpit and reredos Jacobean.

SHORWELL *(St. Peter)*
The church is charmingly set in the lovely well-wooded village of old stone-built thatched cottages. Mostly of 15th-century date, it contains an extremely interesting wall painting of St. Christopher, depicting not only the usual incident, but many others also concerning his life. There is also a 15th-century stone pulpit with Jacobean tester and many memorials of the Leighs, particularly attractive being that of Sir John Leigh and the 'Little Page' with both large and tiny kneeling figures.

YARMOUTH (*St. James, Apostle & Martyr*)
Jacobean Gothic (1626); remarkable statue to Sir Robert Holmes (1692).

YAVERLAND (*St. John the Baptist*)
Woodland setting next Elizabethan manor-house; Norman work.

Herefordshire

INTRODUCTION

THIS SECRET, partly Welsh, county is so deeply silent in its many remote places and, comparatively, so undamaged by pylons, poles, factories, aerodromes, and villadom, that those who know it cannot be blamed for wishing to protect its rustic beauty from the crowds. Medieval farms, half-timbered and tiled, are isolated down narrow hilly lanes; railways are still used and single tracks wind picturesquely past oil-lit stations in lush meadows, hopfields and cider orchards; many churches and houses are spared electricity; Victorian Hereford of Kilvert's diary survives; the hills of almost empty Radnorshire and the bare Black mountains of Brecon and Monmouth diversify its western horizon and the Malvern hills are its eastern: the Rivers Wye, Lugg, Frome and Arrow create rich valleys in its pastoral heart. And in the centre is the city and county town, with Cathedral, assize court, hospital, market and eponymous Viscount all complete.

From the south of this county the Welsh were never driven out by the Saxons and they assimilated the Normans in their own way, for here is that curious group of Norman churches of which Kilpeck is the best known, where the carving of fonts, tympana and capitals seems to be Celtic and unlike any other Norman work in England. Besides Norman churches, red fields, red Herefordshire cattle, cider, hops and barley, a chief feature of this woody landscaped county is the prevalence of old half-timber buildings. These are rarely thatched but have roofs of old tiles. Weobley, Eardisley and Pembridge are complete villages of them. Building stones are many and were used chiefly for churches and they vary from the pale pitted tufa to red sandstone. There are few big country houses. Moccas by Robert Adam, Berrington by Henry Holland are fine classic examples, Downton Castle (1780–5) built by Richard Payne Knight, the exponent of the 'picturesque' theory, and Hampton Court, Hereford, are 'Gothick'. Eastnor Castle by Sir Robert Smirke 1808 is a very early example of Norman revival.

The Cathedral of Hereford, still largely Norman, is square and west-country looking and is not so much admired as Gloucester and Worcester with which it is usually compared. The county itself contains grand churches of every age, from Norman to early 20th century, of every style, that is except 15th-century Perpendicular, and this is odd since most of the medieval churches of the rest of England were added to in this century and in many counties, the most impressive parish church is wholly 15th-century. Hereford was not a rich county in the last century so that Victorian 'restorations' are cheap and ugly or else the churches were spared restoration altogether. For its size there is more 17th-century woodwork and Georgian box-pewing in Herefordshire than elsewhere. The county seems to have gone straight from 'High Church' to Evangelical and 19th-century Tractarianism is rare, with the notable exception of Monkland. As may be expected in so unspoiled a county, the settings of almost all the churches are attractive and in the Welsh districts the old parish church is, Celtic fashion, some way off from the village. There is no 'typical' Herefordshire church. The churches are either curiously beautiful or dull inside. No county has a church so wonderful as Abbey Dore, that solemn Cistercian Early English Abbey with its 17th-century woodwork making a rich contrast, nor is there parochial Decorated to compare with the S. aisle of Leominster. No county has so delicately moulded and joyfully coloured example of Georgian as the Rococo-Gothick church of Shobdon, and for unrestored remoteness there is little to compare with Clodock and Richard's Castle. Brinsop so excitingly restored by Sir Ninian Comper, Brockhampton, Lethaby's bold design in the Arts and Crafts William Morris manner, Teulon's strange Victorian effort at Hoarwithy, are all possessions which help to make the county so full of the unexpected. My own memory of the perfect Herefordshire is a Spring day in the foothill of the Black mountains and finding among winding hilltop lanes the remote little church of St. Margaret's, where there was no sound but a farm dog's distant barking. Opening the church door I saw across the whole width of the little chancel a screen and loft all delicately carved and textured pale grey with time.

J.B.

SELECTED LIST OF CHURCHES

by David Verey, F.S.A.

ABBEY DORE *(Holy Trinity & St. Mary)*
Here surrounded by the small orchards of the Golden Valley are the presbytery with its wonderful square red sandstone ambulatory and chapels, and the crossing and transepts of a great conventual church of the Cistercian order, alight with colour from the 17th-century glass in the lancet windows, a perfect example of Early English architecture with 17th-century fittings. The great oak screen was designed by John Abel for Viscount Scudamore in 1634 when he restored the Abbey as a Parish Church, thus saving for posterity one of the most beautiful buildings in Herefordshire.

ACONBURY *(St. John the Baptist)*
Part of 13th-cent. priory of Austin Nuns.

ACTON BEAUCHAMP *(St. Giles)* CL
Rebuilt, 1816; Classical.

ALMELEY *(St. Mary)*
Early 14th cent.; painted Tudor nave roof.

ASHPERTON *(St. Bartholomew)*
Early 14th cent.

ASTON *(St. Giles)*
Norman; N. doorway with *Agnus Dei*.

ASTON-INGHAM *(St. John the Baptist)*
Lead font, 1689.

AYMESTREY *(*St. John Baptist & St. Alkmund*)
The red sandstone church with spacious plastered interior was enriched in the 16th century by the most lovely tall rood-screen. The modern electric light fittings are notably excellent.

BACTON *(*St. Faith*)
A pretty place buried in the Golden Valley where once lived Blanche Parry, maid-of-honour to Queen Elizabeth I. Her alabaster effigy can be seen in the church kneeling before a contemporary statue of the Queen. A charming inscription ends 'Allwaye wythe maeden quene a maede dyd ende my liffe'.

BICKNOR, WELSH: *see Welsh Bicknor.*

BIRLEY *(*St. Peter*)
Has a pretty red sandstone church mottled with yellow lichen but alas! a scraped interior. The chancel arch is enriched with ball flower, the airy S. chapel with three windows is Perpendicular and there is a lovely Norman font. The artificial lighting is entirely done by candles.

BISHOP'S FROME (*St. Mary*)
Largely rebuilt Norman.

BISHOPSTONE *(*St. Lawrence*)
The church has an unusually broad nave with a fine Jacobean roof. Great Transitional stone arches lead to the transepts. Just N. of the Jacobean reredos is a sculptured monument by Peter Hollins 1842. The interior of the church is plastered. Modern stone bell turret. Pretty country churchyard but no signs of any village.

BODENHAM (*St. Michael & All Angels*)
Lofty 14th-cent. arcades.

BOSBURY *(*Holy Trinity*)
A large red sandstone church with late Norman arcades, a Perpendicular chapel and two very grand Elizabethan tombs in the chancel. Detached 13th-century tower. Churchyard Cross. Set in the middle of the black-and-white village, one of the chief hop growing centres.

BRAMPTON BRYAN (*St. Barnabas*)
Setting; rebuilt after Civil War; hammer-beam roof; 14th-cent. effigy.

BREDWARDINE (*St. Andrew*)
Setting; partly tufa built large Norman church with Georgian tower of small coursed stones.

BRIDGE SOLLERS (*St. Andrew*)
Norman.

BRINSOP *(*St. George*)
A not altogether promising exterior set in an orchard, the interior shows every sign of love having been lavished on it for many generations. 14th-century screen, 14th-century glass, carved Norman tympanum of St. George and the Dragon, windows in memory of Wordsworth, the glowing alabaster reredos by Sir Ninian Comper, everything, new and old, is beautiful.

BROCKHAMPTON-BY-BROMYARD (*All Saints*) GR
1790.

BROCKHAMPTON-BY-ROSS *(*All Saints*)
Modern and very well composed, built in 1902 by W. R. Lethaby with a central tower and thatched roof, a temple of the Arts and Crafts movement.

BROMYARD (*St. Peter*)
Norman.

BYFORD (*St. John Baptist*)
Mostly 13th cent.; S. transept.

CANON-PYON (*St. Laurence*)
13th-cent. arcades; 14th-cent. tower; misericords.

CAPLE, KING'S: *see King's Caple.*

CASTLE FROME *(*St. Michael & All Angels*)
Set in hop country the church contains a 12th-century font richly carved with the four evangelistic creatures and the Baptism, which can be compared with the font at Eardisley, by the same hand; also 17th-century alabaster effigies.

CASTLE, RICHARD'S: *see Richard's Castle.*

CLODOCK *(*St. Clydog*)
On the edge of the Black Mountains and on the banks of the Monnow the church is broad, aisleless and altogether delightful, It has late 17th-century furniture, a gallery. a three-decker pulpit and box-pews.

COLWALL (*St. James the Great*)
13th cent.; S. arcade.

COWARNE, MUCH: *see Much Cowarne.*

CREDENHILL (*St. Mary*)
Setting; 14th-cent. glass.

CROFT *(St. Michael & All Angels)*
The pretty little church quite dwarfed by the huge house of Croft Castle, stands close by the front door and contains a magnificent tomb of Sir Richard Croft who died in 1509 after fighting in many battles of the Wars of the Roses, and his wife who was the widow of a Mortimer. There is 17th-century panelling and a gallery.

DILWYN *(St. Mary the Virgin)*
A spacious church full of light, as only the chancel has stained glass, with lofty 13th-century arcades and a clerestory. The tower is part of an older church, c. 1200, with a small 18th-century spire.

DINMORE *(Chapel of St. John of Jerusalem)*
Setting; 14th-cent. spire.

DORMINGTON *(St. Peter)*
Norman door knocker of bronze.

EARDISLEY *(St. Mary Magdalene)*
The centre of a large parish in which medieval houses abound, hidden away in the orchards, the church has a wonderful font carved in, c. 1150; it is a cup-shaped bowl with cable necking and bands of interlacement and figures in relief representing the Harrowing of Hell, two men with sword and spear fighting, and a large lion. The figures are shown in quilted garments and the work is by the same carver as the Castle Frome font.

EASTNOR *(St. John Baptist)*
Church and Rectory designed by Sir Gilbert Scott in 1852 and very good. The church has a medieval tower but apart from that and some 12th-century stones, it is Scott's 'Middle Pointed' with a Kempe E. window, and contains various treasure such as a Crucifixion attributed to Van Dyck, and an altar frontal from Venice mounted on richest red velvet, used during Trinity instead of green. Terra-cotta panels in churchyard and on village green, and picturesque thatched cottages; and hidden (in this Victorian setting) under the church tower relics of the 18th century, some very good sculpture by Thomas Scheemakers.

EATON BISHOP *(St. Michael & All Angels)*
A spacious church with tall 13th-century arcades; like some Cotswold churches, it has a window over the chancel arch; but the glory of the church is the early 14th-century glass in the E. window.

EDVIN LOACH *(St. Mary the Virgin)*
Ruined Saxon church; pink herringbone masonry and white tufa quoins.

EDVIN RALPH *(St. Michael)*
Restored 12th cent.; medieval effigies.

ELTON *(The Blessed Virgin Mary)*
Restored Norman.

EVESBATCH *(St. Andrew)*
Norman font with 17th-cent. cover.

FOWNHOPE *(St. Mary)*
Setting; Norman tympanum; large Trans. church.

FOY *(St. Mary)*
Setting; 17th-cent. glass and monuments.

FROME, BISHOPS: *see Bishops Frome.*

GARWAY *(St. Michael & All Angels)*
A wonderful little Norman church on the hill slopes above the Monnow. The chancel arch has three orders of richly carved chevrons carried on shafts with water-leaf capitals. The 13th-century detached tower was joined to the church by a passage in the 17th century. Below it, is the circular stone dovecot of the Knights Templar.

GOODRICH *(St. Giles)*
14th-cent. broach spire.

HENTLAND *(St. Dubricius)*
Setting; late 13th-cent. N. arcade; broad nave with scissor-beam roof continuing into chancel.

HEREFORD *(All Saints)*
Mostly late 13th or early 14th century, with a spacious interior entered directly from the street like a real City church. It has an elegant 14th-century spire, a chained Library, and fine choir stalls.

HOARWITHY *(St. Catherine)* GR
A 19th-century church built by S. S. Teulon, 'the fiercest, ablest, and most temerarious of contemporary architect adventurers'. Here the stones of Venice can be seen on the banks of the Wye. Both Italians and local craftsmen were employed. Marbles, lapis lazuli, and gold mosaics.

HOLME LACY *(St. Cuthbert)*
14th-cent. arcade dividing nave from equally broad aisle; 16th–17th cent. monuments.

HOLMER *(St. Bartholomew)*
Large 12th cent. with lancet windows having concave splays; detached tower

with later timber-framed belfry; chancel with hammer-beam roof.

HOPE-UNDER-DINMORE (*St. Mary the Virgin*) GR
'Decorated' nave, 1878, refurbished 1896; monument by Roubiliac.

HOW CAPLE *(St. Mary)*
Church and Court set in a beautifully wooded slope in a loop of the Wye. Church contains a wooden screen supporting the arms of William III and two pulpits with red-lined canopies, also much fine new woodwork.

KENCHESTER (*St. Michael*)
Norman; 16th-cent. roof truss.

KILPECK *(St. Mary & St. David)*
Apart from a corner of the nave which is Saxon, some medieval windows and a 19th-century restored bell-cote, it all dates from the third quarter of the 12th century, and is a particularly rich example of the late Romanesque style showing strong Scandinavian influence. The S. doorway has carvings of Welsh warriors in peaked Phrygian caps. There is a carved corbel table. The chancel arch has draped and nimbed Apostles, and much more. (*See Plate 4*)

KING'S CAPLE (*St. John the Baptist*)
14th-cent. spire.

KINGSLAND (*St. Michael*)
14th cent. with clerestory; chantry chapel.

KING'S PYON (*St. Mary*)
Setting; early 14th-cent. roof in nave and in S. transept; 14th-cent. effigies.

KINNERSLEY (*St. James*)
Saddle-back tower; late 15th-cent. S. arcade; 17th–18th-cent. monuments.

KINSHAM (*All Saints*)
Early 18th-cent. gallery and pulpit.

KNILL (*St. Michael*)
Setting; font; hatchments; churchyard Cross.

LEDBURY (*St. Michael & All Angels*)
Setting; mostly early 14th cent.; detached tower with Georgian spire; monuments; windows by Kempe.

LEINTHALL EARLS (*St. Andrew*)
Norman.

LEINTHALL STARKES (*St. Mary Magdalene*)
Norman.

LEOMINSTER *(St. Peter & St. Paul)*
Has three aisles or naves; on the N. the old monastic church with fine Norman arches, in the centre the 13th-century parish church, on the S. the 14th-century aisle with superb Decorated windows ornamented with a profusion of ball flower both inside and out. Built of local sandstone it has a large tower at the W. end with a 12th-century doorway.

LETTON (*St. John the Baptist*)
Norman; tufa and sandstone; early 18th-cent. pulpit.

LINTON BY ROSS (*St. Mary the Virgin*)
Setting; 14th-cent. spire.

LLANDINABO (*St. Tunabius*)
Early Renaissance screen.

LLANVEYNOE (*St. Beuno & St. Peter*)
10th-cent. Crucifixion.

LUGWARDINE (*St. Peter*)
Tower, *c.* 1400.

LYONSHALL (*St. Michael & All Angels*)
13th cent.; setting.

MADLEY *(The Nativity of St. Mary the Virgin)*
A superb large sandstone church built in the 13th and 14th centuries and structurally unaltered; the long arcaded nave and the apsidal chancel with a wealth of 14th-century glass in the E. window are rare and beautiful. The village has black and white houses.

MARCLE, MUCH: *see Much Marcle.*

MARDEN (*St. Mary the Virgin*)
Setting; 14th-cent. apsidal chancel.

MATHON (*St. John the Baptist*)
Medieval tower; 14th-cent. roof trusses.

MICHAELCHURCH (*St. Michael & All Angels*)
Norman.

MICHAELCHURCH ESCLEY (*St. Michael & All Angels*)
Mostly early 16th cent.

MIDDLETON-ON-THE-HILL (*St. Mary the Virgin*)
Norman.

MOCCAS *(St. Michael & All Angels)*
Set in the park of the Adam house Moccas Court, a Norman church with rounded apse, most lovingly restored. Built of calcareous tufa in the second quarter of the 12th century. Some 14th-century glass.

33. Suffolk bench ends. Ufford. 15th century

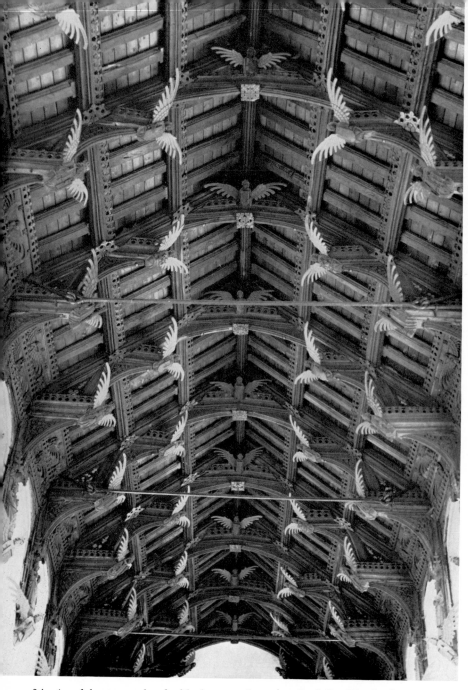

34. Angel hosts on the double hammer-beam roof of St. Wendreda, March, Cambridgeshire. c. 1500

35. West country woodwork. 15th century screen. Kenton, Devon

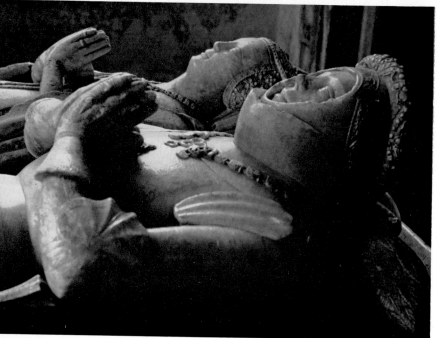

36a. An angel ringing bells in St. John's, Stamford, Lincolnshire. 15th century
36b. Alabaster effigies of Lord and Lady Bardolph (c. 1450) on a table tomb
in St. Margaret's Chapel, Dennington church, Suffolk

37. *The head of St. Anne in the East window of All Saints, North Street, York. 15th century*

*38. 14th century brass of a vestry priest and a layman.
Shottesbrooke, Berkshire*

*39. East Anglian early Renaissance. The terra-cotta screen at the entrance
to Bedingfield chapel, Oxborough, Norfolk, 16th century*

40. *Manx Baroque. Ballaugh Old Church, Isle of Man. Early 18th century*

41. *Wren's city steeples. St. Vedast, Foster Lane, 1670-97, and St. Mary-le-Bow, 1670-80, in the background. City of London*

42. *Rural isolation. Martindale, Westmorland. Mostly 1633 and early 19th century*

*43. Commercial prosperity. Christ Church, Spitalfields, London.
Nicholas Hawksmoor, 1723-9*

44. *A 17th century squire, Sir Thomas Lucy, and his wife. Erected 1648. Charlecote, Warwickshire*

45. The Fettiplace monuments. 17th century. Swinbrook, Oxon.

46. The Renaissance in London. Wren's domed interior of St. Stephen Walbrook

*47. The Renaissance in the country. Gayhurst, Buckinghamshire,
1728. Monument by Roubiliac*

48. *The nobleman's church. Great Witley, Worcestershire. Rebuilt in 1735 ; refurnished 1860. Built for Lord Foley*

49. The squire's chapel. Babington, Somerset. Mid-18th century

50. 18th century fantasy. The nave ceiling at West Wycombe,
Buckinghamshire

51. *Pews for sermon-tasters. 18th century interior of Whitby
Parish Church, Yorkshire*

LEI·CHE·L·CIEL·NE

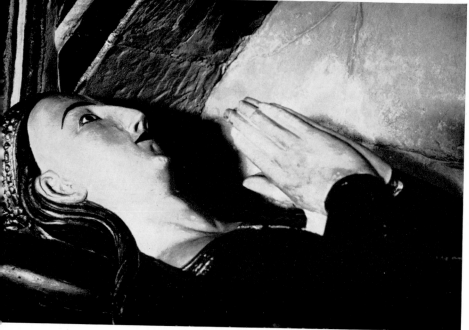

52a. *Classic grief. Penelope Boothby (d. 1791), by Thomas Banks.*
Ashbourne, Derbyshire
52b. *Mediæval piety. Princess Elizabeth of Lancaster.*
Burford, Shropshire. Early 15th century.

53. Monument to Dr. Plot, historian (1696). Borden, Kent

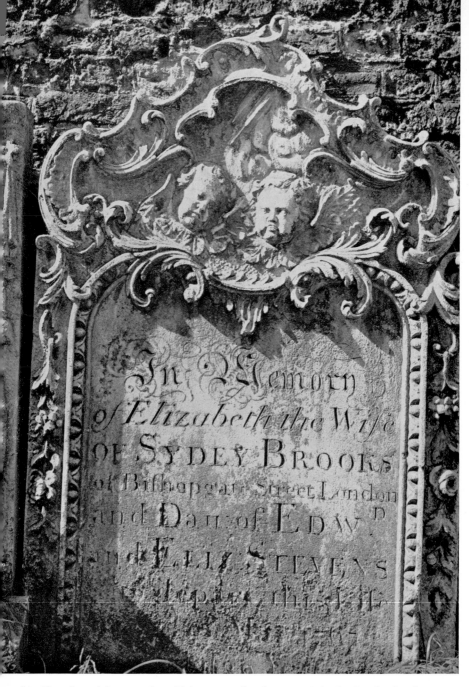

54. Churchyard Rococo; late 18th century headstone. Wisbech, Cambridgeshire

55. 18th century Gothic. Tetbury, Gloucestershire. Francis Hiorne, 1781

56. Greek Revival. St. Pancras, London. W. & H. W. Inwood, 1819-22

57. Late Georgian Gothic Revival. St. Luke's New Church, Chelsea. J. Savage, architect, 1820-34

58. Tractarian originality. All Saints, Margaret Street, London.
W. Butterfield, 1849

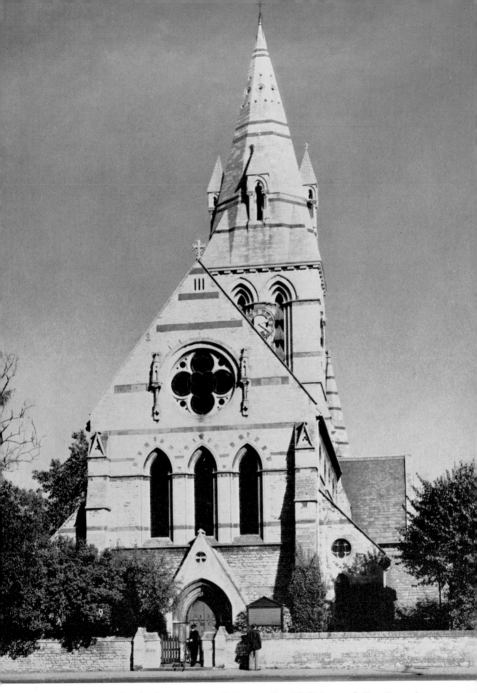

59. *Bringing the faith to married Dons. St. Philip's and St. James'
Church, Oxford. G. E. Street, 1860-66*

60. Seaside High Church. St. Bartholomew, Brighton, Sussex.
Edmund Scott, 1874

61. Vistas and vaulting. St. Michael, Croydon. J. L. Pearson,
1880-85

62. Arts and crafts Gothic. St. Andrew, Roker, Co. Durham.
E. S. Prior, 1906

63. The exterior, St. Andrew, Roker

64. *Unity by inclusion. Gothic and Classic blended in one by Sir Ninian Comper. St. Mary, Wellingborough, Northamptonshire. Consecrated 1908, completed 1931*

MONKLAND (*All Saints*) GR
Chancel and nave rebuilt by G. E. Street, 1856; spire added to 13th-cent. tower for the Rev. Sir Henry Baker, compiler of Hymns A. & M.

MONNINGTON-ON-WYE *(*St. Mary the Virgin*)
Set in lush water meadows by the Wye and built in 1679, the church is a period piece with delightful oak benches, pulpit and a Royal Arms of Charles II. The timber-framed lych-gate is of the same date; but the church tower is 15th century.

MUCH COWARNE *(*St. Mary the Virgin*)
The church, set in undulating hop country has a tall, graceful Early English arcade between nave and S. aisle, in which are the early 17th-century effigies of Edmund Fox and his wife lying on an altar tomb of fine design. The interior is lime-washed and beautiful.

MUCH MARCLE *(*St. Bartholomew*)
Setting. 13th-century nave, clerestory, central tower, very long chancel. Contains very fine monuments; alabaster effigies of 1650; a lovely mid-14th-century woman; a late-14th-century couple and a wooden yeoman.

MUNSLEY (*St. Bartholomew*)
Norman.

NEWTON, WELSH: *see Welsh Newton*.

ORLETON (*St. George*)
Norman font.

PEMBRIDGE *(*St. Mary*)
Fine example of early Decorated style, with detached belfry which inside resembles a dark forest of ancient timbers. Set in a compact village most of the houses of which are very old and timber-framed.

PENCOMBE (*St. John*) GR
'Trans.-Norman', 1864.

PETERCHURCH *(*St. Peter*)
Norman with double chancel and an apse, all with tall Norman arches. The black-smith-made modern electric light fittings are excellent in design and proportion for this strong, severe church, but the walls are bare of plaster and badly pointed.

PIXLEY (*St. Andrew*)
Small 13th-cent. church with 14th-cent. screen; set in a farmyard.

PUTLEY (*dedication unknown*) GR
Rebuilt, 1876, by Thos. Blashill; 14th-cent. churchyard Cross.

PYON, KING'S: *see King's Pyon*.

RICHARD'S CASTLE *(*St. Bartholomew*)
Set on the hill near the earthworks of a Norman castle on the Shropshire border near the woods haunted by Milton's Comus, the detached early 14th-century tower is a splendid foil to the great bulk of the church. Inside there are 17th-century box-pews and the family pew in the N. chapel where there is also some 14th-century glass *in situ*, and the E. window has the most lovely flowing tracery. Funeral hatchments. Over the border in Shropshire is an enormous Gothic church by Norman Shaw with some details copied from this church.

ROSS-ON-WYE (*St. Mary the Virgin*)
14th-cent. spire; 15th-cent. glass; 16th and 17th cent. monuments.

ROWLSTONE *(*St. Peter*)
On the hills between the Monnow River and Dulas brook, a 12th-century church with carved S. doorway, tympanum and chancel arch. The capitals of the door are carved with birds and intertwining foliage as is the chancel arch. Late 15th-century candle-brackets.

ST. MARGARET'S *(*St. Margaret*)
On a lonely hill top, a small church with plastered walls containing an exquisitely carved pre-Reformation screen and rood loft.

SARNESFIELD *(*St. Mary*)
A very pretty grey stone 12th-century church with lime-washed interior, elegant candelabra and wall monuments. Church-yard tomb of John Abel, 1577–1674.

SELLACK (*St. Tyssilio*)
Jacobean gallery, pulpit and communion rails; 14th-cent. spire.

SHOBDON *(*St. John the Evangelist*) GR
Mid-18th-century rococo-Gothic with enormous pews painted white. The whole effect is extremely pretty and is now much admired, though in the past antiquarians have suffered anguish because its Romanesque-Celtic predecessor was despoiled.

STOKE EDITH (*St. Mary the Virgin*) CL
1741; 14th-cent. spire.

G

STRETFORD *(St. Cosmas & St. Damian)*
Almost as broad as it is long with a 13th-century arcade in the middle, dividing the chapel and aisle from chancel and nave. The whole covered by one roof constructed about 1540. Two early 16th-century screens go right across the church and a Jacobean pulpit is in the middle. Two sets of 14th-century effigies.

STRETTON GRANDISON *(St. Lawrence)*
14th-cent. spire.

STRETTON SUGWAS *(St. Mary Magdalene)* GR
Rebuilt, 1880; contains Norman sculptured tympanum and 15th-cent. incised slab monument.

SUTTON ST. MICHAEL *(St. Michael)*
Norman.

TARRINGTON *(St. Philip & St. James)*
Partly Norman.

TURNASTONE *(St. Mary Magdalene)*
13th cent.; waggon vaulted roof.

TYBERTON *(St. Mary)*
Rebuilt in 1720, it retains a late Norman doorway. Built of brick with a pretty tower surmounted by a stone cornice, pediments and urns, the exterior has been spoiled by ugly modern windows. Inside, however, there is a magnificent early 18th-century reredos carved with the symbols of the Passion, in a spirit of mysticism and communion most unusual for the period. The other furnishings are contemporary and there are monuments to the Brydges family.

ULLINGSWICK *(dedication unknown)*
13th cent.

UPTON BISHOP *(St. John the Baptist)*
Late 14th-cent. tower.

VOWCHURCH *(St. Bartholomew)*
The roof of this medieval church was reconstructed, about 1613 by John Abel, on oak posts with the most delightful result. The screen and communion rails are the same date. The nave is plastered and the chancel scraped, offering a good opportunity for comparison.

WALTERSTONE *(St. Mary the Virgin)*
Setting; peasant-rococo wall tablets.

WELLINGTON *(St. Margaret)*
Norman tower.

WELSH BICKNOR *(St. Mary)* GR
1858; 14th-cent. tomb of Margaret Montacute.

WELSH NEWTON *(St. Mary the Blessed Virgin)*
Rare stone screen.

WEOBLEY *(St. Peter & St. Paul)*
Spire; monuments; setting.

WESTON-UNDER-PENYARD *(St. Lawrence)*
Setting; Norman arcade.

WIGMORE *(St. James the Apostle)*
Saxon masonry.

WITHINGTON *(St. Peter)*
14th-cent. spire.

WORMSLEY *(St. Mary)*
Setting; Norman.

YARPOLE *(St. Leonard)*
Detached medieval tower.

YATTON *(dedication unknown)*
12th-cent church; disused in farmyard.

Hertfordshire

INTRODUCTION

AT FIRST sight Hertfordshire has little to offer in the way of churches: due to a number of reasons there are, with the exception of Hemel Hempstead, no fabrics of the first rank in the county. Indeed, like the landscape in which they are set, these churches are distinguished rather for their seemliness and moderation than for more dramatic qualities.

Physically Hertfordshire is a county of undulating chalkland with some deposits of glacial clay in the river valleys of the south and east. The only strongly marked features are the Chiltern Hills; entering the county in the south-east above Tring they form a diagonal ridge across to the north-east dying away beyond Royston into the Essex uplands. Because of the geological formation there is, except for flint rubble, no building stone, and the cost of transporting stone precluded its use, except for piers, tombs, window tracery and dressings. Where stone was used it was generally Tottenhoe or other clunches from the lower and middle chalk and because of their poor weathering qualities there is very little original stonework to be seen externally. To this replacement is due a certain hardness in appearance of many of the old churches.

Formerly the county was heavily wooded, large areas being covered by the Chiltern, and Middlesex and Essex forests. This had more effect on secular than ecclesiastical work and, apart from roofs and screens, timberwork is generally confined to porches.

Historically and socially Hertfordshire suffered from three things: first, the Abbey of St. Albans; secondly, good roads which divided the county; and thirdly, the lack of any strong central influence.

It might have been expected that St. Albans Abbey – one of the wealthiest in the country – would have been the dominant source of architectural influence in the area. This, however, was not the case: due to the constant mismanagement of its finances and estates the Abbey was kept in a state of chronic insolvency, and the county in a state of incessant agrarian disturbances. No Abbot was ever able to embark on any very vigorous building programme which might have influenced local masons.

The second and third factors are, to a large extent, interrelated. Except for the ancient Icknield Way, the main roads of the middle ages, which followed the lines of the older Roman roads – Watling St., Ermine St., Stone St., Akeman St., and the later Great North Road – all ran roughly north-south.

195

Even today cross-country journeys are awkward and inconvenient; in the Middle Ages they must have been almost out of the question. The result has been that the county has developed architecturally in strips. The best buildings are to be found in the long one-street towns and villages. Family traits are found in groups of churches along one road which are not found in churches along the others. This has led to comparatively unspoilt areas between the main traffic lanes: once away from these roads the county retains much of its rural character unchanged.

Admittedly there are bad patches: the road from London out through Waltham Cross is an eyesore; the Middlesex border has been badly savaged; New Towns are spreading; and Watford has been raped by the 20th century – a fact of which the Corporation appears inordinately proud. On the whole, however, Hertfordshire has been luckier than might have been expected from its proximity to London.

Today few country churches are so convincingly the 'village-church' as those of Hertfordshire. Fabrics are generally in good repair; churchyards, by present-day standards, not ill kept; and services seldom sufficiently extreme to render the Book of Common Prayer useless. The most striking feature is generally the tower, sturdy and battlemented, with usually a taller stair turret and crowned with the ubiquitous spirelet, known locally as a 'snuffer'.

Most churches in the county can show something of interest – often in the shape of magnificent monuments of the 16th, 17th and 18th centuries. The many country houses – especially those of retired London merchants – meant a number of wealthy, if not always distinguished dead, whose taste for tombs of a modest piety has led to many fine and not a few extraordinary examples of funereal sculpture.

Woodwork, too, is widespread and interesting, and often – as at Hitchin – of a very high standard. Of pre-Reformation figure carving there is little, and of old glass even less. Brasses are to be found in most churches.

The Victorians were, on the whole, kind to Hertfordshire. Restorations, if lacking in character, are seldom out of period or locality, and there is a merciful absence of what was piously believed to be 13th-century detailing from the Nene Valley. Most of the great names of the period are represented, but seldom in a manner to cause comment.

Of the four or five Gothic revival churches of merit one is outside the scope of this inquiry: as, however, it is not only the finest in the county, but also one of the finest products of the movement in the country, the Roman Catholic Church of the Holy Rood at Watford – by Bentley – should not be missed. And, of course, the seeker after curiosities is bound to visit St. Albans for the work of Lord Grimthorpe. After all there is nothing like it anywhere else.

H.G.S.

SELECTED LIST OF CHURCHES

by H. Gordon Slade, A.R.I.B.A., *and Sir Albert Richardson*, P.P.R.A., F.S.A., F.R.I.B.A.

ABBOTS LANGLEY (*St. Lawrence*)
12th-cent. nave arcades; 14th-cent. chapel; frescoes in chancel; 1732 Raymond monument.

ALDBURY (*St. John the Baptist*)
Pretty village; stone screen with 15th-cent. tomb; 16th-cent. wood lectern.

ALDENHAM (*St. John the Baptist*)
14th and 15th cent. nave; Tudor vestry; chest; 13th-cent. font; Crowder tombs, 14th–15th cent.

AMWELL, GREAT: *see Great Amwell.*

ANSTEY *(*St. George*)
A strangely impressive building which appears larger at first sight than it actually is. The lower stages of central tower, *c.* 1200, show the transition from Romanesque to Gothic. The chancel is a roomy 13th-century design with 16th-century stalls and misericords and an unusual sedilia and piscina. The transepts with squints to the chancel are 13th century. The nave is of 14th-century design with clerestory and a 15th-century roof. A pleasant surprise to find such a church which has escaped restoration. In the churchyard is the 15th-century lych-gate.

ARDELEY (*St. Lawrence*)
Largely restored by F. C. Eden who designed the village hall, forming a stylish group.

ASHWELL *(*St. Mary*)
This magnificent 14th-century church belongs to East Anglia. Both its design and the clarity of light, due to a lack of stained glass, remove Ashwell in feeling from the Home Counties. The W. tower is remarkable for its height, its buttresses, the use of clunch as a facing material, and its extremely elegant timber and lead spirelet. The interior shows a steady development from E. to W., the large aisleless chancel having been begun, *c.* 1340, and the nave being finished, *c.* 1380. The narrow W. bay of the nave was formed between the western buttresses of the tower which were decorated with blind full height arches. There are 15th-century sedilia, 15th-century screens in the aisles, and a 17th-century pulpit and Communion Table. In the tower are two interesting graffiti. A lovely church crying out for restoration from which, thank Heaven, it has been largely spared. The village is in every way worthy of it.

AYOT ST. LAWRENCE *(*New St. Lawrence*)
A Greek temple with flanking pavilions and linking screens, designed 1778–9 by Nicholas Revett, to terminate a view in the park where the old church was left to be a Gothick ruin. It is an exercise in the application of Greek detail to a Palladian composition. Internally the classicism is of Rome and not of Greece: a Rome, however, which has been tempered to the unexceptionable Anglicanism of the 18th century. The rectangular nave is entered from the vestibule though a columned screen. The nave has a coffered ceiling and is flanked by two deep arched recesses, and the E. end is a coffered apse.

BALDOCK (*St. Mary the Virgin*)
Spacious; arcaded; 15th-cent. screens and roofs; conservatively restored by Butterfield.

BENGEO (*St. Leonard*)
Unspoilt survival; 12th cent. and later; apsidal chancel; remains of wall-paintings and tiles.

BENINGTON (*St. Peter*)
Village; simple 13th–15th cent. church; lovely N. chancel chapel; fine tombs.

BERKHAMSTED (*St. Peter*)
Large and handsome; cruciform; dark inside despite clerestory; restored by Butterfield rather absent mindedly, 1871; brasses.

BISHOP'S HATFIELD *(St. Etheldreda)*
To the Glory of God and the House of
Cecil. Handsome W. tower. The enormous
unaisled nave is a 19th-century rebuilding
on the original lines. Transepts are unusual
in possessing Western chapels. Transepts
and chancel are 13th century, S. chapel
15th century with good arcades. N. chapel,
1618, separated from chancel by arcade
carried on Tuscan columns. Monument of
Robert Cecil, 1st Earl of Salisbury; effigy
on slab carried by four kneeling virtues
with cadaver below (Maximillian Colt,
c. 1612). Very chaste. The same cannot be
said of the scheme of decorations per-
petrated by the 3rd Marquis in 1871.
Lovely 18th-century iron screen from
Amiens. Excellent modern fittings.

BISHOP'S STORTFORD *(St. Michael)*
Externally this large 15th-century church
shows an amusing contrast between the
solidity of the original work and the flimsi-
ness of the upper stages of the tower and
spire, which were added in 1812. It dominates the town in a manner unusual for the
county where the churches are generally
rather self-effacing. The roofs are original –
that of the nave having finely traceried
spandrels, and resting on stone corbels
carved as Apostles and shield-bearing
angels. In the aisles a more secular note is
struck, and the corbels include a cook, a
woodman, and a gardener. The label-stops
of the nave arcade still bear their original
head carving. The greater part of the richly
carved rood-screen and the original quire
stalls survive with carved misericords and
traceried backs.

BROXBOURNE *(St. Augustine)*
Attractively set on a bank of the River
Lea, flint-walled except for ashlar-faced N.
chapel and vestry, 1522, tiled and leaded
roofs largely 15th century. Inside, the nave
and chancel are of six bays without a break
and with the original roofs. The altar-tomb
in the chancel of Sir John Say and his wife
(1473) has brasses and much original
colour. Other and later Say tombs in
chancel, among them the 16th-century
tomb of Sir William Say. There are a number of brasses and monuments, and the
S. door is an exuberant piece of work of
c. 1640 with pilasters and segmental pediment.

BUNTINGFORD *(St. Peter)*
Brick cruciform, 1614–26; unfortunately

restored, 1899; an attractive neighbour to
Ward's Hospital.

BUSHEY *(St. James)*
Good 19th-cent. enlargement by Scott;
15th-cent. nave roof; 13th-cent. chancel;
unusual tympanum with Royal Arms; 17th-
cent. pulpit; very nasty graveyard.

CHIPPING BARNET *(St. John the Baptist)*
Mostly an over-hearty Butterfield rebuilding of 1875; 17th-cent. Ravenscroft monuments.

ESSENDON *(St. Mary the Virgin)*
Lovely Wedgwood font, *c.* 1780.

FLAMSTEAD *(St. Leonard)*
13th-cent. nave; stiff-leaf capitals; 15th-
cent. screen; best wall-paintings in county
except for St. Alban's Cathedral; monuments by Stanton, *c.* 1670 and Flaxman,
1762.

FLAUNDEN *(old church, St. Mary Magdalene)*
13th-cent. ruins on Greek cross plan.

(St. Mary Magdalene) GR
Setting; Gilbert Scott's first church, 1838.

GILSTON *(St. Mary)*
13th-cent. rood-screen; Gore monuments
17th cent.

GREAT AMWELL *(St. John the Baptist)*
Picturesque setting above 1800 water-
garden of New River (Robert Mylne architect); attractive country church; Norman
apsidal chancel; Georgian monuments in
churchyard.

GREAT GADDESDEN *(St. John the
Baptist)*
A comparatively unspoilt building – but its
development is obscure. Probably a 12th-
century fabric enlarged in succeeding centuries. S. nave arcade shows stiff-leafed
capitals similar to Flamstead and Offley.
Clerestory and roof, 15th-century N.
chapel – a particularly mean little building
of 1730 built to house the remains of the
Halseys of Gaddesden Place, to whose
memory there are at least twenty-two
monuments in the church. As most of them
are white marble it is not surprising that it
seems a chilly little place.

HARPENDEN *(St. John)* GR
F. C. Eden, *c.* 1920; enlightened Perp.
revival.

HATFIELD, BISHOP'S: *see Bishop's Hatfield.*

HEMEL HEMPSTEAD *(St. Mary)*
This large 12th-century town church with central tower and 14th-century timber spire is the finest in the county. Fortunately it stands at the end of the old town farthest removed from the New Town development. Begun *c.* 1140 and about forty years in building it is, except for the porches, vestries and spire, all of the one period. The nave of six bays with aisles is unusual in possessing a clerestory. The quality and elaboration of decoration show that the nave and transepts are later than the chancel, which has a remarkably early ribbed vault. The nave and transept roofs are unassuming 15th-century work. Appalling decorations by Bodley, *c.* 1885.

HERTFORD *(All Saints)* GR
Grand and unexpected north country Perp. by Austin and Paley, 1895–1905; open and pastoral setting.

HERTINGFORDBURY *(St. Mary)*
Cowper monuments, one by Roubiliac, *c.* 1727; bench-ends of incredible vulgarity.

HITCHIN *(St. Mary)*
Externally this was until recently, over-whitened, a most pleasantly textured building showing something of every material. There is an unfortunate piece of gardening of the 'Willow-waly' school which lies to the E. The woodwork is without equal in the county. The N. aisle roof mid-14th century; the remaining roofs 15th century as are screens, pulpit and font. The tower is 12th and 13th centuries. The size of the church and the richness of its surviving fittings show that Hitchin was a town of some wealth. The medieval street plan and a number of good old buildings survive.

KING'S LANGLEY *(All Saints)*
Very fine alabaster altar-tomb of Edmund of Langley.

KNEBWORTH *(St. Mary & St. Thomas of Canterbury)*
Setting; 15th-cent. benches; Strode monument, 1662; Lytton memorials in N. chapel.

LANGLEBURY *(St. Paul)* GR
Woodyer, 1865; wooden shingle spire; interior rich in carved angels and decoration.

LANGLEY, ABBOTS: *see Abbots Langley.*

LANGLEY, KING'S: *see King's Langley.*

LITTLE GADDESDEN *(St. Peter & St. Paul)*
Monuments.

LITTLE HORMEAD *(St. Mary)*
Remote; 12th-cent. ironwork on N. door.

MIMMS, NORTH: *see North Mimms.*

MUCH HADHAM *(St. Andrew)*
Originally a 12th-century church. Rebuilding started with chancel, *c.* 1220, S. aisle, *c.* 1250, N. aisle, *c.* 1300 and culminated with tower, 1380. In the 15th century the clerestory, the roofs, S. porch and many windows were renewed. The roofs are very good and have hardly been touched since they were first built. The screen and chancel stalls are 15th century, and there is a sprinkling of brasses. The village is an excellent one, with hardly any intrusions.

NORTH MIMMS *(St. Mary)*
Almost all 14th cent.; including fine brass, *c.* 1360.

OFFLEY *(St. Mary Magdalene)*
Nave 12th cent.; stiff-leaf capitals; 15th-cent. benches; monuments in 18th-cent. chancel by Sir Robert Taylor and Nollekens.

OXHEY CHAPEL *(dedication unknown)*
1616; simple with contemporary reredos and font; buried in building estates.

REDBOURNE *(St. Mary)*
15th-cent. rood-screen; 18th-cent. monuments in chancel, and font.

RICKMANSWORTH *(St. Mary)* GS
Tower; Laudian Gothic, 1630; interior mostly competent Arthur Blomfield Perp.

ROYSTON *(St. John & St. Thomas)*
Large, Victorianised; 13th cent. and later.

ST. ALBANS *(St. Michael)*
Nave originally Saxon with 12th-cent. arcades; monument to Sir Francis Bacon, *c.* 1626.

(St. Stephen)
Brass eagle lectern of 16th cent., looted from Holyrood.

ST. PAUL'S WALDENBURY *(All Saints)*
Exuberantly Classical chancel and screen of 1727; 14th–15th cent. nave.

SANDRIDGE *(St. Leonard)*
Stone screen, *c.* 1400.

SARRAT (*Holy Cross*)
12th–13th cent. cruciform; enlarged later; traces of paintings.

SAWBRIDGEWORTH (*St. Mary the Great*)
Spacious with screen; monuments; brasses.

STANSTEAD ABBOTS *(*St. James*)
Completely unspoilt interior with 18th-century box-pews and three-decker pulpit. N. chapel, brick of 1577. Nave 12th century, chancel 13th century. Tower and timber S. porch 15th century. Some quite good memorials of first half of 19th century.

STEVENAGE (*St. Nicholas*)
Of various dates from 12th cent.; 15th-cent. roofs, screens and stalls.

STORTFORD, BISHOP'S: *see Bishop's Stortford.*

TRING (*St. Peter & St. Paul*)
Well-designed 16th-cent. bays; Bodley restoration 1880–2; Gore monument, 1707.

WARE *(St. Mary)*
Very large, very handsome, and externally very much restored. Inside, what one can see today dates from the late 14th century and early 15th century. It is unusual that the transepts should be carried to full nave height and endowed with clerestories. The nave arcades are particularly handsome, with the main mouldings running unbroken to the floor. Between the chancel and S. chapel is a handsome fan-arch similar to one occurring at Luton. The S. chapel also possesses some fine 17th-century panelling with openwork scrolling and 17th-century communion rails and table. The octagonal font of *c.* 1380 is the most elaborate in the county with panelled sides in high relief. The carving has considerable vigour, well above the usual 'shop work' standard. Exterior suffers from proximity of some 'God wottery' gardening.

WATFORD *(St. Mary)*
An oasis of quiet in Hertfordshire's largest, ugliest, and noisiest town. The churchyard has 16th-century almshouses and an 18th-century Free School round it. The church is over-restored outside, but this treatment is not so apparent inside. Basically a large 13th-century church to which clerestory, new arcades and S. chancel chapel were added in the 15th century. Of the 13th-century there remains the chancel arch, the arches and responds of the S. arcade and the beautiful double piscina in the chancel.

The pride of St. Mary's is the Essex Chapel (1595) separated from the chancel by a Tuscan arcade. The Morryson tombs, largely of alabaster, are the work of Nicholas Stone. Both show semi-reclining life-size figures under rich canopies, with kneeling mourners. Originally there was a fine central tomb, but this was removed some years ago to lie in Ducal isolation at Chenies.

The woodwork except for the 15th-century nave roof and late 17th-century pulpit is generally 19th century, very good of its period, and quite unusual restraint is shown in the design.

WHEATHAMPSTEAD (*St. Helen*)
13th cent. onwards; N. transept; reredos.

Huntingdonshire

INTRODUCTION

PERHAPS BECAUSE it is small – the third smallest in England – and because its scenery is uneventful, either flat or very gently rolling, and because it has few recognized 'beauty spots', this delightful county has been less able to defend itself than others against the more hideous and cheap manifestations of modern 'progress'.

The Great North Road bisects it from north to south. This and other main roads account for some splendid medieval bridges like those at Huntingdon and St. Ives, St. Neots and Spaldwick, and for several old inns like the 'George' and 'the Fountain' in Huntingdon itself, the 'Lien' and the 'George and Dragon' at Buckden, the 'Bell' at Stilton, the 'Haycock' at Wansford Bridge and others, some of which have reverted to private houses. But the soulless anonymity and the garish adjuncts of motor traffic have slashed the gentle landscape across and across; aerodromes have made wide scars on it and the deserted huts and blocks of service departments still spot its unlucky face. And, of course, in a county where there is so much sky in the landscape, pylons and poles are particularly intrusive.

Yet it still has much beauty. In the west and south its remote hilly landscape has many oaks and ash trees. About a century and a half ago the Huntingdonshire elms (*ulmus glabra*) originated here. The churches and cottages in the west and south are of yellowish-grey limestone and approach the excellence of those in neighbouring Northants. From St. Neots to St. Ives, near the slow windings of the sinuous Ouse, are willowy meadows and villages of reed-thatched cottages where the churches are the only old stone buildings, the stone having been brought here by water in medieval times. The north-west tip of the county is brick-fields with Fletton as their capital and the north-east is fen 'when first drained (and much Hunts. fen was drained in the last century) the spongy peat stood some feet above the rivers and channels, but it has so shrunk that a water-course may now be higher than your head. It is a new land, and though the soil is rich, much of it coloured with flowers and vegetables, it has a bleak empty look. The villages are modern and poor . . . ' (Andrew Young, *A Prospect of Britain*).

Huntingdonshire has five attractive old towns. St. Neots, St. Ives, Huntingdon linked with the old red brick of Godmanchester by a bridge and meadows, and Kimbolton, two parallel streets, one Georgian and the other medieval with the great Vanbrugh house of the Dukes of Manchester at one end of them.

201

The brick industry is long established in the county and old red-brick houses make a happy contrast with silvery medieval stone and humbler plaster-walled cottages and inns.

When it is remote, Huntingdon is more remote and countrified than anywhere in England and there is, to me at any rate, a strong atmosphere in the county of the Civil War. The towns, one feels, stand for Parliament, the villages for the King. Oliver Cromwell was born at Huntingdon, where a chapel spire is higher than the church towers. He has a statue at St. Ives and several of his chief supporters came from the county. The 17th-century high church movement is represented by George Herbert, who rebuilt and refurnished his village church at Leighton Bromswold in 1620, and Nicholas Ferrar who founded an Anglican religious community, of which Little Gidding church survives as a tender memorial. In the Civil War, Barnabas Oley, Vicar of Great Gransden, smuggled the Cambridge College plate through Huntingdonshire to Charles I at Nottingham.

J.B.

SELECTED LIST OF CHURCHES

by R. Stanley-Morgan, A.R.I.B.A.

ALCONBURY *(St. Peter & St. Paul)
The village watered by Alconbury Brook running down the long village green, with the church on the Northern fringe of a cluster of colourwash-and-tile cottages. The inside of the 13th-century chancel noble and serene, enhanced by an attached arcade along each side, the 15th-century roof marrying well with the older work. Good contrast between the plaster of the chancel and the pebbly walls of the nave where the plaster was stripped. The tower has one of the many good broach spires of the county.

ALWALTON (St. Andrew)
Cruciform church with good mixture of medieval styles.

BARHAM *(St. Giles)
Tiny church – dark and unspoilt inside. A N. aisle built on in 1850 but surprisingly filled, like the rest of the nave, with box-pews in the Georgian fashion.

BLUNTISHAM (St. Mary the Virgin) GS
Symmetrical church of 14th and 15th cent.

BRAMPTON (St. Mary Magdalene) GS
Tower of 1635, in the old Gothic tradition.

BUCKDEN *(St. Mary)
The church has a graceful steeple overshadowed by the 15th-century brick tower of Buckden Palace nearby. The bulk of the nave in a good sober Perpendicular and the double-storey S. porch has a workmanlike vault. Inside, the plaster has been scraped away showing the coarse rubble beneath and throwing into prominence the ashlar of a lofty arcade. Some interesting 16th-century panels with Passion scenes have been imported. 15th-century roofs and painted glass.

BUCKWORTH (All Saints)
Very broad steeple with 14th-cent. broad spire.

CHESTERTON *(St. Michael)
The county is short of 18th-century work but here is a countryman's version of a Roman chancel added to an unexceptional pointed nave: also a S. porch with a 'Gibbsian' rusticated door. A clever indirect lighting effect gained by blocking the top of the chancel arch (and displaying a hatchment thereon) so that most of the incongruous E. window is hidden from the congregation in the nave. This hidden light

filters through three arches of a charming wooden chancel screen in a Roman Doric order. An impressive Jacobean monument to the Beville family is in the N. aisle.

CONINGTON (*All Saints*)
House nearby Gothicised to make a picture with the church tower which is rich and late 'Perp.' as is the whole fabric.

DENTON (*St. Mary Magdalene*)
Various 17-cent. dates; quaint.

ELTON (*All Saints*)
Lofty Perp. W. tower with the low church wrapped around it on three sides.

EYNESBURY (*St. Mary*)
The church stands boldly at a road intersection and is typical of the haphazard way the parish church has grown, assimilating Norman and Pointed work (of three different periods), a massive 'Gothic Survival' tower of 1687 on the S. side and a Victorian reshaping of the chancel to give the features thought necessary by the Ecclesiologists. This last change sacrificed an old E. window over the chancel arch and made the E. end unnecessarily dark. The N. aisle has retained a series of playfully-carved benches from the 1500s.

FEN STANTON (*St. Peter & St. Paul*)
Very good Decorated chancel.

FLETTON *(*St. Margaret*)
This has a good share of Norman work, not over-plentiful in the county, but is chiefly remarkable for a series of Saxon carvings worked into the buttresses on the outside of the chancel, which are now beginning to suffer from their centuries of exposure.

GIDDING, LITTLE: see *Little Gidding*.

GLATTON (*St. Nicholas*)
Vaulted vestry and noble 15th-cent. tower; wall-paintings.

GODMANCHESTER (*St. Mary the Virgin*) GS
Tower of 1623; rest mainly 13th–15th cent.; stalls with misericords late 15th cent.

GRAFHAM (*All Saints*)
Tiny and whitewashed, with dormers.

GREAT PAXTON *(*Holy Trinity*)
A dark and cavernous church of the Conqueror's time conceived on a thrilling scale – the arches of the crossing stupendous when compared with the man-sized nave arcade. No hint of all this outside,

since the central tower has disappeared and there is now a stubby 14th-century steeple at the W. end. Most of the interior is rendered in cement.

HAMERTON (*All Saints*)
14th cent. refashioned in late 15th cent.; good tower.

HOUGHTON (*St. Mary*)
Pleasant white village. 14th-cent. steeple has sensitive silhouette.

HUNTINGDON (*St. Mary*)
Broad and solid tower of late 14th cent.

KIMBOLTON (*St. Andrew*)
Good little town – and the church has some medieval wood-carving and painting.

LEIGHTON BROMSWOLD *(*St. Mary*)
George Herbert rebuilt the nave and tower in 1626 in an individual style best described as 'Norman'. He sacrificed the old aisles and married his new nave to the medieval transepts, which perform their proper function in giving breadth and freedom to the whole design. The church has in fact become a true Protestant 'preaching space'. The roof design is bold with sturdy tie beams. Delightful 17th-century furnishings of particular interest: twin pulpits or ambones, choir stalls and the tiniest of chancel screens all off a Jacobean turner's lathe.

LITTLE GIDDING *(*St. John*)
In undulating country relieved from the extreme flatness of the Fens, and sheltered by a grove of trees, the tiny church survives the depopulated village and the hall, now levelled to the ground. Little Gidding will always be linked with Nicholas Ferrar and his unique experiment in the contemplative life. From outside the red brick is disappointing, but within there is richness. The present fabric is mainly early 18th century. The tiny nave and chancel fitted out as a miniature college chapel. The walls lined throughout with a striking classical arcading in timber, the barrel ceiling ribbed and panelled. Lectern, font, and chandelier good and appropriate.

ORTON LONGUEVILLE *(*Holy Trinity*)
13th and 14th century with S. aisle of 1675; box-pews; St. Christopher wall-painting early 16th cent.

PAXTON, GREAT: see *Great Paxton*.

RAMSEY *(*St. Thomas of Canterbury*)
The church a monastic relic from the old

Abbey so, as one would expect, standing on the fringe of the compact little town with space to admire the Perpendicular symmetry of the nave. Nave arcades late 12th century. The only projection from this 15th-century rectangle is the late Norman chancel – very light and gracious with an Angevin vault, plastered to give the ribs their full dramatic power. The W. tower is an anachronism – from 1672.

ST. IVES (*All Saints*)
Stately Perp. with rich painted rood-screen; loft and organ-case on it, all by Comper.

ST. NEOTS *(St Mary)*
Good small market community with medieval bridge over the Ouse and a well-proportioned market square, but the church tucked away on the fringe of the town. A luxurious 15th-century building with perhaps the finest tower in the county. The church faced in ironstone and pebbles with ashlar dressings; an agreeable contrast in colour and texture. The roof almost flat – not over elaborate but very English and most satisfying. Almost everything a good town church should be.

SAWTREY (*All Saints with St. Andrew*) GR
Dark and correct Gothic of 1880, A. W. Blomfield.

TILBROOK (*All Saints*)
12th–16th cent.; vaulted rood-screen with figure painting.

WARBOYS (*St. Mary Magdalene*)
Early broach spire; Norman chancel arch.

WOODSTON (*St. Augustine of Canterbury*)
Nave of 1844 in a hard Norman style.

YAXLEY *(St. Peter)*
Some agreeable colour in the village, with black-and-white timber cottages thrown against brick and tile. The church, noble and large for the size of the community. An elegant steeple with flying buttresses crowns an impressive composition, the many components – aisles, transepts and porch – massing together most fittingly. The plan is complex, with an aisled chancel and transepts, all of differing roof levels. Inside a series of medieval narrative wall-paintings and a good 15th-century East Anglian chancel screen. E. window, altar and reredos by Sir Ninian Comper.

Isle of Man

INTRODUCTION

THE ISLE OF MAN is rich in variety of natural scenery. It is a mixture of Ulster and Cornwall to look at; there are mountains and moors down its middle, whence streams splash to the sea through wooded glens. High fuchsias and veronicas grow by stone cottages, sub-tropical trees and shrubs flourish in those parts which are sheltered from the prevailing south-west gales. The building stone of most of the island is slate of various colours and there is a certain amount of soft red sandstone in Peel and good grey limestone at Castletown. The northern point of the island has a rich swampy district called the Curragh which tails off into a flat sandy tract. Elsewhere the coast is mostly high cliffs.

The Celtic Church was founded in the Isle of Man about the 5th or 6th century, and influenced by missionaries from Ireland. Their churchyard crosses survive and all the seventeen old parish churches of the island, despite many rebuildings, have retained the plain, rectangular plan of Celtic times. In the 8th and 9th centuries the island was invaded by Scandinavian pagans; soon converted, their cross-slabs display both pagan legends and Christian themes. The crosses at Kirk Maughold and the Thor Cross at Kirk Bride and the Odin Cross at Kirk Andreas are particularly interesting. Under the Norwegians the western islands of Scotland (Sodor) and the island of Man became a single diocese c.1135, and Man remained Norwegian until 1266. Its Church was controlled directly by Rome until the Reformation. Only two considerable medieval buildings remain. They are St. German's Cathedral on an island off the west coast of the fishing port of Peel, and Rushen Abbey. But both are ruins. The Manx Gothic was more like Irish Gothic than English.

The Reformation proceeded slowly in Man, and its Church remained 'high' church until the beginning of the 19th century. Church architecture, as opposed to antiquities, begins with Georgian times. The famous and saintly bishop, Thomas Wilson, who occupied the see from 1698 until his death in 1755, and his successor Bishop Hildesley, were responsible for the restoration and refitting of all old churches. In Bishop Wilson's time there was a Manx baroque style that may be seen in the west front of Ballaugh Old Church. The Gothic Revival came early to the Island and may have received its impetus first from the castellated building by George Steuart, built as a house for the Duke of Atholl, the island's owner and governor at the end of the 18th century,

205

and now known as the Castle Mona Hotel, Douglas. People who fell into debt used to flee to the Isle of Man at this period and build themselves castellated mansions. A Manx Gothic Revival style established itself, and Castletown Church is an early example, while the work of John Welch in the 1820s and '30s is really distinguished.

After the debtors, the visitors: Douglas in the 19th century became the chief town, and Castletown, the old capital with its Georgian streets, remained Manx. With the new holiday traffic, new churches in North-of-England Victorian style appeared all over the island, and those which seem most distinguished are listed.

Man is 227 square miles, slightly bigger than Rutland, and has 17 parishes. Its Bishop has a say in the government of the island and a seat in the Tynwald Court, and consequently no vote but only a seat in the House of Lords. Its churches are many and small. Though none of the earlier ones may have much architectural distinction, they have a storm-resisting, prayer-soaked holiness about them. Most old churches were heavily restored, and only two retain their Georgian fittings.

J.B.

SELECTED LIST OF CHURCHES

by John Betjeman and Basil Megaw, F.S.A.

BALLAUGH, OLD CHURCH (*St. Mary*)
An old church to which Bishop Wilson added a front in 1717, in a simple and strange Baroque style. (*See Plate 40*)

BALLAUGH, NEW CHURCH *(St. Mary)*
By John Welch, 1832. Exterior an impressive attempt in local stone to produce Boston Stump reduced in scale.

CASTLETOWN *(St. Mary)*
By Thomas Brine, 1826. The high pews, galleries, wall tablets, high pulpit and liturgical arrangements here make this a pre-Tractarian church.

DALBY (*St. James*)
Remote hamlet on W. coast; church, 1840, in the style of John Welch, pinnacled without and unrestored within.

DOUGLAS *(St. George)*
1761–80. By a local builder who was sent to Whitehaven to copy the church there. The interior was much restored in 1910 when the upper galleries were removed and the church extended.

(*St. Matthew*)
By J. L. Pearson, 1895–1902; mysterious and dark, lofty and intricate; the chancel has a mosaic floor which was supervised by M. H. Baillie Scott.

(St. Ninian)
By W. D. Caroë, 1914. A sensitive local stone rendering of late Gothic freely treated. Spacious and impressive interior.

(*St. Thomas*)
1849; a big-boned building of local stone by Ewan Christian.

KIRK BRADDAN, NEW CHURCH (*St. Braddan*)
By J. L. Pearson, 1876. Austere Early English. It looks very English in this wooded valley by the old church. As in all Pearson's churches, the proportions are fine and the detail bold.

KIRK BRADDAN, OLD CHURCH *(St. Braddan)*
The mother church of Douglas in a beautiful wooded valley by the River Dhoo. The churchyard is full of Georgian headstones and dominated by an obelisk

designed by Steuart to Lord Henry Murray. Tower, 1773. Interior high pews, galleries, clear glass and monuments on walls.

KIRK MALEW (*St. Lupus or Lua*)
What all the old Manx churches were like before Victorian restoration; outside a white-washed rectangle in fields; inside box-pews and Georgian fittings. North transept 18th cent.

LEZAYRE (*Kirk Christ or Holy Trinity*)
By John Welch, 1835; an attempt in local stone to look like a spired country church of the English midlands; contemporary woodwork inside.

RAMSEY (*St. Paul*)
1822 Classic with galleries; architect unknown.

Kent

INTRODUCTION

THIS IS the county which seems the longest inhabited in historic times. The Romans lived here, St. Augustine landed here, Saxons and Normans have left their mark. The two ancient sees of the county, Canterbury and Rochester, were both founded in the reign of the Saxon King Ethelbert (*d.* 616). The shrine of St. Thomas à Becket in Canterbury Cathedral was the greatest place of medieval pilgrimage in England, and even today, when London has engulfed the north-west corner of the county, there is a feel of Kent about its suburban corner and of pilgrims setting out down the Old Kent Road. The long civilization of the county is summarised in the soaring stateliness of Canterbury Cathedral whose architecture from Norman to Perpendicular is magnificent, and whose 13th-century glass in quality, if not quantity, equals that of Chartres and Bourges.

Kent has always been the doorstep of England from the Continent, it is the county one thinks of when invasion is threatened, from Roman times till the Battle of Britain. And seen first, after arrival home from abroad, the white chalk cliffs, the hops and orchards and oast houses, the warm red tile hung houses and timbered yeoman's farms, the oaks and filbert copses of the Weald, the flint and ragstone churches are a graceful sight. Right across the county from west to east runs a high range of chalk hills, from Surrey to Dover, cleft in two places by Kent's chief rivers, the Medway and the Stour, with Maidstone on the Medway and Canterbury on the Stour. On the hilly Sussex borders was ironstone and once an iron industry. On the northern border along the Thames Estuary are marshes with old-fashioned towns like Gravesend, Sheerness and Whitstable and the Medway ports of Strood and Chatham, all of which are still weather-boarded and Dickensian in their older side streets. Far away in the south-east corner is the Romney Marsh, a flat sheep-nibbled kingdom with oak posts and rails and few trees and windswept salty churches. The rest of the county inland is what it is always called, 'The Garden of England'.

Kent's oldest towns are associated with pilgrims, beer and the sea. In late Georgian and early Victorian days, the coast became popular as a seaside resort. Herne Bay, Margate and Ramsgate and Dover have their stucco, Brighton-style terraces. Later Folkestone was developed as a mid-Victorian resort. In this century the electrification of the railways has turned all the parts of the county on the London border into a near suburb, and many an

208

old cottage and farmhouse has been saved from destruction by the business man in search of country life.

   After the splendour of Canterbury Cathedral, the rest of the Kent churches, Rochester Cathedral itself included, are an anticlimax. In the weald and the west the churches are built of Kentish rag, on the Sussex borders near the chalybeate 17th-century spa of tile-hung Tunbridge Wells, sandstone is used, and on the chalk hills flint and clunch. Few of the churches have clerestories. Roofs are steep and large enough to cover nave and aisles in one. The Early English style predominates and tracery is a county speciality in the old churches. The largest group of comparatively 'unrestored' churches is that on Romney Marsh.

                                                                    J.B.

SELECTED LIST OF CHURCHES

by Anthony Barnes, John Betjeman, Rupert Gunnis and the Ven. E. Maples Earle

ADDINGTON (*St. Margaret*)
Chapel has painted ceiling; brasses and fragments of tombstone with a Lombardic inscription.

ADISHAM (*Holy Innocents*)
E.E. arcade c.f. Alkham.

ALDINGTON (*St. Martin*)
Fine tower; stalls with misericords.

ALKHAM (*St. Anthony*)
E.E. in N. chapel as at Cheriton, W. Hougham.

ASH-BY-SANDWICH (*St. Nicholas*)
Large 13th–15th cent. church with imposing central tower whose over-encumbered nave gives place to a chancel free of furnishing.

ASH-BY-WROTHAM (*St. Peter & St. Paul*)
13th-cent. nave; 15th-cent. tower and roof.

ASHFORD (*St. Mary*)
Cruciform with magnificent central tower; monuments.

AYLESFORD (*St. Peter*)
Norman tower and 15th-cent. nave and aisle; Culpeper tomb.

BADLESMERE *(St. Leonard)*
A quarter of a mile E. of Ashford-Faversham road, three miles N. of its crossing Maidstone-Canterbury road. A small church with a pretty belfry, box-pews rising in level at the W. end, three-decker pulpit, choir stalls and Victorian oil-lamps which do no harm to a complete 18th-century interior of rare beauty. The walls and choir stalls are older and this may account for one's feeling that this church is the best because the most varied of its kind in the county. The twin E. lancets are a local feature.

BAPCHILD (*St. Laurence*)
Norman 13th and 15th cent.; wall-paintings *c.* 1300.

BARFRESTONE *(St. Nicholas)*
The best Norman church in Kent and virtually unaltered though much restored in 19th century. The carved decoration within and without is of surprising elaboration; note especially the S. doorway with its striking tympanum. (*See Plate 7*)

BARMING (*St. Margaret*)
Norman windows in E. wall; 14th-cent. Flemish choir stalls with rich carving in deep relief and on the round.

BECKENHAM (*St. George*)
A Gothic revival Perp.-style rebuilding in grand manner.

BELVEDERE (*St. Augustine*) GR
1916 Temple Moore from designs by C. Hodgson Fowler.

BETTESHANGER (*St. Mary the Virgin*) CL
Scheemaker monument in a ghastly copy of Barfrestone.

BEXLEY (*St. Mary*)
A restored 13th-cent. church.

BEXLEY HEATH (*Christ Church*) GR
T. Knight 1877; very stately Early French Gothic; simple, lofty and stone roof of banded slate, apsidal in Kentish rag.

BIDDENDEN (*All Saints*)
The interior does not fulfil the promise of the exterior and the lovely village.

BORDEN (*St. Peter & St. Paul*)
Attractive exterior but interior over restored; tower 12th cent.; arcades 13th cent.; rest mainly 14th and 15th cents.; wall painting of St. Christopher 15th cent.; monument to Dr. Plot, the historian of Oxfordshire and Staffordshire, *d.* 1696, who was born and died here. (*See Plate 53*)

BOUGHTON ALUPH *(All Saints)*
Is a large cruciform church mainly 13th and late 14th century and most distinguished.

BOUGHTON MALHERBE (*St. Nicholas*)
Medieval church on the edge of the cliff of the High Weald.

BOUGHTON-UNDER-BLEAN (*St. Peter & St. Paul*)
Hawkins monument by Epiphanius Evesham.

BRABOURNE (*St. Mary the Blessed Virgin*)
Fine Norman work; richer in details than in general effect; restored by Sir Gilbert Scott.

BRENCHLEY (*All Saints*)
16th-cent. carved screen; hammer-beam roof in chancel; 13th cent. and later.

BROMLEY (*St. Andrew*) GR
Sir C. Nicholson, 1930.

(*St. John the Evangelist*) GR
G. Truefitt 1880; well grouped and built of Kentish rag and brick; ugly and full of character.

(St. Peter & St. Paul)
The marvellously restored tower stands as a link with the past and is wedded onto the new Gothic-style building by J. Harold Gibbons.

BROOK *(St. Mary)*
Unaltered early Norman church with 11th-century (and later) paintings, a good screen and pulpit, and old tiles. This is a massive church which carries its longevity more convincingly than many older and tidier churches.

BROOKLAND *(St. Augustine)*
Picturesque and quite unspoilt with long low roofs and two E. gables; 13th century and later. Remarkable detached timber belfry with conical cap. The 12th-century lead font is one of the show-pieces of Romney Marsh. King post roofs, box-pews and clear glass.

CANTERBURY (*St. Martin*)
Norman font.

CAPEL-LE-FERNE (*St. Mary*)
Triple chancel arch with rood above.

CHARING *(St. Peter & St. Paul)*
Stands among the ruins of the archbishop's manor-place and is approached down a lane off the pretty main street. The tall W. tower leads one to expect an impressive interior and we are not disappointed. Both ensemble and detail are good. Chiefly 13th and 15th century restored after a fire in 1620. Vaulted porch and 17th-century bench-ends.

CHARLTON-IN-DOVER (*St. Peter & St. Paul*) GR
Soaring Early English by J. Brooks, 1897.

CHARTHAM (*St. Mary*)
Brass of Sir Robert Stevans 1306 and large monument by Rysbrack to Sir Wm. Young 1751; glass; mainly 14th cent. and of cruciform plan.

CHATHAM (*Christ Church, Luton*) GR
E. R. Robson 1884, in the style of A. W. Blomfield.

(*St. John*) CL
Sir R. Smirke, 1821; interior spoiled 1869.

(*St. Mary*) GR
Largely rebuilt 1896–7; and 1908 by A. W. Blomfield; effective tower; fine interior.

CHELSFIELD (*St. Martin*)
15th cent. with some Norman work; brasses and memorials; modern E. window by Moira Forsyth.

CHEVENING (*St. Botolph*)
Impressive, severe interior; Stanhope chapel.

CHIDDINGSTONE (*St. Mary*)
13th-cent. stone carving; hatchments.

CHIDDINGSTONE CAUSEWAY (*St. Luke*) GR
By J. F. Bentley, Perp. of 1897–8; Bath stone; nave and chancel; N. tower; simple, solid, distinguished.

CHILHAM *(St. Mary)*
The village, castle and church stand on high ground, set round a large square, with black-and-white houses; enchanting, even if for a moment it reminds one of Victorian and Edwardian pictures of Meets, Squires, Christmas festivities and Marcus Stone. The church, chiefly Perpendicular, contains a remarkable series of monuments, including two early 17th century ones of nielloed black-and-white Bethesden marble; a group by Chantrey; two children by Munro; and most unusual of all, a pillar to Lady Digges with the four Cardinal Virtues seated around it, the work of Nicholas Stone, and erected in 1631.

CHISLEHURST (*The Annunciation*) GR
J. Brooks, 1873; tower by E. J. May.

(*St. Nicholas*)
Yew avenue; some box-pews; Scadbury Chapel; Sidney monuments.

CLIFFE-AT-HOO *(St. Helen)*
On the Hoo peninsula. Remote and large among trees above the marshes of the Thames estuary. Cruciform with aisles and long transepts, W. tower, 13th century with 14th-century chancel and 15th-century porch; magnificent 14th-century sedilia, stalls and screen. On the sturdy pillars are the remains of painted bands of colour.

COBHAM *(St. Mary)*
Here are the finest collection of brasses in the county including some twenty adult and forty children of the Cobham family and a carved and painted 'altar' tomb set immediately before the altar and rich in 16th-century work. The 13th-century chancel itself is of spacious proportions to accommodate the members of the adjoining college which survives as an almshouse.

COWDEN (*St. Mary*)
Remote village; timber tower and spire.

CRANBROOK (*St. Dunstan*)
One of the best of the Weald churches with a municipal air about it; mainly late medieval; baptistery of 1725 for immersion of adults; porch and tower vaulting.

DARENTH (*St. Margaret*)
Two-storey chancel; Norman font.

DARTFORD *(Holy Trinity)*
Tower 12th century with 15th-century top; rest mainly 13th and 14th century. On the E. wall of S. chapel is large 15th-century mural painting of St. George; a sculptured tomb commemorates Sir John Spielman (1626), founder of the first paper mill in Kent.

DAVINGTON (*St. Mary Magdalene & St. Laurence*)
On outskirts of Faversham and formerly church of a Benedictine nunnery of which considerable remains survive in S.; only nave and aisles remain and are 12th cent., restored by Willement in 1845; interior has monastic severity in keeping with its origin.

DEAL (*St. George*) CL
1715; classical; Nelson worshipped here and William IV erected a tablet to his memory; carved civic pew.

(St. Leonard)
Medieval but largely rebuilt 1684 and enlarged 1819. The uneasy mixture is redeemed by the charming Queen Anne gallery given by the pilots of Deal.

DOVER (*St. Mary in Castro*)
Saxon and of cruciform plan; heavily restored by Scott and Butterfield; adjacent is a Roman pharos (lighthouse).

DYMCHURCH (*St. Peter & St. Paul*)
Norman work.

EAST LANGDON (*St. Augustine*)
Medieval cope; font.

EASTRY (*St. Mary the Blessed Virgin*)
Large relief by J. Bacon, R.A., of Glorious First of June on monument of Capt. Harvey.

EAST SUTTON (*St. Peter & St. Paul*)
Large brass of Sir Edward Filmer 1629 by Edward Marshall; mainly late 14th cent.

ELHAM *(St. Mary the Virgin)*
To many this is the most beautiful parish church in Kent and this is a tribute to the careful restoration by the late F. C. Eden. The 13th-century arcades were pierced through the Norman walls when the aisles were added, the clerestory is Perpendicular and the Early English chancel has a triplet in the E. wall. There are good corbels, old tiles, text-boards and a profusion of excellent furnishings, mostly modern.

ELMSTED (*St. James the Great*)
Very remote; beams.

END, SOUTH: see South End.

EYNSFORD (St. Peter & St. Paul)
Norman with later alterations; slim spire and spacious apse.

FAIRFIELD *(St. Thomas of Canterbury)
A tiny barn-like structure of timber and plaster with brick walls standing in a field on Romney Marsh surrounded by ditches and sheep. 14th century refashioned in 18th century and carefully restored by Caroë in 1913. Inside are original roof timbers, textboards, box-pews, three-decker pulpit and altar rails in white edged with black.

FAVERSHAM (Our Lady of Charity)
Large cruciform; transepts; Norman and 14th cent.; nave rebuilt by elder Dance 1755; present W. end 19th cent.; brasses, misericords, wall-paintings.

FAWKHAM (St. Mary)
12th–13th cent.; 14th-cent. porch and small timber tower; fading murals.

FOLKESTONE (St. Saviour) GR
Neo-Perp. done in brick and very impressive.

FORDWICH (St. Mary)
A small structure of Norman origin, unusually attractive with good texture outside and inside, tall narrow 13th-century tower arch, old tiles, box-pews, well-furnished sanctuary and 1688 Royal Arms. Some 14th-century painted glass and Saxon sarcophagus.

FOUR-ELMS (St. Paul) GR
Edwin T. Hall 1881; reredos by W. R. Lethaby.

FRINDSBURY (All Saints)
High above Medway; view to Rochester; on Norman window splays some 13th-cent. paintings including one of St. William of Perth, the baker saint, whose shrine was in Rochester Cathedral.

GILLINGHAM (St. Augustine) GR
Temple Moore 1916; one aisle; square columns.

(St. Mary)
12th–13th cent.; church on green; roof corbels; stone carvings.

GODMERSHAM (St. Lawrence the Martyr)
Old and cold in pretty surroundings.

GOUDHURST *(St. Mary the Virgin)
Is a good example of a Weald church, with its long low nave, yellowish stone and distinguished monuments.

GRAVENEY *(All Saints)
Stands in a pretty churchyard and is well-weathered; Norman in origin but now chiefly 14th century and later, with good nave roof and charming S. porch. Most of the glass is clear and the woodwork is pale so that the interior is light and seems more spacious than it really is. There are old tiles, screens, sedilia, Grinling Gibbons pulpit, chest, good stalls, box-pews and two brasses.

GRAVESEND (St. George) CL
Old church 1731 by Chas. Sloane; a brick and stone building no longer used as a church, and in the Dickensian part of the town near the river.

(St. James) GR
1852; S. Dawkes; impressive exterior.

GROOMBRIDGE (St. John)
A brick building erected by William Cranfield in 1625. The interior has windows by Kempe and one containing 17th-century glass; the chandeliers and font are of the same period. Seated effigy of Philip Packer, 1686, showing him with broken neck, just as his corpse was found in a nearby lake.

HALSTOW, LOWER: see Lower Halstow.

HARBLEDOWN (St. Nicholas)
Norman and 13th cent.; free from Victoriana; roof, font, seating and capitals.

HARDRES, UPPER: see Upper Hardres.

HARTY (St. Thomas the Apostle)
In the remotest corner of Sheppey; medieval.

HASTINGLEIGH (St. Mary the Virgin)
Medieval in situation and date.

HAWKINGE (St. Michael & All Angels)
Tiny medieval church.

HERNE (St. Martin)
A large village church of 13th cent. origin refashioned in 14th cent. with some later details; interior heavily restored; note late medieval screen and stalls; good 15th cent. heraldic font; Bishop Ridley became vicar in 1538. (See Plate 13)

HEVER (St. Peter)
14th-cent. tower and shingle spire; barrel roof; Boleyn brass and Jacobean pulpit; curious wrought-iron lectern made locally with monstrous ingenuity.

HIGH HALDEN (*St. Mary the Virgin*)
14th-cent. wooden porch; big beams in tower.

HILDENBOROUGH (*St. John the Evangelist*) GR
Ewan Christian 1844; anti-Tractarian interior; broad and low, and in advance of its times.

HOLLINGBOURNE (*All Saints*)
Large; Culpeper chapel; 17th and 18th cent. monuments.

HORSMONDEN (*St. Margaret*)
Perp. tower and clerestory; and a tablet to the discoverer of the Stomach Pump.

HORTON, MONK'S: *see Monk's Horton.*

HOTHFIELD (*St. Margaret*)
Medieval church in good setting.

HUNTON (*St. Mary*)
16th-cent. tomb of Sir Thomas Fane and his wife; medieval glass.

HYTHE *(St. Leonard)*
A Norman fabric largely rebuilt in 13th century with further refashioning in 14th century; tower 18th century; the chancel has the best Early English work in any parish church in Kent. The crypt contains vast quantities of bones.

IGHTHAM (*St. Peter*)
Mostly 14th cent. but with some Norman remains; 17th-cent. box-pews; Dutch glass with Henry VII and his Queen; Cawne monument; mural monument to Dame Dorothy Selby by Marshall; 17th-cent. embroidery.

INGHAM (*St. Mary*)
Old door with carvings of faces and flowers; good tracery; massive five-bayed screen; 15th-cent. pulpit; canopied aumbry and piscina.

IVYCHURCH *(St. George)*
It is a long low building with tower and turret covered with lichens of different colours, and forlorn in its tiny hamlet. The large number of churches in Romney Marsh is always surprising (four are ruins) and Ivychurch alone could contain most of the inhabitants of the marsh. After the flying-bombs had damaged it, it did contain a high percentage of the sheep and birds there, but the necessary restoration has been done without impairing its strange beauty. Mainly Late Decorated but tower rather later.

KEMSING *(St. Mary)*
The church of Norman origin with later additions is full of beautiful craftsmanship. Most of the modern work is by Sir Ninian Comper (1902). The screen is 15th century restored and provided with rood figures by Comper. 13th-century stained-glass medallion, early 14th-century brass, Jacobean font cover.

KILNDOWN (*Christ Church*) GR
Carpenter, Butterfield, Willement, under the supervision of Beresford Hope 1841; the Royal Martyr in stained glass; a museum of the Camden Society and a precursor of All Saints, Margaret Street.

KNOWLTON (*St. Clement*)
Narborough monument by Grinling Gibbons.

LAMBERHURST (*St. Mary*)
14th–15th cent.; nave roof shingled; remains of consecration crosses painted on walls.

LANGDON, EAST: *see East Langdon.*

LANGLEY (*St. Mary*) GR
1853–5 Wm. Butterfield; small; distinguished; very fierce alabaster and tiles; contemporary glass; cruciform with aisles and central tower.

LEAVELAND (*St Laurence*)
Massive beams in tiny church.

LEIGH (*St. Mary*)
Like the village, was given fancy dress in 1861.

LENHAM *(St. Mary)*
A village rich in old and picturesque houses; church chiefly 13th and 14th century and full of good things, pulpit with tester, carved stalls, font, mural painting of the Weighing of Souls, window tracery. The fittings are more notable than the fabric.

LINTON (*St. Nicholas*)
Cornwallis chapel; monuments, including Horace Walpole's to Galfridus Mann.

LOWER HALSTOW (*St. Margaret*)
Medieval church almost afloat in the Medway. Lead font with figures.

LULLINGSTONE *(St. Botolph)*
In the grounds of Lullingstone Castle is this white little church rising from the lawns. It is almost a family chapel and mausoleum with the monuments of the ancestors of the Hart-Dykes. 14th century

with 16th-century N. chapel and early 18th-century porch; the early 16th-century rood-screen complete with coping and early 18th-century open parapet. There is old English and foreign painted glass and a decorated plaster ceiling.

LYDD (*All Saints*)
Longest parish church in Kent; chiefly 13th cent. with lofty 15th-cent. tower and Saxon remains; brasses and 14th-cent. effigy.

LYMPNE *(St. Stephen)*
Superb view over Romney Marsh. The church which groups well with the medieval house on W. is chiefly Norman and Early English with massive axial tower; king-post roof.

LYNSTED (*St. Peter & St. Paul*)
The village abounds in Tudor cottages and Elizabethan manor-house; the church, mainly Dec. and Perp., is a mausoleum of Roper and Hugesson monuments; Teynham monument by Epiphanius Evesham.

MAIDSTONE *(All Saints)*
A large town church formerly collegiate, situated above the Medway and flanked by the archbishop's manor-place and the former college, a wonderful medieval group. 15th century and of admirable proportions. Misericords, sedilia with contemporary painting behind, monuments.

(*Holy Trinity*) CL
John Whichcord 1825.

(*St. Luke*) GR
W. H. Seth-Smith 1896–7; art nouveau Gothic of Methodist type and glass to match; strange coupled columns in nave.

MARDEN (*St. Michael & All Angels*)
Pleasant Weald of Kent church.

MARK BEECH (*Holy Trinity*) GR
1852 D. Brandon, chancel Bodley 1892.

MEREWORTH *(St. Lawrence)*
Built for John Fane, Early of Westmorland, about 1740, by an unknown architect. A Tuscan nave and W. portico of real elegance; the spire is a copy of St. Giles-in-the-Fields, London; the interior is Doric with a painted barrel vault in the nave and plaster ceilings to the aisles; there is a finely-carved tombstone and splendid golden 18th-century armorial glass.

MERSHAM (*St. John the Baptist*)
One of the many churches around Ashford which are worth a visit (Sevington and

Willesborough are two others) and after Brook, probably the best; mainly 13th and 15th cent.; glass.

MILTON (*St. Andrew*) GR
G. E. Street, 1872.

(*Christ Church*) GR
Originally by R. C. Carpenter 1856; rebuilt 1935; saddleback central tower; Kentish and plain.

MILTON REGIS *(Holy Trinity with St. Paul)*
Church is in unattractive surroundings, but is a handsome building with a Saxon core and massive W. tower – the best flint tower in the county. Chiefly 14th century. It has some good window tracery and brasses.

MINSTER-IN-THANET (*St. Mary the Virgin*)
Cruciform; tower, nave and aisles 12th cent.; chancel and transepts 13th cent. with stone vaulting; stalls with misericords.

MONKS' HORTON (*St. Peter*)
A small and pretty medieval church reminiscent of the richer parts of Sussex; 13th cent.

MURSTON (*All Saints*) GR
1874 W. Burges; distinguished and in dull surroundings.

NETTLESTEAD *(St. Mary)*
Stands a little apart near Nettlestead Place with its 14th-century gateway and immense barn. The church itself is 15th century with older tower and has a wide aisleless nave. Most of the windows contain 15th-century painted glass of high quality. Early 17th-century mural monuments.

NEWCHURCH (*St. Peter & St. Paul*)
One of the spacious churches of Romney Marsh surrounded by barns, haystacks and a few cottages; chiefly 13th and 14th cent. with a Perp. tower, font and screen.

NEWINGTON-ON-THE-STREET *(St. Mary the Virgin)*
A long and lofty church with a magnificent flint and stone tower rising through the cherry trees, it is as distinguished inside as out, with its tombs, screen, wall-paintings and the capitals in the chancel. Mainly 13th and 14th century.

NEW ROMNEY *(St. Nicholas)*
Is the only town church in Romney Marsh. It is a splendid building, mostly Norman and 14th century. The tower and W. door

and the geometric tracery of the E. window, the Norman arches of the nave and the whole atmosphere of the church give it a pre-eminence of its own among the famous Romney Marsh churches, although it is less romantic than Ivychurch, less picturesque than Old Romney and less eccentric than Fairfield or Brookland.

NORTHFLEET
(*All Saints, Perry Street*) GR
J. Brooks, 1870; big-boned and simple.

*(*St. Botolph*)
One of the larger parish churches of Kent with a fine clerestory. Chiefly Decorated and Perpendicular but with some Saxon long and short work and plain tower of 1628. Stalls, 14th-century chest and some brasses.

(*St. Mark, Rosherville*) GR
1853; fancy Gothic to go with the pleasure garden.

OLD ROMNEY *(*St. Clement*)
There is no village, but a number of pretty houses and the tumbledown church, with box-pews, text-boards and many other delights. Few churches are more picturesque (and there is a pleasant sense of tension while one is in it – 'Will the walls fall this time or not?') Chiefly 13th century with 14th-century S. chapel.

OTFORD (*St. Bartholomew*)
Timbered porch and Norman tower; hatchments and Royal Arms; lit by candles from brass candelabra.

PATRIXBOURNE (*St. Mary*)
Good Norman door and W. window; 16th–17th cent.; Swiss glass.

PECKHAM, WEST: *see West Peckham.*

PEMBURY, OLD CHURCH (*St. Peter*)
A Norman tower and shingled turret; fine oak roof.

PENGE (*St. Paul*) GR
G. Bassett Keeling, 1865; very mad Gothic.

PENSHURST (*St. John Baptist*)
13th cent. and later. S. door has its original ironwork; carving of praying woman built into wall is one of several coffin fragments; Sidney memorials in chapel rebuilt *c.* 1820 by J. B. Rebecca; 17th-cent. heraldic glass in W. window.

PETHAM (*All Saints*)
Has been burnt in this century and so is free from Victoriana; good tower and position.

PLAXTOL (*no dedication*)
In a village rich in old houses and one of the few churches built during the Commonwealth; Gothic survival with hammer-beam roof; much enlarged in 1894; note the ancient reredos of foreign provenance.

PRESTON-NEXT-FAVERSHAM (*St. Catherine*)
High and distinguished amongst railways and breweries.

QUEENBORO' (*Holy Trinity*)
Decayed and charming port; church has 17th-cent. painted roof worthy of restoration.

RAINHAM *(*St. Margaret*)
Chancel late 13th century with traces of Norman work; rest mainly 14th and 15th century. The N. and S. doors are medieval, the former retaining its bolt block. The E. bay of nave roof is panelled and coloured to form a canopy of honour for the screen. Some of the consecration crosses remain on the walls and there are other remains of wall-paintings. There is an admirable 15th-century parclose screen and a chest six hundred years old.

RAMSGATE (*St. George*)
Built by H. T. Kendall from designs by H. Helmsley in 1825–7; very distinguished Georgian version of Perp. without and within.

(*St. Lawrence-in-Thanet*)
Large cruciform fabric with 12th-cent. core much rebuilt in 13th cent. with 15th-cent. windows and screen.

ROLVENDEN *(*St. Mary the Virgin*)
Is best approached from the E. It is a fine church, mainly Decorated and Perpendicular built in stone that is almost chocolate-coloured, and its three eastward gables are the best example of a common effect in Kentish churches (c.f. Stone-in-Oxney). Gibbon family pew; they were cousins of the historian.

ROMNEY, NEW: *see New Romney.*

ROMNEY, OLD: *see Old Romney.*

ST. MARGARET-AT-CLIFFE *(*St. Margaret of Antioch*)
Has few traces of anything but Norman work. The ornament is rich, with a fine W. door, arcades along the whole length of the nave at clerestory level, and, inside, rich decoration above the arches of the nave.

ST. MARY-IN-THE-MARSH *(*St. Mary*)
Exhibits all the texture typical of a Marsh
church. Mainly 14th and 15th century with
an earlier core. Clear glass, white walls, old
tiles and early 18th-century furnishings.

ST. NICHOLAS-AT-WADE (*St. Nicholas*)
Attractive setting by a farmyard; large and
impressive fabric with clerestoried nave;
the core is Norman but as a whole it is now
mainly 13th and 14th cent.; carving on
capitals, Jacobean pulpit and holy table as
well as a brass and a handsome chandelier;
the exterior has a strong East Anglian
flavour.

SANDWICH (*St. Clement*)
Norman central tower; rest mainly 14th
and 15th cent.; heraldic font; stalls with
misericords.

(*St. Mary*)
Norman origin, much rebuilt after fall of
tower in 1667.

(*St. Peter*)
13th and 14th cent. with 17th-cent. brick
tower.

SHOREHAM (*St. Peter & St. Paul*)
Pleasantly sited in the Darenth Valley.
Mainly 15th cent.; a great split oak forms
arch of porch; famous screen running the
full width of the church, one of best in
England; panelled doors give access to the
platform or pulpitum on top; Burne Jones
window; monuments with portrait busts by
Cheere.

SMARDEN (*St. Michael*)
Church handsome outside and in unusually lovely village; the span of the roof
is incredible.

SOUTH END (*St. Barnabas, Downham*)
GR
Sir C. Nicholson, 1930.

(*St. Luke, Downham*) GR
Sir C. Nicholson, 1938.

SOUTHFLEET (*St. Nicholas*)
14th cent.; brasses; sculptured sedilia; in
the chancel are two paintings, probably
17th cent. of Latimer and Ridley; Sir John
Sedley (1603) monument.

SPELDHURST (*St. Mary*)
1871. A good Gothic Revival church on
site of older building; Burne-Jones windows and decent furnishings; base of
tower 15th cent.; unspoilt village.

STELLING (*St. Mary*)
Good 14th-cent. window tracery; altar
rails, box-pews and pulpit 18th cent.

STONE *(*St. Mary*)
Believed to have been built by the masons
of Westminster Abbey. Has a perfect harmony of proportions and is richly decorated; all 13th century. Chancel vault by
Street. Exterior covered by dust from
cement works. There is a brass of John
Lombard, 1408, a canopied tomb to Sir
John and Lady Wyllshire (16th century)
and mural paintings, but the architecture
is the main glory of the building. (*See
Plate 12*)

STONE-IN-OXNEY (*St. Mary the Virgin*)
Good situation, good exterior (especially
from E.), with a lofty nave and a Mithraic
altar.

SUTTON, EAST: *see East Sutton*.

SWANLEY (*St. Mary*) GR
1901–2. Brick, aspidal, lofty, unfinished
nave; Dudley Newman.

SWANSCOMBE (*All Saints, Galley Hill*)
GR
1894–5. R. Norman Shaw; boldly moulded;
spacious neo-Perp. in stone and flint.

TENTERDEN (*St. Mildred*)
A 13th-cent. church recast in 14th and 15th
cent.; the noble tower is the best parochial
example in Kent.

TEYNHAM *(*St. Mary*)
A cruciform church with immense transepts standing between the cherry orchards
and the sea; aisles prolonged each side of
W. tower. 13th century with 15th-century
arcades and chancel arch. Texture is good
and the white interior is effective. King
post roof, enormous E. window and several
brasses.

TONGE (*St. Giles*)
Pleasant situation; Norman with 13th cent.
and later refashioning; a single king-post
roof covers nave and aisles making the
outside look like a great barn; old painted
glass, carved stalls, 13th-cent. ironwork
on tower door, and a wall-painting of St.
Christopher.

TROTTISCLIFFE (*St. Peter & St. Paul*)
The W. wall is an amazing example, comparatively modern, of squared flint work;
communion rails 17th cent.; the high-
canopied and carved pulpit came from
Westminster Abbey in 1824.

TUNBRIDGE WELLS (*St. Barnabas*) GR
J. E. K. and J. P. Cutts, 1893; brick, lancet-style.

(*Holy Trinity*) GR
1829, Decimus Burton; individual Perp. in local sandstone; impressive interior.

*(*King Charles the Martyr*)
The oldest church in the town erected 1676 and enlarged twenty years later; it possesses a beautiful moulded plaster ceiling for which alone it would be well worth visiting.

UPPER HARDRES *(*St. Peter & St. Paul*)
Is one of those small parish churches with a host of beautiful possessions, in this case medieval glass, W. gallery, unusually good roof, monuments including one with the Chilham-style flower decoration, and good texture.

WAREHORNE (*St. Matthew*)
On the edge of Romney Marsh and in the spacious manner of that district. 13th cent. and refashioned later with 18th-cent. porch and tower in brick; the absence of modern stained glass is characteristic of the Romney Marsh churches and adds to their charm; arcades of Sussex marble; fragments of 13th-cent. glass.

WESTERHAM (*St. Mary the Virgin*)
13th-cent. tower with timber spiral staircase; Royal Arms of Edward VI.

WEST PECKHAM (*St. Dunstan*)
Norman lower and partly Saxon walling; remarkable squire's pew is the finest in Kent.

WESTWELL *(*St. Mary*)
It has been called a village cathedral and is certainly one of the most exciting churches in Kent from the architectural point of view. 13th century with a few later alterations including 16th-century timber-framed porch. The lofty chancel is vaulted and in place of a single chancel arch there are three tall and narrow openings with cusped heads and round columns; lovely sedilia and remains of painted glass and stalls.

WEST WICKHAM (*St. John Baptist*)
Now engulfed in suburbia but still a village church with the old court beside it; rebuilt *c.* 1490 by Sir John Heydon; organ chamber and some fittings by J. D. Sedding

who spent the last three years of his life here; late medieval glass and rood-screen.

WINGHAM *(*St. Mary the Virgin*)
Large village with many timber-framed houses and others with elaborate brick ornament and the handsome spired church in the middle. Chiefly late 13th and 15th century with a wooden arcade between nave and aisle. Once a collegiate church; the stalls with carved misericords survive as well as the screen base, 17th-century monuments, and iron screen to Oxenden chapel.

WOODCHURCH *(*All Saints*)
Village green and the church spire rising behind. The church has been called one of the most beautiful in Kent and it is in the main a masterly work of the 13th century with some later alterations. The arcades of Bethesden marble have alternate round and octagonal columns. The triple lancets at the E. end with banded marble shafts are most effective. Priest's brass 1320, late Norman font of black marble, 13th-century glass and manorial pew.

WROTHAM *(*St. George*)
The tower rises straight off the old London road and has a vaulted passage beneath it from N. to S. The church is 13th century, refashioned in 15th century. There is a vaulted porch with room above and the massive door has a lock block of oak and a key nearly a foot long. The screen is 15th century. There is an interesting series of brass and the Lady Chapel reredos is by Sir Ninian Comper. E. Window from Wren's St. Alban, Wood Street, London.

WYE *(*St. Martin & St. Gregory*)
A little town with many old houses and the patched but still impressive church grouping well with the adjacent 15th-century college. The fall of the central tower in 1685 destroyed a spacious chancel and chapels which were replaced about twenty years later by the present surprising and delightful apsidal chancel with a massive brick and flint S. tower. The lofty 15th-century nave has a grand timber roof.

YALDING (*St. Peter & St. Paul*)
Cruciform and with a strong atmosphere of the late Middle Ages.

Lancashire

INTRODUCTION

LANCASHIRE, ALONE among our counties to be charged with giving itself the airs of a continent, perhaps does so because it is the only one to contain two of Europe's great cities. Alternatively, it may be led into hubristic excess (one of its recurring characteristics, as, for example, at Blackpool during the summer holidays of the cotton towns) by the extraordinary variety which, like England itself, it comprehends within its area. About no other county is it so difficult to generalise. The river that marks its boundaries in the north-west is the River Duddon, which rises near the three-shire stone Lancashire shares with Westmorland and Cumberland, and drops through a cascade of Wordsworthian sonnets to Morecambe bay. In the south-east steam rises from the black waters of the River Tame as it sings, according to Haslam Mills, of cops and twists and counts and mills upstream 'stopped for bobbins'.

The River Irwell began to run with muck and money in the 16th century and much more or less filtered effluent has since then flowed under its bridges, past Manchester's neo-Venetian warehouses, into the Mersey, which for periods merges its identity with the Manchester Ship Canal, one of the many world's wonders of engineering that occur, without achieving communication, between Manchester and Liverpool. Both cities rise on the carboniferous and red sandstone plain, a northern extension of Cheshire round the millstone grit of the forest of Rossendale, the westward projection of Pennine moorland. The landscape of the coalfields is typical of its kind, spindly trees, blown to an eastern slant, roads paved with setts, paths with cinders, fences of large upright flagstones, low-pitched roofs, though there are some picturesque surprises, such as the wooded oasis of Worsley, with its black-and-white timbered halls, or the lung provided by that most Lancashire of great houses, Knowsley.

The plain becomes agricultural as it sweeps up the west to the limestone beyond Lancaster, whose skyline of castle and church arising over Harrison's bridge across the Lune summarises the long history of the County Palatine from old John of Gaunt to the mill chimneys of today, sparse here compared with those in the south-east where they are agglomerated in the area aptly defined as moorland and milltown. There the mills dominate the industrial scene, with their accompanying contributions to the landscape, of the red-brick co-op and institute, of town halls and civic centres, the great glass boxes of modern schools, and the chapels and bethels of non-conformity. The various medieval churches have been much rebuilt. Some small churches of the 17th and 18th century have been more fortunate: Hoole (1628), Billinge (1717), Tarleton (1719), Edenfield (Ramsbottom 1778), Holy Trinity, Warrington (1758), and others. The 19th century achieved an occasional miracle of beauty such as the exquisitely slender 300 feet marble spire of the Early English style church of St. Walburghe, Preston. It was designed by J. Hansom, inventor of the cab.

The prevailing tone, however, is set by the churches of the Million Pound Act, signatures everywhere of Pugin, Gilbert Scott, Street, Medland Taylor, Austin and Paley and other ecclesiologists of the Gothic revival. The greatest achievement of this movement is in Manchester where, in addition to the incomparable Rylands library, Waterhouse's Town Hall, in Albert Square, turns the corner by means of Vincent Harris's 1938 extension which links it to his superb Classic Library, facing Lutyens' Cenotaph in St. Peter's Square, in a sequence which is the finest demonstration imaginable, of architectural good manners. A dramatic group of buildings, forming the heart of Liverpool, includes St. George's Hall, described by Sir Charles Reilly as the best 'Greco-Roman' building in Europe, the climax of a long movement. It is among the finest Renaissance buildings in the world. Sir Robert Rawlinson and C. R. Cockerell continued, after the death of Harvey Lonsdale Elmes, the designs with which he had won the competition at the age of twenty-five. A similar and even younger triumph at the age of twenty-one, was that of Sir Giles Gilbert Scott, whose cathedral, still a-building, is the glory of modern gothic.

The gulls from the great port soar upwards to where the tower swims into the sky, and from the back bedrooms of decayed Georgian houses nearby the lodgers may see the light of the sun as it sets over the sea, reflected from the mountains of Lancashire-beyond-the-sands, north of Morecambe Bay.   F.S.

SELECTED LIST OF CHURCHES

by Peter Fleetwood-Hesketh

ASHTON-UNDER-LYNE *(*St. Michael*)
Important painted glass, *c.* 1500.

ASTLEY, NEAR TYLDESLEY (*St. Stephen*) CL
Tree-sheltered, a little to the north of the Liverpool-East Lancashire road. A small brick church rebuilt in 1760 and enlarged 1834, 1843 and 1847. Nave, chancel, aisles, and an embattled tower with Romanesque-looking round-topped openings. Very Georgian inside with square pews, galleries, coved plaster ceiling and Royal Arms. Plain glass in the big arched windows and a

good 18th-century wall tablet. Modern oak pulpit. Opposite stands the picturesque, gabled vicarage.

AUGHTON *(*St. Michael*)
Of grey-brown stone, standing low, among shady lanes S. of Ormskirk. The spire, centrally placed on the N. side and rising from the octagonal upper stage of an otherwise square tower, as copied at Ormskirk and Halsall, is pre-1350 Decorated. Early English nave and 16th-century N. aisle (with round-topped windows) and N. chapel. Victorian chancel. Wall recess with

cusped and moulded arch under tower. 17th-century brass plates. Westmacott's memorial to Rev. G. Vanbrugh. Sundial, 1736.

BILLINGE *(St. Aidan)* CL

In a long hill-top village near open-cast mining. The greenish-cream limestone church (1717; keys at No. 42) has urns along its embattled parapet, on gate piers and on the clock turret over the W. door; a huge bell in the Cupola above; unusual stone 'Gothick' tracery in the round-headed windows and a Gothic flavour in the small modern transepts (of more pinkish stone). Otherwise Classic; Doric columns, pilasters and entablature, and a long stone roof.

The light arcaded interior is quiet save for the loud, slow ticking of the clock in its turret behind and above us. Round arches upon stone Doric columns divide the church into nave and aisles. Plastered walls and ceiling, segmentally barrel-vaulted over the nave, where hangs a splendid two-tier brass chandelier. No pews, only chairs; but the old W. gallery remains, with panelling beneath it and all round the walls. Apse, with Corinthian pilasters. A decorative panel records the rebuilding. A tiny convex brass commemorates James Sceasbrick† and his wife, 1721. Marble tablets to Meyrick Bankes, 1827 (his hatchment hangs in a spandril of the arcade), and to Thomas and Anne Snape (with a sculptured group) signed by Farnceys (sic)‡ and Spence. Both clear and coloured glass (rich blue Victorian and later); and some tinted, opaque and ugly.

BURTONWOOD *(St. Michael)* CL
Georgian; well restored, 1939.

BURY *(St. John)* CL
Georgian.

CARTMEL *(St. Mary the Virgin)*
Among the fields of a pleasant little town, in a wide valley of the Cartmel Peninsula. Lancashire's greatest medieval parish church, once part of a long-vanished priory. It is a massive cruciform building basically late 12th-century Transitional, with Perpendicular windows inserted in the 15th, when the diagonally-set upper stage of the central tower was added. The great central arches and those in the aisles and

† for Scarisbrick.

‡ see also St. Ann, Manchester and St. Luke Farnworth.

triforium are pointed, but the chancel arcades are round. The S. choir aisle is a rebuilding of c. 1350 with good Decorated windows. Walls mainly of limestone and slate rubble, with red sandstone and mill-stone grit for the pillars, and Caen for the great Perpendicular E. window. The others are red sandstone. Simple embattled para-pets and small stepped-up corner pinnacles. Small belfry and huge buttresses at W. end. Magnificent Renaissance screens and stall-canopies, erected by George Preston of Holker during his restoration of the church, begun in 1618, when it had stood roofless for eighty years. Among many beautiful memorials are the lovely 14th-century Harrington monument (with recumbent effigies), whose canopy is built up from contemporary fragments, and that of Dame Katharine Lowther, a fine baroque work of 1700. Good brass chandeliers.

CARTMEL FELL *(St. Anthony)*
A little low roughcast church on the fell-side, built 1503. Low mullioned windows and low saddle-back tower. The floor slopes down to the altar, conforming to the fall of the ground. Two screened pews and a three-decker pulpit of 1698. Some good medieval glass, English and Flemish, and a carved and once gilt pre-Reformation figure of Christ (much damaged), from the vanished rood-screen. This is one of the two pre-Reformation crucifix figures existing in England. The flat ceiling has gone, to reveal the rafters, and the plaster has been removed round the tower arch, exposing the rough stonework.

CATON *(St. Paul)*
Norman doorway blocked with medieval cross slabs.

CHIPPING *(St. Bartholomew)*
1506; well restored 1872.

COLNE *(St. Bartholomew)*
Monuments by Sir Robert Taylor (c.1746); 16th-cent. roof.

CROSTON *(St. Michael)*
Village; Victorian and modern glass; rectory; setting.

DEANE *(St. Mary)*
'Perpendicular horizontality.'

ECCLESTON, NEAR ST. HELEN'S *(Christ Church)* GR
Tree-shrouded by a quiet road. A prim red sandstone church founded and designed by Samuel Taylor, 1838, with a spire and tall

pinnacles. Within, a dim religious light, and saints in each lancet window. The sharply pointed chancel arch stands out against a subdued radiance that surrounds the altar. The pews have doors and there is foreign-looking carving – dark rococo panels, much older than the church – incorporated here and there; Doric columns support the oak gallery and the spandrils of the hammerbeam roof are carved. Arthur Fincham's memorial – two white plaques on a black ground – tells us that he died in 1856 aged thirty-one and that this was erected by his parents. The lower plaque, oval, bears the following inscription: 'The workpeople of Ravenhead add this tribute of affection and respect to the memory of one who during his short career ever proved himself their zealous and attached friend.'

EDENFIELD *(no known dedication)* CL
In a straight stone village north of Ramsbottom, high among the East Lancashire moors. Rebuilt of small dark masonry in 1778. Galleries, square pews lined with red baize, mostly clear glass. Like Tarleton, its atmosphere is unspoilt, unspruced Georgian.

EUXTON *(no known dedication)*
A rhododendron-bordered path leads under a simple modern lych-gate to the embowered, ancient-looking little church of rough pink stone that stands high above the main road. It comprises an aisleless nave, largely rebuilt in the 16th century, with small Decorated windows (restored), a square 18th-century corbelled belfry, and chancel of 1837. Iron tie rods must unfortunately reinforce the excellent Tudor roof. There is a double piscina, and no plaster on the outward-leaning walls. Sundial, 1775.

FARNWORTH (WIDNES) *(St. Luke, formerly St. Wilfrid)*
An ancient church of red sandstone, at the top of the village street, now included in the chemical town of Widnes but with open country to the north. Good Tudor wooden ceilings in chancel and S. transept. A thin, regrettable roof over the nave, put in when the old one was needlessly destroyed in 1855. Bold chapel, rebuilt c. 1855, with good monuments (Chantry Tenerani, etc.: and earlier 17th and 18th centuries). Handsome Atherton sacrophagus monument in chancel by Franceys† and Spence of Liverpool. Many hatchments. Royal Arms, 1661.

† See also St. Ann, Manchester, and St. Aidan, Billinge.

FLIXTON *(St. Michael)* CL
Georgian.

FORMBY *(St. Peter)* CL
Built in 1736 of brick and stone; with bell-turret, large round-topped windows and W. gallery; Gothic chancel and side-chapel of 1873. A good light for reading is admitted by the clear glass of the Georgian side windows, while the stained glass in the E. window prevents any unpleasant glare from that direction – an object lesson in the use of clear and coloured glass. The church stands behind trees, not easily found in this residential place near the sandhills and the sea.

GREAT SANKEY *(St. Mary)*
W. of Warrington, by the main Liverpool road. A small embattled church of mellow brick, rebuilt in 1765 and probably altered later; 'Gothick', with a little spire. Marble tablets, 1800–50 but in an earlier tradition, are well spaced between the flat-pointed windows. Glass.

HALSALL *(St. Cuthbert)*
An important W. Lancashire village church of buff-coloured dressed stone inside and out. Spire, 15th century early Perpendicular, rising from a tower whose upper stage is octagonal. Steep roofs to nave, c. 1320 and chancel c. 1350; buttressed and pinnacled and of exceptional beauty. Spired turrets (one with a rood-loft stair) on either side of chancel arch and sanctus bell-cote on the gable above. Finely-ornamented 14th-century tomb recess in N. wall, containing a later, mutilated effigy. In the same wall and also 14th century, a beautiful Decorated doorway of three continuous moulded orders, with its original panelled and traceried oak door. Effigies and brass of Halsall family. General restoration in 1886.

HEYSHAM *(St. Peter)*
Setting; antiquity; Anglo-Saxon relics and 10th-century hog-back.

HINDLEY *(All Saints)* CL
In a large colliery village near Wigan. Brick Georgian, 1766. Round-headed windows, with 'Gothick' tracery and a good doorway. Black and gold interior with gallery on fluted frieze.

HOLME *(St. John)* CL
Georgian, altered 1897.

HOOLE *(*St. Michael*)
Near the River Douglas and the Ribble estuary in low, pastoral country. It stands opposite a pleasant farm-house by a stretch of the old Liverpool-Preston road that has been by-passed and left as a quiet lane, some distance from the small, elongated hamlets of Much and Little Hoole. The embattled stone tower was built in 1720 and the corner urns are no doubt of this date, but the rest, of pink brick, with low stone mullioned windows whose lights are round-headed, is 1628, save for the chancel of 1859. There are box-pews, a gallery, a hatchment, a curious two-decker pulpit of 1695, and Victorian glass. Jeremiah Horrocks, astronomer, was curate here when he discovered the Transit of Venus in 1639; he lived at Carr House.

HORNBY (*St. Margaret*)
Octagonal tower, 1514.

HUYTON (*St. Michael*)
Georgian pinnacles; screen *c.* 1500.

KIRKBY *(*St. Chad*) GR
Paley and Austin, 1870; 12th-cent. font.

LANCASTER (*St. John*) CL
Georgian.

*(*St. Mary*) Parish Church
1431 (tower 1759). Position; length; stalls; Roubilliac.

LEIGH (*St. Mary the Virgin*)
Tower 1516; remainder rebuilt by Austin and Paley, 1873, and enlarged 1910. Samuel Green organ case, 1777, in vestry.

LIVERPOOL

(*St. Bride*) CL
Handsome Greek Stucco Ionic, by Rowland, 1830.

(*St. Catherine, Abercromby Square*) CL
By John Foster, 1831, with a portico, damaged by bombing.

(*St. James*) CL
A very good rectangular brick church standing high above St. James's Street, built in 1774 by Cuthbert Bisbrowne, a speculative builder, with round-headed windows and a square embattled tower. Galleries on Gothick iron pillars; good internal plaster cornice; painted and gilt Royal Arms; wall tablets; wrought iron staff-rests from another church, with gilt liver bird. But later roof and chancel, no original pews, and dreary glass.

(*St. Luke, Bold Street*) GR
Magnificent 'Perp.' of darkened grey stone, by John Foster, 1811-30; badly bombed.

(*St. Margaret, Prince's Road*) GR
G. E. Street, 1869.

(*St. Nicholas*. By the landing stage) GR
Its stone Gothic tower and openwork spire, by T. Harrison, *c.* 1815, survived the bombing, but the rest (Joseph Brook's 'Gothick' of 1774–5, with a collection of interesting memorials) was gutted and is now rebuilt to another design.

*(*St. Anne, Aigburth*)
Stands, like a country church, low and long, with fields behind it sloping down to the river. The style is 'Norman' (in the manner of P. F. Robinson – little round arches and wall arcades, even on the gateposts); the material, smooth red sandstone; the date, 1837; the architects, Cunningham and Holme, of Liverpool. The tower has a clock and scalloped overhanging parapet. The spacious interior has a W. gallery, and galleries in the wide transepts. The stained glass is of many periods and gaily coloured, excepting the pleasant vine pattern design in the S. chancel windows.

*(*All Hallows, Allerton*) GR
'Late Decorated' in rock-faced sandstone, by G. Enoch Grayson, 1872–6; in quiet, park-walled Allerton Road. The tower, with large pinnacles and tall perforated windows, diminishes upwards in five stages. Interior mostly of Storeton stone, enriched with a beautiful display of Burne-Jones glass, made by William Morris and set in windows whose tracery is constantly varied. The designs, sparkling with pink, blue, green and gold, made yet more brilliant by very narrow borders of white glass, are remarkable for their wonderful arrangements of lines. Chancel panelled in red and green jasper, with stone and alabaster stripes above, and a wooden-panelled ceiling, arched and gilt-ribbed, with supporting golden angels. Marble sculptured group by F. Fabiani in S. transept, a replica of one at Genoa (trumpet damaged). Wyncote House, opposite, and a cottage, are pleasant early 19th-century 'Tudor'.

(*St. Margaret, Anfield*) GR
W. and J. Audsley, 1873; dark brick with aisles, apse and high saddle-back tower at crossing.

*(*All Saints, Childwall*)
The medieval church, partly rebuilt, a

Gothick inn and cottages, all of sandstone, form a secluded, tree-shaded group on the side of a ridge overlooking the country E. of Liverpool. Tower and spire 1810; white lych-gates and gates in porch; table-tombs in the churchyard, which slopes down to where the modern marble crosses are. Gascoyne pew, 1740, now the vestry. Hatchments of Gascoynes, Hardmans, Asshetons and Lord Salisbury; Royal Arms, 1664; monument to Rev. T. Kelsall, 1734, and others; brasses of Norris and Percevall families, c. 1524 and c. 1700; panel recording Lady Gerard's gift, 1722, and others; ancient font altered from octagon to round, Stanley crest on cover; glass c. 1856 in chancel and in Bibby chapel (by W. Warrington), and c. 1908 in N. aisle (rebuilt 1906). Pews 1853, with doors. Organ well placed in W. gallery; six bells, from 1700. Hearse house c. 1810.

(St. Dunstan, Edge Hill) GR
By Aldrich and Deacon, 1899. Successful use of bright red pressed brick with terra-cotta decoration. Proportions; surfaces; harmonious effect of well-designed stained glass in lancet windows of various sizes.

(St. Mary, Edge Hill)
'Gothick', 1812–13. An embattled brick church on top of a hill among late Georgian terraces. The tower, with small pinnacles and a recessed top, affords distant views. The flat-ceilinged interior is lit by pointed windows with wooden tracery and clear glass, except that in the E. window, and in two others that have some red and blue at the top. The gallery, supported on clustered columns, has a very pretty cusped front, now cut down. Its pews are original, but not those below, though the old panelling remains round the walls. N.B. stairs, with Gothick spandrils; wide, well-proportioned doors with cusped panels; organ case; ceiling decoration over altar; cornices and other details. Monument to Edward Mason, the founder, 1814, with figures and drapery; and other tablets a little later. Clock in tower given by his daughter, 1819, made by James Condliff; and two bells recently rehung on wooden frames. Outside are handsome iron gates and a lamp, but barbed wire replaces the churchyard railings that have, like those round the tombs, been taken away.

(St. Benedict, Everton) GR
Brick and terra-cotta, by Aldrich and Deacon, 1886; curious.

(St. George, Everton) GR
On top of a hill. Thomas Rickman's light iron Gothic of 1812–14, whose tower has traceried battlements. Corresponding tower- and chancel-arches. Glass 1863–1952, the rest plain (replacing what was bombed). Good pinnacled iron grave enclosure near gate, and several others, some broken and many gone. Gothick Kilshaw tomb. Opposite is a handsome public reading room and technical school of 1896, and a picturesque modern 'Tudor' inn.

(St. John the Evangelist, Knotty Ash) GR
Stone Gothic of 1835, with a lych-gate and a spire; good details and original latticed panes in those windows that have not been filled with stained glass.

(St. Agnes, Sefton Park) GR
J. L. Pearson, 1883. A red brick church with well-disposed buttresses, sandstone dressings and steep red roof from which rise a lead flêche and the two stone spirelets that flank the polygonal apse. Stained glass in single and double lancet windows bejewels the entirely *stone* interior, which has sharply pointed arches and gives an impression of size and scale much greater than its really quite small dimensions. Nave, aisles, transepts, chancel and ambulatory are stone rib-vaulted throughout. There are grilles and polished gates and many holy lamps; a cream and red and gold reredos; and, on the altar, a gilt metal cross of great delicacy. The adjacent vicarage is in a corresponding style.

(St. Michael-in-the-Hamlet, Toxteth) GR
The secluded 'hamlet' of St. Michael lies between Aigburth Road and the river – a latticed and stuccoed oasis amid later streets of small red houses. All, or most, is 'Gothick' of the early 19th century, including Rickman's church of 1815. Its low square tower has openwork battlements and tall pinnacles of cast iron, the material also used for the pillars separating nave from aisles and for the window tracery. The stucco which originally covered the walls and was painted uniformly with the iron-work, has been removed, exposing the mellow brick but leaving the treatment of the iron parapet and pinnacles a problem not solved by painting them red as they are now, and perhaps insoluble. In the church is a monument to Jeremiah Horrocks, the astronomer (see Hoole).

(St. John the Baptist, Tue Brook) GR
G. F. Bodley, 1868–71.

(Our Lady, Walton-on-the-Hill) GR
The mother church of Liverpool, and a high-standing landmark as seen from the Mersey. Bombed 1940, leaving only the sandstone tower of *c.* 1830 (J. Broadbent), with large crocketed pinnacles. Body now rebuilt in a different style. Mullioned school-house, 1613.

(St. Bridget, Wavertree)
E. A. Heffer's 'Early Christian' basilica, 1868–71, with an elegant campanile. Dark red brick, striped with black. Its beautiful outline is noticeable from a distance; its interior is unspoilt. Arcades with closely-spaced red marble columns separate the narrow, semi-vaulted aisles from the nave, whose flat, coffered ceiling has plaster decoration, pink, cream and blue, with touches of gilt at the E. end and a blue semi-dome over the apse. In the narrow clerestory windows are saints in coloured glass, just right for this church. Other windows plain except three, inferior and later, in the apse; and a small 1914–18 memorial window at the W. end. Mosaic of the *Last Supper* behind the altar. Bow-fronted organ-case whose gilt pipes have good stencil designs.

(Holy Trinity, Wavertree) CL
By John Hope, 1794, now Liverpool's best Georgian church and a prominent landmark. The early Georgian rectory stands to the N.; to the S., the modern Bluecoat School (1906). An old mounting block stands by the new houses opposite this church of fine grey ashlar with a balustraded parapet, a Classic steeple in the Wren tradition, its upper stages soon to be rebuilt; and a light interior – grey, white, light blue and green – whose flat ceiling has a gilt central rosette and small dentil cornice. Sir Charles Reilly's skilful alterations in 1911 included the present extended chancel with square columns, urns and shallow apse; the low, comfortable pews; and the removal of the gallery, save at the W. where it remains, upon its Gothick pillars. Good mahogany Georgian pulpit; corresponding modern litany desk and lectern; 1880 glass in apse windows. Good, simple marble wall tablets, especially James Worthington (*ob.* 1799) and his wife. But in the churchyard too many graves of white marble and black.

(St. Jude, West Derby) GR
Rickman, 1831; new round window and chancel arch by James Brooks, 1882.

LOWTON (*St. Luke*) CL
1732. Box-pews; galleries; clear glass.

LUND (*St. John Ev.*) GR
1825–52. Roman altar used as font.

MANCHESTER
(St. Ann) CL
A fine city church of 1709–12, in the style of Wren, with low-church Whig and anti-Jacobite associations; where Wesley preached in 1733 and 1738. It stands across one end of St. Ann's Square – long and wide like an ancient market-place, with the cathedral tower visible at the other end – and is of red sandstone with a square W. tower whose cupola was demolished as unsafe in 1777, and a handsome E. apse with good carving in the frieze and tall Corinthian pilasters that are repeated inside, where their fluting and capitals are gilt on a cream ground. An arcaded, galleried interior with flat coved ceiling. Much of the woodwork, including pew backs, and the magnificent pulpit (now strangely sunk), is original, and that in the side chapel is also contemporary. Marble font, 1711. 'Descent from the Cross' by Annibal Carracci. Monuments, including Rev. Samuel Hall by Franceys† of Liverpool, 1813; and several churchwardens' staves. Late Victorian and Edwardian glass. This is a peaceful oasis in a busy city. Close to are the Georgian-fronted District Bank in King Street and the gutted, but still architecturally charming Cross Street Chapel.

(St. George) GR
This splendid cluster of fat stone pinnacles in the middle of a great open square is Francis Goodwin's Gothic of 1826–7. It is of grey ashlar in large smooth blocks, with a narrow, heavily pinnacled tower and very massive, large-scale details. The beautiful galleried interior (key at 12 Wenlock Street, a short distance to the N.E., whence we see some interesting early warehouses by the Bridgewater Canal) has a ribbed plaster ceiling, and a tower arch that is tall and narrow. Richly coloured glass – blue and red, with golden pinnacles – has survived in the upper parts of the E. window which was otherwise shattered in World War II. There is a very handsome organ-case, an oak pulpit that was made by the choir-boys,
† See also Billinge and Farnworth.

and pew ends, no two, it seems, alike. Only the gates are left of the beautiful ironwork that used to enclose the graveyard, where, since this was a garrison church for the local barracks, are many interesting graves of the Crimean and other wars, one of the best being that of the Honourable George Berkeley Molyneux, 1841.

(*St. Matthew*) GR
Mission church only remaining (*Barry's* fine Gothic church of 1825 having been demolished in 1952); brick Gothick, 1829; rounded end, rounded windows.

(*St. Philip*) GR
In a district much devastated by bombing. Do not be discouraged, by the steeply pointed limestone exterior built in small, rough courses, with a corner spire, from entering this pleasant Victorian church; whose well-proportioned arcades have alternate round and octagonal pillars with good capitals, whose roof is excellent, and whose details everywhere are good. It was built by the Birley family in 1860; designed by Shellard and Brown. Most of the aisle windows are filled with good contemporary patterned glass, and there are two in the N. chapel, richly coloured, one with prophets, the other with saints; and a splendid modern E. window by the firm of William Morris that replaces one shattered in the war and depicts local activities upon a rich blue background. The floor tiles are patterned in red, yellow, black and blue. Good colour on walls and roof of chancel. Excellent modern electric lighting that shines E. from the aisle roofs.

*(*St. Thomas, Ardwick Green*) CL
By one of Manchester's pleasanter open spaces. A brick rectangle of 1741 whose two eastern-most bays were skilfully and almost imperceptibly added later, and whose fine campanile is later still, perhaps 1840. Within, superimposed Doric columns support galleries whose fronts are well detailed, with a dentil cornice; and a wide flat ceiling whose coffers are painted blue. The glass in the round-headed windows, and the chancel furniture, are Victorian; but the panelled pews and most other fittings are untouched Georgian, including the organ by Samuel Green, in its mahogany case.

*(*St. Luke, Cheetham*) GR
A most elegant clerestoried Gothic church by T. W. Atkinson, 1839; grey stone, with a spire that seems to lean slightly. A galleried interior, quite un-spoilt, whose E. end is excellently decorated with wall tracery and small canopies, like lace; and a picture. A high pulpit with figures beneath it, and good Victorian glass, especially on the S. side; and a magnificent organ-case at the W. end. Good street railings, gates and gate piers. An altogether remarkable and unspoilt church, perhaps the best of its kind in Manchester.

(*St. Mark, Cheetham*) CL
This small, almost hidden brick church of 1794, in spite of altered windows and later W. porches, retains much of its Georgian character, in pews and panelling and gallery, all of fine quality and detail. The churchyard is full of excellent gravestones, well lettered and ornamented, and several splendid monuments, of which the most magnificent is that of Adam Murray who died in 1818, a sarcophagus enclosed by Ionic columns, though one is missing and its railings have been taken away. While the removal of those round the graveyard has brought the inevitable desecration caused by dogs and others.

*(*St. Matthew, Crumpsall*) GR
By Isaac Taylor, 1910. A 'country' church in this high northern suburb of Manchester, grey and small and low (but not 'rustic'), with a square tower, aisles and visible low-pitched roofs of small grey slates. Good masonry and finish. Worshippers in the wide, pleasant interior of stone and cream-coloured brick can imagine they are in some little church in N. Lancashire or Westmorland. There is some stained glass at the E. and W. ends, all of it good and suitable.

*(*St. James, Didsbury*)
On a slight elevation of smooth grass and yews, looking westward over the low Mersey meadows. It was rebuilt in stone in 1620, as recorded on the tower whose pinnacles are tall, with weather-vanes, and whose parapet is scalloped. The light-painted interior, which has grown eastward in stages (1770 and 1871) contains both round and pointed arches. The arcaded alabaster Mosley monument (1612), with kneeling figures, is important, and there are others, John Bland (1715) and Lady Bland (1736), in a Gibbs design. Ugly, elaborate marble and alabaster of 1911 in chancel. External stone refacing, 1855. Across the lane is the former rectory, with a brick wall.

(*St. Michael & All Angels, Wythenshawe*)
GR
Star-shaped brick and concrete church built in the 1930s by Cachemaille-Day and Lock.

MELLING-WITH-WRAYTON (*St. Wilfred*)
Rural medieval.

MIDDLETON *(St. Leonard)*
Resembles Deane; position; wooden bell-chamber; brasses; glass.

ORMSKIRK *(St. Peter & St. Paul)*
Tower 1540 and earlier spire; effigies.

OVERTON (*dedication unknown*)
Remote; Norman; Georgian bits.

PENDLEBURY *(St. Augustine)* GR
Bodley and Garner, 1874.

POULTON-LE-FYLDE *(St. Chad)* CL
In the middle of this old market town. A stone rebuilding of 1752–3, retaining its early 17th-century Perpendicular tower, with a Romanesque chancel of 1868. Pedimented Doric doorways lead to the Georgian interior. Galleries with square pews and original candle sockets are reached by a good contemporary staircase, and there are many hatchments; also some brasses and marble tablets. Baptistery enclosed by 17th-century screen formerly part of Hesketh pew; carved Jacobean pulpit, lately restored. 18th-century brass chandelier. Fleetwood and Hesketh vault with pedimental porch, dated 1699.

PRESCOT (*Our Lady*) CL
Classic steeple; Jacobean roof; memorials.

PRESTON (*St. George*)
An 1884 rebuilding of an early 19th-century 'Norman' church; stone; good use of glass, especially in baptistery (pictorial) and in apse (white).

(St. Peter) GR
Rickman, 1822–5; stone and iron Gothic among the brick streets of Preston. An unusual, upstanding building whose parts compose well together, though the spire, at the S.E. angle, is later (1851). The original belfry at the W. end remains, and there are flying buttresses. Everything inside is cusped – the iron arcade supporting the gallery (with Royal Arms), the panels of the doors and even the door handles. The great iron-traceried E. window is filled with the coats-of-arms of local families.

RIBCHESTER (*St. Wilfred*)
Locality; E.E.; Georgian pews; clear glass.

RIVINGTON *(Holy Trinity)*
A charming little church on a knoll in this moorland village. Built, *c.* 1540; remodelled, *c.* 1666. Late Perpendicular screen. Linen-fold pulpit. Brass chandelier. Brass inscriptions of 1627 and 1650 and a copy of the Pilkington genealogical picture. Mullioned windows with good modern (*c.* 1900) glass. Detached 16th-century belfry, now a tool-house.

ROCHDALE (*St. Chad*) Parish Church
Position; monuments, one by Coleburne.

(*St. Mary*) GR
Almost rebuilt by Comper, *c.* 1910.

RUFFORD (*St. Mary*) GR
In flat W. Lancashire, between the white-washed village and the station. A perfect small brick and stone Victorian church (1869; Danson and Davies) with a spire suggesting a child's box of coloured bricks. Low aisles lit by small pointed windows mostly filled with good contemporary pictorial glass, and a new one by Kaye and Pemberton. The capitals of the pillars are carved with boldness and originality. Memorials in the Hesketh chapel and elsewhere (mostly from an earlier church) include an alabaster slab with figures (1458), a brass of 1541, a table 1of 1778 with a verse by William Cowper, a Flaxman of 1817 and a recumbent figure by Matthew Noble. Royal Arms and brass chandelier, both 1763.

SALFORD
(Christ Church) CL
Classic, 1830. An unspoilt Georgian church with a front of darkened stone. Portico and graceful 'Wren' steeple. Galleried interior with Grecian columns; segmental ceiling with rosettes. Magnificent woodwork. Box-pews throughout, with mahogany book-rests. High mahogany double-decker pulpit, centrally placed. Wide mahogany organ-case. Apse with Corinthian columns. Outside are three sarcophagus tombs; the other gravestones flat.

The church faces Acton Square, quiet, Georgian and sett-paved. N.B. No. 1, and terrace opposite, with fanlights. Also good Georgian houses all along the Crescent, Chapel Street (including Hulme Place), looking northwards over the Irwell valley towards Broughton. Behind Christ Church is the Canal. Demolished 1958.

(*St. John the Evangelist, Broughton*) GR
Gothic, 1836–9; R. Lane; with galleries;
chancel 1846, J. E. Regan; decorating and
glass by Pugin. Grey ashlar. Narrow tower
with tall pinnacles. Situation. Unspoilt
graveyard with Gothic railings, standing
headstones and trees, surrounded by sett-
paved streets. N.B. houses in Bury New
Road, behind.

(*St. Paul, Kersal*) GR
Irregular stone Victorian Gothic by A.
Trimen, 1851, altered by A. H. Davies
Colley, 1885. By the side of the spire is the
little spire of a corner turret. Pleasant in-
terior. Landmark.

(*St. Philip*) CL
Sir Robert Smirke, 1825, Greek. Similar to
his church of St. Mary, Wyndham Place,
London, but all is ashlar here instead of
brick and stone. As there, a domed cylindrical steeple rises from a semi-circular
Ionic peristyle on the S. side of the church,
closing the vista from Bank Place. Nice
railings. Pleasant interior; renovations.

*Parish Church (Sacred Trinity) CL
Classic, with a pinnacled Gothick tower.
A little Georgian church of 1751 among
great low railway bridges. Its railings have
gone and traffic rumbles near, while
pigeons flutter on the parapet and cornice
of the grey ashlar walls, pierced by two
rows of round-topped windows. Within,
the rich simplicity of darkened oak and
white plaster; like the chapel of some great
house. Banners hang from the dark roof,
which is modern (flat ceiling removed,
1886); the gallery fronts are enlivened by
heraldic shields and adorned with a pair of
marble tablets to the Drinkwater family
(one, 1797, signed S. Hope) and the Royal
Arms. More coats of arms in carved
cartouches on pew-ends; floor paved with
memorial flagstones; black and gold dona-
tion (etc:) boards and silver-topped staves.

(*St. Thomas, Pendleton*) GR
Gothic, 1831. Style of Barry. Pinnacled
grey ashlar with a tower, and a graveyard
whose excellent railings have fortunately
survived. Skylit galleries; plaster rib-
vaulting. Deep blue glass in top of E.
window.

SAMLESBURY (*St. Leonard*)
In a low situation near the Ribble. A very
neat stone church comprising 16th-cent.
clerestoried nave and aisles, and tower,
c. 1900 on the N. side. No chancel. The

17th and 18th century box-pews have been
lowered and the three-decker pulpit is now
a two-decker. Geoffrey Hornby's fine
monument is by J. Kendrick, 1801, with an
urn and draped figure. Funeral helmet,
sword and shield of the Southworth family.
Plain Norman font. Alabaster slab of Sir
William and Lady Atherton, 1440. Jacobean altar rails. Royal Arms over E. window. Plaster unfortunately removed from
the crude rubble walls.

SANKEY, GREAT: *see Great Sankey*.

SEAFORTH (*St. Thomas*) GR
Gothick; pinnacled stucco, built by Sir
John Gladstone in 1815; enlarged later.

SEFTON *(St. Helen*)
Among flat meadows N. of Liverpool. The
large 14th-century spire rises from its
buttressed tower, their tapering outlines
unified by fat corner finials or spirelets,
their brown-grey stone reflecting the
mellow sunlight. The church is otherwise
late Perpendicular (*c*. 1535–40) with long,
horizontal lines and an almost flat roof
behind an embattled parapet. It is divided
into nave and aisles, chancel and N. and
S. chapels, and contains much splendid
early 16th-century wood-carving that includes a canopied rood-screen (restored
1820 and '42) similar screens N. and S. of
the chancel and to the N. and S. chapels,
and the screen of Lord Sefton's pew. Canopied pulpit, 1635. The monuments of the
Molyneux family comprise the best medieval
series in Lancashire, ranging from a mailed
effigy of *c*.. 1296 to a table tomb with
brasses of 1564. There are some good later
monuments and handsome chandeliers.

SOUTHPORT (*St. Cuthbert*) CL
The parish church of North Meols; stone,
rebuilt 1730 and enlarged later – Tower and
spire 1739; Nollekens monument and
others; carving by Richard Prescot (*c*. 1704),
brought from St. Peter's, Liverpool.

(*Holy Trinity*) GR
1837 church rebuilt 1903–14 by Huon
Matear; very grand town church of pink
brick and sandstone, whose lofty tower
is a landmark; style French; interior
dramatic like a cathedral, with organ case
and rood screen combining to enhance this
effect; nave has pointed, ribbed barrel vault
and chancel roof has flamboyant stone
tracery; 1850-ish glass from old church,
and good modern; at N.E. a dark mysterious chapel.

STAND (*Whitefield*) *(*All Saints*) GR
Sir Charles Barry, 1822–6; a tall and many-pinnacled landmark on high ground, built from 'Waterloo' fund; grey ashlar with strong vertical emphasis; entered through high, open arches in base of narrow tower (as at Barry's church of St. Peter, Brighton); galleried interior with clustered columns and plaster rib-vaulting; rich glass in E. windows, blue, red and gold predominating, good modern rood screen; charming early 19th cent. rectory, mildly Gothick.

STANDISH *(*St. Wilfred*)
1582–4; Gothic with Classic detail; tower rebuilt 1867; fine roofs, font, pulpit, table tombs and later monuments (Nollekens 1778, Sephton 1752, J. Bacon Jr. 1806). Hatchments. Rich Victorian glass.

STIDD *(*St. Saviour*)
12th cent.; archaic; small; remote.

TARLETON *(*St Mary*) CL
The old church, 1719; brick, with a stone turret and cupola of 1824, and porch and vestry of that date. It has corner urns and a semi-octagonal E. end, and stands by the Liverpool-Preston road, descending to cross the Douglas where there is a picturesque brick and stone warehouse. The churchyard has some good stone graves and some ugly modern ones. Clear glass windows, ivy-fringed, amply light the simple interior. Square pews (one with the name-plate of 'Geo.Anthy Legh-Keck' who lived at nearby Bank Hall), old benches, gallery and a black stove. For the dark days and evenings, three oil lamps.

TUNSTALL (*St. John Bapt. formerly St. Michael*)
An ancient church in pastoral country; large buttresses; antiquities.

UPHOLLAND (*St. Thomas*)
14th cent. with remains of Benedictine priory.

URSWICK (*St. Mary*)
Massive 13th-cent. tower; box-pews and gallery; wall plaster and ceiling removed *c.* 1910.

WARRINGTON (*St. Elphin*)
Chancel 1354; remainder, with huge spire, mostly 1860; memorials.

(Holy Trinity) CL
1758. A splendid town church in the style of Gibbs, who designed Bank Hall nearby. Smoke has darkened the stone rustications

and Ionic pilasters, but the small cupola (it looks later) is usually freshly painted. Good plasterwork inside and excellent woodwork, including galleries (behind columns) and balustraded pulpit. Brass chandelier from old House of Commons, given in 1801.

WARTON (*St. Oswald or Holy Trinity*)
15th cent., restored; Washington arms; scenery.

WHALLEY *(*St. Mary*)
Large 13th century with 15th-century tower, clerestory and aisle windows. The splendid carved woodwork includes the 15th-century canopied stalls from the adjacent Abbey, screened pews of the 17th and 18th centuries and the organ of 1729, originally in Lancaster parish church. Chancel walls scraped.

WIDNES (*St. Mary*) GR
Austin and Paley, *c.* 1910; clear glass except in E. window.

WIGAN (*All Saints*)
The medieval parish church, largely rebuilt 1845–50; the recent whitening of the interior contributes much to its beauty; important Bradshagh memorials and others.

(*St. George*)
Georgian Classic.

WINWICK (*St. Oswald*)
14th cent. Position; roof; Legh monuments; Pugin chancel.

WOODPLUMPTON *(*St. Anne*)
At the S. end of this quiet village. The low Fylde landscape, green and wooded, falls gently westward. The long, low building that we see – warm cream-coloured stone with touches of pink, octagonal-domed belfry (with fish weather-vane), Classic doors and windows, and embattled parapet above the cornice – is the 1748 rebuilding of the S. and W. walls of a 15th-century church. The low, wide interior (three aisles under separate roofs) retains its ancient Gothic arcades. The modern-looking roof over the central aisle, with dormers, and other modern oak fittings (pews and the long low screen across the great width of the church) are entirely in keeping. Stained glass above average. Marble tablet to Henry Foster, navigator and astronomer, 1844, and those of Worthington and Kitchen (slate, lozenge-shaped) and Threlfall families. Table-tombs in churchyard. One of Lancashire's most attractive and best cared-for churches.

Leicestershire

INTRODUCTION

WHAT DOES 'Leicestershire' mean to you? To most outsiders it stands, I think, for a flat, featureless country strangely beloved by hunting men, for boots and shoes, and a kingdom of red brick. The truth is different. Far from being flat, the county stretches up on its eastern side to the high wolds that it shares with Lincolnshire – part of the limestone spine of England; and on the west it has its own, unique Charnwood Forest, whose granite hills rise to 900 feet above the sea. The hunting country lies mainly in the east and south, and nobody who has walked it (or driven to Leicester by the great road from Grantham, with its swinging, majestic descent into Melton Mowbray) will ever wonder why the hunting men should love it.

This is where Stilton cheese comes from; but Leicestershire lets the glory go to Stilton – where it was merely sold, never made. That is a characteristic wry Leicestershire joke, and it goes for other things in the county too. Belvoir – an incredible castle, standing up on its hill like something in a fairy-tale – is popularly supposed to be in Lincolnshire, or in Rutland. And when it comes to great men, Leicestershire cheerfully allows twaddle to be talked about Wycliffe at Lutterworth, provided nobody mentions its real worthies, like Latimer and George Fox, the first Quaker.

There, indeed, is a hint of the county's character: plain, self-effacing, firmly Puritan. There is no great Roman Catholic family here, though a Cistercian monastery hides in Charnwood Forest. And in Leicester itself Puritanism goes with political Radicalism. But it is a moderate, a Midland Radicalism: content with the city's fat prosperity and the hideous buildings that now go with that, yet all the time secreting, behind the shopping streets and the harsh red brick, an old town with five ancient churches, a medieval guildhall and castle, and one of the grandest stretches of Roman wall in England.

J.S.

SELECTED LIST OF CHURCHES

by Jack Simmons

APPLEBY MAGNA (*St. Michael*)
Village; good 14th-cent. fabric; monument and glass 14th cent.

ASFORDBY (*All Saints*)
Strange plan; 13th–15th cent.; nave roof.

ASHBY-DE-LA-ZOUCH (*St. Helen*)
Monuments.

ASHBY FOLVILLE (*St. Mary*)
Monuments.

AYLESTONE (*St. Andrew*)
Great chancel; Elizabethan brass.

BARKBY (*St. Mary*)
Village; fine fabric mainly 13th and 14th cent.

BOTTESFORD *(*St. Mary*)
The approach to the church is delightful, across a brook and through a screen of trees. The nave and the spire are handsome 15th-century work, reminiscent of several over the Lincolnshire border, a few miles away. The chancel was rebuilt in the 17th century, to accommodate the magnificent monuments of the Earls (later the Dukes) of Rutland, whose home, Belvoir Castle, looms up on the hills to the S. The monuments completely fill the chancel, blocking the sight of the altar from the nave. They afford a fascinating view of changing aristocratic taste in the 16th and 17th centuries.

BREEDON-ON-THE-HILL *(*St. Mary & St. Hardulph*)
Stands within a great Iron Age camp on top of the hill, keeping watch on the Trent Valley. The hill itself is being steadily quarried away, the workings now approaching close to the edge of the churchyard. There was a Saxon monastic foundation here. The present church is Norman and 13th century: its nave has been destroyed. From the Saxon church came the wonderful 8th-century carved stones, now set high up under the clerestory, in the S. aisle, and inside the tower (see especially the figure let into the wall on the first floor). The N.

aisle contains monuments and a Jacobean canopied pew of the Shirley family of Staunton Harold.

BRENTINGBY (*dedication unknown*)
17th cent.; spire 13th cent.

BROOKSBY (*St. Michael & All Angels*)
Villiers and Beatty memorials.

BUCKMINSTER (*St. John the Baptist*)
Village; stately fabric, mainly 14th cent.

CASTLE DONINGTON (*St. Edward*)
Situation; 13th cent. in origin, refashioned in 14th and 15th cent.

CHURCH LANGTON *(*St. Peter*)
The tower is a landmark to the traveller entering Leicestershire from London by the Midland line. It is a very fine composition, tapering by stages from the ground and panelled at the sides. The proportions of the building throughout are excellent: the characteristic Leicestershire nave, short and high, is seen here to perfection. The fabric is almost wholly of the 15th century. The interior is a little chilly, from over-zealous restoration: but that enables one to concentrate attention on the architectural outlines, which are the most important thing here.

CLAYBROOKE *(*St. Peter*)
Good Perpendicular nave, of the conventional tall Leicestershire type. The chancel is perfect early 14th-century work, as beautiful inside as out. The best exterior view is from the S. side of the churchyard, where the treatment of the walls and the flowing tracery of the windows can be studied.

COLEORTON (*St. Mary the Virgin*)
Glass; woodwork.

COTESBACH (*St. Mary*) GR
1812.

CROXTON KERRIAL (*St. John the Baptist*)
Woodwork, village.

DALBY, GREAT: *see Great Dalby.*

EASTWELL (*St. Michael*)
Stone screen.

EDMONDTHORPE (*St. Michael*)
Chancel; monuments.

EVINGTON (*St. Denys*)
Window tracery in N. aisle.

FENNY DRAYTON (*St. Michael & All Angels*)
Monuments.

FOSTON (*St. Bartholomew*)
Monument.

GADDESBY (*St. Luke*)
Perhaps the most exciting medieval church in the county, dating mainly from about 1290 to 1340. The ornamentation of the exterior of the S. aisle is unique – a brilliant and riotous exhibition of the 14th-century stone-carver's art. The elaborate decoration of the parapet is incomplete. The interior has been sympathetically and lightly restored, leaving the old (partly medieval) seating and brick floors. The light pours in through clear glass, illuminating the wide empty spaces of the nave. In the chancel is a life-size statue of Colonel Cheney on his horse at Waterloo, removed from the Hall near by.

GALBY (*St. Peter*)
1741; Gothic and classical.

GREAT DALBY (*St. Swithin*) GR
Village; 17th-cent. Gothic church with earlier remains.

HALLATON *(St. Michael*)
The main body of the church is 13th century, including its delightful tower and spire. The aisles are a 14th-century addition: at the E. end of the N. aisle there is an elaborately decorated turret, surmounted by a little spire. There is a Norman tympanum in the porch. The interior is less distinguished, though there is good 13th-century ornamentation in the chancel. The N. aisle has a small crypt.

HUMBERSTONE (*St. Mary*) GR
Rebuilt, except tower, by J. R. Brandon, 1858.

KEGWORTH *(St. Andrew*)
The lower part of the tower is 13th century, the whole of the rest of the building early 14th century, giving it a striking architectural coherence. Chapels at the E. end of the aisles look like transepts and help to build up the impressive external view from the E. The interior is somewhat bare: good late 17th-century Royal Arms. The church stands well, in the centre of the little town, on a hill above the water-meadows of the Soar.

KING'S NORTON *(St. John the Baptist*)
Entirely rebuilt by the younger Wing of Leicester, 1760–75. The church should first be seen from across the fields to the S., its lofty windows giving it a grandeur unusual in 'Gothick' buildings. The approach from the W., up a series of ascending levels, is impressive. Inside, the church is dominated by the pulpit, placed centrally (an arrangement now very rare in England). The fittings are 18th century throughout. Here again, it is the windows that give the building its special distinction. All that is missing, to realise the architect's soaring conception, is the spire, which was destroyed by lightning in 1850.

KIRBY BELLARS* (*St. Peter*)
Beautifully placed on rising ground above the little River Wreak. Best seen from the road leading from Melton Mowbray or from the N. across the river. Tall and elaborately ornamented broach spire. The ironstone and limestone combination appears here to great advantage. The building is of the 13th century, enlarged and embellished in the 14th, when it became the church of a small collegiate foundation.

LEICESTER *(All Souls*)
This was one of the last works of G. F. Bodley and was finished in 1907. It was damaged by fire in 1940 but has been well repaired since. Severe exterior of brick, without a tower. The interior is cool in white and green, lofty (though in fact the building is on quite a small scale), and admirably lighted. There is a window by Sir Ninian Comper at the E. end of the N. aisle.

(*St. Leonard*) GR
F. W. Ordish, 1875.

(St. Margaret's)
The most handsome of the city churches. The S. doorway and the S. arcade of the nave are 13th century, the rest of the church 14th and 15th century. The tower and the chancel are particularly good examples of Perpendicular work. By the altar is the alabaster tomb of Bishop Penny (d. 1520). As a composition the church appears best from the N.-E. corner of the churchyard.

*(*St. Martin's*)

Although the ground plan is medieval (including the unusual outer S. aisle), the building was so frequently and drastically restored in the 19th century that the fabric must be regarded as mainly Victorian. Its best feature is perhaps the steeple, which was substituted for another – of a wholly different kind, resting on four Norman arches – by J. R. Brandon in 1867. In conception it owes something to Ketton, but it is distinguished from any medieval spire of the kind by its great size. It is 220 feet high, intended to soar above the whole town; and in spite of the competition of ferro-concrete and neon lighting, it still does so with perfect assurance. Excellent Swithland slate monuments in the churchyard and inside, in the N.E. (Herrick) chapel. This church is now the Cathedral.

*(*St. Mary de Castro*)

The church stands on the edge of the Castle Green. Its good spire (15th-century design, much rebuilt and repaired) dominates the river front of the old town. Except on days of brilliant sunlight, the interior is gloomy and mysterious. The history of the fabric is complicated, and at some points perplexing. There is Norman work in the nave, and the chancel dates entirely from the end of the Norman period, with splendid contemporary sedilia. The wide S. aisle is mainly 13th century (roof 15th century) and originally formed a separate church, walled off from the older building. The tower is 'engaged' into this aisle, its ground floor forming a baptistery.

(*St. Matthew*) GR
Scott, 1867.

(*St. Nicholas*)
Saxon work in N. wall.

(*St. Paul*) GR
F. W. Ordish, 1871.

LOCKINGTON *(*St. Nicholas*)
Until the recent extensive restoration, the most interesting 'unrestored' church in the county. See the photographs, taken before the restoration, in the library of the Leicestershire Archaeological and Historical Society, The Guildhall, Leicester.

LOUGHBOROUGH (*All Saints*)
Handsome town church, 14th and 15th cent.

LUBENHAM *(*All Saints*)
Virtually unrestored. Plaster and white-wash still cover the walls, and even the 13th-century piers and capitals of the nave. The early 19th-century box-pews survive as a set, together with a little medieval seating in the chancel. The N. aisle was used as a National School from 1815 to 1859 when it was thrown into the main body of the church.

LUTTERWORTH (*St. Mary*)
'Doom' painting; spurious Wycliffe relics; mainly 14th and 15th cent. with traces of earlier work.

MARKET HARBOROUGH (*St. Dionysius*)
Steeple and chancel 14th cent.; nave 15th cent.

MELTON MOWBRAY *(*St. Mary*)
A grand cruciform town church with a central tower (lower stage 13th century, upper stage about 1500), marred only by a very clumsy external stair-turret on the N. side. The best view is from the S.W. At the W. end there is a Galilee porch. This, like the whole of the interior, has suffered much from bad restoration: the chancel is dingy and almost wholly without interest now. The transepts have E. and W. aisles, a rare extravagance denied to many cathedrals. There is a fine set of 18th-century chandeliers.

NEVILL HOLT (*St. Mary*)
Chapel; 14th and 15th cent.; Jacobean pulpit.

NOSELEY (*St. Mary*)
Chapel; late 13th cent. with 15th-cent. roof and E. and W. windows, font, heraldic glass and stalls.

NORTON, KING'S: *see King's Norton.*

PEATLING MAGNA *(*All Saints*)
Not a church of great note from the outside, though well seen from the road to the E. Mainly 14th and 15th century. Inside, the walls have been 'scraped', but the pearly colour and texture of the stone are as delightful, in their different way, as plaster. The windows in the chancel are deeply set and show fine mouldings. The woodwork includes some 15th century and some Jacobean seats, and a fine 17th-century pulpit and altar rails. Incised slabs, mounted on altar tombs, in the chancel to members of the Jarvis family.

QUENIBOROUGH (*St. Mary*)
Spire.

ROTHLEY (*St. Mary the Virgin*)
Saxon cross in churchyard.

SAXBY (*St. Peter*) CL
1788.

STAPLEFORD *(*St. Mary Magdalene*)
GR
In a glade of the woods of Stapleford Park. It should be seen in the spring when the daffodils are out. The church was wholly rebuilt, to the designs of George Richardson and at the expense of the Earl of Harborough, in 1783, in the 'Gothick' style. The interior is distinguished. The seats face inwards, as in a College chapel. All the original fittings remain, and the woodwork is good, especially in the W. gallery. A 15th-century brass and Caroline monument survive from the earlier church, both of high quality. On the N. side of the chancel is a monument by Rysbrack. The glass is clear throughout, but there is constant colour and movement in this church from the play of the trees outside.

STAUNTON HAROLD *(*Holy Trinity*)
The private chapel of Staunton Harold Hall, set at an oblique angle to it, on a grass bank rising from the lake. The chapel was built at the expense of Sir Robert Shirley in 1653–65, as an Anglican gesture of defiance to the Commonwealth Government. Though not the only church in England built during the Cromwellian period, it is unique in preserving all its original fittings, including pews, painted ceilings, altar hangings, and plate. The 17th-century pale green glass survives in some of the windows. Early 18th-century organ; iron chancel screen, probably by Robert Bakewell. The chapel is now in the hands of the National Trust.

STOCKERSTON (*St. Peter*)
Glass; 17th-cent. incised slab, probably by Nicholas Stone.

STOKE GOLDING *(*St. Margaret*)
A building of exceptional perfection, showing 'Decorated' design and carving at its best, both outside (openwork parapet, buttresses, etc.) and inside (especially the S. arcade of the nave, with clustered columns and capitals carved with foliage). The windows are notable throughout, particularly

the 'Geometrical' E. windows of the nave and aisle, and the N. windows, with their flowing tracery, which are a little later. The building may be dated about 1300–40.

STONTON WYVILLE (*St. Denys*)
Monuments.

THORNTON *(*St. Peter*)
In a charming situation, on the side of a hill falling steeply down to a reservoir. Walk up the hill and across the village street, and you are on the edge of the Leicestershire coalfield. The church has been very little restored, retaining its plastered walls, old floors and seating, tympanum last painted in 1820, and enormous S. door with medieval ironwork. In the S. aisle the traceried heads of the E. window contain 14th-century glass. The W. window of the N. aisle is of the 'ox-eye' design. The shallow chancel is Victorian. The levels of the floor fall markedly towards the E.

TILTON (*St. Peter*)
Exterior, limestone and ironstone.

TUR LANGTON (*St. Andrew*) GR
1866, J. Goddard. Red brick.

TWYCROSS (*St. James the Great*)
13th-century. French glass.

WARTNABY (*St. Michael & All Angels*)
Norman wall-painting.

WISTOW *(*St. Wistan*)
A small church on the edge of the park at Wistow Hall, formerly the home of the Halfords. 15th-century tower, but the appearance of the fabric is now mainly of the 18th and early 19th centuries. Good altar rails of painted ironwork. Look at the church from the E., as F. L. Griggs did for his fine drawing, reproduced in *Highways and Byways in Leicestershire*.

WITHCOTE *(*dedication uncertain*)
A very small rectangular building, serving as the chapel for Withcote Hall, which it adjoins, and dating probably from about 1520–30. The windows are filled with rich early 16th-century glass. 18th-century reredos, incorporating monuments on either side of the altar. The building is overcrowded with poor seating and a large and ugly font of 1858.

Lincolnshire

INTRODUCTION

THIS IS the second largest county in England and the least appreciated. The broad estuary of the Humber cuts it off from Yorkshire, so that it is on the way to nowhere except to the city of its glorious cathedral and its own fishing port of Grimsby. It has pleasure resorts like Skegness on a very few of those ninety miles of low sandy coast, extremely rich agricultural towns like Spalding and Boston among their flat fields of bulbs and roots, the industrial borough of Scunthorpe. The county town and cathedral city of Lincoln is ancient on the hill and industrial in the valley. Only the south-west corner of this little-known county is bothered by the through traffic from London to the north. A.1 roars through the limestone town of Stamford with its fine churches, stone-tiled roofs and substantial 17th-century and Georgian houses built in hilly streets. A.1 goes on to Grantham whose elegant 14th-century spire rises above the old red-brick and red-tiled roofs of the town.

Those who think of Lincs as dull and flat are wrong. The scenery runs from north to south down the whole length of the county in varied bands. Along the inland western border is a limestone cliff extending from Stretton in Rutland to Winteringham on the Humber. Along its ridge runs the Ermine Street in a straight line, and known locally as The Ramper, and on the slopes below are the country houses, parks and feudal villages. From this ridge was quarried the beautiful white Ancaster and Lincoln limestone, of which so many of the churches were built. From Barton-on-Humber almost as far as the forgotten port of Wainfleet, extend the chalky hills known as the wolds, which are an unexplored variant of the Sussex downs. Here at Somersby, near the old red-brick town of Louth with its silver spire, Tennyson was born. The limestone ridge looks west, and the chalky heights look east to

> Calm and still light on yon great plain
> That sweeps with all its autumn bowers,
> And crowded farms and lessening towers,
> To mingle with the bounding main.

The 'great plain' is the fen and the marsh north of it between the wolds and the sea. The coast is mostly dunes and samphire moss against the cold North Sea. In fen and marsh the landscape is three-quarters sky as it is in so many of Tennyson's poems. A further type of Lincolnshire scenery is the heath between the chalk and the limestone. In places it creates something as unex-

234

pected as Woodhall Spa, that half-timbered Bournemouth-like settlement, among silver birches, heather and rhododendron.

The county has 700 churches and is divided into three parts, Lindsey the northern half of the county, and Kesteven and Holland the south-western and south-eastern quarters. Then these parts are sub-divided into sokes and wapentakes and the whole county is Anglo-Saxon, though largely Scandinavian in dialect and place-names. Except for the Cathedral and Louth, the old churches of Lindsey are smaller than those in the south of the county, and on the wolds and heath, where there was only local sandstone, they consist only of nave and chancel, the weathered sandstone churches of the wolds having a crumbled and patched look. Kesteven, being full of limestone and a prosperous wool district, abounds in splendid 14th-century churches most of which have enormous towers and spires. The part known as Holland was navigable fen, and stone was brought here by water to build some of the finest late-medieval churches in England, such as Boston, Spalding, Gedney and Long Sutton, which look all the more magnificent for the flatness of the landscape.   J.B.

SELECTED LIST OF CHURCHES

by the Rev. Canon P. B. G. Binnall, F.S.A.

ADDLETHORPE *(St. Nicholas)*
One of a group of late 15th-century churches in the marsh, shorn of its chancel by a former rector in 1706. Some of the medieval stained glass can still be seen. Much of the original woodwork, 'possibly the best of any village church in the shire' remains in screens and pew-ends.

ALFORD *(St. Wilfrid)*
A good 14th-century church notable for three things: the chamber over the S. porch, the fine alabaster monument of members of the Christopher family (temp. Charles II) and a drastic restoration by Gilbert Scott in 1869, when a second N. aisle was added and the tower was heightened.

ALGARKIRK *(St. Peter & St. Paul)*
One of the most stately churches in the N. Fenland, in a fine natural setting. Cruciform with double aisles to the transepts. Restored by R. C. Carpenter (the architect of Lancing College) in 1850.

ALKBOROUGH *(St. John the Baptist)*
This church stands in a commanding position in the N.W. corner of the county, and from the top of the tower one can see York Minster, Lincoln Cathedral, Beverley Minster, Spurn Lighthouse and Hull Docks. The lower part of the tower is probably pre-Conquest. The nave arcades are 13th century and the chancel was rebuilt by J. O. Scott in 1887.

ALTHORPE *(St. Oswald)*
15th-cent. church on Trent bank; 14th-cent. brass of priest.

ALVINGHAM *(St. Adelwold)* and NORTH COCKERINGTON *(St. Mary)* two churches in one churchyard.
Alvingham, font; medieval glass.
North Cockerington, Norman work.

ANCASTER *(St. Martin)*
Medieval architecture; setting.

ANWICK *(St. Edith)*
Possesses one of the 14th-century broach spires typical of the Sleaford district. When the chancel was restored one hundred years ago a Madonna figure was found which still bears traces of its original colour, in one of the walls.

APPLEBY *(*St. Bartholomew*)
In a picturesque setting at the end of an avenue of trees. The church was largely rebuilt in 1800 and is mainly notable for the traces of funeral black on the inside walls, which were put into mourning on the death of a former Lord St. Oswald, and have never quite recovered. There are some fragments of masonry from Thornholme Priory in this parish, where St. Hugh used to feed blue-tits.

ASGARBY, NR. SPILSBY (*St. Swithin*)
Setting; church measures 25 ft. by 16 ft.; early 19th cent.

ASLACKBY (*St. James*)
Setting in a valley; 15th-cent. tower.

AYLESBY (*St. Lawrence*)
Medieval features and monuments.

BAG ENDERBY *(*St. Margaret*)
A sandstone church in a remote village in the heart of the wolds, with a 14th-century nave, chancel and windows, and 15th-century tower, porch and E. window. The font has carvings of a Pietà and emblems of the Passion. Medieval glass includes the arms of Crowland Abbey. Monuments to Andrew Gedney, 1591, and William Langhorne, 1739.

BARDNEY (*St. Lawrence*)
Fine proportions; late medieval chancel of brick; remains brought from Abbey can be seen in the church.

BARKSTON (*St. Nicholas*)
Pretty village; good medieval architecture.

BARKWITH, EAST: *see East Barkwith.*

BARLINGS *(*St. Edward, King & Martyr*)
This church is pleasantly placed in a green field near the ruins of the Premonstratensian Monastery whose Abbot was hanged for his share in the Lincolnshire Rising in 1536. There is a Norman doorway and some 13th-century work. In 1876 a scheme of 'restoration' was undertaken and the E. bay of the nave was heightened. Fortunately funds ran out before the work could be completed. The church has a curious hump-backed appearance.

BARNETBY-LE-WOLD *(*St. Mary*)
A lovely, forlorn little church on a hill top, with a Norman lead font, Saxon work in the S. wall and a unique sculpture depicting an unidentified animal rather like a cat. There is also a good modern church in the village.

BARROW (*Holy Trinity*)
Norman arcades.

BARTON-ON-HUMBER *(*St. Mary*)
Originally a chantry chapel, this is one of the most magnificent churches in the county with an elaborate Norman N. arcade, early 14th-century S. arcade, 15th-century clerestory, and a number of memorials including a brass (1433) to the memory of Simon Seman, a London alderman.

*(*St. Peter*)
The tower with its W. extension is the earliest piece of ecclesiastical architecture in the county and is similar in type to that of Earls Barton, Northants. St. Chad founded the original church here in the 8th century. Apart from the Saxon work most of the present building is 14th century surmounted by a fine Perpendicular clerestory. Perhaps the most notable feature is the unglazed E. window of the N. aisle which bears the crucifix and attendant figures on its three mullions.

BASTON (*St. John the Baptist*)
Medieval architecture; parish chest.

BAUMBER (*St. Swithin*)
Medieval church enclosed in brick.

BELLEAU (*St. John the Baptist*)
On edge of a wooded hill, overlooking site of manor-house formerly occupied by Sir Harry Vane, the younger.

BELTON, NR. GRANTHAM (*St. Peter & St. Paul*)
Brownlow memorials; pretty estate village.

BELTON IN ISLE OF AXHOLME (*All Saints*)
Perp.

BENINGTON *(*All Saints*)
The church was restored by James Fowler in 1876 and has good lancet windows in the chancel, a 14th-century nave and late 15th-century tower and clerestory.

BICKER (*St. Swithin*)
Pre-Conquest carved stones; Norman and 16th-cent. features.

BIGBY *(*All Saints*)
A small church in a beautiful setting at the foot of the wolds near Brigg. Apart from the nine-sided font the most interesting features are the monuments, including one dated 1518 to Sir Robert and Elizabeth Tyrwhit, which bears figures of their

twenty-two children, and a brass of 1632 to Edward Naylor 'a faithfull and painefull minister of God's word'.

BILLINGBOROUGH (St. Andrew)
Setting picturesque; spire.

BILLINGHAY *(St. Michael)
This church should be visited by anyone wishing to see an excellent example of recent restoration work. There is a good spire and a 15th-century chancel screen. Oak pews, the work of a local craftsman have recently been provided.

BINBROOK *(St. Mary with St. Gabriel)
Is notable for a fine aerodrome and the best church designed by a much criticised architect, James Fowler of Louth. It was built in 1869 replacing one of the two former churches, both of which were demolished. Fowler's church has a well-proportioned spire but is perhaps a trifle too ambitious and cathedral-like for a village in the heart of the Lincolnshire wolds.

BISCATHORPE (St. Helen)
Pretty setting; brick, cased with cement, imitating Louth in miniature.

BLYBOROUGH *(St. Alkmund)
Pleasantly set in a well-wooded park. Has a ridiculous tower, but is worth visiting for the sake of the early 15th-century tomb of a former rector, Robert Conyng, who is represented in Eucharistic vestments, and also for the interesting Rood, set on a beam brought from Thornton Abbey. Part of the figure of Christ was lying amongst lumber in the church several years ago, and the rest was dug up in the rectory garden.

BONBY *(St. Andrew)
Attractive 13th-century church with an early 18th-century tower, at the foot of the Cliff hills, near Brigg. Part of the head of an early churchyard cross lies on a window-sill.

BOSTON *(St. Botolph)
One of the largest, and in some respects the grandest, of all the parish churches of England. Almost entirely 14th century and an unrivalled example of late Decorated architecture. Magnificent S. porch, sixty-four carved stalls in the choir and a series of monuments ranging in date from the 13th–17th centuries. In recent years a vast amount of restoration work has been successfully undertaken, largely through generous help from the United States of America. A particularly pleasing feature of this modern work is the gilded and painted roof. Loftiest tower in England. (See Plate 22).

BOTTESFORD *(St. Peter's Chains)
This was once a picturesque village but is now a suburb of Scunthorpe. The church, with its rare dedication, is full of interest but the most striking features are the lancet windows in the chancel, said to be the longest in any parish church in England, and the small bronze sanctus bell which was found enclosed in a wall during the restoration of 1870. The N. transept, formerly known as the Morley choir, was long used as the burial place of this ancient family, which consistently adhered to the Stuart dynasty and the Roman Catholic faith. The last representative died in humble circumstances in 1865 and was buried in the churchyard as near as possible to his ancestors within the building.

BOURNE *(St. Peter & St. Paul)
This is one of the few surviving monastic churches in Lincolnshire, although the present building contains only the nave of the Abbey church. The nave arcades are good examples of 12th-century work, there are twin W. towers of which one is incomplete, and a 15th-century clerestory. New altars have improved the appearance of the church.

BRACEBY (St. Margaret)
Small with Dec. and Perp. features.

BRANSTON (All Saints)
Saxon tower with spire; continental glass.

BRANT BROUGHTON* (St. Helen)
In large, attractive brown-brick and red-tile village rise the Decorated tower and spire. 13th-century arcades and Perpendicular clerestory. Good modern carved wood and wrought iron, executed by local craftsmen working under Bodley, who restored the whole church beautifully and rebuilt the chancel in 1876.

BROCKLESBY (All Saints)
Pelham memorials.

BROUGHTON *(St. Mary)
Has a Saxon tower with an external turret stairway. Most interesting features inside church are two 14th-century brasses, two fine alabaster effigies of members of Redford family, about 1380, and large inelegant monument of Sir Edmund Anderson, Lord Chief Justice of the Common Pleas, 1671.

BURGH-LE-MARSH *(St. Peter & St. Paul)*

The lofty tower of this handsome late 15th-century church serves as a sea-mark near Skegness. Unusual parapet and exceptionally fine windows in the bell-storey. Unfortunate restoration of 1865, but chancel screen was reconstructed from surviving woodwork in 1891. The N. doorway is earlier than the rest of the church and belongs to the period of the Black Death; the S. porch, now used as a vestry, was built of brick in 1702, and is picturesque but incongruous. Leonard Palmer brass (1610). Font and pulpit (1623). Excellent modern oak doors to the tower by a local craftsman.

BURTON-ON-STATHER *(St. Andrew)*

The church has little to commend it in the way of architecture, but it is worth going a long way to see the view over the confluence of the Trent and Ouse to form the Humber, and across the Plain of York. Monuments of the Sheffield family were brought here from Owston in the Isle of Axholme, including an early 14th-century figure of a knight in armour.

BURWELL *(St. Michael)*

On a hill, approached through an avenue of yew trees; Norman chancel arch; font, 1468.

BUSLINGTHORPE *(St. Michael)*

1835; brick; early brass; effigy of knight in stone and part of an incised figure of a priest in lintel of W. window.

BYTHAM, LITTLE: *see Little Bytham.*

CABOURN *(St. Nicholas)*

Saxon tower; Norman tub font.

CADNEY *(All Saints)*

Has a late Norman S. arcade, but most of the church is early 13th century. The E. window is Perpendicular. There is a Norman font, 16th-century alms box on a shaft and a 12th-century stone coffin lid. Best of all is the parclose screen round the chantry chapel in the S. aisle, bearing traces of its carved inscription.

CAENBY *(St. Nicholas)*

Setting.

CAISTOR *(St. Peter & St. Paul)*

The lower stage of the tower is late Saxon or early Norman, the nave arcades are 13th century and the N. arcade bears corbels identical with those in the choir aisles

of Lincoln Cathedral. There is a noble Early English S. door. In the Hundon chapel at the E. end of the N. aisle there are some 13th and 14th century stone effigies, and on the chancel floor is a brass to John Ousteby and his wife Joan (1461). The vestry contains a coloured alabaster monument to Sir Edward Maddison who died at the age of one hundred in 1553.

CAMMERINGHAM *(St. Michael)*

Saxon stone.

CARLTON SCROOP *(St. Nicholas)*

The lower part of the tower is Norman, the upper, 14th century. The nave arcades and porch are 13th century. The E. window contains figures of the donor and his wife in medieval glass. Handsome Jacobean pulpit.

CARLTON, GREAT: *see Great Carlton.*

CARLTON, LITTLE: *see Little Carlton.*

CAWTHORPE, LITTLE: *see Little Cawthorpe.*

CAYTHORPE *(St. Vincent)*

A church of much interest with its nave divided into two by an early 14th-century arcade. The central tower is surmounted by an exceptionally tall crocketed spire, rebuilt by Gilbert Scott in 1860 after having been struck by lightning. There are remains of a Doom painting over the tower arch, and late 17th and early 18th century memorials to the Hussey family.

CHERRY WILLINGHAM *(St. Peter)*

Built 1753, is the best example of its period in the county. Recently restored to something like original form. Large memorial to founder, Thomas Becke, 1757, on N. wall.

CLEE *(Holy Trinity & St. Mary)*

A cruciform church with Saxon tower. Both arcades are Norman, the N. earlier than the S. On a pillar is a tablet recording the dedication of the chancel and transepts by St. Hugh in 1192. Good Norman font.

CLIXBY *(All Hallows)*

This was the chancel of an early 13th-century church and was ruinous until restored in 1889. On the floor is a stone with an incised cross and chalice and the remains of a Lombardic inscription, to the memory of Robert Blanchard, priest.

COATES, GREAT: *see Great Coates.*

COATES, LITTLE: *see Little Coates.*

COATES-BY-STOW *(St. Edith)*

One of the smallest churches in the county,

excellently restored by Pearson in 1884. It contains a Perpendicular rood-screen complete with loft and tympanum. Some of the boards of the latter have been renewed but traces of the painted figures can still be seen on the older wood. The pulpit and bench-ends are also 15th century and there are some fragments of medieval glass. There is an alabaster monument of the Commonwealth period to Brian Cook.

COCKERINGTON, SOUTH: *see South Cockerington.*

CONINGSBY (*St. Michael & All Angels*)
Tower with pathway through it; Perp. window in S. aisle; huge one-handed clock.

CONISHOLME *(St. Peter)*
The small, mainly 14th-century church has been rescued from decay and admirably restored. Pantiles have been substituted for the cracked lead on the roof, and the walls plastered and whitened inside and out. There is a brass (1515) to John and Anne Langholme and their fourteen children.

CORBY (*St. John the Evangelist*)
Glass; wall-paintings.

COVENHAM
A restful spot, with two churches close to each other, on either side of a stream.

(St. Bartholomew)
Has lost its N. transept, is 14th century with an unusual and beautiful font, bearing figures of the Blessed Virgin Mary and the twelve Apostles. The bowl is held up by carved angels. There is a brass of Sir John Skypwyth, 1415, and in one of the windows are remains of its original stained glass.

(St. Mary)
Is possibly a little later and has an octagonal font, with carved emblems of the Passion on suspended shields.

CROFT *(All Saints)*
A lovely church near Skegness, full of good 15-century woodwork including screens and bench-ends. Pulpit, 1615. Brass eagle lectern, found in the mud at the bottom of a moat some years ago, is late pre-Reformation. Among the excellent monuments is a small brass in the S. chapel, showing the upper part of a knight in chain mail, which is one of the oldest in England. In an unusual position, against the S. jamb of the chancel arch, is a monument to William Bonde, 1559, erected by his son Nicholas, President of Magdalen College, Oxford.

CROWLAND *(St. Mary with St. Guthlac & St. Bartholomew)*
The great abbey church must have been a magnificent building, but little remains except the W. front, N. aisle and N.W. tower. After many vicissitudes, two successful restorations were carried out in the 19th century by Sir Gilbert Scott and J. L. Pearson respectively. The lower part of the W. front is late 12th century, the upper part two hundred years later. The church itself, including the tower, is early 15th century. A unique triangular bridge in the town, built about 1390, once spanned streams which now run beneath the road.

CROWLE (*St. Oswald*)
Saxon cross-shaft.

CROXBY *(All Saints)*
This church is so isolated in the heart of the wolds that it might easily be missed, which would be a pity. Most of the building and the font are Norman. There is some 13th-century arcading in the walls and a few 15th-century pew-ends. There is a two-light window on the S. side, the sandstone masonry of which was eroded and beyond repair and has been cleverly reproduced in limestone.

CROXTON *(St. John the Evangelist)*
A good example of modern restoration; stonework pointed as it should be, rain-water disposed of properly, and walls plastered and lime-washed. The church, mainly 13th century was in very bad condition and the restoration which cost £1,000 reflects great credit on a very small parish. A few years ago a panel of medieval glass, depicting the Crucifixion, was restored to the church.

DEEPING ST. JAMES *(St. James)*
Originally the priory church, this well displays every architectural style from Norman to 18th century. It was originally cruciform, but the transepts have gone. The tower and spire were built in 1717. The late Norman font is adorned with a design of intersecting arches.

DONINGTON-ON-BAIN (*St. Andrew*)
Memorial to 17th-cent. vicar.

EAST BARKWITH *(St. Mary the Virgin)*
A typical village church, mostly late 15th century. The W. window of the S. aisle is a lancet with widely-splayed jambs, found in 1868, having been bricked up. There were traces of fittings for a shutter and no

grooves for glass, so it may have communicated with an anchorite's cell. There is an original Madonna over the porch, about 1380. The font, with emblems of the Passion, is almost identical with that of Covenham St. Mary. The N. aisle was added in 1868.

EAST KEAL *(St. Helen)
14th-century font decorated with curious grotesque head. Between E. and W. Keal the view towards Boston is the finest in the county.

EAST KIRKBY (St. Nicholas)
Easter sepulchre.

EDENHAM (St. Michael & All Angels)
Perp. tower of Somerset type; window tracery.

EWERBY *(St. Andrew)
The spire is one of the best of its date in England. It is 172 feet high and engaged by the aisles. The church is Decorated architecture at its finest. The font is contemporary with the church but appears to be mounted on the inverted bowl of a Norman font. There is some good woodwork in the chancel and a late 14th-century effigy in the N. aisle. The altar rails are probably Laudian and the windows contain exceptionally good early 19th-century glass. The church was restored by Hodgson Fowler in 1895.

FISHTOFT (St. Guthlac)
Perp. screen.

FLEET *(St. Mary Magdalene)
Fine 14th-century Fenland church with tower and spire detached from rest of building. Chancel rebuilt in 1862. Remainder of church is Decorated except for Early English arcades and Perpendicular W. window.

FOLKINGHAM *(St. Andrew)
A picturesque village, once a town of importance, on a hill-side, with an enormous market-place and an old coaching inn. The church, which is surrounded by noble trees, has a splendid rood-screen and chambered S. porch. The arcades are 14th century and the windows early 15th century. The chancel is Early English with traces of Norman work. The late Perpendicular tower, one of the best in the county, is a conspicuous landmark.

FRAMPTON (St. Mary the Virgin)
Broach spire; 'Ricardus in angulo' stands for ever in his corner on the N.E. of the church.

FRISKNEY *(All Saints)
This church, on the edge of the Fens, contains architectural features of all periods from Norman onwards, good Perpendicular screen-work and a Commonwealth pulpit. Some particularly interesting wall-paintings were discovered here in 1879 when Butterfield was restoring the church; but they have almost disappeared.

FRODINGHAM (St. Lawrence) GR
Conservative treatment in early days of Gothic revival; rebuilt, except tower, 1841; altar, 1635.

FULBECK *(St. Nicholas)
A particularly attractive village, claimed to be the prettiest in Lincolnshire. The church, approached by a long path between rose-beds, has a fine tower, the parapet of which is very much like that of Burgh-le-Marsh at the other end of the county. There is a late Norman font.

GAINSBOROUGH *(All Saints)
The tower is late Perpendicular, but the rest of the church was rebuilt about 1735 and provides a good example of the period, although it was unfortunately 'improved' internally in 1864–9. Close to the church is the Old Hall, a large old house now a Folk Museum.

GAUTBY (All Saints) CL
18th cent.; setting; Vyner memorials.

GEDNEY *(St. Mary Magdalene)
'More glass than wall', possesses an Early English tower surmounted by an unfinished Perpendicular spire. The E. window is an example of 14th-century work of a continental type. There is some 14th and 15th century stained glass in the N. aisle. The S. porch has an upper storey, approached by a turret stairway. The monuments include a late 14th-century brass, some coloured alabaster effigies of members of the Welby family and a 13th-century figure of a knight in armour.

GLENTHAM *(St. Peter)
The tower was rebuilt in 1756 and the church, though heavily restored in 1855, is a 15th-century building of considerable charm which, after several years of neglect, is now undergoing another restoration. Two notable features of this church are the Pietà over the door of the S. porch and the brass effigy of Elizabeth Tournay, 1452, in the chapel at the E. end of the N. aisle.

GLENTWORTH (*St. Michael*)
Saxon tower; Wray monument, 1592.

GOLTHO (*St. George*)
Setting; remote early brick church.

GREAT CARLTON *(St. John the Baptist)*
In a particularly pleasant setting, surrounded by fine trees. Rebuilt, except for the tower, in 1860–2; an example of good Gothic Revival work. Those who look at the 15th-century tower are bidden, by a carved inscription, to pray for the soul of Robert Schadworth.

GREAT COATES *(St. Nicholas)*
A grand Perpendicular tower with eight pinnacles. Brasses to the Barnardiston family. The nave arcades are Early English and the chancel is Decorated. The chancel was restored by James Fowler of Louth in 1865.

GREAT GONERBY (*St. Sebastian*)
Imposing position beside the Great North Road.

GREAT PONTON (*Holy Cross*)
Village; church mostly 1519; fiddle-shaped weather-vane.

GREAT STURTON *(All Saints)*
Obscure and tiny village on edge of Wolds, with a church conservatively restored on anti-scrape principles by Micklethwaite in 1904. Within built-up N. arcade is an unusual painting of Time and Death.

GRIMOLDBY (*St. Edith*)
Mainly late 14th cent.

GRIMSBY *(St. James)*
This stately church was thoroughly restored by R. J. Withers between 1874 and 1885; it was severely damaged by enemy action during the last war, but has now been restored. The main fabric is 13th century and the tower was rebuilt in 1365.

GONERBY, GREAT: *see Great Gonerby.*

GOXHILL (*All Saints*)
15th-cent. tower; E.E. chancel.

GRAINTHORPE *(St. Clement)*
Has fine spacious nave and aisles, early Decorated, with a good Perpendicular tower. There are high pews, and a brass on the chancel floor consisting of a cross with an elaborate head. The stem is lost but part of the foot remains and stands on a rock in some water, wherein fish are swimming.

GRANTHAM *(St. Wulfram)*
This is from an architectural point of view one of the most important town churches in England and must have been a wonderful sight inside in the 15th century. It is set among Georgian houses in a quiet close of its own. The tower and spire present the very best of 14th-century workmanship, the main body of the church is 14th and 15th century, but the N. aisle is earlier. There are six late Norman pillars, a beautiful N. porch of late Decorated work, a late Perpendicular chantry chapel in the N. aisle and an early 16th-century S. porch. The font is rich and unusual, with carved panels of scriptural subjects. There is also a vaulted 14th-century crypt.

GRASBY (*All Saints*) GR
Well rebuilt under Charles Tennyson Turner, brother of Tennyson.

HACKTHORN (*St. Michael*)
Hall, park and village setting; church conservatively rebuilt, 1849.

HAINTON (*St. Mary*)
Heneage memorials.

HALTHAM-ON-BAIN *(St. Benedict)*
A small church in a water meadow in a pretty village containing an inn thatched with Norfolk reeds. The S. door is Norman and has a carved tympanum. There is an Early English N. arcade, a fine Decorated E. window, a six-sided font and an ogee-headed priest's door. The woodwork and internal arrangements are a curious mixture of medieval and 18th-century work. There is no tower, but the bell-cote, which is covered with lead, is dignified and well-proportioned. A church not to be missed.

HALTON HOLGATE *(St. Andrew)*
Stands on one side of the Hollow Gate and commands one of the best views in the county. It is entirely 15th century with a noble tower. It has been much, but carefully, restored at various times. An effigy of a knight in armour was found under the floor.

HARPSWELL *(St. Chad)*
A small church at the foot of the Cliff hill. It has a Saxon tower with an inscription stating that the clock was given to commemorate the Battle of Culloden, but the original clock was removed to the stables of Aswarby Park, near Sleaford, and the present one substituted for it. There is a 14th-century S. aisle and the N. arcade has

been built up. In 1891 an incised effigy of a priest was found in the floor. There is also a 14th-century effigy of a rector and a memorial to another, William Harrington, who died in 1697. This last is inscribed on the ancient altar slab.

HAUGH (*St. Leonard*)
Bolle monuments.

HAXEY (*St. Nicholas*)
Monuments; tower.

HECKINGTON *(St. Andrew)*
A most famous Decorated church, perfect from outside but a little disappointing inside, except for the wonderful Easter sepulchre and the beautifully carved sedilia. By an unusual arrangement, the transepts come W. of the easternmost bay of the nave. The medieval proportions cannot be properly appreciated because of the loss of the chancel screen and the modern glass is a poor substitute for that which must originally have enriched the windows. The tracery design of the E. window is an unsurpassed piece of artistry of which a somewhat similar, but smaller, edition can be seen at Navenby.

HELPRINGHAM (*St. Andrew*)
Tower and spire.

HOGSTHORPE (*St. Mary*)
Tower; 18th-cent. brick porch.

HOLBEACH *(All Saints)*
A little later than Heckington and marks transition from Decorated to Perpendicular. Magnificent tower and spire, and a fine W. window, unaccountably described in Murray's *Guide* as 'ungraceful'.

HORBLING *(St. Andrew)*
A cruciform church whose tower has Norman work at the bottom and Perpendicular work at the top. There is a lot of 14th-century work and a good font with emblems of the Passion, and in the N. aisle is an unusual medieval effigy of a kneeling knight and lady.

HORNCASTLE (*St. Mary*)
Memorial on canvas to Sir Ingram Hopton, killed in Battle of Winceby, 1643.

HOUGH-ON-THE-HILL *(All Saints)*
Has a Saxon tower with an exterior turret. There are two 13th-century arches on the N. side of the chancel giving access to a chantry chapel. The Early English pillars of the aisle arcades are lofty and graceful

and are surmounted by a 15th-century clerestory, and there is a 13th-century font of an unusual type. King John spent the last night of his life in a small Priory at Hough after over-indulging himself on an unwise diet of peaches and new cider at Swineshead.

HOWELL *(St. Oswald)*
A very prettily situated church in a tiny parish near Heckington. The architectural details are Norman, Transitional and Decorated. Notice the 14th-century bell-gable, the font (1373) with shields, and an incised memorial to John Croxby, a 15th-century rector.

HUMBERSTONE *(St. Mary)*
The church was built at a cost of £3,000 in 1720–1 and is attached to a 15th-century tower. It still possesses much of its original charm, but has suffered somewhat from attempts at Gothicising. In the N. and E. walls of the chancel are some remains of Saxon carving.

INGOLDMELLS *(St. Peter with St. Paul)*
One of a group of impressive churches near Skegness, with a 15th-century porch and a wealth of notable woodwork. Like Addlethorpe, Ingoldmells lost its chancel at the beginning of the 18th century through the negligence of the same incumbent. A unique feature is a brass to the memory of William Palmer 'wyth the stylt', 1520, on which he is represented as a civilian in a long-sleeved gown with his 'stylt' or crutch beside him.

IRNHAM *(St. Andrew)*
This is a particularly interesting church, standing in a wooded park, and displaying architectural styles from the 13th–15th centuries; there is a fine brass to Sir Andrew Luttrell, 1390. Parts are missing but the figure of the knight and the cusped canopy over his head are specially good examples. The manor belonged for many generations to the Roman Catholic family of Thimbleby to whom there are some monuments.

KEAL, EAST: *see East Keal.*

KEDDINGTON (*St. Margaret*)
Early gable cross inside church; medieval wood eagle lectern.

KELSTERN (*St. Faith*)
Setting; South family memorials; modern glass.

KINGERBY *(St. Peter)*
An extremely picturesque church, standing by the roadside opposite a wood which is carpeted with aconites in springtime. There is a very solid tower and a S. door both of the 12th century. Reared against the S. wall is a specimen of what Boutell described as 'semi-effigial monuments'. It shows the head and shoulders of a civilian, beneath which is a floreated cross in relief, with the feet of the figure protruding from its base and resting on a dog. There are four shields, one bearing the arms of the Disney family, to which the subject of the monument belonged.

KIRKBY, EAST: see East Kirkby.

KIRKBY-ON-BAIN *(St. Mary)*
Setting; Queen Anne Arms.

KIRKSTEAD *(St. Leonard)*
Part of monastic buildings of the important Cistercian Abbey of Kirkstead displaying best type of Early English design. During the 18th century the chapel was used by Presbyterians whose pulpit now adorns the old church at Walesby. Well restored in 1914.

KIRMINGTON *(St. Helen)*
Copper spire, 1838.

KIRTON *(St. Peter & St. Paul)*
Cruciform; Central tower moved to W. early 19th cent.

KIRTON-IN-LINDSEY *(St. Andrew)*
Massive Early English tower with pilaster buttresses and S. door of same period, porch of which has been converted into vestry. Late Norman priest's door in chancel with tympanum of knot work. Tower arch divided by central pillar was uncovered during restoration in 1860.

KNAITH *(St. Mary)*
Part of priory; font.

KYME, SOUTH: see South Kyme.

LANGTON-BY-PARTNEY *(St. Peter & St. Paul)*
Dr. Johnson used to worship here when he visited his friend Bennet Langton at the Hall, and on one celebrated occasion he took off his coat and rolled down a grassy hill. If he revisited the church now, he would still feel at home in it, although the E. end would probably surprise him. An early 18th-century building, with tiered seats, facing N. and S., a three-decker pulpit and a gallery, all unspoiled by restoration.

LAUGHTON *(All Saints)*
One of the best examples of thorough, but conservative restoration by Bodley. There is a Perpendicular tower, which used to have a single-handed clock. The N. arcade is Norman and Transitional, the S. 14th century. In the E. bay of the S. aisle is a table-tomb with a 14th-century brass of a knightly member of the Dalison family, which has been made to serve as a memorial to two 16th-century descendants.

LEA *(St. Helen)*
Glass; stone effigy.

LEADENHAM *(St. Swithin)*
A notable church, mainly 14th century with an impressive tower and magnificent crocketed spire, forming one of the string of distinguished churches between Lincoln and Grantham. Attractive Flemish glass was inserted in the E. window in 1829.

LEAKE *(St. Mary the Virgin)*
A notable Fenland church suffering from settlement of walls by reason of continuous land drainage. Mainly 15th century with a spacious nave of six bays and N. and S. porches. Over the newel staircase to the rood-loft there is an unusual and handsome octagonal turret which has been damaged by the use of iron cramps. See also the alabaster figure of a knight and an ancient poor-box.

LINCOLN *(St. Benedict)*
A small church, in the High Street, which narrowly escaped demolition about thirty years ago, when various 'improvements' were being made to the city, and the old corporation church of St. Peter-at-Arches was pulled down and re-erected on a housing estate at the top of the hill. St. Benedict's is an early 13th-century building and contains two alien memorials, the Grantham monument from Goltho and a large marble tablet with a portrait in relief of W. A. Nicholson, one of the founders of the R.I.B.A., which was brought from the old burial ground of St. Swithin's.

(St. Mary le Wigford)
The oldest church in the city, with a Saxon tower of unusually slender proportions; a Roman tombstone is built into its W. side. There is much Early English and Decorated work. The font is 15th century.

LINWOOD *(St. Cornelius)*
Brasses.

LITTLE BYTHAM *(St. Medard)*
A picturesque church in a pretty village near Stamford. It has some Saxon work at the S.E. corner of the nave. Over the S. door of the chancel is a unique tympanum, thus described by Keyser 'In the centre is a sunk circular medallion said to have once contained the skull and arm-bone of St. Medard, the Patron Saint. On either side is an eagle within a circle, and below an animal adoring, and some interlaced circles. On the lintel is a pattern of rectangular figures enclosing leaves'.

LITTLE CARLTON *(St. Edith)*
Setting; quaint 1837 with spirelet.

LITTLE CAWTHORPE *(St. Helen)* GR
Gothic Revival in red brick, by R. J. Withers; setting.

LITTLE COATES *(St. Michael)*
Small Perp.; skilfully enlarged, 1913.

LITTLE STEEPING *(St. Andrew)*
Charming 14th–15th cent.

LONG SUTTON *(St. Mary)*
One of the most famous Fenland churches, with an Early English tower and spire almost detached from the main building. The lead spire is the oldest and best example in the county. There is a handsome 15th-century S. porch of two bays, and to the N. of the chancel is a 14th-century two-storey addition. Inside the church notice a medieval brass eagle lectern.

LOUTH *(St. James)*
This magnificent church, whose spire reaching a height of 294 feet is a landmark, is one of the last great medieval Gothic masterpieces. It was rebuilt of Ancaster stone between 1501 and 1515. 'For fifteen years, with scanty labour and scantier means, the work was carried on. They borrowed from the gilds and the richer inhabitants, they pledged their silver crosses and chalices. From the richest to the poorest all seem to have been affected with a like zeal.' *The First Church Warden's Book of Louth*, Dudding, 1941. The great pride of the townspeople in their achievement and their fear for its fate were largely responsible for the outbreak of the Lincolnshire Rising in 1536. The church was restored by James Fowler in 1869 and a reredos designed by him was erected in 1877. Much of the wood-carving in the church was the work of a local craftsman in the 19th century.

LUDBOROUGH *(St. Mary)*
Largely rebuilt by James Fowler, 1858–60; lancet E. windows; medieval glass.

MALTBY-LE-MARSH *(All Saints)*
14th and 15th century church recently restored. Original building evidently had no tower and the lines of W. window can be seen within tower arch. Beautiful 14th-century font with carved figures of angels holding open books, at its angles.

MANBY *(St. Mary)*
Setting; mainly late 16th cent.; Saxon carvings.

MARKBY *(St. Peter)*
Only thatched roof in Lincs.

MARTON *(St. Margaret)*
Has a Saxon tower with herringbone masonry, a Norman chancel arch, low-side window and a niche for the figure of a saint (probably St. Margaret, the Patron) in the chancel.

MESSINGHAM *(Holy Trinity)*
Henry Vincent Bayley, vicar from 1811 to 1818, found the church in shocking state of disrepair and effected thorough restoration, using fragments of woodwork and stained glass which had been thrown out of other churches. He has been most unjustly stigmatised by Dr. Cox and others as the 'robber Archdeacon', but he did not rob to enrich his church and he did not become Archdeacon until several years after he ceased to be vicar here. The glass includes a variety of pictures, etc. collected from different churches.

MIDDLE RASEN *(St. Peter & St. Paul)*
The finest part of this church is the Norman S. door, which came from the destroyed church of Middle Rasen Drax, in the same parish. There is a 15th-century screen and a 14th-century figure of a priest holding a chalice. The tower and the windows of the S. aisle are good Perpendicular work.

MORTON-BY-GAINSBOROUGH *(St. Paul)*
Well rebuilt by Micklethwaite; Burne-Jones and Morris windows.

MOULTON *(All Saints)*
A magnificent Fenland church with a late Perpendicular tower and spire and many other features of great beauty, such as the stiff-leaf foliage capitals and the W. window, above which are canopied niches containing figures of saints.

NAVENBY *(*St. Peter*)
The tower and spire fell two hundred years
ago and the former was replaced by a poor
substitute, but the remainder of the church
is beautiful. The six-light Decorated E.
window, somewhat resembling that at
Heckington, is amongst the best of its
kind. There is also an Easter sepulchre on
the N. side of the chancel, beneath which
the sleeping soldiers are depicted and the
Marys appear above. At the E. end of the
S. aisle is a disused font with a handsome
carved cover designed by Charles Kirk of
Sleaford and shown at the Great Exhibition of 1862.

NETTLEHAM *(*All Saints*)
One of the few Lincolnshire villages with a
stream running through them, and beside
the stream is the church, mainly 13th
century, with a chancel admirably rebuilt
by Bodley and Garner. In the splays of the
nave arcades are extensive traces of medieval wall-painting.

NETTLETON (*St. John the Baptist*)
Saxon tower.

NOCTON (*All Saints*) GR
Good; Sir Gilbert Scott.

NORMANBY-LE-WOLD (*St. Peter*)
Setting.

NORTHORPE *(*St. John the Baptist*)
A small church full of detail with two
Norman arcades, some scraps of medieval
glass and two late brasses. The best feature
is the early 14th-century S. doorway, enriched with a design of naturalistic foliage.
The little picturesque village contains the
ruins of a 16th-century manor-house.

NORTH SOMERCOTES (*St. Mary*)
17th-cent. repairs in brick; woodwork;
paved floor.

NORTH THORESBY (*St. Helen*)
Modern E. window.

OSBOURNBY *(*St. Peter & St. Paul*)
The church here is principally 14th century
and possesses fine sedilia and much 15th-
century woodwork, including bench-ends
depicting Adam and Eve, St. George and
the dragon, and a fox preaching to geese.

PANTON (*St. Andrew*)
Stalls and pulpit of mahoo wood; mutilated effigy.

PICKWORTH (*St. Andrew*)
Tower and spire; screen; wall-paintings.

PINCHBECK (*St. Mary*)
Restored by Butterfield, 1863.

PONTON, GREAT: *see Great Ponton.*

RAND (*St. Oswald*)
Monuments.

RASEN, MIDDLE: *see Middle Rasen.*

RASEN, WEST: *see West Rasen.*

REDBOURNE (*St. Andrew*)
Incised memorial, 1401. Unique trans-
parency in E. window by John Martin;
Georgian coloured glass.

RIPPINGALE *(*St. Andrew*)
A pretty village in north Kesteven. The
architectural details of the church are
worth studying, and include a series of
medieval monuments, two knights in chain
mail, a 15th-century deacon, an effigy of a
lady and altar-tomb with figures of Roger
de Quincey and his two wives.

RISEHOLME (*St. Mary*) GR
S.S. Teulon, 1851.

ROPSLEY *(*St. Peter*)
The church still contains parts of the original Saxon work, including carved crucifix
at N.W. angle. One chancel window and N.
arcade are late Norman work, tower and
spire are 14th century and the S. chapel is
Decorated. Medieval glass and benches in
the nave. S. porch, 1483. In S. arcade a
pillar (1380) commemorates its rebuilding.
At E. end of N. aisle is a stone 'bridge'
which formerly led to a rood-loft.

ROTHWELL (*St. Mary*)
Setting; Saxon tower; Norman arcades.

ROUGHTON *(*St. Margaret*)
A church of considerable beauty in a small
wooded village on the banks of the Bain. It
contains traces of early medieval work but
was largely rebuilt at the beginning of the
16th century in brick. The tower, which
also serves as a porch, is of unusual design.
On the N. wall is a memorial to Norreys
Fynes, a lay Non-juror, 1736.

ROXBY (*St. Mary*)
Window tracery.

SALTFLEETBY *(*All Saints*)
Originally a late Norman church, rebuilt
early in the 13th century. The lower stages
of the tower, the nave arcade, the N. wall
of the chancel and its two-light window are
all 13th century. In the 15th century the
upper stages of the tower were added and

the unusual windows in the N. side of the nave were put in. The nave roof was repaired in 1611 and the chancel rebuilt in 1873. In the S. porch is the coat of arms of John Grantham, Patron of the church, flanked by shields bearing a crucifix and emblems of the Passion. Most of the 15th-century rood-screen remains. On the E. wall of the side chapel is one of the five stone reredoses in Lincs and there is a good 13th-century font.

SAPPERTON (St. Michael)
Font. Female effigy.

SAUSTHORPE *(St. Andrew)
A handsome and well-proportioned church built of white brick by Charles Kirk of Sleaford in 1844. It has a tower and spire more or less modelled on Louth and forms a conspicuous and charming feature of the landscape on the road from Horncastle to Skegness. The church is a very remarkable example of good work in an unpromising medium, by an architect who was also a practical builder.

SCAWBY (St. Hibald)
Setting; Nelthorpe and other memorials.

SCOTTER *(St. Peter)
A church which contains work from Saxon to Perpendicular. The S. door and tympanum are pre-Conquest and the arcade between the nave and the N. aisle is a perfect example of Early English work. There is a 15th-century rood screen and there are some interesting memorials. Under the tower is the earliest known set of ringers' rules in verse.

SCOTTON (St. Genewys)
Spacious with early Neville monuments.

SCOT WILLOUGHBY (St. Andrew) GR 1826; one of earliest Gothic Revival churches in Lincs; 13th-cent. font.

SCRIVELSBY (St. Benedict)
Marmion and Dymoke memorials; setting.

SIBSEY *(St. Margaret)
A fine church on the edge of the Fens, recently restored. There are two Norman arcades and a grand tower whose lower stages are 13th century. Over the chancel arch is the original gable for the sanctus bell.

SILK WILLOUGHBY *(St. Denis)
Everything about this church is beautiful. 14th-century tower is surmounted by a slender and graceful spire with flying buttresses. Most of building is late 14th century and the S. door, with ball-flower moulding, is particularly charming. Chancel well rebuilt in 1878. The woodwork includes 14th-century pew-ends, 15th-century rood-screen and 17th-century pulpit.

SKEGNESS (St. Clement)
Very late Perp. almost Tudor; small 18th-cent. pan-tiled brick porch.

SKIRBECK *(St. Nicholas)
Standing on the bank of the Witham, this church is notable for its Early English nave and a tower, c. 1450, with a magnificent W. window. The Norman chancel was pulled down in 1598 and a beautiful new one was erected a few years ago to the designs of Temple Moore. There is a handsome Elizabethan pulpit of elaborate design.

SLEAFORD *(St. Denys)
The half-timbered Vicarage dated 1568 and the W. end of the church with its broach spire form a delightful group on the E. side of the market-place, in striking contrast to the modern buildings near by. In the church notice the double N. aisle, the beautiful late 14th-century windows, the Perpendicular clerestory and the font. Rood-loft by Sir Ninian Comper.

SNARFORD *(St. Lawrence)
This church stands in a grass field near an old farm-house, partly built from the remains of a manor-house of the St. Paul family, numerous members of which are commemorated by a remarkable series of monuments. It is, in fact, little more than a mausoleum, but should on no account be missed by anyone interested in the monumental sculpture of the 16th and 17th centuries.

SOMERBY-BY-BRIGG (St. Margaret)
Cumberworth effigy.

SOMERCOTES, NORTH: see North Somercotes.

SOMERCOTES, SOUTH: see South Somercotes.

SOMERSBY *(St. Margaret)
A small 15th-century church in the heart of the wolds, standing opposite to the old Rectory house in which Alfred Tennyson was born. This is one of the prettiest and most peaceful spots in England. In the churchyard is a famous 15th-century cross.

SOTBY (St. Peter)
Modern pulpit; alabaster figures.

SOUTH COCKERINGTON (*St. Leonard*)
Setting; consecration crosses; Scrope memorial.

SOUTH KYME *(St. Mary & All Saints)*
Small church near the keep of an old castle. Village is intersected by a stream and is in well-wooded country. Church once formed S. aisle of a Priory church, and has a Norman door, but main part is 14th century. It was much altered in 1805, restored in 1869 and again in 1890.

SOUTH SOMERCOTES *(St. Peter)*
'The Queen of the Marsh' with a tall, graceful spire rising from a wide flat landscape. There is a font with emblems of the Passion.

SOUTH WILLINGHAM (*St. Martin*)
Early chancel windows, with plate tracery; restored screen; view.

SPALDING *(St. Mary & St. Nicholas)*
The church is mainly 14th and 15th century and has double aisles on each side of the nave, with a tower and spire at the S.W. corner. The N. porch has a vaulted roof. There is a chantry chapel at the S.E. corner. The whole church was restored by Gilbert Scott who added a N. aisle to the chancel in 1864–6. Spalding is a prosperous Fenland town with many Georgian and earlier buildings.

SPILSBY (*St. James*)
Market town; Willoughby monuments; 18th and early 19th cent. headstones in churchyard.

STAINFIELD *(St. Andrew)*
A delightful Queen Anne church, largely unspoilt and traditionally though incorrectly said to have been built by Sir Christopher Wren. Panels of 17th-century needlework and some pieces of late medieval armour. The church stands N. and S. instead of E. and W. The surrounding country is thickly wooded and the grass field next to the church contains mounds which mark the site of a Benedictine Nunnery.

STALLINGBOROUGH (*St. Peter & St. Paul*) CL
Mid-18th cent.

STAMFORD
Is one of the most delightful towns in England and is built entirely of local limestone. It has six churches, four of which are outstanding.

(All Saints)
Principally Early English with Perpendicular tower and vaulted porch and a series of brasses.

(St. George's)
Associated with the Order of the Garter; and with monuments.

(St. John's)
Mid-15th century with contemporary glass, woodwork and brasses. (*See Plate 36a*)

(St. Mary's)
Early English, Decorated and Perpendicular, possessing monuments and a tower with broach spire.

STEEPING, LITTLE: *see Little Steeping*

STOW *(St. Mary)*
This wonderful church is frequently, but incorrectly, called the mother of Lincoln Minster. It is built in the form of a Greek cross with a low central tower. The latter stands on massive 11th-century arches and the spacious chancel is a perfect example of Norman work, displaying the original curious arrangement of windows at the E. end. The main W. door is notable Norman work and the font is one of exceptional beauty, with a dragon carved beneath it to represent the defeated devil. On the E. wall of the N. transept are remains of a wall-painting which represented St. Thomas of Canterbury. Altogether this is the finest Norman church in Lincolnshire.

STURTON, GREAT: *see Great Sturton.*

SURFLEET (*St. Lawrence*)
Leaning tower; mainly 14th and 15th cent.

SUTTERTON (*St. Mary the Virgin*)
Cruciform; W. window.

SWATON *(St. Michael)*
The main structure of this recently restored church is Decorated but it was obviously built at different times. The great W. window is fine. The 15th-century woodwork includes parts of a screen in the S. transept, and in the N. aisle is a 14th-century figure of a lady.

SWINESHEAD *(St. Mary)*
On the tower is a lantern from which springs a short spire. The main body of the church is Decorated but the N. aisle is Perpendicular and the chancel was rebuilt in 1847.

TALLINGTON (*St. Lawrence*)
Saxon work; Norman S. door; font cover; sanctus bell.

TATTERSHALL *(Holy Trinity)*
Standing near the famous castle, this church was entirely rebuilt in the middle of the 15th century and is of noble proportions. It was a collegiate church and the chancel is divided from the nave by a heavy stone screen built in 1528. In the N. transept are some good 15th and 16th century brasses of continental manufacture. Tattershall church strikes the visitor as being too light and a little bleak, an effect which is produced by the absence of stained glass. Originally every window was filled with contemporary glass but most of it was removed in 1737 and twenty years later was taken to Stamford, where it may still be seen in St. Martin's Church and in the dining-hall of Burghley House. The little that remains in the church was transferred from the transepts to the E. window. Here twenty-eight panels occupy seven lights in the lower half of the window, mostly consisting of isolated parts of various series representing the sacraments, saints, angels and the corporal acts of mercy.

TEALBY *(All Saints)*
This medieval church is notable for the beauty of its setting on a slope above an attractive stone-built village and looking across to the park and enormous ruins of Bayons Manor.

THEDDLETHORPE *(All Saints)*
The main body of this attractive building is 14th and 15th century, although other periods are represented. In the E. chapels of the aisles there are Perpendicular windows, while those in the clerestory are unspoilt Decorated. The rood-screen and the stone reredos in the S. aisle are both of the 15th century. There are two parclose screens belonging to the 16th century and some 18th-century monuments. There is also a brass of 1424 and fragments of medieval glass. On the aisle walls which retain some of their original plaster there are traces of early colour decoration. The tower, like that of Horncastle, is surmounted by a curious pinnacle.

(St. Helen)
Almost completely rebuilt in 1866, but famous for the medieval stone reredos at the E. end of the N. aisle. This consists of beautiful cusped and canopied work and no doubt originally contained a group of carved figures.

THORESBY, NORTH: *see North Thoresby.*

THORNTON CURTIS (*St. Lawrence*)
Tournai marble font.

THORPE ST. PETER *(St. Peter)*
Has 14th-century porch, although most of the building is one hundred years later. Jacobean pulpit and late Perpendicular screen with carvings of birds. The well-proportioned 13th-century font has a trefoiled arcade.

THRECKINGHAM *(St. Peter)*
A church which is notable for its tower and 14th-century broach spire, characteristic of the district. The chancel is late Norman and the remainder of the building is Decorated, containing some fine mouldings. There are mutilated effigies of members of the Trikingham family.

THURLBY-BY-BOURNE (*St. Firmin*)
Setting; 13th-cent. font.

TOFT-BY-NEWTON (*St. Peter & St. Paul*)
Setting with village green; effigies in chancel.

TORRINGTON, WEST: *see West Torrington.*

TYDD ST. MARY *(St. Mary)*
A 14th-century Fenland church with a 15th-century brick tower and stone spire. The arcades are 12th-century relics of a former church. The 14th-century chancel has some striking tracery in the windows. The 15th-century font is decorated with shields held by angels.

UFFINGTON *(St. Michael & All Angels)*
A noteworthy church with a Perpendicular tower surmounted by a crocketed spire, a 14th-century W. door with ball-flower ornament, early 13th-century arcades, largely rebuilt in 1865, and a chantry chapel on the N. side. There are some monuments to members of the Manners family and a 14th-century figure in armour. This is a pretty village close to Stamford with many fine trees and a 16th-century manor-house, Casewick Hall.

ULCEBY, NR. GRIMSBY *(St. Nicholas)*
An attractive village with a tortuous main street and some pretty cottages. The proportions of the tower and spire are peculiar

but not unpleasing. The church, much restored in 1852, 1879 and 1887, still retains among other things, a 13th-century font. Spires are exceptional in this part of the county.

WALCOT *(*St. Nicholas*)
Very attractive with 13th-century broach spire. Note the late 15th-century carved pew-ends with shields and other devices, the round Early English font and some fragments of medieval glass.

WALESBY *(*All Saints*)
There is a good modern church in the village by Temple Moore but the old one stands in solitary dignity on the top of a hill. For a long time it was practically a ruin, but it was completely restored, by the generosity of the late Canon N. S. Harding, about twenty years ago. The arcades mark the transition from Norman to Early English. The substantial tower with stepped angle-buttresses has double lancet windows. There is a restored 15th-century chancel screen; a 17th-century pulpit was formerly used by the Presbyterians at Kirkstead. When the church was restored the ravages of dry rot necessitated the removal of the box-pews, but a few of these are preserved in the N. aisle. The view from this church across the valley of the Ancholme is superb.

WELBOURN *(St. Chad)*
Tower and spire; porch.

WELL *(*St. Margaret*)
A delightful piece of 18th-century landscape gardening. A brief for £1,201 for its erection was issued in 1732. The surrounding country which is undulating and well-wooded is exceptionally beautiful and the church, which has a portico like a temple, is an attractive example of early Georgian work.

WESTBOROUGH *(*All Saints*)
A tiny village which was evidently once much larger, and is distinguished by a truly magnificent church. This was originally cruciform, but has lost the S. transept. The greater part of the building is Early English and there are some lancet windows in the chancel. The vestry was originally a chantry chapel and its stone altar still remains. The tower was rebuilt in 1752.

WESTON *(*St. Mary*)
Almost entirely Early English with 14th-century transepts and 15th-century tower.

The splendid S. porch has an arcade on either side. The font is circular and divided into eight sections on each of which is a device of foliage in deep relief.

WEST RASEN *(All Saints)* GR
Rebuilt, 1829; curious turrets for pinnacles. Clerestory.

WEST TORRINGTON *(St. Mary)*
Norman font.

WHAPLODE *(*St. Mary*)
A large and interesting church with a Norman chancel arch and a tower begun in the 12th century and finished in the 14th. The chancel was rebuilt in 1818. The tower stands in an unusual position at the E. end of the S. aisle. There is a striking monument to Sir Anthony Irby, 1593, and his wife Alice, 1625, on the base of which their five children are shown kneeling.

WIGTOFT *(St. Peter & St. Paul)*
Woodwork.

WILLINGHAM, SOUTH: *see South Willingham.*

WILLOUGHBY *(St. Helen)*
Setting; mainly 14th and 15th cent.

WILSFORD *(*St. Mary*)
Church has a graceful 15th-century spire, traces of Saxon work, two Norman pillars, a 13th-century N. arcade and a 14th-century S. arcade. It is beautifully situated among trees.

WINTERINGHAM *(All Saints)*
Impressive; late Norman arcades; E.E. chancel; effigy of knight.

WINTERTON *(All Saints)*
Saxon tower; E.E. arcades; brass, 1504.

WINTHORPE *(*St. Mary*)
A late 15th-century church with a great expanse of glass and a magnificent collection of original woodwork, including a rood-screen, carved pew-ends with poppy heads, very beautiful choir stalls and parclose screens at the ends of the aisles. There are also some early 16th-century brasses. The churchyard cross has been carefully restored.

WISPINGTON *(St. Margaret)* GR
Setting; rebuilt, 1863.

WOLD NEWTON *(All Saints)*
Setting; modern figures of saints.

WRANGLE *(St. Mary the Virgin & St. Nicholas)*

Early English, Decorated and Perpendicular with a grand 14th-century E. window and an Elizabethan pulpit. The glass was inserted between 1345 and 1371, and contains figures of kings and prophets, St. George, St. Cecilia, St. Lucy, St. Laurence, St. Barbara and other saints. There is also an altar-tomb of Sir John Read, 1626, whose family was for many generations resident here. Near the font is a leger stone, dated 1705, commemorating William Erskine, a non-juring incumbent who built the present beautiful vicarage.

WYBERTON *(St. Leodegar)*

Thoroughly and conservatively restored by G. G. Scott (junior) in 1881. Its principal features are a 15th-century tower and roof with angels in the bosses. The church stands on the edge of a well-wooded park belonging to a handsome 17th-century mansion, which was, until recently, the Rectory.

YARBURGH *(St. John the Baptist)*

Tower with sculptures of the Fall round W. door, c. 1500.

London

INTRODUCTION

LONDON, WHICH includes the City of London and the County of London,
which has raped much of Middlesex and parts of Essex, Kent and Surrey,
cannot be treated in the same way as other districts. The only big medieval
churches, old St. Paul's, Westminster Abbey, St. Bartholomew's, Smithfield,
St. Katherine by the Tower (demolished 1825), The Temple Church, and the
various religious foundations along the banks of the Thames were built
mainly of imported stone brought by water from as far as Caen and Purbeck,
since there was no available good local stone. The few medieval parish churches
surviving in the boroughs of the County of London are not exceptional
architecturally. Middlesex had a humble perpendicular style rather like that of
Herts and South Essex. Surrey and the parts of Kent now within London had
no fine parish churches except St. Mary Overy, Southwark, which is now
Southwark Cathedral.

London's first great church-building period after medieval times (and there
were about a hundred churches in the square mile of the City before the fire
of 1666) was in the 17th and 18th centuries. With few exceptions, the chief
churches of these times were classic. Sir Christopher Wren built fifty in the
City, of which nineteen were destroyed to pay for new suburban churches,
and fifteen were destroyed by the Germans, leaving only sixteen Wren churches
now surviving in the City. Of the sixteen City churches built since the time of
Wren, half have been destroyed to pay for suburban churches. This is a great
loss, as they were almost all more impressive and original, at any rate internally, than the lesser Wren churches. All the post-Wren survivors have escaped
destruction by the Nazis. In Westminster and Southwark and just outside the
City, several handsome churches were built in the 18th century. These were
in the classic style. The usual building material in these parts for 17th and 18th-
century churches was Portland stone. This is well suited to the London climate,
and weathers black and brilliant white so that it gives an effect of shadow on
the greyest day. Brick was also used, and London brick in the 17th and early
18th centuries was always of a variety of red and brown shades which have
stood up to the soot remarkably well. Wren built lead steeples to some of his
churches.

The next big phase of building was after the Napoleonic campaigns (*see*
pp. 65–67) when the usual materials were white stock brick for walls and Bath
stone for portico, steeple and dressings.

251

Finally, there is the biggest church building period in London since medieval times, from the mid-19th century onwards. The churches of this period vary greatly in merit, and only exceptionally fine ones are listed. Because London churches cannot be arranged like those of an agricultural county, they are put under Boroughs, in a manner which, we hope, will fulfil the same purpose as the other lists.

J.B.

SELECTED LIST OF CHURCHES

by John Betjeman

CITY *(All Hallows by the Tower)*
Medieval, largely destroyed by war, re-constructed 1956–7 by Seely and Paget who added elegant spire to 17th-century tower. Grinling Gibbons font cover.

(All Hallows, London Wall)
Designed by George Dance, Junior, 1765–7. The exterior is modest and apparently windowless. Inside the church is elegance itself, a barrel-vaulted ceiling decorated with flower pattern in Adam style, the plasterwork being lit by large semi-circular windows above the broad frieze which binds the whole interior together, and below which are the Ionic pilasters and sur-prisingly and effectively there is no cornice above the frieze. Above the panelled apse is a coffered semi-dome. Dance probably copied his method of lighting a church sur-rounded by high buildings from Hawks-moor's at St. Mary, Woolnoth, and his apse from Gibbs' St. Mary-le-Strand but he interpreted their themes in the restrained manner of the later Georgian age. The fittings are unobtrusive and unexceptional. The church is still (1958) out of use.

(St. Andrew-by-the-Wardrobe)
Wren, 1686–93. Renaissance. Gutted 1940, not yet rebuilt (1958).

(St. Andrew, Holborn)
Wren, 1684–1704. Renaissance. Gutted 1941, not yet rebuilt (1958).

(St. Andrew, Undershaft)
Built 1520–32 in late 15th-century style. Nave and aisles. Stuart style glass in W. window. Panelled roofs. Ironwork of altar rails by Tijou. Stow monument 17th century.

(St. Anne & St. Agnes, Aldersgate)
This inconspicuous church is justified by its interior. The plaster-vaulted ceilings are on the same plan as St. Mary-at-Hill and St. Martin, Ludgate, except that the centre of the Greek cross has a wide cross vault in-stead of a dome. Some of the old wood-work remains of which the best is the elegant altar-piece. It is still (1958) out of use.

(St. Bartholomew-the-Great, Smithfield)
This great Norman church would be im-pressive anywhere. The 17th-century brick tower, containing the oldest ring of bells in England and old brick Verger's house built against the N. wall, with the flint and Portland stone refacing added by Sir Aston Webb at the end of the last century, give the outside an East Anglian look which the interior belies. This is vast, dark and Romanesque with a triforium and apsidal end. Charmingly the Perpendicular tomb of Rahere, founder of the great hospital, and a perpendicular watching window in the triforium opposite are inserted between rugged Norman columns. A cross-vaulted ambulatory leads round the church past an E. Lady Chapel. The church is the choir and transepts of a monastery whose nave was on the sight of the present churchyard. The ancient W. gatehouse survived, and one side of the cloister. (*See Plate 9*)

(St. Bartholomew-the-Less)
Medieval tower. Body of church octagonal Gothick by George Dance the Junior, 1789, not improved in 1822 and 1865. Repaired after World War II by Seely and Paget.

(St. Benet, Paul's Wharf)
The red-brick exterior with stone dressings
and swags above the windows, old tiled
roofs, tower and lead dome and lantern
look very well on the steep slope S. of
Queen Victoria Street. It was finished by
Wren in 1683. The interior with galleries,
W. organ and the usual carved Renaissance
altar-piece, pulpit and wainscotted walls is
one of the least altered City interiors.

(St. Botolph, Aldersgate)
Rebuilt in the style of G. Dance, Junior, in
1790. Square pillars on each side support
a gallery from which rise Corinthian
columns themselves supporting an arched
ceiling delicately ornamented with bands
and flowers. The ceiling is lit by semi-
circular windows as in Dance's church of
All Hallows, London Wall. There is an
apsidal E. end, and the W. end with its
organ-case is an elegant composition. The
pulpit and sounding board are also of
the same date and the beautiful transparency of Our Lord in the Wilderness in
the E. window was painted by James
Pierson in 1788. The rest of the glass in the
church is deplorable.

(St. Botolph, Aldgate)
George Dance, Senior, 1744. Aisled and
galleried heavy Classic redecoration by
J. F. Bentley in the '80s with plaster work
and balusters.

(St. Botolph, Bishopsgate)
James Gold, 1728. Aisled and galleried
City classic with tower and inside nave, an
1820 cupola.

(St. Bride, Fleet Street)
Wren, 1671–1703. Gutted 1940. Restored by
Godfrey Allen and re-opened 1958. Elegant
wedding-cake steeple of diminishing stages.
Interior arcaded and once galleried is now
replanned on collegiate lines.

(St. Clement, East Cheap)
Wren, 1683–7. Small much-restored and
plain classic.

(St. Dunstan-in-the-East)
Gothic steeple after St. Nicholas, New-
castle-on-Tyne, by Wren, 1670–99. Body of
church rebuilt by Laing 1810 in good
Georgian Perp. was destroyed in 1940.

(St. Dunstan-in-the-West)
By John Shaw, 1832. Tower a reduced
version of Boston, Lincs. Body of church a
spacious Gothic octagon.

(St. Edmund, the King & Martyr)
Wren (?), 1670–1708. Elegant tower and
steeple on Lombard Street. Interior plain,
except for font cover and Etty's Moses
and Aaron paintings.

(St. Ethelburga, Bishopsgate)
This modest old church is interesting because it is like what many of the hundred
and more small churches in the City must
have been before the Fire. It consists of
nave and S. aisle with an arcade of Perpendicular columns. It is well furnished and
was sympathetically restored by Sir Ninian
Comper.

(St. Helen's, Bishopsgate)
A large irregular plan. Fabric mostly late
13th century. Inside are impressive 17th-
century monuments including that to Sir
John Spencer, a rich Lord Mayor and late
17th-century woodwork and doorcases.

(St. James's, Garlick Hythe)
Finished by Wren in the same year as St.
Benet's. The best exterior feature is the
Portland stone steeple on the tower. The
interior columned, wainscotted and plaster-
vaulted with much Renaissance woodwork,
is grand and stately. Its plan is more
medieval than most of Wren's City
churches.

(St. Katherine Cree)
1628. The only Laudian church in London.
E. window has Catherine Wheel set in
square head. Aisled with Gothic vaulted
ceilings sprung from classic columns.

(St. Laurence, Jewry)
Wren, 1671–7. Renaissance. Gutted 1940.
Restored 1957 by Cecil Brown. Wren's
panelled vestry did not survive 1940 but
the building is again sumptuous Renaissance as befits it being the Lord Mayor's
official church. E. wall outside based on
Wren's 'Model Design' for St. Paul's.

(St. Magnus the Martyr, London Bridge)
The beautiful Portland stone tower and
steeple mark the entrance to old London
Bridge and are now best seen from the
river. Inside is a wealth of magnificent
woodwork and ironwork – W. screen,
gallery and organ-case, doorcases, pulpit,
altar-piece, sword rests and Communion
rails. Restored in this century by Martin
Travers and Laurence King.

(St. Margaret, Lothbury)
One of Wren's later works in Portland
stone with a tower and lead spire. The

interior has a N. aisle and ingenious clerestory to the broad nave. It is filled with old woodwork from City churches destroyed by the Victorians. A Flemish-looking screen from All Hallows' the the Great (a Wren church) stretches across the E. end. The rich pulpit and sounding board are also from All Hallows'.

(St. Margaret Pattens)
The stone tower with obelisks as pinnacles and a tall lead spire is a beautiful contrast with Wren's stone spire of St. Dunstan's-in-the-E. near by. Inside the church is like St. Margaret's, Lothbury, and has an attractive organ gallery.

*(St. Martin, Ludgate)
The lead spire of this stone church is an elegant foil to the dome of St. Paul's as one sees it from Fleet Street. The interior, though much rearranged in the last century, still contains its woodwork and the vaulted ceiling is a Greek cross in plan like St. Anne and St. Agnes and St. Mary-at-Hill.

*(St. Mary, Abchurch)
The brick tower, lead spire and plain brick exterior are pleasant, but the inside is magnificent. It is one of the most richly decorated of Wren's churches, a great square room roofed by a dome springing from eight pendentives. The dome is painted by Sir James Thornhill. The woodwork of altar-piece, pulpit and font cover is richest English Renaissance.

(St. Mary, Aldermanbury)
Wren, 1670-6. Renaissance. Gutted 1940, not yet rebuilt (1958).

(St. Mary, Aldermary)
This is Wren Gothick. Its fine tower is like the one he designed for St. Michael, Cornhill. The inside is chiefly remarkable for Wren's Gothick plaster ceilings consisting of a series of shallow domes supported on pendentives made to look like fan vaulting. Unfortunately the Classic woodwork which would have harmonised with this half Classic, half Gothick architecture has disappeared and there is much dull Victorian woodwork.

*(St. Mary-at-Hill)
The plain exterior gives no idea of the riches within. Four fluted columns support broad arches over transepts and E. and W. ends. Above the middle of the Greek Cross thus formed rises a central dome from four pendentives adorned with plaster work. The plaster work throughout is rich and bold, but best of all are the wood and ironwork particularly over the W. gallery and on the pulpit and altar-piece. The iron sword-rests of various Georgian dates are the best in the City. The woodwork is mostly 17th century with skilful 1847 additions in the Renaissance style. The high pews survive.

(St. Mary-le-Bow)
Wren 1670-80. Gutted 1940. Has the most elaborate and famous Wren steeple rising from a tall tower with Roman Doric doorways set in a rusticated plinth and adorned with cherubs. The brick church, set back from the tower, was square with narrow aisles and wide nave and is not yet (1958) rebuilt. Norman crypt. (*See Plate 41*)

(St. Mary, Somerset)
Wren, 1686-95. Tower only and a very splendid one, surrounded by 'a great crop of obelisks and blazing urns twenty feet high' (E. & W. Young: *Old London Churches*).

*(St. Mary, Woolnoth)
This church designed by Wren's talented clerk Nicholas Hawksmoor, 1716-27, is original and impressive within and without. The W. tower is divided at its summit into two turrets surmounted by balustrades. The N. front is a splendid example of how to make a windowless wall interesting. The N. wall is quite plain because it originally had buildings against it. Inside, the church is square and for so small a site gives an amazing impression of sumptuousness and height. The effect is created by the fluted Corinthian columns rising in groups of three in the four corners of the church. They support a bold entablature and cornice above which rise semi-circular clerestory windows. There is a strongly-moulded flat plaster ceiling. The altar-piece has twisted columns and a canopy of wood with imitation tassels. The only projecting gallery to survive is at the W. end. Organcase, pulpit, gallery fronts and wrought iron Communion rails are all fine and part of Hawksmoor's compact design.

(St. Michael, Paternoster Royal)
Wren, 1686-1713. A steeple not unlike the western towers of St. Paul's. It is octagonal and curved, a deliberately ornate contrast with plain stone tower. Plain interior, not yet repaired (1958).

(St. Nicholas, Cole Abbey)
Wren, 1671–7. Gutted 1940. Handsome
stone exterior with highly original thick
lead steeple rising from a tower with urns
at corners. Plain interior. Not yet rebuilt
(1958).

(St. Olave, Hart Street)
c. 1270 and 15th century. Gutted 1941.
Restored 1955. Clerestoried nave and two
aisles.

*(St. Peter, Cornhill)
The brick tower with its leaded cupola and
spire with an enormous key as a vane is
hard to see among high buildings. Inside
the irregular oblong shape of the church to
which a regular Classic design of arcades
and arched roofs has been applied, gives it
a distorted appearance. But the woodwork,
screen, organ gallery and pulpit are beautiful and make it one of the most complete
City church interiors.

*(St. Stephen, Walbrook)
There is a stone tower with an elegant
steeple but the glory of this church is its
interior. As G. H. Birch says in *London
Churches* (1896) 'Nowhere else could one
find a simple parallelogram . . . so
admirably arranged'. Corinthian columns
on stone bases divide the church into bays,
aisles and sanctuary leaving an open space
in the middle to support a large coffered
dome which is lit by a lantern. The plaster-
work of the dome is arranged in horizontal
bands, the broad and rich bands in the
middle breaking up any effect of monotony. The organ-case, font cover and altar-
piece and pulpit are Renaissance, woodwork richly carved. The church was much
damaged in the war but fortunately lost its
inappropriate stained-glass windows. The
Victorian mosaic floor is unworthy of this
splendid church. *(See Plate 46)*

(St. Vedast, Foster Lane)
Wren, 1670–97. Gutted 1940. The simple
baroque stone tower and steeple is light,
airy and elegant, built as though to contrast
with nearby St. Mary-le-Bow and to show
the latter up as too elaborate. Plain interior
nave and S. aisle originally not square, now
rebuilt square 1958 by S. Dytry Bow. *(See
Plate 41)*

BATTERSEA *(Ascension, Lavender Hill)*
By James Brooks, 1873. Severe Tractarian.
Early English in red brick.

(St. Mary) Parish Church
By Joseph Dixon, 1775–6. Stock brick and

Classic with W. portico, tower and spire
beside the river. 17th-century glass. Monuments.

BERMONDSEY *(St. Mary Magdalene)*
Playful stucco Gothic outside by G. Porter.
Inside Wren-style Classic, mostly late 17th
century.

(St. Mary, Rotherhithe)
Brick Classic, 1714–47. Among wharf-
enclosed remains of riverside village.

BETHNAL GREEN *(St. John)*
By Sir John Soane, 1825–6. A very odd and
Soane-like stone bell-cote on brick church.
Inside unfortunately remodelled by Vic-
torians.

(St. Matthew)
By G. Dance, senior, 1743–6. Classic.
Severely bombed.

CAMBERWELL *(St. Chrysostom, Peckham)*
Architect unknown, 1813. Flimsily attractive Gothic. Galleried interior. Little
spoiled within or without.

(St. Faith, Herne Hill)
By Greenaway and Newberry, 1907. Lumpy
new-art Gothic.

(St. George)
By Francis Bedford, 1822–4. Greek Doric
by Surrey Canal. Interior attractively decorated by Basil Champneys in '90s and later.

*(St. Giles) Parish Church
By Sir Gilbert Scott, 1844. A stately and
correct essay in Middle-Pointed cruciform
with spire. Well proportioned within.

*(St. Marks, Coburg Road)
By R. Norman Shaw, 1880 and later. Unexpectedly spacious interior, nave and aisles.
Wooden vaulting throughout. Panelled
walls and columns. Wooden screen painted
stone colour fills chancel arch.

CHELSEA **(Holy Trinity, Sloane Street)*
By J. D. Sedding, 1888–90. Free and origi-
nal Perpendicular. The cathedral of the
Arts and Crafts movement.

*(All Saints)
Mainly 17th-century brick. Totally destroyed in late war. Being rebuilt. Monuments.

*(St. Luke, Sydney Street) Parish Church
By J. Savage, 1820–34. Ashlar faced. Tower
and portico sumptuous King's Chapel
style within. Galleries; stone-vaulted chancel roof. *(See Plate 57)*

CLERKENWELL *(Holy Redeemer)
By J. D. Sedding, 1887–8. Campanile by
H. Wilson later. Italianate without and as
impressive as a big Wren church within.

*(St. James)
By J. Carr, 1788–92. Attractive Wren-style
steeple in Portland stone of unusually old-
fashioned design for its date. Interior with
double W. galleries very splendid.

FINSBURY (St. Barnabas, King's Square)
By T. Hardwick, 1826. Ionic front and odd
thin spire well related to wide late Georgian
square. Interior refurnished after bad war
damage. Galleries and pews removed.

(St. Luke's, Old Street)
By G. Dance, senior, 1732–3. The spire is a
fluted obelisk of Portland stone. Very
strange. Interior wealthy 18th-century city-
style. Ionic columns, galleries, pulpit, altar-
piece and organ-case.

GREENWICH *(St. Alfege)
By N. Hawksmoor, 1711–14. A massive
four-square Portland stone building whose
pedimented E. end on the main street looks
like an entrance. Strong plain pilasters remind one of Wren's original design for St.
Paul's. A broad frieze and cornice bind the
building together. The tower and spire
added by John James, 1730, seem feeble by
contrast. Interior a square-galleried room
with flat ceiling resting on corbels. Shallow
chancel under depressed arch. Almost all
fittings modern copies made after bomb
damage.

(St. Andrew & St. Michael, Dreadnought
Street)
By B. Champneys, 1900–2. Stock brick with
stone dressings. Late Gothic freely treated.

*(St. Luke, Charlton)
A 17th-century brick country church surviving in charming old churchyard in hill-
top village at entrance to Charlton House.
17th-century monuments and glass. Comparatively unspoilt interior with hatchments
and plaster.

HACKNEY (St. Barnabas)
By Sir Charles Reilly, 1910. Hidden by
high buildings. Yellow stock brick within
and without. Byzantine. Impressive interior with screen, large chancel, apse and
E. ambulatory. Concrete vaulting.

(St. John) Parish Church
By James Spiller, 1792–7. An astonishing
yellow brick building in the shape of a
Greek cross with Portland-stone steeple,
broad eaves and semi-circular porches on
each of the four sides like Paddington (St.
Mary). The interior, burned out in 1956, is
enormous, its shallow-vaulted roofs having
no interior supports. The medieval tower
only of the old church standing in a corner
of it. Large churchyard.

*(St. Mary of Eton)
By G. F. Bodley, 1880. A picturesque group
on Eastway with gate tower leading to
court of Eton Mission buildings. The
church inside has a broad nave with
painted roof, tall narrow aisles and a S.E.
chapel. It is full of vistas of arcades with
strong simple mouldings.

HAMMERSMITH (Holy Innocents)
By J. Brooks, 1887. Austere and lofty brick
lancet-style.

(St. John the Evangelist, Glenthorne Road)
By W. Butterfield, 1856. Stock brick
church. Sincere and simple with saddle-
back tower. Interior whitened and coloured.

(St. Peter)
By E. Lapidge, 1827. Greek with strange
heavy tower. Interior less altered than
many of this date.

HAMPSTEAD (St. John, Church Row)
    Parish Church
By H. Flitcroft. Stock brick with castellated
steeple. In churchyard Constable and many
famous artists, actors, architects and
writers are buried. Many 19th and 20th
century architects and decorators worked
on the galleried interior with its vaulted
ceiling and Ionic columns. The effect is rich
and Victorian looking E., but looking W. it
is still 18th century. Pulpit, c. 1750.

(St. John, Downshire Hill)
1818. Simple Classic stucco proprietary
chapel with bell-cote in district of neat
stucco houses. Evangelical interior with
high pews.

(St. Mary, King Henry's Road)
By W. P. Manning, 1873. Red brick lancet-
style. Apsidal-ended. Lofty whitewashed
interior. Has work by Bodley, Bayes,
Kempe and Comper and was centre of
Percy Dearmer's liturgical experiments.

*(St. Stephen, Rosslyn Hill)
By S. S. Teulon, 1876. Highly original and
weird within and without. Brick with plate
tracery and many curious projections including the tower. Interior rich with decoration and carving, which no 'good taste'
could ever tame into insipidity.

ISLINGTON (*St. George's, Tufnell Park*)
By G. Truefitt, 1868. A polygon with
ambulatory round all sides but the E.
which has an apse. Detached tower never
completed.

(*Holy Trinity, Cloudesley Square*)
By Sir Charles Barry, 1826. A very cheap
version of King's College Chapel, Cambridge. Worth seeing outside for its happy
proportions to the late-Georgian square
that surrounds it.

(*St. James', Pentonville*)
By A. H. Hurst, 1787. A builder's brick box
in Adam style. Galleries and their surrounding walls taken away before the war.
Interior plain and attractive.

(*St. John the Evangelist, Holloway Road*)
By Sir Charles Barry, 1826. Commissioners
Perpendicular in yellow stock brick. In-
terior with all its original fittings.

(*St. Mary's*) Parish Church
Spire by L. Dowbiggin, 1751–4, is light and
elaborate in Portland stone. Body of church
destroyed in the war, rebuilt by Seely and
Paget.

(*St. Mary Magdalene*)
By W. Wickens, 1812. Plain brick without
with square tower. Interior galleried and
with much Georgian woodwork.

*(*St. Saviour, Aberdeen Park*)
By W. White, 1859. Red-brick cruciform
with low octagonal lantern tower. The interior red brick with low aisles and painted
chancel is beautifully proportioned. The
levels at the E. end being skilfully arranged,
the light throughout the church being
modulated, the effect of the building
though small is of mystery and size.

KENSINGTON *(*St. Cuthbert, Philbeach
    Gardens*)
By Roumieu Gough, 1884–7. This big red-
brick Gothic building overshadowed now
by the Earls Court Exhibition Building is
chiefly remarkable for its interior decoration, where S. and W. Kensington Tractarian devotion has given jewels, pictures,
carving and inlay work for all available
space. Amid all this sumptuousness Father
Geldart's rich reredos and the altar rails
and strange lectern by W. Bainbridge
Reynolds are particularly prominent.

*(*Holy Trinity, Kensington Gore*)
By G. F. Bodley, 1902. The plain stone
three-gabled front gives little idea of the
soaring and complex interior which consists of nave with aisles of varying widths

and differing arcades. The windows have a
variety of elaborate Perpendicular traceries
and the glass is Kempe-ish. The reredos
and fittings are expensive and good. Prevailing colours olive green and brownish-
red with gold and brass. Chairs not pews.
Bodley's swan song.

*(*St. John the Baptist, Holland Road*)
By James Brooks, 1889. A comparatively
humble entrance leading to the stone-
vaulted impressiveness of this English
Cistercian interior. Nave and transepts are
separated from apsidal E. end by a stone
screen and rood.

(*St. Mary Abbots*) Parish Church
Rebuilt by Sir Gilbert Scott, 1869–72.
Correct Victorian middle-pointed, well
suited to the correct rich middle-class
suburb of its time. Spire and tower nobly
proportioned. Attractive cloister from road
to S. door by Micklethwaite and Somers
Clarke, 1889–93. Dark lofty interior
damaged in war and inexpensively restored.

LAMBETH (*St. Agnes, Kennington*)
By G. G. Scott, junior, 1877. At the time of
writing (1956) the considerable ruins of
this beautiful church, the first and foremost example of the neo-Perpendicular
Revival in England, are still standing. The
red brick with stone dressings. The wooden
vaults, screen and pulpit remain and are
now (1958) partly incorporated in a mean
successor.

(*All Saints, Rossendale Road*)
By G. H. Fellowes Prynne, 1888–91. Lofty
apsidal ended vaulted, with side chapel.
Grand late Tractarian Gothic in brick with
stone tracery. Perched on a steep slope.
Unfinished at W. end.

(*St. Anselm, Kennington Road*)
By Adshead and Ramsey, 1913. Tall,
simple, neo-Byzantine. Yellow stock brick
without. White with low aisles within. It
rises high above a charming neo-Regency
estate by the same architects.

*(*St. John the Divine, Kennington*)
By G. E. Street, 1874. Red-brick Geometric with apsidal chancel cleverly united
to nave by canted bay. Lean-to aisles. W.
tower and stone spire. The whole gutted by
Germans and rebuilt.

(*St. Luke, West Norwood*)
By Francis Bedford, 1822. Portico and
tower and steeple Corinthian Greek. Interior 'Lombardised' by G. E. Street in

I

1878, a try-out for what he was to do in the Guards Chapel, Wellington Barracks.

(*St. Mark, Kennington*)
By Roper, 1822. Greek Doric gutted by Germans.

*(*St. Matthew, Brixton*)
By C. F. Porden, 1822. Finely sited at an important road junction on rising ground. Tower at E. end. Portico at W. Galleried interior, until unfortunate introduction of a side chapel in 1930s, was pure Doric throughout without a curved line anywhere.

*(*St. Peter, Vauxhall*)
By J. L. Pearson, 1863–5. The first French Gothic church by this great architect. Of yellow stock brick within and without. Broad nave and apsidal chancel. Brick-vaulted with stone ribs. Triforium arches in chancel. Massive low pillars in nave and narrow aisles. Transepts. Decoration and glass throughout by Clayton and Bell. This is a most restrained and beautiful building to which later generations have done no harm.

LEWISHAM *(*St. Andrew, Catford*)
By P. A. Robson, 1904. The latest and lumpiest phase of the Arts and Crafts Movement at its best. Outside towerless and massive, dark red brick on a hill top. Inside spacious with brick piers, wide nave and the buttresses showing in the narrow aisle. Thick and original tracery with glass to match.

(*St. Hilda, Stondon Park*)
By Greenaway and Newberry, 1907. Lumpy art Gothic. Attractive brick work but naked and yellow-tinted within.

(*St. John, Bromley*)
By Sir Charles Nicholson, 1928. Light and airy suburban Perpendicular. In stock brick.

(*St. Swithin, Hither Green*)
By Ernest Newton, 1892. A Domestic architect using the manner of Bodley. Red brick with late Decorated tracery, mainly lit at E. and W. Inside the relation of arcading to clerestory above is well managed by mouldings.

PADDINGTON *(*St. Augustine, Kilburn*)
By J. L. Pearson, 1870–80. Pearson's largest London church. Its red-brick tower and white ashlar spire rise more than 250 feet over a drab neighbourhood. The church is red brick and cruciform with a lead flèche at the crossing and all is Early English. Inside one's first impression is of a multiplicity of brick-vaulted vistas with stone ribs and of varying heights. There are double aisles pierced through the buttresses, a triforium right round the church and carried across transepts by bridges. The low baptistery at the W. end and low ambulatory behind the three-bayed chancel increase the sense of height in nave and choir. The windows by Clayton and Bell, the paintings and ironwork are all in keeping. The way to see this church is to walk right round the inside, watching arch cutting into arch giving a different vista with every step.

*(*Holy Trinity, Latimer Road*)
By R. Norman Shaw, 1887–9. Though Shaw described himself as 'a house man and not a Church man' this, with mission house attached, is an original and beautiful group in red brick. The church is lit only by two vast and broad windows at E. and W. ends with highly original tracery, the mullions being nearly as thick as buttresses. There are no aisles and the church is all under one big roof. Inside the roof is panelled and comes down low. To compensate for lack of stained glass the leading of the clear glass is arranged in elegant patterns suited to the tracery. The reredos is by Lethaby and Hamilton Jackson as at Leek and Ilkley.

(*St. Mark*)
By Bassett Keeling, 1864. Self-conscious originality in brick Gothic with plate tracery and cast-iron columns inside. Black and weird.

*(*St. Mary*) Parish Church
By J. Plaw, 1788–91. Shaped like a Greek Cross with a shallow dome on top. Yellow brick walls, Portland-stone semi-circular porches on three sides and a Venetian window at the E. end. A most satisfying exterior on its green mound on Paddington Green. Inside is an octagonal gallery round three sides and the chancel on the fourth. As John Summerson says: 'The thing is thoughtfully worked out and quite undeserving of the scorn which later church builders heaped upon it.'

*(*St. Mary Magdalene*)
By G. E. Street, 1868–78. Tall thin brick and stone steeple is visible for miles. The church, hard to find in dismal streets, has its high brick apse neatly fitted into the acute angle of two of them. The interior is

tall and dark and very high in all senses of that word but the thing to see is the crypt under the S. aisle by Comper, 1895, designed to hold the Blessed Sacrament in days of persecution. The crypt is all gold with a singularly rich reredos, a blue ceiling with gold stars, gilded Scottish-Gothic tracery in the arches, a delicate screen, and a painted organ-case, all lit by Comper's stained glass.

(*St. Peter, Kensington Park Road*)
By T. Allom, 1852. The last gasp of Georgian Classic by the designer of the heavy Italianate Ladbroke estate. Corinthian and galleried inside.

POPLAR (*All Saints*) Parish Church
By C. Hollis, 1821–3. With brick parsonage opposite by same architect and in ample green space. Expensive Greek revival (Ionic) in Portland stone with steeple over Ionic portico designed as a variation on George Dance Senior's at St. Leonard's, Shoreditch. Interior looks awkward now that galleries have been removed.

(*St. Mary, Bow*)
Medieval and 17th century. Weather-beaten stone and brick, islanded by traffic. Well restored by Goodhart Rendel. Countrified interior.

(*St. Mathias*)
1776. Ridiculous Victorian outside, but inside wooden Tuscan columns support wooden cross vaults.

ST. MARYLEBONE *(All Saints, Margaret Street)*
By W. Butterfield, 1850–9. The dark brick church, Vicarage and Choir School form a Tractarian oasis among furriers. The tall unbuttressed tower with its slate and lead spire, the polychromatic brick and original style had never been seen in London before, and this is the pioneer church of the phase of the Gothic Revival which ceased to copy medieval but went on with new materials like cast iron and stock brick from where the medievals left off. For the smallness and confined nature of the site the effect of space richness, mystery and size is amazing. The original plan was strictly Tractarian – one altar visible from all parts of the church, no screen, light from the W. end and the chancel more sumptuous than anywhere else. The side altars by Comper are wisely not in Butterfield's style and excellent in themselves do not compete with the huge mouldings and violent con-

trasts of texture and colour which make this building so memorable. The decoration on the N. wall is by Dyce, the S. aisle and clerestory window are by Gibbs (the latter reminded Prebendary Mackay 'of a good hand at bridge' but they are just right for their setting). The roof, to quote John Summerson, 'is like a huge ingenious toy'. The effect of this building is all achieved by scale – the huge but low arcades, the lofty chancel arch and reredos beyond. The thought and care over detail in this building are best appreciated after long familiarity. (*See Plate 58*)

(All Souls, Langham Place)
By J. Nash, 1822–4. As Portland Place falls too far W. to be in line with Upper Regent Street, Nash built a church 'whose nave swings erratically to the N.E., but whose circular vestibule, crowned by a quaint colonnaded spike, makes a lovely terminal feature to the northward stretch of Regent Street' (J. Summerson). Inside, this stone church is a galleried Corinthian hall with flat ceiling, all tastefully restored by H. S. Goodhart-Rendel since the 1939 war, and very Evangelical.

(The Annunciation, Marble Arch)
By Walter Tapper, 1913. Cliff-like buttressed brick exterior. Inside with N. aisle and clerestory nave, tall, grey and imposing, with rich woodwork and delicate E. window, late Gothic.

(St. Cyprian's, Clarence Gate)
By Sir Ninian Comper, 1903. The brick buttressed outside, with its wide late-Perpendicular windows, with their bottle-glass panes, contrasts with the sumptuous interior. Simple, stone-vaulted arches under a W. gallery open on to a wide nave and aisles without pews and whose polished wood floor surface reflects graceful arcade piers and the gold screen and loft which, with a lace-like tracery, stretches across the whole width of the E. end. Parcloses divide the E. end into chapels. Altars, hangings, statues, light fittings, font cover and stained glass are all by Comper.

(*St. John's Wood Chapel*)
T. Hardwick, junior, 1814. Elegantly sited on the crest of a hill near Lord's. Ionic Portland-stone portico and turret above, Tuscan interior, all white. Galleries glazed from nave.

(*St. Mary*) Parish Church
T. Hardwick, junior, 1817. An expensive Corinthian church in Portland stone,

whose portico and steeple terminate Nash's stucco York Gate leading out of Regent's Park. There are Corinthian side entrances and three vestibules and at the E. end two entrance projections set diagonally. The galleried interior was over-decorated in later Victorian times.

(St. Mary, Wyndham Place)
By Sir Robert Smirke, 1823. A circular tower on the S. side fits well into Wyndham Place, otherwise a correct Commissioners' Classic church, redecorated by Victorians.

*(St. Peter's, Vere Street)
By J. Gibbs, 1724. A humble brick exterior with Tuscan portico and bell turret. Singularly exquisite inside, tall columns rise past the galleries and support a carved ceiling with 'spritely plaster-work by Bagutti' (Pevsner). The stained glass by Burne-Jones and painted altar-piece by him, though hardly suited to this miniature St. Martin's-in-the-Fields, have their own merit.

(St. Benet, Kentish Town)
C. G. Hare, 1908. Lofty Bodley-esque interior, simple and square-ended.

(St. James', Hampstead Road)
By T. Hardwick, 1791. Brick, Adam style, with cupola. Galleried interior.

(St. Luke, Kentish Town)
By B. Champneys, 1868–70. Early-pointed red brick, with saddle-back tower, on a steep hillside. Apsidal ended. Narrow lean-to aisles, glass by H. Holliday in apse and Morris and Co., in clerestory.

(St. Martin, Gospel Oak)
E. Buckton Lamb, 1866. Extraordinary outside and in. Thin tower with spire-like newel turret. Cruciform, with apse. Transept windows with strange tracery. All in Kentish rag. The interior is aisle-less, low and stranger still, with hammer-beam roof supported on brackets and the transepts seeming to be more important than the nave. No one could call this imitating medieval.

(St. Mary, Brookfield)
By W. Butterfield, 1876. A noble nave in polychrome brick leading to an anti-climax of a chancel by G. E. Street, 1881.

*(St. Mary Magdalene, Munster Square)
By R. C. Carpenter, 1849–52. The spire has never been built and the church consists of a spacious nave with separately gabled aisles, all correct Middle-pointed. Inside,

slender arcades of clustered columns give views of Hardman glass designed by Pugin, frescoes by Daniel Bell, paintings and elegant screen and rood by Micklethwaite and a perfect Camden Society chancel. A faint smell of incense completes the elegant early ritualistic effect of this restrained and scholarly building.

*(St. Michael, Camden Town)
By G. F. Bodley and Garner, 1876–81. Of stock brick with Bath stone dressing, this is in the Decorated style. Austere, tall, structural, this is thought to be Bodley's best work. 'The strong individuality of its architect shines through its adoptive 14th-century style, as Wren's shone through the adoptive Palladian style' (Bumpus). The clerestoried interior, with large windows high up at E. and W. ends, is solemn, high and vast.

ST. PANCRAS **(St. Pancras, New Church)*
By W. and H. W. Inwood, 1819–22. The most expensive and the best of all English Greek Revival churches. Outside it is of Portland stone, with portico, steeple, apse and two square projections at the E. end, that on the N. containing an elegant oval vestry and surrounded on the outside with caryatids. The portico is Ionic and the steeple an adaptation 'free and astonishingly successful' (Summerson) of the Tower of the Winds. Rich Greek detail from the Erectheum adorns the outside and is in terra-cotta. At the W. end there are three impressive entrance lobbies, two for gallery staircases, and that in the middle an attractive Doric octagon under the tower. The interior is a vast flat-ceilinged hall, terminated by an Ionic apse and surrounded on three sides by galleries supported on columns decorated with lotus leaves. Even though lately re-decorated, the church is needlessly dark because of Victorian stained glass introduced to dispel the 'Pagan' effect, as it was thought in those days, of the Greek detail. It is worth turning on the lights to see the detail of mahogany pulpit, oak pews, and original altar now in Lady Chapel. (See Plate 56)

(St. Pancras, Old Church)
Medieval and 1838 Norman Revival, embellished inside by Martin Travers, 1930.

*(All Hallows, Gospel Oak)
By J. Brooks, 1889. The formidable, towerless and buttressed exterior of Kentish rag rises from red Victorian villas. Inside it is

aisled, with very tall circular piers branching into ribs which support no vaulting, for the roof was completed after Brooks's death. The church is lit by bold lancets high in the side aisles and a rose W. window. The chancel was completed in 1913 by Sir Giles Gilbert Scott, who also designed the massive stone font. It is a spacious interior, admirably suited to ceremony and is sparing in its detail. Its cathedral-like effect is created by massiveness, simplicity and proportion.

(St. Silas, Kentish Town)
By E. Shearman, 1912. Tall, very simple Gothic of pleasant pale brick. Many-vistaed interior, with bold woodwork, ambulatory, aisles and side chapels, owes something to the later style of Temple Moore.

SHOREDITCH (St. Chad, Haggerston)
By J. Brooks, 1868. Cruciform, red brick with a lofty brick interior, vaulted chancel and side chapel, clerestoried nave, with thick stone columns and narrow lean-to aisles. All the essentials of a grand church without fuss.

*(St. Columba, Kingsland Road)
By J. Brooks, 1867–71. Gaunt and noble. In red brick with vicarage and hall to match. Interior cruciform with lofty clerestoried nave, low arcades and lean-to aisles, opening on a vaulted crossing and tall square chancel with double windows between a buttress as an E. end. This, the best of a great church architect's works, has unfortunately been whitewashed inside.

(St. John, Hoxton)
By F. Edwards, 1825–6. Commissioners' Ionic in brick and Bath stone; galleried interior.

(St. Leonard) Parish Church
By G. Dance, senior, 1736–40. A ponderous, City-style church in red brick and Portland stone, with a portico like Hawksmoor and a steeple imitating Wren, and which has an elegant outline above the E. London chimney-pots. The inside denuded of side galleries, old stained glass and famous E. window, is best seen looking W., where there is a beautiful Chippendale-style gilt clock case in the gallery front.

(St. Michael's)
By J. Brooks, 1863–5. School, vicarage and convent, the latter completed by J. D. Sedding, was once a charming Tractarian enclave. The church and vicarage survive.

The former of brick, lofty, unbuttressed and plate tracery.

SOUTHWARK (All Hallows)
By G. G. Scott, junior, 1880. A soaring brick masterpiece by the most scholarly and original Gothick Revivalist. Gutted in the war and like its predecessor, St. Agnes, Kennington, in this diocese, only to be rebuilt on mean lines.

(St. George)
By J. Price, 1734–6. Brick with Portland-stone steeple, galleried interior under ceiling of cherubs and clouds by Basil Champneys, 1897.

(Holy Trinity)
By Francis Bedford, 1823–4. Commissioners' Corinthian with Doric steeple above. Its plain interior was made dramatic and catholic by Martin Travers in 1927.

(Lady Margaret Church, Walworth)
?1889. Red brick small mission church, whose interior, with apse and low nave arcades, is happily proportioned, simple, mysterious and full of atmosphere.

(Lady Margaret Church, Walworth)
?1880. Humble mission church. Red brick within and without. The low arcades and wide apse make a happily proportioned interior.

(St. Peter, Walworth)
By Sir John Soane, 1823–5. Soane was not a church man and this is his first and best. Ionic outside with stone steeple, plain galleried interior, light and wide and with original altar at E. end.

STEPNEY *(St. Anne, Limehouse)
By N. Hawksmoor, 1712–24. Another majestic masterpiece in Portland stone, lighter than Christ Church, Spitalfields, and with a tower composed of diminishing oblongs, emphasised horizontally by heavy cornices, and vertically by deep recesses for holding shadow. At the W. end is a beautiful pilastered apse, with semi-dome. From all sides, and particularly above the docks and small E. London houses, this building looks magnificent. The interior, burnt in 1850, was beautifully restored by P. Hardwick. It is galleried, with a great oval ceiling hanging over the nave and a chancel whose E. window by Clutterbuck, dark and rich, is most surprisingly sympathetic to Hawksmoor's style and grand scale.

*(Christ Church, Spitalfields)
By N. Hawksmoor, 1723–9. A huge, heavy

galleon of white Portland stone anchored among the red-brick Queen Anne houses of the weavers. Two flights of steps lead to immense portico with barrel vault in the middle; oblong tower and spire on top of this. The body of the church is a separate composition, but towers, spire, portico and church hang together as one walks by. Everything is massive, simple and gigantic, 'the body of the church support with static and imposingly regular detail the enormous weight of the spire' (E. and W. Young). The aisled and columned interior is rich and grandly gloomy. A clerestory lights the flat and coffered nave ceiling; from the arcades below, the arches open on to transverse coffered tunnel vaults which overhang the aisles. E. and W. the great rectangle of the church is interrupted by transverse motifs, a huge beam on Corinthian columns, with a Royal Arms above, turning the E. end into a chancel, beyond which the walls curve to make a sanctuary. Eyes must be lifted from poor Victorian work at ground level to appreciate the grandeur. (*See Plate 43*)

*(*St. George's-in-the-East*)
By N. Hawksmoor, 1715–23. 'Still a ruin from the war, though the white castellated tower and turrets seem to sail like a battleship over the houses when one is steaming down the river. In winter the river winds yell through the deep funereal arches in this mighty tower and past the ruthless keystones, each as big as a child's coffin. Charred woodwork creaks and flaps below. It is a waste of time describing such a building, drawing attention to the complex ground plan or analysing the elements in the harmony of the tower, describing how the interior was – Greek Cross, Tuscan giants, depressed elliptical vaults, diagonal emphasis: the only thing is to go, and gape at what remains' (E. and W. Young).

(*St. John, Wapping*)
By Joel Johnson, 1756. Dark brick tower, clock turret and cupola, alone survive.

(*St. Paul's, Shadwell*)
By J. Walters, 1817. Surprisingly Wren-like steeple for the date. Stock brick rectangle, with galleried and domed interior.

(*St. Philip*)
By Arthur Cawston, 1883. Red brick and unfinished outside, pale stock brick and brick-vaulted throughout inside, with baptistry, aisles, transepts, side chapels and

ambulatory leading round to Lady Chapel behind high altar. Clerestory and triforium below. Very much in the style of Pearson. Impressive, many-vistaed and incense-laden.

STOKE NEWINGTON *(*St. Matthias*)
By W. Butterfield, 1851. Though bombed and sparingly repaired, this great brick church is Butterfield at his boldest and simplest. From all angles the outside, with its saddle-back tower over the chancel, its high nave and lean-to aisles and low sanctuary E. of the tower, looks well. A grand bastion of the Faith in a sad district. Inside the effect of solemn grandeur is caused by two great transverse arches of low pitch over the chorus cantorum, the W. narthex, the severe nave arcades and roof modelled on Ely lit by a clerestory. The whole church cost only £7,000.

(*St. Mary, New Church*)
By Sir Gilbert Scott, 1855–8. Sumptuous Middle-pointed with spire 1890 by J. O. Scott.

(*St. Mary, Old Church*)
Small medieval in park setting, 1580 and 1830 additions.

WANDSWORTH (*All Saints*) Parish Church
Tower, 1630. Nave, 1780. N. aisle, 1724. Chancel, 1891. Barrel-vaulted interior with columns and impressive, ponderous chancel. 'Galleries, shining with gilded records of benefaction, lurk far back in wide aisles, and there is a fine sweeping staircase going up to them. Font and pulpit are original and a square churchwardens' pew survives.' (E. and W. Young.)

(*All Saints, Putney*)
By G. E. Street, 1874. Burne Jones glass.

*(*All Saints, Tooting Graveney*)
By Temple Moore, 1905–6. A large brick and stone church in late Decorated, with tower, long nave, choir of seven bays and square-ended Lady Chapel beyond, all rising among small villas. Inside are double aisles divided by slender columns of grey Forest of Dean stone. The roofs are wooden and vaulted. High altar is Baroque. Elegant iron screens. Many vistas and cathedral-like interior proportions.

(*St. Anne*)
By Sir Robert Smirke, 1822. Commissioners' Greek, set high on a hill. Interior Victorianised.

*(Christ Church, Streatham)
By J. Wild, 1842. A graceful basilica in yellow brick with red-brick dressings. Obelisks guard the W. front. The detached campanile has a spire. The tall, galleried interior has an E. apse, Decorated by Owen Jones. In 1891, Walter Crane did the E. windows of the aisles.

*(Holy Spirit, Clapham Common)
By H. P. Burke Downing, 1911. Tall, Bodley-esque, stock brick, with N. aisle and nave only, all lit by lancets and a rose W. window. Interior lofty and impressive and restrained.

(Holy Trinity, Clapham Common)
By Kenton Couse, 1775. Stock brick, islanded on the flat common. The chancel by Beresford Pite, 1902.

(Holy Trinity, Roehampton)
By G. Fellowes Prynne, 1898. Early Deck, with spire, and huge stone chancel screen.

(St. Leonard, Streatham)
1831 and earlier. Monuments.

(St. Luke, Balham)
By W. White, 1883. Byzantine.

(St. Paul, Clapham)
By C. Edmonds, 1815. A brick simple classic in crowded old churchyard in the original village of Clapham. Monuments. Interior Victorianised.

(St. Paul, Putney)
By J. Micklethwaite and Somers Clarke, 1877. Red brick and towerless in rich, leafy suburb. Surprisingly simple and 'arty and crafty' for its date. Perpendicular tracery. Broad, spacious light interior with octagonal piers.

WESTMINSTER (St. Barnabas, Pimlico)
By T. Cundy, 1850. Small and crowded Tractarian Middle-pointed interior, with a S.E. chapel by Comper.

(St. Clement Danes)
By Wren, 1680–2. Steeple by J. Gibbs, 1719. Gutted, 1941. Restored, 1958. The galleried interior has a vaulted ceiling and curved E. end, once adorned with rich Baroque sculpture, probably by Wren's mason, Edward Pierce.

(St. George's, Hanover Square)
By John James, 1712–24. Massive Corinthian portico. Heavy square windows and a weak steeple. Light and well-upholstered interior has beautiful 16th-century Flemish

glass brought here in 1840 from a convent at Malines.

(Grosvenor Chapel)
Built and possibly designed, by B. Timbrell, 1730. Brick exterior with spire and portico, all looking American colonial behind Dorchester Hotel. Light, white interior with galleries and attractive vaulted ceilings and a great screen across the E. end by Sir Ninian Comper, who did the altars beyond it.

(St. James's, Piccadilly)
By Wren, 1682–4. Restored by Sir Albert Richardson, 1953. Modest old brick exterior with tower and steeple. Outdoor pulpit by Temple Moore. Pale, light, galleried interior, de-Victorianised. Columns rise from galleries to carry elegant barrel vaults. Marble font by Grinling Gibbons who also carved reredos swags. Organ-case from Chapel Royal, Whitehall.

*(St. James-the-Less)
By G. E. Street, 1858–61. No copy of medieval, but a highly original work in coloured brick. Detached tower has slate steeple into which pinnacles fade. Round E. end with plate tracery. Cloistered porch. Built of brick because London is a brick town. Inside, red granite columns with well-carved capitals. Sculptured pulpit over arch of brick-vaulted chancel is a Doom by G. F. Watts. Walls enlivened by patterns in brick, stone and marble. Glass and roof painting by Clayton and Bell.

*(St. John, Smith Square)
By T. Archer, 1714–28. Gutted, 1941. The four Baroque corner towers rise from graceful pedimented compositions on N. and S. façades and flank more dominant projections on the other two. Thus, this bold and strange church, islanded in the middle of a red-brick Queen Anne square, presents a different Portland stone and temple-like termination to each of the four streets that enter the square.

(St. Margaret)
1504 and later. Much restored late Gothic. Graceful aisled interior with early 16th-century Flemish glass E. window of Crucifixion.

*(St. Martin-in-the-Fields)
By J. Gibbs, 1722–6. Trafalgar Square was made a century later so that the awkward way the Portland-stone steeple bestrides the Corinthian portico was not apparent, and the church was glimpsed through

narrow streets in parts, not as a whole. Both steeple and porticoed body of the church are compact and elegant as separate units. Much-visited interior has galleries, tall columns, supporting vaulted nave ceiling with graceful plasterwork, especially over chancel arch and shallow domes over aisles. The E. end is an anti-climax.

(*St. Mary's, Bourne Street*)
By R. J. Withers, 1874. Small and stately apsidal-ended brick mission church, with 1920-ish Baroque fittings, and N. chapel by H. S. Goodhart-Rendel.

*(*St. Mary-le-Strand*)
By J. Gibbs, 1714–17. Intended as the westerly termination of two narrow streets, now swept away, the church looks like something in Rome and the steeple is an afterthought. Outside, the effect is two-storeyed, bound round with strong cornices. Inside, the two-storey effect is less happy, for there are no galleries, and the large first-floor windows have ugly glass and detract from the rich, vaulted ceiling. Deep chancel is even richer than the nave and with even uglier glass, but it is a beautiful little church, islanded in traffic.

(*St. Matthew*)
By Sir Gilbert Scott, 1853. Competent Middle-pointed with Bodley and Comper furnishing.

(*St. Paul, Covent Garden*)
Rebuilt by T. Hardwick, junior, 1795, after Inigo Jones. A huge, brick barn with wide eaves and Tuscan E. portico.

(*St. Stephen, Rochester Row*)
By Benjamin Ferrey, 1845–7. Correct and expensive English Middle-pointed revival.

WOOLWICH (*Holy Trinity, Beresford Square*)
By J. D. Hopkins, 1833. Modest classic with unspoiled galleried interior.

(*St. Luke, Eltham*)
By Temple Moore, 1906. Spacious, light interior. Wagon-roofs. Consciously simple piers. S. aisle by J. Tolhurst, *c.* 1930 (Pevsner).

(*St. Mary Magdalen*) Parish Church
1733. Stock brick with tower but Victorian chancel and interior.

(*St. Michael*)
By W. Butterfield, 1875–8. A vast clerestoried nave. The church has later additions.

Middlesex

WESTMINSTER WAS once the centre of this county, and its Guildhall is still in Parliament Square. But in 1889 Middlesex lost all its London territory (the City was always independent). From Hammersmith to Temple Bar, from Stoke Newington to Bishopsgate, the County of London was formed, and even the heights of Hampstead, those Middlesex-looking uplands, were included. If a Londoner would see how beautiful this part of what once was Middlesex looked, let him walk over Parliament Hill Fields to Kenwood, where he will see the wooded hills, ponds, willows, oaks and grassy hollows, leading to a landscaped park and Adam house. This is the Middlesex which Keats, Constable and Leigh Hunt knew.

Today the county, the second smallest in England, has over two million inhabitants, and many of them do not realise they live in Middlesex. Aerodromes, reservoirs and factories occupy the rich, flat, market-gardening land in the south-west corner along the north bank of the Thames. Suburbs fill up most of the rest. But there are still villages where the original Middlesex may be seen – Shepperton, Stanwell, Harmondsworth, Harefield, Norwood Green, and South Mimms are some of the least spoiled, their modest churches rising among weather-boarded cottages and the rust-coloured brick mansions of the cit who sought his 18th-century *rus in urbe* among walnut trees and cedars in his miniature park hidden behind brown brick walls. There are still great houses: Hampton Court (with its Wren chapel), Syon, Osterley, Chiswick, Breakspear, Wrotham, Dyrham, and Trent. The Georgian Canons has disappeared. In Enfield Chase are still some fields, there are farms and country inns in the Harefield district, Littleton seems hidden and remote under its great reservoir. Harrow village preserves its hilltop quiet, looking from its elmy height over miles of roof and railway. With an effort of imagination one can see Uxbridge as it once was, a country market-town, and along the old turnpikes that cross the county to the City the vestiges of Georgian coaching days and Victorian market gardens and the Cockney's bona-fide taverns persist.

Middlesex was a rich agricultural county which supplied London with food before London ate up its fields. Its medieval churches, except Westminster Abbey, were never much. There was no local building stone, for Middlesex is nearly all clay. But bricks were made early, and the old Tudor red bricks of Middlesex, and the dark-brown and purple and red ones of the 17th and 18th

265

centuries, are varied and beautiful. The old parish churches were often added to or rebuilt when Londoners moved out into the country. Original hamlet churches survive at Perivale and Northolt. They are humble South Essex-like buildings in keeping with the old wooden barns of the county which remain – the barn at Harmondsworth is one of the biggest in England.

What seems surprising at first is that there are so few major churches of the Gothic Revival period, when all these suburbs started to fill the county. This is, I think, because the sort of Tractarian squire who would rebuild his village church and use the best London man was not a Middlesex dweller. The county was too suburban for him, and the new large Victorian villas were often built by Nonconformists who had made their money in the City and West End. It was not until the present century when 'Greater London' called for missions that the more interesting modern buildings were erected.

Looking for Middlesex is even more fun than looking for Middlesex churches, and of the latter Harefield is to me the most undisturbed and exciting. Tottenham parish church, so imaginatively enlarged by William Butterfield who is buried in its cemetery, is the most remarkable.

J.B.

SELECTED LIST OF CHURCHES

by Michael Robbins

BEDFONT (*St. Mary*)
Village green; 12th cent. and later; wall-paintings *c*. 1300.

BEDFORD PARK (*St. Michael & All Angels*)
Norman Shaw, 1875; 'Queen Anne' with Gothic tracery; group with bank and inn.

BRENTFORD (*St. Faith, Windmill Road*) GR
G. F. Bodley and C. G. Hare, 1907.

COWLEY (*St. Laurence*)
Tiny and primitive; double-decker W. gallery.

CRANFORD *(St. Dunstan)*
In a remote situation for Middlesex, in a park by the stables of demolished Cranford House. Chancel and tower 15th century; intervening nave modest red brick, 1716; chancel floor 17th-century marble. Monuments to Berkeley family, Thomas Fuller (of 'The Worthies'), Sir Roger Aston (William Cure, 1612, very grand) and Lady Elizabeth Berkeley (Nicholas Stone, 1635, Berniniesque).

DRAYTON, WEST: *see West Drayton.*

EALING (*The Ascension, Hanger Hill*) GR
Seely and Paget, 1939.

(*Christ the Saviour, formerly Christ Church, Ealing Broadway*) GR
G. G. Scott, 1852; renovated by G. F. Bodley, 1908; windows by Hugh Easton, 1952.

(St. Peter, Mount Park Road)
Upper-class suburban church of the nineties (J. D. Sedding, 1893; completed by H. Wilson). Highly original design, with great W. window trisected by buttresses; spirelets, and two rows of little turrets along roof.

ENFIELD (*St. Andrew*)
Medieval town church on market-place.

FELTHAM *(St. Dunstan)*
A rustic building of 1802 with round-headed windows, short tower, and shingled spire; aisles of a 'Norman' cast were added in 1856. The interior is simple; a W. gallery stands on wooden columns, the panelling

filled with charity inscriptions in elegant script. Box-pews.

FINCHLEY (*St. Mary*)
15th-cent. church with outer S. aisle, 1932.

FRIERN BARNET (*St. John the Evangelist*) GR
J. L. Pearson, 1891.

GOLDERS GREEN (*St. Alban*) GR
Sir Giles Gilbert Scott, 1932; central tower.

GREENFORD (*Holy Cross*)
Gallery.

(*Holy Cross, new church*)
A. E. Richardson, 1939; timber with brick facings.

HAMPSTEAD GARDEN SUBURB (*St. Jude on the Hill*)
E. L. Lutyens, 1910; 'basilica' type.

HAMPTON (*St. Mary*) GR
E. Lapidge, 1831; white brick.

HANWELL (*St. Mary*) GR
G. G. Scott and W. B. Moffatt, 1841; setting.

HAREFIELD *(*St. Mary*)
Pleasantly set, away from the village by the vanished manor-house. A modest medieval church, chancel 13th century, S. aisle early 14th century, N. aisle and tower (N.W.) soon after 1500; chancel altered by Henry Keene, 1768, with remarkable plaster ceiling. The glory of Harefield is its monuments: a gallery of sepulchral art from the 15th century to 1800 which yet does not overwhelm the church. The Newdigate and Ashby families are commemorated by William White (1614), Grinling Gibbons (1692), Sir Robert Taylor (1760), John Bacon, Jr. (1800) and others unknown. The grandest monument is a canopied tomb to Lady Derby (1636), with columns, stone curtains, and much heraldry. The pulpit, communion rails, reredos, and font-cover are fine 17th and 18th century carving, some from Flanders.

HARLESDEN (*All Souls*) GR
E. J. Tarver, 1879; octagonal, timber-braced roof.

HARMONDSWORTH (*St. Mary*)
Brick tower *c.* 1500; village; tithe barn.

HARROW *(*St. Mary*)
Splendidly situated 400 ft. up on Harrow Hill, the finest setting in Middlesex; the pale grey exterior and the slim lead-and-timber spire can be seen for miles above the suburban villas. Lower part of tower *c.* 1130; chancel, nave, and aisles early 13th century; transepts *c.* 1300; clerestory and nave roof *c.* 1450; spire rebuilt 1765. The whole church was fiercely restored by Gilbert Scott, 1846–9, when the 'Decorated' style was introduced. The interior is consequently hard, and the outside walls flinty. Brasses from 1370; monuments, principally to headmasters of Harrow School.

HARROW, NORTH: *see North Harrow.*

HAYES (*St. Mary*)
Good roofs; centre-swinging lych-gate; roses in churchyard.

HENDON (*St. Mary*)
15th-cent. church; two S. aisles added 1915, Temple Moore.

HENDON, WEST: *see West Hendon.*

HILLINGDON (*St. John the Baptist*)
Monuments.

HORNSEY (*St. Mary*) GR
James Brooks, 1888; Perp.

ICKENHAM (*St. Giles*)
Little village church.

KENTON (*St. Mary*) GR
J. H. Gibbons, 1936.

KINGSBURY (*St. Andrew*) old church
Tiny ancient church. 12th cent. and later.

LALEHAM *(*All Saints*)
A 12th-century village church in country and river setting. Matthew Arnold buried in churchyard. Restored interior; has bold S.W. window by Miss Geddes.

LITTLETON *(*St. Mary Magdalene*)
Medieval church of a tiny village, now almost overshadowed by a gigantic reservoir. Some 12th-century work, with 16th-century brick clerestory above; chancel longer than nave, with mausoleum of 1705 on N. side; tower has open top stage of same date. Good old pews, screens, rails (Flemish), pulpit; twenty-four colours of Grenadier Guards hanging in nave.

MILL HILL (*John Keble Church, Dean's Lane*)
D. F. Martin-Smith, 1936; square plan.

MIMMS, SOUTH: *see South Mimms.*

NORTH HARROW *(*St. Alban, The Ridgeway*)
The best Middlesex church of the 1930s, by A. W. Kenyon, in yellow brick, over a

reinforced concrete frame with bold high tower. The interior is plain and serious, cement-finished, with barrel roof contracting at chancel and sanctuary; the only colour is at the altar.

NORTHOLT *(St. Mary)
Standing on a knoll by the old village green, the churchyard sloping on the other side to a by-pass road. A simple aisleless building, with chancel off centre; whitewashed exterior with brilliant red roof tiles; bell-turret with little spire, the best of a typical W. Middlesex family. Interior plain, light, and charming; wooden W. gallery of 1703.

PERIVALE (St. Mary)
Rustic setting; 13th cent. and later.

POTTERS BAR (King Charles the Martyr) GR
F. C. Eden and R. Marchant, 1941.

ROXETH (Christ Church, South Harrow) GR
G. G. Scott, 1863; coniferous Victorian churchyard.

RUISLIP (St. Martin)
Good roofs.

SHEPPERTON (St. Nicholas)
Galleries; group with rectory and inn.

SOUTHGATE (Christ Church) GR
G. G. Scott, 1863; Burne-Jones and Rossetti glass.

SOUTH MIMMS *(St. Giles)
Village church, lying between the old main street and Telford's Holyhead Road of 1826. Bold W. tower with square-headed windows and projecting newel turret of typical 15th-century Middlesex type; 13th-century chancel, nave c. 1400, N. aisle early 16th century, all sound work; red-brick N. chapel, c. 1530. Splendid Frowyck monuments, with canopied tomb-chests of 1500 and 1530. Some delicate early 16th-century painted glass. The whole renovated in 1877 to G. E. Street's designs of twenty years earlier.

STAINES (St. Peter, Laleham Road) GR
G. H. Fellowes Prynne, 1893; handsome late Victorian.

STANMORE (St. John, old church)
Brick, 1632; a dramatic ruin.

STANWELL *(St. Mary)
A village church with slender spire standing up from the flat plain of S.W. Middlesex. Nave arcades, c. 1260; most of the rest 14th century; N. aisle by S. S. Teulon, 1862. Imposing Knyvett monument by Nicholas Stone, 1622.

SUNBURY (St. Mary)
Stephen Wright, 1752; polychromatically overlaid by S. S. Teulon, 1856.

TEDDINGTON (St. Alban) GR
W. Niven, 1889; a vast fragment.

(St. Mary)
Modest old brick jumble; mainly 18th and 19th cent.

TOTTENHAM (All Hallows)
Brick S. porch, c. 1500; E. end Wm. Butterfield, 1875.

TWICKENHAM (St. Mary)
J. James, 1715, with 15th-cent. stone tower; riverside setting.

WEST DRAYTON (St. Martin)
15th cent.

WEST HENDON (St. John, Algernon Road) GR
Temple Moore, 1895; fine-drawn Perp.

WHITCHURCH *(St. Lawrence, Little Stanmore)
A nobleman's church of 1715, built for the opulent Duke of Chandos, of Canons, by John James; the tower, 16th century, survives from the previous church. The red-brick exterior nothing special; inside frescoed all over with panels and grisaille, probably by Louis Laguerre and Antonio Bellucci, c. 1720. Many original fittings; the ducal pew at the W. end like a theatre box surmounted by a fresco after Raphael's Transfiguration. On the N. side the Chandos chapel (James Gibbs, 1735); enormous tomb with statues by Gibbons. Organ by Jordan, c. 1720.

Norfolk

INTRODUCTION

THE BEST way to approach Norfolk is from the west across the skiey levels of Marshland. The roads are high above the fields which have settled on account of the drainage of the land into the dykes and rivers. The distances are immense and everywhere there are church towers. The Walpoles and the Wiggenhalls, the Terringtons and the Tilneys – some of the most splendid churches in East Anglia and a wonderful introduction to the many glories that are ahead.

Lynn is visible from a long way off but once there it is difficult to leave for, as the late Hilaire Belloc once wrote, 'all the roofs of Lynn and all its pavements are worthy (as though they were living beings) of individual names' and it would take many years to know them all. There is the wide expanse of the 'Tuesday Market' surrounded by dignified and stately houses, the more intimate little square between St. Margaret's Church and the marvellous flint flush work Guildhall, and then the superbly beautiful Renaissance Customs' House – the work of one of the greatest of all the great men of Lynn, Henry Bell (c. 1653–1717).

Bishop's Lynn in the Middle Ages, it became King's Lynn at the Reformation, but more than ever 'King's' in the time of Edward VII who made his home nearby at Sandringham, set amid the lovely upland heaths and woodland of West Norfolk which falls steeply away to the coast, to the strange layers of red and white in the cliffs at that essentially Edwardian resort, Hunstanton.

Where the Royal Family had given the lead others were not slow to follow and by the beginning of the present century The Midland and Great Northern had linked Cromer and Sheringham, Yarmouth and Norwich with 'The Sheers'. Wonderful yellow and blue engines (with an achievement of arms on their tenders blazoned with fishes and keys in saltire as if they were 'by appointment to the Holy See' but in reality an amalgamation of the arms of King's Lynn, Sutton Bridge, and Spalding) drew dark red Midland trains from Leicester and from Nottingham; and with its locomotive works at Melton Constable the M. and G.N. turned a tiny North Norfolk village into a miniature Derby.

Between The Midland and Great Northern and the sea comes a lovely stretch of country, now, alas, the site of so many aerodromes. But though the peace is shattered by the hideous scream of the jet-aircraft, there are the splendours of Houghton and Holkham in their great parks, here and there the

269

smaller well-wooded estate, and every mile or so the fresh brick and flint cottages clustered into a village, or set in groups round some great medieval remain as at Castle Acre, or in separate and distinct townships as with The Burnhams, or creeping down to the sea along the edge of an estuary as at Cley and Blakeney; and always the grey flint church tower, squat and circular or square and soaring up to a parapet of flint and stone. Sometimes set in the midst of the cottages but often a little apart and solitary among the fields.

Again and again one sees the solid Georgian farm house set amid its capacious buildings, a witness of the enclosure movement of a century-and-a-half ago, and every ten miles or so a good comfortable Market Town – Fakenham, Holt, Aylsham, North Walsham – all showing abundant testimony of the prosperity of those times and still far enough away from the county capital, and from each other, to have a very real life of their own and a considerable importance for their own immediate locality.

But after North Walsham the country makes a sudden change. The churches still are of flint but the cottages are plastered and thatched with reeds, and you descend, but so slowly that you are not conscious of descending, to a new and a different flatness. Not the brown flatness of Marshland but the luxurious green flatness of the Broads.

The Broads are very tantalising. You do not see anything of them unless you are actually on them and you can wander for miles along twisting lanes, and often within a few yards of a Broad, but it is not until you see a sail sliding through what appears to be green meadows that you realise that there is water there at all.

Only occasionally do the Broads reveal themselves as a wide landscape. On the high ground at Ludham and at Martham. A landscape which broadens in one direction towards the sea, where the trees are fewer, where the Broads (Hickling and Horsey) are larger and shallower, where the church towers stand vividly against the skyline, and beyond, at the utmost limit of sight, the long low line of sand dunes. But the other way the Broads become smaller and deeper, the rivers are lined with gardens and thick trees as Broadland narrows inwards towards its capital, which is also the capital of Norfolk, Norwich.

The best way to visit Norwich, is to look down upon it, as George Borrow loved to look down, from the heights of Mousehold Heath, and it is impossible not to share his enthusiasm. 'A fine old city . . . Yes, there it spreads from north to south, with its venerable houses, its numerous gardens, its thrice twelve churches . . . its grey old castle upon the top of that mighty mound.'

Though Norwich has its share of that sameness which the 20th century has impressed upon the outskirts of every city in England, its industries and its suburbs are well planned. But may the planning stop short at the city itself, for to do away with the narrow streets and winding alleys, with a church at every corner, would be to destroy the character of Norwich as a medieval city – a medieval city which is like a gothic building. Upset its delicate poise, knock the keystone out of the vault, and its beauty has gone for ever. But within the city walls Norwich is still a rural capital, a medieval town which is really an agglomeration of villages with their old country names – St. Miles Coslany, St. Clement's-at-the-Fye Bridge, St. John's Timberhill, St. James-in-Pockthorpe – and in the middle the quietest 'parish' but with the mightiest church, the marvellous Cathedral with its soaring spire and solid Norman arches rising to a superbly beautiful vault with flying buttresses, set amid the calm though – now, alas, with many of the fine 18th-century houses converted into offices – somewhat commercial oasis of the Close.

Ascend 'the mighty mound' of the Castle and the parochial map of Norwich is clearly visible with the village clustered about their church towers; and the Castle itself is well worth a visit for the Museum, which is one of the best provincial museums in the country; and for the beautifully planned galleries which contain a magnificent collection of the Works of those painters of Norwich whose Society is unique in the History of English Art, and who depicted the ever varying Norfolk countryside with an accuracy and invigorating freshness that has never been surpassed.

Whichever way you go out of Norwich you are in company with Old Crome. North-east to Mousehold Heath. Westward to Earlham Park which looks much the same as it did in the days when he taught the Miss Gurneys to draw; and on through his *Marlingford Grove* into that neat and well-wooded district of central Norfolk which has a character that is all its own. A prosperous and well-kept region watered by the slow stream of the Wensum. A land of comfortable-looking Parks and Halls which has been immortalised by the everyday doings of Parson Woodforde and his friends whose names are recorded in so many of the churches and churchyards of those villages which are gathered about the towns of Dereham and Hingham, Reepham and Foulsham, and Swaffham away to the west on the edge of the Breck.

The southern part of this region is watered by the Yare which after Norwich becomes, for East Anglia, a mighty stream and now and again one can still see a wherry, with a great spreading sail such as Old Crome knew, making its way down to Yarmouth. Yarmouth is best approached by water across the wide expanse of Breydon, and it is a seaside town which has a season of one sort or another going on nearly all the year round.

On the other side it is a pleasure resort with the solid and ornate Edwardian houses at the northern end still catering for the more staid holiday maker who comes by train to spend a week or two, and just a little earlier perhaps than the vast crowds who come day by day by train and bus to the Fun Fair at the southern end of the Promenade in August and September.

On the other side of the town is the continuous bustle of the port, and then the Denes with mile upon mile of nets drying and repairing in readiness for the herring season in October when Yarmouth becomes a turmoil of lorries, shouting, mountains of fish boxes. When the Scots fisher girls cut and slash at a never-ending torrent of herrings and the 'YH' of the Yarmouth boats is interspersed with the 'GY' and 'PD' of those from Grimsby and Peterhead and from even farther afield.

East Norfolk is so utterly different from West that in passing from one to the other it is difficult to believe that one is in the same county, but the most different region of all is the south-western, the Breckland; and this has changed more perhaps than any other part of Norfolk in recent years. Time was when corn grew on those light lands and older sportsmen tell of how the last

Buzzard was shot on Thetford Chase. But now it is mile upon mile of fir trees, for Breckland has been called upon to supply the North of England and South Wales, and – from the appearance of Brandon station – the whole world with pit props. Here and there are glimpses of old Breckland with groups of pines round the lovely inland meres – Langmere, Ring Mere, Thompson Water – but conifers thick and black are advancing like files of embattled troops, and the troops themselves have engulfed much of Breckland in their battle area. Tottington and Thompson, Stanford, Buckenham and West Tofts are uninhabited. The churches gaunt and unused. The cottages tumbling into ruins with their gardens and fields yellow with charlock. This part of Breckland shows what is meant by 'scorched earth' and the visitor who wants to see Breckland at its best, and enter into the spirit of it, had better go over the border and – avoiding yet another huge and ghastly aerodrome – see that part of it which is in Suffolk – but not before he has visited the capital of Breckland, the town of Thetford.

Thetford is like a miniature Norwich with a castle mound looking down upon an agglomeration of villages, and though London is reported to be overspilling so far north into a new town here, let us hope that the old one, which stands on the remains of an even earlier and Saxon Thetford, will remain inviolate. Here, as at Norwich, are the winding streets and narrow lanes, a fine Market Place, all merging into a most attractive regency quarter for alone among the East Anglian country towns Thetford made determined, though not very successful, attempts to be a spa in the early years of the 19th century with its Pump Room situate beside a shady walk on the bank of the river.

Just one more region of Norfolk remains apart from that southern region which is the best introduction to Suffolk. That indeterminate region between the Breckland and the West Norfolk heights. A land of arable fields and heathland merging into Breck, and the little wooded valley of the Wissey with its green meadows. A land where the villages are centred upon Northwold, Methwold, Downham Market and Stoke Ferry. A land which, as with all the other regions of Norfolk, changes suddenly, but again almost imperceptibly, into the Fens; into the Isle of Ely with the great west tower of the Cathedral visible in the far, far distance.

C.L.S.L.

SELECTED LIST OF CHURCHES

by the Rev. C. L. S. Linnell

ACLE (*St. Edmund*)
11th-cent. tower; 15th-cent. belfry; screen.

ACRE CASTLE: *see Castle Acre.*

ACRE SOUTH: *see South Acre.*

ACRE WEST: *see West Acre.*

ALDERFORD *(St. John the Baptist)*
Carefully maintained this church with its seven-sacrament font – a design which is almost an East Anglian speciality as all but two of the forty known examples are in Norfolk and Suffolk – has little of later periods which mars the simplicity of the small medieval village church.

ASHWELLTHORPE (*All Saints*)
17th-cent. furnishings; alabaster tomb for Sir Edmund de Thorpe, 1446.

ATTLEBOROUGH *(St. Mary)*
The Norman E. end is a little gloomy for it is really the crossing of this once cruciform church, the chancel having disappeared. Lofty 15th-century nave with a wonderful screen and loft. More complete even than the famous one at Ranworth though the painting is less remarkable. Probably early 16th century, and all along the front of the loft are blazoned the arms of the twenty-four English sees then existing. Above, on the W. wall of the central tower, are well-restored figure paintings – the background to the rood.

AYLSHAM (*St. Michael*)
15th cent.; brasses; 17th-cent. monument to Bp. Jegon of Norwich; late medieval screen paintings.

BACONSTHORPE (*St. Mary*)
14th-cent. Easter sepulchre.

BALE (*All Saints*)
15th-cent. glass in S.E. window of nave.

BANNINGHAM (*St. Botolph*)
Hammer-beam roof.

BARNHAM BROOM (*St. Peter & St. Paul*)
15th-cent. screen with paintings.

BARNINGHAM, LITTLE: *see Little Barningham.*

BARNINGHAM, NORTH: *see North Barningham.*

BARSHAM, EAST: *see East Barsham.*

BARTON TURF *(St. Michael & All Angels)*
This church is remarkable for one of the finest screens in East Anglia. Enriched with gesso work and paintings of the nine orders of angels with Saints Appolonia, Sitha, and Barbara. St. Appolonia, whose intercessions were especially efficacious against toothache, is vividly represented holding a formidable molar in a pair of pincers.

BARTON BENDISH (*St. Andrew*)
Small Jacobean box-pews.

BAWBURGH (*St. Mary & St. Wolstan*)
Screen with painting of the local St. Walstan – his well, N. of church.

BEESTON - NEXT - MILEHAM *(St. Mary)*
15th-century arcade, clerestory and hammer-beam roof, but in the main this church is a wonderful example of the 14th-century East Anglian style. So alike is it in proportions, and in the design of the window tracery, to Great Walsingham that it is tempting to believe that one man was responsible for both.

BESSINGHAM (*St. Andrew*)
Early circular tower.

BINHAM *(St. Mary)*
Only the nave, deprived of its aisles, remains of the great Benedictine priory church standing in the meadows. All around are the remains of the conventual buildings recently excavated by the Office of Works. The side aisles and the great W. window were complete until the early years of the 19th century. After a century of neglect this church has begun to live again. The W. front is certainly the most

splendid example of the 13th-century style in Norfolk.

BLAKENEY *(St. Nicholas)
Shows how happily the medieval builders could combine two differing architectural styles. The 13th-century chancel with groined roof and well-restored stalls and return stalls has, with the careful rebuilding of the rood-screen and loft, the appearance of a separate church. Yet it blends very well with the great 15th-century nave. The W. tower, of a simpler design than some of the period, stands in a commanding position above the village. The small tower at the N.E. corner of the chancel may have been used as a lighthouse to Blakeney Harbour but it is clear that its original purpose was to provide a staircase to the chamber above the chancel.

BLICKLING (St. Andrew)
Brasses; monument (G. F. Watts) for the Marquis of Lothian.

BLOFIELD (St. Andrew)
15th cent.; W. tower.

BOOTON *(St. Michael & All Angels)
Perhaps the most enthralling ecclesiological curiosity in Norfolk. Designed in the 1870s by the then incumbent, the Rev. Whitwell Elwin, an amateur architect, it is a riot of the 'middle pointed'. Outside is a veritable forest of pinnacles which, along with the rest of the masonry, were unfortunately made of bath stone which weathers badly in the East Anglian climate. The nave, copied from Temple Balsall in Warwickshire, is very impressive but the chancel, with which Mr. Elwin was at pains to be scrupulously 'correct', is a little lifeless. The hammer-beam roof is perhaps somewhat massive for a church of this size, and the angels project so far forward that one is not surprised to learn that they were made by a man whose real occupation was the making of figure-heads for boats.

BRACON ASH (St. Nicholas)
18th-cent. tomb house N. of the chancel.

BRESSINGHAM (St. John the Baptist)
Carved bench ends in nave.

BRINTON (St. Andrew)
15th-cent. nave roof; bench-ends, 1544.

BRISLEY *(St. Bartholomew)
The chief glory of this church is in the 15th-century W. tower standing superbly on the rising ground in the centre of the village. For the rest, though this church is in a deplorable condition the medley of 15th-century woodwork worked up into box-pews and a three-decker, and the uneven flooring with big square tiles interspersed with blue leger stones, give the feeling of a Rowlandson print. A church in which one can visualise Dr. Syntax preaching! As at Foulsham there is a clerestory in the chancel as well as in the nave.

BURGH-NEXT-AYLSHAM (St. Mary)
Unusual chancel with 13th-cent. arcading.

BURLINGHAM (St. Edmund)
15th-cent. pulpit; wall-paintings.

BURNHAM NORTON *(St. Margaret)
In this, the best of all the Burnhams, no attempt has been made to cover up the remains of those medieval ornaments that have been removed, with the result that in this church one gets the feeling of what a small medieval church looked like inside. The pulpit is one of the finest 15th-century pulpits in existence, hexagonal with paintings of the Latin Doctors.

BURNHAM THORPE (All Saints)
Nelson's church; canopied brass in chancel for Sir William Calthorpe, 1420.

CAISTOR (St. Edmund)
Among ruins of 'Venta Icenorum'; Roman tiles in walls.

CARBROOKE (St. Peter & St. Paul)
15th-cent. nave and W. tower.

CASTLE ACRE *(St. James)
15th-century pulpit and screen, spoilt by ruthless 'pitch-pine' restorations.

CAWSTON *(St. Agnes)
'God spede the plow and send us ale corn enow our purpose to make at crow of cok of the plowlete of Sygate be merry and glede war good ale yis work mad'. Church ales have given way to fêtes but the Plough and the sign of the Plough Inn of Sygate stand beneath this inscription on the balustrade of the tower gallery showing that Cawston was, and still is, an agricultural rather than a 'wool' church. The roof is one of the most splendid of all the East Anglian hammer-beams. Good Sir John Schorne is numbered among the Apostles on the screen as he is at Suffield and at Gateley. He was Rector of North Marston, Bucks., and a water diviner. He discovered a well most beneficial against the gout and

hence in his picture he conjures the devil of pain out of a leg. The good land of Norfolk is all around in Cawston church, and the good people have never let their church go out of use. Not even in the great rebuilding of the 15th century, as the decoration round the base of the tower inside as well as out shows that it was built separately while the rest was a-building.

CLEY *(St. Margaret)
'A very beautiful lady but deplorably dressed.' Yet the poverty of the furnishings of Cley church bring out the splendour of its proportions even more. So splendid that even the Middle Ages could not realise it to the full. Surely they would never have been content with the little 13th-century tower cowering in the N.W. corner with a weather mould on the inside E. wall showing how small was the original Cley church before the architect – and surely he must have been an architect of no mean ability – set out the new building in the 14th century.

CORPUSTY (St. Peter)
Small 15th cent.

CREAKE, NORTH: *see North Creake.*

CREAKE, SOUTH: *see South Creake.*

CRESSINGHAM, GREAT: *see Great Cressingham.*

CROMER (St. Peter & St. Paul)
15th cent.; more impressive outside than in.

DEOPHAM (St. Andrew)
W. tower of west country rather than East Anglian type.

DEREHAM, EAST: *see East Dereham.*

DEREHAM, WEST: *see West Dereham.*

DUNHAM, GREAT: *see Great Dunham.*

EARLHAM (St. Mary)
Little changed since Percy Lubbock's *Earlham.*

EAST BARSHAM (All Saints)
Memorial with portrait bust of Mary Calthorpe, 1640, by John and Matthias Christmas.

EAST DEREHAM *(St. Nicholas, originally St. Withberga)
As at Beccles in Suffolk there is a big 15th-century detached bell tower. The church is cruciform with a lantern over the crossing. Nave and transepts of splendid proportions and in the chancel an interesting piscina, sedilia, and Easter Sepulchre.

There is a notable seven-sacrament font, and in the N. transept a memorial by Flaxman for the poet Cowper. No memorial could express better the character of the person it commemorates and of the person who put it up – Cowper's friend and first biographer William Hayley. As at Wymondham the church stands a little apart from the town and close to the bell tower stand Bonner's cottages with rich pargetry work unusual in Norfolk. At Dumpling Green on the east side of the town and down a lane stands a neat and many-sashed farm house looking much the same no doubt as it did when George Borrow was born there in 1803.

EAST HARLING *(St. Peter & St. Paul)
The 15th-century furnishings of this church, one of the finest in south Norfolk, are some of the richest in the county. Considerable remains of a wonderful screen and lofty 15th-century canopied tombs, and the glass in the E. window is some of the best of the 15th-century school in East Anglian glass painting.

EDGEFIELD (St. Peter & St. Paul)
14th-cent. hexagonal tower stands a mile away; church moved in 1882 by J. D. Sedding.

ELHAM, NORTH: *see North Elham.*

ELLINGHAM, GREAT: *see Great Ellingham.*

ELSING *(St. Mary)
14th century throughout this church is of the most amazing width – nearly forty feet. It contains one of the finest font covers in Norfolk, and the brass in the chancel to Sir Hugh Hastings (1347), the founder, is one of the most remarkable military brasses in England.

EMNETH (St. Edmund)
15th cent.; monument in S. aisle to Sir Thomas Hewar, 1632, by Nicholas Stone.

ERPINGHAM (St. Mary)
15th-cent. W. tower; military brass for Sir Thomas Erpingham, 1416.

FELBRIGG *(St. Margaret)
This church standing in Felbrigg Park is particularly remarkable for its many memorials. The brass in the nave for Sir Simon de Felbrigg (1416), standard bearer to Richard II, and his wife, Lady-in-Waiting to Queen Anne of Bohemia, is one of the best military brasses in England and one of the five representing a Knight

of the Garter. The style of post-reformation brasses is well represented by those to Thomas Windham and Mrs. Coningsby; and among the many memorials of a later period is the large and stately 'marmor modestum' for Thomas Windham, by the Norwich sculptor Martin Morley, and the fine bust of William Windham by Joseph Nollekens (1810).

FERSFIELD (*St. Andrew*)
Small with Jacobean furnishings in chancel. (Rev. Francis Blomefield's leger stone.)

FINCHAM (*St. Martin*)
Early 15th-cent. tower; screen.

FOXLEY *(St. Thomas the Apostle)*
After much neglect this church is receiving a careful restoration which has wisely retained the W. gallery. The 15th-century screen with pictures of the four Latin doctors is a most vigorous example of medieval figure-painting. St. Augustine in particular in a big furred almuce gives the impression of high relief with the perspective most skilfully executed – as if he were about to step into the nave!

FRENZE *(St. Andrew)*
Has numerous brasses to the Blennerhassett family. Down a lane and almost in a farmyard this church is most welcoming in its unrestored condition, and has the appearance of a snug little private chapel with large Jacobean pew and pulpit.

GATELEY *(St. Helen)*
As at Frenze this church has to be approached through a farmyard. It contains a 15th-century screen (*see* Cawston) and the monument to Mrs. Elizabeth Segrave (1727) – 'in her conjugal life not so happy as deserving' – is an excellent example of the work of the Norwich sculptor, Robert Page.

GLANDFORD *(St. Martin)*
Entirely rebuilt in the early years of the present century this small church is filled with so much – hammer-beam roof, screen, elaborately carved dado all round, and exceedingly beautiful windows by Bryans – that it is overwhelming. The whole, the gift of Sir Alfred Jodrell, is a marvellous example of the Edwardian richness at its very best and most elaborate. It stands most beautifully in a neatly kept churchyard and on a little hill overlooking the Glaven Valley. Close by is a neat little building in the Flemish style, housing a collection of shells and many other objects most of which are more curious than beautiful.

GOODERSTONE *(St. George)*
A most lovely medieval interior with 15th-century benches and a square-headed screen so different from the usual East Anglian style. Two-decker Jacobean pulpit.

GREAT CRESSINGHAM (*St. Michael*)
Well proportioned 15th-cent. church and W. tower.

GREAT DUNHAM (*St. Andrew*)
Partly pre-Conquest with axial tower.

GREAT ELLINGHAM (*St. James*)
Spacious 14th cent.; 15th-cent. additions.

GREAT SNORING (*St. Mary*)
15th cent. with 17th-cent. furnishings.

GREAT WALSINGHAM (*St. Peter*)
14th-cent. chancel destroyed; excellent 15th-cent. seating.

GREAT WITCHINGHAM (*St. Mary*)
14th–15th-cent. chancel, nave, and tower; S. porch with flint flush work and Annunciation carving.

GREAT YARMOUTH *(St. George)*
Even in a county of large medieval churches the destruction during the late war of the great church of St. Nicholas was a grievous loss, but the loss of St. George's would have been even worse and one cannot but be too thankful that this, one of the three best Georgian churches in Norfolk, (Gunton, North Runcton and St. George's, Yarmouth), escaped almost without damage. Built by John Price in 1714 St. George's is a most perfect example of the 'auditory' church of the early 18th century with galleries all round, classical reredos and pulpit, and wide plaster ceiling in the nave.

GUESTWICK (*St. Peter*)
Alignment altered in 15th cent.; 11th-cent. tower.

GUNTON *(St. Andrew)*
There are few examples of 18th-century church buildings in East Anglia but this one, built by Robert Adam in 1769, is unquestionably one of the most attractive that could be found anywhere. Palladian W. front and inside it is furnished as a college chapel with contemporary organ on a W. gallery, and each of the stalls beneath is supplied with a magnificent folio Prayer

Book in blue morocco with gilt tooling, for the use of the Harbord family who caused all these beautiful things to be made. The great house is partly ruined, the park tangled and overgrown, but the former glory has not departed from Gunton church which preserves the spirit of the period better than any other such church in the eastern counties.

HALES (St. Margaret)
11th cent. with contemporary ornament round the apse.

HAPPISBURGH (HAZEBORO) (St. Mary)
Tower and screen.

HARLING, EAST: see East Harling.

HARPLEY (St. Laurence)
S.W. tower; W. nave window; screen rather garishly repainted.

HEYDON *(St. Peter & St. Paul)
With a mortuary chapel against the N. wall of the chancel and a series of tombs railed off in the N. aisle the whole church has something of the feeling of a mausoleum. But it has many points of interest – in particular a most exceptional 'tub' font – and both church and churchyard are beautifully kept and have a perfect setting along one side of the most attractive village greens in Norfolk.

HINDRINGHAM (St. Martin)
14th cent.; church chest.

HINGHAM *(St. Andrew)
This must have been quite the noblest 14th-century church in Norfolk but is a fearful example of how 19th-century restorers by their very 'correctness' could take the very life out of a building. Perched up on a flight of steps the high altar is particularly unhappy but one's attention is taken away from this by the most beautiful Flemish glass in the great E. window. In the chancel a beautiful canopied tomb for Lord Morley. With its many 18th-century houses Hingham is one of the most attractive country towns in Norfolk.

HOLT (St. Andrew)
E. window by Bryans.

HORSHAM ST. FAITH (St. Mary & St. Andrew)
Pulpit (1480) and screen (1528).

HOVETON (St. Peter)
Small church (1624) with contemporary fittings.

INGHAM *(Holy Trinity)
Originally the collegiate church of the Trinitarian Canons. There are considerable remains of the stone pulpitum dividing the collegiate chancel from the parochial nave. The founder, Sir Oliver de Ingham (1344) lies on a bed of pebbles in the chancel as does Sir Roger de Kerdiston at Reepham St. Mary. Both nave and chancel are of soaring height as if Sir Oliver, using the stones for his pillow, had seen a ladder rising heavenwards. So magnificent are the proportions of this building with its fine W. tower that it is almost possible to forget the poor 19th-century furnishing. The enormous organ fills two bays of the N. aisle! A little unnecessary, one feels, in a village church.

KELLING (St. Mary)
Easter Sepulchre.

KENNINGHALL (St. Mary)
Arms of Elizabeth I.

KETTERINGHAM *(St. Peter)
This is a most attractive church completely restored in the very early 19th-century gothic style. Two large pews in the chancel, box-pews in the nave, western gallery and three-decker pulpit all in the same style as Ketteringham Hall which was rebuilt about the same time by the Boileau family. The church has the appearance of a private chapel standing almost within the gardens of the Hall.

KING'S LYNN *(St. Margaret's)
Looks so splendid without, but a little disappointing within, the nave having been rebuilt in 15th-century gothic as that style was understood in the 18th century. The 13th-century chancel has been aggressively 'gothic-revivalised', and though G. F. Bodley's altar piece is very fine, one regrets the disappearance of Henry Bell's beautiful classical reredos. The organ case is most beautiful and in the S. choir aisle are the famous Braunche and Walsoken brasses, without exaggeration two of the most magnificent of such memorials in the world.

*(St. Nicholas)
For sheer size it is overwhelming. Quite the most spacious of all the great churches of East Anglia. The 13th-century tower looks very small in the S.W. corner trying to assert itself against this enormous nave and chancel (which are continuous with no chancel arch) with a modern spire.

KNAPTON *(*St. Peter & St. Paul*)
It is worth going a long way to see the wonderful double hammer-beam roof here. The gift of John Smithe in 1503 it has an enormous span of 30 ft. 6 in. and retains much of its original colour. The 13th-century purbeck marble font has an attractive cover (1704) with the palindromical inscription

ΝΙψΟΝ ΑΝΟΜΗΜΑ ΜΗ ΜΟΝΑΝ ΟψΙΝ
(wash my sins and not my face only).

LANGHAM (*St. Mary & St. Andrew*)
15th-cent. W. tower; Burne-Jones glass in N.E. nave window.

LETHERINGSETT *(*St. Andrew*)
The eminent Mr. William Butterfield was given *carte blanche* with this church with the result that the 13th-century nave has a very pleasing Victorian interior with windows by Kempe and some beautiful candelabra. The chancel, however, has been raised out of all proportion to the size of the building and there is an overwhelming reredos by Messrs. Pietro and Niccolo Bazzanti of Florence. Just beneath the parapet of the 12th-century circular tower can be seen traces of small round windows.

LITCHAM (*All Saints*)
15th-cent. screen and pulpit; 17th-cent. brick tower.

LITTLE BARNINGHAM (*St. Andrew*)
Shrouded skeleton holding hour-glass on corner of large pew, dated 1640, 'for couples joined in wedlock'.

LITTLE WALSINGHAM *(*All Saints*)
Is rather over-restored, but has, with the exception of Walsoken, the finest of all the seven-sacrament fonts surmounted by a graceful 17th-century cover presented by Sir Henry and Lady Sidney who have a well-designed monument in the N. chapel. After four centuries pilgrims have again come to Walsingham. Probably in greater numbers than ever before to the Anglican shrine in Little Walsingham and to the Roman Catholic 'Slipper Chapel' – a perfect little early 14th-century building and so similar in design to the gatehouse of the ruined priory at Burnham Norton. The slipper chapel is in the adjoining village of Houghton St. Giles where the church has a 15th-century screen.

LODDON *(*Holy Trinity*)
With continuous nave and chancel this is a good example of the 15th-century East Anglian town church. Of the many points of interest, perhaps the most remarkable, is the vivid figure painting on the screen, one of the panels representing the martyrdom of little St. William of Norwich crucified against two stakes.

LOPHAM, SOUTH: *see South Lopham.*

LUDHAM *(*St. Catherine*)
Has the unusual feature of the emblem of the patron saint, the wheel, worked into the tracery of the spandrils of the arch-braced roof. St. Appolonia with her tooth again appears on the screen together with St. Mary Magdalene, St. Stephen, St. Edmund, Henry VI, the Latin Doctors, Edward the Confessor, St. Walstan and St. Laurence. An arduous but very attractive approach to this church is by water to Womack Broad, or along the Thurne to St. Benet's Abbey, where the gatehouse remains as the base of a windmill, and then across the meadows and into the town by way of Johnson Street.

LYNN, KING'S: *see King's Lynn.*

MATTISHALL (*All Saints*)
Hammer-beam roof; W. tower.

MORSTON (*All Saints*)
Mainly 14th-cent. church with 15th-cent. octagonal font with the four Evangelists, interspersed with the Evangelistic Symbols, on the panels; the Evangelists and their symbols appear again on the 15th-cent. screen together with the four Latin Doctors; the screen was probably the gift of the Rector, who was also Bishop of Clogher, *c.* 1475; a good alabaster monument in the S. aisle. (*See Plate 10*)

MULBARTON (*St. Mary Magdalene*)
Curious memorial; two copper plates opening bookwise; 15th-cent. glass.

MUNDFORD *(*St. Leonard*)
A most lovely restoration by Sir Ninian Comper, though without colour. The chancel is especially attractive with black-and-white paving and divided from the nave by a beautifully proportioned rood screen and loft.

NARBOROUGH (*All Saints*)
Spelman monuments; that to Clement Spelman, 1679, attributed (though this is non-proven) to C. G. Cibber.

NECTON (*All Saints*)
Hammer-beam roof.

NORTH BARNINGHAM *(St. Peter)*

Isolated in the fields this dilapidated building is in danger of being written off as 'redundant'. Yet it contains the most exquisite 14th-century carving in the grouped piscina and sedilia; two arresting portrait busts of Sir Austin Palgrave and his wife set in what he was pleased to call the 'small monument' which fills the E. end of the aisle; a charming memorial in the chancel to Sir Austin's sister, Mrs. Pope; and a 'wheel window' design in brick and stone in the paving of the central aisle.

NORTH CREAKE *(St. Mary)*

There are many points of interest – 15th-century nave roof, exceptionally fine 14th-century grouped piscina and sedilia in the chancel, a brass (1500) to Sir William Calthorpe, a great benefactor holding a model of the church – but the whole effect is a little dull owing to an uninspired 19th-century restoration.

NORTH ELMHAM *(St. Mary)*

14th–15th cent.; remains of Saxon Cathedral to N.

NORTH RUNCTON *(All Saints)*

With the exception of GUNTON this church, built by Henry Bell who designed the famous Customs House at King's Lynn, is the finest 18th-century church building in the county. Four graceful Ionic columns in the nave rise to a square dome with intersecting vaults. W. tower in keeping with the rest of the building, surmounted by urns at the corners and a classical flèche, and in the chancel oak panelling beautifully carved. This lovely church was evidently a labour of love on the part of Henry Bell who not only designed it but subscribed much of the cost of building.

NORTHWOLD *(St. Andrew)*

Easter Sepulchre.

NORWICH *(St. Andrew)*

Early 16th century with tombs in the N. aisle to the Suckling family and a stately font cover (1637).

(St. Catherine-in-Mile Cross)

Well proportioned modern church (1935).

(St. George-in-Colegate)

A 15th-century church where Old Crome lies buried in the S. aisle and the church remains with all its early 19th-century fittings just as he would have known it, pews, pulpit, W. gallery with organ on top, and a handsome classical reredos.

(St. George's-in-Tombland and St. John's-on-Timberhill)

As in most cities the churches of Norwich are rich in monumental sculpture, not only in the works of great masters (like Nicholas Stone in St. George's - in - Tombland) but also in the works of local sculptors more than a century before its more famous school of landscape painters. Of these one might mention the monument in St. John's-on-Timberhill to the sculptor Robert Page, designed by himself.

(St. Giles)

15th-cent. W. tower and nave.

(St. Gregory)

Remarkable painting of St. George on the W. wall of the N. aisle.

(St. Helen's)

Chapel for the Great Hospital in Bishopgate.

(St. John Maddermarket)

Classical reredos and brasses.

(St. John de Sepulchre)

W. tower at top of Ber Street.

(ST. JOHN'S-ON-TIMBERHILL): see St. George's-in-Tombland.

(St. Laurence)

15th-cent. town church.

(St. Michael-at-Coslany)

Depressing within, but without has the most elaborate flint flush work that can be seen anywhere.

(St. Peter Mancroft)

The finest of all the large town churches of the 15th century where, as at Framlingham (Suffolk) and at Ringland, the hammer-beams of the roof are covered with false vaulting, where the great E. window is filled with contemporary Norwich glass and the font stands beneath a huge canopy supported by carved posts at the corners. With its great W. tower panelled in stone it stands in a dominating position above the Market Place; close by in the Haymarket is a statue of its most famous parishioner, Sir Thomas Browne, smiling benignly down musing upon his urn, and in the vestry is a portrait of him by H. Morland.

(St. Stephen)

16th cent.; tower rebuilt 1601.

OULTON-NEXT-AYLSHAM *(St. Peter & St. Paul)*

14th–15th cent. with earlier features.

OUTWELL (*St. Clement*)
15th cent. well restored.

OXBOROUGH *(St. John the Evangelist)*
Is a sign and a portent of the danger to so many country churches unless something is done to preserve them and that soon. The tower and spire (one of the two medieval stone spires in Norfolk) fell in 1948 and demolished the nave. The chancel remains and fortunately the Bedingfield Chantry Chapel at the E. end of the S. aisle was undamaged with its terra-cotta work exactly similar to that of the Ferrers memorial at Wymondham, and reminiscent of that at Layer Marney, Essex, and of Torrigiani's work in Henry VII's chapel at Westminster. The Rev. Charles Parkyn, the continuator of Blomefield's *History of Norfolk*, has a monument in the chancel describing him as 'indefessus . . . contra errores papisticos' which are still close at hand in the very beautiful 19th-century Roman Catholic Chapel just inside the Park near the W. front of the marvellous 15th-century Oxborough Hall. The chapel has a German triptych above the altar. (*See Plate 39*)

OXNEAD *(St. Michael)*
The glory of this little church has departed along with Oxnead Hall of which – the most splendid house of the Pastons – only one wing is left, and down towards the Bure are considerable remains of the gardens and terraces. But the church is worth seeing for the very lovely bust of Nicholas Stone to Lady Katherine Paston 'whose tomb was arch'd about with weeping eyes, whom sorowe's blasts did likewise crystallise'.

PASTON (*St. Margaret*)
Wall-painting.

POTTER HEIGHAM (*St. Nicholas*)
14th-cent. arcades, hammer-beam roof and screen. 15th-cent. brick font; wall-paintings.

PULHAM *(St. Mary the Virgin)*
This church, beautifully restored by G. F. Bodley, shows how well he understood the spirit of the 15th-century style. In the centre of the attractive village is a medieval building called Pennoyer's School. Once the chapel of St. James and now a class-room in the present day Primary School.

RANWORTH *(St. Helen)*
The screen makes this one of the most remarkable churches in Norfolk. Complete with its loft and vault, lateral altars, nearly all its original colour and marvellous figure painting it is unquestionably one of the great treasures of medieval art in England. The painting of St. Michael, to mention only one of the panels, is a most perfect example of the work of the medieval artist in this style. Neither must one forget the 15th-century lectern and the priceless Sarum Antiphoner, given to Ranworth in the 15th century, which is one of the most beautiful of such illuminated books in existence. And yet, exceptional though it is today, Ranworth was probably little more so than many a village church in all its 15th-century splendour.

REDENHALL (*St. Mary*)
W. tower identical in design to W. tower of Wymondham Abbey.

RINGLAND *(St. Peter)*
Beautifully situate on the rising ground above the village and overlooking the Wensum, this church has a wonderful roof like St. Peter Mancroft, Norwich and Framlingham (Suffolk). 14th-century arcades rising to a lofty 15th-century clerestory containing much contemporary glass.

RUNCTON, NORTH: *see North Runcton.*

SALLE *(St. Peter & St. Paul)*
In this church the 15th-century style reached its apotheosis before it hardened into the rather formal 'perpendicular' of the lofty town churches of East Anglia. The wonderful proportions of the nave, chancel arch (with much of the canopy of honour above the rood remaining), transepts, and long chancel (complete with its stalls and return stalls), N. and S. porches with chambers above, make it not only the most marvellous church in a county of marvellous churches but one of the most beautiful in all England. Standing alone in the fields, superbly placed on the highest ground in the district, it is the great offering of the families (the Boleyns, the Briggs, the Fountaines) who owned the land. Stand in the tower gallery above the huge font cover (supported by a bracket from the gallery rail) and you appreciate to the full the size of the building, and the incredible daring of the carpenters who spanned this wide nave with a simple arched-braced roof with the wall posts brought down upon corbels which are

really the principal rafters of the aisle roofs carried right through the nave walls, thus stepping out the weight of the nave roof on to the aisle walls. Stand in the chancel and look up at the enormous wooden bosses depicting the Life of Our Lord, and look back at the soaring tower arch and you realise again that all the superlatives you can muster are inadequate to describe the stupendous majesty of this church. However often one visits Salle there seems to be always something fresh to wonder at and admire and every visit is an heartening experience. 'Sursum Corda' and Salle Church in all its glory never fails to supply the answer.

SALTHOUSE *(St. Nicholas)
This church, built by Sir Henry Heydon of Baconsthorpe between the years 1491-7, replaced an earlier building of which the W. tower alone remains. Standing in the most exposed position facing the North Sea, above the village that was once a port, this large and rather gaunt church resembles a ship of which only the hull remains. A battered rood-screen is all that is left of its medieval furnishings and on the back of it inattentive choir boys in the 16th and 17th centuries have left interesting records of the sort of ships they would have seen on the 'Salthouse Mayne Channel' in their time. Salthouse has waged many battles against the sea and now much of the village lies in ruins after the most terrible inundation in all the many centuries of its history – on 31st January, 1953.

SAXTHORPE (St. Andrew)
14th cent. with early square tower.

SCOTTOW (All Saints)
17th-cent. organ case and reading desk.

SEETHING (St. Margaret)
Early round tower; wall-painting; seven-sacrament font.

SHELTON *(St. Mary)
Though of a very familiar and formal 15th-century East Anglian design this church has a character of its own, being built mostly of brick and it is somewhat of a shock to come across it at a turn in the road. This red church is in the middle of the Norfolk countryside. The W. tower is of the usual Norfolk flint.

SHERINGHAM, UPPER: see Upper Sheringham.

SNETTISHAM (St. Mary)
Medieval stone spire; W. Galilee porch.

SNORING, GREAT: see Great Snoring.

SOUTH ACRE *(St. George)
A gem. Nestling among the trees this lovely little church has recently received a careful and sympathetic restoration in which much of the old woodwork has been preserved.

SOUTH CREAKE *(St. Mary)
A splendid example of the spaciousness of a great East Anglian 15th-century church when all unworthy furnishings have been cleared away revealing the pillars of the arcades not, as is so often the case, struggling through a devastation of unsightly pewing, but coming right down to their bases which in this case have been widened for seats. Here one can see the nave of a big 15th-century church restored to much of its original appearance. A 15th-century pulpit still remains. (See Plate 15)

SOUTH LOPHAM (St. Andrew)
Norman central tower.

SPARHAM (St. Mary)
Screen panels showing cadavers (probably the donors) with St. Thomas of Canterbury and St. Walstan.

STODY *(St. Mary)
The most attractive of a group of three churches – Stody, St. Mary-in-Coslany, and St. Peter's, Hungate, Norwich, now a museum of ecclesiastical art – of a most unusual design and probably the work of one man. As at St. Mary-in-Coslany, Stody is a 15th-century cruciform church attached to an 11th-century W. tower, and the treatment of the roof at the crossing in all three cases is most remarkable. Arched beams taken right across from corner to corner intersecting with a large boss in the middle.

SWAFFHAM *(St. Peter & St. Paul)
Again an example of a great 15th-century church, very splendid without but a little disappointing within. The hammer-beam roof is magnificent, but the crowded pewing in the nave and poor furnishing of the chancel do much to detract from the very lovely proportions of the building. Swaffham is an 18th-century town with a wide Market Place in the centre of which stands a palladian Market Cross surmounted by a figure of Ceres holding a sheaf of corn.

SWANNINGTON (*St. Margaret*)
13th and 14th cent. nave arcades with
inset tower; well restored in 17th-cent.
manner with altar table of 1635.

SWANTON MORLEY (*All Saints*)
Spacious 14th–15th cent.; inset tower and
crypt at E. end of chancel.

SWARDESTON (*St. Mary*)
E. window by Bryans to Nurse Edith
Cavell.

TERRINGTON (*St. Clement*)
Largest in Marshland; detached bell
tower.

(*St. John*)
14th-cent. nave; box-pews; font cover,
1632.

THOMPSON (*St. Martin*)
14th-cent. W. tower and chancel.

THORPE MARKET *(St. Margaret*)
Built in 1795 this church is unquestionably
one of the best examples of the period in
Norfolk. It would be difficult to find a more
attractive church of the 'paste-board
scenery' type of Strawberry Hill gothic,
with two open-work screens at either end,
two 'gothick' porches, and four small
turrets at the corners. In the chancel are
memorials to the Rant family taken, it
seems, from the earlier church. The
romantic revival feeling is enhanced by the
way in which the church stands framed in
foliage at the end of a long avenue leading
towards Gunton Park.

THURNING *(St. Andrew*)
Just the nave remains and the N. aisle,
each bay of which contains a box-pew. The
wainscot work of these, and the three-
decker pulpit and three-sided Communion
rails came from the chapel of Corpus
Christi College, Cambridge, in 1825.

TIBENHAM *(All Saints*)
This church is especially remarkable for its
17th-century woodwork, especially the
great double-decker Buxton family pew in
the S. aisle erected in pursuance of a faculty
granted by Archbishop Laud in 1635.

TITTLESHALL *(St. Mary*)
The interest here is chiefly monumental
with the memorials to the Coke family,
among which is one of the finest of all
Nicholas Stone's effigies to Sir Edward
Coke, Lord Chief Justice (1634), and the
memorial for Lady Coke (1805) by
Nollekens.

TOFTS, WEST: *see West Tofts.*

TRUNCH *(St. Botolph*)
A beautiful 14th-century building. Hammer-beam roof with most elaborate
traceried spandrils. Most remarkable of all
is the font cover standing on carved posts
like the one at St. Peter Mancroft,
Norwich.

TUNSTEAD *(St. Mary*)
A 14th-century church which is full of
interest and at present undergoing a
thorough and careful restoration. A most
unusual feature is the extraordinary stone
platform at the E. end of the chancel
behind the altar.

UPPER SHERINGHAM (*All Saints*)
Screen; rood-loft and seating.

UPWELL *(St. Peter*)
This building is remarkable for the fact
that it was necessary to crowd even this
enormous 15th-century building with pews
in every available place; nave (where even
the central gangway is filled with benches),
aisles, and in the galleries. In the chancel
is a particularly delightful quadrangular
brass to Sinulphus Bell (1618) and Mrs.
Bell 'who never delayde by deeds and good
usage to give him content'. Fortunate Mr
Bell! In the churchyard are crowds of
exceedingly fine 18th-century headstones
beautifully preserved. Until fairly recently
visitors could travel from Upwell along the
banks of the river to Outwell and on to
Wisbech by means of what must now be
considered a venerable antiquity – a steam
tram. With the church towers, windmills,
and rows of houses flanking the river banks
Outwell and Upwell are typical fenland
villages and almost Dutch in appearance.
A landscape Hobbema might have painted.

WALPOLE (*St. Andrew*)
Jacobean pulpit; altar rails now the
balustrade to tower gallery.

(St. Peter)
Undoubtedly the finest church of the fens.
Other great churches of the 15th century
leave one spell-bound at their magnificence
as buildings, but here in addition it is the
number of things to see in the way of
furnishings which are so remarkable.
Especially of the post-reformation period
for which the Jacobean screen right across
the W. end and the 'sentry box' for the
protection of the clergyman officiating at
the grave-side in inclement weather,
require particular mention.

WALSINGHAM, GREAT: see Great Walsingham.

WALSINGHAM, LITTLE: see Little Walsingham.

WALTON, WESTON: see West Walton.

WARHAM *(St. Mary)

Enormous figures of Popes and Cardinals, Prophets and Kings in the rich and glowing Flemish glass (interspersed with fragments of English medieval) contrast a little oddly, and supply a blaze of colour in this church which though medieval really belongs to the 18th century. With its towering three-decker, box-pews, and 'bird-bath' font this is another 'Rowlandson' church and the spirit of the period is enhanced by the Royal Arms above the chancel arch, and the mouldering tomb house on the N. side of the chancel for the Turner family of King's Lynn who were the patrons of the famous local architect Henry Bell.

WELLINGHAM *(St. Andrew)

The church itself is in no way exceptional, but the base of the screen has panels (dated 1532) with some of the most lovely and best preserved medieval figure painting in Norfolk. St. Sebastian, St. Michael weighing the souls with Our Lady putting a rosary in the balance in favour of the departed, the Resurrection with the instruments of the Passion and Pilate vigorously washing his hands. But most remarkable of all is the very vivid picture of St. George slaying the dragon, so perfect in detail, with the princess leading her lamb and her parents, the King and Queen of Silene, looking on anxiously from one of the towers of the city, and so exactly similar is it, though much smaller, to the painting of St. George in St. Gregory's, Norwich, that it is impossible not to believe that if one man was not responsible for both, one of the pictures was inspired from the other or copied perhaps from the same illuminated illustration.

WEST ACRE *(All Saints)

Worked up in the 17th century from the priory church.

WEST DEREHAM (St. Andrew)

17th-cent. woodwork; memorials for Thomas Dereham, 1723, and Col. Edmund Soame, c. 1714, by R. Singleton of Bury.

WEST TOFTS (St. Mary)

Chancel restored by A. W. N. Pugin, who refitted the whole church.

WEST WALTON *(St. Mary)

For a large building of the 13th-century period this church is unsurpassed, certainly by any church in Norfolk with the exception perhaps of the W. front of Binham. But at West Walton one sees the glory of the 13th-century style in its completeness. The carving of the arcades is reminiscent of that of the same period in Lincoln Cathedral. A most remarkable detached bell tower standing 60 feet S. of the church. A 17th-century feature which has an interest for present-day East Anglia is the board on which is painted a prayer of thanksgiving for preservation from the dangers of floods.

WESTON LONGUEVILLE *(All Saints)

Parson Woodforde's church, but there is little that he would recognise apart from the 15th-century screen and the grand pew in the S. aisle for the Custance family. A most interesting 'Jesse Tree' wall painting in the N. aisle. Woodforde has a pleasing memorial in the chancel and there is a contemporary portrait of him, by his nephew Samuel Woodforde R.A., in the vestry.

WICKHAMPTON *(St. Andrew)

Stands in a bleak position overlooking the wide expanse of Breydon towards Yarmouth. Two early 14th-century tomb recesses with canopies in the chancel, but the church is most remarkable for the best of all the East Anglian examples of the wall-painting representing the Three Living and The Three Dead.

WICKMERE (St. Andrew)

14th–15th cent. well restored; modern table tomb and effigy by Esmond Burton for Lord Walpole.

THE WIGGENHALLS

The woodwork of these three churches is unsurpassed by many in Marshland.

*(St. German)

The bench-ends have especially vivid representations of the Seven Deadly Sins.

*(St. Mary Magdalene)

Much wonderful 15th-century glass.

*(St. Mary the Virgin)

A pre-Reformation lectern (1518) and in this church as well as St. German's are Jacobean pulpits with hour-glass stands.

WIGHTON (All Saints)

Large 14th cent. with earlier tower.

WITCHINGHAM, GREAT: *see Great Witchingham.*

WIVETON *(St. Mary)*

Though this church has the most horrible pewing, and glass in the nave which casts a mustardy hue over everything, one cannot but admire the lovely proportions of the building. The lofty nave arcades and the arcading of the aisle windows where the sills are lowered for seats – so common a feature in East Anglia. For a 15th-century church all of one period Wiveton is hard to beat and though not so magnificent as Salle it represents in the same way the highest achievement of the 15th-century style before it became formalised into the often rather too regular 'perpendicular' of the latter half of the century. Wiveton stands on the banks of the Glaven overlooking Cley. Two villages spreading along green meadows which until little more than a century ago were a navigable estuary. Just below the church is a high-arched 14th-century bridge on the road to Cley.

WOOD DALLING *(St. Andrew)*

15th-cent. wedge-shaped tower; E.E. chancel with lancets.

WORSTEAD *(St. Mary)*

One of the finest 'wool' churches of East Anglia. A typical and very lofty East Anglian rood-screen, the gift of John Arblaster in 1511. Like Brisley, it is a medley of 15th-century woodwork worked up into 18th-century seating. Beautiful W. tower from which the heavy Victorian pinnacles have been wisely removed, and the lofty font cover has recently received a careful restoration. As at Cawston there is an inscription along the front of the tower gallery. 'This werke was made in ye yer of God MCCCCCL at ye proper cost of ye benefactors of ye chyrch of Worstead callyd ye bachellers lyte yt God preserve wth all ye benefactors of ye same now and ever. Amen.' How wonderful of the 'bachellers' to make this beautiful thing in so uncertain a time in the history of the church as 1550!

WYMONDHAM *(St. Mary & St. Thomas of Canterbury)*

Norman arcades and triforium incased in wonderful 15th-century work rising to a lofty clerestory and one of the most beautiful of all the East Anglian hammer-beam roofs. The ruined tower at the E. end does not stand over the crossing of the former Abbey church, which in its glory must have ranked with Tewkesbury, Malmsbury and other great conventual churches of England, but two bays westward. As was often the case the sharing of the church by the parish caused endless difficulties and disputes between the monastery and the parishioners. The triumph for the monastery resulted in the central tower being placed westward into the parochial nave and the stone pulpitum being carried right up to the roof. Against this is Sir Ninian Comper's wonderful screen and tester, one of the most striking examples of all his beautiful work which has done much to revive this particularly lovely church which for all its parochial status is better considered among the Cathedrals and great monastic churches of the country. The N. aisle was rebuilt in the 15th century and also has a hammer-beam roof but the S. aisle is a little disappointing and was put together after the Reformation out of fragments of the conventual buildings only little of which remain. The extent of the choir can easily be traced in the churchyard to the east of the church, and the E. end of the Chapter House stands on the edge of the churchyard and alongside a sunk fence which in the early years of the 19th century was cut right through the site of the cloister!

YARMOUTH, GREAT: *see Great Yarmouth.*

Northamptonshire

INTRODUCTION

THE IMPRESSION made by Northamptonshire, a too little regarded county, is of an assured and beautiful use of stone for country houses, farms, cottages, outbuildings and above all for churches. Competent masonry has gone on since the middle ages. The county is on the limestone belt and the building stone varies from a pale silvery limestone to a deep-brown ironstone, with every shade of yellow and gold between. Medieval masons delighted to arrange the stone to give decorative effects to the outside of walls, as at Finedon, Irthlingborough and Woodford. Old roofs are tiled with stones graded from small at the ridge to large at the eaves on barns, manor houses and most old buildings, and of these stone tiles, the best are those known as Colleyweston slates which come from this county.

If ever the word 'steeple chasing' needed explanation, this is the county to describe what it means, for it abounds in steeples. Broach spires whose chamfered sides rise to a graceful point like a sharpened pencil from a tower which seems part of the same design as at Stanwick, crocketted spires of immense height as at Oundle and Higham Ferrers, dumpy spires which are almost pyramids, towers and spires in which it is hard to say which lends more grace to which as at Raunds and King's Sutton – these rise generally out of elms on hills and in valleys, so that not even the pylons and poles of our own age can quite extinguish their effect. There are few eminences in the pastoral parts of this mildly undulating country from which one can see less than three church spires. More times than not one finds clustered about the church an attractive stone-built village, though terrible havoc has been done in most of them by medical officers of health who would sooner pull down an old cottage than allow it to be enlarged and restored.

Norfolk has larger churches and grander woodwork, Somerset has more lacelike towers, but Northampton above all counties has variety and originality and elegance in its architecture, from the strange Saxon long- and short-work on the tower of Earls Barton to the stone octagonal lantern with its flying buttresses on the top of the late Perpendicular tower of Lowick. Northampton's medieval church builders seem to have been conscious architects and not mere builders. This quality in their church towers and spires, particularly in the 13th and 14th centuries, together with the fact that 'Early English' and 'Decorated' were regarded as pure and perfect respectively, made the spires of the east and north of the county and of S. Lincs, the model for Victorian church architects. So Northamptonshire spires may be seen rising out of the suburbs of London and other big cities and even over the roof tops of foreign and dominion capitals where there is an Anglican church.

Naturally, churches so deservedly popular with the Victorians came in for a good deal of 'restoration' at their hands. Many have been ruined internally by having the plaster stripped from their walls and the stone picked out in cement to give an 'ancient' effect, shiny tiles have replaced old stone or brick floors, and cheap pews and church furnishings have completed the devastation. We have listed here those medieval churches which are wholly or compara-tively unharmed by Victorians. But there is hardly a medieval church in the county which is without beautiful stonework somewhere, either in the many mouldings of an arch or in a lively piece of carving acting as capital, corbel or waterspout.

The county has suffered more than most in the South Midlands from 19th-century and modern industry. It was never grim, so that factories, pylons and power stations ill become its gentle landscape. The boot and shoe industry caused a rash of hard bright brick villas in the last century in Northampton itself, and Rushden, Wellingborough and Irthlingborough. But these villas are Midland-looking and have no affinities with London. In the present age great harm has been done to its loveliest scenery by the iron and steel industry whose huge dredgers pick their way like prehistoric animals over the farms, digging up the earth and raising mountains and bringing poles and wires and mineral lines in their trail. Recent legislation, however, has made restoration compulsory, and this is being done very well.

THE SOKE OF PETERBOROUGH

THE SOKE of Peterborough is independent of Northamptonshire though coloured the same on maps. In the east it is fen country, becoming hilly and wooded as it stretches westward to Stamford. Outside the limestone walls of this lovely Lincolnshire town stand the park and immense Elizabethan house of Burghley in the Soke. The Manor of Burghley and other lands in the Soke, (together with wide jurisdictional rights over the whole area) formerly belonged to the abbots of Peterborough, and were granted by Elizabeth I to her treasurer Lord Burghley. His descendant, the Marquess of Exeter, who is styled Lord Paramount of the Soke, still has his own court of Quarter Sessions, but his powers are now only nominal. Until 1812 this court had the right of hanging people. The Soke has its own separate county council and police force. The industrialised city of Peterborough is not half so dull as those who pass through it in the train or on the Great North Road may think. It is a grey town, grey limestone, lightish grey and grey-yellow brick. The west front of the Cathedral was described by Fergusson, that best of architectural critics, as 'the grandest and finest in Europe'. Norman nave and roof and the splendid 'New Building' in Perpendicular at the east end, the tree-shaded ramifications of the close, are all hidden from the main road, so is the excellent local museum.

The churches of the Soke and their villages are almost all in local limestone and with stone spires. Vestiges of Norman work in many of the churches recall the influence of the Benedictine Abbey.

J.B.

SELECTED LIST OF CHURCHES

by R. Stanley-Morgan, A.R.I.B.A., and Gyles Isham

ABINGTON (*St. Peter & St. Paul*) GR
Early 19th cent.

ALDWINKLE *(All Saints)*
Set in meadowland in a tree-shaded spreading stone village with two churches. All Saints has a striking 15th-century tower, pinnacled and delicately moulded. The church, with aisles and S. chapel, is disused and the first glimpse from the N. door shows how well a 13th and 14th century church can look without pews. The old plaster and floors remain and the old clear glass is in most of the windows, with a few pieces of medieval stained glass. The pillars and arcade are elegant.

APETHORPE *(St. Leonard)*
In a well-kept stone village with well-designed Edwardian and later cottages. Tower, aisles and S. chapel. Inside whitewashed, cut-down box-pews, 18th-century altar-piece and 18th-century glass of Last Supper above. In S. chapel Mildmay Monument, 1621, one of the most sumptuous in England, effigies lying under domed four-post bed in marble. Chapel decorated to match, with 1621 E. window, Dutch-style glass, blues and deep greens and pretty scene of Garden of Eden. Fane tablets in this chapel.

AYNHO *(St. Michael)*
A delightful settlement at the S. tip of county, characterised by the unfenced front gardens gracing the village street. The church retains a rich 15th-century tower but the body of the building was transformed in 1723, after the manner of Vanburgh, by a local carpenter-cum-architect,

Edward Wing. Wing's alterations are uncompromisingly domestic in style with windows in two storeys, and illustrate one of the phases of history of English churches which the Victorians tried to pretend had never existed.

BADBY (*St. Mary*)
Charming orchard village; 14th cent. on an eminence; tower, 18th-cent. Restoration.

BARNACK *(St. John the Baptist)*
A church with a Saxon core still evident in the base of the steeple and in the form of the tower arch and other details. The church has since acquired the characteristics of the succeeding centuries and so is typical of that inspired architectural hotch-potch which is the English Parish Church. The Barnack stone quarries fed the greatest of the medieval building projects in the Nene Valley and further afield.

BARTON, EARLS: *see Earls Barton.*

BENEFIELD (*St. Mary*) GR
Rood and reredos by Comper.

BRAMPTON ASH (*St. Mary*)
Unspoilt medieval work.

BRIGSTOCK (*St. Andrew*)
Saxon work.

BRINGTON, GREAT *(St. Mary*)
A good sober 13th-century church with the conventional arcades and small country church clerestory and with a modest 'English-type' timber ceiling. The canopied tomb of Sir John Spencer, 1522, is therefore of unexpected magnificence as are also the other Spencer monuments. The Perpendicular chancel is dark with recent stained glass which somewhat dims its glories.

BRIXWORTH *(All Saints)*
The church of this industrialised village has been described as 'probably the most impressive early Saxon building in the country'. This is not an exaggeration. Most of the surviving building dates from the end of the 7th century. Roman tiles were used by the Saxons for the abaci and the arches, otherwise they built in stone rubble. The suggestion that they adapted a Roman secular building to Christian use is nonsense, although it has sometimes been made. When the church was founded, the district had only just been Christianised and the narthex at the W. end of the church, part of which survives under the tower, was probably used for the instruction of the grown-up converts or catachumens. The church was monastic, a daughter house of Peterborough. It is possible that the church was extensively damaged in the Danish raids in the late 8th or early 9th century, and the church was rebuilt in the late 10th or early 11th century. Part of the existing sanctuary, and the circular turret with vaulted stair, was built against the tower at this time. An upper chamber was made in the tower to which this staircase gave access, and the chamber had a window made into the nave. This room was used, as at Earls Barton, by persons of 'distinction'. Various alterations took place in the Middle Ages and in the 14th century the belfry and spire were added. In the mid-19th century some of the medieval accretions were removed, including a 15th-century chancel. The early remains of the church were explored, and the apse restored on its old foundations. This work was fairly well done, but recent experimental efforts to restore the Saxon stonework have been less successful. These efforts have now ceased.

BUGBROOKE *(The Assumption or St. Mary)*
15th-cent. chancel screen.

BURTON LATIMER *(St. Mary the Virgin)*
12th–15th cent.; screen 15th cent.; wallpaintings 14th cent.

CARLTON, EAST: *see East Carlton.*

CASTOR *(St. Kyneburgha)*
The village, now a small one, stands near a Roman settlement and in Norman times was evidently still important, to judge by the fine tower of the period, crowned with a stumpy Germanic spire. Few Norman Cathedrals had a more richly-wrought steeple than this, with all four walls of the tower panelled in two stages of characteristic Romanesque detail. There are fragments of even older carving, both inside and outside and a pretty transept, once used as the village school.

CHIPPING WARDEN (*St. Peter & St. Paul*)
The principal parts are 15th-cent. work.

COTTESBROOKE *(All Saints)*
A secluded church in a hollow amongst Irish yews, not in itself remarkable, save for the extraordinary 17th-century Langham pew, in two storeys with fireplace, and the three-decker pulpit opposite. The other fittings, including the box-pews in the nave, have managed to survive the Gothic mania which attacked less lonely spots in the last century.

CRANSLEY (*St. Andrew*)
River setting; medieval church of various dates.

CRICK *(St. Margaret)*
Much Decorated work including an enriched steeple of the period.

CROUGHTON (*All Saints*)
Medieval furnishings and wall-painting.

DAVENTRY *(Holy Cross)*
There are some charming Georgian streets in this town, in keeping with a typical mid-18th-century church by David Hiorn of Warwick, after models provided by the works of Flitcroft and Gibbs in London and Derby. There is a gallery in each aisle peeping behind the Tuscan columns. The plaster vault springs from a heavy abacus at the head of each of these columns, which are in reality wooden casings of stone piers. There is no portico outside but a bulky tower surmounted by a 'rather gouty Georgian finger pointing the way to Heaven' as Marcus Whiffen calls the steeple.

EARLS BARTON *(All Saints)*
No student of English architecture is allowed to be unaware for long that Earls Barton's tower is Saxon, and an outstanding example of their robust but repulsive surface decoration, and of long-and-short work at the quoins. This fortress-like tower, nevertheless, gives a strong feeling of solidity and permanence. This is a church built by the local lord, thoroughly

secular in character and with no monastic associations such as Brixworth had. It contrasts with the overgrown industrialised village, largely of red-brick homes. The plastered face of the tower is in agreeable contrast too with the coursed rubble of the rest of the building, just as the tiny Saxon openings contrast with the characteristic Northants ogee windows of the aisles. Later work includes a good Norman entrance door, a 15th-century screen and a mid-17th-century tower clock. You can light up the chancel by putting sixpence in the slot-meter.

EAST CARLTON (*St. Peter*) CL
Classical features including box-pews.

EASTON MAUDIT (*St. Peter & St. Paul*)
Monuments and a steeple with flying buttresses.

EASTON NESTON *(St. Mary the Virgin)*
Fittings and monuments of classical character; box pews. Hatchments.

ETTON (*St. Stephen*) GR
1874 rebuilt.

EVENLY (*St. George*) GR
Rebuilt 1864. Good village and setting.

FAWSLEY (*St. Mary*)
In park; Knightley monuments.

FINEDON *(St. Mary)* and RUSHDEN *(St. Mary)*
Two churches either side of Higham Ferrers with many features in common, the most curious a strainer or relieving arch across the nave in front of the chancel. There may have been a structural reason for this in one case, but hardly in both! Each church has a modest W. steeple, a porch at the S.W. corner and transepts. The windows are sober yet elegant. Ironstone gives a rich texture to the exteriors.

FOTHERINGAY *(St. Mary & All Saints)*
A charming village with a fine old inn. The fragment of a great 15th-century collegiate church of which only the nave remains, in itself an impressive landmark to this part of the Nene Valley, with flying buttresses and a great deal of glass. The great octagonal lantern is such as Wyatt must have dreamed of when working on his Gothic skyscraper tower at Fonthill Abbey. The base of the tower at Fotheringay opens three ways into the body of the church and is fan-vaulted. Inside, the 18th-century fittings include an attractive reredos with decalogue, creed,

etc. in gold after the fashion of the time. The early 16th-century pulpit and Perpendicular font are noteworthy. (*See Plate 19*)

GEDDINGTON (*St. Mary Magdalene*)
Medieval work; Eleanor Cross in village. (*See Plate 17*)

GREAT HOUGHTON (*St. Mary*) CL
1754, but altered.

GRETTON (*St. James the Great*)
Box-pews and pulpit, etc.; good setting.

HARTWELL (*St. John the Baptist*)
In Norman style; 19th cent.

HIGHAM FERRERS *(St. Mary)*
An old limestone town in which a narrow side street gives the first view of the rich crocketed steeple with its pierced parapet, flying buttresses and deep Early English mouldings. The 13th-century W. tower of the church has a carved doorway reminiscent of the style of Westminster Abbey, *c.* 1260. Inside, the church is a double building, that on the S. being 13th century and that on the N. 14th century. There is much good carved woodwork, old and modern, the latter by Comper. In 1362 Henry Chichele, Archbishop and founder of All Souls College, Oxford, was born here and built Chichele College (1422) and on the S. side of the churchyard the Bede House (1423) with its Infirmary Hall and chapel at the E. end, gave the stalls and the choir-screen to the church and endowed the Grammar School W. of the church toward the end of his life. This is luscious and beautiful Perpendicular with undercut mouldings and windows increased to reduce the flat wall-surface to a minimum.

HOUGHTON, GREAT: *see Great Houghton.*

IRTHLINGBOROUGH *(St. Peter)*
One of the boot and shoe towns of Northants but wedded to the country tradition, it retains a market cross and a great bridge across the Nene, as well as the medieval church. The tower is practically divorced from the rest of the building and, with its octagonal lantern, is reminiscent of a lighthouse.

KETTERING *(St. Peter & St. Paul)*
The steeple, soaring above the busy town, is visible from the railway and so is justly famed. This tower and spire are from the same school of design as Oundle and while the treatment is more restrained, the

K

silhouette is probably more satisfying. The body of the church is long and low by comparison: clean horizontal lines at the eaves without pinnacles and the lead roofs and Barnack limestone blend well together. Do not miss the elaborate Montagu tombs from 16th and 17th centuries.

KING'S SUTTON *(St. Peter)
Near the Oxfordshire border and visible from the Western Region railway line, this spire is more famous than most. Richly ornamented and rising 100 ft. above the flying buttresses at its base, it is hardly surpassed in the county in its soaring grace. It cannot be expected that the rest of the church should reach the same standard but there is interest for the student of 19th-century work in the chancel and screen by Scott, one of whose problems was the incorporation of a new organ into the ancient church.

LOWICK *(St. Peter)
A small village, its glory evidently departed save for the 15th-century church, with a pinnacled lantern tower, dominating the group, which takes in transepts and double chancel. Survivals from the Middle Ages include some extensive glass fragments of the 14th century and the remarkable effigies on the monuments of the Greenes, who were Lords of the Manor of Drayton. Among the later sculpture is a Westmacott work of 1843 commemorating the 5th Duke of Dorset.

MARSTON TRUSSELL (St. Nicholas)
18th-cent. pulpit, etc.

MIDDLETON CHENEY (All Saints)
Perp. spire above thatched village.

NASSINGTON *(St. Mary the Virgin & All Saints)
A rich 14th-century crocketted steeple.

NORTHAMPTON *(All Saints)
Only the tower survives of the much larger medieval church. The rebuilding after a fire in 1675 is ascribed to Henry Bell of King's Lynn. The domed classic interior owes something to Wren's St. Mary-at-hill in the City of London, but it is a homely provincial version, much 'restored' in the 1860's and later by Scott.

*(Holy Sepulchre)
Opinions may differ as to which is the most beautiful church in the town, but this is certainly the most curious – one of the five surviving round churches in England, owing its character and its dedication to the inspiration of the Crusaders. The round part of the church is the original nave, dating from the early 12th century, while the present nave was added a half century later and formed the choir to which aisles were added during the next two centuries. The result is a disjointed exterior, but the interior has the peculiar fascination that belongs to any rarity. The clerestory is a 15th-century rebuild, but the columns supporting it remain the old Norman fashion. The present chancel and all the outer walls except the round part and the S. aisle are 19th-century work (Gilbert Scott).

(St. Lawrence) GR
Impressive E.E. red brick by Burden and Baker; late Victorian.

(St. Mary) GR
By Holding; stone-vaulted interior.

(St. Matthew) GR
By Holding, in the manner of J. L. Pearson.

*(St. Peter)
Predominently Norman in style, this church has a rich arcade, aisles rebuilt in the 14th century and chancel arches. The stocky tower was rebuilt in the 17th century and has cut into the symmetrical Norman arcade; it is itself adorned with Romanesque arcading. The chancel is a weak invention of Scott, in whose time the church was smartened up to suit the conventions of the 19th century.

ORLINGBURY (St. Mary) GR
Good village; 19th-cent. church.

OUNDLE (Jesus Church) GR
Arthur Blomfield, 1879.

*(St. Peter)
The small unspoilt town of stone and slate is a natural centre for the northern parishes of Northants, though little known outside except for the famous school. The church large and opulent, its chiefest glory is in its steeple – a true piece of architecture, with the massive surfaces of the tower panelled vertically to carry the eye to the spire above. The composition of the church, with transepts and deep S. porch is of picturesque massing – as in other Northants churches selected, there is an intriguing medieval pulpit. The interior spoilt by scraping and repainting the masonry.

OVERSTONE (St. Nicholas) GR
Neat Gothic church of George III's reign; box-pews.

PETERBOROUGH (*All Saints*) GR
By Temple Moore; 19th cent.

PLUMPTON (*St. John the Baptist*) GR
Remote stone hamlet.

POLEBROOKE (*All Saints*)
One of the best 13th-cent. broach spires.

RAUNDS (*St. Peter*)
Good early broach spire; wall-paintings.

ROCKINGHAM *(*St. Leonard*)
The wide village street climbs up from the
Welland to Rockingham Castle with thatch
and stone cottages set against wooded
background. The church is a 19th-century
rebuild but preserves the 17th and 18th
century Watson monuments and a piece of
carving by James Paine. The memorial by
William Palmer to Margaret Watson is one
of the few Baroque monuments by an
English sculptor.

ROTHWELL (*Holy Trinity*)
Large; cruciform; mainly 13th cent.

STAMFORD (*St. Martin Without*)
Stately late 15th cent.; rich Cecil monu-
ments, the most splendid being that of Lord
Treasurer Burghley.

STANFORD-ON-AVON *(*St. Nicholas*)
A light and spacious church with the nave
cleared of pews, and hatchments used
intelligently as decoration, but most remarkable for the 17th-century organ-case
and its discreet W. gallery. The monuments
of the Cave family have been well restored.
Archbishop Laud was once rector here.

STANWICK (*St. John the Baptist*)
Lofty Nene Valley spire on an octagonal
tower; 13th cent.

STEANE *(*St. Peter*)
A quaint little 17th-century chapel set in
the Great Park and raised in 1620 by Sir
Thomas Crewe; it appears at a quick
glance to be complete with buttresses,
pinnacles and all the authentic signs of the
Middle Ages but is approached from the
road between a formal avenue of trees.
Services are held here only once or twice a
year, the village, Hinton-in-the-Hedges,
having its own Norman church. Steane is
remarkable inside for the box-pews and
two-decker pulpit left behind by the Age of
Reason. There are 17th- and 18th-century
monuments to the Crewe family on the N.
side of this tiny building, which is equally
divided by an arcade of two bays only.

STOKE DOYLE *(*St. Rumbald*)
A rustic Georgian church by an unknown
artist, retaining pulpit, pews and font of
the 18th century. Contemporary monuments, including a Rysbrack, sustain the
atmosphere of the time.

STOWE NINE CHURCHES (*St. Peter &
St. Paul*)
Good stone village; the church an assembly
of many periods from the Saxons onwards.

SULGRAVE (*St. James*)
Washington pilgrims should visit. Compact medieval village church.

SUTTON, KING'S: *see King's Sutton.*

THORNHAUGH (*St. Andrew*) GR
Norman and E.E. well restored Micklethwaite, 1889. Monument early 17th cent.

TICHMARSH *(*St. Mary the Virgin*)
A quaint unspoilt village with 16th-century
almshouses. The church remarkable for a
noble Perpendicular tower, curiously West
Country in character, with coupled windows in the upper storey and the pinnacles
rich and profuse. The Pickering family pew
is a 17th-century curiosity, sited above the
porch. Dryden was bred here and loved to
return in after years.

WARKTON (*St. Edmund*)
Fine Perp. tower; Montagu monuments by
Roubiliac, van Gelder and Campell.

WARMINGTON *(*St. Mary*)
With one of the justly famous Northants
broach spires, this church is a consistent
Early English structure. The ribbed-vaulted
nave ceiling is in timber throughout and is
a pleasant medieval conceit. It was a useful
precedent for those Victorians who wanted
boarded ceilings for cheapness: the woodwork including the rood, a painted pulpit
and some old benches, is 14th century with
the addition of a good Jacobean screen to
the N. chapel.

WELDON (*St. Mary the Virgin*)
18th-cent. tower with cupola on medieval
nave.

WELLINGBOROUGH (*All Saints*)
The old church of the town; 600 years old
in part.

(*St. Barnabas*) GR
Victorian town church.

*(*St. Mary*)
Comper's 20th century answer to the
challenge of the incomparable Nene Valley

churches is a tall Perpendicular fan-vaulted building. There is a bold tower, contrasting on the skyline with the spire of the medieval church but utilising the same traditional ironstone. The fittings are sumptuous with a good deal of colour and a characteristically forceful rood. (*See Plate 64*)

WHISTON *(St. Mary the Virgin)*
The church pleasantly sited on a wooded hillside. The tower a heady design from the early 16th century with the stone dressings and parapet light in contrast to the dark facing of the rest of the tower. The rest of the building sober by comparison, with characteristic timber ceilings and the ample Perpendicular windows of the time. The plan is box-like without a structural chancel. Fittings include some original benches, and classical monumental sculpture by Nollekens.

WHITTLEBURY *(St. Mary)*
A characteristic village setting; 13th cent.; stumpy broach spire; chantry sculpture inside.

WICKEN *(St. John the Evangelist)* GR
Mid-18th-cent. Gothic by T. Prowse; plaster fan-vault; thatched village.

WITTERING *(All Saints)*
Late Saxon work inside and out.

WILBARSTON *(All Saints)* GR
Victorian additions by Bodley.

Northumberland

INTRODUCTION

THE LAST seaward miles of Tyne and Tweed, Cheviot and Pennine tops, a seventy-mile-long stretch of coast – and, within them, the most northerly county of England; Northumberland. In the south-eastern corner a tangle of heavy industry, coalmining, shipbuilding, engineering: a conurbation: sullen, soiled and sordid, but containing, nevertheless, England's finest industrial city, the provincial capital, Newcastle. The industrial area less than a tenth of the county, yet carrying 80 per cent of its population; and the county, even so, one of the least populous of all in relation to its size – which gives some indication of how quiet the rest is. It is by far the largest tract of deeply quiet country in England. Outside the industrial corner, only three small country towns, less than half a dozen villages, and the rest of the population in scattered hamlets and in farmhouses and cottages. The coast lined by golden sands, sand dunes, basalt cliffs, with rocky islands off-shore. The coastal plain, where the main-line railway goes to Scotland, stock-rearing and mixed-farming country. The hills (and all over the county you are conscious of the hills) high, wide and lonely; not whale-backed and heathery (except the Pennines in the south-west) but mostly grassy hills, pitching into individual summits. The richly-wooded valley of the Tyne in the gap between Cheviots and Pennines: narrower dales running up into the folds of the hills. A great national forest making a new kind of country out of the mid-stretch of Cheviot. A very varied county: a very individual county.

Its history and frontier-feeling character are shown, inevitably, in its old buildings. In the Roman wall striding along the top of the crags above the waters of dark loughs. In scores of castles and peel-towers, vast like Alnwick, small like Holy Island, ruined like Simonburn: in fortified rectories, as at Corbridge and Elsdon: and in semi-fortified churches, too, as at Edlington. And in what has gone as well as in what remains. Bolam church, with its Saxon tower, standing in complete solitude where once was a town with a castle and 'two-hundred slated houses enclosing a green'. Bywell, also once a flourishing town, with, now, *two* churches, a castle, a medieval market cross, a hall, a vicarage, all in a wooded loop of the Tyne, and not another building in sight.

Old, wild, wide, quiet, remote. That is the Northumberland beyond the conurbation.

THOMAS SHARP

293

SELECTED LIST OF CHURCHES

by L. C. Evetts

ALNHAM (*St. Michael*)
12th-cent. work; font, 1664.

ALNWICK *(*St. Michael & All Angels*)
Beautifully situated on the top of a hillside.
The church embodies the most important
15th-century work in Northumberland.
Aisles extend to total length of chancel,
thus forming a plan rather square in
character. 14th-century effigies of great
beauty. 15th-century fragments of glass,
including a delightful example of a Pelican
in her Piety. Royal Arms, painted, first
Hanoverian period.

ALWINTON (*St. Michael & All Angels*)
13th cent.; chancel raised above nave by
sloping site.

ANCROFT (*St. Anne*)
Norman with a 'Vicar's Pele', i.e. a 14th-
cent. fortified tower built into W. end.

BAMBURGH *(*St. Aidan*)
Spacious setting on coast. 13th, 14th and
15th century structure. A fine 13th-century
crypt beneath chancel. The architectural
character of the interior is marred by very
inferior stained glass of the 19th century.
There is one good window, 20th century, by
Ballantine of Edinburgh. Royal Arms
painted on canvas, third Hanoverian
period. Burial place of Grace Darling.

BELLINGHAM (*St. Cuthbert*)
Small, towerless; fine 13th-cent. chancel,
barrel-vaulted; remodelled, 1609; whitewashed interior.

BELTINGHAM (*St. Cuthbert*)
Small Perp. Tudor building.

BERWICK (*Holy Trinity*)
A mixed Gothic and Classical building of
considerable architectural interest. It was
built during the Commonwealth. Internally
its character is somewhat spoiled by the
introduction of stained glass in the 19th
century which is of a Gothic style. The
lettering on one or two small brass plates
of 18th-century date is worth noting.

BIRTLEY (*St. Giles*)
Small; aisleless, *c.* 1200; pre-Conquest
incised stone.

BLANCHLAND *(*St. Mary the Virgin*)
Premonstratensian foundation. Massive
13th-century stonework in what was N.
transept of Abbey Church. Pretentious
19th-century woodwork. Fragments of late
medieval glass, some of which are in a
window of adjoining inn. Monumental
slabs. Rare churchyard cross. Beautiful
village largely rebuilt in the 18th century
consistent in form and materials. Stone
walls and roofs now mellowed in colour by
oxidation and lichen.

BOLAM *(*St. Andrew*)
Pre-Conquest tower of lovely proportion.
Much Norman work. Mutilated recumbent
effigy of knight, 14th century. Plain lead
glazing of beautiful character, 19th and
20th centuries. The setting, like the church
itself, is one of the most pleasant in
Northumberland. Although situated in the
midst of undulating parkland the church
was, almost within the span of living
memory, a part of a village renowned for
its saddlery. The village and the craft have
disappeared.

BOTHAL *(*St. Andrew*)
13th and 14th century structure in a most
beautiful setting. Extensive fragments of
medieval glass *in situ*: one tracery light contains a magnificent rayed rose. Good 17th-
century altar rails. Alabaster table-tomb of
Ralph, Lord Ogle and his lady, 16th century. Good 18th-century headstones in
churchyard.

BRANXTON (*St. Paul*)
Norman chancel arch.

BRINKBURN *(*Priory Church of St.
Peter & St. Paul*)
Augustinian foundation, set near the banks
of the Coquet in wooded countryside.
Complete late 12th-century structure well
restored by Thomas Austin in 1858. Long

lancet windows. Fragments of 13th-century grisaille glass, similar in character to York work. The mill-race still flows near by.

BYWELL *(St. Andrew & St. Peter)*
Two parish churches sited closely together in beautiful wooded setting near River Tyne. St. Andrew has pre-Conquest tower. St. Peter has splendid E. window of three lancets.

CHILLINGHAM *(St. Peter)*
Sited on gentle elevation sheltered from the North. Simple stone church dating from the 12th century. Chief interest lies in magnificent 15th-century Grey tomb. Font and cover 1670; 17th-century pulpit.

CHIPCHASE *(dedication unknown)* CL
18th-cent. chapel with contemporary pulpit.

CHOLLERTON *(St. Giles)*
Roman monolithic columns; 12th-cent. S. arcade.

CORBRIDGE *(St. Andrew)*
Characteristic Northumbrian country town built of stone. Main body of church 13th century. Good lancet windows. Pre-Conquest tower with stilted tower arch of simple masonry.

CORSENSIDE *(St. Cuthbert)*
Remote moorland setting; small Norman undecorated structure.

CULLERCOATS *(St. George)*
Beautiful church by J. L. Pearson, 1884. Built in the 'Early English' style but quite original in structure. Ashlar stonework. Very dignified interior. Glass in clerestory of apse by Kempe, in strong range of colour.

DODDINGTON *(St. Mary & St. Michael)*
13th cent.; much restored.

EARSDON *(St. Alban)* CL
1836–7, by J. and B. Green; dominating position; some heraldic glass from Hampton Court.

EDLINGHAM *(St. John Baptist)*
Medieval and 16th–17th cent.

EGLINGHAM *(St. Maurice)*
13th-cent. work amongst much post-medieval.

ELSDON *(St. Cuthbert)*
Bare Northumbrian village built around a large green. Church of rubble stonework of 12th and 14th century date. Very fine

renaissance tablet affixed to a column in the nave. Plain lead glazing of good character, particularly E. window which looks out on a beautiful tree.

EMBLETON *(Holy Trinity)*
13th-cent. nave arcades; medieval tower of good design; fortified vicarage.

ETAL *(St. Mary the Virgin)* GR
1858, by W. Butterfield.

FELTON *(St. Michael & All Angels)*
13th–14th cent. structure; 15th-cent. nave roof.

FORD *(St. Michael & All Angels)*
13th cent.; beautiful open countryside.

GOSFORTH *(All Saints)* GR
1887, by R. J. Johnson.

(St. Nicholas) CL
1799, by John Dodds.

HALTON *(dedication unknown)*
Norman chancel arch; rest mainly early 18th cent.

HALTWHISTLE *(Church of the Holy Cross)*
Towerless church in pleasant setting on slope in the midst of this country town. Entire main structure of 13th century. Irregular masonry in stone containing a considerable amount of iron. Plastered interior, consistent and pleasing. Stepped sedilia. Medieval monuments, including Blenkinsopp effigy, c. 1389. Massive 18th-century headstones in churchyard.

HARTBURN *(St. Andrew)*
In delightful setting near the Hart burn. 13th-century structure with later rebuilding. Nave floor slopes down towards E. Long chancel. 13th-century font. Many excellent 18th-century headstones in churchyard.

HAYDON BRIDGE *(St. Cuthbert)*
Medieval work remaining; font made from Roman altar.

HEDDON ON THE WALL *(St. Andrew)*
Built on hillock quite close to the Roman Wall. Very complete church of early work. Vaulted sanctuary 12th century. Interesting 'long and short' work. Fine zig-zag chancel arch.

HEXHAM *(St. Andrew)*
Of great historical importance as foundations of Wilfrid's church of the 7th century survive. Roman dressed stones used in structure. Barrel-vaulted crypt of great

austerity and grandeur, on the stones of which can be seen some Roman inscriptions. Chancel late 12th century. Transepts 13th century. Unique survival of night staircase. Nave by Temple Moore in 1908. Pre-Conquest Frith stool. 15th-century wooden pulpit. Painted screen, Thomas Smithson, prior, 1491–1524. Stalls and misericords 15th century. Chantry chapel and effigy of Prior Leschman. Many effigies. Royal Arms, painted, first Hanoverian period.

HOLY ISLAND (*St. Mary the Virgin*)
Late 13th cent.; long chancel and bell-cote; rebuilt, 18th cent.

HOUGHTON, LONG: *see Long Houghton.*

HOWICK (*St. Michael*) CL
1746; Normanized, 1849.

INGRAM (*St. Michael*)
Early medieval; 17th-cent. font.

KIRKHARLE (*St. Wilfred*)
14th cent.; heraldic font, 15th cent.

KIRKHAUGH (*Holy Paraclete*) GR
1868–9; designed by the Vicar, the Rev. Octavius James.

KIRKNEWTON *(St. Gregory)*
Set at the foot of hill country near Cheviot. Small low chancel of early date with unusual vault which springs a few feet from the floor to a rounded point at apex; beautiful stone carving on N. side of chancel arch depicting Adoration of the Magi, which, on iconographical grounds antedates medieval types.

KIRKWHELPINGTON *(St. Bartholomew)*
Set in small village at the foot of vast moorland. Originally cruciform. Good 12th and early 13th century work remaining in N. tower and S. porch. Nave of rubble stonework. Chancel of 18th century with plastered walls and ceiling, sash glazing. Splendid lettering on 18th-century ledgers in chancel floor.

LONG FRAMLINGTON (*St. Mary the Virgin*)
Late 12th-cent. nave and chancel.

LONG HOUGHTON (*St. Peter*)
Chancel arch dates about time of Conquest; S. aisle, *c.* 1200.

MITFORD *(St. Mary Magdalene)*
Church in lovely setting near ruined castle.

12th-century nave of massive stonework. Long and distinguished 13th-century chancel.

MORPETH (*St. James*)
By B. Ferrey, 1843–6; neo-Norman.

(St. Mary the Virgin)
A good example of 14th-century work so little seen in Northumberland. The E. window depicting Tree of Jesse with scenes from the life of Our Lady in the tracery lights represents the most complete medieval glazing in the county, though not escaping the hands of the 19th-century restorer. There are other fragments of medieval glass.

NEWBIGGIN (*St. Bartholomew*)
Now perilously near the sea due to eroding coast; 13th cent.; later medieval work; Royal Arms, painted, first Hanoverian period.

NEWBURN *(St. Michael & All Angels)*
Beautiful church of rubble stonework now happily stripped of a good deal of its 19th-century fussiness but still plastered. Norman tower. N. aisle early 12th century, circular arches. S. aisle, 13th century.

NEWCASTLE (*St. Aidan*) GR
Fine structure in medieval style by Messrs. Hicks and Charlewood, 1888–9, a feature of whose work is unity of design achieved by omission of a chancel arch.

(All Saints)
Elliptical 18th-century auditory church by David Stephenson. Contemporary radial pewing in mahogany. Unusual placing of the clerk's seat. Thornton brass, 15th century. Two windows containing 18th-century painted and enamelled glass. Impressive city church virtually bereft of its parish.

(St. Andrew)
12th-century chancel arch and nave arcading. 15th-century unpainted font cover of elaborate design. Early Georgian S. porch. Royal Arms, carved and painted, third Hanoverian period, of most skilful design. Walls now stripped of their plaster but likely to be replastered in the future.

(St. Ann)
Rectangular 18th-century church with apse. Colonnaded portico at W. Contemporary painting shows church of light stonework against background of green fields; now black encompassed by mass of houses and industry.

*(St. John the Baptist)
Medieval church. Font cover 15th century. Impressive 17th-century pulpit. Fragments of medieval glass, chief among them a 14th-century shield of arms of Newcastle. How many cities may boast a 14th-century record of their arms? Also 15th-century shields of Thornton and Percy in glass.

(St. Matthew) GR
By R. J. Johnson, c. 1900; Bodleyesque Perp.

*(St. Nicholas)
One of the great parish churches of England, now the Cathedral, with a wonderful lantern tower of the 15th century. The body of the church is chiefly 14th century. Heraldic font and cover, 15th century. Monuments 17th century. Organ-case late 17th century. Roundel of 15th-century glass, depicting Virgin and Child, probably work of York school. Royal Arms, carved and painted, Temp. Charles II.

NORHAM *(St. Cuthbert)
Imposing small town formed of rows of cottages dominated by a magnificent castle. Church of reddish stone has a Norman chancel and arch, and S. arcade. Massive stonework for a church of this scale. 14th-century effigy. Royal Arms, carved, unpainted, Stuart.

OLD BEWICK *(Chapel of the Holy Trinity)
Set in remote and beautiful hill country in the North part of the county. Small Norman apsidal chancel and nave, relatively complete.

OVINGHAM *(St. Mary the Virgin)
The village has little architectural beauty other than that provided by its magnificent church and delightful vicarage dating from the 15th and 17th centuries. The church has a pre-Conquest tower and a 13th-century nave, transepts and chancel. The interior, with its plastered walls, high columns, and long lancet windows gives one the impression of immense vertical strength. Royal Arms; painted, second Hanoverian period.

PONTELAND *(St. Mary the Virgin)
12th-century work in tower. 13th-century N. transept of great individual character with long lancets deeply splayed. 14th-century windows in chancel containing many fragments of contemporary glass, chiefly heraldic. Beautiful undecorated

14th-century font. Royal Arms, painted, third Hanoverian period. Plain lead glazing of great beauty, c. 1861.

ROCK *(St. Philip & St. James)
In parkland setting, so well recorded in the drawings of David Jones, 1932. Small Norman church, rather suffering from 19th-century addition.

ROTHBURY (All Saints)
Delightful Northumbrian township set amongst hills; medieval features in church, but much restoration; chancels and transept 13th cent.; part of early cross.

ST. OSWALD-IN-LEE (St. Oswald) CL
Chapel of 1737; Gothicised, 1878; moving view over bare hills to N. Here St. Oswald won the decisive battle of Heavenfield (635) against the heathen Britons.

SEATON DELAVAL *(Our Lady)
Set in grounds of Vanburgh's house. Small Norman church of great beauty. Delaval effigies, 14th century. Eight medieval stone shields of arms of outstanding merit.

SIMONBURN *(St. Mungo)
Set in a beautiful village in the North Tyne Valley in an enormous parish containing a vast area of moorland. Church dates from 13th century. Double piscina. Numerous fragments of early stonework. 17th-century monument to Cuthbert Ridley, rector.

STAMFORDHAM (St. Mary the Virgin)
13th cent.; medieval effigies and 14th-cent. carving of crucifixion; carved shield of arms in porch.

THOCKRINGTON (St. Aidan)
Small Norman church with medieval alterations set on hillock in open sweeping country; chancel of exquisite proportion in plain masonry, with vaulted ceiling.

TYNEMOUTH *(Christ Church)
18th-century structure in ashlar stonework, with plastered interior. Its beauty was concealed somewhat by 19th-century furnishings and memorials which have for the most part been removed. The original font of wood has been reinstated, and many windows of dreary stained glass have been replaced by plain windows with their leading based on the traditional Northumbrian pattern. Organ now in W. gallery.

WARDEN (St. Michael & All Angels)
11th-cent. tower; 13th-cent. transepts.

WARKWORTH *(St. Lawrence)
Church and castle set at opposite ends of a

long broad street. Norman chancel arch, vaulted chancel 12th century. 15th-century porch with room above. Exquisite wrought-iron rails, 17th century. Fragments of 15th-century glass, small figures and badges. Royal Arms, painted, *Temp.* James II.

WHALTON *(St. Mary Magdalene)*
Very long village on S. slope of hillside. Norman work in tower and tower arch. 12th-century nave and chancel. Royal Arms, painted, second Hanoverian period.

WHITTINGHAM *(St. Bartholomew)*
Pre-Conquest work in tower. Plain massive arch of tower towards nave. Medieval work elsewhere much altered. Plain lead glazing best of 19th-century redecoration.

WIDDRINGTON *(Holy Trinity)*
Embodies 14th-cent. work; N. arcade late 12th cent.

WOODHORN *(St. Mary the Virgin)*
A church with considerable archaeological interest but the expansion of industry has spoiled its environment. 11th, 12th and 13th centuries. Spacious light chancel. Beautiful stone effigy of lady, 13th century. Royal Arms, painted, Victorian.

Nottinghamshire

INTRODUCTION

NOTTINGHAMSHIRE SOUTH of the Trent, along the Foss Way, is of a piece with Leicestershire, with gentle hills, ridged meadows and bramble and dog-rose hedges; many of the villages here have shrunk during the past two centuries, and some of the churches have been shorn of aisles. The western part of the county lies on coal and is well populated; some of the colliery villages are nicely grouped on hilltops round new or enlarged churches, but in the main the scenery is unattractive apart from a few square miles in the upper Erewash valley and the pure medieval landscape which contains the ruins of Beauvale Priory. On the limestone of the north-west both buildings and landscape are more austere, with dry stone walls in the Derbyshire manner and even a quite precipitous gorge at Creswell Crags. The mining settlements to the north of Worksop are scarcely distinguishable from their neighbours in the West Riding. The 'Carrs' of the north-east are rich fens. In the east, along the Lincolnshire border, the Trent flows through a fairly rich mixed agricultural landscape which is dominated by the distant west front of Lincoln Cathedral and enlivened by the Great North Road and its attendant railway; the houses here are of good brick and many of them are roofed with pantiles. Two enormous electricity works have been put here, heated by coal from the west of the county and cooled by Trent water; more are to come. The one near Newark has earned its architect a prize, but the new industrial haze is beginning to shorten the view in this open landscape and to alter the quality of the light. The centre of the county, between Mansfield, Worksop and Tuxford, presents a curious contrast between the intense vitality of the new colliery villages and the air of death which hangs about the last oaks of Sherwood Forest and the few remaining great houses of the Dukeries.

In its landscape and in the character and dialect of its people Nottinghamshire belongs partly to the Midlands and partly to the North. What unity it has comes from the county town, whose undisputed supremacy within the county borders, since the time when they were the boundaries of a Danish military district, contrasts markedly with the far shakier authority of its neighbours, Lincoln, Derby, and York. The wise men of Gotham still sell their cheeses in Nottingham; and the city's cattle market, the agricultural shows at Wollaton Park and the annual Goose Fair still bring in the country folk from the whole of the southern half of the county. It is, of course, an industrial town; but most of its industries are of the kind which make no smoke and which occupy enormous numbers of young women. Most of the county's men are employed in the collieries to the north-east, and hundreds of buses cross the city's north-eastern boundary each weekday in each direction. The small towns of the north, Mansfield, Sutton, Worksop and Retford, play a similar role in the life of the county; but they are infinitely poorer than Nottingham, both in their architecture and in their entertainments. Newark, in the south-east, is a wholly admirable town; it cooks good food and brews good beer for travellers on the Great North Road; its castle and its Civil War fortifications are impressive; and its market-place deserves a book to itself.

There are few large churches in the county. Southwell Minster is, of course, in a class of its own, and the only two parish churches of impressive size are St. Mary, Nottingham, and St. Mary Magdalene, Newark. Worksop and Blyth are in the separate category of 'monastic remains' and are easily the two finest churches in the north of the county. The small churches are often well-sited and the Nottinghamshire village of red-brick and pantiled cottages grouped round its grey church makes an attractive picture. Spires punctuate the rolling landscape south of the Trent, but in the north the medieval churches are normally low-towered, squat and rather square. There are no grand and urbane classical churches of the Derby Cathedral type, but merely a few quite good 18th-century rectangles, put up to replace, as modestly as possible, decayed medieval structures. But there are three examples of this period, Papplewick, Ossington and Markham Clinton, which have a very individual right to attention. Victorian building and rebuilding were extensive; after the grey-brick 'regulation' churches of the early 19th century (*e.g.* St. Saviour, Retford, and Christ Church, Newark), red-brick was widely used. The new colliery towns grew quickly and churches were put up quickly to meet the need; few are worthy of attention. Of the famous Victorian architects only three are worthily represented: Pearson by the splendidly lavish St. Paul's, Daybrook; Bodley by Clumber and Sneinton St. Alban; and Comper by inspired restoration work in various places. Churches are still being built. The walls of New Clifton are rising; Broxtowe's 20th-century experiment houses 17th-century fittings; and even in Clipstone, which the guide-books accuse of being churchless, one may worship in the fine and well-ordered church of All Saints, built in 1928.

Good fittings are disappointingly meagre. The best fragments of medieval alabaster are now in the Castle Museum in Nottingham. There are no spectacular wall-paintings. In fact the sober 'workaday' atmosphere of the Midlands is faithfully reproduced in its places of worship; and we find, therefore, a homely, unspectacular beauty which is very appealing.

C.B. & N.H.S.

SELECTED LIST OF CHURCHES

by the Rev. Charles Bayes and N. Horton Smith

ANNESLEY (*All Saints*) GR
1874, T. G. Jackson, and 1908.

BALDERTON (*St. Giles*)
Woodwork; Norman doorway.

BLYTH *(*St. Mary & St. Martin*)
A Priory fragment, beautifully sited on the village green, and visited by hundreds for its rugged late 11th-century nave. This has a fine altar with the medieval screen as reredos. Note also the medieval paintings and admire the fortuitous external design of the shortened E. end.

BUNNY (*St. Mary the Virgin*)
14th cent.; lavish.

CARLTON-IN-LINDRICK (*St. John the Evangelist*)
Saxon tower; much Norman work.

CARLTON-ON-TRENT (*St. Mary*) GR
G. G. Place, 1851.

CLIFTON, NR. NOTTINGHAM (*St. Mary the Virgin*)
Mostly 14th cent.; N. transept full of Clifton tombs; medieval gable crucifix.

CLUMBER (*St. Mary the Virgin*) GR
Bodley, 1886; sumptuously pious.

CODDINGTON (*All Saints*)
Bodley and Wm. Morris fittings, 1865.

COLSTON BASSETT (*St. John the Divine*) GR
A. W. Brewill, 1892; expensive.

EAST LEAKE (*St. Mary the Virgin*)
Well-mannered medieval medley; a real 'shawm'.

EAST MARKHAM *(*St. John the Baptist*)
This is the county's Thaxted, though not so vast, so famous, or so complete. It is Perpendicular, clerestoried, and large for a village. One enters on a stone-flagged floor, where rush-bottomed chairs in pale oak (with blue hassocks) are discreetly grouped. The Comper E. window and the wide High Altar are in complete accord, and the whole church is faithful to the principles of the 'English Kalendar'. The little grey chamber-organ has little gilded pipes, there are tapers on brackets, and enough antiquity in wood, brass and glass to fascinate the historically-minded. The church gains much in spaciousness from the absence of a screen. The baseless Jacobean pulpit and the miraculously-unearthed altar mensa are appropriate.

EDWINSTOWE (*St. Mary*)
Mainly 13th cent.; massive, strong spire.

EGMANTON *(*St. Mary*)
The modest, porchless, exterior gives no hint of the pious gaiety within. Here, sponsored by the Duke of Newcastle and executed by Comper, is Anglo-Catholic romanticism at its best. The canopied rood screen dominates the interior, and the colour is repeated on organ-casing, font-cover and openwork pulpit. Beyond the screen is less colour and more mystery: a candled shrine, and, in front of Comper's E. window, a hanging pyx. The antiquarian will admire the Norman doorway and font, the 17th-century altar, and the fragments of old glass.

ELSTON CHAPEL (*dedication unknown*)
Entirely unrestored; 12th and 14th cent. with 1820-ish interior.

FLEDBOROUGH (*St. Gregory*)
Mainly 13th–14th cent.; some very old glass; lonely site.

GEDLING (*All Hallows*)
Unusual spire; E.E. chancel.

GROVE (*St. Helen*) GR
C. Hodgson Fowler, 1882.

HAWTON *(*All Saints*)
Seen from the W., across the open unhedged fields, this church appears as it must have done 500 years ago. Its 15th-century tower is noble and has a fine carved and inscribed door. Within, the simple old pews in the nave are well-spaced; but the eye is led on to the chancel, with its curvilinear E. window and superb 14th-century

stonework. The Easter sepulchre is the best in the country. Its figures are slightly mutilated, but the detail decorations are magnificently abundant and various. This, and the sedilia, are of a deep golden stone; and the similarity to Southwell, both in material and intricate workmanship, is obvious. The sheer magnificence is surprising in an ordinary village church, and emphasises the present mean and meagre ritual arrangements.

HOLME (St. Giles)
A small, rather inaccessible church by the Trent which richly rewards the finder. It is Nevil Truman's chef d'oeuvre as a piece of gentle and sensitive restoration. Its charm lies in its loneliness, its leaning walls and in the tasteful ordering of its ancient furnishings. There is simple old woodwork in screen and benches, and the altar rails are Jacobean. The E. window is a medieval medley and very lovely.

HOLME PIERREPONT (St. Edmund)
17th-cent. work in a semi-Gothic style.

KEYWORTH (St. Mary the Virgin)
Striking 14th-cent. tower.

KINGSTON-ON-SOAR (St. Wilfrid)
16th-cent. chantry.

KINOULTON (St. Luke) CL
1793. Red brick.

LANGAR (St. Andrew)
13th-cent. cruciform; Renaissance monuments and Jacobean woodwork.

LAXTON (St. Michael the Archangel)
Large. Note late Perp. clerestory and 1532 screen.

LEAKE, EAST: see East Leake.

MANSFIELD (St. Mark) GR
Temple Moore, 1897.

MARKHAM CLINTON; CL
Smirke's mausoleum of 1832; used until recently as parish church; now sadly neglected.

MARKHAM, EAST: see East Markham.

MARKHAM, WEST: see West Markham.

MUSKHAM, NORTH: see North Muskham.

NEWARK *(St. Mary Magdalene)
A town church (15th century) in the grand manner with transepts, aisles, nave and choir, and a splendid landmark of a spire. Within, one sees thick poppyheads up to

the black medieval screen, and the pews in the transepts look pulpitwards. But all is different beyond the screen. Comper's great gilded reredos (1937) shines triumphantly above the High Altar and gives a needed focus to an otherwise over-darkened interior; around it are brassily furnished chantry chapels, and beyond it three good altars. The E. window of the S. aisle is a gay medieval jumble of glass, and the two painted panels of the Dance of Death are alone worth a long journey to see. In a queer position (W. wall of S. transept) is the 1939–45 War Memorial, a Pieta by R. Kiddey; it is an incised slab, and good modern work of the post-Gill era. The prayer-script before it is very inappropriately written. Notice, too, the old library in the S. parvise, and the dim, effective oratory in the N. porch.

NORMANTON-ON-SOAR (St. James the Great)
13th cent.; spire over crossing.

NORTH MUSKHAM (St. Wilfrid)
20th-cent. restoration in Perp. style.

NORWELL (St. Lawrence)
13th–15th cent. medley; good tracery.

NOTTINGHAM (St. Alban, Sneinton) GR
Bodley, 1886–7; red brick.

(Holy Trinity, Lenton) GR
Stevens, 1892; superb Norman font in unworthy setting.

*(St. Mary)
A huge cruciform Perpendicular church in crumbling stone, stifled by large factory-blocks, in the oldest part of this old town. The splendid bronze doors by Wilson (1904) in the S. porch lead one to the vast, quiet, multi-windowed interior. It is all impressively homogeneous both in structure and furnishing. The latter is nearly all good Victorian with Bodley as a pervasive influence; the stained glass is encyclopedic in its range of designers. The E. end is illogical but satisfying. A large colourful Prince Consort memorial window of 1863 is partly blocked by the towering gilded Bodley reredos of 1885; and the two wings of this reredos can never be closed because of the English 'four-poster' altar erected beneath them! Fragments of old glass and alabaster may be found in the Temple Moore S. choir aisle. Other details are the medieval vestry, the incomplete rood-screen, the wall monuments (as thick as

stamps in an album, but less colourful), the rows of tattered flags, and the spirited wood-carved Lion and Unicorn of 1710. S. chapel by Temple Moore, 1912.

(*St. Paul, Daybrook*) GR
J. L. Pearson, 1896.

*(*St. Stephen, Sneinton*)
'Bodleyism' at its most complete, although in fact nearly all by C. G. Hare (1912), who rebuilt the Rickman church of 1839, retaining the central tower and crossing. Proportions are good, and the main axial vista leads from a tall-canopied font through the coloured rood to the gorgeous Oberammergau High Altar. But not all beauties are apparent at first glance: each transept is differently and effectively treated; the gold and green organ-casing stands on a screen between S. transept and crossing. There are modern continental statues, and a vigorous set of Stations of the Cross (1926). The 15th-century oak stalls (from St. Mary's, Nottingham) are beautifully arranged in the choir; there are eight misericords. This externally sombre cruciform 20th-century town church is surprisingly sited in a large walled and wooded churchyard.

OSSINGTON (*Holy Rood*)
1782; note Deist monument.

PAPPLEWICK (*St. James*)
The county's best example of Georgian Gothick. It lies in a wood half a mile from the village, at the end of a lane, guarded by two sets of gates. The tower is 14th century, but the rest is 1795. We enter through a porch as high as the nave. Inside the church is very light, with cream walls and plastered ceiling. A gallery, with fireplace, extends over the N. side of the nave and gives a cramped but cosy effect. Period features are the pulpit, the Royal Arms at the W. end, and the painted two-light E. window. The shallow font basin is smaller than many a medieval stoup. Lighting is by candles only – ideally they should be in silver sconces; actually they are in wrought-iron undulations down the underside of the gallery – a very 20th century 'arty-crafty' touch.

PERLETHORPE (*St. John the Evangelist*) GR
A. Salvin, 1876.

RATCLIFFE-ON-SOAR (*Holy Trinity*)
15th–17th cent. alabaster Sacheverell tombs.

REMPSTONE (*All Saints*) CL
1773. Neat classical with many original furnishings.

RETFORD, WEST: *see West Retford.*

SCARLE, SOUTH: *see South Scarle.*

SIBTHORPE (*St. Peter*)
Glorious 14th-cent. chancel and mean 18th-cent. nave.

SOUTH SCARLE (*St. Helen*)
Perp.-Norman mixture; rich 12th-cent. N. arcade; nave roof 15th cent.

STOCKWITH, WEST: *see West Stockwith.*

STRELLEY (*All Saints*)
Unspoiled village in woods. Apart from the base of the tower (13th cent.) and the clerestory (15th cent.) the whole building belongs to the second half of 14th cent. Best ancient screen in the county, a Jacobean pulpit with tester and Strelley monuments.

SUTTON-ON-TRENT (*All Saints*)
Fine late Perp.; note Mering Chapel, *c.* 1525; screen 16th cent.

TEVERSAL *(St. Catherine*)
The village is a rural oasis in the coal-producing area of the Nottinghamshire-Derbyshire border, and its 12th and 13th century church is remarkable for its unrestored 17th and 18th century interior. From the W. gallery with its modest organ to the narrow Laudian altar with its central alms-dish, all (except a 1908 reading-desk) is solid traditional Anglican furnishing. The pulpit is low, for there were never side galleries; and the box-pews have seating strips of red baize. The Molyneux pew in the S. aisle is roofed and has barley-sugar columns; four red velvet cushions, emblazoned with a cross motive on a blue shield, are provided for the books of the noble family; a 1784 Prayer Book and an 1822 Bible are covered in similar style. Eight hatchments display the Molyneux arms in various quarterings; and the Royal Arms dominate the chancel arch. In the choir are miniature three-a-side box-pews and three vast wall monuments. This little church has a deep peace and a sweet smell of roses and honeysuckle.

THURGARTON (*St. Peter*)
Priory fragment; 13th cent. with Victorian chancel.

UPPER BROUGHTON (*St. Luke*)
Setting; 13th cent. and later.

WEST MARKHAM (*All Saints*)
Derelict until recent years; self-consciously simple and 'folkcrafty' restoration; 12th-cent. font.

WEST RETFORD (*St. Michael & All Angels*)
Spire; mainly 14th and 15th cent.

WEST STOCKWITH (*St. Mary the Virgin*)
CL
1722; brick classical.

WILLOUGHBY-ON-THE-WOLDS (*St. Mary & All Saints*)
13th–15th cent. Willoughby monuments.

WOLLATON (*St. Leonard*)
Mainly 14th cent.; reredos *c*. 1660; monuments 15th and 16th cent.

WORKSOP *(St. Mary & St. Cuthbert*)
The twin-towered W. front with its fine doorway is the feature of the exterior. Within, the long and narrow nine-bay nave, late-Norman with lofty triforium, serves as choir also. The E. end has been limewashed. Rebuilding has been drastic, continuous and interesting. Sir Gilbert Scott's E. window is now in the N. transept, where his coloured reredos looks like an uncomfortable, but commodious, sedilia. There are many good small objects of devotion, including paintings. The rebuilt Lady Chapel (Brakspear, 1922), though simple in design, has a mysterious peace. There is a small Calvary and a 'baroque' Madonna.

WYSALL *(Holy Trinity*)
12th-century core; chancel 14th century with 15th-century roof. Pulpit, screen and stalls all 15th century.

Oxon

INTRODUCTION

OXON IS the most diversified of all inland counties. In the north it is the Midlands with hints of oncoming Birmingham when one sees the pinkish brick villas in the Banbury district bringing a 19th-century industrial atmosphere into the medieval and Georgian brown ironstone of the older groups of buildings. 20th-century industry turns Midlands-wards too, for the Morris and Pressed Steel Works at Cowley have noisy long links with Coventry and Brum. In the west, Oxon is the Cotswolds with that perfect limestone town of Burford which strangers fancy is in Gloucestershire.

The City and University are largely a limestone Cotswold town, at any rate in their surviving ancient streets. The south-eastern peninsula of the county, slipped between Berks and Bucks, is Chiltern scenery, near-suburban, with beech woods and steep chalk hills and scenario-writers' hide-outs in valleys, and pleasure-seekers' villas by the broad Thames where Salter's steamers ply. The capital of this part of the county is the old red-brick town of Henley, and Watlington is its isolated poor relation.

There is the flat Upper Thames country of willows and distant elms and limestone churches and cottages. Around Stanton Harcourt and Eynsham this scenery is full of Matthew Arnold and by Bampton and Kelmscott it is full of William Morris. There are the wide and unvisited inland marsh of Otmoor, all aeroplanes and bombs: the remote medieval park of Wychwood: the picturesque planted park of Blenheim where the palace spreads its curious outline above the lake: there is a remote mid-Oxon associated with the books of Flora Thompson and with the landscaped village of Great Tew. Then in the north-west corner, with Northants and Warwicks near, is a land of little hills and golden brown churches and cottages which looks like a medieval manuscript scene.

The finest old churches are not in the chalky southern end but where the quarries are in the north and west whence the stone could be floated down the Thames and its tributaries to Oxford and Dorchester.

The great medieval churches of the county, Adderbury, Bloxham, St. Mary the Virgin, Oxford, New College Chapel and cloisters, Oxford, Horley, Thame, Dorchester, Stanton Harcourt, Burford, Cropredy, Witney and Bampton are all midland in character, with the exception of the complete late-Norman church of Iffley,which is on its own. The Gloucestershire masons influenced the Perpendicular work which is abundant in the county. But

Oxon is also a country of great houses: Blenheim, Ditchley, Middleton, Nuneham, Shirburn, Stonor, Thame Park, and smaller stone manor houses like Kelmscott, Yarnton, Chastleton, Garsington – in fact most of the stone villages have gabled manor houses. The churches, therefore, often have the look of family chapels, and in some instances, not content with grand baroque monuments or a new aisle, a tasteful squire would wholly rebuild a church in classic style as at Chislehampton or Wheatfield. The best of all private chapels, excluding the college chapels in Oxford itself, is that at Rycote with its 17th-century furniture.

J.B.

SELECTED LIST OF CHURCHES

by John Piper and John Betjeman

ADDERBURY *(St. Mary the Virgin)*
Large hilly village of golden ironstone Georgian houses and old cottages among greens and elms with a magnificent Decorated and Perpendicular church to match. The imaginative corbel table on N. wall, of musicians, the lovely late Perpendicular chancel in the style of the Divinity Schools at Oxford, the tower and spire and windows make its exterior about the finest in the country. The inside is rather too restored but retains screen and brasses.

ASTHALL *(St. Nicholas)*
Village; Dec. tomb; glass.

BAMPTON *(St. Mary)*
Setting; tower and spire and proportions.

BANBURY *(St. Mary)* CL
S. P. Cockerell, 1793.

BLOXHAM *(Our Lady of Bloxham)*
A golden ironstone village with thatched cottages, and on a hill above it the church whose 14th-century spire is seen for miles over the elms. Handsome N. and S. porches. Clerestoried interior, aisled and spacious but harshly restored by Street. Splendid 15th-century S. chancel. Thornycroft monument, 1725, by A. Carpenter. Painted panels in screen.

BRIGHTWELL BALDWIN *(St. Bartholomew)*
Setting; glass; brasses; tombs; barrel organ.

BROUGHTON *(St. Mary)*
Park and castle; screen; glass; monuments; wall-paintings.

BUCKNELL *(St. Peter)*
E.E. details.

BURFORD *(St. John the Baptist)*
'Model old English town' (J. Piper) of Cotswold stone with church at bottom of hill on River Windrush. The churchyard is rich in sculptured table tombs, Georgian and earlier. The church with spire and tower and parvised porch is cruciform of various dates with chapels added, interior effect largely 15th century. Sylvester and Tanfield tombs and some old glass.

CASSINGTON *(St. Peter)*
Spire and tripartite Norman plan. Norman corbels. Dark impressive interior with Jacobean woodwork and old foreign glass.

CHALGROVE *(St. Mary the Virgin)*
Village; 14th-cent. chancel; tracery; paintings.

CHARLTON-ON-OTMOOR *(St. Mary the Virgin)*
Glass; screen; tower.

CHECKENDON *(St. Peter & St. Paul)*
Norman apsidal interior; wall-paintings; tablets.

CHINNOR *(St. Andrew)*
Glass; mouldings.

CHISLEHAMPTON *(St. Katherine)*
On the edge of a small park stands this 1763 little white church which is classic. Bell-cote and vane and clear glass, round-headed windows. Inside box-pews, carved

wooden altar piece and tablets and candles make unspoiled Georgian interior.

CHURCH HANDBOROUGH *(St. Peter & St. Paul)*
A tall spired building of stone, extended through the centuries since Norman times, whose combined effect makes a charming village church. 12th-century S. door carvings, font, 15th-century nave arcades, pulpit and screen across chancel and aisles with coloured rood loft over aisles, and tomb recesses.

CHURCHILL *(All Saints)* GR
1862 Gothic, copied from Magdalen, Oxford.

COGGES *(St. Mary)*
Setting; glass; monuments; modern furnishings.

COMBE *(St. Lawrence the Martyr)*
Unspoiled village; Perp. glass; paintings.

CROPREDY *(St. Mary the Virgin)*
Churchyard; stately Perp.; screens and woodwork.

CUDDESDON *(All Saints)*
A diocesan village; cruciform; vistaed interior.

DEDDINGTON *(St. Peter & St. Paul)*
Dec. and Perp.; good proportions.

DORCHESTER *(St. Peter & St. Paul)*
Main-road village with remaining traces of the distinction proper to one of the oldest of English cities. Abbey church, approached through a Butterfield lychgate, is splendid in its proportions and detail. Mostly Decorated, it has earlier and later parts. The Jesse window, some of its stonework imitating tree-branches, has its original figures in glass and stone, and there is much old glass in other windows too. Among the tombs is the justly celebrated stone effigy of a late 13th-century knight, which has inspired many sculptors, including modern ones. (*See Plate 16*)

DUCKLINGTON *(St. Bartholomew)*
Village; Flamboyant N. aisle.

EASINGTON *(St. Peter)*
Farmyard church, rustic; Jacobean pulpit.

ENSTONE *(St. Kenelm)*
Village; furnishings; monument, 1633.

EWELME *(St. Mary the Virgin)*
Flint and brick village where watercress grows in Chiltern foothills. Castellated 15th-century church, patched with brick, stone and flint rises above old brick almshouses. It is all late distinguished Perpendicular, not village building. Inside effect is East Anglian with screen, spired font cover and old roofs, that in S.E. chapel painted. Pleasant early 19th-century poppy head pews. Chaucer and Suffolk tombs, old floors and many brasses.

FILKINS *(St. Peter)* GR
G. E. Street 1857; simple and subtle in local stone of attractive village.

FOREST HILL *(St. Nicholas)*
Tractarian furnishings.

FREELAND *(St. Mary the Virgin)* GR
J. L. Pearson, 1867.

GARSINGTON *(St. Mary)*
Village and setting.

GREAT HASELEY *(St. Peter)*
Good mouldings; large Dec. and Perp.

GREAT MILTON *(St. Mary the Virgin)*
14th-cent. tracery; Dormer tomb, 1618; glass.

GREAT ROLLRIGHT *(St. Andrew)*
Perp. tower; 12th-cent. carving.

GREAT TEW *(St. Michael & All Angels)*
Village; setting; mouldings; texture outside; spacious inside; brasses; late monuments.

HANWELL *(St. Peter)*
An untouched orange ironstone place whose hidden church of the same stone is remarkable for its lively rustic carvings on corbels outside and capitals within.

HOOK NORTON *(St. Peter)*
Village; spacious; Norman font; wallpaintings.

HORLEY *(St. Etheldreda)*
A north Oxfordshire ironstone village whose spacious church of various dates has been made distinguished by sympathetic modern furnishing and restoration. Wallpainting of St. Christopher; rather touched up; rood loft and screen by T. Lawrence Dale, 1949, stone floors, with oriental carpets.

HORNTON *(St. John the Baptist)*
Village; wall-paintings.

HORTON-CUM-STUDLEY *(St. Barnabas)*
Butterfield, 1867.

IDBURY *(St. Nicholas)*
Village; Perp. and woodwork.

IFFLEY *(*St. Mary the Virgin*)*
A late Norman (1170) show piece, and rightly so, within and without. W. front rich in beakhead and zigzag carving. Dark aisled interior shows eastward view of two elaborate Norman arches with vaulting between, leading to contrasting light Early English vaulted W. end. Unfortunate Victorian woodwork. (*See Plate 6*)

KELMSCOTT (*St. George*)
Village; wall-paintings; William Morris tomb in churchyard by Philip Webb.

KIDLINGTON (*St. Mary the Virgin*)
Spire; glass; screens and stalls.

KINGHAM (*St. Andrew*)
Decorative 1853 refurnishings.

LANGFORD *(*St. Matthew*)*
Stone village in flat willowy Upper Thames setting. The church is on a grand scale, very early Norman, of which the tower and the relief carving on the E. side of the S. porch of the Crucifixion and the proportions of the church are evidence. Distinguished work of later dates, especially chancel and W. end which are Early English.

LEAFIELD (*St. Michael & All Angels*) GR
Village; stone spire; well-proportioned; Gilbert Scott, 1860.

LEWKNOR (*St. Margaret*)
Setting; font; monuments 17th–18th cent.; Rossetti glass.

LITTLE FARINGDON (*dedication unknown*)
Village; Norman and later.

LITTLE ROLLRIGHT (*St. Philip*)
Farmyard setting; simple rustic.

LOWER HEYFORD (*St. Mary*)
Village; screen; glass.

MARSTON (*St. Nicholas*)
Woodwork.

MERTON (*St. Swithun, Bishop of Winchester*)
Large and light; Jacobean pulpit.

MILTON, Nr. Banbury (*St. John the Evangelist*) GR
Butterfield, 1856.

MILTON, GREAT: see Great Milton.

MILTON-UNDER-WYCHWOOD (*St. Simon & St. Jude*) GR
G. E. Street, 1854.

MINSTER LOVELL (*St. Kenelm*)
Village and setting; Perp.; vaulted under central tower.

NEWINGTON (*St. Giles*)
Setting; spire; screen; glass.

NEWINGTON, SOUTH: see South Newington.

NORTH LEIGH (*St. Mary*)
Effigies; vaulted chantry; glass; painting.

NORTHMOOR (*St. Denys*)
Village; texture; monuments.

NUNEHAM COURTNEY (*All Saints*) CL
Park setting; 'Athenian' Stewart, 1764; Greek; domed.

ODDINGTON (*St. Andrew*)
Furnishings.

OVER WORTON (*Holy Trinity*) GR
Rich Victorian, 1844; Derrick, architect.

OXFORD *(*All Saints*)*
A classic and Civic church in the High Street, 1707–8, said to have been designed by Dean Aldrich, its tower and rather heavy spire on an axis with Trinity College chapel and gates in Broad Street. The oblong body of the church is bound together externally by a heavy moulded cornice below clerestory windows and articulated with flat Corinthian pilasters, broken into by a pedimented porch. The interior is more successful and repeats the exterior scheme. The attic storey supports a flat ceiling carved at the side and rich in plasterwork. 18th-century pulpit, altar piece, much woodwork and candelabra and W. gallery and organ case remain. But the whole interior has been 'rearranged' by Victorians including the window glass.

(*St. Barnabas*)
Byzantine with campanile, 1869, all by A. W. Blomfield; brick in a brick district and spacious within.

(*St. Giles*)
Countrified church; 12th cent. and later.

(*St. John the Evangelist, Iffley Road*) GR
Bodley, 1896; for the Cowley Fathers; austere and refined.

*(*St. Mary the Virgin*)*
The 14th-century spire (last rebuilt 1897–8 and pinnacled) of this large church, its 15th-century windows and baroque porch by Nicholas Stone, 1637, with twisted columns and 18th-century ironwork gates, make it the grandest parish church in Oxford, a focus on the skyline and a glory of the High Street. Inside the clerestoried and aisled nave is rather untidy and furbished up, though steeped in

history. The noblest thing inside is the chancel, *c.* 1467, with its clear old glass and 17th-century communion rails and niched E. wall.

(*St. Mary Magdalen*) GR
Wide and 'high'; vigorous Victorian glass of all dates.

(*St. Michael*)
Pre-Conquest tower.

(*St. Paul*) CL
1835, by H. J. Underwood; Ionic.

(*St. Peter's-in-the-East*)
Hidden setting by old walls New College garden; headstones; vaulted late Norman chancel and 17th cent. and earlier glass in E. window; early Norman crypt with cushion-capped pillars.

*(*St. Philip & St. James*)
By G. E. Street, 1860–6. Cruciform with apse and oblong tower with spire. Bold and simple external mouldings. Bands of a pink sandstone bind the composition together. W. front original and delightful as seen from Leckford Road. Inside too dark because of unfortunate stained W. window, but nave arcades narrowing towards tower arch to give effect of length, nave roof caps and stonework are all bold and strong. Tractarian plan with High Altar visible from all parts of church. (*See Plate 59*)

ROLLRIGHT, GREAT: *see Great Rollright.*

ROLLRIGHT, LITTLE: *see Little Rollright.*

ROTHERFIELD GREYS (*unknown*)
Magnificent Elizabethan Knollys monument.

ROUSHAM (*St. Leonard & St. James*)
Manor house setting; Jacobean pews; monuments; tablets; hatchments.

RYCOTE *(*St. Michael and All Angels*)
In a park near a lake this remote mid-15th-century domestic chapel near Thame is of ashlar with tower and buttressed nave and chancel, clearly the work of an architect. Inside it is remarkable as containing nothing later than Laudian times and all things up till then, sumptuous – 15th-century benches and screen base, early 17th-century family and royal pews, one domed and the other of two storeys, blue ceiling with gold stars, late 17th-century altar-piece and communion rails. Clear old glass. Queen Elizabeth and Charles I worshipped here when on visits.

SARSDEN (*St. James*) CL
Rebuilt 1760; classical with cruciform plan.

SHILTON (*Holy Rood*)
Village; Norman font with 14th-cent. carving.

SHIPLAKE (*St. Peter & St. Paul*)
Old French glass.

SHORTHAMPTON *(*All Saints*)
A tiny hamlet church near Charlbury. It is a small and simple building, aisleless and bell-coted, of various dates from Norman till 1820, when it was furnished in carpenter's style with box-pews and high pulpit and the chancel rebuilt. The plaster walls show signs of wall-painting and the appeal of the building is its remoteness and feel of rustic worship.

SOMERTON (*St. James*)
Village; screens; Fermor tombs, 16th cent.

SOUTH LEIGH (*St. James the Great*)
Much medieval painting (retouched)

SOUTH NEWINGTON (*St. Peter ad Vincula*)
Perp. porch; paintings.

SPELSBURY (*All Saints*)
Village; monuments, 18th cent.

STANTON HARCOURT *(*St. Michael*)
A grand cruciform church near other old buildings and reflected in ponds; the Early English and Perpendicular details are delicate and well thought out. The inside is little spoiled and much enhanced by its old stone and marble floor. Early English screen with painting, old glass and Harcourt monuments 17th–19th century in Perpendicular S.E. chapel.

STANTON ST. JOHN (*St. John the Baptist*)
Village; glass, 14th cent.

STOKE LYNE (*St. Peter*)
Village; 12th-cent. carvings; modern furnishings.

STRATTON AUDLEY (*St. Mary & St. Edburga*)
Village; Borlase tomb, 1688.

SWINBROOK (*St. Mary the Blessed Virgin*)
Village; Fettiplace tombs. (*See Plate 45*)

SWYNCOMBE (*St. Botolph*)
Setting; Norman.

TACKLEY (*St. Nicholas*)
Village; cruciform; monuments, 18th cent.

TEW, GREAT: *see Great Tew.*

THAME *(St. Mary the Virgin)*
The fine church of an attractive brick and flint and plaster market-town. It is cruciform and developed from Norman origins in later styles in a consistent manner. Notice S. porch, window tracery, Decorated screen, brasses, and many monuments, especially that of Lord Williams in middle of chancel.

WARBOROUGH (*St. Lawrence*)
Tower; font; wall-painting.

WATERPERRY *(St. Mary the Virgin)*
A remote village in meadows. The church is against the manor house, and nothing much outside. But inside are old glass of good quality, box-pews, a monument by Chantrey, hatchments and old stone floors.

WATERSTOCK (*St. Leonard*)
Armorial window; tomb, 1370.

WESTWELL (*St. Mary the Virgin*)
Headstones; glass.

WHEATFIELD *(St. Andrew)*
A remote place from which the glory has departed – a stable, a park, a walled garden, and on a slope of the park, the church. This originally medieval, was classicised in 1750 and inside are hatchments, tombs, two-decker pulpit, old pews, clear glass, with fragments of old stained glass, a Peter Scheemakers tomb, 1739, and rich classic altar and rails.

WHEATLEY (*St. Mary*) GR
Spired; G. E. Street, 1857.

WIDFORD *(St. Oswald)*
Approached by footpath only and in the Windrush Valley below Burford, a tiny medieval church with wall paintings, box-pews, clear glass and bits of Roman pavement.

WITNEY (*St. Mary the Virgin*)
Setting; headstones; spire; large.

WOODEATON (*Holy Rood*)
Setting; 18th-cent. woodwork and fittings.

WORTON, OVER: *see Over Worton.*

WROXTON (*All Saints*)
Village; Georgian Gothic tower; effigies; 18th–19th-cent. monuments.

YARNTON *(St. Bartholomew)*
Manor house, vicarage and church form a group. To the 13th-century church were added in 1611 an ashlar tower with mellifluous bells, a porch and a S.E. chapel by Sir Thomas Spencer, all late Perpendicular. In the church is much old woodwork in pews, a Jacobean screen to the Spencer chapel which has painted walls and roofs and grand 17th-century monuments. In chancel is alabaster 15th-century reredos and in aisle a medievalist brass of 1826, and in the windows fragments of old glass, English and Flemish.

Rutland

INTRODUCTION

TWO STONE quarries of Ketton and Clipsham, which have been worked since medieval times and are still in use, and centuries of prosperous agriculture, make this, which is the compactest and smallest county of England, the richest in old stone buildings, whether churches, barns, country houses, farms or cottages. The scenery is hilly and its wide uplands are thus described by Dr. W. G. Hoskins in his guide to Rutland; 'limestone walls shining from afar in the clear winter sun and the rows of stacks in the corners of the great ploughed fields; fields that themselves gleam like a rich, brown velvet, ready for the barley and the wheat. It is very like the Cotswold country – indeed it is the same stone underneath – but without the self-consciousness of so much of that well-known land'. The stone varies from what he aptly calls 'sheep-grey' limestone in the east of the county round Ketton and Clipsham where the finest churches are, to golden brown, yellow and orange in the west. Between 1150 and 1350, the villages of Rutland seemed to have vied with each other as to which could build the finest church, and as Dr. Hoskins says, 'no county in England can show so many fine churches in such a small area, except perhaps the neighbouring area of South Lincolnshire . . . '.

In later centuries most of Rutland was parcelled out among four great landlords, the Finches at Burley-on-the-Hill, the Noels at Exton (their land is now sadly scarred with iron-ore workings), the Heathcotes at Normanton (only the classic church remains with its 1911 nave and chancel by Romaine Walker) and the Cecils who still live over the border in the Elizabethan splendour of Burghley House by Stamford town. There were also smaller squires with their houses and modest parks. In the last century the county became popular with hunting people who like the old way of life, no wire, good inns and ample stables. Thus Rutland today still retains an atmosphere of having been cared for by landlords. The two chief towns of Oakham and Uppingham are small enough to be what old-fashioned landowners would describe as 'the village'; once more to quote Dr. Hoskins, 'Everywhere in the villages one sees the hand of the same benevolent despotism, and one sees too frequently also the impact of a new form of society in the broken-down stone walls which no one can afford to put up again, in the Colly Weston roofs (Colly Weston slates are of dark brown stone which attracts moss and lichen) patched with corrugated iron, in the big house which is more often than not a hospital or a school'. There is really only one blemish on the face of Rutland, and that is the strings of overhead wires that bedevil every village in profusion.

J.B.

SELECTED LIST OF CHURCHES

by W. G. Hoskins

BARROWDEN *(St. Peter)*
Attractive limestone village in rich meadows of Welland Valley. Church mainly 14th century: graceful tower and spire. Some 15th-century enlargement (clerestory, E. window, etc.). Remarkable width of church, even by Rutland standards where wide churches are common. Renaissance monument (1588).

BROOKE *(St. Peter)*
Remote in the gentle valley of the Gwash: sweeping limestone uplands all around. 13th-century tower, some Norman work inside, but much rebuilt about 1579 and this gives the feeling. Looks as though nothing had changed since then, with complete screen, benches, and stalls of that period. Beautiful Renaissance tomb of Charles Noel (1619), retaining original colouring.

CASTERTON, GREAT: *see Great Casterton.*

CASTERTON, LITTLE: *see Little Casterton.*

CLIPSHAM *(St. Mary)*
Much excellent 16th–19th century village building in limestone. Note village school, 1849. Large, beautiful 14th-century church on edge of small well-tree'd park. Fine tower, with broach spire of unusual design. Interior originally Norman: N. arcade has massive 12th-century capitals, S. arcade 13th century. Much reconstruction in 14th century (e.g. window tracery). Usual 15th-century clerestory. Some medieval glass behind organ. But most striking feature of Clipsham is exterior view from S. Important medieval (and modern) quarries near village.

COTTESMORE *(St. Nicholas)*
Imposing 14th cent., but 'scraped'.

EDITH WESTON *(St. Mary)*
Pleasing exterior; good village.

EGLETON *(St. Edmund)*
Rich Norman work; good village.

EMPINGHAM *(St. Peter)*
Rutland at its best: large attractive limestone village above Gwash Valley and a splendid church over all. Three adjacent churches of Empingham, Exton, and Ketton hard to beat as a trio anywhere in England. Empingham is nobly proportioned: note the W. tower and crocketed spire, and W. front (all 14th century). Internally, nearly all Early English – both arcades, and especially S. transept, almost in original condition with some medieval colouring. Substantial changes in 15th century (e.g. new windows, clerestory, new roofs). Early English chancel has beautiful double piscina and triple sedilia – even for those who usually blench at these antiquarian details.

ESSENDINE *(St. Mary)*
Close to site of a Norman castle, of which it was the chapel. Original parish church went long ago. Considerably repaired and rebuilt, but substantially a Norman building still, remodelled in 13th century. Striking S. doorway, *c.* 1140, often photographed. Trees and meadows all around.

EXTON *(St. Peter & St. Paul)*
Another noble church, in the park of what was formerly one of Rutland's great houses. Excellent limestone village outside park. Drastic rebuilding of church after damage by lightning (1850) explains incongruity of details, but general effect still fine. Tower and spire especially notable. But the monuments to the Noels, Haringtons, and others connected with them, are the really splendid thing about the church. Here we have the memorials of a dead civilisation. Notice especially the tabletomb with alabaster effigies of John Harington (1524) and wife, the appealing

monument to Sir James Harington (1591) and wife in the chancel, the splendid tomb of Robert Kelway (1590), and the Noel monuments and sculpture by Grinling Gibbons and Nollekens: and read the gorgeous rolling epitaphs aloud. Exton is intoxicating.

GREAT CASTERTON *(St. Peter & St. Paul)*
Right beside the hellish din and fury of the Great North Road, but all is peace within. Those who like completely unrestored churches – all 13th century here – will like Great Casterton very much. Tower added 15th century. Church large, plastered, and whitewashed; clear glass, Georgian pulpit. Good collection of Ketton headstones (carved with winged cherubs' heads, etc.) in churchyard.

GREETHAM (*St. Mary the Virgin*)
14th-cent. tower and spire.

HAMBLETON *(St. Andrew)*
Stands well on an eminence in village: views over the rich Vale of Catmose. 13th-century tower and stumpy spire (these are a very characteristic sight in Rutland). Mainly 12th century inside. Chancel (14th century) much restored and adorned by late 19th-century rector. Much foreign woodwork of this period (pulpit, lectern, organ-case, etc.). Interesting as a good period piece of late Victorian High Anglicanism.

KETTON *(St. Mary)*
Stands in a large, attractive village (built of local honey-coloured limestone) with the exquisitely beautiful tower and spire rising above the trees and the sepia Colly Weston slate roofs. W. front fine example of late 12th-century work (Norman evolving into Early English); rest of church almost entirely 13th century with very lofty and dignified arcades. Spacious chancel practically rebuilt, 1863, but still striking because of great size, panelled roof (now newly painted in medieval colours), and E. window and altar by Comper (1907). Notable collection of carved Ketton headstones in churchyard – a local art now dead.

LANGHAM *(St. Peter & St. Paul)*
Yet another noble 14th-century church dominating (in this case) a rather messed-up village. Tower 13th century: Decorated spire added early 14th. Internally, a

spacious 14th-century building with plastered walls and much clear glass. Some 15th-century enlargement (e.g. clerestory and transepts). Fine proportions best seen looking W. from altar steps. Some good glass by Comper – chancel 1904 and S. transept 1908.

LITTLE CASTERTON *(All Saints)*
Long, low and grey in meadows by the Gwash, beside tree-shadowed rectory. No tower, but W. bell-cote which is characteristic of smaller Rutland churches. N. arcade about 1190: S. arcade a little later. Usual clerestory. Some 14th-century wall-painting especially in recess of W. window. Fine double brass (under carpet in chancel) to Sir Thomas Burton (1381) and his wife Margaret (1410).

LUFFENHAM, NORTH: *see North Luffenham.*

LYDDINGTON *(St. Andrew)*
A grand church, mostly Perpendicular, in a village full of good building in ironstone. Lyddington belonged to the medieval bishops of Lincoln, who had a palace here of which the 15th-century great hall remains. Tower and chancel of church belong to older building, 1320–40, but nave and aisles were rebuilt about 1500, by one of the bishops. The height and symmetry of this work make it of great beauty. Note medieval wall-paintings; but especially the 17th-century arrangement of the sanctuary, with altar enclosed by rails on all sides. Medieval brasses. Acoustic jars in chancel.

MANTON (*St. Mary the Virgin*)
W. front.

MARKET OVERTON (*St. Peter & St. Paul*)
Late Saxon tower arch.

NORMANTON *(St. Matthew)*
Stands entirely alone, sailing like a white ship across the wide green seas of the park. The big house of the Heathcotes now demolished. The little railed-in oval churchyard looks far and wide over the gentle Rutland landscape. Original church built 1764. Dignified W. portico and tower added 1826 (the tower a copy of those of St. John's in Smith Square, Westminster). Georgian nave and chancel replaced in 1911 in a style conforming to tower. Medallion bust by Rysbrack to the first Sir Gilbert Heathcote. Church locked: key kept at house in park.

NORTH LUFFENHAM *(St. John the Baptist)*

Large unspoiled limestone village, and a large church to go with it, a little way off among trees. Mostly 14th-century work (tower and broach spire, window tracery), arcades are good 13th century. Medieval glass in chancel; E. window by Kempe. Particularly long, lofty chancel. Fittings.

OAKHAM *(All Saints)*

Attractive little country town, full of old-fashioned shops and trades, with a magnificent church that rises like a central jewel in all distant views of the Vale of Catmose. Noble 14th-century tower and spire of ashlar limestone. Lofty interior of same date with notable sculptured capitals (various subjects depicted) and arcades. Usual enlargements in 15th century (clerestory, good Perpendicular windows). Note the treatment of W. front of tower.

RYHALL *(St. John the Evangelist)*

A pleasant village by the Gwash, and one of the best churches in Rutland with an exquisite tower and spire, 13th century. Very wide nave and aisles again: N. arcade is about 1200, S. arcade a little later. Chancel rebuilt in 15th century. Tablet (1696) to an infant genius, aged two. St. Tibba (patron saint of falconers) lived and died here about 690. Against W. wall of N. aisle are remains of a medieval hermitage associated with her cult, possibly the burial place of the saint against which the first church was built.

SEATON *(All Hallows)*

Norman work, especially chancel arch.

STOKE DRY *(St. Andrew)*

Unsophisticated, charming little church on hillside bordering remotest Leicestershire: new reservoir (1940) below adds to delightful scene. Norman work visible here and there, but building mainly 13th century (S. arcade) and 14th, with the usual 15th-century clerestory, porch, and window tracery. The Digbys made Stoke Dry their principal seat (15th–17th centuries) and their three tombs (1496, 1540, 1590–1602) are notable, especially the table-tomb of Kenelm and Anne Digby. Chancel-screen 15th century. Better series of wall-paintings than usual, 15th century. Priest's chamber over N. porch said to be where Gunpowder Plot hatched (an Everard Digby hanged for complicity in 1606) but story not true.

TEIGH *(Holy Trinity)*

Tower 14th century, but plastered over in 1782 (and a few details added) when rest of church rebuilt. Externally, a pretty little Gothick church: internally a pure 18th-century ensemble. Box-pews face each other. At W. end, a triple grouping of pulpit, reading desk, and clerk's desk, with Lord's Prayer and Creed on either side. Commandments on E. wall. Small font used to be fixed to altar rails (very characteristic of period) but recently removed by someone with lack of knowledge. Plastered ceilings. Gothick window tracery, mostly clear glass. Those who like 18th-century churches will like Teigh very much. Usual pleasant little limestone village amid rich grassland.

TICKENCOTE *(St. Peter)*

Just off the Great North Road. Everybody knows the photograph of the famous 12th-century chancel arch here, but the original is even more impressive. A staggering thing in five orders, each carved with a different design. Most of the 12th-century church was rebuilt in 1792 in the Norman style, but the vaulted chancel is largely the original. Good 13th-century font.

TIXOVER *(St. Luke)*

A happy surprise in the meadows of the Welland Valley, far from village and everything except grass, buttercups, and bull-rushes. Mostly Norman, with a magnificently solid, untouched tower, and inside an imposing tower arch (all about 1140). Rest of church mostly 13th century, windows altered in 17th. Original medieval stone seats along chancel walls. Marble monument to lord of manor, 1623. Lit by oil-lamps and candles: evensong at Tixover in Rutland has an imploring note about it. Unfinished list of men serving in 'the war of 1914' in the porch in fading ink. One feels that life at Tixover stopped about then. (*See Plate 8*)

WARDLEY *(St. Botolph)*

Decayed and melancholy church amid beautiful rolling landscape.

WHISSENDINE *(St. Andrew)*

Near the Leicestershire border: too much red brick and slate in village. But a splendid church, with notable 14th-century tower (fine even by Rutland standards). Spacious, light interior, with wide nave and aisles so characteristic of the county. N. arcade 13th century. Rest of church 14th and 15th.

Remarkable 15th-century roof with carved figures. Early 16th-century screen in S, transept came from St. John's College. Cambridge in 1869, where Scott was 'restoring' and throwing things out. Much good modern woodwork. At W. end, a model of church made from 'the pith out of rushes which grew in the village brook' by an old lady a century ago: a charming Victorian oddity.

Shropshire

INTRODUCTION

THERE IS not one sort of scenery which can be called characteristic of the varied and beautiful landscape of Shropshire. This agricultural county, comparatively free from modern factories, is bisected by the Severn. Shrewsbury, the capital, Ludlow and Bridgnorth and Whitchurch are its attractive old towns. Its Cheshire borders are flat and pitted with ponds: Wenlock Edge with its 'forest fleece' and the Clee Hills give wonderful outline to the pastoral country south of the spires and towers of Shrewsbury: wooded combes like Devon descend to orchard land on the borders of Worcestershire: the north-west corner of the county round Oswestry has a Welsh quality: the Long Mynd, Stiperstones and Clun Hills on the edges of Montgomery and Radnor, to the west, have the grand and under-populated look of a border country and there the few old churches are fortress-like. Scenery is more memorable in Shropshire than buildings, castles are prominent and if a generalisation is possible about the medieval churches, it is that most of them are small (with the exception of St. Mary, Shrewsbury, and Ludlow), and the gradual growth of ages. The prevailing materials are a good sharp pink sandstone and half-timber. Timber-framed churches have been much repaired and the most complete example, Melverley, does not look as old as its origin.

'Fear God and honour the Corbets' is said to be a Shropshire motto and the non-Welsh half of the county is diversified with the seats of hunting squires who did much church rebuilding and repair in the 18th century. The Myttons, Clives, Hills, Cottons, Hebers, Bougheys, Plowdens and Smythes are other Shropshire families and they do not seem to have been markedly Puritan but either old-fashioned High Church before becoming Tractarian in Victorian times, or Roman Catholic. Two-bottle squires hung on in the Newport neighbourhood until this century.

To this remote county, in late Georgian times, came that early industrialism of pottery at Coalport and iron at Coalbrookdale, which turned the chasm-like Severn valley north of Bridgnorth into a brick semblance of the Stroud Valley in Glos. Ironbridge, Broseley and Madeley are its romantic survivals. The industrial churches here are either severe classic by Telford the engineer or starved looking 'early pointed' in brick. Methodism flourished.

In Victorian times ironmasters from Wolverhampton, like the Sparrows, and manufacturers from Kidderminster, Birmingham and Manchester discovered Shropshire much as London discovered Surrey and Sussex. Norman Shaw and Eden Nesfield built them houses, Street, Pearson and Scott 'restored' old churches for them or built new ones.

Shropshire, more than most English agricultural counties, is remarkable for its 18th-century and Victorian churches. Its older churches are more impressive for their fittings, monuments, hatchments and liturgical arrangements than for their architecture. Shropshire is a county where the scenery is splendid and the churches for the most part are unobvious. This is the reason why later ages than the medieval predominate in the selections given below.

J.B.

SELECTED LIST OF CHURCHES

by John Betjeman and Robert Wakeford

ACTON BURNELL (*St. Michael*)
Setting; good 13th cent. but heavily 're-stored'; 18th-cent. Smythe monuments.

ADDERLEY *(St. Peter)*
This early 19th-century romantic Gothick church is large and cruciform with a sturdy classic tower. It stands on the edge of parkland. The windows are pointed and most of the panes are clear crown glass. The tracery is an outstanding example of the iron window-tracery that is typical of this part of Shropshire at the date. In the chancel there is a newly discovered palimpsest brass. The N. transept was a manor pew, and has a Jacobean screen and early 19th-century armorial glass.

ALBERBURY (*St. Michael*)
Norman in origin but with work of all medieval periods; massive saddleback tower at N.E. of nave and handsome 15th-cent. roofs, that of aisle with embellishments added, *c.* 1840; 14th-cent. glass and 19th-cent. pews; Leighton monuments.

ALVELEY (*St. Mary*)
Setting; Norman with much recasting during the medieval period and Georgian top to tower; still rewarding in spite of A. W. Blomfield's restoration 1878; arcades, late 15th-cent. clerestory, nave roof and wall-paintings.

BATTLEFIELD *(St. Mary Magdalene)*
The site of the battle in 1403 between Henry IV and Harry Hotspur, who was beaten and killed, is now a peaceful off-the-main-road setting for this stately church. The outline is Perpendicular, but three of the windows have reticulated tracery. By the 19th century the nave had lost its roof, and the restoration of 1861–2 has left the inside very ugly. There is foreign glass of pre-Reformation date in the vestry, and a lovely wooden Pieta placed on one of the sedilia in the chancel.

BERWICK (*dedication unknown*) CL
17th–18th cent.; box-pews.

BOLAS, GREAT: *see Great Bolas.*

BRIDGNORTH (*St. Mary Magdalene*) CL
Thomas Telford, 1792–4; tower; interior spoiled.

BROMFIELD (*St. Mary the Virgin*)
Riverside setting; Priory remains; painted chancel ceiling, 1672; Bodley restoration, 1890.

BURFORD (*St. Mary?*)
Setting; Cornwall effigies, one of triptych form and late 16th cent. (*See Plate 52b*)

CALVERHALL (*Holy Trinity*) GR
W. Eden Nesfield, 1879; glass.

CHESWARDINE *(St. Swithun)*
J. L. Pearson rebuilt this church so well that the 13th-century N. chapel which he merely moved, stone for stone, seems to fit in appropriately with the rest, which is Early English of 1886–9. The dog-tooth

mouldings, stiff-leafed foliage and banded shafts are first-class, and so are the proportions. Interesting 19th-century glass. Old brasses.

CHETWYND (*St. Michael & All Angels*) GR
B. Ferrey, 1865–7; spire; graceful and impressive interior.

CLAVERLEY (*All Saints*)
Black-and-white houses and parsonage. The handsome church is of Norman origin as is shown by tower base and N. arcade; rest late 13th–15th cent. Wall-paintings over N. arcade *c.* 1200 call to mind the Bayeux tapestry. Nave and chancel roofs; 15th and 16th cent. monuments.

CLEOBURY NORTH (*St. Peter & St. Paul*)

CLIVE (*All Saints*)
Setting; mainly C. J. Ferguson, 1885–94, with medieval core.

CLUN (*St. George*)
Restored and partly rebuilt by Street in 1877; Norman with later alterations including 13th-cent. N. aisle with noble 15th-cent. collar-braced roof, fortress-like tower, arcades and wooden canopy over altar; early 18th-cent. lych-gate.

COLEMERE: *see Lyneal-cum-Colemere.*

EDSTASTON (*St. Mary the Virgin*)
Textured exterior; three Norman doors; medieval roof.

ERCALL, HIGH: *see High Ercall.*

GREAT BOLAS (*St. John the Baptist*) CL
John Arlldig, 1726–9; box pews.

HALSTON (*private chapel*)
This timber-framed chapel belongs to the owners of Halston. The interior is one of the most interesting in the county. It is fully panelled and retains other original fittings of mid-16th century date, but there is no evidence to show whether the building was put up shortly before the Dissolution by the Knights of St. John of Jerusalem, or, soon after, by the Mytton family (the Jack Mytton portrayed by Nimrod was squire of Halston). On both sides of the small recess which contains the altar are large square pews in one of which a pulpit was erected in 1725 without destroying the pew.

HEATH CHAPEL (*dedication unknown*)
Setting on the hills; Norman; box-pews, two-decker pulpit and three-sided altar rails.

HIGH ERCALL (*St. Michael & All Angels*)
12th-cent. carving over N. door; capitals; wooden effigy.

HODNET (*St. Luke*)
Chiefly 14th cent. with octagonal tower and Norman doorway. Monuments; chained books.

HOPTON CANGEFORD (*dedication unknown*) CL
18th cent.; clear glass; apse; brick floors; manor pew.

KINLET *(St. John Baptist*)
Set in parkland, a mile down a drive near brick and stone 1729 hall, now a school. The medieval stone church with Norman features is near a walled garden. A timber-framed Victorian clerestory prepares one for Victorian, but not bad, furnishings within. E. window has beautiful and well-restored 14th-century glass. Big collection of monuments, next best in the county after Tong, from 14th century onwards to Blount, Childe and Baldwin families. Of these the best is canopied Blount tomb.

LANGLEY CHAPEL *(dedication unknown*)
Beautiful and remote, set beside gateway of Langley manor-house S. of Acton Burnell. 17th-century stone built with bell tower. Inside untouched. Old floors, stone for nave, brick for chancel. Plastered walls; benches with turned knobs and doors; carved and canopied desk for daily offices facing nave. Table away from E. end with kneelers round it.

LEATON (*Holy Trinity*) GR
Pountney Smith, 1859; tower and spire, 1872; well proportioned within and without.

LEEBOTWOOD *(St. Mary the Virgin*)
On a wooded eminence stands this plaster-covered old church among many handsome Georgian headstones, particularly the similar series to the Corbett family. Inside has clear glass except for cheerful and bright early Victorian E. window; box-pews with iron hat pegs in them and some 17th-century panelling; two-decker pulpit; a chancel division, *c.* 1800 which is a sort of screen; Corbett and Plymley tablets in chancel; W. gallery. Unfortunately there are harsh tiles on floor and the old roof was cheaply repaired with pitchpine.

LLAN-Y-BLODWELL *(St. Michael)
Beautifully sited on the edge of Wales. A 19th-century incumbent, the Rev. John Parker, almost rebuilt, and entirely redecorated the church between 1844 and 1860. The outline of the fine spire is curiously convex. Inside, all is colour, red, blue and gilt. The screen is 15th century repainted. The altar is copied from an Italian model. There are some texts on the walls. The effect is rich and pleasing, but not to those who dislike decoration laid over architecture.

LONGNOR *(St. Mary the Virgin)
Late 13th-century stone church in tree-shaded proximity to brick 17th-century Longnor Hall. Entirely unrestored by Victorians. Outside stairway to W. gallery. Gothick E. iron window tracery; original clear glass. Inside box-pews, galleries, hatchments, reading-desk and pulpit, old floors, plastered walls.

LUDLOW *(St. Laurence)
A very grand 15th-century town church whose pinnacled tower dominates the hill up which climb houses, brick and Georgian, half-timbered and quaint. Ludlow is the Burford of Salop, a show town and no disappointment. The church inside is large and lofty and cruciform, with 14th-century nave and transepts. Expensive restoration by Sir Gilbert Scott in 1859 and Sir Arthur Blomfield later has taken away some of its old texture, but beautifully carved choir stalls, 1447, reredos and screens remain in the splendid Perpendicular chancel which retains some original glass. Monuments.

LYDBURY NORTH *(St. Michael)
Well restored by J. T. Micklethwaite, 1901, when the fine 15th-century nave roof was revealed. Cruciform on plan and Norman of two periods with 14th-century N. transept and 17th-century S. transept. Delightful texture within and without. Rood-screen with plastered tympanum above on which are inscribed the Commandments, great array of 17th-century box-pews, Norman font with 17th-century cover, stone altar in N. transept and late 17th-century altar rails.

LYNEAL-CUM-COLEMERE *(St. John the Evangelist)* GR
G. E. Street, 1870; bold, small and simple; of contrasting ashlar.

MADELEY *(St. Michael)* CL
Thomas Telford, 1794–6; tower and octagonal nave; cast-iron tombs in churchyard.

MALINS LEE *(St. Leonard)* CL
Thomas Telford, 1805; tower and octagonal nave.

MELVERLEY *(St. Peter)
This timber-framed church is probably 15th century; the supports are numerous, and the divisions between them narrow. Inside, a frame of the building divides chancel from nave, and another frame makes a W. division, with gallery over and vestry and lobby beneath. Of the three divisions the chancel is the largest, and the frame, looking like a chancel-screen, produces an odd effect. The River Vyrnwy is near enough to be a danger to the building, and the distant views are magnificent.

MINSTERLEY *(Holy Trinity)* CL
1690, brick and stone; pulpit with domed tester.

MORE *(St. Peter)
A hamlet church by a farm in remote flat landscape between hills of the Welsh border. It was built in 1845 in a countrified Gothic style and has been little disturbed since and is full of the piety of early Tractarianism. Timbered roof with stars over chancel; low box-like pews; glass and fittings all early Victorian.

MORETON CORBET *(St. Bartholomew)
Setting by huge ruined early 17th-cent. manor-house; Corbet monuments; altar and glass by Comper, 1905.

MUNSLOW *(St. Michael)
Setting; 16th-cent. glass in N. aisle; restored, c. 1840: 1835 E. window; Dec. tracery.

ONIBURY *(St. Michael)
In a valley, aisleless and Norman with stone tower and pebble-dash nave and chancel. Interior most sensitively restored by Detmar Blow in 1902 on sound anti-scrape principles. Rough hewn oak W. gallery with square front and Edward VII carved arms; old simple roof; rough hewn oak pews with oak posts supporting iron lanterns for electric light; plaster walls with hat pegs; 1902 Commandment boards; red hangings; box-pews at W. end. A loving recapturing of village simplicity.

PITCHFORD *(St. Michael)
Yew surrounded and beside splendid half-timbered manor hall with 17th-century summerhouse in a tree, old roofs and brick

chimneys. Church, with lake at W. end, is of pink sandstone, medieval and little restored. Inside are 17th-century box-pews and pulpit and communion rails. Wooden effigy of knight in chain mail, c. 1230, fragments of 14th century and 18th century (armorial) glass; Tudor incised slabs; hatchments.

QUATT (*St. Andrew*)
Glass; Elizabethan and 18th-cent. monuments; 18th-cent. brick tower and nave; W. gallery.

RICHARD'S CASTLE *(*All Saints*)
Built by Norman Shaw, 1891–2, in green free stone on a hill. It has a large and chaste tower. The window tracery on the outside is copied from that in the old church which is across the border in Herefordshire (q.v.) only it is larger. Inside the church is vast and bare except for the E. end to which the eye is naturally led. Nothing is mean about this building and what impresses one most is its sense of size, mouldings, arches, proportions of nave and chancel and aisles seem vast. This achieved because the architect was a master of scale.

ST. GEORGE (*St. George*) GR
G. E. Street, 1862; highly original.

ST. MARTIN'S *(*St. Martin*)
Almshouses of 1810 form a pretty setting to this old-fashioned and unspoiled church. Much of the fabric is 13th century but it is the furnishings that are its chief claim to distinction. An inscription over the vestry door records the building of the vestry and the re-pewing of the church in 1810. These box-pews, some oak and some deal, remain; the double-decker pulpit is hung with Georgian velvet. W. gallery, Royal Arms, turned rails round three sides of the altar. Rich and dark two-light window by D. Evans, c. 1840.

SHIFNAL (*St. Andrew*)
Large and of many periods with Norman core; Elizabethan hammer-beam roof in nave and monuments, 16th and 17th cent.

SHREWSBURY (*St. Alkmund*) CL
Perp. tower and tall spire; nave and chancel 1795; Strawberry Hill Gothick by J. Carline and Tilley; E. window a transparency by Egginton after Guido Reni.

*(*St. Chad*)
One of the great Georgian churches designed by George Steuart 1790–2, architect

of Attingham, Lythwood Hall and Wellington Church in Salop. It is of pale yellow ashlar and its free standing square tower and circular steeple add grace to the spired skyline of Shrewsbury. The building stands high in public gardens known as the Quarry and is approached by a late-Georgian street. Its plan is two intersecting circles, the smaller forming an entrance hall, the larger a vast galleried auditorium. The interior plaster and original woodwork is in low delicate relief and Adamesque. Unfortunately the high pews have been cut down and the altar arrangements and stained glass are of a later and less sympathetic era.

(*Holy Cross*)
Abbey Church; Norman and E.E.; chancel by Pearson, 1887.

(*St. Julian*) CL
Medieval tower; nave by T. Pritchard 1750, with columned aisles; D. Evans glass c. 1840.

*(*St. Mary*)
Large sandstone town church of all dates from Norman to 15th century. Though its inside is scraped, its stained glass puts it into the top class. Most of the glass in the windows is excellent 15th and 16th century of Flemish origin, but the E. window, loveliest of all, has 14th-century English glass climbing from a recumbent stained glass Jesse.

(*St. Michael*) CL
J. Carline, 1829–30, in yellow brick; elegant tower.

STOKE ST. MILBOROUGH (*St. Milbruga*)
Setting; aisleless; spacious. Note roofs and Norman chancel arch.

STOKESAY *(*St. John the Baptist*)
The churchyard borders the moat of Stokesay castle, a fortified manor-house with timbed-framed 17th-century additions. The church, damaged in Civil Wars, was largely rebuilt and refurnished afterwards. Many of the 17th-century furnishings remain, including pews, one canopied and of two storeys, and wall texts.

STOTTESDON (*St. Mary*)
Setting; Norman font; 12th-cent. carvings; noble Dec.; tracery and columns.

TONG *(*St. Mary the Virgin with St. Bartholomew*)
Large and grand, almost all of 1410.

Though inside it is scraped, harshly red-tiled on floor and filled with greenish glass, its monuments are some of the best in England. There are screens with remains of painting, brasses, and the 'Golden Chapel' built in 1515 on the S. as a chantry by Sir Henry Vernon, retains its old stencilled walls, and its gilt fan-vaulted ceiling and the beautiful effigies of the Vernon family. Notice, too, 15th-century Pembruge effigies by choir screen.

TUGFORD (*St. Catherine*)
Village; textured exterior; charming modest interior. (*See Plate 24*)

UPTON CRESSET (*St. Michael*)
Steep orchard setting; Norman chancel arch and S. door.

WELLINGTON (*All Saints*) CL
G. Steuart, 1790; Adam-esque stone exterior.

WHITCHURCH *(St. Alkmund*)
Built 1712–3 after the old church fell down. William Smith of Warwick did the rebuilding, but John Barker, a carpenter and joiner by trade, may have been the architect. The church is handsome outside and has a splendid red sandstone tower. Inside, it has been drastically restored, and almost all the large circular-headed windows filled with stained glass. Some good woodwork still remains, although pews and pulpit have been cut down and organ moved. Fine Tuscan arcades to the nave. Interesting tombs. The whole setting is attractive, with pleasant streets leading up to the church, which is on an eminence.

(*St. Catherine*) CL
1836; Greek Revival; tower.

WHITTINGTON (*St. John the Baptist*) CL
Tower 1747; nave 1805–6 by T. Harrison; E. window and woodwork by F. C. Eden, 20th cent.

WISTANSTOW (*Holy Trinity*)
Norman in origin but now largely 14th cent. and later. Roofs of nave (late 14th cent.) and chancel (17th cent.), box-pews (1801); 17th-cent. wall texts and attractively lettered headstones in churchyard.

WORTHEN (*All Saints*)
Wide with 17th-cent. seating throughout; 1761 chancel.

WROXETER (*St. Andrew*)
Roman columns at gate; Norman font; brick floor; coloured effigies in chancel; excellent 17th–18th cent. woodwork.

L

Somerset

N O COUNTY really comes up to Somerset for medieval churches and of these three-quarters are 'Perp' (15th century). As A. K. Wickham said, 'the boundaries are natural, and have from very early times also been those of the diocese. . . . It is not of course suggested that the local style ceased at the county borders or even that the medieval builders were conscious of them, but merely that they provide today a casket, as it were, in which these jewels can most easily be compared and admired'. Churches are mentioned first here because they are the most prominent sights in Somerset, despite the wide variety of its scenery. This variety contains: sea coast along the Bristol Channel; heathery hills on Exmoor; rich valleys in the south-west full of orchards; elmy steep combes round Bruton and Shepton Mallet; a bare and comparatively churchless area on the west where the Brendons rise to 1,707 feet at Dunkery Beacon, and the friendlier Quantocks rise nearly as high between Bridgwater and Taunton; a silvery gorge like Cheddar in the Mendips; on the east, Radstock, where coal is quarried; and in the middle of the county the flat alluvial basin providing a fen district where the Axe, Brue and Parrett flow into the Bristol Channel; and hills rise like blue islands from the flat. Nor are the towns less varied: Bath so 18th-century with its limestone crescents and terraces and squares, Wells whose towers rise from a hollow in the Mendips, a city where the cathedral predominates and the atmosphere is medieval in the sound of bells; Taunton, Yeovil and Bridgwater chain-stored and industrialised; Ilminster, Crewkerne and Axbridge, old fashioned market towns with grand 'Perp' churches. Over orchards and elms and willows, wherever you are in Somerset, you can hear church bells, for few towers contain less than six of them and this is the chief county of ringers.

The variety of stones gives the county a colour. Bath quarries provide pale-yellow stone. Doulting stone from which Wells and the Mendip churches are built is silvery-grey, around Somerton and the Polden hills the quarries yield blue lias which looks particularly good with the old red curly tiles on cottages, and in the west is red sandstone. Finest of all stone is that from Ham Hill in the south. On the Dorset border the old cottages and churches are a rich golden-yellow.

It was after the Black Death and at the end of the 14th century that the great rebuilding of Somerset churches started and I know of no better summary of these buildings than that of the Victorian antiquarian Freeman, 'The typical form is a lofty and elaborate W. tower, disengaged from the aisles, often vaulted within, and nave and aisles with or without clerestory; very commonly a S. porch as high as the aisles, a high roof, and a comparatively insignificant chancel of earlier work, with Perp. chapels on each side. Polygonal turrets are frequent. The roofs are various, but different forms of the coved roof are typical. The interiors are rich in screens and other woodwork. The work is generally superior in the north to that in the south part of the county, owing to the superior quality of the stones admitting more delicate chiselling. The towers, which are the great glory of the county, may be ranked under three typical forms. (1) The Taunton type with a staircase turret at one corner, and double buttresses at the others, all the pinnacles being of equal height, the tower being divided into stages by horizontal string courses: e.g. St. Mary Magdalen and St. James, Taunton; Isle Abbots; Bishops Lydeard; and Huish. (2) The Bristol type, with a prominent turret, crowned with a single spirelet rising above the rest. (3) The Wrington type, which dispenses with staircase turret and horizontal divisions and is panelled with two enormously lofty belfry windows, with pinnacled turrets of the same height: Wrington; St. Cuthbert's, Wells; St. John's, Glastonbury; and North Petherton. Spires are very unfrequent and where they exist are sometimes imperfect . . .

To these glorious towers, built by Somerset people for themselves and essentially non-monastic, the Victorians did little harm. They seem to have been overawed into leaving them alone and confined their attentions to interiors, but even here their 'restorations' were generally mild.

J.B.

SELECTED LIST OF CHURCHES

by E. T. Long

AXBRIDGE *(St. John Baptist)*
A large cruciform church with handsome central tower and the pierced parapets so characteristic of N. Somerset. The interior is notable for the fine plaster ceiling (1636) in the nave, good panelled roofs in the aisles, Prowse monument (1670) and an embroidered 17th-century frontal. The fabric is mainly 15th century but the plan suggests an earlier core. The little town is attractive with some interesting houses with overhanging upper storeys.

BABINGTON *(St. Margaret)*
The 18th-century church and manor-house form a charming group away from all other habitations. The church is the most completely unaltered Georgian example in Somerset. Apsidal sanctuary and small W. tower with octagonal cupola. The interior

has good moulded plaster work on the roof and apse. Box-pews, curved holy table, gated altar rails, two-decker pulpit, pedestal font and clear glass. (*See Plate 49*)

BACKWELL *(St. Andrew)*
It stands on high ground just off the busy road from Bristol to the S.W., pleasantly backed by woods. The church is a fine fabric with work of every century from the 12th to the 17th. The noble 15th-century tower was repaired in the 17th century which accounts for the unusual appearance of the top storey. Note the 15th-century chantry and tomb on N. of chancel, early 16th-century screen and fine 18th-century brass chandelier.

BAGBOROUGH *(St. Pancras)*
The little 15th-century church stands on

the lower slope of a wooded hill hard by the late Georgian manor-house. The interior is rich in Comper fittings and glass and there is a fine display of the early 16th-century bench-ends so characteristic of the Quantocks. The genius of Sir Ninian Comper has made it an ideal village church.

BANWELL *(St. Andrew)*
One of the many fine churches of N. Somerset. The approach is between two rows of cottages leading direct to the graceful W. tower. A 14th-century core, but now mainly 15th century as so often with the greater Somerset churches. The usual pierced parapets of the district. The interior is impressive with noble roof, magnificent vaulted screen, many old bench-ends, stone pulpit and painted glass, all 15th century. The W. gallery is said to have been made from an Elizabethan manorial pew.

BATCOMBE *(St. Mary)*
Pleasantly sited in the hilly country north of Bruton away from main roads. The fabric is mainly 15th century with an outstandingly impressive tower. The chancel is 14th century with 17th-century E. window and on the N. a picturesque 18th-century vestry. Note the pierced parapets and, within, the aisle roofs, fan vault to tower, 17th-century altar rails and brass and the recently inserted altar and hangings by W. H. Randoll Blacking. *(See Plate 23)*

BATH ABBEY *(St. Peter & St. Paul)*
One of the last big Perpendicular monastic churches to be built. Begun, 1499, on site of earlier building. Not completed by the time of the dissolution of monasteries, 1539, when glass and lead were sold and the building became mother church of Bath. Nave completed in 17th century by public subscription and windows glazed. A tall cruciform building with oblong tower and impressive W. front showing angels descending and ascending by ladders. 'The icy regularity of Bath Abbey' described by Ruskin, is emphasised by Sir Gilbert Scott's restoration of 1864–73. Scott removed 'incorrect' 17th-century work and substituted stone vaulting to nave and put in rich pews and stalls to choir. Interior effect, owing to removal of organ and screen into a transept, rather barren and unmysterious. 18th-century tablets to Bath fashionables a pleasing feature of walls. For reasons connected with propor-

tions and hard restoration, Bath Abbey is less effective than comparable buildings like St. George's Chapel, Windsor, St. Mary Redcliff, Bristol, or King's College Chapel, Cambridge.

BATH *(St. Mary Magdalene, Holloway)*
Unaisled, late 15th cent.

(St. Michael) GR
1835–7, by G. P. Manners. An entire rebuilding in a crudely effective E.E. style with a graceful vaulted and aisled interior.

(St. Swithun, Walcot)
Rebuilt by John Palmer, 1777–80; tower and spire 1790; Ionic classic; interior galleried and with free-standing Ionic columns; monuments; Victorian pews; shallow chancel.

BATHWICK *(St. Mary)* GR
1820, by J. Pinch; rich and effective Somerset-style stone tower of three stages, with strong mouldings; bold mouldings round pinnacled and battlemented exterior; inside, a sumptuous Tractarian rearrangement and new chancel by G. E. Street in 1873.

BISHOPS LYDEARD *(St. Mary)*
A large village pleasantly sited at the foot of the Quantocks and built of the local red sandstone. Here, as often in the more prosperous parts of Somerset, the church was rebuilt in the 15th century with one of the beautiful towers for which the county is justly famous. Within is a noble roodscreen restored to its former glory by the genius of Sir Ninian Comper with the Rood and its attendant figures all gold and colour. Comper altars and glass make glorious the chancel and chapel and there is a fine array of the richly-carved bench-ends so characteristic of the region. Note the finely-carved churchyard cross.

BRENT, EAST: *see East Brent.*

BRENT, SOUTH: *see South Brent.*

BROOMFIELD *(All Saints)*
W. country Perp.; roofs and seating early 16th cent.

BRUTON *(St. Mary)*
The noble two-towered church stands near the site of the former Augustinian Abbey on the edge of a little town full of charming old houses. It was rebuilt in the 15th and 16th centuries but the present chancel is fine Georgian work which the 'restorers' mercifully spared. The W. tower is distinguished even in Somerset; the other

which is much smaller is over the N. porch. Note the rich tie-beam roof of the nave, Georgian reredos, Jacobean screen in tower arch, 15th-century embroidery and 17th-century Berkeley monuments.

BRYMPTON D'EVERCY (St. Andrew)
14th–15th cent.; monuments and stone screen; setting with manor-house and outbuildings.

BUCKLAND DINHAM (St. Michael)
12th cent.; later enlarged and refashioned; porch has fan vault.

CADBURY, NORTH: see North Cadbury.

CAMELEY *(St. James)
A lonely hamlet church with an old farmstead to keep it company. The small fabric of chancel, nave, S. porch and W. tower is of 12th-century origin refashioned in 15th century. The interior is perhaps the most 'atmospherick' in Somerset with white walls, clear glass, box-pews, canopied pulpit, gated altar rails and galleries. Note, also, 15th-century wagon-roof in nave and mural monument to Cadwallader Jones (1692).

CHARTERHOUSE-ON-MENDIP (St. Hugh) GR
1913 by W. D. Caroë; small mission church in local stone and style; attractive rustic interior with excellent fittings in restrained arts and crafts manner.

CHEDDAR (St. Andrew)
W. country Perp.; tower, stone pulpit and woodwork 15th cent.; remains of 15th-cent. painted glass.

CHEDZOY (St. Mary)
Tower, 15th cent.; arcades 13th cent.; bench-ends 16th cent.; medieval embroidery.

CHEWTON MENDIP *(St. Mary Magdalene)
A pleasant stone village on a plateau in the Mendips. The church is of 12th-century origin and to this period belong the chancel and nave. The S. chapel and E. part of the aisle were added in 13th century and the latter extended westward in 14th century. Some refashioning in 15th century. The glorious tower is 16th century and has an elaborate parapet and panelled middle stage of the Gloucester type with original sculpture on W. front. Note 12th-century N. doorway, late 15th-century bench-ends, 17th-century lectern and holy table. Complete medieval churchyard cross.

CHURCHSTANTON *(St. Peter & St. Paul)
In a lane more than a mile from the centre of population and close to the Devon border. The church is typical West Country Perpendicular, largely refitted c. 1800. The base of the tower is 13th century. An unspoilt interior with box-pews, W. gallery, much clear glass and fragments of medieval painted glass. The front of the gallery is formed of early 16th-century bench-ends.

CLEVEDON (All Saints) GR
Victorian Gothic; Comper fittings and glass.

COMPTON MARTIN *(St. Michael)
An unusually imposing Norman village church with aisled and clerestoried nave and vaulted chancel. The tower is good 15th-century work. The interior has, unfortunately, been scraped. Note the 15th and 17th century parclose screens and spiral column of S. arcade. The tower has numerous canopied niches, pierced parapet and panelled arch.

CONGRESBURY (St. Andrew)
15th cent. with earlier core; spire to tower; roof 15th cent.; font 12th cent.; screen on stone base 15th cent.

CREWKERNE *(St. Bartholomew)
An imposing and spacious Perpendicular town church with central tower, unusually large N. transept with E. chapel and short but lofty clerestoried nave. The W. front with angle turrets and niched figures flanking the doorway is a masterly composition. Good roofs. Interior over-seated as so often in town churches.

CRICKET MALHERBIE (St. Mary Magdalene) GR
Rich Tractarian interior; Camden perfection.

CROSCOMBE *(St. Mary)
A handsome church in the centre of a large village which lies in a pleasant valley running down from Shepton Mallet to Wells. Mostly 15th or early 16th century. The tower has a stone spire. The interior was largely refitted early in 17th century with lofty screen, canopied pulpit and box-pews which mingle pleasantly with the earlier bench-ends. The chancel roof is dated 1664 and is a post-medieval version of tie-beam construction. Note, also, the two-storeyed vestry, 13th-century S. doorway, fragments of late 15th-century painted glass and two 18th-century chandeliers.

CROWCOMBE (*Holy Ghost*)
Somerset Perp.; bench-ends 16th cent.; font 15th cent.; screen 18th cent.; churchyard cross 15th cent.

CULBONE (*St. Culbone*)
Remote and small; 15th cent. screen and seating.

CURRY MALLET (*St. James*)
15th cent.; tower; 17th-cent. monument.

CURRY, NORTH: *see North Curry.*

CURRY RIVEL *(St. Andrew)*
The church well sited above the main part of the village is mainly 15th century but with a large 14th-century N. chapel. The fine tower, though rebuilt, is probably a faithful reproduction of the original. Note S. porch, aisle roofs, 15th-century screen and painted glass, 16th-century bench-ends and 17th-century monuments.

DITCHEAT (*St. Mary Magdalene*)
Cruciform with central tower; 14th and 15th cent.; nave roof 15th cent.; reading desk 17th cent.; wall-painting 15th cent. (restored).

DUNSTER *(St. George)*
A large cruciform fabric, the E. portion of which was the conventual church of a Benedictine Priory which stood to the N. and of which there are still some remains. The fabric is 12th century in origin with contemporary W. doorway. Chancel much renewed 13th-century work. The rest mainly 15th century. Nave and aisles have good 15th-century roofs. Note the Luttrell monuments 14th, 15th and 16th centuries and above all the splendid parochial rood-screen running right across nave and aisles. The village is delightful and the whole is dominated by the castle.

EAST BRENT *(St. Mary)*
This parish is associated with Archdeacon Denison who was rector for more than fifty years and a vigorous Tractarian. The church possesses an ancient and graceful stone spire and is mainly 15th century. The tower retains interesting figure sculpture on its W. face. The interior is rich in old fittings and the elaborate plaster ceiling of the nave (1637) recalls that of Axbridge. Note the late 15th-century bench-ends, painted glass and wooden lectern together with the 17th-century pulpit and gallery.

EAST PENNARD (*All Saints*)
15th cent.; roof; 17th-cent. pulpit.

EVERCREECH (*St. Peter*)
14th–15th cent; tower and nave roof 15th cent.

GLASTONBURY *(St. John Baptist)*
A spacious town Perpendicular church with one of the finest towers in Somerset exhibiting in its elaborate parapet and panelled middle stage the influence of Gloucester. Handsome two-storeyed vaulted porch. Within, note the sumptuous tie-beam roof of the nave, tower vaulting, 15th-century stone pulpit, late medieval painted glass, portions of a medieval vestment and early 16th-century altar-tomb.

HAM, HIGH: *see High Ham.*

HAM, LOW: *see Low Ham.*

HEMINGTON (*St. Mary*)
12th cent.; later refashioned and enlarged; 15th-cent. tower.

HIGH HAM *(St. Andrew)*
A pleasant upland village with some comely houses and attractive prospects. Adrian Schaell, an Elizabethan incumbent, wrote a lengthy memoir of the parish in the register in 1598 where he states that the church except the 14th-century tower was rebuilt in 1476 by the Abbot of Glastonbury, John Dyer the rector, Sir Amias Poulett and others. This date agrees with the architectural evidence. It is an accomplished specimen of Somerset Perpendicular with clerestoried nave, sumptuous roofs and vaulted rood-screen. Note, also, the fine display of carved bench-ends, Norman font, Jacobean lectern and some medieval painted glass.

HINTON BLEWITT *(All Saints)*
Approached by winding lanes in the remote country north of the Mendips. The church which stands high is mainly 15th century with a N. aisle added, *c.* 1530. The interior as a result of careful restoration in 1928 is one of the most charming in the district with stone floors and mainly clear glass. Note roofs, 12th-century font, fragments of 16th-century painted glass, canopied pulpit dated 1638 and early 16th-century seating.

HINTON ST. GEORGE (*St. George*)
Somerset Perp.; setting; roof 15th cent.; monuments 16th and 17th cent.

HOLCOMBE *(St. Andrew)*
Stands alone in the fields, the village having

moved a mile away where there is a Victorian church. The old fabric is of 12th-century origin, refashioned in 16th century and later. Interior very 'atmospherick' with box-pews, hat pegs, two-decker pulpit, gallery and clear glass.

HUISH EPISCOPI (*St. Mary the Virgin*)
12th cent. in origin with a good contemporary doorway; refashioned in 14th cent. and 15th cent; splendid 15th cent. tower with many niches and elaborate pinnacled parapet; screen 15th cent.; Stuart Royal Arms and Jacobean pulpit. (*See Plate 21*)

ILMINSTER *(St. Mary)*
One of the great Somerset churches. Mainly 15th century and of cruciform plan with very handsome central tower and elaborate N. transept as at Crewkerne. The nave arcades rebuilt and aisles raised early in 19th century to accommodate galleries. E. sacristy is a Somerset feature. Fine Wadham monuments 15th, 16th and 17th centuries including that of the founders of Wadham College, Oxford. Note, also, fan vault of tower, 17th-century pulpit and screen and 18th-century chandelier. The little town is attractive with some interesting houses including the Chantry and Tudor Grammar School.

ISLE ABBOTTS *(St. Mary)*
The stately Perpendicular tower rises from the flats through which meanders the River Isle. The chancel is good early Decorated work with contemporary windows. The rest is 15th century and early 16th with fan-vaulted porch and a tower with niches retaining most of its figure sculpture. Note panelled roof of aisle, Norman font and 15th and 17th century screens. (*See Plate 28*)

KILMERSDON (*St. Peter & St. Paul*)
12th cent. and later; tower, aisle roof and stone screen, 15th cent.

KINGSBURY EPISCOPI *(St. Martin)*
A large village of Ham stone in the marshy basin of the River Parret set about with willows. Many attractive old cottages and farmsteads. The imposing church is mainly 14th and 15th century with one of the most satisfying of the great Somerset towers. The lofty chancel has splendid transomed windows and an E. sacristy. Note the fan vaulting of the tower, 15th-century screen and fragments of late medieval painted glass.

LANSDOWN *(St. Stephen)* GR
1840–5 by James Wilson; prominent tower of elegant and original outline; interior conventional.

LARKHALL (*St. Saviour*) GR
By John Pinch, 1829–32; impressive late Georgian attempt at Somerset Perp. in ashlar; galleried interior, Victorianised in 1882.

LEIGH-ON-MENDIP (*St. Giles*)
15th cent.; tower; glass and seating 15th cent.

LONG SUTTON *(Holy Trinity)*
The spacious village green is surrounded by lias-stone houses of many periods above which looms the lofty tower of the late 15th-century church. It is a spacious and impressive fabric in the best Somerset manner with clerestoried nave and a magnificent tie-beam roof of the local type. Note the 15th-century pulpit and rood-screen, both with rather garish Victorian colour, 17th-century pulpit and 15th-century tower vaulting.

LOW HAM (*unknown*) GS
17th cent.; Somerset Perp. with contemporary screen and some glass.

LYDEARD, BISHOPS: *see Bishops Lydeard.*

MARTOCK *(All Saints)*
A small town not far from the famous Ham Hill quarries which provided the stone for its noble church and many interesting houses. The church has a 13th-century chancel but the rest is good Somerset Perpendicular, though the tower is hardly worthy of the great clerestoried nave with its rich parapets. Within, the principal feature is the wondrous tie-beam roof of the nave, perhaps the finest of its kind. There are canopied niches in the clerestory with 17th-century paintings of the Apostles.

MELLS *(St. Andrew)*
One of the best villages in Somerset – which is saying a good deal – with a stately church, a mellow Tudor manor-house and a wealth of charming cottages and farmsteads. The church was rebuilt in the 15th century with a noble tower and a profusion of carved detail. The interior, also, is beautiful in spite of excessive 'restoration'. Note the nave and chapel roofs, the Norman font, fragments of medieval painted glass and various monuments, including that of Edward Horner by Munnings and Lutyens.

MIDDLEZOY (*Holy Cross*)
14th–15th cent.; tower; bench-ends early
16th cent.; glass 15th cent.; pulpit 17th
cent.; screens 15th and 17th cent.

MILBORNE PORT (*St. John Evangelist*)
12th, 15th and 19th cent.; tower; screen
15th cent.; stalls 20th cent.

MUCHELNEY (*St. Peter & St. Paul*)
15th cent.; tower; 17th-cent. nave roof and
seating.

NORTH CADBURY *(*St. Michael*)
The church, a splendid example of Somerset Perpendicular groups well with the
manor-house which is Tudor on N. and
Georgian on S. The chancel, which is particularly impressive, was built for the use
of a college and once possessed fine stalls.
Note roofs, early 16th-century seating and
15th-century painted glass in W. window.
The large village is rich in old houses from
16th century onwards.

NORTH CURRY
   *(*St. Peter & St. Paul*)
A large village on the low ridge which
stands out into Sedgemoor, east of Taunton.
The church is a fine cruciform fabric with
octagonal central tower and pierced parapets. The N. doorway is 12th century and
the base of the tower 13th century. Largely
rebuilt in the 14th century and considerably
refashioned in the 15th century, to which
belong the clerestory and most of the windows. The roofs though mostly modern are
traditional and good. The porch and crossing are vaulted. Note remains of 14th-
century clerestory below the later one,
12th century chest, two effigies, fine chandelier dated 1809 and glass of Burlison and
Grylls.

NORTH PETHERTON *(*St. Mary*)
A large and rather dull village on the main
road from Taunton to Bridgwater not far
from the edge of Sedgemoor. The church
amply compensates for the village and is
mainly 15th century with a superb tower
retaining most of its original figure
sculpture and crowned with a rich pinnacled
parapet. There is an eastern sacristy as in
several other important Somerset churches.
Within, note the roofs of nave and aisles,
the 15th-century font and pulpit and 17th-
century manorial pew.

NORTON-SUB-HAMDON (*St. Mary*)
Late 15th cent.; tower; embattled aisles;
attractive village beneath Ham Hill.

PAWLETT *(*St. John Baptist*)
Standing on high ground above the rich
pasture land of Pawlett Hams. A medieval
church with a highly 'atmospherick' interior. With a 12th-century core it was refashioned and enlarged in 13th and 15th
centuries. Note the 12th-century font, 15th-
century screen and a fine display of 17th-
century fittings – three-sided altar rails,
box-pews, font cover, pulpit and reading
desk. Windows mostly with clear glass in
rectangular leading.

PENNARD, EAST: *see East Pennard.*

PENNARD, WEST: *see West Pennard.*

PETHERTON, NORTH: *see North Petherton.*

PILTON *(*St. John Baptist*)
A pleasant rambling village on a hillside
with the great 14th-century tithe barn on
the opposite slope. The church is of 12th-
century origin refashioned and enlarged in
15th century. Clerestory to nave and chancel. The tower stair turret terminates in an
unusually tall crocketed finial. Note the
late 12th-century arcade, the splendid 15th-
century roofs, parclose screens, portion of
15th-century cope, fragments of late medieval painted glass and a fine chandelier
dated 1749.

PORLOCK (*St. Dubricius*)
13th cent.; later refashioned; low tower
with timber spire; 15th-cent. monument;
reredos by W. H. R. Blacking.

QUEEN CAMEL *(*St. Barnabas*)
A large and pleasant lias-stone village with
wide street at the N. end of which is the
impressive 14th and 15th century church
with a charming 18th-century portico
porch which somehow escaped the Victorian 'restorers'. The interior has unfortunately been scraped but is still interesting
with a fine tie-beam roof to the nave, lofty
vaulted screen, font with much figure
sculpture and some 18th-century embroidery.

REDLYNCH (*St. Peter*)
18th cent. with clear glass windows; pulpit
and reredos contemporary.

RODE (*St. Laurence*)
15th cent. with 19th-cent. rebuilding; aisle
roofs and wall-paintings 15th cent.; altar
rails late 17th cent.

ST. CATHERINE (*St. Catherine*)
Setting; 12th cent. refashioned late 15th
cent.; painted glass and pulpit 15th cent.;
monument 17th cent.

SELWORTHY *(All Saints)*

Superbly situated on the side of a wooded hill overlooking the rich country which here borders Exmoor. White cottages with thatched roofs and round chimneys rising towards the typical 15th-century W. Somerset church with its plastered walls and squat tower. Within are rich wagon-roofs, medieval and Comper glass, carved bench-ends, 15th-century pulpit with 17th-century tester, 18th-century gallery, manorial pew and monument by Chantrey. The fabric is of 14th-century origin enlarged early in 16th century.

SOUTH BRENT *(St. Michael)*

On the lower slopes of Brent Knoll, an isolated hill rising out of the Somerset flats. We enter by a good Norman S. doorway and there are some remains of 13th and 14th century work including the S. chapel, but the fabric was mainly rebuilt in the Perpendicular period. Good roofs in nave and aisle. Note striking set of late medieval bench-ends and fine monument bright with colour to John Somerset (1663) and his two wives.

STAWLEY *(St. Michael)*

Among lanes in hilly country on the Devon border. One of the few churches in that area which virtually escaped Victorian 'restoration'. The fabric is 13th century and late medieval but the fittings are mostly 18th century and include box-pews, altar rails, pulpit with domed tester and clear glass.

STOGURSEY *(St. Andrew)*

A spacious cruciform church with central tower crowned with a lead and timber spire. The E. portion served as the quire of a small Benedictine Priory of which the only visible feature is a circular dovecote. The church is largely of two periods in the 12th century. About 1500 the transepts were incorporated in the reconstructed chancel chapels and the windows mostly renewed. There was a drastic mid-19th century 'restoration' when the levels were altered and the roofs renewed. Interior much improved of late. Note good Norman detail, 14th and 15th century monuments and 16th-century bench-ends.

STOKE ST. GREGORY *(St. Gregory)*

Cruciform with octagonal central tower; 13th cent. and later; bench-end 16th cent.; pulpit 17th cent.

STOKE-SUB-HAMDON *(St. Mary)*

The village in two sections lies, as its name suggests, below Ham Hill, famous from time immemorial for its quarries of golden stone. The church is at East Stoke and is one of the most notable Norman fabrics in Somerset and its restoration by Ferrey was restrained. The base of the tower serves as the N. transept. The chancel and nave are 12th century while the tower, S. transept and most of the windows are 13th century. Note the good Norman and Early English detail, the 15th-century nave roof and 17th-century pulpit.

SUTTON MALLET *(unknown)*

A small village at the foot of the Polden Hills amid the rhynes and willows of Sedgemoor. The little church, highly 'atmospherick', was rebuilt in 1829 and retains its box-pews, gated altar rails, three-decker pulpit and W. gallery.

SWELL *(St. Catharine)*

At the bottom of a narrow lane leading from the Langport and Taunton road stands a lovely group of buildings dominated by the medieval and Tudor manor-house. The little church is approached through a farmyard. It is of 12th-century origin, recast in the 15th century when the panelled chancel arch and the present windows were inserted. The interior is delightful with clear glass and lovely fragments of late medieval glass, 15th-century seating, 17th-century altar rails, font cover and pulpit and 18th-century box-pews. There is no tower but only a timber bell-cote.

TAUNTON *(St. Mary Magdalene)*

A large town church with the highest and most elaborate of the Somerset parochial towers. The tower was rebuilt in the old form in 1862, pink sandstone being used in place of the friable grey material of the original work. The body of the church was rebuilt in the 15th and early 16th century with double aisles to the nave. Very rich two-storeyed porch. Within, note the roofs especially that of the nave of the local tie-beam type, the niches over the arcades and an especially large one on one of the pillars, and fragments of late medieval painted glass. Fine though the interior is, extensive restoration and overcrowded seating have deprived it of its atmosphere.

TINTINHULL *(St. Margaret)*

A most attractive village rich in old houses, especially round the green. The church is mainly 13th and 14th century with N. lateral tower. Though rather heavily restored the interior still possesses much character. The *pièce de resistance* is the glass in the E. window by F. C. Eden depicting the Fons Vitae. Note, also, the Jacobean pulpit with tester, 15th-century brass, 16th-century bench-ends and Comper churchyard cross.

TRULL *(All Saints)*
The 15th-century church is a treasure house of late medieval art – rood-screen, pulpit with figures of the Doctors, a fine array of carved bench-ends and an unusually extensive display of late 15th-century glass.

WATCHET *(St. Decuman)*
Mostly 15th cent.; tower; roofs 15th cent.; gated altar rails 17th cent.; monuments 16th and 17th cent.; pulpit with tester 17th cent.; screens late 15th cent.

WEDMORE *(St. Mary)*
A large and imposing cruciform church with lofty central tower. The core is late 12th century to which belong the tower arches, parts of the chancel and the inner S. doorway. There is a 14th-century window in S. chapel. All other features are Perpendicular. The later additions have absorbed the transepts. Note roofs of chapels, one with original colour, ironwork on S. door, early 16th-century wall-painting of St. Christopher, Jacobean pulpit and three 18th-century chandeliers.

WELLOW *(St. Julian)*
A fine Perpendicular church with a chancel by Bodley standing at the end of the long village street amid the hills between Radstock and Bath. The interior has been recently restored with much care and is now exceedingly attractive and 'atmospherick'. Note the roofs, especially those of nave and chapel, screens, seating and some late 15th-century wall-paintings recently brought to light.

WELLS *(St. Cuthbert)*
A large town church of 13th-century origin, refashioned and enlarged in 15th century. There was originally a central tower which was replaced in the 15th century by the superb structure at the W. end and among the finest in Somerset. There are good roofs, that of the nave being of the local tie-beam type. Rich Carolean pulpit. In the transepts are sadly mutilated but still beautiful stone reredoses. Some remains of

medieval painted glass. Early 17th-century monument and medieval font cover.

WESTON-SUPER-MARE *(All Saints)*
This beautiful church by Bodley is probably the finest of entirely modern foundation in Somerset. The S. aisle and chapel were added by Eden. The tower is not yet built. The stately Decorated arcades and boarded wagon-roofs are excellent. The rood-screen by Bodley needs a loft with more projection and is inferior to that of the S. chapel. There is some exquisite Eden glass and a lovely embroidered Tree of Jesse reredos in the S. chapel. The Gothic font is Bodley's but the Classic Comperesque cover is by Eden.

WESTON ZOYLAND *(St. Mary)*
In the heart of Sedgemoor the great 15th-century tower looms over the marshland with the lines of willows marking the dykes. One of the great Perpendicular churches of Somerset satisfying within and without, the interior having benefited by Caroë's careful restoration. The chancel is 14th century and out of scale with the rest. Note the splendid tie-beam roof of the nave, the 15th-century bench-ends, 16th-century heraldic glass, Jacobean pulpit and decent modern fittings.

WEST PENNARD *(St. Nicholas)*
A large lias-stone village with a network of lanes almost in the shadow of Glastonbury Tor. The handsome church was completely rebuilt in the second half of 15th century with chancel, clerestoried nave, aisles, S. porch and W. tower with timber and lead spire. Fine and richly-carved roofs throughout. Note the parapets, square framed rood-screen, late 15th-century painted glass (Coronation of Our Lady, etc.). Georgian Royal Arms and churchyard cross with emblems of the Passion on the base.

WINSCOMBE *(St. James)*
A good stone village which culminates in the fine 15th-century church with its graceful tower, pierced parapets and elegant rood stair turret. Within there is a good panelled roof in the N. aisle. Note the Norman font, carved bench-ends and extensive display of late medieval painted glass.

WITHAM *(St. Mary, St. John Baptist & All Saints)*
A little late 12th-century French church, apsidal and stone vaulted. It was here that

the first English Carthusian monastery was founded by Henry II, and St. Hugh, later Bishop of Lincoln, came from Burgundy as Prior, probably erecting this church in the style with which he was familiar; W. end modern but convincing. Note the Comper glass in several windows, a little medieval glass and the Jacobean pulpit.

WIVELISCOMBE *(St. Andrew)*

The church of this little town rebuilt in 1829 has been described as a 'tasteless building with a showy semi-Italian interior'. It is nothing of the sort, being in fact a most interesting structure in a free rendering of Perpendicular and has of late been relieved of certain Victorian blemishes which had been intruded and has now a delightful interior. Box-pews, gated altar rails and W. gallery. Monument with effigies to Humphry Windham and wife, 1622. The architect was Richard Carver of Bridgwater.

WOOLLEY *(All Saints)* GR

18th-cent. Gothick with apsidal sanctuary and W. cupola; clear glass in rectangular leading.

WRINGTON *(All Saints)*

Pleasantly situated in the Yeo Valley between two low ranges of hills. The church possesses one of the best of the many noble Somerset towers; with its long and graceful belfry windows it belongs to the class of Evercreech and St. Cuthbert's, Wells. The 15th-century nave and aisles are worthy of the tower but the earlier chancel is somewhat out of scale. Note the fine roofs, screen, 15th-century font and stone pulpit.

WYKE CHAMPFLOWER *(Holy Trinity)*

A chapelry of Bruton. The fabric which is a small aisleless parallelogram is attached to the manor-house and was rebuilt in 1623 in Jacobean Gothic. It has entirely escaped Victorian 'restoration'. Note the box-pews, hat pegs, altar rails, holy table and stone pulpit. Decent font dated 1945.

YATTON *(St. Mary)*

A large village in the fertile Yeo Valley with many interesting houses including the medieval rectorial manor place. The church is one of the most impressive in Somerset with a central tower crowned with a truncated stone spire. As so often in Somerset the chancel is out of scale with the nave, being, like the transepts, a relic of the earlier fabric which was not rebuilt in the 15th century though a handsome chapel was added on the N. Noble porch and W. front in the best Somerset manner. Good 14th and 15th century monuments. Nave and aisles have contemporary roofs. A pall is made up from a late 15th-century dalmatic.

Staffordshire

INTRODUCTION

STAFFORDSHIRE IS believed by many people to be 'just the Black Country and Potteries', which only proves how unknown the county is. If it were not famous for heavy engineering, pottery and coal, it would still deserve a measure of fame for the charm and variety of its landscape and architecture. Four centuries ago, Camden's *Britannia* described the county in terms still fairly relevant: 'The north part is mountainous and less fertile; but the middle, which is watered by the Trent, is fruitful, woody and pleasant, by an equal mixture of arable and meadow grounds; so is also the south, which has much pit-coal and mines of iron; but whether to their loss or advantage, the natives themselves are the best judges . . . '.

Few people apart from the natives realise that there is a large part of the Peak District in the county. In fact, it is said that 'the best parts of Derbyshire are in Staffordshire' – the hundred square miles between Dovedale and the Dane Valley, across the Leek moors. To the west, the crag of Mow Cop, the birthplace of Primitive Methodism, overlooks the Cheshire plain; in the north, the Weaver Hills overlook Alton Towers and Castle with their exciting Pugin skylines. In the centre and south there are the old Royal Forests of Cannock Chase and Kinver, and to the east is Needwood Forest with its great estates – and Bodley's masterpiece at Hoar Cross. In the central undulating lowlands lies Lichfield, and the Cathedral of St. Chad.

A county for over a thousand years, Staffordshire still forms a rather separate and independent region, across which runs the Watling Street, leading the Romans and everyone else through the county rather than into it.

Culturally conservative, the county seems often to have woken late but vigorous to its tasks, witness the notable architecture of the 19th-century churches, especially the outstanding work of Bodley, Norman Shaw, Street – his own favourite church design is at Denstone – and Pugin – his ten churches here include St. Giles, Cheadle, with its fabulously coloured interior.

But to begin at the beginning, there is fine Norman work at Stafford and Tutbury, besides less considerable remains in seventeen other churches; good 13th-century at Brewood, Coppenhall, Weston-on-Trent tower, and, of course, the nave of Lichfield Cathedral; much fine Decorated, notably in the Lichfield Lady Chapel, and at Clifton Campville and Checkley; and the usual amount of 15th-century work, the most complete examples being St. Peter's, Wolverhampton, and Penkridge. Very late Gothic occurs at Barton-under-Needwood (1533), Blurton (1636) and Broughton (1633), small, isolated, and

332

one of the most charming churches. The building materials are usually local stone and tiles, though timber arcades are found at Betley and Rushton. Towers are the rule, though a few good spires exist.

Among the Renaissance churches are Ingestre by Wren, Patshull by Gibbs, and Burton-upon-Trent by Francis Smith.

This is no place for too archaeological or historical an approach, whether to churches or the architecture of the county – the guide books can tell about the ancient forts, castles, abbey ruins, the great houses set in their parkland, and the architectural details of churches, such as tracery, screens, woodwork, and the characteristic Staffordshire incised stone tomb-slabs. But if a list were made of the significant details to make a pilgrimage to see, it should include the tympanum at Kingswinford, the squire's pews and the three-decker pulpit at Baswich, the stone pulpit with the lion at Wolverhampton, the fonts at Ilam, Armitage and All Saints, Leek, the Gerrard tomb at Ashley, and the great figure of Christ at Swynnerton.

In landscape and architecture Staffordshire is a good average, with numerous high spots. There is quiet, remote country especially in the centre and north: there is much industrial building in certain parts: and both in the towns and the countryside there are many churches which well deserve to be loved more widely.   D.B.P.

SELECTED LIST OF CHURCHES

by D. B. Peace, A.R.I.B.A.

ACTON TRUSSELL (*St. James the Great*) 15th cent.; tower, 1566.

ADBASTON (*St. Michael & All Angels*) 12th–15th cent.; mid 15th-cent. alabaster incised slab.

ALREWAS *(All Saints)* Tower and exterior mainly Perpendicular, the clerestory being raised directly over the aisle and chancel walls: 13th-century chancel. The interior high and spacious and with fine 16th-century roofs. Good fittings – 17th-century pulpit, 15th-century font, sedilia, stalls, Kempe glass, and a good W. door of 1627 with appropriate ironwork.

ALSTONFIELD *(St. Peter)* Pleasant setting in the Peak District limestone country near Dovedale. Outer walls of attractive checkered sandstone and limestone. Plain and serene inside: Norman, Decorated and Perpendicular. Excellent box-pews including Charles Cotton's more richly done, and two-decker pulpit, all c. 1637.

ASHLEY *(St. John the Baptist)* Late Gothic tower, early 17th-century; pedestrian exterior of 1861. The interior, by Bodley, completed 1910, surprisingly good. Chancel divided from nave by rood-screen after only two bays; good reredos and the altar well lit; the whole effect enlivened by many brass candelabra. Magnificent alabaster tomb of Lord Gerrard at N., 1617, and at the S. several impressive Victorian marble memorials to the Kinnersleys.

ASTON, LITTLE: *see Little Aston.*

BARTON-UNDER-NEEDWOOD   (*St. James*) 1533; glass; heraldry; apsidal chancel.

BASWICH *(Holy Trinity)* 1739 (£336) by Richard Trubshaw and Richard Jackson. A small brick church with medieval stone tower overlooking Stafford. Light and simple interior, the eye caught by the three-decker pulpit and the two Levett family pews just beyond the medieval chancel arch, one raised on spindly columns and the other on stout Doric ones. Heraldic table tombs and pleasing modern glass.

BETLEY *(St. Margaret)*
The exterior has the interest of a Gothic tower of 1693 and timber-framed clerestory and porches. Quite impressive work inside – timber columns, arcades and trusses in the nave; good roof and parclose screen. Gallery, 18th century, with box-pews. Good monument, 1610.

BILSTON *(St. Leonard)*
Francis Goodwin, 1826. Classical, like a grey fortress, with a charming octagonal domed tower; nice ironwork on top. The good Soane-ish gate piers and the iron tomb-slabs are more appropriate to the setting than the modern stone flagged garden and figure. Good gently coloured Greek interior with galleries (Ewan Christian, 1883) and modern work by Bernard Miller.

BLITHFIELD *(St. Leonard)*
Isolated setting by the Hall, home of the Bagots since the 14th century. Simple 14th-century tower; lofty nave and clerestory, 13th and late 15th century screen; and 40 benches, 15th century; glass 14th and 16th century; and the Bagot tombs and memorials.

BLORE (*St. Bartholomew*)
14th–15th cent.; screen; benches; Bassett tomb; glass; stalls.

BLURTON (*St. Bartholomew*) GS
1626 and later; roof.

BLYMHILL *(St. Mary)*
A Street 'restoration' of great originality and interest with some old work left, including the tower. A fine conglomerate work of art. Windows with bold plate tracery and high relief figures; the Adoration of the Magi carved by Street as his gift to the church; his stone, woodwork, iron, brass and gilding at their best. In the chancel, a small and lovely old carved wooden Nativity with oxen, shepherds and heavenly horsemen; on the S. side outside, a great lioness; dormered clerestory. School by Street by the churchyard gate.

BOBBINGTON (*Holy Cross*)
12th and 13th cent.; chest.

BRADLEY *(All Saints)*
A church of great antiquarian interest.

Tower, 15th century, and a nave generously lighted, bold and box-like outside, graced inside by a fine nave arcade, *c.* 1260; chancel arcade earlier. Carved Norman tub font, rood stair (modern rood-screen), some good glass fragments, and late 16th-century alabaster effigies.

BREWOOD *(St. Mary)*
A largish church with a spire in an attractive village. The nave simple and quite good Perpendicular, the chancel mid–13th century, the S. side, gabled, by Street. The Giffard tombs are excellent, 16th–17th century – 10 recumbent effigies in alabaster, Sir Thomas and Sir John being unusually good; countless small figures. Also at the W. end, a small and charming wall monument to the Moretons, 17th century.

BRIERLEY HILL (*St. Michael*) CL
1765.

BROMLEY, KINGS: *see Kings Bromley.*

BROMWICH, WEST: *see West Bromwich.*

BROUGHTON *(St. Peter)*
Stands isolated by the road, opposite the big timber-framed Elizabethan Hall. A little late-Gothic gem of 1630. Unspoiled. All of a piece with box-pews, well placed memorials, 14th and 15th century glass, all excellent. Unique font like a vast stoup.

BURTON-UPON-TRENT *(St. Chad)*
Bodley's last church, 1910. Tall tower and good massing, a simple nave and Lady Chapel fronting the dull street. (On the other side, an octagonal vestry like a chapter-house, by C. G. Hare.) The tower with pierced stonework to the openings, is separated from the church by a low, vaulted passage, a perfect foil to the big, simple interior. Slender columns, wooden barrel vault, the chancel defined in it by only a projecting fringe of pierced woodwork. Well detailed, and no memorials to disturb the serenity.

(St. Modwen) CL
Francis Smith, 1726.

(St. Paul) GR
Lord Grimthorpe and J. M. Neale, 1874; alterations and fittings by Bodley.

CANWELL (*St. Mary, St. Giles & All Saints*)
Temple Moore 1910; an exquisite little church in Hollington stone with vaulted roof, contemporary fittings and a window by Geoffrey Webb.

CAVERSWALL (*St. Peter*) GS
1637; pulpit and pews.

CHEBSEY (*All Saints*)
11th–15th cent.; a 'rewarding' church.

CHECKLEY *(St. Mary & All Saints*)
The best medieval church in North
Staffordshire. A bold tower (Norman and
Perpendicular), embattled nave and chancel, N. and S. porches; and Saxon cross-
shafts (A.M.'s) in the churchyard. The nave
lofty 13th century, clerestory and roofs
17th century, the chancel very good 14th
century. (Tracery, 14th-century glass,
sedilia, 16th-century stalls and tomb
effigies.) Parclose screen, glass, and English
altar by Comper.

CHEDDLETON (*St. Edward the
Confessor*)
13th–15th cent.; Burne Jones and Rosetti
glass.

CHURCH EATON *(St. Editha*)
Bold 12th-century tower, slender 15th-
century spire and simple long roof line.
E. end dominated by great window span-
ning the whole width. The interior a nice
mixture of late Norman and Perpendicular
with pleasant late 19th-century glass. Bold
Street-ish font and pulpit.

CHURCH LEIGH *(All Saints*)
A. W. N. Pugin, 1846. Cruciform, bold
central tower, the exterior generally well
detailed. The interior simple and very good
but over-pewed, with much excellent
Victorian (and some medieval) glass. Good
tomb with effigies, 1523.

CLIFTON CAMPVILLE *(St. Andrew*)
Perhaps the best medieval parish church
in the county, mainly 13th and 14th
century with a small vaulted N. transept.
Tall spire, the tower being pierced at the
base with large windows and a high arch
to the nave. Spacious, light, authentic, the
church has all the interest of craftmanship
and design that an old church should have.
Queen post roof, carved stone heads, wall-
painting, a little old glass, tombs, memorials
of many periods, screens, misericords – all
good.

COLTON (*The Blessed Virgin Mary*)
13th century and Street, 1861.

COPPENHALL (*St. Laurence*)
c. 1220; small, complete and almost
unspoilt.

CROXALL (*St. John the Baptist*)
13th–15th cent.; 15th and 16th cent.
incised slabs.

DENSTONE *(All Saints*)
Street, 1862. A bold, original and dramatic
composition, especially when seen from
the north; the round turret and high
chancel very well composed. Stonework,
iron, brass, marble, stained glass, light
fittings and lettering all designed with
great skill and verve.

DILHORNE (*All Saints*)
13th and 18th cent.; old octagonal tower;
13th and early 16th cent.; holy table and
rail, 1639.

EATON, CHURCH: *see Church Eaton.*

ECCLESHALL *(Holy Trinity*)
Sited at the end of the pleasant market
town; a fine pinnacled tower. Entered by a
big vaulted porch, the church has a spacious
nave, mostly late 15th century, and a 13th-
century chancel. Tombs of four Bishops of
Lichfield – Eccleshall Castle was a Bishop's
palace till the 19th century. Bishop
Overton's 17th-century memorial is especially good. Sgraffito angel over priest's door,
mass clock and arrow whets on S. side.

ELFORD *(St. Peter*)
At the end of an avenue, in the lee of the
big Georgian hall. Tower, 1598, the rest
mostly by Street, 1870. Rich detail on the
side facing the hall. Usually visited for the
tombs, including the charming child effigy
with the tennis ball, *c.* 1460, but also
architecturally interesting – roof with an-
gelic and heraldic corbels, carved, coloured
and gilt capitals, red and blue lettering
round the arches, harmoniously done for
once, altar rail with brassy angels, good
ironwork on the door.

ELLENHALL (*St. Mary*)
15th cent.

ENVILLE (*St. Mary the Blessed Virgin*)
12th–14th cent.; tombs; misericords; good
tower by Scott.

FORTON *(All Saints*)
Association of Georgian and medieval
nicely handled. The tower, stocky but
handsome 15th century, and the E. end,
Decorated, are joined by a S. wall and nave
of 1721. The N. aisle is medieval. A good
table tomb, with effigies, 1633. Hall near
by, 1665.

GNOSALL *(Collegiate Church of St. Lawrence)*
A cruciform church on the fringe of a scattered village, mainly 13th and 15th century. The great Norman crossing scarcely checks the flow of nave to chancel. Flamboyant E. window with quite impressive 20th-century memorial glass. Some nice Norman detail.

GRINDON *(All Saints)* GR
1848; spire; massing; setting.

HAMSTALL RIDWARE *(St. Michael)*
An isolated village church of supremely simple silhouette; spire, with tower, gateway and dovecotes of old manor-house nearby, mainly 14th and 15th century. The nave, simple and lofty, flows straight into the chancel without a break – a perfect setting for the old glass, parclose screens, tombs, memorials, and medieval painted panels in the reredos.

HANBURY *(St. Werbergh)*
13th cent.; monuments.

HARLASTON *(St. Matthew)* GR
1883; half-timbered turret and porch; early tower base.

HAUGHTON *(St. Giles)* GR
J. L. Pearson, 1887; tower and N. side medieval.

HIGH OFFLEY *(St. Mary the Virgin)*
12th–17th cent.

HIMLEY *(St. Michael & All Angels)* CL
1764; screen and panelling.

HOAR CROSS *(Church of the Holy Angels)*
Bodley, 1876. Great architecture. Original, well massed, well sited, well detailed; essentially English. Like Broughton, Patshull and Ingestre, a family church, near the Hall, and architecturally all of a piece, in this case under the beneficence of the Meynell-Ingrams. The perfect association of splendour and intimacy architecturally expressed. Deeply buttressed tower, nave severe outside, chancel high and richly done. Perfectly handled contrasts within. Glass, Stations of the Cross, tombs, woodwork, stone vaulting, good craftsmanship everywhere.
Down the road at Hadley End, there is a mission church also by Bodley, 1901. Simple composition relieved by bell turret and figure of Virgin and Child at W., and by a Calvary in a tall arch at the E. end

outside. Derelict (1958) and eminently worth repairing.

HOLLINSCLOUGH *(St. Agnes)*
In the upper Dove Valley in the Peak District, on the gritstone but against a background of lovely limestone hills. Church and school built as one, 1840. Domestic in scale and character, apart from the bell turret astride the ridge and the tall pinnacles of the gables. Stone-slated roof. High, well proportioned interior with a gallery; painted texts on starchy ribbons, 1890 Lombardic. Clear crown glass, and views of the hills and sky.

HOPWAS *(St. Chad)* GR
John Douglas, 1879; timber-framed; vigorous massing, with flèche.

HORTON *(St. Michael)*
Mainly 16th cent.; screen and brass.

INGESTRE *(St. Mary)*
Sir Christopher Wren, 1676. Till recently, the private chapel for the Hall – fine 16th-century front just adjoining. The church being just below the road, the proportions of the tower are affected, the base appearing too squat. To correct this, look from the N.W. over the wall, not through the ironwork and gates. A good general view is from the S.E. Square plan plus chancel, engaged Tuscan columns with single abacus. The most elaborate country church of its time described (? by Wren himself) as 'not great, but uniform and elegant . . . The *Chancell* within paved throughout with Black and White marble, the *Windows* illustrated with *Armes* and matches of the *Chetwynds* in *painted glass*: and the *Ceilings* with the same in *Fretwork* . . . an elegant *skreen* of *Flanders Oak*, garnisht with the *Kings Armes* . . . the Ironwork about it curiously *painted* and *guilt* . . . '.

KINGS BROMLEY *(All Saints)*
11th–15th cent.; stalls and glass.

KINVER *(St. Peter)*
14th–15th cent.; brass 16th cent. and pulpit, 1625.

LAPLEY *(All Saints)*
12th–15th cent.; Dutch font.

LEEK *(All Saints)*
Norman Shaw, 1887. A large squat-towered church reminiscent of North Yorkshire, here set among Victorian houses. Generous porch; unexpectedly light interior. A nice contrast between the intimate scale and great arches. Splendid

green marble font; chancel panelling and reredos by Lethaby (painted by F. Hamilton Jackson). Murals in chancel by Gerald Horsley. Good pulpit and lectern (? Lethaby).

(*St. Edward the Confessor*)
14th cent. and chancel by Street. Huge gallery like an escalator. Saxon crosses.

LEIGH: see Church Leigh.

LICHFIELD (*St. Chad*)
13th–14th cent.; good setting; St. Chad's Well.

LITTLE ASTON (*St. Peter*) GR
G. E. Street, 1874; good marble work.

LONGDON (*St. James the Great*)
12th–14th cent.; Stoneywell chapel; glass.

LONGSDON (*St. Chad*) GR
Gerald Horsley, 1903; fine tower and stumpy spire.

MARCHINGTON (*St. Peter*) CL
Richard Trubshaw, 1742.

MAVESYN RIDWARE *(St. Nicholas)*
Unusual composition of medieval tower and N. aisle (the Trinity Chapel) and a brick Gothic box of a nave, 1782. The interior is also interesting – the N. aisle has two knights' effigies and 16 incised slabs with figures and heraldry – 4 only are old – and a helmet, gauntlets and shield hung up. Ten hatchments, and numerous shields dotted around the walls. Good heraldic window of 1870. Communion rails cast-iron, font Norman. All very odd.

MAYFIELD *(St. John the Baptist)*
Pleasant setting in the Dove Valley; somewhat apart from the village. Good tower of 1515, the chancel 14th century, with a jolly scalloped parapet. Late Gothic porch and Norman doorway lead into spacious Norman nave: pews, pulpit and communion rails all 1633, the latter round N., S. and W. of the holy table. Two nice 18th-century memorials. Font, 1614.

MEERBROOK (*St. Matthew*) GR
Norman Shaw, 1870.

MUCKLESTONE (*St. Mary*) GR
C. Lynam, 1883; 14th-cent. tower.

NEWBOROUGH *(All Saints)*
Oldrid Scott, 1901. Slender octagonal pinnacled tower and spire of great beauty and originality. The rest simple and serene. The whole well massed and detailed.

NEWCASTLE - UNDER - LYME (*St. Giles*) GR
Scott, 1876; tower 13th cent.

NORBURY *(St. Peter)*
Excellent simple nave and chancel of about 1340, with the original roof. The tower, brick Georgian Gothick. Four sedilia, founder's tomb with painted figure and exciting carvings in the arch-spandrels, marble Scrymsher monument of 1708, odd font, 1738. Good carved heads to drip moulds.

OFFLEY, HIGH: see High Offley.

OKEOVER (*All Saints*)
14th–15th cent.; screen; brass; glass; setting.

PATSHULL *(St. Mary)*
James Gibbs, 1743. A simple composition in a parkland lakeside setting. Octagonal cupola on a square tower. Symmetrically disposed S. nave front, with large figure on the roof at the chancel end. Interior a little coarse; contains the Astley tomb of 1687, with standing figures and mourners below; also the Astley table tomb, *c.* 1600. Pulpit and good gilt screen.

PATTINGHAM *(St. Chad)*
Norman, Early English, and Decorated, and a spire of 1871. Lofty nave with Norman arcade; double N. aisle. Chancel 13th century. Good archy views.

PENKRIDGE *(Collegiate Church; now St. Michael & All Angels)*
A good simple tower, most of the exterior 16th-century Perpendicular. The interior high and spacious, with 13th-century arcades. Dutch wrought-iron screen of 1778. Two fine table tombs and one two-storeyed tomb of the Littletons, 16th and 17th century – nine recumbent effigies, many small ones and much heraldry. Two incised slabs with figures, 15th and 16th century.

PENSNETT, BRIERLEY HILL (*St. Mark*) GR
L. Stride, 1849.

RANGEMORE (*All Saints*) GR
Butterfield, 1867.

RANTON (*All Saints*)
13th cent.

ROLLESTON (*St. Mary*)
14th cent.; tombs; glass.

RUSHTON *(St. Laurence)*
In isolation on a ridge, with a view of the fringes of the Staffordshire and Cheshire Peak District. A church of rare interest and individuality: gritstone and stone aisle slate, mostly 17th and 19th century outside, with a weather-boarded bell turret and high gabled dormers. Inside, the original timber-built nave (?1203), spanned by low beams with a text in good Georgian lettering; hefty posts and struts like low, spreading trees; king posts and Gothic arched ceiling and a Georgian minstrel's gallery; Jacobean pulpit and Squire's pew, hatchments above, big Tables of the Law, and oil lamps. Everything friendly and domestic, clearly the *House* of God.

SALT *(St. James the Great)* GR
1843; screen by A. W. N. Pugin from Alton Towers.

SANDON *(All Saints)*
On a hill in Sandon Park. Mostly 14th century, the tower massing and fenestration generally odd and full of interest. The interior is dominated by the screen supporting the family pew of the Harrowbys: this and the 17th-century pulpit are both good. In the chancel are the Erdeswick tombs, notably that of Sampson Erdeswick, 1601, to his own design: also wall-paintings of heraldic shields hung on trees – family trees.

SEDGLEY *(All Saints)* GR
Thomas Lee, 1828.

SEIGHFORD *(St. Chad)*
A church of much antiquarian interest with some architectural detective problems. Seen from the road it appears mostly brick Gothick, with a western tower – 1754, by Wm. Baker. But the chancel and the N. side are medieval, and the interior mostly early Norman. Good Jacobean pulpit; tomb and effigies, *c.* 1593; monuments, hatchments, scraps of old glass and wall-painting; and a memorial tablet *c.* 1938 by Eric Gill.

SHARESHILL *(St. Mary of the Assumption)* CL
c. 1740: old tower; two stone effigies.

SHEEN *(St. Luke)* GR
Butterfield, 1852; good rectory.

SHENSTONE *(St. John the Baptist)* GR
John Gibson, 1853; well massed gabled composition; old tower near.

SLINDON *(St. Chad)* GR
Basil Champneys, 1894.

SMETHWICK *(Old Church)* CL
Georgian chapel of ease to Harborne Church.

STAFFORD
(Collegiate Church of St. Mary)
Cruciform with central octagonal tower (no spire since 1594). The most prominent views are of the W. – a rough design – and the S. – mainly young Scott, 1840–44 reproducing the original work. The N. side is good, and the Decorated N. transept is the best part of the generally fine interior, mainly 1180–1490. Tudor nave roof. Unique type of Norman font, alabaster tomb effigies, many good simple memorials rightly placed, and one lancet window (at N.W.) by A. W. N. Pugin. Near the W. end, the original stones mark the site of St. Bertelin's shrine, the small beginnings of the county town; remains of Saxon and earlier wooden church and cross, excavated 1954.

(St. Chad)
Formerly hidden behind the shops of Greengate Street, St. Chad's was restored and refaced by Scott, 1874. Almost all the interior is grand bold Norman with an unusually rich chancel arch. Chancel and crossing longer than the nave. Builder's name inserted on W. pier of tower. Fine fake-Norman font.

STOKE-ON-TRENT, HANLEY *(All Saints)* GR
Gerald Horsley, 1911.

STONE *(St. Michael)* GR
Wm. Baker, 1753: early Georgian Gothick.

STOWE-BY-CHARTLEY *(St. John the Baptist)*
12th–14th cent.; 16th-cent. alabaster tomb.

STRETTON, NR. TUTBURY *(St. Mary)* GR
Micklethwaite and Somers Clark, 1897.

SWYNNERTON *(St. Mary)*
12th–15th cent.; huge medieval figure of Christ.

TAMWORTH *(Collegiate Church of St. Editha)*
The pinnacled church tower and the castle dominate the silhouette of this largely Georgian town. Grand immediate effect inside W. door beneath the tower, rich Baroque monument by the door, with figures, heraldry, urns, swags, etc., *c.* 1680.

Open stone screen at E. of tower extends full height of nave. The church is generally of 'noble and ample proportions', mostly late 14th century with 15th century clerestory and roofs: 18th-century wrought-iron screen (spoiled by being made higher in recent years). Norman work in the choir. Recumbent effigies, some Pre-Raphaelite glass, unique double spiral staircase in tower.

TATENHILL (*St. Michael & All Angels*)
13th–15th cent.

TIPTON (*St. Martin*) CL
1797.

TITTENSOR (*St. Luke*) GR
T. Roberts, 1881; random stone, brick and tile walling.

TRENTHAM (*St. Mary & All Saints*) GR
Sir Charles Barry, 1844; Norman piers re-used; screen 1633; monuments.

TUTBURY *(Priory Church of St. Mary)*
Sited overlooking the town, near the castle. An important Norman church. Some confusion in design outside belies the excellent interior. Rich W. front and fine doorway of seven orders, including the earliest English alabaster work: tower at the S.W. with an insignificant top storey. Street's apsidal E. end (1868) is a serene effort at keeping in keeping without copying; inside, though, the chancel arch and apse are somewhat unhappy. Tall hefty arcade of *c.* 1100, old triforium now serving as a clerestory. Good W. wall. Fine ironwork on the doors.

WALSALL (*St. Matthew*) GR
Francis Goodwin, 1821; good cast-iron arcades and windows; 15th cent. chancel.

(*St. Paul*) GR
J. L. Pearson, 1893.

WARSLOW (*St. Lawrence*) CL
1820; 1908 chancel with Pre-Raphaelite glass; mosaic and fabric.

WATERFALL (*St. James & St. Bartholomew*)
12th and 15th cent.

WEST BROMWICH (*Christ Church*) GR
Francis Goodwin, 1827.

WESTON-ON-TRENT (*St. Andrew*)
Fine tower, 1210; the rest 19th cent.

WESTON - UNDER - LIZARD (*St. Andrew*)
14th–15th cent.; 1702, and Street, 19th cent.; monuments and glass.

WOLVERHAMPTON *(Collegiate Church of St. Peter)*
Well sited on a hill. A large, well-massed composition of tall 15th-century central tower, two-storey vaulted porch, high transepts and good Victorian chancel. Mostly 1480, spacious and lofty: light transepts, dark chancel. Very fine stone pulpit integral with main structure, with jolly lion on the balustrade. Some good woodwork – W. gallery of 1610, choir-stalls and parclose screen; some excellent monuments – especially the bronze standing figure of Sir Richard Leveson by Le Soeur, *c.* 1625. Carved circular cross-shaft, *c.* 850, in churchyard (a cast is to be seen in the Victoria and Albert Museum).

(St. John)
Wm. Baker, 1755. Set in a decrepit Georgian square. Good W. front. The tower and spire nicely handled – octagonal spire, with stone bands and pierced. Pedimented E. end with blind arches. The interior Doric with galleries. Nice gate piers and ironwork.

WOMBOURN (*St. Benedict Biscop*) GR
G. E. Street, 1867; medieval tower and spire.

WYCHNOR *(St. Leonard)*
Rather isolated, overlooking the plain. Mostly 14th century with a 16th-century tower partly in brick. A bold and friendly building, with good, big, square-headed, traceried windows and richly coloured and textured stone. A little heraldic glass.

YOXALL (*St. Peter*)
14th and 19th cent.; monuments.

Suffolk

INTRODUCTION

SOUTH NORFOLK glides almost imperceptibly into Suffolk. Beginning with that leafy countryside just south of Norwich, where Old Crome found that king among trees – 'The Poringland Oak', and proceeding down the valley of the Tas, the white-washed cottages and farms, timber-framed with wattle and daub and high-pitched roofs, become more and more frequent. Villages like Saxlingham Nethergate begin to have wide greens with the cottages dotted about round the edge like so many villages in Suffolk. Little towns like Loddon, Long Stratton, and Pulham Market are similar places to Debenham, Stradbroke, and Laxfield; and though Harleston and Diss are on the Norfolk side of the Waveney Valley they are but smaller versions of their Suffolk, though more northerly, neighbours Bungay and Beccles.

Then as one proceeds farther into the Suffolk countryside the villages appear more remote. In comparison with Norfolk there are fewer aerodromes and the ear-piercing screech of the jet-aircraft less frequent. There are few main roads and, now that so many branch lines have been abandoned, fewer railways. Neither does one often encounter in the narrow lanes the 'Eastern Counties' red bus which seems to have found its way into most Norfolk villages.

The brick and flint give way to colour-wash and thatch, the villages have a softer appearance, the fields smaller, the woodlands thicker and the trees larger, so that by the time one has left Harleston and Fressingfield behind, or penetrated into the quiet villages just inland from the coast at Southwold or Aldeburgh, one has the feeling of being in the depths of the country as nowhere else in East Anglia.

What may be said of the villages may also be said of the towns. They are more compact, quieter, and more retired. No 'A' road runs into Framlingham, Lavenham, or Eye, and those which are on some important line of communication seem to have kept themselves apart from the main stream of traffic, like Woodbridge where the by-pass helps it to remain as a perfect example of an old country town spreading along the main street and thickening about the Market Place in the middle.

As for the towns, so for the capital. Norwich is an industrial city and country capital all in one. Suffolk has intensified both but kept them well apart. Ipswich is the industrial capital, with the result that the parochial distinctions of the old medieval city are less evident; and Bury the country market town where the industries are kept in the background.

So also for the coast. Like Yarmouth, Lowestoft is both a pleasure resort and a fishing town but smaller, quieter, more restrained, and the same sort of comparison could be made between Cromer and Southwold, Sheringham and Aldeburgh, and between Hunstanton and Felixstowe.

The Suffolk rivers are smaller but they have longer estuaries which penetrate for a long distance inland. The Ore follows the coast for ten miles and more before it decides to turn inland as the Alde; Woodbridge is on the tidal estuary of the Deben but it is a long way from the sea. The Gipping is a quiet little stream until at Gippeswick (Ipswich – the creek of the Gipping) it becomes the long estuary of the Orwell; and the same may be said of the Stour which Suffolk shares with Essex on its southern border.

It is to the Stour Valley that one comes after the remote country of East Suffolk and, though it is apparent at once that Constable's country is near enough London to have been discovered by the week-ender, it is a lovely district with a character that is all its own and with its own capital; another collection of medieval villages which is the town of Sudbury with a statue of Gainsborough in the Market Place.

Gainsborough and Constable. How often did those painters set their figures against the background of a Landscape Park and that is exactly what the Stour Valley is as you see it spread out beneath the high ground at Stoke-by-Nayland or at Bures. A Park which continues right on through Sudbury to that wonderful village of Parks and Halls, Long Melford.

West of Long Melford, Suffolk becomes Essex and though Clare is on the Suffolk side of the Stour it is essentially an Essex country town with the houses rich in pargetry work. But north and east of Melford one is back again in the heart of Suffolk. Even 'B' roads are few and far between so that with no map, and with all the signposts destroyed (as patriotic East Anglians both in Norfolk and Suffolk were most instant in doing in the early days of the late war), 'the man in the moon who came down too soon' to Shimpling or to Hawkedon, Thorpe Morieux, Nedging Tye, or Kettlebaston, would find it difficult 'to find his way to Norwich', as the saying goes, and would be more likely to get hopelessly lost in the maze of lanes and footpaths. But it is a country in which one would be quite content to get lost for sometime or another all the roads lead to the local metropolis which is not only the most lovely town in Suffolk, but one of the most beautiful in all England – Lavenham.

To enter into the spirit of the country the traveller in East Suffolk will find it almost essential to be equipped with the Works of George Crabbe, and for the highlands of West Suffolk he will be well advised to seek out some faded copy of the poems of the contemporary Robert Bloomfield, who, though a more pedestrian poet, could at times describe the spirit of a place even better than Crabbe himself. He depicts the rolling grassland of Euston Park and the wide upland fields of Honington, of Troston, and of Sapiston, around which he had plodded as a 'Farmer's Boy', and with the foliage of spring, the shimmering heat of summer, the falling leaves of autumn, and the hard cold of winter, with the accuracy of a steel engraving.

West Suffolk, too, has a distinct character but the various districts are not so sharply distinguished from one another as they are in Norfolk. If Suffolk melts into Norfolk along the Tas, and into Essex in the valley of the Stour, so also the chalky heights of West Suffolk blend into the white chalk of Cambridgeshire; the cottages, and the churches too, are built of hard chalk or clunch, and one can make one's way over the Gog Magogs into the Midlands without meeting the barrier of the Fens.

C.L.S.L.

SELECTED LIST OF CHURCHES
by the Rev. C. L. S. Linnell

ACTON (*All Saints*)
One of the finest military brasses in England (Sir Robert de Bures, 1302). Jennens monument (1726) in S. aisle.

ALDEBURGH *(*St. Peter & St. Paul*)
This spacious 15th-century church has lost its chancel but has a long S. porch extending from the church to the main road, with wide arches on the E. and W. for the passage of processions round the church. In the N. aisle is a bust of the Rev. George Crabbe by the local sculptor, T. Thurlow of Saxmundham. But even without this lovers of Crabbe will recognise Aldeburgh church instantly as the church of 'The Borough' standing on its hill overlooking the sea with the town below. But Aldeburgh is no longer the 'two parallel and unpaved streets, running between mean and scambling houses' that Crabbe knew, but a neat and pleasant little seaside resort with an annual Festival of Music and the Arts.

AMPTON *(*St. Peter*)
Hidden in the trees this lovely village takes a little finding. In the church is the chantry chapel of John Coket (1479) but it is the Calthorpe family who are chiefly commemorated. Henry Calthorpe and his family have a monument in the chancel signed by the East Anglian sculptors John and Matthias Christmas who were also wood carvers and did much of the embellishing of King Charles I's great ship *The Sovereign of the Seas*. In the nave is the kneeling figure of Dorothy Calthorpe – 'a virgin votary oft in snares'. She 'troubles no man's dust' and prays that 'other men may be as just'. Her gift to the parish was the handsome row of Almshouses to the E.

of the church. The great treasure of this church is one of *The Sealed Books of Common Prayer* of which neither the British Museum nor the Bodleian possesses a copy.

ASHBY (*St. Mary*)
Tower, round at base and octagonal above with lancet windows.

ASHFIELD MAGNA (*All Saints*)
17th-cent. pulpit; altar table (1619).

ASSINGTON (*St. Edmund*)
S. doors; Gurdon monuments.

ATHELINGTON (*St. Peter*)
15th-cent. bench-ends.

BACTON *(*St. Mary*)
A good example of the East Anglian stone and flint work in the clerestory with Latin inscription on the exterior commemorating the donors, Robert and Agnes Goche, and James and Margaret Hobart and their parents.

BADINGHAM *(*St. John the Baptist*)
This lovely church set in a little wooded valley has a graceful hammer-beam roof and one of the finest of the seven-sacrament fonts in East Anglia. In the panel representing penance the evil spirit is vigorously portrayed as a devil with horns.

BADLEY (*St. Mary*)
Unspoilt interior; 17th-cent. woodwork in box-pews. (*See Plate 29*)

BARDWELL (*St. Peter & St. Paul*)
14th-cent. glass with kneeling figure of benefactor, Sir William Berdewell.

BARHAM (*St. Mary*)
18th-cent. reredos with altar rails.

BARKING (*St. Mary*)
15th-cent. font cover, rood and parclose screens.

BARNBY (*St. John the Baptist*)
Wall-paintings.

BARNINGHAM (*St. Andrew*)
15th-cent. rood screen; 17th-cent. screen doors, pulpit and tester.

BARSHAM (*Holy Trinity*)
Well restored; early circular tower.

BARTON, GREAT: *see Great Barton.*

BARTON MILLS (*St. Mary*)
14th-cent. glass.

BEALINGS MAGNA (*St. Mary*)
15th-cent. carved S. doors; 17th-cent. pulpit.

BECCLES *(St. Michael)*
This large church with detached bell tower is a little dull inside but is of splendid proportions. Grand 15th-century S. porch. Its most treasured possession is a beautiful copy of the Prayer Book of 1549. Beccles is a good country town with fine 18th-century houses. The church stands well on ground falling away steeply to the Waveney.

BEDINGFIELD (*St. Mary*)
Double hammer-beam roof; 17th-cent. altar table.

BERGHOLT, EAST: *see East Bergholt.*

BILDESTON (*St. Mary*)
Lofty with graceful arcades; Suffolk type tie-beam and hammer-beam roof.

BLAKENHAM MAGNA (*St. Mary*)
S. porch.

BLUNDESTON (*St. Mary*)
Small 11th-cent. circular tower; 11th-cent. S. door.

BLYFORD (*All Saints*)
Elizabethan altar table.

BLYTHBURGH *(Holy Trinity*)
'In the Name of Blessed Jesus, the Holy Trinity, and to the Honour of Holy Mary, Anne, and Katherine this church was rebuilt'. But shorn of much of its 15th-century splendour it looks a bit gaunt like Salthouse in Norfolk – a great ship stranded among the remains of the town that was once a port. But inside there is a warmth of feeling that comes of the beautiful 15th-century woodwork now turned a beautiful silvery-grey colour with age. The marvellous cambered tie-beam roof with arch-braces was too high for the most devilish of 17th-century iconoclasts, William Dowsing, to destroy and though he did his worst with arrows and shot, much of the original colour remains. The 15th-century bench-ends in the nave have vivid representations of the Seven Deadly Sins and in the chancel are splendid stalls with carved figures of the Apostles. These once served the purpose of school desks in the Hopton chapel on the N. side of the sanctuary and a scholar has cut his name on one of them – 'Dirk Lowersen Van Stockholm 1665'. The front of these stalls with the carved figures was evidently the front of the rood-loft. With all these things and much much more Blythburgh Church is one of the most interesting in Suffolk.

BOULGE (*St. Michael & All Angels*)
Edward Fitzgerald buried here.

BOXFORD *(St. Mary*)
Standing in the middle of a pretty village this church is remarkable for the unique 14th-century wooden N. porch with beautiful wooden vaulting. The S. porch has a representation of the Annunciation and there is a 17th-century font cover with doors that fold back revealing on the inside texts painted on scrolls. One stands in the S. aisle in wonder and admiration at the monument to a lady who died at the age of 113. In the S. aisle is a delightful 17th-century brass to an infant, David Birde, asleep in his little cot.

BOXTED *(All Saints*)
One of the most class-conscious of churches with ornate private pews for the Poley family filling the aisle N. of the nave and raised well above the common people. In the pews themselves there are well-defined partitions between the accommodation for the family and that for their retainers. There is good 17th-century woodwork and fine monuments, particularly the alabaster figure of Thomas Poley (1638) in elaborate armour.

BRADFIELD COMBURST (*All Saints*)
Wall-paintings.

(*St. Clare*)
17th cent.; altar table.

(*St. George*)
17th cent.; woodwork.

BRADLEY MAGNA (*St. Mary*)
Norman S. doorway with tympanum; 17th-

cent. altar table; 18th-cent. pulpit and tester.

BRAMFIELD *(St. Andrew)*
This little church has a very early circular tower standing by itself S.W. of the church. Inside is a beautiful screen with vaulting, the best of its kind in Suffolk. In the chancel is Nicholas Stone's exquisite effigy of Mrs. Arthur Coke (1634), certainly his masterpiece and one of the great treasures of Renaissance art in England.

BRAMFORD *(St. Mary)*
A 14th–15th century church which must have been aglow with the most wonderful glass before 1644 when Mr Dowsing destroyed '841 superstitious pictures'. Yet there are many things remaining. Good hammer-beam roof, 13th-century piscina and sedilia and a 16th-century font cover like the one at Boxford but more elaborate.

BREDFIELD *(St. Andrew)*
Single hammer-beam roof with canopy of honour for rood.

BRENT ELEIGH *(St. Mary)*
Pleasing 18th-cent. interior box-pews containing 17th-cent. carving; 17th-cent. pulpit and altar table with three-sided communion rails.

BRETTENHAM *(St. Mary)*
Font; 17th-cent. woodwork, especially in lectern; Baskett Bible (1716).

BRICET MAGNA *(St. Mary & St. Laurence)*
Remains of transeptal chapels; 12th-cent. font with interlaced arcading; 14th-cent. glass.

BROME *(St. Mary)*
Victorian 'restoration' in all styles of Gothic; Cornwallis monuments.

BRUNDISH *(St. Laurence)*
Woodwork and 15th-cent. glass; engraved brass (1360) of a priest.

BUNGAY *(Holy Trinity)*
Early circular tower; 17th-cent. woodwork.

(St. Mary)
Tower; 14th-cent. N. aisle.

BURES *(St. Mary)*
An attractive little town with the Stour, dividing Suffolk from Essex, running through the middle of it. The church is chiefly remarkable for its 14th-century wooden N. porch, 15th-century armorial font, and for its monuments. In particular the early 14th-century wooden effigy of a knight, a member of the de Cornard family. Standing in the fields just off the main road on the way to Sudbury is the extremely interesting 'Chapel Barn' now furnished most beautifully as a private chapel with a neat stone altar. The building can sometimes be seen through the courtesy of the owner at 'Chapel Barn Cottage' and is well worth a visit. It is 13th century with lancet windows – a triple lancet towards the E. 14th and 15th century De Vere tombs from Earls Colne Priory.

BURGATE *(St. Mary)*
Tomb with canopied military brass (1409) for Sir William de Burgate and his wife.

BURSTALL *(St. Mary)*
15th-cent. wooden S. porch; simple 14th-cent. parclose screen; 14th-cent. nave arcade.

BURY ST. EDMUNDS *(St. John)* GR
This interesting Gothic Revival church, built in 1891, is a good example of the scrupulously correct 'Early English' style of the period.

(St. Mary)
A noble church with a marvellous late 15th-century hammer-beam roof in the nave and a wagon-roof in the chancel. Before the high altar was buried John Reeve of Melford, the last Abbot of Bury. The N. chapel, restored in memory of men of the Suffolk Regiment, is beautifully furbished by Sir Ninian Comper. The S. chapel was the chantry of John Boret and the monument to Boret himself (1467) has a grim cadaver effigy. His motto 'Grace me Governe' appears in the wonderfully painted roof. To the E. of St. Mary's lie the remains of the Abbey of St. Edmundsbury situate in a beautifully kept public park and to the W., just outside the abbey gate, a wide square with 18th-century houses. Bury is the capital of W. Suffolk and though industrial has not lost the feeling of a country market town.

BUXHALL *(St. Mary)*
Well-proportioned 14th cent.

CAVENDISH *(St. Mary)*
One of the most beautiful villages in Suffolk. Many thatched cottages round a village green rising up towards the church with its lofty clerestory panelled in flint flush work very similar to that at Long Melford. In the 14th-century tower the

ringing chamber is furnished as a living room with fireplace and with windows having their original wooden shutters. In the church are two magnificent lecterns, a 15th-century eagle of brass and a 16th-century two-sided wooden lectern.

CHEDISTON (*St. Mary*)
Arched-braced roof; pulpit (1637) and communion rails.

CHELSWORTH (*All Saints*)
Remains of Doom painting.

CLARE *(St. Peter & St. Paul)*
Since Mr. Dowsing 'brake down 1000 superstitious pictures' (his record!) it is not surprising that there is only a little heraldic glass in the E. window. There is much 17th-century woodwork especially in the S. aisle gallery and as at Cavendish there is a 16th-century lectern designed to be used also as a money-box. Eden glass. Clare is a spacious market town with many of the houses, especially that to the S. of the church, rich in pargetry work.

COCKFIELD (*St. Peter*)
14th-cent. canopied tomb in chancel; in N. aisle 12th-cent. niche embellished with foliage in low relief.

CODDENHAM (*St. Mary*)
Rebuilt, 14th–15th cent.; earlier work visible, especially in chancel; parts of 16th-cent. screen with unusual representations of prophets.

COMBS *(St. Mary)*
There is much of interest in this church but most interesting of all is the beautiful glass in the S. aisle representing the Old Testament Kings and Prophets in the genealogy of Christ, the Works of Mercy, and – most vivid of all – the scenes from the Life of St. Margaret of Antioch. She is represented as a shepherdess, standing in judgment before a King with the devil standing on a pedestal at his side, being cast into prison; in prison she is being swallowed by the devil in the guise of a dragon but escapes and the picture shows her giving the devil a good birching! and, last, she is stepping lightheartedly into a cauldron of boiling oil.

COTTON (*St. Andrew*)
Lofty 14th-cent. nave; double hammer-beam roof; S. door.

COVE, NORTH: see *North Cove.*

COVE, SOUTH: see *South Cove.*

COVEHITHE *(St. Andrew)*
Only the shell is left. The tower remains and joined to it a tiny church built in 1672 within the nave arcade. Here and there a few pieces of flint flush work remain on the towering walls of this vast church which the inhabitants could not possibly maintain. A few cottages are all that remain of the village itself along the lane that runs down to the sea.

CRATFIELD (*St. Mary*)
One of the finest seven-sacrament fonts. 17th-cent. woodwork includes desk lectern; 15th-cent. chest in N. chapel.

CREETING (*St. Peter*)
Wall-paintings of St. Christopher and a mermaid; 15th-cent. pulpit; 17th cent. altar table.

CRETINGHAM (*St. Peter*)
17th-cent. interior with three-decker, three-sided Communion rails and altar table; box-pews probably 18th cent.

CULFORD (*St. Mary*)
Monument to Lady Bacon and her grandchildren (1654) by Thomas Stanton.

DALHAM *(St. Mary)*
In this, the loveliest village of W. Suffolk, the road runs alongside the stream – each house having its separate bridge – and then up a steep lane through a tunnel of foliage to Dalham Hall, a marvellous 17th–18th century house standing superbly on a raised parterre overlooking mile after mile of the 'Suffolk Highlands'. Down the valley opposite sweeps a fine avenue of trees. The church stands to the right of the Hall and is not visible at first but it is a spacious 14th–15th century building with 15th-century roof and screen. The series of wall-paintings is very much decayed. Of modern furnishings a very fine window by Bryans. There is an inscription to the effect that the 'Steepl' was 'reedified' in 1625.

DALLINGHOO (*St. Mary*)
17th-cent. woodwork.

DEBENHAM (*St. Mary*)
Magnificent W. porch; 15th-cent. nave arcade with hammer-beam and tie-beam roof.

DENHAM (*St. John the Baptist*)
Palimpsest brass, on one side the figure of Anthony Bedingfield (1574), on the other part of a flemish brass.

(*St. Mary*)
Monument to Sir Edward Lewkenor by John and Matthias Christmas (1638).

DENNINGTON *(St. Mary)*
This wonderful church is chiefly remarkable for its aisle and parclose screens complete with their lofts and parapets. 17th and 18th century pulpit and box-pews in the nave, together with beautiful 15th-century bench-ends, one of which represents a Skiapod, a fabulous human being lying on his back and using his enormous webbed feet as a sunshade. In the S. chapel is a monument with alabaster effigies of Lord Bardolph (who fought at Agincourt) and his wife Joan, *c.* 1450. A most interesting feature is the cover for the hanging pyx (in which the Blessed Sacrament was reserved) suspended in front of the altar. (*See Plate 36b*)

DENSTON *(St. Nicholas)*
One comes across this church almost by accident at a turn in the road. It is situated in a beautiful position on the rising ground above the village and, late 15th century throughout, its interior has undergone little change since the 17th century. Fine arch-braced roof with cambered tie-beam like Blythburgh together with very good choir stalls and seven-sacrament font. In Denston church, more than anywhere else in the county, can one get the feeling of what this Suffolk type of 15th-century church was like in its original splendour.

DRINKSTONE (*All Saints*)
15th-cent. rood-screen.

EARL STONHAM *(St. Mary)*
This is a 'problem' church showing many evidences of an earlier building with a central tower but rearranged and rebuilt during the 14th century. A splendid hammer-beam roof, the hammer posts supporting the arch-braces above having richly-carved bosses. In this, better perhaps than in other roofs of this type, one can see the method of its construction and appreciate its solidity. A 17th-century pulpit equipped with four hour-glasses. The one on a bracket measures the full hour as does the largest of a group of three on a shelf behind the pulpit. The two smaller ones are designed for less formidable exhortations of a quarter and a half-hour in length.

EAST BERGHOLT (*St. Mary*)
Bells hung in cage at ground level in churchyard. They are counterweighted and are pushed over by hand instead of being pulled by ropes. Mainly late medieval.

EASTON (*All Saints*)
18th–19th cent. interior; 14th-cent. glass; 17th-cent. altar table and Communion rails.

EDWARDSTONE (*St. Mary*)
17th-cent. pulpit and tester; brass to a Mr. and Mrs. Brand, *c.* 1620 with odd inscription.

ELEIGH, MONKS: *see Monks Eleigh.*

ELMSETT (*St. Peter*)
Three-sided 17th-cent. Communion rails.

ELMSWELL (*St. John the Divine*)
Monument by Maximilian Colt for Sir Robert Gardener (1619), Lord Chief Justice.

ELVEDEN (*St. Mary & St. Patrick*)
W. D. Caroë, early this cent.; Prince Frederik Duleep Singh memorial.

EUSTON *(St. Genevieve)*
One of the most splendid examples in East Anglia of a 17th-century church. It was built by Lord Arlington in 1676. Well might Evelyn describe it as 'most laudable'. The church is embellished with beautiful panelling and a magnificent reredos by Grinling Gibbons, and there is a plaster ceiling in the S. aisle. The church is set amid the rolling grassland of Euston Park where Charles II used to enjoy watching 'the jolly blades racing'. Henry FitzRoy, first Duke of Grafton, the natural son of Charles II, married the daughter of the Earl of Arlington and the magnificent heraldic sign of the Grafton Arms, in the neat and well-kept village street, bears the Royal Arms with bar sinister in the first quarter.

EYE *(St. Peter & St. Paul)*
The main line from Ipswich to Norwich passes through Diss and though Eye has a rail connection from Mellis, this no longer operates, so the town has been passed by and left as a very pleasant country town little more than a big village. The church is especially remarkable for the splendid 15th-century W. tower, panelled in flint and stone and with octagonal buttresses. The fine rood-screen has interesting but cruder figure painting than most of the East Anglian screens. The most remarkable feature of the screen is the beautiful rood

and loft restored by Sir Ninian Comper in 1925.

EYKE (*All Saints*)
Base of 12th-cent. central tower with fine arches; the church Key has wards cut to spell the name of the village I K E.

FELSHAM (*St. Peter*)
15th-cent. N. porch with flint flush work.

FRAMLINGHAM *(*St. Michael*)
One could spend many months, and years, in this the most interesting of the country towns of Suffolk, for Framlingham is like Ely, Windsor, Tewkesbury, Warwick, a town which enshrines the History of England in epitome. The castle with its tall Keep and curtain walls, one of the principal possessions of the great families, the Bigods, the Mowbrays, and the Howards, is, in the words of Bernard Barton 'a Fall'n dismantled Pile'. But even so it is one of the most majestic of such remains in the country. It was here that Bishop Ridley was arrested by order of Queen Mary Tudor. It was to this place that Mary herself rode post haste from Kenninghall in Norfolk in the summer of 1553 to be proclaimed Queen; and it was within these walls that many of the most famous of the Roman Catholic recusants were imprisoned in the time of Queen Elizabeth. On one side the town comes right up to the castle, and on the other the high walls look down over mile upon mile of the quiet, undulating, leafy Suffolk countryside. The church is remarkable for the large aisled chancel rebuilt after the Reformation to house the tombs of the Howard family brought from Thetford Priory. These tombs must be counted among the great treasures of the monumental art of the period in England. In particular that to Henry Fitzroy, Duke of Richmond (1536) with the sides panelled in high relief sculpture similar to Torrigiani's work in Henry VII's chapel at Westminster. The painted alabaster tomb to Thomas Howard, Duke of Norfolk (beheaded in 1572) is by William Cure, Master Mason to the Crown, and that to Sir Thomas Hitcham (1636) by the East Anglian sculptor Francis Grigs. Notice should also be taken of the monument to Jane Kerridge by the great 18th-century sculptor L. F. Roubiliac. The chancel itself is beautifully furnished with an altar and reredos by Sir Thomas Jackson, R.A., and with the magnificent organ

by Thalmar of Peterborough (1674). This was originally in the chapel of Pembroke College, Cambridge, and was presented to Framlingham in 1708. It used to stand in the nave in a W. gallery which has fortunately been preserved and re-erected in the old grammar school buildings – a fine 17th–18th century block – within the castle walls. The nave and W. tower are examples of the East Anglian 15th-century style with hammer-beam roof, the hammer-beams enclosed in false vaulting as at St. Peter Mancroft, Norwich, and at Ringland in Norfolk. The church and churchyard are set high above the market-place which slopes steeply down to the river, and in going up the other side of the road towards Dennington it is somewhat of a shock to be faced with towering red-brick buildings of Framlingham College (Suffolk's memorial to Prince Albert in 1865) in the hardest of the hard Revival Gothic. But, as is often the case with buildings of this period, they are not unimpressive when seen from a distance.

FRAMSDEN (*St. Mary*)
15th-cent. double hammer-beam roof; altar table (1628).

FRESSINGFIELD *(*St. Peter & St. Paul*)
In this church is the superb 15th-century woodwork in chancel and nave roofs, and in particular the marvellous series of benches in the nave, one appreciates as perhaps nowhere else the beautiful silvery-grey colour of the oak. Unspoiled by the horrible practices of staining and oiling, the wood has been allowed to mellow of its own accord and for all its venerable colour it is as good as when it was first cut and carved by the wonderful craftsmanship of the 15th-century workmen. Fressingfield is a great church so very peaceful and quiet brooding over its village and facing it on the N. side but at the bottom of the little valley stands the neat and many-sashed Georgian rectory. Along the S. side of the churchyard runs the brick-and-timbered Guildhall, now the 'Fox and Goose', the N.E. corner-post of which has a carving of St. Margaret of Antioch trampling on the dragon. In the churchyard, in the angle of the aisle and S. porch is a simple table-tomb for William Sancroft the non-juring Archbishop of Canterbury, a native of this village.

FRITTON (*St. Edmund*)
Very interesting early church with circular

tower and very small Norman apse; 15th-cent. wall-painting of St. Christopher and 17th-cent. three-decker pulpit and altar table.

GAZELEY (*All Saints*)
13th-cent. E. window; 16th-cent. glass in the N. clerestory and wagon-roof in the chancel.

GISLINGHAM *(*St. Mary*)
This well-restored church, in which the 18th-century three-decker pulpit and box-pews on the N. side of the nave have fortunately been preserved, has a marvellous double hammer-beam roof. The few remains of the screen are enough to show that it must in its glory have been something like the magnificent one at Ranworth in Norfolk. The most unusual peal board for 1822 has not only the names of the ringers against the bells they rang, but the instruments of their trades. The tower itself is 17th century, rebuilt in 1639 of red brick.

GLEMHAM, GREAT: *see Great Glemham.*

GORLESTON *(*St. Andrew*)
This church, in what is virtually a suburb of Great Yarmouth, has been much restored but is well worth a visit for the seven-sacrament font, the Stuart Royal Arms, huge paintings of Moses and Aaron, a 14th-century Easter sepulchre, and the brass to a member of the Bacon family, *c.* 1320.

GREAT BARTON (*Holy Innocents*)
Spacious; 13th-cent. chancel; 15th-cent. hammer-beam roof in nave.

GREAT GLEMHAM *(*All Saints*)
In the church is an example of a simple 15th-century arch-braced roof and a seven-sacrament font on which the detailed carving of the panels is exceptionally well preserved. The three 15th-century bells in the town were made by the Norwich bell-founder Richard Brasyer, and one of them has the lovely inscription *Sum Rosa Pulsata Mundi Maria Vocata* – when rung I'm called Mary, the Rose of the world. Though the church has been much restored it still seems to contain the spirit of the Rev. George Crabbe who was once parson here:
    'How stately stand yon pines upon the
      hill,
    How soft the murmurs of that living
      rill!

And o'er the park's tall paling,
  scarcely higher,
Peeps the low church and shows the
  modest spire.'

GREAT SAXHAM *(*St. Andrew*)
This church has been much restored but is worth a visit for the fine portrait bust of John Eldred (1632), and there is a fine brass showing Eldred in the robes of an alderman of London. As the inscription relates he was a great traveller in the Levant as a spice merchant.

GRUNDISBURGH (*St. Mary*)
Double hammer-beam roof.

HADLEIGH *(*St. Mary*)
To the W. of the church stands the 15th-century red-brick tower of the Deanery, for Hadleigh is a 'peculiar' with a Dean instead of a Rector and outside diocesan authority and directly subject to the Archbishop of Canterbury. There is a spacious nave but perhaps the church is more remarkable for the furnishings it contains. A 14th-century font with good modern cover (1925), some good stalls with miserere seats in the chancel which also contains a beautiful organ-case, the upper parts of which are by the 17th-century Father Smith; some good bench-ends, one of which shows a wolf holding in his jaws the head of St. Edmund. Also many brasses, the most remarkable of which is a palimpsest showing on the one side one of the Deans of Hadleigh, the Protestant martyr Rowland Taylor (1560) and on the other a portion of a Continental (probably Flemish) brass from which it was cut. Along the S. side of the churchyard is the fine range of the 15th-century Guildhall.

HARKSTEAD (*St. Mary*)
Norman doorway and windows; 14th-cent. Easter Sepulchre.

HARTEST (*All Saints*)
Setting; 15th-cent. pulpit.

HAWKEDON *(*St. Mary*)
This carefully restored church, in which the W. gallery has wisely been retained, has 15th-century bench-ends and 17th-century altar table, pulpit, chair, and Communion rails. The church is set in the middle of a wide village green, one of the most attractive places in the district.

HAWSTEAD (*All Saints*)
Splendid alabaster monument in chancel for Elizabeth Drury (1610) by Gerard

Christmas with Latin epitaph, by Dr. John Donne.

HELMINGHAM (*St. Mary*)
W. tower, 1543. Tollemache memorials and one by Nollekens to the Countess of Dysart.

HENGRAVE (*St. John Lateran*)
Now the private chapel of Hengrave Hall; monuments to Margaret Countess of Bath and her husbands John Bourchier and Sir Thomas Kitson; beautiful alabaster monument for Lord Darcy; round tower 12th cent. and remainder 15th cent.; Eden glass.

HENSTEAD (*St. Mary*)
Norman S. door.

HEPWORTH (*St. Peter*)
15th-cent. font cover.

HERRINGFLEET (*St. Margaret*)
12th-cent. circular tower.

HESSET *(*St. Ethelbert*)
A 15th-century tower with elaborate parapet. Wall-paintings representing St. Barbara, St. Christopher, the Seven Deadly Sins – where the sinners are being gobbled up into the jaws of hell – and the remarkable but very faded Christ of the Trades with pincers, hammer, scythe, spade, and pitch-fork. Two most interesting possessions of this church are the 15th-century Pyx Cloth (for covering the Blessed Sacrament) and Burse.

HIGHAM (*St. Mary*) GR
Sir Gilbert Scott, 1861.

HITCHAM (*All Saints*)
15th-cent. double hammer-beam nave roof; 17th-cent. roofs in chancel and aisles; screen panels.

HOLBROOK (*All Saints*)
Consecration Crosses; monument to John Clenche, 1607.

THE ICKLINGHAMS (*All Saints*)
Standing on a hill above the village, has a beautiful 14th-century nave and five-light E. window. There are fragments of 15th-century seating and a 17th-century altar table and rails. There are original kneelers cut from thick tufts of reeds from which the work 'hassock' has been derived.

IKEN *(*St. Botolph*)
The church is in no way exceptional but it has the most perfect setting of any in Suffolk. At the end of a lane amid a grove of trees on top of 'Iken Cliff' overlooking the wide expanse of the Alde estuary with Aldeburgh in the distance. One is not surprised to learn from a tombstone in the churchyard that one incumbent, the Rev. Arnold Wainewright, was content to remain in this delectable place for fifty-five years.

IPSWICH *(*St. Augustine*)
A modern church by Mr. Munro Cautley, the greatest living authority on the churches of Suffolk.

*(*St. Margaret*)
Fine double hammer-beam roof in the nave.

*(*St. Mary Quay*)
Possesses one of the finest continental-type brasses in the country for Thomas Pownder (1525), Bayly of Ipswich and a Merchant Adventurer.

*(*St. Mary-le-Tower*)
Principal church of the town. Practically rebuilt by R. M. Phipson, the most active Gothic revival architect in East Anglia.

*(*St. Nicholas*)
14-century nave, 15th-century aisles and 17th-century pulpit and Communion rails.

IXWORTH (*St. Mary*)
15th-cent. tower and nave roof; 13th-cent. double piscina.

IXWORTH THORPE (*All Saints*)
15th-cent. benches; 17th-cent. altar table, Communion rails, and pulpit.

KEDINGTON *(*St. Peter & St. Paul*)
Though a medieval fabric with a simple 16th-century hammer-beam roof the atmosphere of this church is of the 17th and 18th centuries. Much of the beautiful woodwork of that period remains and at that time also parts of a 15th-century screen were worked up into a magnificent canopied pew in the easternmost bay of the N. arcade next to the beautiful Jacobean chancel screen. Most beautiful three-sided Communion rails surrounding a sanctuary paved with black-and-white marble in which stands a magnificent altar table, early 17th-century or possibly Elizabethan. A handsome three-decker pulpit and tester with an hour-glass in a stand at the top stage and a wig block at the next, the reading desk, stage. There is a W. gallery, c. 1750, and 18th-century box-pews in the aisles, and further remains of the furnishing of that period is the fluted design and marbling painted on the shafts of the piers

of both arcades. Near the pulpit is a wide entrance down into the spacious Barnardiston vaults. There are four of these approached from a subterranean vestibule 10 ft. by 6 ft. in size, and the deceased (there are more than fifty lead coffins, some of them moulded to the exact shape of the body) were kept very comfortable for there is a fireplace in one of the vaults! Beautiful 15th-century benches in the nave and in the aisles and in the chancel splendid monuments to the Barnardiston family. Notably that for Sir Thomas and Lady Barnardiston (1526) with life-size effigies, and the alabaster monument for Sir Nathaniel Barnardiston (1653). One of the finest of the Puritan churches.

KENTFORD (*St. Mary*)
Wall-painting.

KERSEY *(St. Mary)*
This church has a beautiful setting at the top of a village street running through a water-splash and then up the hill between neat red-brick and colour-washed houses. There is a 15th-century tower but inside the church has been most fearfully restored. But there are many points of interest, in particular a piscina in the N. chapel and in the N. aisle some panels of the rood-screen with figure-painting. The S. porch has a 15th-century roof.

KESSINGLAND (*St. Edmund*)
14th-cent. font.

LAKENHEATH *(St. Mary)*
Lakenheath is in that border region of W. Suffolk where the land merges into the Brek on the one side and slopes away to the Fens on the other. The church contains a wonderful series of 15th-century benches in the nave and a cambered tie-beam roof. A lovely 13th-century font with foliage carved in high relief.

LANGHAM (*St. Mary*)
15th-cent. screen with remains of loft.

LAVENHAM *(St. Peter & St. Paul)*
Not unjustly described as 'an almost unspoilt example of a medieval town in England' with its splendid half-timbered houses at every turn. Notably the marvellous Guild-hall and the houses in Pump Court, Mill Hill, Barn Street, Bolton Street, Prentice Street, Shilling Street, and in Water Street leading down to the river. This lovely 'wool' town has the most splendid of all the 'wool' churches of East Anglia,

towering above the village with its colossal W. tower, 141 ft. high, and no tenor bell has a sound more impressive than the deep tone of the great tenor of Lavenham made by Miles Graye in 1625 and weighing 23 cwt. But though the proportions of the church are so splendid the late 15th-century Perpendicular has a worldliness about it akin to St. Peter Mancroft in Norwich. Thomas Spring, a wealthy clothier, was a great benefactor and there is a lovely 'Spring Chantry Chapel' in the N. aisle. Some of the original stalls and return stalls remain in the chancel, together with a 14th-century chancel screen. Also in the chancel a marble and alabaster monument to Dr. Copinger (1622), Rector for forty-five years. The beautiful 'Branch Chapel' (1500) is at the E. end of the S. aisle. Some of the 19th-century restorations have been unfortunate, particularly some especially virulent stained glass.

LAXFIELD *(All Saints)*
The birthplace of William Dowsing, the iconoclast of execrable memory who certainly did not forget his own parish church, a fine building but most terribly mutilated. But it is worth seeing for the fragments of 15th-century benches worked up into the box-pews, the W. tower with flint flush work, and the splendid seven-sacrament font. There is a 17th-century pulpit and reading desk.

LEISTON (*St. Margaret*)
13th-cent. font.

THE LIVERMERES
Park-like setting to both villages. The father of M. R. James, ghost story writer, was rector here.

MAGNA (*St. Peter*)
Interesting remains of wall-paintings.

PARVA (*St. Peter & St. Paul*)
Restored in a Strawberry Hill manner; 18th-cent. box-pew.

LONG MELFORD *(Holy Trinity)*
This enormous church is set most beautifully on the rising ground at the end of the 'Long' straggling village of Melford at the top of the village green with the 16th-century brick of the Cordell Hospital in the foreground. With its very large nave and almost separate, and most exquisite, Lady Chapel for daily offices and celebrations it is of cathedral proportions. The great W. tower, which encases an 18th-century one

of brick, is a rather unfortunate early 20th-century attempt by G. F. Bodley to reproduce the West Country type of tower. The nave with slender columns rising to a lofty clerestory has in the E. window, and in the W. windows of the aisles, some of the most superb 15th-century glass in the county. The huge monument to Sir William Cordell (1580), Master of the Rolls and founder of the Hospital at Long Melford, is one of the finest examples of the work of Cornelius Cure, Master Mason to the Crown and the maker of the monuments to Queen Elizabeth and Mary, Queen of Scots, in Westminster Abbey. Through the N. aisle and past the fine brasses to the Clopton family, there is an entrance by way of a vestibule with vaulted roof into the Clopton Chantry Chapel with its magnificent roof, on the freize of which is painted on scrolls a poem by Lidgate, a monk of Bury. Directly behind the high altar comes the vestry and beyond the marvellous 15th-century Lady Chapel surrounded by an ambulatory with a wonderful cambered tie-beam roof all the way round. At Long Melford one is amazed by the size of the nave but, as in a Cathedral, that is by no means all and this wonderful building leads you on through aisles and chantry and chancel to the Lady Chapel which is the most magnificent and yet at the same time the most intimate of all.

LOUND *(St. John the Baptist)
A most lovely church, exquisitely restored. The screen with its loft and rood, and the wonderful organ-case and font cover are all the work of Sir Ninian Comper. The organ-case at the W. end of the church is especially magnificent and above the font the beautifully decorated beam supporting the cover.

LOWESTOFT (St. Margaret)
15th cent.; flint flush work, especially fine in the panelling of the S. porch; 14th-cent. font, badly mutilated.

MARLESFORD (St. Andrew)
Norman arcade; monument N.

MELFORD, LONG: see Long Melford.

MELTON (St. Andrew)
15th-cent. seven-sacrament font.

MENDLESHAM *(St. Mary)
Very fine W. tower and 17th-century woodwork; pulpit, reading desk and font cover all made by John Turner of Mendlesham

in 1630. But the unique feature of this church is the collection of 16th and 17th century armour in the chamber above the S. porch which has been used as the parish armoury since 1593.

METFIELD *(St. John the Baptist)
The most interesting feature of this church is the canopy of honour above the rood formed by decorating the easternmost bay of the nave roof. The rood itself has disappeared and only the base of the screen remains.

MILDEN (St. Peter)
Pleasant setting; pulpit, 1685; monument to James Allington, 1626.

MILDENHALL *(St. Mary)
This is without doubt the most splendid of all the churches of Suffolk and in the nave and aisle roofs the marvellous achievement of the Suffolk type of heavy carpentry reached its zenith. Without exaggeration the nave roof is the most wonderful example in existence of the cambered tie-beam construction interspersed with arch-braced hammer beams. In the aisles are hammer-beam roofs and the wealth of carving on that of the N. aisle in particular is unsurpassed. One cannot be too thankful that here, as at Blythburgh, it was too high for the devilish Mr. Dowsing to shoot down. There is much 13th-century work in the fabric of the church which was preserved in the great rebuilding of the 15th century. At the N.W. extremity of the county the great W. tower, 113 ft. high, stands as an impressive landmark across mile upon mile of Fens. Approached from this direction Mildenhall is indeed a wonderful and a splendid introduction to the many glories of the church architecture of Suffolk.

MONK SOHAM (St. Peter)
Hammer-beam roof, seven-sacrament font; 17th cent.; altar table.

MONKS ELEIGH (St. Peter)
W. tower; 17th-cent. woodwork.

MUTFORD (St. Andrew)
11th-cent. circular tower with 15th-cent. octagonal belfry; remains of 14th-cent. W. (Galilee) porch; fragments of wall paintings and a figure of St. Christopher overpainted with 17th-cent. Lord's Prayer and Creed; 15th-cent font. This most interesting church was much neglected and then

poorly restored in the 19th cent. (*See Plate 20*)

NAYLAND (*St. James*)
16th-cent. screen panels; Constable picture of Christ instituting the Eucharist.

NEDGING (*St. Mary*)
Norman doors.

NEEDHAM MARKET *(*St. John the Baptist*)
One stands aghast at the nave roof, the most astounding example of the marvellous ingenuity of the 15th-century craftsmen. Yet somehow it is not so pleasing as some of the other and simpler types of roof. It is a most remarkable instance of the way the carpenters dealt with the difficult problem of bridging a wide span with the minimum amount of outward thrust. Wide hammer-beams carry tall posts strengthened by lateral struts and support cambered tie-beams. The posts are carried up above the tie-beams to provide a clerestoried lantern. The soaring vaults set by the medieval masons are wonderful and more than wonderful. One stands amazed at the roof of Needham Market for the tremendous daring of the craftsmen in wood.

NEWTON (*All Saints*)
Canopied tomb in chancel with effigy of Margaret Boteler (1310).

NORTH COVE (*St. Botolph*)
Norman S. door.

NORTON (*St. Andrew*)
Misericord seats.

OCCOLD (*St. Michael*)
Pulpit and tester (1620).

ORFORD *(*St. Bartholomew*)
Is like Aldeburgh. A 'Borough' and a little town that was once a port and the river, the Alde, now become the Ore, runs between it and the sea. Aldeburgh has its Martello Tower and Orford has the wonderful remains of an earlier fortress in the Castle – one of the best Norman Keeps in England. There is more beautiful Norman work in the church in the ruined chancel. The top stages of the tower have collapsed but the nave is 14th-century work with beautiful tracery in the aisle windows and quatrefoil clerestory lights.

PAKEFIELD (*All Saints & St. Margaret*)
Well restored after damage by enemy action.

PALGRAVE (*St. Peter*)
15th-cent. hammer-beam roof with much original colour.

PARHAM (*St. Mary*)
17th-cent. woodwork.

PLAYFORD (*St. Mary*)
Military brass for Sir George Felbrigg (1400).

POLSTEAD *(*St. Mary*)
Standing by itself in a well-wooded park this church is the only one in Suffolk having a medieval stone spire. The church was rebuilt in the 14th century but much 12th-century work remains. Especially in the nave arcade where the arches are of 12th-century brick work with the remains of brick clerestory windows above.

PRESTON (*St. Mary*)
Late 16th-cent. triptych when closed displays series of texts and Decalogue; when open reveals most remarkable and elaborate painting of Royal Arms of Elizabeth I.

RAMSHOLT (*All Saints*)
Riverside setting; the early tower is oval.

RATTLESDEN *(*St. Nicholas*)
A 'problem' which shows the rebuilding and alterations which took place in all periods from the 13th century onwards. The 15th century providing a hammer-beam roof, bench-ends, and screen (only the lower part of which remains). To the 14th century belongs the magnificent font and the aumbry on the N. side of the chancel.

REDGRAVE (*St. Mary*)
Note especially memorials for Nicholas and Anne Bacon (1616) by Bernard Johnson with effigies by Nicholas Stone; portrait brass for Anne Butts (1609); and splendid 18th-cent. monument for Lord Chief Justice Holt (1719) by Thomas Green of Camberwell.

THE RICKINGHALLS
Two pleasant villages in the quiet undulating country of N. Suffolk near the Norfolk border.

Inferior *(*St. Mary*)
A 12th-century circular tower extended, as is often the case, into a pleasing 15th-century octagonal belfry. Also a beautiful 14th-century S. aisle with remarkable geometrical tracery in the S.E. window.

Superior *(*St. Mary*)
Another 14th-century church with 15th-century additions, and a W. tower with flint flush work on the parapet.

RISBY (*St. Giles*)
Round Norman tower and Norman chancel arch; 17th-cent. pulpit and altar table.

ROUGHAM *(St. Mary)*
Very well proportioned 14th–15th century building with early 16th-century N. aisle with inscriptions on the buttresses giving the date (1514) and the names of the people who built it. 15th-century hammer-beam roof with contemporary seating in the nave.

RUMBURGH *(St. Michael)*
Once a Benedictine priory and there are considerable remains of the conventual buildings. There is an unusual 13th-century rectangular W. tower with three lancet windows towards the W. Only the bottom stages remain and the top has been finished with a hipped barn roof with tiles. Most lovely screen on which some of the original colour remains.

RUSHBROOKE *(St. Nicholas)*
The interior of this church was refurnished in the 19th century with seats facing one another and return stalls at the W. end in the manner of a college chapel. All in the 'paste-board' Gothic style. A most remarkable possession is the Royal Arms of Henry VIII.

SANTON DOWNHAM *(St. Mary)*
The attraction of this place is in the churchyard which is most beautifully kept with all the 18th-century headstones carefully cleaned – a model of the treatment these beautiful memorials ought to receive. The church has evidences of very early workmanship especially in the S. door of the chancel.

SAXHAM PARVA (*St. Nicholas*)
Norman round tower and S. door with tympanum.

Saxham, Great: *see Great Saxham.*

SAXSTEAD (*All Saints*)
Hammer-beam roof; 17th cent.; altar table and Communion rails; parish stocks and whipping-post in S. porch.

SHADINGFIELD (*St. John the Baptist*)
15th-cent. font; altar table with actual altar cloth used on it, kept in its contemporary box.

SHELLAND *(King Charles the Martyr)*
With box-pews and a three-decker pulpit this little church has one of the most attractive 18th-century interiors in Suffolk. The parish is in the unusual position of being a 'donative' – the personal possession of the patron who institutes the incumbent.

SHOTLEY (*St. Mary*)
Nave and aisles 14th cent. with late 15th-cent. clerestory and roof; chancel 18th cent. Classical with woodwork of same date.

SNAPE (*St. John the Baptist*)
Setting; 15th-cent. font.

Soham, Monk: *see Monk Soham.*

SOMERLEYTON (*St. Mary*)
15th-cent. painted screen.

SOUTH COVE (*St. Laurence*)
N. and S. Norman doorways and door to rood-loft stair with painting of St. Michael.

SOUTHWOLD *(St. Edmund)*
With the exception perhaps of Blythburgh this is the most splendid of the great 15th-century churches of E. Suffolk. With much of its 15th-century fittings complete, of which the wonderful stalls and return stalls and screen require especial mention. The screen stretches right across the church with magnificent figure-paintings on the panels representing, in the N. aisle the Nine Orders of Angels, in the nave the Twelve Apostles, and in the S. aisle the old Testament Prophets. There is also a magnificent 15th-century pulpit. The whole building with continuous nave and chancel is a great 15th-century church of the Norfolk type with the lovely slender columns of the arcades rising to a lofty clerestory and hammer-beam roof, that portion above the screen being arranged as a canopy of honour for the rood. Lofty W. tower richly panelled in flint. Southwold is one of the great churches of East Anglia and it had little of that 'worldliness' which is so often the feeling of the rather formal 'Perpendicular' churches of the period. It has been most beautifully restored.

STANNINGFIELD (*St. Nicholas*)
Norman doorway; picture of Doom above chancel arch with Our Lord in Majesty seated upon the rainbow, as in Byzantine art.

STOKE-BY-CLARE (*St. John the Baptist*)
15th-cent. pulpit; wall-paintings.

STOKE-BY-NAYLAND *(St. Mary)*
The finest church of 'The Constable Country' standing amid its little town with many half-timbered houses. A most beautiful one stands to the W. of the church and

M

to the E. a well-proportioned red-brick Georgian rectory. The W. tower 120 ft. high with diagonal buttresses panelled with niches, with deeply recessed windows, a marvellous W. door with the arms of Tendring and Howard in the spandrils, and with brick and stone dressings is one of the most stately church towers of Suffolk and is beautifully situate on the high ground above the Stour Valley. The S. porch has two doors embellished with tracery and niches and in the chamber above is a 16th and 17th century library. A beautiful soaring nave with splendidly proportioned arcades and there are many interesting memorials. Magnificent brasses. Notably the fine military brass for Sir William Tendring (1408) and the exceptionally fine and superbly engraved figure of Katherine Howard (1452) in heraldic cloak. In the N. chancel aisle is the fine monument to Sir Francis Mannock (1634) which, together with the portrait brass to Lady Mannock, has been attributed to Nicholas Stone. In the S. chapel another fine monument with alabaster effigy for Lady Ann Windsor (1615).

STONHAM, EARL: *see Earl Stonham.*

STOWLANGTOFT *(St. George)*
One does not connect the leaders of the Tractarian revival with Puritan East Anglia but in addition to the famous meeting at Hadleigh, at which the 'Tracts for the Times' were agreed upon, 'that clever young gentleman from Oriel', Mr. Newman, often visited Mr. Rickards, the Rector of Stowlangtoft who had been one of the Fellows of Oriel who had elected him. The 'silvery tones' of thin, bespectacled Mr. Newman were often heard in this church which is shrouded in that 'dim, religious light' so beloved of the Tractarians, and the church has been rather heavily restored. Among the modern furnishings, however, are a series of Flemish carvings in the panelling of the E. wall. 15th-century screen and return stalls with misericords. Arch-braced roof with cambered tie-beam and with a canopy of honour for the roof similar to that at Metfield. Wall-painting of St. Christopher on the N. wall of the nave.

STOWMARKET *(St. Peter & St. Paul)*
14th and 15th cent.; wig rack, 1675.

STRADBROKE *(All Saints)*
W. tower; mainly 15th cent.

SUDBOURNE *(All Saints)*
18th-cent. fittings; 16th-cent. monument.

SUDBURY *(All Saints)*
A 15th-century pulpit, parclose screens in the chancel and an unusual painting, 17th century, representing the pedigree of the Eden and Waldegrave families.

(St. Gregory)
A magnificent font cover, a 15th-century roof with canopy of honour for the rood. The 14th-century chancel was built by Archbishop Simon de Sudbury, the Archbishop of Canterbury murdered at the time of the Peasants Revolt in 1381. His skull is enclosed in a glass case. Only one original screen painting remains, that of the water diviner Sir John Schorne who also appears at Cawston, Gateley, and Suffield in Norfolk.

(St. Peter)
Stands above the market-place; it has been much restored but has fine parclose screens in the chancel where there are also interesting paintings of Moses and Aaron, part of a classical reredos, the work, c. 1730, of a local painter, Robert Cardinall, who was a pupil of Kneller. A most interesting possession of this church is an early 16th-century funeral pall of dark red silk-velvet with green and gold fringe and embroidered with floral designs and kneeling figures in shrouds. There is also a 17th-century pulpit cloth embroidered with the arms of James I.

SWEFFLING *(St. Mary)*
Village; medieval leather chalice case.

TANNINGTON *(St. Ethelbert)*
The particular interest of this church is the series of 15th-century bench-ends very similar to those at Wiggenhall St. German's in the Norfolk Marshland. They have representations of the Sacraments, the Evangelistic Symbols, and the Seven Deadly Sins — on one of the benches the sinners are being swallowed up into hell's mouth. There is also a canopy of honour to the rood.

THORINGTON *(St. Peter)*
Circular tower.

THORNHAM PARVA *(St. Mary)*
14th-cent. retable with paintings.

THORPE MORIEUX *(St. Mary)*
15th-cent. wooden S. porch.

THURLOW MAGNA (*All Saints*)
12th-cent. font and 17th-cent. chest, pulpit and chair.

THURLOW PARVA (*St. Peter*)
17th-cent. woodwork; altar table and three-sided Communion rails; the Soame chapel monument to Sir Stephen Soame, 1619.

TUDDENHAM (*St. Martin's*)
Norman door; 15th-cent. benches and pulpit.

(*St. Mary's*)
14th-cent. church with 15th-cent. hammer-beam and arched-braced roof.

UFFORD *(*St. Mary*)
This beautiful church in a quiet retired village surrounded with trees has many points of interest but that feature which is of breath-taking beauty and magnificence is the marvellous – and more than marvellous, but no superlatives can describe it – telescopic font cover. Unquestionably this is the most beautiful of its kind in existence. Even Mr. Dowsing was compelled to admire it. 'Ufford. There is a glorious cover over the font, like a Pope's triple crown, a pelican on top picking its breast, all gilt over with gold'. It has lost all its colour but even so it is one of those priceless treasures of medieval art which one can see over and over again and still remain spellbound at its beauty and at the wonderful devotion and consummate skill of the people who made it. (*See Plate 33*)

WALBERSWICK (*St. Andrew*)
15th-cent. W. tower and S. aisle remain.

WALDRINGFIELD MAGNA (*St. Laurence*)
17th-cent. woodwork in chancel from St. Michael's Cornhill.

PARVA (*St. Laurence*)
Tudor brick porch; 14th-cent. font.

WALSHAM-LE-WILLOWS *(*St. Mary*)
A spacious 15th-century church with Suffolk-type tie-beam and hammer-beam roof. In the E. window a considerable quantity of 15th-century glass and a most unusual feature is the maiden's garland hanging in the nave. 'For Mary Boyce 1685'.

WANGFORD (*St. Denis*)
12th-cent. doorways.

(*St. Peter*)
17th-cent. pulpit and reading desk from Henham Hall.

WANTISDEN (*St. John*)
Tower; Norman S. door.

WASHBROOK (*St. Mary*)
14th-cent. Easter Sepulchre; arcading in chancel.

WENHASTON *(*St. Peter*)
There are many things of interest to see here – 15th-century font and nave roof, and 17th-century altar table and pulpit – but everything else is eclipsed by the wonderful painting of the Doom. Originally the tympanum within the chancel arch but now re-erected against the N. wall of the nave. Better perhaps than any other example does the Wenhaston Doom show how this tympanic filling of the chancel arch provided the painted scenery background to the rood. The position of the great rood itself, with its attendant figures of Our Lady and St. John, are clearly visible and behind (on the tympanum itself) came on the one side Our Lord seated on the rainbow, and on the other Our Lady and St. John the Baptist. Below St. Peter, in papal tiara, receives a group of figures naked except for their headgear – crowns, mitres, and cardinal's hats – and on the other side of the central pillar of the rood St. Michael weighing souls with the devil in the background. At the extreme left the dead are rising from graves and walking upstairs and on the extreme right the damned are being dragged by a chain into hell's mouth. The painting is of wonderful freshness and vigour but below come three lines of black letter inscription reminding us of the spoliation of this amazing thing at the time of the Reformation, for it refers to the veneration the government of the day required to be given to the Royal Arms which must have been superimposed on the tympanum in place of the rood and picture of the Doom.

WESTHALL *(*St. Andrew*)
A most interesting 'problem' church showing how the original 12th century was altered in the 13th and again in the 14th century. The 15th century provided a rood-screen and seven-sacrament font, the 16th a N. porch and in the 17th century the tower was made higher. The figure-paintings on the screen are especially interesting. On one triple panel is the only known representation of the Transfiguration on a medieval screen.

WETHERDEN (*St. Mary*)
Double hammer-beam roof, hammer-beams dependent from the arch braces above; on wall posts (also pendants!) are carved figures in canopies.

WICKHAMBROOK (*All Saints*)
Monument to Thomas Higham (1630); 17th-cent. altar table and Communion rails.

WILBY *(*St. Mary*)
This church has a W. tower with flint panelling round the base and a lofty parapet. In the nave is a series of 15th-century benches with carvings representing the Sacraments, the Seven Works of Mercy and the Seven Deadly Sins. Also a 17th-century pulpit and tester.

WINGFIELD *(*St. Andrew*)
Wingfield is set deep in the quiet countryside and yet it takes you back at once into that 'scambling and unquiet time' the 15th century, and here as at Framlingham one has the history of England in miniature with the fortunes and the remains of the great family of De La Pole. The S. front of Wingfield Castle, built by Michael de la Pole in 1384 – who died at the siege of Harfleur in 1415 and has a wooden effigy in the church – stands facing a wide moat. Then the beautiful farm-house, once the Wingfield College, facing the fish pond, laid out by the Canons of Wingfield who maintained a boarding school for 'the sons of gentlemen' in the 15th century. Then the wonderful collegiate church, the original parclose screens separating the aisle chapels from the collegiate chancel with its miserere stalls. The piers and arches of the S. chancel arcade are richly decorated with shields. Then there are the magnificent medieval tombs. As at Walpole St. Peter in Norfolk there is a 'sentry box' for the use of the clergyman officiating at the graveside in inclement weather.

WISSETT (*St. Andrew*)
11th-cent. round tower; Norman doorways.

WISSINGTON *(*St. Mary*)
This little church in the heart of the Stour Valley has had the most virulent 19th-century restoration, which is a marvellous example of how the Gothic Revivalist has to make everything conform to one period. In this case the Norman – even to Norman Communion rails! The apse – such a rarity in East Anglia – has been poorly restored and the chancel is divided from the nave by two fine Norman arches which show that there was once a central tower. There is a most unusual 12th-century S. doorway with a tympanum in the nave. Though faded, the series of wall-paintings give one a very vivid idea of what a small country church looked like inside in the 13th century. There is an especially attractive one showing the Wise Men in bed being warned in a dream not to return to Herod. Also a picture of St. Francis preaching to the birds, two women gossiping with devils eagerly encouraging them, and a series of paintings of the Nativity, the Adoration of the Magi, Herod, the Presentation in the Temple, St. Michael and St. Nicholas.

WITHERSDALE
*(*St. Mary Magdalene*)
A most lovely little 17th-century interior with pews, pulpit with tester, altar table and rails complete. All a perfect example of an unspoilt village church of the period.

WITHERSFIELD (*St. Mary*)
Series of poppy-heads in nave.

WOODBRIDGE *(*St. Mary*)
A stately town church of the 15th-century East Anglian type with continuous nave and chancel and a W. tower with flint flush work and octagonal buttresses. The interior has been wonderfully improved of late by a beautiful E. window by Martin Travers. As is often the case in a town church there are interesting 17th and 18th century memorials but the most unusual of these is to be seen not in the church but in the stable of the Bull Inn (on the opposite side of the market-place) to George Carlow, an ostler, who preferred to be buried there in 1738.

WOOLPIT *(*St. Mary*)
This church has one of the most splendid East Anglian double hammer-beam roofs and the most interesting canopy of honour that can be seen anywhere. Against the wall above the chancel arch it is covered over with vaulting which is taken back at the corners to the easternmost hammer-beams of the roof. A feature of the church is the extreme narrowness of the aisles which suggests that they were intended to be used only for processional purposes and not for seating. There is a 15th-century S. porch; splendid 15th-century seating.

WORLINGWORTH (*St. Mary*)
15th-cent. S. porch with flint flush work; 17th-cent. seating, pulpit, and altar table into which has been inserted the medieval stone mensa.

WORTHAM (*St. Mary*)
Largest early circular tower.

WYVERSTONE (*St. George*)
15th-cent. hammer-beam roof and screen with paintings; 16th-cent. pulpit with linenfold panelling and 17th-cent. Communion rails.

YAXLEY *(St. Mary)*
Another 15th-century porch on the N. side. The screen of the same period has been badly mutilated but there are some beautiful figure-paintings on the panels enriched with gesso work. There is a beautiful richly carved pulpit and tester (1635) and a 'Sexton's Wheel' not unlike the one at Long Stratton St. Mary in Norfolk – a sort of revolving calendar indicating festivals and fasts.

YOXFORD (*St. Peter*)
Setting; brasses.

Surrey

INTRODUCTION

FOR CENTURIES the small area of Surrey was little regarded. It was an unattractive district to the Romans and it has few extensive medieval remains. The 17th century found profit from its rich meadows in the Thames Valley and there were once fields round Mitcham and Carshalton, redolent with lavender, mint, camomile, penny royal and other herbs for supplying London herb-sellers. Battersea, now part of London, was famous for asparagus and Chertsey for carrots. In the 18th century the heights of Richmond Hill, Cooper's Hill and St. Anne's Hill, looking over the winding Thames, were favoured for country seats by the nobility; as Denham said of Cooper's Hill, the view was

> Though deep, yet clear; though gentle, yet not dull;
> Strong, without rage; without o'erflowing, full.

Through the middle of the county, east to west, runs a narrow high ridge of chalk which links the north downs of Kent with Hampshire. And the views from the Hog's Back and Box Hill have long been famous. Leith Hill, on the greensand, is 965 feet, the highest eminence in this part of England.

But for the most part Surrey was regarded in polite circles as a barren county of heaths, firs and unprofitable soil. It was not until Victorian times that its scenery came to be much admired, except by a few romantics in advance of the public taste. But when it *was* admired, much happened to Surrey. Rich City gentlemen built themselves houses on its heights and less affluent citizens built themselves villas, so that the county today is almost peasantless. As land was cheap and unfertile, Government departments found it desirable for barracks, orphanages and asylums. Schools, too, were built on its sandy commons among the conifers. Today, threaded by many electric railways from the metropolis, Surrey is thickly populated, and it is impossible to walk far among its pinewoods without spying a human habitation through the trunks.

The county has great natural beauty and though one regrets its overdevelopment, the outline of its hills, the wide views, the safe wildness, safe now from the footpads and highwaymen of two centuries ago, the ponds, the timbered cottages and the new villas with their lovingly tended gardens, the gorse, bracken and heather, the sheepy valleys still to be found on the southern slopes of the Downs, make one wish one had known it before it was discovered.

Several old towns of real beauty survive – Guildford, Dorking, Farnham and Reigate and Bletchingley in particular. Even Croydon, which is now joined to London by houses, still has the atmosphere of a country town, divorced from the Metropolis.

The story of the churches of Surrey is mostly one of heavy restoration, of unpretentious fabrics or of new Victorian buildings. But there was wide variety of local stone, such as Bargate stone, which gives the older churches delightful texture. Most of the finest churches are 19th century, for here lived the great Victorian church architects, Woodyer and G. E. Street, and between them they left their mark upon Surrey churches and their imitators and pupils did not let them down.   J.B.

SELECTED LIST OF CHURCHES

by the Rev. B. F. L. Clarke

ABINGER (*St. James*)
12th and 13th cent.; well restored by F. Etchells, 1950.

ADDISCOMBE *(St. Mary Magdalene)*
By E. B. Lamb, 1869, in Kentish rag. It was built for a schismatic congregation but consecrated in 1878. It is very striking and original within and without, and the detailing is all clever, but not to contemporary (1955) taste. The tower top by H. Mackintosh (1926) is of its date and contrasts with the rest of the church. The effect of space inside is tremendous, and is created by a wonderful timber roof.

ALBURY *(St. Peter & St. Paul)*
Henry Drummond, one of the Apostles of the Catholic Apostolic Church, built a new parish church outside the park, and a Catholic Apostolic Church in another part of it – both designed by William McIntosh Brooks of London. The old church was dismantled in 1842: the chancel is ruinous. It was of Norman nave-tower-chancel plan: late 13th-century S. aisle, and chancel now Perpendicular. Transept by Pugin. The tower has an 18th-century shingled dome.

ALFOLD (*St. Nicholas*)
13th cent. and later; Norman font; timber belfry; 17th-cent. pulpit.

BEDDINGTON *(St. Mary)*
Rebuilding began in the 14th century. In 1387 Sir Nicholas de Carew left £20 towards the work. Carew chapel, tower, S. aisle and porch 15th century. Additional N. aisle and restoration, 1852: restoration and re-decoration, 1869. A handsome, flint-faced exterior: the outline of the tower rather like a Kentish church. Interior made solemn by Victorian decoration and glass. Pulpit 16th century. Carew brasses and monuments. Organ-case by Wm. Morris. Modern E. window by Nuttgens.

(*St. Michael & All Angels*)
1907, W. D. Caröe; full of cleverness and built on whims.

BENHILTON (*All Saints*)
S. S. Teulon, 1864–5. Keeping very quiet.

BETCHWORTH *(St. Michael)*
The village street, with the church at the end of it, has been painted by Sutton Palmer. The church is mostly 13th century. The tower, early Norman, was originally central, but was rebuilt on the S. in 1851. Font by Eric Kennington.

BLACKHEATH *(St. Martin)*
By C. Harrison Townsend, 1893. A pretty village with hardly any peasants, and the church exactly suited to such a place. It is Italian-looking outside, with deep eaves and very low walls. The interior is a charming little barrel-vaulted chapel made mysterious by a screen and hidden lighting behind the wide and rounded arch of the marble sanctuary. There is a sparing and

wise use of decoration entirely painted by Mrs. Lea Merritt, who is famous for her picture 'Love Locked Out'.

BLETCHINGLEY (*St. Mary*)
Norman, 13th and 15th cent.; 18th-cent. Clayton monument by Richard Crutcher.

BOOKHAM, GREAT: *see Great Bookham.*

BURHILL, WALTON-ON-THAMES (*St. Mark*) GR
1919, Walter Tapper; in Whiteley Village; Yorkshire rustic Gothic; deliberately 'good taste', whitened inside.

BURSTOW (*St. Bartholomew*)
Early Norman; 15th-cent. aisle; timber tower.

BUSBRIDGE (*St. John Baptist*) GR
By G. G. Scott, Jnr., 1865–7. Surrey style; ironwork rood by Lutyens.

BYFLEET, WEST: *see West Byfleet.*

CARSHALTON *(All Saints*)
Nave, chancel, central tower and S. aisle remain of the old church. The surviving arcade is 13th century with capitals of stiff-leaf foliage. The wall of the S. aisle was raised in 1723, when the church was beautified: the N. wall, which no longer exists, was raised in 1725. 18th-century monuments, including Sir William Scawen (1722), by Rysbrack, and Sir John Fellowes (1724). A large new Perpendicular church was built to the N. from designs by A. and R. Blomfield: begun in 1893, completed in 1914. Re-decorated and improved by Sir Ninian Comper. (But ought he to have gilded and painted the 18th-century altarpiece in the old chancel?)

(*The Good Shepherd*)
1930, Martin Travers; good baroque and clever stained glass; Hispano-Italian.

CATERHAM (*St. Lawrence*)
Unrestored; unused; Norman enlarged in 12th–13th cent. Roofs.

CHALDON (*St. Peter & St. Paul*)
Norman, enlarged later; 13th-cent. painting on W. wall; 13th-cent. bell.

CHARLWOOD (*St. Nicholas*)
11th-cent. nave, central tower and chancel; 14th-cent. screen at W. of S. chapel; wall-paintings.

CHEAM (*St. Dunstan*)
Lumley Chapel and monuments.

CHERTSEY (*St. Peter*) GR
Rebuilding, 1806–8 (but for tower and chancel) begun by R. Elsam, but finished by Thomas Chawner; Gothick, with window-frames and mullions of artificial stone; iron columns encased in wooden piers.

CHIPSTEAD *(St. Margaret*)
A 13th-century cruciform church with central tower. G. E. Street read a paper before the Ecclesiological Society in 1850 maintaining that this church, Merstham, Merton, and Gatton, in Surrey, and Cliffe at Hoo and Brasted in Kent, were the work of the same guild of architects. He called Chipstead and Merstham well-nigh perfect in their way, and not the less lovely from their great simplicity. Screen 15th century; pulpit 17th.

COMPTON *(St. Nicholas*)
A very interesting church. Tower and parts of the walls are 11th century. The arcades and aisles, and chancel and tower arches, c. 1170. A two-storied sanctuary was constructed – the only one remaining in England: the lower stage groined, the upper with a contemporary wooden balustrade. 17th-century pulpit, rails, and screen (now at the W. end).

COULSDON (*St. John the Evangelist*)
13th cent.; very little restored on a new estate.

CROYDON (*St. John the Baptist*)
Large Perp.; rebuilt by Scott, 1867. Whitgift monument, 1604, and Sheldon monument, 1677, by Jasper Latham.

(St. Michael & All Angels)
By J. L. Pearson, 1880–5, and one of his loveliest churches. Outside, it is of red brick; but inside, of stock brick with stone ribs for the vaulting. In one of the E. chapels there is Pearson's usual trick of using tall, slim columns, two of which are functionless from the vaulting point of view, but make a screen to suggest complexity. The transepts are most magnificent on a small scale (*See Plate 61*)

(*St. Peter*) GR
1851, G. G. Scott; Middle pointed; ornate and pretty throughout.

CROWHURST (*St. George*)
12th–13th cent.; timber tower; monuments, one of cast iron.

DITTON, LONG: *see Long Ditton.*

DORKING (*St. Martin*) GR
Rebuilt Woodyer, 1868–77.

DUNSFOLD (*St. Mary & All Saints*)
c. 1300; 15th-cent. timber belfry.

EGHAM (*St. John the Baptist*)
Rebuilt Henry Rhodes, 1817–20; plain Grecian; yellow glass skylight over sanctuary; marble altar; the altar painting by Westall – almost entirely burned, 1949; refitted in 19th century; re-Georgianised in 1948–9.

ENGLEFIELD GREEN (*St. Jude*) GR
1859, E. B. Lamb; by a large cemetery, with the look of an abnormal Victorian cemetery chapel; peculiar plan, and eccentric details; lined with strange mixture of stone and brick.

ESHER *(St. George)*
Not used for regular worship, but carefully kept. A most lovable, unrestored church. The brick transept with gallery pew was built in 1725–6: the gallery has been taken down. Upper W. gallery 1840–2. Altarpiece by Sir Robert Ker Porter: according to an early 19th-century writer, the figure of Christ 'has all the beauty and dignity which, we have reason to believe, characterised the superior classes of the Hebrew race in ancient times.' Picture of the Apotheosis of Princess Charlotte, by A. W. Devis, and marble monument to her by F. J. Williamson.

EWHURST (*St. Peter & St. Paul*)
Picturesque on a hill; cruciform 13th cent.; partly rebuilt by Robert Ebbels after fall of tower in 1837.

FARLEIGH (*Blessed Virgin Mary*)
Small 12th cent.

FARNHAM (*St. Andrew*)
12th-cent. work; enlarged 13th–15th cent.

(*St. James*) GR
1876, Henry Woodyer.

FELBRIDGE (*St. John*) GR
By W. White, 1865; unconventional stone and brick; well thought out interior detail.

FETCHAM (*St. Mary*)
Pre-Conquest walling; 12th-cent. S. aisle and tower; 13th-cent. N. aisle and transept.

GATTON *(St. Andrew)*
Stands in the park. Modernised by the 5th Lord Monson (1834), and fitted with woodwork and glass from the Continent – Aürschot, Burgundy, Nuremberg, Tongres, Ghent and Rouen. Screen from an English church. A most impressive interior.

GODALMING *(St. Peter & St. Paul)*
Some pre-Conquest remains. Central tower, chancel and transepts Norman. Aisles added in the 13th century, chancel aisles rebuilt in the 14th. The tall, lead-covered spire is 14th century. Lengthened westwards in the 15th century. Repaired in 1840 (John Perry of Godalming) and restored in 1879 (Sir G. G. Scott).

GRAFFHAM *(St. Andrew)*
In Bramley. By H. Woodyer, 1864, in Bargate stone, in the Early English style. The church was Woodyer's parish church, paid for by him. He is buried in the churchyard. St. Andrew's cross and the letter A run through the design. There is good Hardman glass. The solid screen supports the roof and was put there by Woodyer because Sumner, then Bishop of Winchester, refused to consecrate churches with screens, so Woodyer made this one structural, and got his way.

GREAT BOOKHAM *(St. Nicholas)*
Arcades 12th century of differing dates: the chancel was built by John Rutherwyke, Abbot of Chertsey in 1341 (inscription). S. aisle widened in 15th century. Timber tower, with shingled spire, on stone base. Restored by Carpenter (1845) and Butterfield (1885): E. window glass designed by Butterfield and executed by O'Connor. Monument of Col. Thomas Moore, 1735.

GUILDFORD *(Holy Trinity)*
The pro-Cathedral. Tower fell in 1740 and wrecked the old church. The new church – opened in 1763 – was almost certainly designed by James Horne, architect of St. Catherine Coleman, Christchurch, Southwark, and St. Mary's, Ealing; a rather uninspired architect. A solid red-brick church with battlemented tower.

1869, galleries removed and windows altered by Woodyer. E. end, 1888, by Sir A. Blomfield, who also made plans for the remodelling of the whole church. Pulpit and gallery remain.

Monuments of Abp. Abbot (1633), by John and Matthias Christmas, and the Hon. Arthur Onslow, Speaker of the House of Commons, 1768.

Its inside has an enormous span of ceiling without intermediate supports, broader than any London church. As in all Horne's churches, the ironwork and joinery are very good, particularly the pulpit here. Archbishop Abbot's tomb is of alabaster with pedestals of columns made of piles of books. A pretty churchyard slopes up S. of church.

*(St. Mary)
The central tower is late pre-Conquest. Transepts added and chancel rebuilt early 12th century: c. 1160, nave and aisles, apsidal chapels, and chancel remodelled (the apse has been taken down). Aisles widened in the 13th century; 13th-century paintings in the N. chapel.

(St. Nicholas)
Rebuilt, 1875, by Ewan Christian after plans by S. S. Teulon; solemn interior, Clayton and Bell glass.

HALE (St. John the Evangelist)
1844, Benjamin Ferrey; Norman; solemn and tall inside.

HASCOMBE *(St. Peter)
One of the prettiest villages in Surrey. Church by H. Woodyer, 1864, is a Tractarian work of art. The exterior is plain, and the richness of interior effect is gained by gilding and painting on roofs and reredos, and by the richly moulded interior arches of coupled windows. There is good dark Hardman glass throughout, except for E. window by Clayton & Bell. The nave walls are painted all round with St. Peter's net.

HASLEMERE (St. Christopher) GR
1902-3, by Charles Spooner.

HERSHAM (St. Peter) GR
J. L. Pearson, 1887; unfortunately whitewashed.

HINDHEAD (St. Alban) GR
1905-6, finished 1915 and 1931; J. D. Coleridge; odd and arty; Perp-ish.

HOLMBURY ST. MARY (St. Mary)
Beautifully set against a hanging wood; a model village church by G. E. Street, 1879, who lived here and built it of local stone in memory of his wife.

HORSLEY, WEST: see West Horsley.

KEW *(St. Anne)
Consecrated, 1714. Enlarged in 1766, plans by J. J. Kirby. Enlarged again in 1810; plans by Robert Browne. 1822, new gallery and organ. Enlarged again by Sir Jeffery Wyatville in 1837. Mausoleum moved farther E. and apsidal chancel with dome, S. chapel, vestry and organ chamber by H. Stock, 1883-4.

KINGSTON-UPON-THAMES (All Saints)
Mostly 15th cent.; 18th-cent. brick tower;

restored by Brandon (1862) and Pearson (1886-8); bright Victorian glass.

KINGSWOOD, LOWER: see Lower Kingswood.

LEATHERHEAD (St. Mary & St. Nicholas)
Fine scale given by chalk wall to small chancel arch; 14th-cent. transepts; 15th-cent. tower.

LIMPSFIELD (St. Andrew-on-the-Chart) GR
Hertfordshire Gothic by R. Blomfield, 1895; reredos H. Wilson.

(St. Peter)
13th cent. and later; restored by Pearson.

LINGFIELD *(St. Peter & St. Paul)
A College was founded in 1431 by Sir Reginald Cobham; the church was rebuilt at this time. Stalls, screen, and lectern with chained bible. An excellent series of monuments of the Cobham family.

LONG DITTON (St. Mary) GR
Good routine job by G. E. Street, 1878.

LOWER KINGSWOOD (The Wisdom of God)
Sidney H. Barnsley, 1892; replica of a Balkan church with narthex and apse, and much material brought from Balkan ruins; unique in England in its thorough-going Byzantinism.

LOWFIELD HEATH *(St. Michael)
Wm. Burges, 1867, in a French Gothic style consisting of nave, chancel, and S.W. tower. This is a most beautiful little church, made so by the extraordinary vigour of the sculpture and the sensitivity shown in the placing of it.

MALDEN (St. John the Baptist)
Small brick church; nave, chancel and tower, rebuilt in 1610; new nave and chancel added on the N. in 1873 – T. G. Jackson architect.

MERSTHAM (St. Katharine)
13th-15th cent.; 13th-cent. tower with shingled spire.

MICKLEHAM (St. Michael)
Wooded slopes behind; massive tower 12th cent.; after earlier restoration in 1822 by P. F. Robinson, partly rebuilt by Ewan Christian in 1872, in massive Victorian Norman.

MORDEN (*St. Lawrence*)
Rebuilt, 1636; red brick with tower; E.
window glass of Moses and Aaron; altar
rails; pulpit, 1720.

NEWDIGATE (*St. Peter*)
13th and 15th cent.; timber tower.

NORWOOD (*St. Luke*) CL
Greek revival by F. Bedford, 1822–5, remodelled by G. E. Street, 1878; a try-out
for the Guards' Chapel.

NORWOOD, SOUTH: *see South Norwood.*

NORWOOD, UPPER: *see Upper Norwood.*

OCKHAM *(*St. Mary & All Saints*)
Among the trees in Ockham Park. 13th-
century work, including the beautiful E.
window of seven lancets. S. side of nave
14th century; tower 15th. Brick mausoleum
of the King family; faculty, June 1734.
Monument of Peter, 1st Baron King, 1734,
and Ann, 1767, by Rysbrack. Bust of Peter
7th Baron King, 1783, by R. Westmacott,
jnr. Voysey casket opposite King tombs, a
strange contrast.

OTTERSHAW (*Christ Church*) GR
1864, by Scott; 13th-cent. style, polychrome brick; conspicuous.

OUTWOOD (*St. John Baptist*) GR
1869, by Wm. Burges; tower M. P.
Manning, 1876; all well-proportioned.

OXSHOTT (*St. Andrew*) GR
1912, W. D. Caroë and Passmore (mostly
latter).

OXTED (*St. Mary*)
14th-cent. work in chancel.

PEPER HAROW (*St. Nicholas*)
Restoration by Pugin, 1848.

PETERSHAM (*All Saints*)
J. Kelly, 1902; red-brick romanesque;
expensive.

*(*St. Peter*)
A Thames-side village with many 18th-
century houses. A beautiful unrestored
church. S. transept and tower were built in
the 17th century. Faculty for building a
N. transept, 1703. Pulpit, 1797. S. transept
rebuilt, 1840 – Meakin, architect. Pews and
galleries remain.

PYRFORD (*St. Nicholas*)
On hill overlooking Newark Priory ruins;
Norman; celure over the former rood;
remains of wall-painting; 17th-cent. pulpit.

RANMORE (*St. Barnabas*)
A rich man's church with prominent spire;
1859, by Scott, who paid no regard to local
style. On a beautiful common.

REDHILL (*St. John the Evangelist*) GR
1842, by J. Knowles; Giles Hesketh, 1867;
enlargement by Pearson, 1889; tower and
spire, 1895.

REIGATE (*St. Mary Magdalene*)
Arcades with stiff-leaf capitals, *c.* 1200.
Chancel and chapels 14th cent., tower 15th.
Chancel and chapels restored by Woodyer;
a later restoration by Scott in 1874–8;
monument of Richard Ladbroke (1730) by
J. Rose.

RICHMOND *(*St. Luke*) GR
Goldie, Child and Goldie, 1890: fierce
suburban Gothic; screen by Sir Robert
Lorimer.

*(*St. Mary Magdalene*)
The tower was built in 1624, by Henry
Walton, freemason. The rest of the church
is said, in the guide books, to have been
rebuilt in 1750. In fact, a N. aisle of brick
was added at the beginning of the century
(faculty 1699); and a faculty was granted in
1749 for the addition of a S. aisle to match
the N. Chancel and chapels, 1904, by G. F.
Bodley. Many 18th-century tablets.

(*St. Matthias*) GR
1858, Scott; his first pointed style at its
most characteristic.

SHACKLEFORD (*St. Mary*) GR
1865–6 by Scott; early 13th-cent. style;
satisfying.

SHERE *(*St. James*)
A beautiful village on the Tillingbourne,
discovered by cyclists, *c.* 1900, and its
praises sung in the guide books of the
time; much visited by motorists now.
Cruciform 12th-century church; S. aisle
and top of tower good 13th-century work;
some work of the 14th and 15th centuries;
a shapely shingled spire. Carefully restored
by S. Weatherley in 1895.

SOUTH NORWOOD (*Holy Innocents*) GR
Large and delicate, by G. F. Bodley (1894).

STOKE D'ABERNON *(*St. Mary*)
The S. wall is pre-Conquest, with a blocked
doorway 12 ft. from the ground. N. aisle
late 12th-century chancel remodelled, and
vaulting built, in the 13th. Norbury Chapel
15th century. A destructive 'restoration' –

which certainly qualifies for inverted commas – by Ford and Hesketh in 1866: the interior has been, to some extent, de-restored. In the chancel are the magnificent brasses of Sir John D'Abernon (1277) – the earliest surviving brass in England; and of his son, Sir John (1327). Remains of 13th-century painting in the chancel. Monuments in the Norbury Chapel. Imposing early 17th-century pulpit with tester; hour glass.

THURSLEY *(St. Michael & All Angels)
Pre-Conquest windows have been discovered. An impressive 15th-century wooden tower supported by oak piers in the centre of the nave.

TITSEY (St. James) GR
1861; Pearson; simple E.E.

UPPER NORWOOD *(St. John the Evangelist)
By J. L. Pearson, 1875. Strikingly situated on a steep slope with woods to the W. of it. In Pearson's usual Early English style, of stock brick and stone ribs. There is less complexity here than in later churches and an effect of breadth is given by the wide nave and spreading E. end.

VALLEY END (St. Saviour) GR
1867, by G. F. Bodley; of brick, in the simplest Middle Pointed style; though an early Bodley church, it shows the emergence of his later style.

WALTON-ON-THE-HILL (St. Peter)
Leaden Norman font.

WEST BYFLEET (St. John the Baptist) GR
1910, W. D. Caröe; very lanky.

WEST HORSLEY (St. Mary)
Pre-Conquest and later work; Nicholas monuments.

WEYBRIDGE (St. James)
1847–8, by J. L. Pearson, his first church; good Middle pointed; enlarged, 1864.

WITLEY (All Saints)
Uncannily pretty like all Witley; largely 13th cent.; restored in 1899 and enlarged by Aston Webb.

WOKING *(St. Peter)
Late 11th-century W. doorway, with door and ironwork; tower and chancel, 13th century; aisle, 14th; brick porch, 1622, gallery and pulpit.

WONERSH *(St. John the Baptist)
Secluded wooded setting. There are designs in the Adam collection, dated 1767, for a new church. This was not carried out. The church was mainly rebuilt in brick in 1793–4. It was restored in 1901–2 by Sir Charles Nicholson. The regard for texture within and without, shown by Sir Charles, the organ-case by Bentley, the brass chandeliers and good modern glass by Archibald K. Nicholson make it a model of conservative restoration of this date.

WORPLESDON (St. Mary)
13th–14th cent.; 15th-cent. tower; 18th-cent. rails, pulpit and font; glass.

WOTTON *(St. John the Evangelist)
Beautifully situated among large trees. The tower is 11th century, with a top that suggests Monmouthshire. The rest of the church is 13th century. The N. chapel is the burial place of the Evelyn family: a brick 'dormitory' was added in 1778. Many monuments of the Evelyns.

Sussex

INTRODUCTION

SUSSEX STRETCHES along the English Channel from Rye on the east to Thorney Island on the west. The coastline has been made hideous from end to end by the desire of London's overspill to have a house by the sea or at least spend the week-end there. The only unspoilt part is between Eastbourne and Seaford, which belongs to the National Trust and is therefore immune. Parallel with the coastline run the South Downs, referred to in Sussex villages as 'the hill' – low and wooded in West Sussex, higher and treeless in East Sussex. They enter the sea at Beachy Head, but are interrupted by four out of the five Sussex rivers – the Arun, Adur, Ouse and Cuckmere. Behind the Downs is the Weald – a belt of heavy clay and greensand which in early medieval times was dense forest.

The churches of Sussex are many and various. They are not among the most magnificent since, unlike East Anglia and Gloucestershire, there was no flourishing local industry here when Gothic architecture reached its zenith in the 15th century, and of the many religious foundations with churches or chapels only the great Priory Church of Boxgrove survived the Dissolution. It is true that throughout all the Middle Ages and up to 1811 when Ashburnham Forge closed down, Sussex was the centre of the iron industry; but disappointingly little evidence is to be found in the churches, and the iron screen at Ashburnham and the grille at Arundel are the only important examples of iron-work in church furniture.

There is a great deal of Norman and Early English architecture, very little Decorated and not much Perpendicular. Very few churches were rebuilt in the 18th century; Glynde is the only one of architectural interest. Most were scraped, refurnished and mercilessly 'cleaned up' in the 19th century; there is a certain amount of medieval church furniture still surviving – but very few 18th-century box pews. A characteristic feature of Sussex churches is the shingled spire. Oak shingles are thin 'slates' of wood, which are – or should be – cleft, not sawn. They are still made, though cleavers are not easy to find. They last about 100 years. Elegant and graceful shingled spires are Playden, West Hoathly, Cuckfield and Horsted Keynes. A humbler version of the spire, known as the 'Sussex cap', is found on many smaller churches such as Wivelsfield, East Chiltington, Bishopstone. There are four stone spires – Chiddingly, Northiam, Dallington and East Preston – of which the first two are the best. There are also in the Ouse valley three round towers – St.

Michael's, Lewes, Southease and Piddinghoe – the only ones outside East Anglia. West Sussex churches are, on the whole, smaller and more rustic than those in East Sussex. East Sussex was more generally prosperous than West where several feudal lords, the Dukes of Norfolk and Richmond, and Lord Leconfield owned and own large tracts of country, and many villages were small hamlets with no squires or people of any consequence.

Another local feature is Horsham stone. These large, thin slabs are used for roofing on many of the larger churches in the centre of Sussex within twenty-five miles of Horsham; they are not found in the extreme west or east where tiles, often of a warm golden red, as at Amberley and Playden, take their place.

There are a large number of oak medieval roofs, mostly of a simple trussed and raftered type. There is one more elaborate Elizabethan roof at South Harting.

There were many churches with frescoes on the walls. Some were destroyed during 'restorations' but good examples survive at Trotton, Hardham and West Chiltington.

The stone used in churches is mostly of local origin. Downland churches are often built of flints and sometimes chalk is used in the arches as at Litlington; the tower at Southover, Lewes and the Tudor church of Twineham are of brick. Roman brickwork occurs at Westhampnett, St. Olaves, Chichester, Bosham, Eastergate and Hardham.

W.S.M.

SELECTED LIST OF CHURCHES

by W. S. Mitchell and John Betjeman

ALFRISTON *(St. Andrew)
Handsome flint church (1360) with central shingled spire, in form of Greek cross, standing aloof across a meadow from the huddled street of tile-hung cottages, half-timbered smugglers' inns and dilapidated market cross. Inside scraped and refurnished but with fine proportions and unusually high arches at the crossing. Chancel has triple sedilia and piscina on S. side, Easter sepulchre on N. Georgian arms. Circular churchyard.

AMBERLEY *(St. Michael)
Pretty village overlooking Arun Wild Brooks. Cottages of flint and stone, many of them thatched. Handsome church, 12th and 13th centuries, with tile-capped tower forms medieval group with the castle, former palace of Bishops of Chichester. Steeply-pitched tiled roof sweeps over nave

and S. aisle. Early Decorated S. door has capitals of vine and oak leaves. Inside scraped and refurnished. Chief feature is handsome Norman chancel arch with triple chevron moulding. Well spaced Early English windows in chancel. Late Norman arcaded font.

ARDINGLY (St. Peter)
Perp. oak screen; Dec. canopied tomb; Perp. tomb with brasses; 16th-cent. brasses.

ARLINGTON (St. Pancras)
All styles from Saxon to Perp.; British urn and Roman tiles found beneath nave.

ARUNDEL (St. Nicholas)
Perp. arcades; wrought iron grille; wall-paintings.

ASHBURNHAM *(St. James)
A family church next to the now deserted house of the Ashburnhams in park laid out

by Capability Brown. Rebuilt in 1663 except for Tudor tower. Banners, armour and altar-tombs to Ashburnhams; also painted and gilt iron screen (Jacobean) probably made locally as this was centre of Sussex black country. Unusual Command-ments (1676) painted on canvas in carved gilt frame with white doves and cherubs. Carolean oak staircase in tower to gallery and complete 17th-century seating.

BATTLE (*St. Mary*)
Handsome; 13th–15th cent. Trans. Nor-man arcades; scraped and refurnished; alabaster tomb, 1548.

BERWICK *(St. Michael & All Angels)*
Farming hamlet at foot of Downs. 13th-century church scraped by Victorians, but recently adorned with wall-paintings by Vanessa Bell and Duncan Grant – effective, colourful and warm.

BIGNOR (*St. Cross*)
Chancel screen 14th cent.; plain Norman or Saxon chancel arch; early Norman bowl font.

BISHOPSTONE (*St. Andrew*)
Saxon work, including sundial on porch; Dec. niche inside porch; Norman tower built in four diminishing stages.

BOGNOR (*St. Wilfrid*) GR
1909, by Fellowes Prynne; seaside Perp.; spacious parti-coloured interior.

BOSHAM *(Holy Trinity)*
Seafaring place overlooking the mud creeks of Chichester Harbour. Oldest seat of Christianity in Sussex. Church, in midst of fishermen's cottages, appears crudely in Bayeux tapestries. Saxon tower with shingled broach spire, high Saxon chancel arch and E. window of five lancets rising to the centre (13th century). Chancel has a recessed tomb (13th century) with recum-bent figure of a girl. Roof and furnishings modern; walls throughout scraped bare of plaster with consequent effect of coldness and discomfort.

BOXGROVE *(St. Mary & St. Blaise)*
Stately relic of Benedictine Priory church. Choir and transepts remain with central tower tile-capped and battlemented. Nave ruins also stand. Transepts and E. bays of nave are Norman. Choir is pure Early English (1235) at its best – with vaulted roof, clerestory with Purbeck marble shafts, and rich arcades, each pair within a large round containing arch. Splendid chantry tomb built by Lord de la Warr who was buried at Broadwater; richly decorated, carved and coloured (1532). Each transept has a high oak gallery, simi-lar to those in Spanish convents for lay members to hear Mass.

BREDE (*St. George*)
16th-cent. monument; old glass; brasses.

BRIGHTLING (*St. Thomas à Becket*)
13th and 14th cent.; scraped and refur-nished; squire's pew and W. gallery with barrel organ.

BRIGHTON *(St. Bartholomew)* GR
Vast brick Gothic, 1874, by Edmund Scott, a local and unknown architect. It is aisle-less and 135 feet high. Interior adorned with baldachino, silver side altar and pulpit all by H. Wilson, an architect and crafts-man of the 'nineties. (*See Plate 60*)

(*St. Margaret*) CL
1824; Stucco 'restored' internally, 1874.

(St. Martin, Lewes Road) GR
Brick Early English by Somers Clark, 1875. The arcaded nave slopes down from a raised W. end to a vast chancel enriched and gilded. The reredos, font cover and pulpit are also by Somers Clark. This is one of the most impressive interiors of the Gothic Revival in England.

(St. Mary) GR
1877–9, by Sir William Emerson; brick building in French Gothic style with in-genious and impressive E. end.

(*St. Michael*) GR
Originally a small brick Decorated church by G. F. Bodley, 1858–62. In 1893 the enormous nave and N. aisle designed by W. Burges, were carried out after his death by J. S. Chapple. Their style is French Gothic and the reredos and chancel deco-rations are by Romaine Walker. There is glass by Burne-Jones, Ford Madox Brown and Rossetti in the Bodley part of the church.

(*St. Nicholas*)
Old parish church of small seaport town on windy hill; well restored by R. C. Carpen-ter, 1852; Kempe stained glass; Perp. screen of East Anglian type; font 12th cent.

(*St. Paul*) GR
1848, by R. C. Carpenter, spire by his son R. H. Carpenter; interior correct, mysterious and Middle-pointed Dec.

(*St. Peter*) GR
The new parish church by Sir Charles
Barry in Commissioners Perp., 1824; in-
genious W. end with tower; chancel by
Somers Clark, 1906.

BROADWATER *(*St. Mary*)
Handsome, spacious, cruciform church in
N. suburb of Worthing. Mostly 12th and
13th century. Tower arches have rich
chevron and beak-head mouldings. Vaulted
13th-century chancel with carved oak stalls
and misericords. Two 16th-century tombs
to de la Warrs.

BURTON *(*dedication unknown*)
Small medieval church sheltered by trees in
park near 18th-century house. Old rough
walls with traces of Norman herringbone
work and miniature tile-capped tower.
Inside quite untouched and very rich in
interest. 15th-century painted screen, old
oak seating, hatchments, large Royal Arms
painted on plaster. Painted figure on splay
of window. Two handsome canopied 14th-
century tombs – one in chancel with recumbent figure of girl, another in nave with
good brasses. Very early bowl-shaped font.

CHICHESTER *(*St. John*)
A Greek-style parallelogram with campanile built in 1813. This is like the proprietary chapels which once abounded in
the Church of England. It is pure Georgian
within. The three-decker pulpit rises to a
great height in front of the Communion
Table. The lessons and service are read
from the second tier; the sermon, for those
good at heights, is preached from the pulpit above which commands the galleries.
The service is extreme Evangelical.

(*St. Peter*) GR
Stately early Dec. revival by R. C. Carpenter, 1852.

CHILTINGTON, WEST: *see West Chiltington.*

CHIDDINGLY (*unknown dedication*)
13th, 14th and 15th cent.; tall stone spire,
one of four in Sussex; 17th-cent. monument.

CHITHURST *(*unknown dedication*)
Small, aisleless church, standing on a
mound. Ancient and rustic. Rough irregular texture of outside walls. Within – plain
early Norman chancel arch with squint, old
solid oak seating, handsome oak canopy to
font.

CLAPHAM (*St. Mary*)
15th-16th cent. brasses; 1550 tomb.

CLAYTON (*St. John the Baptist*)
Mostly 12th and 13th cent.; wall-paintings;
Saxon chancel arch.

CLYMPING (*St. Mary*)
Trans. Norman tower and chevroned doorway.

COOMBES *(*unknown dedication*)
Hidden up a combe in the Adur Valley.
Low and barn-like with small tiled bell-
cote. Inside ancient and rustic. Timber roof
with king-posts, rude Norman chancel
arch. Extensive remains of frescoes, un-
covered, 1953, in nave and chancel. Two
good Perpendicular windows of green
sandstone.

COWFOLD (*St. Peter*)
13th and 15th cent.; remarkable brass,
10 feet long, to Prior Nelond of Lewes.

CUCKFIELD *(*Holy Trinity*)
Spacious 14th and 15th century church
with graceful shingled spire and panorama
of Downs. Screen and pulpit by Bodley,
and two good windows in N. aisle by
Kempe. Unusual 15th-century painted roof
with tie-beams and bosses of Nevill family.
Monuments by Flaxman and Westmacott.
Georgian Royal Arms.

DANEHILL (*All Saints*) GR
Handsome church in commanding position; Bodley and Garner, 1890; windows
by Kempe; reredos and fittings.

DEAN, EAST: *see East Dean.*

DEAN, WEST: *see West Dean.*

DIDLING *(*St. Andrew*)
Small and lonely in a field beneath the
Downs. Inside has massive 13th-century
seating; Jacobean pulpit and altar rails.
Rough tub-shaped Norman font. Oil lamps
and simple country charm.

DONNINGTON (*Holy Trinity*)
13th cent.; no interest except for modern
furnishings by Etchells.

EASEBOURNE (*St. Mary*)
12th cent.; partly rebuilt (1876); tombs,
16th and 18th cent.; monument by Chantrey.

EASTBOURNE *(*St. Mary*)
Large handsome 13th and 14th century
church, timber-framed Lamb Inn, medieval rectory and a few Georgian houses

are all that remain of the small town that gave its name to the demure modern seaside resort. Massive Perpendicular tower. Inside spacious and well proportioned with good vistas. Nave has clerestory and 13th-century arcades. Chancel arch Transitional with zigzag ornaments. Chancel has Transitional pointed arcades with chevron mouldings. Hatchments, large Georgian arms in white and gold frame, triple sedilia, 14th-century parclose screens. Good modern glass in E. windows.

(St. Saviour) GR
1870, by G. E. Street; lean-to aisles; apsidal end; ingenious relation of nave to chancel; a splendid building.

EAST DEAN, East Sussex *(St. Simon & St. Jude)*
12th and 13th cent.; pulpit and sounding board; 1623; Norman basket work font.

EDBURTON *(St. Andrew)*
13th cent.; pulpit and altar rails presented by Laud; 12th-cent. leaden font.

ETCHINGHAM *(St. Mary & St. Nicholas)*
Stands on low ground near the Rother. Stately grey church with massive tile-capped tower between nave and chancel – once surrounded by a moat. Built by the Barons of Etchingham in 1360 and containing some of the best Decorated work in Sussex. Inside scraped and refurnished except for chancel which has screen, carved stalls and misereres. Good Decorated tracery, particularly in chancel, and flamboyant E. window; many fragments of old glass. Large canopied brass (1444) to Sir Thomas de Echyngham and his parents, and two other brasses to the same family.

FINDON *(St. John the Baptist)*
Flint 13th-century church sheltering against a downland hanger and close to Findon Place. Very unusual plan of twin naves under one roof divided by Transitional Norman arcade was thought by Sir Gilbert Scott to be almost unique. Elaborate oak roof has timbers of exceptional length stretching across the two naves. Walls are scraped and furnishings modern, but a small piece of wall-painting survives, also a battered screen and three medieval seats.

FIRLE, WEST: see West Firle.

FOLKINGTON *(St. Peter)*
Ancient, rustic. Hidden behind park on edge of downland hanger. Lichened, tiled roof, wooden bell-cote, unspoilt flint walls. Good trussed and raftered roof with tie-beams. 18th-century box-pews and pulpit. Two handsome 17th-century wall monuments in chancel.

FORD *(St. Andrew)*
Alone in fields near Arun mouth, and almost hidden by yews and holm oaks. White wooden bell-cote, good texture of flint and sandstone walls. Brick Jacobean S. porch. Raftered oak roof, plain Norman chancel arch, good Decorated tracery in three-light E. window.

FRISTON *(St. James)*
11th, 12th and 13th cent.; 17th-cent. monument.

GLYNDE *(St. Mary the Virgin)*
Classical. Built of dressed flints for Bishop Trevor in 1765 to designs by Sir Thos. Robinson. Groups well with cupolaed 18th-century stables of Glynde Place. Trim and debonair. Box-pews and gallery. Walls hung with patterned linen – brown design in nave, blue in chancel; unusual effect of brocaded drawing-room. Big, ugly Victorian screen – out of proportion.

GREATHAM *(dedication unknown)*
13th-cent.; priest's box-pew and pulpit; Jacobean altar rails.

GRINSTEAD, WEST: see West Grinstead.

HAMSEY *(St. Peter)*
Alone on a hill in a loop of the Ouse. Spared by Victorians and since carefully restored. Hatchments, Royal Arms of George II, Commandments and a few ancient pews. Norman chancel arch, squint and massive Perpendicular tower with gargoyles.

HARDHAM *(St. Botolph)*
Wizen, hoary little church of nave and chancel on the Arun flats near Pulborough. Inside contains Norman chancel arch, heavy medieval oak seating, 18th-century altar rails and a Jacobean settle. Chiefly known for its series of early 12th-century wall-paintings in nave and chancel, shewing episodes in the life of Christ and other subjects. First discovered when the stones of the chancel arch were scraped in 1862. May have been painted by the monks of Hardham Priory, one mile away, for one of whom an anchorite's squint was pierced in the S. wall.

HARTING, SOUTH: see South Harting.

HASTINGS (*Holy Trinity*) GR
Elaborate Gothic by S. S. Teulon, 1851–9.

(*St. Mary in the Castle*) CL
By Joseph Kay, 1826–8; an Ionic portico in a Georgian stucco crescent opens on to a semi-circular galleried interior.

HOVE *(All Saints*) GR
1890–1, by J. L. Pearson. A vast, pale-greenish stone interior, all vaulting and vistas, but differing from the run of this talented architect's churches in being in a distinctly later style of Gothic than his usual Early English.

(St. Andrew, Waterloo Street) CL
This little classic church, 1828, near the front is unimpressive without, and was severely 'Lombardised' by mid-Victorians. Internally it owes most of its beauty to the font and altar and canopy put in by Randoll Blacking in the present century.

HURSTMONCEUX (*All Saints*)
12th and 15th cent.; canopied tomb, 1534.

ISFIELD (*St. Margaret*)
Brasses and altar tomb, 1631.

LAVINGTON, WEST: *see West Lavington.*

LEWES (*St. John the Baptist, Southover*)
18th-cent. brick tower, rest Norman and Perp.; Norman lead coffins.

(*St. Michael*)
Norman round tower; 15th-cent. brasses; monument, 1559.

(*St. Thomas à Becket-at-Cliffe*)
Perp.; two Royal Arms – one Elizabethan, one Georgian; Dutch painting, 1770, of Ascension.

LITTLEHAMPTON *(St. Mary the Virgin*)
Twisting streets still have village atmosphere. Red-brick Gothic church built in 1935 by Randoll Blacking, to replace an 1825 monstrosity, itself the successor of a medieval church. Outside not impressive, but interior elegant, spacious and light. Well furnished with galleried aisles and W. end, pulpit and sounding board. Handsome painted reredos by Randall Jackson. Royal Arms George IV.

LYMINSTER (*St. Mary Magdalene*)
King-posted and raftered roofs; early Norman chancel arch.

MARDEN, NORTH: *see North Marden.*

NEWHAVEN (*St. Michael*)
Norman tower and apsidal chancel.

NEW SHOREHAM *(St. Mary de Haura*)
Stately, grey church of Caen stone in squalid little seaport. Looks monastic, but was always parochial. Mostly 12th and 13th centuries. Only tower, transept, and unusually long choir and aisles remain. Vaulted roofs and lancet clerestory. 12th-century arcades with rich details in carving of capitals and arches of N. arcade. Dogtooth and stiff-leaf mouldings on transeptal arches.

NORTH MARDEN *(St. Mary*)
Minute Norman church of nave and apse, approached through farmyard. Cows wander in and out of churchyard. Dark and mysterious inside. Small, deep Norman windows admit minimum of light. S. door has chevron moulding and Greek cross at crown of arch. Small wrought-iron Georgian Arms (8 in. by 10 in.).

OLD SHOREHAM *(St. Nicholas*)
Looks across Adur to Lancing College. Early Norman cruciform church; central stone-capped tower with Norman arcades and round openings. Good texture of flint and rough-cast walls. Nave roof has kingposts and dog-toothed rood-beam. Tower arches richly chevroned. Early 14th-century screen and painted 19th-century chancel roof. Good oak seating with heavy fleur-de-lys finials.

OVING (*St. Andrew*)
13th cent.; cruciform; glass by Kempe.

OVINGDEAN (*St. Wulfran*)
Saxon chancel arch and windows; Dec. screen.

PARHAM *(St. Peter*)
Small Perpendicular church in deer park near Elizabethan house. Georgian box-pews, pulpit and screen. Special squire's pew with fireplace. Strawberry Hill Gothic vaulting to chancel. Rare leaden font, 14th century, with Lombardic lettering. Small Georgian Royal Arms.

PENHURST *(dedication unknown*)
Small Perpendicular church with tile-capped tower, standing high and alone by a farmhouse of the same date and overlooking Ashburnham Park. Inside walls scraped – but old furnishings remain untouched, including Perpendicular screen, Jacobean pulpit, lectern, altar rails and

elegant font cover. Nave has oak seating with doors, and panelled walls, 17th century. A little medieval glass.

PETWORTH (*St. Mary and St. Thomas*)
Modern plaster roof and reredos; furnishings by Kempe; Percy tombs.

PEVENSEY *(St. Nicholas)*
Now a shrunken inland village but anciently a thriving seaport. Church mostly 13th century looks seaward, a few hundred yards E. of the large Romano medieval castle. Tower has short and unpretentious broach spire. Inside spacious and dignified, built of green sandstone, which casts a grey-green light over all. Good Early English work. Nave arcades have alternate clustered and octagonal pillars. High chancel arch with stiff-leaf capitals. 17th-century alabaster monument to John Wheatley with recumbent figure.

PLAYDEN *(St. Michael)*
Graceful shingled spire, landmark for miles across marshes. Well proportioned inside and out. Roof of golden-red tiles over nave and S. aisle. Late 12th-century arcades divide nave from aisles; beautiful Early English tower arches between nave and belfry. 17th-century wooden ladder to belfry. Perpendicular chancel screen and good Decorated screen with flamboyant tracery behind choir seats. Georgian Royal Arms.

PRESTON (*St. Peter*)
13th-cent. wall-paintings.

PULBOROUGH (*Assumption*)
Chancel 13th cent., rest 15th cent.; Comper glass and tower screen.

ROTHERFIELD *(St. Denys)*
Hill-top Wealden village of brick and tiled cottages. Large sandstone church with tapering shingled spire and groined N. porch. Two restorations have left the inside unspoilt. Good plaster-work, and wall-paintings of Doom over chancel arch and of the Annunciation over entrance to N. chapel. Nave has waggon-roof and is furnished throughout with deal box-pews, slightly raised towards the W. end. Elaborate canopied Jacobean pulpit came from Archbishop of York's private chapel. Font canopy restored in 1876 has carved panels (1533) with arms of Nevills. Large Perpendicular E. window has glass by Burne-Jones, reminiscent of a William Morris wallpaper. Iron tomb slab with double cross. Georgian Royal Arms.

ROTTINGDEAN (*St. Margaret*)
Mainly 13th cent.; Burne-Jones windows.

RYE *(St. Mary)*
Large cruciform town church, crowning low pyramid of russet roofs and approached by ancient narrow streets – some still cobbled. Quarter boys strike the hours on clock. Flying buttresses support E. end. Inside, long gilt pendulum swings across tower space. 13th-century arcades in nave, varying in form and size. Good vistas across to choir aisles. Roof has king-posts and tie-beams. Window by Burne-Jones in N. aisle; two good modern windows in S. transept and W. end. Large Royal Arms (Queen Anne).

ST. LEONARDS-ON-SEA (*Christ Church*) GR
1875, Middle-pointed; by Sir Arthur Blomfield.

(*St. Peter*) GR
1885; severe E.E. brick, by J. Brooks.

SELHAM (*St. James*)
Pre-Conquest chancel arch; 11th-cent. bowl font 31 in. across, made from single stone.

SHERMANBURY *(St. Giles)*
Small church in park rebuilt in 1710 in 'churchwarden' style. Inside countryfied and unspoilt. Good Royal Arms (Queen Anne), old pews with names of farms and manors painted on them and in a glass case the recorders and viol used before the days of organs.

SHOREHAM, NEW: *see New Shoreham.*

SHOREHAM, OLD: *see Old Shoreham.*

SLAUGHAM (*St. Mary*)
Mostly 14th cent.; 16th-cent. brasses.

SOMPTING *(St. Mary the Virgin)*
Overlooks Worthing from S. slope of Downs. Famous Saxon tower with 'Rhenish helm' spire – four-sided and gabled, unique in England. Inside scraped and refurnished, but with unusual features such as vaulted chapel of S. transept, rude 12th-century 'Corinthian' capitals of tower arch, narrow aisleless nave with no chancel arch.

SOUTHEASE *(dedication unknown)*
Small aisleless church on a slope in the Ouse Valley. The round tower has a round shingled spire, like a dunce's cap. Inside walls have unspoilt plaster-work with remains of wall-paintings. Curious wooden chancel arch. Raftered oak roof and a few

old oak pews and pulpit. Commandment boards on either side of altar. Royal Arms (George III).

SOUTH HARTING *(St. Mary and St. Gabriel)*

Large farming village at extreme W. of Sussex Downs. Handsome cruciform church with copper-covered spire well placed in centre of village. Plain 13th-century nave arcades with no capitals. Massive oak spiral staircase from N. transept to belfry. Chancel has elaborate Elizabethan roof, unusual for Sussex. E. end lit by good triplet of lancets. S. transept has tomb to Cowpers with painted recumbent figures, one above the other; a third kneels in prayer behind them. Wall monument by Westmacott to Sir Henry Fetherstonhaugh of Uppark.

STEYNING *(St. Andrew)*

Retires behind long village street of tile-hung and half-timbered houses. Late Norman church – lofty, spacious and massive. Chancel arch 38 feet high. Huge, tile-capped 16th-century tower of flint and stone chequer work. Norman arcades with rich and various mouldings. Royal Arms – Queen Anne.

STOPHAM *(St. Mary)*

12th–15th cent.; monuments; 15th-cent. brasses.

SUTTON *(St. John)*

Choir stalls; old oak seating; late 12th-cent. pillars in nave.

TARRING, WEST: *see West Tarring.*

TICEHURST *(St. Mary)*

14th–15th cent. tracery in aisles; clerestory windows; 15th-cent. font canopy with folding doors and flamboyant tracery; 14th-cent. glass.

TORTINGTON *(St. Thomas)*

Small and rustic, among farm buildings of mellow Georgian house. Flint walls and white wooden bell-cote. Richly-carved Norman S. door, chancel arch of hard chalk with beak heads and grotesques. Jacobean pulpit, 13th-century oak roof, Norman font with arcading and cable moulding.

TROTTON *(St. George)*

Near Little Rother, spanned here by a medieval bridge. 14th-century church has nave and chancel under one roof with no chancel arch – ugly, barn-like effect. Brass

to Lady Margaret Camoys (1310), second oldest in England to a woman. Large altar-tomb with canopied brasses to Thomas, Lord Camoys, an Agincourt hero, and his wife. Whole W. wall covered with large and unusually well preserved wall-paintings. Good oak seating, some box-pews. Georgian Royal Arms, 17th-century cover to Norman font, Jacobean altar rails.

TWINEHAM *(St. Peter)*

Tudor; brick.

UPMARDEN *(St. Michael)*

A few cottages in remote part of W. Downs. Small farmyard church with rare triangular-headed chancel arch, possibly pre-Conquest. Chancel has triplet of lancets and tie-beams with moulded wall-plates. Brick flooring and unspoilt plaster walls. Two box-pews in chancel. General air of emptiness and desertion.

UPWALTHAM *(Holy Sepulchre)*

In a fold of the Downs. Small and rustic. Nave and Norman apse with later windows. Inside candle-lit with good modern bronze 'spiders'. Plain, solid oak seating.

WADHURST *(St. Peter & St. Paul)*

13th–15th cent.; vaulted porch and shingled spire; inside scraped; thirty inscribed iron tomb slabs, 1614–1790.

WARBLETON *(St. Mary)*

13th–15th cent.; marble wall monument, 1750; brass; squire's pew supported on wooden pillars.

WARMINGHURST *(Holy Sepulchre)*

Small 13th-century church perched on walled bank at end of lane. Complete 18th-century deal furnishings – handsome triple arched screen, pulpit and box-pews. Gay Royal Arms beneath crimson canopy with azure surround painted on plaster above screen. Hatchments, wrought-iron crane for font canopy, two 18th-century wall monuments, brass to Shelleys.

WARNHAM *(St. Margaret)*

13th-cent. restored oak chancel screen; monument, 1613.

WARTLING *(St. Mary Magdalene)*

Box-pews, old plain stained glass.

WEST CHILTINGTON *(St. Mary)*

Pretty village of tiled and whitewashed stone cottages, low stone walls and gardens full of flowers and creepers. Unspoilt medieval church of nave and S. aisle, with short shingled spire springing from roof, overlooks a miniature square. Crooked and irregular in plan and detail; chancel is askew with nave and recess of Decorated W. window has homely, uneven plasterwork. Chevroned N. door and massive Transitional arcades with heavy scalloped capitals. Nave walls and arcades covered with wall-paintings of unusual variety of colours. Curious chancel arch, high, narrow and recessed. Long tunnel squint from S. aisle to altar. Good king-posted roof, 1602. Linen fold pulpit and plain oak seating.

WEST DEAN, East Sussex (*All Saints*)
Downland setting; gabled W. tower, unique in Sussex; 17th-cent. monument; medieval rectory.

WEST DEAN, West Sussex (*St. Andrew*)
Well restored by Etchells, after fire in 1934; Lewknor tomb.

WEST FIRLE (*St. Peter*)
14th cent.; monuments and brasses.

WEST GRINSTEAD *(*St. George*)
Deep among brooks and fields near handsome Jacobean rectory. Stone-slabbed roofs and low, graceful shingled spire. Old, solid oak seating painted with housenames. Pulpit and sounding board, Perpendicular screen. Two altar tombs with brasses 15th century, large monument by Rysbrack, another by Flaxman. Old glass in W. window of S. aisle, two good Victorian windows and one modern by Walter Camm. Monochrome Royal Arms (George IV).

WESTHAM *(*St. Mary*)
Stands just west of Pevensey Castle and basks in its reflected glory, though the church has a glory of its own. Massive early 14th-century tower and good Decorated tracery in windows of N. aisle. Nave has trussed and raftered oak roof. Inside scraped, but has a Perpendicular oak screen to Lady chapel and thirteen small panels of medieval stained glass in E. window.

WEST LAVINGTON *(*St. Mary Magdalene*)
Built in 1850 by Butterfield for Archdeacon, later Cardinal, Manning when he was rector of Wool-Lavington. Small sandstone church with shingled spirelet set in churchyard of flowering shrubs and heathers. Simple and tasteful in style, closely resembling many W. Sussex medieval churches; chiefly remarkable for Butterfield's restraint in design and use of material.

WEST TARRING (*St. Andrew*)
Mainly 13th cent. with 14th and 15th cent. additions; stalls; misericords; modern mosaics.

WILLINGDON (*St. Mary*)
Mainly 13th cent.; alabaster tomb, 1619; brasses.

WINCHELSEA *(*St. Thomas the Apostle*)
Anciently a limb of the Cinque Ports, now a dreamy village of warm brick cottages, guarded by three grey medieval gateways. Houses grouped around large, open churchyard and weathered relic of 14th-century church. Only chancel – choir and two aisles – remains intact. Large richly traceried Decorated windows filled with modern glass by Strachan – good, but too much colour for a building small in proportion to height. Richly canopied sedilia and piscina with crocketed gables. In S. aisle two canopied 14th-century tombs of Alards with recumbent effigies. Three similar and slightly earlier tombs in N. aisle.

WITHYHAM (*St. Michael and All Angels*)
Mostly rebuilt in 1672; altar tomb with effigies and monuments by Flaxman and Chantrey.

WOOLBEDING (*All Saints*)
Saxon nave walls with pilaster strips; medieval glass in nave window; carved tiebeams with wall-plates and corbels.

WORTH *(*St. Nicholas*)
Forms a secluded, sylvan group with the old rectory house. Church has the distinction of being only Saxon cruciform church with untouched ground plan. Outside walls have string course round nave and apsidal chancel. Inside the 22-ft. high chancel arch – largest Saxon arch in England – has a rugged elegance. Transeptal arches, doors N. and S. and two-light windows in nave also Saxon. 16th-century carved pulpit from Germany, altar rails probably of same date and origin. 17th-century oak gallery at W. end in memory of former rector. Chancel candle-lit with good brass 'spiders'.

WORTHING (*St. George*) GR
1868; unusual Gothic of G. Truefitt.

(*St. Paul*) CL
Impressive Doric portico, 1812.

Warwickshire

INTRODUCTION

LEAFY WARWICKSHIRE the guide-books call it, though no one has planted trees in Warwickshire for generations and one day, I suppose, the oaks and elms of Arden will die out. The county was once split between Arden, the woodland of the north, and Feldon, the corn valley of the south. Across the 'sandy grownde' of Arden, 'betar wooded than fertile of corne' now creep the suburban tentacles of Birmingham: out beyond Sutton, Castle Bromwich and Solihull.

Elsewhere in Arden are the homes of the *nouveaux riches*, around Knowle, Lapworth and Ullenhall, the currently fashionable areas, whence this nomadic race of latter-day landed gentry may move on, farther afield, frightened by the prospect of a 'new town' near Alcester. Respectable Leamington is still in favour, despite a genteel shabbiness hanging over the Regency squares – but there is talk of new industry here, too. Theirs are the churches where the fashionable 'county' weddings take place; not shabby like the churches in workaday Warwickshire.

The greater part of the county is quite practical and down to earth and has fewer great estates than other counties. The mining districts of the north-east retain their own character with their blue-brick, mellowing now, after a century, and their man-made landscapes of pit mounds and power stations, the former encountered by surprise among the woods and lanes of a still rural countryside. We find no great churches in North Warwickshire, where, in the Middle Ages there was poverty and meagre population, but some steeples of a local red sandstone pierce the gentle rise and fall of the horizon.

The Bard reigns in the Avon Valley, and the Shakespearean villages and their churches benefit by a constant stream of tourists from the three corners of the world. The remoter villages of the south, with no Shakespearean links, are the poor relations of 20th-century Warwickshire, for here the drift from the land has left the countryside still and quiet. The towns and large villages; Shipston, Alcester, Henley, dream through the weekdays but are shocked into a parody of their ancient bustling life by the internal combustion engine, which invades at weekends, when the ice cream flows as free as the water of Avon.

It has brought, too, the airfields to Wellesbourne and Honily and the Army camps to Long Marston and Kineton. Above all, it has re-created Coventry as one of the boom towns of our day, spreading faster, if not farther, than any

Warwickshire town and pinching-in the narrow green belt between itself and Birmingham. There will soon be new churches in Coventry as well as old to serve a society that worships material things.

If the motor roads are crowded, the canals and some of the railways of Warwickshire are tranquil now – and seedy and nostalgic. Here, and in the villages that are not on the road to anywhere, is a wistful, apprehensive calm; the atmosphere perhaps in any of the hundred Warwickshire villages just before they died in the enclosures of Tudor days – leaving sometimes a dusty, ruined church behind them.

The churches in Birmingham has been described and selected by the Rev. B. F. L. Clarke.

R.S-M.

SELECTED LIST OF CHURCHES

by R. Stanley-Morgan, A.R.I.B.A., and the Rev. B. F. L. Clarke

ALCESTER (*St. Nicholas*) CL
Edward and Thomas Woodward, 1729–30; Classical inside; Gothick outside.

ASTLEY *(St. Mary the Virgin)*
The village a cluster of cottage gardens and elm trees on the fringe of the N. Warwickshire coalfield. The church concocted in 1608 from the 14th-century chancel of the old cruciform Collegiate Church which had fallen into ruin. A tower added at the W. end and a new low chancel at the E. – all in the old Perpendicular tradition. This tower underpinned and a concrete raft inserted to counter mining subsidence. The 15th-century choir stalls, painted with figures of the Apostles, were retained and share the 'nave' with 18th-century box-pews and Victorian benches.

ASTON CANTLOW (*St. John the Baptist*)
Medieval church in 'leafy Warwickshire'; 15th-cent. pulpit.

AUSTREY (*St. Nicholas*)
14th-cent. broach spire.

BARCHESTON (*St. Martin*)
Mid-16th cent.; fabric chiefly late 13th and 14th cent.; Willington tomb.

BEAUDESERT *(St. Nicholas)*
Chosen as typical of a number of Norman churches in the county with narrow nave and chancel, good chancel arches and a later tower at the W. end. Both hamlet and church hidden down a narrow lane off Henley High Street, with a medieval castle mound next to the churchyard. The chancel given a good pseudo-Norman vault by a Victorian restorer in 1865. Nice 15th-century tower.

BERKESWELL *(St. John the Baptist)*
A secluded black, white, and red village with stocks, pump and smithy, threatened as Birmingham and Coventry exert a 'pincers movement' on the country between. This is the richest Norman church in the county with a vaulted crypt beneath the chancel, extending into an octagonal bay under part of the nave. The black and white of the two-storey timber porch enlivens the grey of the masonry – the whole monochrome composition a gift for the amateur photographer.

BILLESLEY (*All Saints*) CL
William and Mary; unspoilt; Classical interior.

BILTON (*St. Mark*) GR
Bodley's rebuild of 1873.

BINLEY *(St. Bartholomew)*
A surprising classical church of 1773 said to be from the hand of Robert Adam and sufficiently like his work at Mistley in Essex to make this seem likely. A sober exterior with an elegant octagonal cupola at the W. to break the skyline. Inside it is

pecked out in Adamesque plaster to resemble a salon of the period. The chancel in a shallow apse with Grecian altar rails in iron and the coloured windows painted naturalistically after the fashion of the time.

BIRDINGBURY (*St. Leonard*) CL
W. elevation Doric, by Richard Trubshaw?

BIRMINGHAM *(St. George)* GR
1820–2, Rickman; a serious attempt at Gothic – the style mid-way between second and third Pointed. Large and imposing. Eastlake considered it a fair specimen of Rickman's ability in design; but found it hard to forgive the iron tracery. The side galleries have been taken down. The E. end was altered in 1884. Rickman is buried here.

(St. Martin)
The old Parish Church of Birmingham. It was cased in brick in 1690, and altered and enlarged several times in the 18th century. The tower and spire, restored by P. C. Hardwick in 1853–5, show scarcely a trace of old work. The rest of the church was entirely rebuilt by J. A. Chatwin in 1873–5. Four medieval monuments remain.

(St. Paul)
Consecrated in 1779; architect Roger Eykyn of Wolverhampton. The steeple (1823) was added by Francis Goodwin. A good example of an 18th-century church, not much altered. E. window glass, 1791, designed by Benjamin West, executed by Francis Eginton. 'Probably the finest remaining example of English 18th-century glass painting.' (Martin Travers.) Fine bust of his father by Peter Hollins.

(St. Peter) GR
1901–2, F. B. Osborne; the successor of St. Peter's, Dale End; large red-brick Perp.

(St. Philip)
Now the cathedral. A mature design by Thomas Archer. The tower is one of the most satisfying pieces of Baroque modelling in England. The churchyard retains none of the 18th-century terraces once surrounding it, but makes a welcome patch of greenery for the office workers at lunchtime. The rusticated outer walls of the church were refaced in the last century, but the tower was left until 1958 in a state of 'pleasing decay'. The chancel is cleverly enriched with free-standing Corinthian columns by the Victorian, J. A. Chatwin.

(St. Stephen) GR
1910, Bidlake. A church which invites to worship; previous building was by Carpenter, 1843.

(St. Peter & St. Paul, Aston)
With the nearby Jacobean 'great house' forming the oasis in a desert of brick and slate. Aston's chief pride is in its monuments – some good 15th-century effigies in alabaster, and later centuries represented by Hollins, Rysbrack, Westmacott, White of Worcester and other artists. The 15th-century tower and spire very good, remarkable for a course of machicolation below the parapet; the rest of the church rebuilt by Chatwin about 1880 onwards in an opulent 14th-century style. Apsidal sanctuary, luxuriant with marble and alabaster.

(St. Paul, Balsall Heath) GR
1852–3, J. L. Pedley architect. Self-confident Victorian early Middle Pointed. There are many other churches of this type, which the enlightened ecclesiologist will appreciate.

(St. Alban, Bordesley)
An expensive Gothic church, 1879–81, by J. L. Pearson in one of the obsolescent parts of the town. The whole of the interior vaulted in this architect's most thoroughgoing manner, terminating in an apse with ambulatory at the E. A good setting for ceremonial. An alien tower added by Reynolds (1938). The exterior in brickwork and disappointing.

(St. Benedict, Bordesley)
1910: Nicol and Nicol; Romanesque.

(Holy Trinity, Bordesley) GR
1820–3, Francis Goodwin – the architect of a good many churches, all much alike, which are usually said by the older guide books to be 'in the later style of English architecture'. They do not attempt to be correct, and might, indeed, be called Gothick. Iron tracery, and many pinnacles: the E. end has a circular traceried window. The interior has been very little altered. An elaborate organ-case, and altar painting by James and George Foggo.

(St. Oswald, Bordesley) GR
1892–3, completed in 1898; W. H. Bidlake; straightforward, lofty, red brick; Dec.

(St. Patrick, Bordesley) GR
1896, Pearson, on a smaller scale than St. Alban's. Of brick, with a N. passage aisle,

S. aisle, and additional aisle of three bays:
at the S.W. is the base of a tower. Wooden
roofed, except for the apsidal chancel,
which is vaulted.

(*St. Basil, Deritend*)
1911; Arthur S. Dixon architect; rather
charming pre-Great War Byzantine.

(*St. Augustine, Edgbaston*) GR
1868; J. A. Chatwin; an elaborate,
prosperous-looking mid-Victorian church.

(*St. George, Edgbaston*) GR
1836–8, J. J. Scoles; E.E.; dignified new
nave and chancel added 1884 – J. A.
Chatwin.

(*St. Germain, Edgbaston*)
1915; Edwin F. Reynolds; Byzantine in
style, though Anglican in plan.

(*St. Barnabas, Erdington*) GR
Rickman and Hutchinson, 1822–3; late
14th-cent. style; iron tracery.

(*Church of the Ascension, Hall Green*)
Queen Anne church; consecrated, 25 May,
1704; plain brick building, enlarged, 1860.

(*Bishop Latimer, Handsworth*) GR
W. H. Bidlake, consecrated in 1904; large
and empty; Low Church, and almost completely without colour.

*(*St. James, Handsworth*) GR
A cheap church of 1838, by Robert Ebbels,
'a dapper, energetic little gentleman', who
specialised in such churches. A large new
church was added by Chatwin in 1894–5.

*(*St. Mary, Handsworth*) GR
Medieval remains of no great interest. Re-
peatedly enlarged in the 19th century and
largely rebuilt by Chatwin in 1874–9. An
unusual number of 18th and 19th century
monuments, including Matthew Boulton,
1809, and James Watt, 1819, by Chantrey.

*(*St. John, Ladywood*) GR
S. S. Teulon, 1852–4, enlarged by Chatwin,
1881. Large and rather vulgar.

*(*St. Aidan, Small Heath*) GR
1893–8; architect F. T. Proud. Brick and
terra-cotta; Perpendicular. Large and lofty,
with wide chancel. The rood and screens,
1912, were designed by F. Bligh Bond. A
successful late 19th-century High Church.

*(*St. Agatha, Sparkbrook*)
1899–1901, W. H. Bidlake, taking the
place of Christchurch in the city. An
exceedingly imposing and successful church.

W. tower with sculptured front, and a projecting baptistery: porches on each side
with carved tympana. The nave has piers
without capitals, a rather tall clerestory and
a simple painted roof: the aisles broaden
out into chapels. The chancel was completely wrecked by bombing. This was the
final flowering of 19th-century Gothic:
there was no more development possible on
these lines, though churches of this type
were built for ten years longer.

BRAILES *(*St. George*)
The village never recovered from a body-
blow dealt by enclosures in the 16th century. The church, known as 'The Cathedral
of the Feldon' is left as memorial to
Brailes' medieval greatness. The 15th-
century steeple a good example of those of
the Cotswold fringe – the nave and aisles
good Decorated work. The interior altered
in 1649 and would have been a Commonwealth rarity but for Gothic face-lifting in
1879. The 14th-century font good and there
is a famous 15th-century carved chest.

CASTLE BROMWICH *(*St. Mary & St.
Margaret*)
The old Georgian brick village by-passed
by new roads and so retaining some character. The old Elizabethan Hall adjoins the
church, with a private path and fine iron
gates between the two. The church a brick
box of 1732, enclosing a medieval timber-
framed chapel, and probably unique on this
account. 18th-century fittings exceptionally
complete: box-pews throughout, very good
two-decker pulpit and wrought-iron altar
rails; neat organ in tiny W. gallery. White
of Worcester was concerned in the design
of the church.

CHARLECOTE
In N. chapel splendid 17th-cent. monuments to three generations of Lucy family,
including Shakespeare's 'Justice Shallow';
church rebuilt 1851 by John Gibson; exterior mellowing, but inside much of harsh,
brittle quality associated with mid-Victorian glass and encaustic tiles; shadowy
churchyard.

CLIFTON-ON-DUNSMORE (*St. Mary
the Virgin*) GR
Bodley's rebuild of 1894.

COLESHILL *(*St. Peter & St. Paul*)
Predominantly Georgian town in Warwickshire red brick. The church crowns the
steep hill, the red sandstone blending well
with the surrounding work. Village pillory

nearby. The church vigorously scraped by the Victorians but still essentially a fine 14th and 15th century town church. The steeple is the finest of a group probably by the same local mason, Henry Ulm or Holme, the others being Shustoke, Sheldon, Curdworth and Yardley and Kings Norton, just over the old boundary in Worcestershire. The chancel very light, as at Stratford. The Digbys were buried here in state and their memorials should be seen. The late Norman font is a work of art.

COMPTON WYNYATES
*(no dedication)
Not to be missed when visiting the famous house. A rare Restoration church, but completely within the old tradition, rebuilt from old materials after damage in the Civil War and untouched by the restorer. A single central arcade nestling down amongst the box-pews – no chancel and the pulpit half-way down the S. side. The white plaster relieved by two ceiling paintings of the firmament – by day and by night. The plainness of the interior shows off the decorative qualities of the hatchments.

COUGHTON (St. Peter)
Early 16th century – with 15th and early 16th-cent. glass; Throckmorton monuments.

COVENTRY (Holy Trinity)
Perpendicular; one of the three spires of Coventry.

(St. John Baptist)
15th-cent. cruciform with central tower.

ETTINGTON (Holy Trinity & St. Thomas à Becket)
Medieval ruins in the park.

FILLONGLEY (St. Mary & All Saints)
Chiefly 14th cent.; good clerestory; restored by Bodley and Garner.

GREAT PACKINGTON *(St. James)
A classic 'mausoleum' by Bonomi 1790, adjacent to the great house. Designed to be seen from the interior by those 'entombed' and made to appear hollowed as from the solid rock. The exterior by contrast disappointing – peppered with semi-circular windows – the pepper-pots standing one at each corner.

GREAT WOLFORD (St. Michael and All Angels) GR
Jas. Trubshawe, 1833.

HALFORD (St. Mary)
Standing in a pleasant rural setting; Norman chancel arch and doorway.

HAMPTON LUCY *(St. Peter ad Vincula)
A good 19th-century hybrid Gothic church, best seen in sunlight across the Avon in Charlecote Park. The tower by Thomas Rickman 1825, the nave and aisles by his partner, Henry Hutchinson, the chancel and N. porch added by G. G. Scott, Snr. in 1858. The nave lofty in proportion to its width with a sensitive plaster vault, giving an impression of a cathedral in miniature. All Rickman's window tracery in cast iron from moulds previously used in his earlier work. Hampton Lucy partly rebuilt as a model village but with an old mill. The cast-iron bridge over the Avon is also by Rickman, 1829.

HARDWICK, PRIORS: see Priors Hardwick.

HASELEY (St. Mary)
Late medieval; box-pews; notable brasses, monuments and old glass.

HENLEY-IN-ADEN (St. John the Baptist)
15th cent. without clerestory; roof.

HONILY (St. John the Baptist) CL
1723.

HONINGTON (All Saints) CL
c. 1690.

IDLICOTE (St. James)
Attractive village with good view; church, Norman, E.E. and later; 18th-cent. arcade to S. chapel; timber bell-cote, box-pews, pulpit with tester and Jacobean screen.

ILMINGTON (St. Mary the Virgin)
Norman and E.E. church on the Cotswold fringe.

KINETON (St. Peter) GR
Fragments of Sanderson Miller's church of 1755.

KNOWLE (St. John the Baptist, St. Lawrence and St. Anne)
Handsome Perp. fabric; good carved screens and stalls.

LAPWORTH *(St. Mary)
A secluded village in wooded undulating country but threatened with dormitory status by the rich of Birmingham. The church remarkable for a steeple connected by passage with N. aisle; built sheer without string courses and with a projecting stair – both unusual features for Warwickshire. The square-headed clerestory rich

and deep. The double-storey annex at the W. end is another curiosity. Largely 13th and 14th century but with traces of possible Saxon work.

LEAMINGTON (*Christ Church*) GR
Norman and curious; Robinson 1825.

LEAMINGTON SPA *(All Saints)*
A fine church though alien to the Regency character of the town; built between 1843 and 1869 in a French Gothic style by a local man, J. G. Jackson. An English tower and W. end perversely added by Sir Arthur Blomfield in 1902. The scale of Jackson's work gigantic throughout, particularly in the two transepts. Internally the church suffers the lack of a vault such as Pearson might have given it, and the Victorian glass and fittings detract from the serenity of the design.

LITTLE PACKINGTON (*St. Bartholomew*)
Medieval wooden bell-cote and late Norman features.

LOXLEY (*St. Nicholas*)
Valley setting; church consecrated in 1286 – chancel still substantially 13th cent., but this small church largely rebuilt early in 18th cent.; most striking external feature is the vestry; box-pews, pulpit high up on the wall and approached from the vestry, altar rails and clear glass.

MANCETTER (*St. Peter*)
Pleasant setting with old houses and plenty of trees; church mainly 13th and 14th cent. with massive 15th-cent. tower; 15th-cent. roof and much 14th-cent. glass in chancel.

MEREVALE (*St. Mary*)
Park setting; the 'capella extra portam' of the Cistercian Abbey; mainly 14th and 15th cent.; considerable remains of 14th–16th cent. glass of high quality; medieval organ loft from abbey church; 13th-cent. effigy and 15th-cent. brass and alabaster table tomb.

MONK'S KIRBY (*St. Edith*)
Imposing 14th-cent. fabric with some 15th-cent. recasting; tower is vaulted and has elaborate 18th-cent. Gothick parapet erected after fall of spire; Feilding monuments.

NEW MILVERTON *(St. Mark)*
A skewbald church of 1879 by the second G. G. Scott in red brick with stone dressings, set in a tidy late Victorian suburb of Leamington. The nave light and spacious, the aisles melting into shallow transepts (this junction badly done externally). Good use of contrasting height between the chancel and the low chapels flanking it. Effective wooden vaults except in nave where there is a boarded barrel roof. The general effect lavish and convincing.

NUNEATON (*St. Nicholas*)
Amongst clipped yews in an industrial town; 13th and 15th cent.; good 16th-cent. monument.

OVER WHITEACRE (*St. Leonard*) CL
Probably by W. and D. Hiorn; steeple of 1850.

PACKINGTON, GREAT: *see Great Packington.*

PACKINGTON, LITTLE: *see Little Packington.*

PILLERTON HERSEY (*St. Mary the Virgin*)
E.E. chancel – rare in Warwickshire; nave roof 15th cent.

POLESWORTH (*St. Editha*)
E.E. abbey church; 13th-cent. effigy of Abbess.

PRESTON - ON - STOUR *(The Blessed Virgin Mary)*
An unspoilt village mixing well the characteristics of the brick, timber and Cotswold stone districts. The church a collector's piece, partly rebuilt in fanciful 18th-century Gothic by Edward Woodward of Chipping Campden for James West, the antiquary, in 1752. The building set about with yews and occupied with the fashionable idea of sublime melancholy, while inside is a deal of 17th and 18th century glass given over to the 'universal dominion of death'. Death is also recorded by monuments carved by Thomas Sheemakers and the Westmacotts, father and son. There is an interesting Gothick gilded ceiling.

PRIORS HARDWICK (*St. Mary*)
Splendid late 13th-cent. chancel with triple sedilia and late 17th-cent. altar rails; nave decently rebuilt in latter part of 19th cent.

ROWINGTON (*St. Lawrence*)
Notable medieval church with central tower in a secluded setting.

RUGBY (*St. Andrew*) GR
Butterfield 1877; medieval tower and part of nave remain.

SHERBOURNE (*All Saints*) GR
Expensive church by Sir Gilbert Scott, 1864.

SHIPSTON-ON-STOUR (*St. Edmund*) GR
G. E. Street, 1854; tower 15th cent.

SNITTERFIELD (*St. James the Great*)
A handsome church much restored and
scraped in 1852; 13th–15th cent.; nave
roof, late medieval work in stalls and 14th-
cent. font.

SOLIHULL (*St. Alphege*)
Good early 14th and 15th cent. cruciform
church with spire.

SOUTHAM (*St. James*)
Good Perp. clerestory and roof; rood-
screen with loft by F. H. Crossley.

STONELEIGH (*St. Mary*)
Norman chancel arch and font; box-pews.

STRATFORD-UPON-AVON *(*Holy
Trinity*)
A good town church of the 15th century
rarely visited for its own sake. The setting
and approach tidied up and idealised for
the reception of Shakespeare-worshippers,
with the addition of cycle stands and all
modern conveniences. A charge of sixpence
has been levied for admission for at least
seventy years. The chancel brilliant when
seen through the dark arches of the central
tower. Towers over the crossing are the
exception in Warwickshire. The massing of
the building best seen romantically from
across the Avon. The steeple is actually a
Georgian pastiche by Wm. Hiorn of
Warwick in 1763.

STUDLEY (*The Nativity of the Blessed
Virgin Mary*)
Chiefly Dec. with assorted features and
fittings from Norman times onwards.

SUTTON COLDFIELD (*Holy Trinity*)
Laudian fittings from Worcester Cathedral
in an altered medieval church; monument
of Bishop Vesey, c. 1554.

TEMPLE BALSALL *(*St. Mary*)
As its name suggests, a foundation of the
Knights Templar, who built here a geometric decorated box, very good of its
kind, which became a favourite with the
Ecclesiologists. The roof, with its parapets
and pinnacles, and also the present bell-
turret were provided by the first Scott in
1849. A Victorian described Scott's tessel-
lated tiles on the chancel floor as 'very
pretty but rather dangerous to walk on'.
The village small but neat with interesting
17th-century almshouses.

TYSOE (*The Assumption of the Blessed
Virgin Mary*)
12th–15th cent.; notable 14th-cent. font;
15th-cent. roof.

ULLENHALL (*St. Mary the Virgin*) GR
J. P. Seddon, 1875; unusual Evangelical
Victorian plan.

WARWICK *(*St. Mary*)
The most interesting of the Warwickshire
town churches. The W. tower over the
roadway frames pleasant views of surrounding Georgian houses. Medieval work re-
stricted to the famous Beauchamp Chapel
and the choir, with its flying vault. The rest
destroyed by fire in 1694 and rebuilt in a
'Gothic Survival' manner by Sir William
Wilson, with some interference by Wren.
The nave and tower out of scale with the
older work but Wilson's interior is noble
and his vaults and arcades a *tour de force*;
there is no clerestory. A fine baroque
organ-case over the W. lobby.

*(*St. Nicholas*) GR
Thos. Johnson 1779 – chancel of 1869.

WASPERTON (*St. John the Baptist*) GR
Scott, 1843.

WELFORD-ON-AVON (*St. Peter*)
Mainly Norman and Perp. in pleasant
setting.

WHITEACRE, OVER: *see Over Whiteacre.*

WILMCOTE *(*St. Andrew*)
The village of little interest but for a good
stone and timber yeoman's house, said to
be that of Shakespeare's mother. The
church, schools and vicarage important in
the history of the Oxford Movement; built
as a group in 1841 by Butterfield before his
individual style developed. Very dim religious light inside the church, so that the
wall decoration, painted on metal sheets, is
barely discernible. A deal of blue and gold
wallpaper. Everything according to the
Ecclesiologists' rules, with triple lancets in
the chancel.

WOLFORD, GREAT: *see Great Wolford.*

WOOTTON WAWEN *(*St. Peter*)
The village retains timber and old brick
cottages and an interesting mill, but is too
near the main Stratford-Birmingham road
for its own safety. The church as yet completely unspoiled with a very strong and

authentic atmosphere of the past. Built in stages about its 11th-century tower, the only Saxon work in the county, each generation has made its own contribution, so that the building now appears as three churches in one, two of them unused and deserted. Fragments of medieval wall-painting and a small 17th-century chained library. 15th-century pulpit and screens and numerous monuments from 15th century onwards.

WORMLEIGHTON (*St. Peter*)
Medieval church – notable 15th-cent. chancel screen.

WROXALL ABBEY (*St. Leonard*)
14th-cent. relic of the Priory with a brick tower added in 17th cent.; 14th-cent. glass.

Westmorland

INTRODUCTION

THE VISITOR who finds, and appreciates, the old and remote churches such as those that lie along the western flank of Cross Fell, the final northern thrust of the Pennines, will not thank the guide who thinks duty done by a time-saving assurance that Cumberland and Westmorland have no outstanding buildings. In some of these little hillside churches, men still pray under arches so crude, so expressive of the earliest Christianity in our land, that they can bring tears to eyes that see them struggling to aspire like prayer itself, from simple men in such a far-off day; and there are windows, innocent of stained glass, through which the full views of valley and running water, of fell side and sky, entering in, are so framed that they seem to some of us glimpses of very Heaven.

There are many of these tiny churches, as at Mardale Green and Martindale, or on the wonderful road that climbs from Brough to Alston. On the east is the great series of fells, Warcop, Burton, Hilton, Marton, Dufton, most of them rising fairly steeply from the plain, with sharp cones or pikes, giving their names to the villages at their feet. Long Marton church, to choose one example, is one of the six churches in the country with one chancel wall built sloping outwards to represent our Lord's head hanging on the Cross. There has probably been a church on this site since the 4th century. One stone has Druid symbols, another an Egyptian birds-head design of great antiquity. Dufton is a typical Westmorland village, with its red sandstone houses, colour-washed, bright with gardens round the village green, facing inwards so as here, as at Milburn and Newbiggin and elsewhere, to form a rough compound in which the cattle could be herded against the raids of the marauders. Besides these tiny churches, there are large and interesting ones at Appleby, Kirkby Stephen, Kirkby Lonsdale and Kendal, but no cathedral, as the county is comprehended in the diocese of Carlisle.

F.S.

SELECTED LIST OF CHURCHES

by Frank Singleton

APPLEBY *(St. Lawrence)*
A large Early English and Perpendicular style church at the foot of the broad main thoroughfare, lined with picturesque cottages, trees and lawns, and dominated at the top by the castle in this delightful miniature county town. Restored, 1655, by the ubiquitous Lady Anne Clifford who also lies here with her mother. Other 17th-century monuments and organ-case. Screens 15th century.

BAMPTON *(St. Patrick)* CL
1726; timber arcades.

BARTON *(St. Michael)*
12th–13th cent.

BEETHAM *(St. Michael)*
Originally Early Norman, now partly mixed styles of Gothic.

BOLTON *(All Saints)*
An ancient little stone edifice which somehow achieves nobility. Late Norman chancel, nave and S. porch with doorway. Another Norman doorway on the opposite side is built up with a window inset and in the wall above it a charming diminutive sculpture of knights jousting – a little medieval treasure. W. turret with two bells is 1693. Font and cover, 1687. Unusual chancel screen of open tracery, probably local work late 18th century.

BOWNESS *(St. Martin)*
Beautiful E. window ingeniously assembled from various dates and sources, with 14th-cent. glass from Cartmel; Flaxman monument.

BROUGH *(St. Michael)*
Large, mostly E.E. and Perp.; stone pulpit, 1624.

BROUGHAM *(St. Ninian)*
Unforgettable. Known locally as 'Ninekirks' it stands surrounded by trees in the middle of a field in a lonely dale by the River Eamont, three miles from the vicarage. If the right of way has been ploughed and sown, drive or walk over it. This is our heritage. This was the site of a Saxon church, then a Norman. Today it is just as Lady Anne Clifford rebuilt it in 1660, plain, whitewashed with oak box and canopied pews, pulpit with sounding board, oak seats with carved arm-rests, and screens (with modern cornice). Over the altar are her initials most memorable of all the remarkable Cliffords of Brougham Castle. Brasses of others lie around.

(St. Wilfrid)
On the border of the parish, over the road from the now dismantled Brougham Hall (former home of the Lords Brougham and Vaux) is this chapel which is run together with St. Ninian's to serve the village of Eamont Bridge. It is an ancient plain little building, chancel, nave and turret with one bell. It also was restored by Lady Anne Clifford and mid-19th century by the first Baron Brougham and Vaux. The contrast between the two interiors is almost unbelievable. Here is rich cathedral opulence. The church is as full as it can be of beautifully carved oak, an elaborate parclose organ casing, pillars, tall pews, screen with rich round posts and beautiful cornice. The reredos is of oak gilt and includes a magnificent 15th-century altar-piece with superb carvings 'in the round'. This is a triptych with a central representation of the Crucifixion and a group below it. It is set under a deep canopy and the sculptured scenes are bordered by medieval woodwork of the finest craftsmanship. Some has been attributed to Dürer. Companion to this continental carving is a locker on which is a representation of Christ rising from the tomb whilst the guardians sleep. It has a magnificent lock and hinges. On the walls of the chapel are wonderfully carved scenes. The pulpit is enriched with medieval carving, the roof of oak is divided into panels each with richly emblazoned shield or crest. The E. and W. windows are stained. The stalls are superb.

There is nothing in Westmorland, or indeed anywhere, to compare with this plain and simple building that might have been compelled by some extraordinary sumptuary law to hide its opulence within.

CLIBURN (*St. Cuthbert*)
12th cent. with late 19th-cent. additions.

CROSBY GARRETT (*St. Andrew*)
The main portion is Norman and later.

CROSBY RAVENSWORTH (*St. Lawrence*)
Originally 11th cent., now 15th cent. and earlier.

GRASMERE *(*St. Oswald*)
Wordsworth and members of his family are buried in the churchyard. The rough, massive old church, 11th, 13th, and 17th century, is notable for a two-storeyed continuous arcade, the lower dating from the 17th century. The resulting jungle of black beams is an object lesson in elementary building, ingenious and almost indescribable except by Wordsworth who had a shot at most things and declared that the roof was upheld

By naked rafters intricately crossed,
Like leafless underboughs, mid
some thick grove,
All withered by the depth of shade
above.

HAVERSHAM (*dedication unknown*)
Norman in origin, refashioned in 14th and 15th cent., and much rebuilt in 19th cent. (1868).

INGS (*St. Anne*) CL
Built 1743 by Robert Bateman, a local Dick Whittington, in Renaissance style with marble floor; epitaph to Bateman on brass by Wordsworth.

KENDAL *(*Holy Trinity*)
The 13th-century nave and aisle have been enlarged till there are now five aisles, mostly in the Early English style and the whole structure is rectangular – a forest of pillars from any view point. Two windows by Bewsey.

KIRKBY LONSDALE *(*St. Mary the Virgin*)
Ancient stone church much modified since its days of Norman greatness from which, however, it still retains three westernmost arches and piers of the N. arcade of the nave, carved and ornamented with striking similarity to those of Durham; also the S.

and W. doorways, the latter a fine example of late Norman work, recessed in four orders and much enriched with zig-zag and other ornament. The chancel was fitted with stalls in the restoration of 1619, and from the same century dates the charming six-sided pulpit. The embattled W. tower was largely rebuilt in 1705. The view from the churchyard is perhaps the finest in the county, praised by Ruskin, painted by Turner, endlessly satisfying. Howgill and Casterton Fells are in front. The Lune flows towards you under their lee and makes a great loop at the foot of the cliffs below the churchyard, enclosing a long V-shape of fertile meadow. The great house of Underley lies across the water amid its meadows and trees. Within the church and around you lie Earls and Countesses of Bective, Cavendish-Bentincks, and many an Olivia, Amelia and Estelle, who have yielded to the girls whom Underley now houses as a school.

KIRKBY STEPHEN *(*St. Stephen*)
Was probably founded in the 8th century, rebuilt 13th and 15th centuries. It has a cathedral-like nave, Early English in style, stately and impressive. Embattled W. tower replaced early in the 16th century, a central Early English tower which fell in the 15th century. Interesting 15th and 16th-century monuments.

KIRKBY THORE (*St. Michael*)
12th–14th cent.; 17th-cent. altar rails and pulpit.

LONG MARTON (*St. Margaret & St. James*)
Early Romanesque; Tympana.

LOWTHER *(*St. Michael*)
Portions of 12th, 13th and 17th centuries, but the keynote of Lowther family piety within is struck by the mausoleum outside, reminiscent of Chesney Wold as depicted by Phiz and one almost looks around for Lady Deadlock.

MORLAND (*St. Laurence*)
Setting and village; large cruciform church with 11th-cent. tower; the rest mainly 13th, 14th and 15th cent.

MARTINDALE *(*St. Peter*)
The old church originally 11th century, was renewed 1633 and again in last century. 17th-century woodwork, good carving in pulpit, massive beams. One of the loneliest churches in Westmorland, 1,000 feet above sea, it was for a time disused. The present

church of St. Peter was erected in Early English style in 1880. (*See Plate 42*)

ORTON (*All Saints*)
15th-cent. nave roof; fabric mainly late medieval.

ORMSIDE *(St. James)*
Strikingly situated on a conical knoll on the west of the River Eden with fine view of Roman Fell. Norman, with strong Scot-repelling tower only 11 feet square. Two beautiful primitive arches with scalloped capitals strangely disturbing. The oak king-post chancel roof is 400 years old. The famous Ormside cup, now at York, a Saxon treasure of gold and enamel, was dug up in the churchyard in 1823.

RAVENSTONEDALE *(St. Oswald)*
Fragments of the old church were incorporated in the present interesting structure

of 1744. It has a three-decker pulpit and the congregation face each other as in some college chapels. The parish running along the border of Yorkshire and Upper Lunesdale is the most extended in the county but the village unto which the church looks is a delightfully tree'd hollow among these moorland heights.

WITHERSLACK *(St. Paul)*
Church built and endowed in 1664 by John Barwick, D.D., a Royalist who became Dean of St. Paul's, restored, 1873. The severe white classical interior, the roof simply moulded, four pillars, two round and two flat at the altar end, is a perfect foil to the romantic setting of hanging woods and limestone out-crop. An infant Stanley in marble sleeps on one window-sill. The canopied pulpit was once a three-decker. The altar table is 17th century.

N

Wiltshire

INTRODUCTION

THIS LARGE oblong county is simple to describe. Two-thirds of it are chalk, one-third is 'cheese'. The chalk runs across the county from east to west. The vale of Pewsey, all elms and flint, and brick and cob cottages and thatch and clear streams, divides the areas of chalk into two. The northern half of the chalk is the Marlborough downs where Avebury stands, a vaster and more impressive pre-historic monument than Stonehenge. The southern half is Salisbury Plain whose cathedral spire gathers the rolling downs around it. The plain is 'like the ocean after a storm, it is continually heaving in large swells. Through all this vast district, scarce a cottage or even a bush appears.' (Rev. W. Gilpin, 1808.) But the valleys in Salisbury plain, particularly the Wylie and the Ebble, contain charming thatched villages with flint and lime-stone churches and small manor houses among elms and beeches under the smooth chalky hills. The plain itself is now much scarred with army camps and manoeuvre ground, and Stonehenge does not seem as remote as it did when Constable painted it. The Marlborough Downs, associated with Richard Jefferies, are bolder and with great hills like Martinsell rising like cliffs, and at their feet the thatched habitations of man. Devizes is the mellow brick capital of the north, Salisbury of the south.

The 'cheese' is a flat limestone dairy country in the north of the county on the banks of the Bristol Avon and the pull of Bristol is felt in it. Chippenham, Cricklade, Malmesbury, Bradford-on-Avon, Calne and Corsham are its most attractive grey stone towns. Here are grand parish churches, like Malmesbury Abbey, Steeple Ashton and Edington. All the great houses of Wiltshire are below the edges of the downs, except for Wilton and Trafalgar, Littlecote and Ramsbury which are in downland valleys. When they were near the downs, their owners planted the bare hills with beech clumps in the 18th century to improve the prospect.

Aubrey summed up the people thus, 'According to the several sorts of earth in England (and so all the world over) the *indigenae* are respectively witty or dull, good or bad. In North Wiltshire (a dirty clayey country) the *indigenae* or aborigines speake drawlinge; they are phlegmatique, skins pale and livid, slow and dull, heavy of spirit; hereabout is but little tillage or hard labour; they only milk the cowes and make cheese; they feed chiefly on milke meats, which cools their braines too much and hurts their inventions. These circum-stances make them melancholy, contemplative and malicious . . . Contrariwise on the Downes, &c, the south part, where 'tis all upon tillage, and where the shepherds labour hard; their flesh is hard, their bodies strong. Being weary after hard labour, they have not leisure to read on or contemplate religion, but goe to bed to their rest to rise betimes the next morning to their labour'.

In the present century many square miles of grassy down have been ploughed: only the army and racehorse trainers have saved some of them. Swindon, where the G.W. railway works are, has grown to be the largest town in the county and factories have transformed the characters of Chippenham and Calne.

The churches of Wilts, except those listed below, were never remarkable as architecture and the county was unlucky in having, in the 19th century, one of the dullest Victorian architects as its chief restorer, Mr. T. H. Wyatt. His hand is heavy on many a once old flint church, and for the only interesting new church he built, the Lombardic one at Wilton, he had to have the assistance of the brothers Brandon, architects of more talent and originality.

J.B.

SELECTED LIST OF CHURCHES

by the late W. H. Randoll Blacking, F.S.A., F.R.I.B.A. and E. T. Long, F.S.A.

ALDBOURNE (*St. Michael*)
12th cent., later rebuilt; tower and roofs 15th cent.; brass 15th cent.; monuments 16th and 17th cent.

ALTON BARNES *(St. Mary the Virgin*)
South of Milk Hill and Wansdyke, and close to the charming cluster of early 19th-century wharf buildings at Honey Street on the Kennett and Avon Canal, this tiny church is little changed since Augustus Hare was rector 125 years ago. Saxon nave, with shallow pilasters; chancel 18th century. Jambs of chancel arch Norman, but the arch rebuilt. Note the painted boards with Royal Arms (James I) and black-letter text beneath which are traces of 15th-century painting.

ALTON PRIORS *(All Saints*)
A stone's throw eastward of Alton Barnes: a disused church, the churchyard of which is knee-deep in grass, yet how much more gracious than marble kerbs and granite chippings!

AMESBURY *(St. Mary & St. Melor)*
Pleasantly situated in the Avon Valley backed by the trees of the park. In spite of somewhat drastic 19th-century restoration this cruciform church is still of considerable interest and charm. It is a 13th-century fabric refashioned in the 15th with fine timber roofs. Note the stone-vaulted chapel off the N. transept, the Norman font, 15th-century screen and some remains of medieval painted glass.

BISHOPS CANNINGS *(St. Mary the Virgin)*
Begun in late Norman times, to which the nave arcade and porch belong, this is a magnificent 13th-century church. The present spire, clerestory, and upper sacristy are 15th century. Nave roof dated 1670. Note early windows at W. end of N. aisle; the fine arcading for recessed altars in transept; and the Chapel of Our Lady of the Bower (rebuilt) with its Ernle monuments and Jacobean holy table. The rich porch doorway is a 14th-century tomb canopy, probably from the S. chapel. In the church is a unique 'carrel', or chair for meditations, also a 17th-century alms-box. Nave walls unfortunately stripped of plaster.

BISHOPS (OR WEST) LAVINGTON: *see West Lavington.*

BISHOPSTONE, S. WILTS *(St. John Baptist)*

Embowered in trees, this is a noble cruciform church wholly remodelled during the 14th century upon a simpler building. C. E. Ponting claimed, with reason, it was designed by William of Edington. Chancel and transept have lovely windows of late 'flowing' Decorated work. Both chancel and S. transept are vaulted; the N. transept and nave, plainer than the rest, have timber roofs with plaster panels. Sacristy on N. side is coeval. S. porch rebuilt. Note the sedilia, almost overweighted with rich carving, and the canopied niches; also the fine Founder's tomb in N. transept. In S. transept is an elaborate tomb-memorial by A. W. Pugin, with glass by Wailes above, in memory of a former rector who brought from abroad the Renaissance woodwork of which the stalls and pulpit are made. Fragments of old glass in sacristy window.

Outside, see brilliant treatment of priest's doorway on S. side of chancel, and the curious building at end of S. transept which has puzzled antiquaries for centuries: it is probably a tomb.

BOSCOMBE *(St. Andrew)*

A little towerless flint and tiled church, 14th-century nave and chancel and shallow 16th-century transept, in a hollow among old brick and flint and cob walls, happily by-passed by the road from Tidworth to Salisbury. Inside are pale white plaster walls, clear glass with a few late medieval fragments, box-pews, high Jacobean pulpit and late Georgian lead altar rails. Richard Hooker was once incumbent, and here he wrote much of his famous *Ecclesiastical Politic.*

BRADFORD-ON-AVON *(Holy Trinity)*

The little town rising steeply in tiers from the Avon and full of beautiful buildings and picturesque corners is essentially a place in which to linger. The parish church near the river is architecturally of great interest and retains some interesting contents. It is a 12th-century fabric enlarged and refashioned in the 14th, 15th and early 16th centuries. The tower has a short stone spire. On either side of the chancel is a 14th-century recessed and canopied tomb, N. of the E. window is a 14th-century wallpainting depicting St. Anne and the Blessed Virgin. Worthy of note, also, is the 17th and 18th century painted glass in one of the nave windows. There is a charming early 14th-century sculptured female head.

(St. Laurence)

The most notable Saxon church in England. For long put to secular use, it was discovered about a century ago, all recollection of its existence having been forgotten. Recent examination of the fabric has led to the belief that it is of two periods and that the lower part of the walls belongs to the church erected by St. Aldhelm, *c.* 700 and mentioned by William of Malmesbury four centuries later. Note the architectural details and sculpture.

BRATTON *(St. James)*

Approached by long flight of steps; cruciform 15th cent.; modern chancel.

BRINKWORTH *(St. Michael)*

Spacious 15th cent.; gallery; pulpit with tester and seating 17th cent.

BROAD CHALKE *(All Saints)*

Another fine cruciform church in the Chalke Valley, where the willow-fringed Ebble flows lazily through water meadows. Here is a notable example of medieval contrivance, for early in the 15th century they took down the arcade dividing the 13th-century nave from its aisles, and put the whole beneath one roof. The E. responds remain. The external treatment of the W. end remarkably like Edington and Bishopstone. Chancel and N. transept late 13th century. John Aubrey, once churchwarden here, described the bells as 'one of the tuneablest rings in Wiltshire'.

BROMHAM *(St. Nicholas)*

12th–16th cent.; central tower with spire; brasses; glass late 15th cent.; monuments 15th, 16th and 17th cent.; screens 15th cent. Thomas Moore is buried in churchyard.

CALNE *(St. Mary)*

12th–15th cent.; tower; nave roof.

CLIFFE PYPARD *(St. Peter)*

15th cent.; modern chancel; monuments 14th and 18th cent.; screen 15th cent.

COMPTON BASSETT *(St. Swithun)*

12th–15th cent.; modern chancel; stone screen with vaulting early 15th cent.

CORSHAM (*St. Bartholomew*)
12th cent. and 15th cent. with some harsh Victorian restoration; monument and stone-vaulted screen 15th cent.

CRICKLADE *(St. Sampson)*
One of the glories of Wiltshire, its great Tudor central tower dominating the little town. It exhibits detail of every century from the 12th to the 16th and recent work by Martin Travers has produced good painted glass, comely altars and other fittings. Note also the tower vault with its fine heraldic display, the late 15th-century S. chapel and 18th-century chandelier.

CRUDWELL (*All Saints*)
12th–15th cent.; seven-Sacrament window and seating.

DEVIZES (*St. John*)
12th cent. enlarged and refashioned 15th, 16th and 19th cent.; stone-vaulted chancel; Norman tower.

(*St. Mary*)
Chancel 12th cent. with stone vault; rest mainly 15th cent.; tower and nave roof.

DILTON *(St. Mary)*
One of the most atmospheric churches in Wiltshire. The fabric appears to be mainly late medieval with the spired stone bell-cote of the county. The interior was re-fitted in the 18th century and has escaped the ravages of the Victorian 'restorers'. Box-pews, gallery, three-decker pulpit with tester and clear glass are here to delight us. There is a plastered tympanum between nave and chancel and the upper storey of the vestry was once a school.

DONHEAD (*St. Mary*)
13th cent. refashioned in 15th cent.; porch has stone vault; font 12th cent.

DOWNTON (*St. Laurence*)
12th–15th cent.; central tower; glass 15th cent.; monuments 18th cent.

DURNFORD *(St. Andrew)*
On reaching Durnford you cannot get farther, thus the place remains unspoilt amidst the willows on the east bank of the Avon. The church is very ancient; the 12th-century nave walls, which have some original roughcast, encase yet earlier ones. N. and S. doorways coeval. Fine 13th-century W. tower. Chancel much rebuilt, c. 1880. Restoration from near-collapse of tower and nave in 1903 by C. E. Ponting, F.S.A.

Note remains of wall-paintings and glass, also early 17th-century pulpit (still retaining its blue-green velvet hanging dated 1657); the lectern with chained copy of Jewel's *Apology*, and communion rails. Old benches beneath W. gallery. One of Wiltshire's most delightful churches.

EDINGTON *(Blessed Virgin Mary, St. Katharine and All Saints)*
Grey flecked with golden lichen, and standing below the steep northern escarpment of the Plain, a stone's throw from the old Salisbury-Bath road, this is not only the best example of a 14th-century Collegiate Church in S. England, but, excepting Salisbury Cathedral, it is the most perfectly proportioned church in the county. Built in nine years, from 1352 to 1361, by William of Edington (the great bishop who planned Winchester nave) for the Augustinian Order of Bonhommes, of which Ashridge was the only other house in England. Cruciform, with central tower, the chancel of three bays formed the monastic quire, the nave serving as the parish church. Nothing now remains of the monastery, but the S. walk of the cloisters was built against the wall of the N. aisle, where the window-sills are made higher for the purpose. Note extreme richness of mouldings in the quire, with comparative absence of carved work, and the plainer masonry in the parochial part. The four canopied niches on side walls of the quire contain mutilated figures of the Four Evangelists, the drapery being of great refinement; these, and the other niches, were elaborately decorated in gold and colour. Traces of a Watching Chamber exist between buttresses outside S. side of quire. The fine 15th-century oak screen and pulpitum has been much restored; originally the open tracery panels were solid and on E. side were returned stalls for the 'Rector' and brethren. Consecration crosses (twelve) both inside and outside. Late Georgian ceiling replaces open-timbered roof of quire. The panelled plaster ceiling in nave is 17th century as also are the fine pulpit and tester, the font-cover, the altar-piece now in N. transept, and the curiously inconvenient communion rails in the quire. Sedilia were much mutilated by erection of beautiful Lewys monument, now moved farther W. In S. transept is magnificent tomb and effigy of an Austin Canon with much of the original colouring. Chantry tomb of Sir Ralph Cheney on S. side; nave

brasses missing. Church contains memorials removed from medieval church at Imber, destroyed with the entire village for army training ground. Considerable remains of 14th-century glass, that in E. window of N. transept especially notable. Careful restoration by C. E. Ponting, c. 1890. The altar in front of the Decorated reredos (1936) in quire corresponds in length with monastic high altar. A church to be visited again and again.

ERLESTOKE (*Holy Saviour*) GR
A characteristic small church by G. E. Street, 1880.

FARLEY (*All Saints*) CL
Built in 1688 possibly from plans of Sir Christopher Wren, and most charming; altar rails, font and cover, pulpit and screens are contemporary.

FISHERTON DELAMERE (*St. Nicholas*)
13th cent.; largely rebuilt, 1833; screen, rood-loft, gallery and seating by F. C. Eden.

FUGGLESTONE (*St. Peter*)
13th cent.; 15th-cent. bell-cote; early 19th-cent. Gothick fittings; altar rails and font with cover 18th cent.

GREAT CHALFIELD *(*All Saints*)
The little church and the adjacent manor-house form one of the most beautiful groups to be found anywhere. Careful restoration of both have greatly enhanced that beauty. The church is of 13th-century origin refashioned in early Tudor days by Thomas Tropenell who also built the great house. Note externally the charming spired bell-cote of local type. Within there is a two-decker pulpit with tester, 15th-century stone screen to the S. chapel and good modern chancel screen of wood. Note in the chapel the sadly mutilated but still beautiful wall-paintings depicting in six scenes the story of St. Catherine.

GREAT SOMERFORD (*St. Peter & St. Paul*)
15th cent. with chancel roof by Comper.

HAM *(*All Saints*)
Consists only of chancel, nave and W. tower; pebble-dashed exterior in retired churchyard full of Georgian altar tombs by yew hedge and brick 18th-century porch. Interior has W. gallery, clear glass, 18th-century chancel rails, box-pews; some of the last slightly Victorianised.

HARDENHUISH *(*St. Nicholas*)
Completely rebuilt on a new site in 1779 by John Wood, Junior, of Bath. A little Georgian gem set on a green hill with apsidal sanctuary, balustraded parapets, Venetian windows and small domed tower; the windows are filled with clear glass.

HEDDINGTON (*St. Andrew*)
13th–15th cent.; font 12th cent. with 17th-cent. cover; organ-case 18th cent.

HEYTESBURY* (*St. Peter & St. Paul*)
A noble cruciform fabric with central tower formerly collegiate. Restored by Butterfield who was less drastic than usual and is said to have endeavoured – alas unsuccessfully – to save the choir stalls. Mainly late 12th, 13th and 15th centuries. Note the immense single lancet at E. end, stone-vaulted 15th-century screen in N. transept and the impressive proportions of the interior.

IDMISTON (*All Saints*)
12th–15th cent.

INGLESHAM *(*St John the Baptist*)
Two houses and a towerless church with N. and S. aisles and a bell-cote and a farm adjoining, all of golden grey Cotswold stone among the wide meadows of the upper Thames above the last lock. William Morris saved this church from Victorian restoration. Inside are vestiges of all dates, medieval wall-paintings, 17th-century paintings on top of them, a few pieces of old glass, remains of painted screens, high pews of differing depths, old uneven floors and clear glass looking on to the churchyard cross and well-carved Georgian tombstones. (*See Plate 32*)

LACOCK *(*St. Cyriac*)
A beautiful church with a rare dedication set in one of the most interesting villages in England with extensive monastic remains and houses from the 14th century onwards. The church belongs mainly to the 14th and 15th centuries and is of cruciform plan with W. tower and spire. The *pièce de resistance* is the N. chapel with its pendant stone vault. Note window over chancel arch, nave roof, brass early 16th century, medieval covered cup, fragments of old painted glass and the Sharington monument mid-16th century.

LAVINGTON, WEST: *see West Lavington*.

LITTLE SOMERFORD (*St. John Baptist*)
13th and 15th cent.; font cover, double-decker pulpit and seating 17th cent.; screen late 14th cent.

LYDIARD TREGOZ *(St. Mary the Virgin)*
A warm and golden church of the 15th century within Lydiard Park. Itself a charming building, it is chiefly notable for its contents. Here are extensive remains of murals; a painted Jacobean screen; much old glass; beautiful wrought ironwork, probably by Edney of Bristol, though maybe by Tijou himself; and above all, the finest Renaissance monuments in any parish church in Wiltshire. See the great canopied tomb of Sir John St. John, and the lovely 'Conversation Piece' of the Mompesson monument near by the same artist. Also the 'Golden Cavalier', and the painted pedigree triptych on the N. chancel wall which opens to disclose portraits of the St. Johns of Elizabeth I's day. The place is wisely kept locked, but the courtesy of the custodian adds to the pleasure of a visit.

MALMESBURY *(St. Mary)*
The present noble church is but the nave and aisles of a vast cruciform monastic fabric of which little else remains; even the W. end is in ruins. It is a Norman fabric refashioned in the 14th century. The S. porch exhibits some of the finest Romanesque sculpture in the country; the arch with eight members contains not only foliage and other decoration but also three bands of figure subjects; on the lateral walls are seated figures of the Apostles, six on either side. Within the massive 12th-century arcades and the elegant 14th-century clerestory are most impressive. The present E. wall rests on the 15th-century stone pulpitum which formerly closed in the monastic quire. In the aisles are sections of the stone rood-screen. Note the 15th-century table-tomb with recumbent effigy said to commemorate King Althelstan who certainly was buried here. To the S. of the abbey is a tower with spire which is the sole remnant of the former parish church of St. Paul. The little town has much of interest including the fine late medieval market cross.

MERE *(St. Michael)*
One of the great churches of Wiltshire which would be notable anywhere and exhibiting in its structure work of many periods. The core may be 12th century, or even earlier, according to the late C. E. Ponting, but the oldest datable work belongs to the beginning of the 13th century and occurs in the chancel. The church was almost rebuilt in the 14th century at various dates and again extensively remodelled, *c.* 1450 when the noble tower was erected. There are seven old screens of various types and the rood-loft has been restored. Note the vaulted N. porch, nave roof, 14th and 15th century brasses, 15th-century painted glass, monument and stalls, 17th-century seating in nave. S. of the church is a 15th-century house and in the little town the Ship Inn with the fine ironwork of its sign should be noted.

MILDENHALL *(St. John Baptist)*
From the outside this pleasant Wiltshire church, Perpendicular tower, aisles and clerestory, plaster covered and in the wide vale of the Kennet east of Marlborough, gives no idea of the glories within. The tombstones have unfortunately been arranged like playing cards around the boundary walls of the churchyard, and gas lighting and clumsy repair to the old roof since the war have not improved an otherwise exquisite building. But inside, Transitional Norman arcades rise from a forest of 'Gothick' box-pews made of the finest oak. There are two 'Gothick' pulpits either side of the chancel arch, 'Gothick' panelling and reredos and pews and communion rails in the chancel, also in finely carved oak. And a little W. gallery above the charming 'Gothick' font, and even the kneelers along the communion rails are of the finest 18th-century leather, and until lately Georgian velvet altar and pulpit hangings survived. This pious refurnishing was done in 1814 and is ascribed to John Pinch, the Bath architect.

NETHERAVON (*All Saints*)
12th cent. and 13th cent., with 15th-cent. windows.

OAKSEY *(All Saints)*
A good example of a Wiltshire village church, 13th century in origin with 14th and 15th century additions and remodelling. The nave has a clerestory but only a S. aisle so that there are two stages of windows on the N. The features of special importance are the wall-paintings discovered a few years ago mainly 15th century and the remains of good 14th-century painted glass.

Note also the 15th-century screen and panels in the choir stalls.

POTTERNE *(St. Mary)

A charming village with several timber-framed houses of which the most notable is Porch House, restored by George Richmond, R.A. The church is of cruciform plan and mostly 13th century with 14th-century central tower and 15th-century parapet. The 13th-century work is beautiful in its simple austerity and worthy to rank with Salisbury Cathedral. Note the inscribed Norman tub font and 15th-century wooden pulpit.

PURTON *(St. Mary the Virgin)

This noble cruciform church, with the lovely Elizabethan mansion next to it, makes an enchanting group. Like Wanborough, there is a central spire as well as a W. tower, though here the spire rises from another tall tower. Building and rebuilding went on from the 13th century until the completion of the W. tower in the 15th century. With its niches and corbels, all once containing coloured imagery, its wall decoration and painted glass, of which many fragments remain, the place is one of the most worshipful in Wiltshire, although some modern adornments are perhaps antagonistic.

SALISBURY
*(St. Thomas of Canterbury)

A fine town church founded in the first half of the 13th century and rebuilt on a spacious plan gradually during the 15th century. Both nave and chancel are clerestoried, the tower is placed on the S. and there is a three-storeyed vestry. The interior though crowded with seating is still most impressive. Over the chancel arch is a splendid Doom painting much restored, and in the S. chapel are mural paintings depicting the Annunciation, Visitation and Nativity. The nave and S. chapel have magnificent roofs. Other features of interest are the late 12th-century font, 14th and 15th century glass, the embroidered funeral pall and the 17th-century monuments.

SHERRINGTON (St. Cosmas and St. Damian)

Medieval, rebuilt 1624, with contemporary fittings.

SOMERFORD, GREAT: see Great Somerford.

SOMERFORD, LITTLE: see Little Somerford.

STEEPLE ASHTON *(St. Mary the Virgin)

Mr. Betjeman likens the church to 'a silvery battleship', and so it is, especially if you approach the once prosperous and still beautiful market town across the dull gault and clay lands from Edington. The great church was built at the height of the cloth-weaving prosperity of the 15th century. First the tower, early in the century, then the noble nave, aisles, E. chapels and porches right at its close (1480–1500). The last late flowering of medieval church building in the county. The small 14th-century chancel was made to serve till 1853, when the present larger but dull chancel replaced it. How distinguished the church must have looked when Leland saw the tower topped with a fine stone spire which almost doubled its present height! The sad tale of the spire's fall, and perhaps of the decreasing prosperity of the town, is told on a brass in the church; another inscription records the happier building of the place. Look at the fine vaulting in the aisles, the chapels, and the S. porch with its great carved boss. It was clearly intended to vault the nave in similar fashion, but this was never done, and instead we have a rich structure of oak and plaster with pendants and bosses, all originally coloured. Compare the masonry with that at Edington, but three miles away. At Steeple Ashton there is a wealth of carving, all of it very bold and virile yet sometimes coarse in craftsmanship; at Edington it is all moulded work, just as direct and sure, but full of sensibility and refinement. Some good monuments and many remains of painted glass, also some good brass chandeliers. Here is an unhappy example of the way in which our fathers encumbered lovely architecture with a far too large organ.

STOCKTON *(St. John Baptist)

Set in a little Close in one of the loveliest of Wiltshire villages, in which thatch predominates, this tree-enshrined church is mainly 14th century. Of great interest is the solid wall, which, save for a central doorway and two squints alongside, completely shuts off the chancel. Though apparently 15th century, the arrangement is curiously like that in an Eastern church. A rood-loft supported on corbels once existed on the W. side, now almost covered with modern woodwork. Norman font with 17th-century cover amidst inharmonious surroundings. Good monuments, including that to John Toppe who built Stockton House.

STRATFORD-SUB-CASTLE (*St. Lawrence*)
13th, 15th and 18th cent.; early 18th-cent. fittings; pulpit with tester 17th cent.

STRATFORD TONY *(St. Lawrence?)*
A plain little church charmingly set upon a mound above the Ebble, here crossed by an ancient trackway with ford and stepping-stones. The chancel a delightful example of pure, simple 14th-century work. The E. window has early glass by Kempe, and below it the old stone altar-slab is still in use. On S. side remains of a tiny low side window for ringing a hand-bell. Nave walls much rebuilt at various times owing to foundations slipping on the hill-side. Tower dates from about 1420. Much of the church's charm due to the retention, though altered, of good 18th-century pews having a broad central passage. E. end marred by floodlight fixed outside above 14th-century window.

TISBURY *(St. John Baptist)*
Pleasantly situated in a small town on the Nadder. It is one of the important cruci-form churches of Wiltshire with an 18th-century top to the central tower replacing a stone spire. The core is late 12th century but the fabric is now mainly of the 14th and 15th centuries. Fine two-storeyed porch and stately, though over-restored chancel. The nave and aisles have good roofs of the 15th, 16th and 17th centuries. Note, also, early 17th-century seating. In the chancel are buried many of the Arundells of Wardour including Lady Blanche, the heroic defender of Wardour Castle in the Civil War.

UPAVON (*St. Mary*)
Late 12th-cent. chancel; font early 13th cent.

UPTON LOVELL (*St. Peter*)
Chancel 13th cent.; rest 1633 in Gothic survival style with nave in medieval manner; effigy 15th cent.

URCHFONT *(St. Michael)*
A charming village under the downs with a pond on the green and a mighty cedar tree. The church is mainly a 14th-century fabric with 15th-century additions. Its most note-worthy feature is the chancel with gabled buttresses and stone vaulting enriched with carved bosses. The porch, also, is stone roofed. Note the lovely 14th-century details in the S. aisle, the round columns of the nave arcades, the 17th-century roof, 14th-century painted glass and 18th-century monument.

WANBOROUGH *(St. Andrew)*
A russet and golden church on the high ground where Ermin Street dives into the Vale. Nave, aisles, and N. porch late 14th century. Fine W. tower 15th century, with chancel and sacristy (with small low win-dow for ringing hand-bell) of the same period. Notable for the hexagonal lantern and tall spire which rise most ingeniously from a shortened bay at the E. end of the nave. An early and rather drastic restora-tion by Sir G. Scott, 1843, with walls stripped of plaster. Two-light window by Christopher Webb. Notice in porch, 'All females are requested to take off their pattens on entering this door'.

WEST (OR BISHOPS) LAVINGTON (*All Saints*)
12th to late 15th cent.; restored, T. H. Wyatt, 1845; monuments.

WESTWOOD *(St. Mary)*
The church and manor-house form a delightful group in this unspoilt corner of Wiltshire. The former has a 13th-century chancel, the remainder of the fabric in-cluding the stately tower with its domed turret and enriched parapet being mainly late medieval, though the nave was re-fashioned in the 18th century when it was provided with its attractive plaster ceiling. The interior has much to delight us in-cluding the chapel roof, a fine display of late medieval painted glass in the chancel, the domed font cover and 17th-century altar rails and pulpit.

WILTON *(St. Mary & St. Nicholas)*
'Lombardy in Wiltshire'. A daring, un-compromising, and extremely expensive design by T. H. Wyatt and David Brandon, notable for being right outside the strict Gothic of the period. Built in 1841–5 for Sidney, Lord Herbert of Lea, who imported from Italy medieval mosaics and marble which the architects have worked into the building and fittings. Remarkable imported late medieval glass, and yet earlier glass in apse windows. The detached campanile is approached by a short cloister; from the surrounding hills it dominates the town in a curiously attractive way, especially under an evening sky in March. Though a

treasure-house of lovely things, the interior seems cold and alien.

WINTERBOURNE BASSETT *(St. Katharine & St. Peter)*

Set amidst foliage on the high ground west of Hackpen, this is an architectural gem. Nave, N. aisle with transeptal chapel, chancel, and S. porch all purest Decorated; only the W. tower and a few minor features are later. Beautiful window and recessed tomb in transept, beneath which is the most lovely and touching thing in the church – a 13th-century tomb-slab with a man and wife hand-in-hand. Late Norman font with 17th-century cover, and much other 17th-century furniture, also good monuments and hatchments. Contrasting 18th and 20th century light fittings at chancel entrance. But how sad are the damp and mouldering walls!

WOODFORD (*All Saints*)

Tower 15th cent.; Comper glass in three windows; gallery and tower screen 17th cent.

YATTON KEYNELL (*St. Margaret*)

15th cent.; tower and stone screen.

Worcestershire

INTRODUCTION

WORCESTERSHIRE IS a small and richly varied county. It is diamond-shaped and, if the simile will be forgiven, it is like a fruit tart. The centre, containing the Severn and Avon valleys with their tributaries, is mostly orchards, miraculously beautiful in spring. The edge of the tart is the hills which surround Worcestershire on all sides. Wherever you are in Worcestershire you can see hills not far off; they are usually flanked with or crowned by trees. The northernmost corner of the fruit tart is burned black, it is part of the black country and extends northwards from Kidderminster towards Birmingham which now extends into Worcestershire. The industrial towns of the county are devoted to ironworking, from founding and engineering through chains down to needles and fish-hooks. In this industrial corner pinkish brick houses and mills and chimneys stretch over hills and valleys and various undistinguished Victorian towers, spires and bell-cotes rise out of them with here and there the weathered iron stone tower of some medieval church, such as the fine ones of Kidderminster and Bromsgrove. A piece of the tart, wholly black country, is broken off and islanded in Staffordshire – the hilltop borough of Dudley with its old castle, chimneys, furnaces, coal mines and factories. This island is the sole survival of many pieces of Worcestershire which were to be found in Warwickshire and Gloucestershire and were relics of monastic landowners of feudal times; there was only one feudal Worcestershire baron, the owner of Dudley Castle, the Church was lord elsewhere.

The rest of the county is a marked contrast. What Surrey is to London, it has become to Birmingham and the Black Country and many an old timber-framed cottage set among orchards or at the foot of steep pastoral hills may be seen on closer inspection to have been saved from destruction by some industrial proprietor who uses it as a week-end hide out. His forbears would have lived on the outskirts of Kidderminster or Dudley or Redditch in some heavy Victorian mansion now divided into flats.

The building materials of houses and churches are as varied as the scenery. Only the big abbeys and priories, in which Worcester was richer than any other county, could afford impressive architecture. Worcester Cathedral (severely but impressively restored by Sir Gilbert Scott) and Great Malvern Priory with its many windows of late medieval and 18th-century glass, and Pershore Abbey which is now only a huge choir with tower crossing, and the stately perpendicular bell tower of Evesham are the chief survivals.

In the fruit districts and where building stones were not easily obtained, the churches were like the old cottages partly of timber construction, often with timber-framed towers or bell-cotes. At the east of the county where the Cotswold hills rise, churches such as Broadway and Church Honeyborne are of a local golden limestone like their villages.

In the west of the county south of the Malvern Hills, churches are of red sandstone and the tower of Martley church is of a brilliant scarlet sandstone which has to be seen to be believed. The church at Shelsley Walsh is of travertine stone, a pale pink stone which was also used in ancient Rome.

As in all midland counties where an industrial life had started in the 18th century, there is much 18th-century church building. Not all of it was swept away by disgusted Victorians – indeed they did well by Great Witley which is the most sumptuous classic interior in England – and there are a Worcestershire baroque style and a Worcestershire Strawberry Hill Gothick style which are individual and charming.

Victorian work in the county is mostly poor, all style and mock construction and this applies to the larger villas as well as the churches.

J.B.

SELECTED LIST OF CHURCHES

by Matley Moore

ALVECHURCH (*St. Lawrence*) GR
14th and 15th cent.; restored interiorly and partly rebuilt by W. Butterfield, 1861.

ASTLEY (*St. Peter*)
12th–15th cent. tower; good monuments to the Blount family 16th cent.

BARBOURNE (*St. Stephen*) GR
Preedy, 1862; well-proportioned, handsome heavy roofs.

BARNT GREEN (*St. Andrew*)
A. S. Dixon, 1809–14; brick Romanesque.

BEOLEY (*St. Leonard*)
15th-cent. tower; good series of monuments to the Sheldons, those to William and Ralph Sheldon and their wives, set between the chancel and chapel under arches, with much heraldry, are outstanding.

BESFORD *(St. Peter)*
14th-century timber-framed nave (rebuilt 1880; all timbers replaced in original position); rood loft; 14th-century bells; 16th-century monument. Remarkable triptych in painted wood, a memorial with

very interesting paintings and much heraldry, probably by Michael Salabos, 1588.

BEWDLEY (*St. Anne*) CL
1746, built by the Woodward brothers of Chipping Campden.

BLAKEDOWN (*St. James the Great*) GR
G. E. Street, 1860.

BREDON *(St. Giles)*
This whole village on the banks of the Avon forms a delightful group, with its street of old houses leading to the church, the rectory as large and stately as a manor house, and one of the finest tithe barns (14th century) in the country. The great church, much of it of the 12th century with its central tower and spire dominates the whole scene. It is full of interest inside; old glass, medieval heraldic tiles, early tombs, a heart burial with a curious slab of a pair of hands holding a heart, an Easter sepulchre and a huge 17th-century monument to Giles Reed whose pride and pomp contrast strongly with the simpler monuments of the earlier ages: it is a fine thing

of its date with the usual litter of offspring in dutiful attendance. All these varied things in the church are of interest and the whole building with its early architectural details and the additions of the different ages offer a vivid comment on the changing interests of the times and the different outlook of the ages which have produced them.

BROADWAY *(St. Eadburgh)*
In spite of the way that it prostitutes its charm, Broadway is a very beautiful village and should be seen in the early morning or late in the evening when the absence of coaches and visitors allows space to enjoy the whole setting. The old church is somewhat away from the village but should be sought out; its quietness and spaciousness, although they gain by contrast with the restless activity of the village, would be remarkable anywhere. Here as much as in any place that I know one senses the peace and devotion of the earlier ages and this so fills the whole building that the details of the architecture and furnishings, all good, fall into their places and, while they contribute to it, are merged into the atmosphere of the whole. Cruciform with central tower; work of all centuries from 12th to 17th. Note altar rails and 15th-century pulpit.

BROMSGROVE *(St. John the Baptist)*
Mid-14th-cent. tower; octagonal spire with crockets; good Talbot and Stafford tombs with effigies in alabaster; on the Talbot tomb was discovered evidence which in 1856 established the claim of Lord Talbot of Ingestre to the Earldom of Shrewsbury; Sir Humphrey Stafford was slain in the Jack Cade rebellion.

CHADDESLEY CORBETT *(St. Cassian)*
Best example of 14th-cent. work in county; 12th-cent. font of pre-Conquest design, interlaced work with dragons' tails twisted into knots; early 14th-cent. monuments.

CROOME *(St. Mary Magdalene)*
A Gothick church of 1763. It is a good and complete example of this fantastic style. The house and park were laid out by Adam and Brown for the 6th Earl of Coventry and the whole group is a silent witness to the state and dignity which were considered essential to the existence of a nobleman of the 18th century. The church at that time was an adjunct to the Great House (much as the stable courtyard and the usual offices were), and enshrined the posthumous greatness of the family: it also formed an eye-catcher from his lordship's windows and vastly improved the scene. Of all these ideas Croome is a fine example . . . within, the church fulfils its function by housing a series of magnificent monuments to the Earls, lying there in their robes and coronets and attended by personifications of the appropriate virtues. Their lordships all show by their expressions that they are consoled in leaving Croome to know that in the heavenly places too there are many mansions. Provision is also made in the church for the worship of God.

CROPTHORNE *(St. Michael)*
12th cent.; contains an equal armed stone cross of about 800, fine example of pre-Conquest art; 17th-cent. monuments with effigies.

CROWLE *(St. John the Baptist)*
Has a late 12th-cent. stone lectern, possibly from Evesham Abbey; 14th-cent. timber porch.

DODFORD *(Holy Trinity)* GR
A. Bartlett, 1908; 'late Gothic freely treated' in brick and rough cast; wooden cloister; open-air pulpit; interior has rood cross by Amy Walford.

DORMSTON *(St. Nicholas)*
Remote situation; 13th–15th cent. with 16th-cent. timber-framed tower.

DUDLEY *(St. Thomas)*
W. Brooks 1817–19. A most interesting example of Regency Gothick, with a very splendid spire and good plasterwork of the style in vaulting and panelling. The arrangement of the decoration of the E. end with statues in niches on the N. and S. walls is unusual. There is a Georgian marble altar and carving of St. Thomas above by Samuel Joseph. The building gains by the loss of most of the dark stained-glass windows of the Victorian time, which were destroyed in the last war. The E. window, which is earlier in date (1821), is painted glass by Joseph Backler. It unfortunately remains and is much admired locally. The subject is the Ascension. In the upper part of the window Our Lord executes an elegant *pas seul* to the admiration of two buxom winged ladies in the base, who look like celestial barmaids but must have been thought by the painter

to represent angels. We have travelled a long way, and in the wrong direction, from the great awe-inspiring figures of the messengers of God as represented in all early art – the mosaics of Italy and the early glass painters of France – a long way from the wistful angels of Botticelli and the 15th-century painters, angels overwhelmed with the burden of their great mission – to the bright young things of Dudley and it is as well, perhaps, that this window does remain, an example of the work and outlook of its own age and a warning to this.

ELMLEY CASTLE *(St. Mary)

The village of Elmley Castle forms a very beautiful group at the foot of Bredon hill, its wide street of pleasant houses leading directly to the church at the end. The church is a charming medieval building, containing much early work, and dominated by a tower with gargoyles: these creatures also inhabit other parts of the building. The font is unusual and fascinating, supported on four writhing monsters of the 12th century, the bowl is 15th century: with shields charged with heraldic and other devices. The most lovely thing in the church, however, is an alabaster tomb to William Savage (d. 1616) and his son Giles (d. 1631) and his son's wife Katherine (d. 1674). She holds an infant in her arms – one of the most beautiful pieces of child sculpture of its own or any age. In contrast to this, and placed just opposite to it, is a great monument (blocking what was a fine Jesse window) to Thomas Lord Coventry, 1699. Equally fine of its kind and not far removed from the Savage tomb in date it seems by its outlook to belong to another age. It was intended for Croome, but owing to a family row was placed here instead. It would have been a fine thing at Croome, and Elmley could well have spared it.

EVESHAM (All Saints)

12th–15th cent.; mortuary chapel to Clement Litchfield (penultimate Abbot of Evesham) with fan vault and pendants.

FLADBURY (St. John the Baptist)

12th–14th cent.; medieval tiles; 15th-cent. brasses; 16th-cent. sanctus bell; 18th-cent. monument to Bishop Lloyd.

GREAT WITLEY *(St. Michael)

Built by the Foleys and enriched by the Dudleys, Great Witley, the finest baroque church in the country, is far too little known. Set in the midst of the Park and formerly attached to the house (now a ruin), among Italian gardens and undulating landscape, the outside suggests southern Europe, and on entering the building one is taken straight there. The whole of the walls and ceiling are adorned with superb baroque plasterwork in white and gold. Set on the ceiling among all this gleaming scrollwork are three paintings by Verrio, which together with the ten windows of painted glass by Joshua Price, were brought by Lord Foley from the Duke of Chandos palace at Canons when it was dismantled. All is exceedingly rich and of great beauty. The woodwork of the seating and other furniture is 19th century and was introduced by Lord Dudley. It is carved magnificently in the Gothic manner, but does not seem out of keeping with the splendours above it. This church is quite equal to many churches on the Continent in this style which people go abroad to see. (See Plate 48)

HALLOW (St. Philip and St. James) GR

W. J. Hopkins, 1869; ambitious Gothic in red and white stone with nave roof supported on transverse arches, the flying buttresses appearing externally above the aisle roofs.

HIMBLETON (St. Mary Magdalene)

Norman origin with 13th, 14th and early 16th cent. additions; early glass; roofs.

HOLT *(St. Martin)

A pleasing group of church (12th century) and castle (14th century) set remote from all other buildings. The church has much rich carved work of the mid-12th century on the doorways and chancel arch. The tower is 15th century, and there is a chapel with remains of 15th-century glass, an Annunciation. The glass is of very fine quality and the drawing of the heads of the two figures is very good indeed. There are several monuments and some 19th-century mosaics, good in quality but badly placed.

HUDDINGTON (St. James)

14th cent.; fragments of heraldic glass.

KEMPSEY (St. Mary)

13th-cent. chancel; important 13th–14th cent. glass; painted tomb to Sir Edmund Wild, 1620.

KIDDERMINSTER (St. Mary & All Saints)

Late medieval much renewed; monuments of great interest, 15th–17th cent.

KNIGHTON-ON-TEME *(St. Michael)
An isolated and remote church mainly
12th century with a good S. doorway set
in a projection with a blind arcade of four
arches over it. Within is a chancel arch
decorated like the S. doorway with on
either side a blind arcade of two arches.
The bell tower is supported on huge timbers
inside the church and there are some
remains of grisaille glass. The whole
building has a strong sense of the peace
and devotion of ages over it; it may be
only its remoteness from the busy world,
but I feel it very vividly and very refresh-
ingly whenever I enter it.

LITTLE MALVERN *(St. Giles)
The presbytery and crossing are all that
remain of this monastic church, the
crossing surmounted by a tower, but all
this work is good and seen, as it is, in
conjunction with the Court adjoining,
which incorporates part of the domestic
buildings of the monastery, against the
background of the hills forms a very
pleasing picture. Bishop Alcock rebuilt
most of the priory, including the church,
at the end of the 15th century at which
time the earlier buildings had fallen in a
state of decay. The late 15th-century glass
in the E. window is most interesting
showing Edward IV and his family. The
figure of the Prince of Wales survives with
part of that of Elizabeth Woodville his
queen and her four elder daughters. The
floor of the church is largely paved with
15th-century tiles.

MALVERN LINK (The Ascension) GR
Walter Tapper, 1903; tall, simple and
Bodley-esque.

MALVERN *(St. Mary & St. Michael)
Mainly of the 15th century, although much
earlier work of the 12th and 13th centuries
can be found, this great priory church is
well known for its choir stalls, its tiles and
above all for its glass, which is of the
greatest interest. The subjects and history
of the windows here is a study in itself.
All the 15th-century tiles were made on the
spot – the kiln was discovered in 1830 near
by – and all have been carefully recorded.
The whole building is very impressive but
the large space between the 12th-century
arcades and the 15th-century clerestory
(there is no blind storey), seems to call for
some decoration to link the two storeys
together. It was probably filled with wall
painting when it was built.

MARTLEY *(St. Peter)
A good building, 12th–15th century, set
just off the village street in the lovely
rich countryside between the Severn and
Teme, it should be seen when the fruit
blossom is clothing all the hills and filling
all the valleys with its beauty: there is
nothing in England to compare with West
Worcestershire in the spring. If we were
really civilized all folk would leave their
work and come and see it and thank God
for so much beauty, and Martley church
would be a good spot in which to do so.
Perhaps the most interesting thing in the
building is the early painted wall decoration. The E. wall has curtain pattern,
probably late 13th century with beasts in
the top loops of the curtain: a fox, a stag,
a hare, and a wolf with four dragons.
Other paintings show an Annunciation
with donor below; St. Martin; Adoration
of the Magi and some lattice work with
the arms of Mortimer and Dispenser in
alternate lozenges. An alabaster effigy of
Sir Hugh Mortimer, 1459, is in the chancel;
the armour is well shown.

NEWLAND *(St. Leonard)
Built in 1864 by the Beauchamp family as
part of a group of almshouses in the style
of the 14th century, this church is of
absorbing interest as showing the ideas of
the time carried out very completely to
show what a medieval church should look
like. The interior is richly decorated: walls
covered with mural paintings, mouldings
decorated in colour, windows filled with
stained glass and coloured marble decoration throughout. It does give a fair idea of
a 14th-century church but, as was usual,
the Victorians were afraid of colour and
the painting of the walls looks washy;
carried out in full colours it would have
been magnificent but as it is, it gives far
more of the spirit of the Middle Ages than
do the stark stone interiors brutally stripped of their plaster and paintings by most
restorers of the 19th century and still
admired by far too many people today.
People 'love that cool grey stone' on the
interior walls of their churches who would
not tolerate bare brick walls in the interior
of their own houses. Newland in 1864
showed the way, but few walked in it.

ODDINGLEY (St. James, Min.)
Largely rebuilt but contains very interesting glass.

OMBERSLEY *(St. Andrew)
A church newly built in 1830 by Rickman

in the 14th century manner; it is a good example of his work. The exterior forms a pleasant group with a well-proportioned spire. It is all the product of one mind, built at one time and worked out after a careful study of the medieval buildings; having a vitality of its own and not becoming, as so many of the churches of that time did, a lifeless academic copy of the work of a past age. Outside, the appearance of a medieval church: inside all is changed and the place looks like the meeting house of a Nonconformist body: galleries, pews and austerity. This can hardly be blamed on Rickman who had to work for the needs of his time and for a generation who had forgotten that churches are shrines first and foremost for the glory and worship of God; and only after that assembly halls for discourses. The only suggestion of a shrine here is the Squire's pew, handsomely fitted. Since this note was written, the interior has been very much improved by the skilful use of colour on walls and ceiling; the galleries unfortunately still remain.

OVERBURY (*St. Faith*)
Good 12th-cent. arcades; bosses in chancel.

PERSHORE *(Holy Cross)*
This great abbey building, when complete, was larger than Worcester Cathedral and much finer work, judging by that which remains. All that does remain is the presbytery and one transept and the central tower. The arcading of the presbytery is beautiful 13th-century work which with its vault is so lovely in its mouldings and proportions that the more we see it, the more we regret that which has been destroyed. The apse at the E. end was built in the 19th century; it is difficult to imagine how anyone seeing what was there could have added this poor work. There are one or two early monuments and two late 16th-century tombs in colour. The transept is dominated by a standing figure representing something or other as a memorial to the 1914 war. Holding a light it would give interest to the foot of the staircase at the Hotel Metropole; it does not add to the glories of this great church.

RIBBESFORD (*St. Leonard*)
Tympanum has early carving of a hunting scene; wooden arcade with octagonal pillars; old glass and 15th-cent. wood carvings from a former rood-screen; bell

13th cent. – undoubtedly the oldest bell in the county.

RIPPLE *(St. Mary)*
An almost unaltered late 12th-century building. It has chancel, central tower with N. and S. transepts, a nave with N. and S. aisles and a N. porch. There is some 15th-century glass and a set of 14th–15th century misericords showing the occupations of the months. A very charming church with a sense of continuity and abiding peace.

ROCK *(St. Peter & St. Paul)*
A great 12th-century church with 16th-century tower and S. arcade, standing practically alone and forming a fine landmark from all sides.

SEDGEBERROW (*St. Mary*)
Complete building of 14th cent.; remained unaltered.

SHELSLEY WALSH (*St. Andrew*)
Church and Manor House here make a good group. The church dates from the 12th and 13th centuries: it was drastically restored in 1859. The walling is mainly of travertine, which is a local stone hereabouts. The late 15th-century screen is the finest in the county, the S. section is returned to form a parclose. There is a good table tomb in wood to Francis Walsh (1596) displaying heraldry, and the floor of the church is mainly 15th-century tiles. A beautiful setting in the Teme valley.

SPETCHLEY *(All Saints)*
A small building, mainly 14th century by the side of the main road from Worcester to Stratford. There is a S. chapel built in 1629 which contains a series of very fine monuments to the Berkeley family, some with good effigies and all with a fine display of heraldry.

STOCKTON-ON-TEME *(St. Andrew)*
Placed on a high ground, which suggests a pagan site, this church contains work of all periods from the 12th century onwards. There is a 12th-century tomb-slab to an early rector and an elaborate wooden 17th-century tomb painted grey to a member of the Walsh family. This is not an outstanding church but makes a picturesque group with the surrounding buildings.

STOKE PRIOR *(St. Michael)*
A fine late 12th-century church with a good tower of the period carrying a modern

shingled spire. The whole building is an interesting early group with its chapel, chancel and sacristy. There are some early monuments within.

STRENSHAM *(St. John the Baptist)
Standing on high ground close to the River Avon and alone in fields; here is richness indeed for the antiquarian. A painted rood-loft front, now set as a gallery front on the W. wall, with 23 saints. A series of monuments of one family from the 13th–19th centuries, most of them of very high quality. Floored with tiles of the 15th century. The whole place is of great interest. There is no parish near by and the church is in urgent need of repairs – it ranks high on the list for help for historic churches.

TARDEBIGGE (St. Bartholomew)
F. Hiorne 1777. Slender classic steeple on commanding site. Victorianised interior.

WARNDON *(St. Nicholas)
A small field church in a parish with no village and almost no roads. It is approached by a field track and gated road. Grouped with farm buildings, this is a very simple little church of 12th century date with a timbered tower, recently roughcast, of the 16th century. Within all is as simple and charming. 17th-century rails and altar table, a seven-sided font, some good fragments of 14th-century glass and encaustic floor tiles, and above all the sense that it has been the homely centre for the worship of simple folk for many, many years and has acquired and retained a real atmosphere of sanctity.

WICKHAMFORD *(St. John the Baptist)
Charming group of Church and Manor

house; church is of the 13th–15th centuries; good woodwork; desk, rails, pews. Main interest, a large double tester tomb in alabaster to two of Sandys family, early 17th century, handsome and interesting piece of work.

WITLEY, GREAT: see Great Witley.

WOLLASTON (St. James, Stourbridge) GR
G. Bidlake, 1860

WORCESTER *(All Saints)
A large and spacious 18th-century church built in the classical manner on an earlier foundation: this building has dignity, space and light to an unusual degree. The lower part of the tower is 15th century, the upper storeys 18th century in the manner of Wren. It has monuments and some good fragments of 15th-century glass from the earlier church.

*(St. Swithun)
Built in 1736 by Edward and Thomas Woodward (who also built St. John's at Gloucester and the church at Bewdley and several others) this building is both within and without a perfectly preserved example of a church of the early 18th century, untouched and with all the furnishings of its time; font, organ, pews, altar and a very fine and imposing three-decker pulpit with the addition of a seat for the Mayor, with mace stand; all as it was originally set up. The ceiling is vaulted in plaster in the Gothick manner. The whole place has nothing incongruous about it and all the woodwork is of very high quality workmanship. No one who appreciates Georgian churches should fail to visit this charming building.

Yorkshire: the East Riding

INTRODUCTION

HERE LIE the broad acres of Yorkshire. With the Wolds as backbone, the Riding stretches from Filey in the north to Spurn Point in the south, and westwards towards Malton and York. There are three distinct regions: (1) The gently undulating Plain of Holderness, a peninsula of distant views and wide skies, whose winding lanes reflect the strong light from the sea. The indigenous cobbles, laboriously gathered from the boulder clay, form the material for its trim churches and old farmsteads. The former culminate in the Gothic splendours of Humberside, where medieval wealth and proximity to navigable water are seen in the village churches of the 'Saxon Line', and in the city of Kingston-upon-Hull.

(2) Dry valleys, ancient barrows and protective belts of trees form the landscape of the Wolds. Except in the Bayle and north-west tower at Bridlington, chalk is principally confined to domestic work. Norman fonts abound in the sturdy churches, evidence of re-building after the Harrying of the North. Beverley, Cottingham, Driffield and the fine Victorian spire at Dalton Holme grace the eastern slopes, whilst the churches of the central Wolds bear the indelible mark of Sir Tatton Sykes' restorers.

(3) The Vale of York, watered by the Derwent, takes on the aspect of the Low Countries. Here, tree-lined lanes lead to remote villages, like Aughton with its melancholy atmosphere, or Scrayingham with its memories of the 'Railway King'. The towers, especially the upstanding one at Holme-on-Spaldingmoor, Bishop Skirlaw's at Howden and Prior Wessington's spire at Hemingborough, are marked features in the Plain.   M.E.I.

SELECTED LIST OF CHURCHES

by M. Edward Ingram

ALDBROUGH (*St. Bartholomew*)
Circular inscribed sun-dial 11th cent.; fine alabaster effigy of knight.

AUGHTON *(All Saints)*
Remote situation in water meadows between River Derwent and earthworks of former Aske residence. Sturdy Tudor tower dated 1536 displaying several shields, enigmatic inscription and carved with an asker or newt. Unspoilt interior: broad Norman chancel arch of three orders surrounded by chevron. Baluster altar rails set back in churchwarden chancel. Contemporary brick N. aisle. Arcaded, untouched Norman font, and brass to Richard Aske and wife, *d.* 1460, possibly brought here from Ellerton Priory at the Dissolution.

BAINTON *(St. Andrew)*
Dominates typical Wold village. Almost purely 14th-century Curvilinear. Nave and aisles with lofty arcades, spacious chancel and W. tower with slightly corbelled-out parapet, once crowned by octagonal spire. Several interesting monuments. In chancel worn brass to Roger Godeale, priest, *d.* 1429. Coloured wall monument to Robert Faucon, 1661, an ejected rector, dated eleven years before his death!

BARMSTON *(All Saints)*
Early 15th-century church stands on forlorn moated site at far end of village, close to remains of Elizabethan red-brick manorhouse, former home of the Boyntons. Church built of cobbles, with squat tower, having pierced battlements, at W. end of S. aisle. In chancel alabaster effigy of knight.

BEEFORD (*St. Leonard*)
Tower similar to Holme-on-Spalding Moor; medieval statue of St. Leonard; priest brass, 1472.

BEMPTON (*St. Michael*)
Early 19th-cent. chancel; post-Reformation wooden arcade and screen incorporating Royal Arms, etc.

BESSINGBY *(St. Magnus, a late misreading of St. Mary Magdalene)* GR
1895, T. L. Moore. Of warm red sandstone

charmingly situated on flank of Wolds. Nave with narrow aisles, chancel and central tower and spire. A successful 19th-century version of a late 14th-century church, preserving fine Norman font (compare Nafferton) and several good monuments, one to Lady Ann Hudson by R. J. Wyatt.

BEVERLEY *(St. John of Beverley, the Minster)*
Superb building exhibiting work of all periods. One of finest Gothic churches in Europe. Formerly collegiate, with double transepts. Choir and main transepts, which have double aisles are principally Early English, and this merges almost imperceptibly into Decorated nave, with elegant Perpendicular W. front and twin towers as crowning glory. Perpendicular altar screen with platform above, and highly decorative Percy tomb to N. Choir stalls with canopies and misereres by Ripon carvers. Great W. door with evangelists and their symbols designed by Hawksmoor, font cover probably by him, lead statues of Athelstan and St. John by William Collins of Driffield, and wrought-iron gates in choir, all date from 1715–40. Choir screen constructed by Elwell of Beverley to designs of G. G. Scott. (*See Plate 14*)

BEVERLEY *(St. Mary)*
Cruciform church. Rich exterior. Nave and tower rebuilt after fall of old 12th-century tower in 1520. Spacious interior. Pier plan and small capitals of arcades recall those at Hull, but bases are exaggerated. Minstrels' pillar on N., with five little figures and label stops here record names of benefactors (1530). Original roofs now repainted under Leslie Moore. 19th-century restorations by A. W. N. and E. W. Pugin. Latter added buttresses to S. transept. Reredos by J. Oldrid Scott. 14th-century stalls with misericords. Charnel house and priest's rooms to N.E. 15th-century font. Many ledger stones and matrices of brasses. Wrought iron altar table, and Wharton monuments belong to 18th century.

403

BIRDSALL (*St. Mary*) GR
1824 and 1879; good modern glass; monuments by Westmacott and Rysbrack.

BISHOP BURTON (*All Saints*)
Setting; Kempe glass in nave; brasses.

BISHOP WILTON (*St. Edith*)
Heavily restored in 1859 by J. L. Pearson.

BOYNTON *(St. Andrew)*
Situated close to Hall gates at end of village street of whitewashed chalk cottages. Late 14th-century tower. Nave and chancel, rebuilt in brick 1768 by John Carr, is delightful Classical structure with Batty Langley Gothick details. Until restoration, 1910, by J. Bilson altar stood beneath architectural baldicchino. Beyond lies Strickland mortuary chapel, containing family monuments, one of which is a cenotaph attributed to William Kent. E. window glazed by William Peckitt. Tower has 'Gothick' plaster vault, and gallery, formerly squire's pew. Unusual lectern and font cover designed by Francis Johnson.

BRANDESBURTON *(St. Mary)*
Shrouded in trees. Built mainly of cobbles (badly pointed at last restoration) with brick clerestory and S. porch. Aisles have simple square-headed windows. Restored, and chancel rebuilt, 1893, by W. S. Weatherbury – good but for strident red-tiled chancel roof. Interior light and spacious, with narrow aisles terminating at W. with curious responds to arcades. Crown glass. In chancel remains of bracket-brass to William Darrell, priest, *d.* 1364, and life-size brass to John St. Quintin, 1397, and wife. Odd half niche projecting from N. wall.

BRIDLINGTON (*Christ Church*) GR
Scott and Moffat, 1840–1; 18th-cent. font and cover from York Minster.

*(St. Mary)
Nave of Augustinian priory. Forms group with 14th-century Bayle Gate. Noble 13th and 14th century arcades with triforium and clerestory, combined on S. side. Beautiful N. porch with interesting capitals and rose ornament. Evidence of rebuilding scheme, *c.* 1480, to which W. end, S.W. tower and three W. bays of S. arcade belong. Suffered two violent restorations in 19th century. In 1846–57 Edmund Sharpe and E. G. Paley partially raised roof pitch. In 1876–1880 G. G. Scott completed W. towers, left unfinished at Dissolution, and filled nave with pitch-pine pewing. Fine

Frosterley marble font, Tournai marble tomb slab, possibly of founder. Re-erected remains of 12th-century cloister arcade in N. aisle.

BUBWITH (*All Saints*)
Fine church beside Derwent; Norman chancel arch; 13th-century arcades and chancel; tower, *c.* 1424; heraldry of Askes and Vavasours; old glass.

BUGTHORPE (*St. Andrew*)
19th-cent. nave; double chancel arch.

BURNBY (*St. Giles*)
Norman and E.E.; three sedilia; brass, 1632; restored by Sir G. G. Scott, 1872.

BURSTWICK (*All Saints*)
Contemporary painting of Execution of King Charles on back of Restoration Royal Arms.

BURTON AGNES *(St. Martin)*
Grouped with medieval manor-house and Elizabethan mansion. Entrance lies through gloomy avenue of overhanging yews. Nave and aisles 13th and 14th centuries. Fine late 15th-century W. tower. Chancel rebuilt, *c.* 1840 by Archdeacon Wilberforce, son of the Emancipator, whose likeness appears on corbel. Mutilated remains of Georgian squire's pew from which fireplace was recently removed. Remains of gallery front incorporated in pewing at W. end. Box-pews. Somerville and Griffith monuments, one has three coffins in place of effigies and two grisly panels of skulls and bones. Boynton monument by H. Cheere.

BURTON FLEMING (*St. Cuthbert*)
Norman churchwardenised.

BURTON PIDSEA (*St. Peter, anciently St. Peter and St. Paul*)
Fine, small Holderness church built of glacial erratics.

CARNABY (*St. John the Baptist*)
E.E. nave; Perp. tower; windows in S. aisle show evolution of crude plate tracery.

CAVE, NORTH: *see North Cave.*

CHERRY BURTON (*St. Michael & All Angels*) GR
Horace Jones 1852–3; setting; striking tower; Kempe windows; iron tablet recording I.C.B.S. grant.

COTTINGHAM *(St. Mary)*
Large cruciform church in overgrown suburb of Hull, but still retaining many fine Georgian houses. Principally 14th

century. Chancel rebuilt and Perpendicular tower with outer stair turret added in following century. W. window has flowing tracery, and that of aisles is Flamboyant. Tracery of chancel windows uninspired. Chancel and nave aisles are battlemented. Little of interest in interior, except wall brass to John Smyth, 1504, and wife, and restored brass to rector Nicholas de Luda, 1383, who built the chancel.

DALTON HOLME *(*St. Mary*) GR
1858–61, J. L. Pearson. Early Decorated cruciform church with aisled chancel; W. tower and spire 208 feet high, which is landmark for whole central Wold area and is reminiscent of Salisbury. Exterior of Steetly stone, and interior Hildenly stone elaborately carved. Details rather prickly, but general effect magnificent. Proportions excellent. Oak furnishings. E. window by Clayton and Bell. Church and furnishings in accord with Ecclesiological principles. In S. chapel, curious Italian-style monument to Sir John Hotham, 1689. Truth, Strength, Justice and Temperance support a semi-recumbent effigy of the knight. Formerly a carved skeleton lay beneath.

DALTON, NORTH: *see North Dalton.*

DRIFFIELD, GREAT: *see Great Driffield.*

DRIFFIELD, LITTLE: *see Little Driffield.*

EASINGTON (*All Saints*)
Weather-beaten E.E.

EAST HESLERTON (*All Saints*) GR
G. E. Street, 1877; windows Clayton and Bell; four figures in tower, designed for Bristol Cathedral, brought here, 1876.

EASTRINGTON *(*St. Michael*)
Outstanding church of commonplace village, with green in front. Norman core with 12th and 13th century work in nave and chancel. Battlemented W. tower and clerestories added in 15th century. Interesting patching to N. chancel arcade following a collapse in 1632; Classical plinth supporting oak framework. Altar-tomb to Judge Portington, *d.* 1456, shewn wearing pigtail, in N. chapel. Incised alabaster slabs; curious crane to 17th-century font cover. In porch large stone carved with eight fantastic beasts.

ELLERTON (*St. Mary & St. Lawrence*) GR
J. L. Pearson, 1847; ancient armorial glass and matrices.

ELLOUGHTON (*St. Mary the Virgin*) GR
J. L. Pearson, 1845; medieval tower; E.E. S. doorway.

ESCRICK *(*St. Helen*) GR
Fine Victorian church, built in Middle Pointed style 1856–7 by F. C. Penrose. Central position in well-planned village, approached through lych-gate. Long nave and chancel terminating at each end in semi-hexagonal apses. At W. this forms baptistry, whose vault is supported on red Devonshire marble. Delicate white marble font, bowl held by two cherubs (male and female) back to back, carved by Gio Tognolt of Rome. Baptistry also houses 18th-century Thompson monuments. Recumbent marble effigy of first Lady Wenlock, *d.* 1868, by Prince Victor of Hohenlohe Langenburg. Lofty tower N. of chancel.

ETTON (*St. Mary*)
Fine Norman church; drastically restored; magnificent Norman tower arch; carved stone royal arms.

EVERINGHAM (*St. Everilda or St. Emeldis*) CL
Shapely Georgian, somewhat Victorianised.

FERRIBY, NORTH: *see North Ferriby.*

FILEY *(*St. Oswald*)
In wooded position overlooking ravine away from town. Cruciform church mainly 12th and 13th centuries. Much restoration work in 19th century. S. aisle doorway with moulded semi-circular head. Miniature medieval effigy, mistakenly described as that of 'Boy Bishop'.

FLAMBOROUGH *(*St. Oswald*)
Stands rather squat and sentinel-like, at approach to village, much spoilt in late years by uncontrolled development. Tower by C. Hodgson Fowler, 1897; structure much restored in 19th century, has rich atmosphere and is foil for early 16th-century rood-screen and loft retaining considerable traces of original colour, the work of Ripon carvers. Medieval parclose screens, one with peascod decoration. Quaint rhyming brass inscription to Marmaduke Constable, *c.* 1520, who fought at Flodden. Monument to 'Wild' Walter Strickland, 1671, whose pardon granted by Charles II is framed in nave. Norman tub font. Medieval crucifix in S. chapel. Maidens' gloves in vestry. Some good modern windows by J. Nuttgens.

FOLKTON (*St. John the Evangelist*)
Early Norman N. doorway, font and chancel arch.

FOSTON-ON-THE-WOLDS (*St. Andrew*)
Norman; E.E.; Curvilinear; position on glacial moraine.

FRIDAYTHORPE (*St. Mary*)
Norman; curious squat tower; restoration by C. Hodgson Fowler, 1902.

GANTON *(*St. Nicholas*)
Setting near foot of N. scarp of Wolds, at top of pretty village street of whitewashed cottages, along which chalk stream flows. Mainly 13th century with S. transept (formerly Legard mortuary chapel), stone-roofed S. porch and W. tower with small octagonal spire. Very fine mid-18th-century monument to John Legard in S. transept. Other monuments by Fisher. Bad modern glass.

GARTON-IN-HOLDERNESS (*St. Michael*)
Head of Janus cross; restored remains of 16th-cent. chancel screen.

GARTON-ON-THE-WOLDS (*St. Michael*)
Norman aisleless church with Perp. chancel; restored and lavishly decorated by G. E. Street, 1872–80; altar frontal by C. E. Kempe.

GOODMANHAM *(*All Saints*)
Simple village church on reputed site of Coifi's heathen temple. 12th-century nave and lower stages of squat W. tower. 13th-century N. aisle and rebuilt chancel. 15th-century belfry and battlements to tower. Low narrow Norman chancel arch. Fine 16th-century octagonal font, similar to that at St. Mary, Beverley, with canopies and shields, standing beside earlier hexagonal one.

GREAT DRIFFIELD (*All Saints*)
Fine 15th-cent. tower; restoration by Sir G. G. Scott and chancel, etc.; rebuilt 1879–80.

GRIMSTON, NORTH: *see North Grimston.*

HALSHAM (*All Saints*)
Curious stone seat beside sedilia; rebuilt Constable chapel in 17th-cent. brick contains alabaster monument.

HARPHAM *(*St. John of Beverley*)
Norman core but completely remodelled in 14th century. Bold W. tower rising above village, and seen from Wolds stands out

against Plain of Holderness. E. end of chancel rebuilt in brick, 1827. Conservative restoration by Temple Moore, 1908–14, when Georgian fittings were retained. Altar rails dated 1726. 17th-century brick porch. Fine collection of medieval and 18th-century monuments to St. Quintin family in N. chapel, including two brasses. Monument N. of sanctuary signed J. Wilton to Charlotte St. Quintin, 1762. Windows of N. chapel have 18th-century heraldic glass by William Peckitt of York.

HAYTON (*St. Martin*)
Trans. arcade with carved 'bell'-capitals; old roofs.

HEDON *(*St. Augustine*)
The 'King of Holderness'. Focal point of small market town. Early English transepts and chancel with Perpendicular E. window. Vestry on S. with Early English arcading on interior W. wall. 15th-century central tower. Fine elevation to N. transept – grouped lancets and recessed doorway, with much display of dog-tooth. Restored and S. transept rebuilt, 1866–8 by G. E. Street. Decorated nave with Recticulated windows, except two W., which are Flamboyant. 14th-century font (compare Holy Trinity, Hull). Elizabethan Royal Arms, 1585.

HELPERTHORPE (*St. Peter*) GR
G. E. Street, 1874–5; windows Clayton and Bell.

HEMINGBOROUGH *(*St. Mary*)
Spacious, light cruciform structure at right angles to village street. Formerly Collegiate. Beautiful, white Tadcaster stone. Low central tower with disproportionately tall spire. Work of 13th and 15th centuries. Decorated chancel with ugly E. window. Tudor S. aisle with clustered shafts and four-centred arches to arcades. Lofty transepts lit by large Perpendicular windows. Medieval parclose screens formerly surmounted by unique Elizabethan cresting. Misericords. 16th-century bench-ends in nave showing Gothic and Renaissance motifs. Early 18th-century pulpit. Hatchment to Dame Lennox Pilkington, frame decorated with skulls and crossbones. Restorations by Ewan Christian, 1885–6, and by Walter Brierly, 1893.

HESLERTON, EAST: *see East Heslerton.*

HESSLE (*All Saints*)
13th-cent. arcade and S. doorway; pretty 15th-cent. stone spire.

HILSTON *(St. Margaret of Scotland)
Simple, modern church by Francis Johnson, set against cold, open sky, and approached by undulating Holderness lane, with hedgerow trees. Interior is sympathetic rendering of Anglican tradition. Very colourful E. window by L. C. Evetts, which with bowed rails and pall frontal exhibits badge and symbols of patron saint. Re-used 12th-century doorway from original church.

HOLME-UPON-SPALDINGMOOR
  *(All Saints)
Position on crest of island hill rising from dead level plain four miles W. of Wold scarp. Pierced, battlemented 15th-century tower emerges from tufted tree-tops and provides landmark for surrounding area. Mainly 15th and 16th centuries with 17th-century brick parapets and porch. Use of variegated stones in fabric indicates complex geological nature of region. Charming unspoilt interior with considerable remains of medieval screen, Jacobean pulpit with tester, 18th-century gallery housing 17th-century barrel-organ by J. Hunton of York, early 19th-century 'Gothic' pews. 15th-century roofs; crown glass; Elizabethan black-letter texts on E. wall. In tower niche ancient crowned figure holding souls in sheet. Restoration by Temple Moore, 1906–11.

HORNSEA (St. Nicholas)
Perp. restored by Sir G. G. Scott, 1867; St. Quintin tomb; effigies and 17th-cent. brass, signed G. Hornbie formerly at Nunkeeling.

HOWDEN *(St. Peter)
Large cruciform church with central tower, dominating small market town and surrounding flat country. 13th-century transepts and nave with W. front (compare E. front of Selby Abbey) finished in first decade of 14th century. Geometric W. window flanked by pierced hexagonal turrets. 14th-century choir of collegiate church, collapsed in 1696, and has been left in ruins. Roofless octagonal chapter house entered through ogee-headed doorway is Perpendicular, and displays arms of Bishop Skirlaw. Central tower built in two stages, spoiled with ugly and incongruous modern roof. 15th-century stone pulpitum with medieval statues gathered from church. Metham and Saltmarshe tombs. Fragmentary brasses nailed to wall, one of knight in plate armour.

HOWSHAM (St. John) GR
G. E. Street, 1860.

HULL: see Kingston-upon-Hull.

HUMBLETON (St. Peter & St. Paul)
13th and 15th cent.; curious tower stair.

HUNMANBY (All Saints)
Very fine Osbaldeston monument, 1770, in chancel by J. Fisher of York; early 19th-cent. fittings; interesting Staveley monument.

HUTTON CRANSWICK (St. Peter, formerly St. Andrew)
Norman S. doorway and chancel arch.

KEXBY (St. Paul) GR
F. C. Penrose, 1852; restored 1924, John Bilson.

KEYINGHAM (St. Nicholas)
Norman core with later medieval additions and reconstruction; low broach spire; iron hour glass stand near pulpit.

KILHAM (All Saints)
Barrack-like Norman nave and S. door; 14th-cent. chancel arch; heraldry; 'Gothick' windows to nave.

KILNWICK-ON-THE-WOLDS (All Saints)
Late 17th-cent. pulpit; Grimston monuments by H. Cheere and J. Fisher.

KILNWICK PERCY (St. Helen)
Norman cleverly reconstructed in 1865; brass of 1584.

KINGSTON-UPON-HULL (St. Augustine) GR
G. G. Scott, jnr., and Temple Moore, 1892.

*(Holy Trinity)
'High' Church. Cruciform town church. Position in market-place with stalls round churchyard walls on market days. Some of earliest medieval brickwork in Decorated choir and transepts. Central tower and nave 15th century. Tall, slender pillars with skimped bands of ornament in place of capitals. Walls are mere screens for glass. Repetition of tracery is monotonous. Much old screenwork, magnificent 18th-century Rococo altar and reredos; good 19th-century pewing with poppy heads. Remains of chantries, some with old glass, a carved Trinity and a votive ship. De la Pole tombs, 15th-century brass, and magnificent ledger stones in choir. Huge 14th-century font (compare Hedon) of different coloured marbles. Church heavily restored by Sir

G. G. Scott, 1842–69, and less so by F. S. Brodrick, 1907.

*(St. Mary)
'Low' church. Small truncated 15th-century town church built in two phases with continuous clerestory. This and nave details imitate those at Holy Trinity. 17th-century brick tower encased with whole of exterior in ashlar, 1860–3 by G. G. Scott, who added second S. aisle. The result is a forest of pillars. Pewing and pulpit by Scott, windows by Clayton and Bell. Striking rood and screens to Temple Moore's design. Tudor wall brass to John Haryson, 1525 and two wives. Dobson monument, 1666, over N. door. Shields of medieval glass in E. window. Atmosphere of constant use and affectionate care.

(St. Nicholas) GR
J. Bilson, 1914.

(St. Andrew, Drypool) GR
Adams and Kelly; very interesting Victorian Royal Arms; 1878.

(St. John, Drypool) GR
T. L. Moore, 1925

(All Saints, Sculcoates) GR
G. E. Street, 1869.

*(St. Mary, Sculcoates) GR
T. L. Moore, 1916, N. aisle contains furnishings and part of structure of demolished 18th-century 'Gothick' church. Includes Tuscan columns from arcades, ledger stones and chandelier. In main church, fine fossil marble font with copper cover. Many 18th and 19th century monuments including several by Hull sculptors, Thomas and John Earle, and one to Mrs. Delmotte in Byrom shorthand.

(St. Paul, Sculcoates) GR
W. H. Dykes, 1896.

KIRBY GRINDALYTHE (St. Andrew)
Rebuilt except for tower by G. E. Street, 1878.

KIRBY UNDERDALE (All Saints)
Setting; 12th-cent. church lovingly restored for Lord Halifax.

KIRKBURN (St. Mary)
Aisleless Norman nave; chancel rebuilt 1856 by J. L. Pearson; later work including reredos by G. E. Street.

KIRK ELLA (St. Andrew)
13th-cent. church; remains of 14th-cent. screenwork.

LANGTOFT (St. Peter)
14th-cent. Flamboyant chancel with canopied sedilia; sculptured Norman font formerly at Cottam.

LANGTON (St. Andrew)
Renaissance monument to Mary Ingram, 1656, N. of sanctuary.

LECONFIELD (All Saints)
Chiefly 13th and 14th cent.; pleasant post-Reformation brick tower; 14th-cent. heraldic glass.

LEVEN (Holy Trinity anciently St. Faith)
GR
R. D. Chantrell, 1843–5; head of Janus cross.

LOCKINGTON *(St. Mary)
Unusually interesting church of well-kept, unspoilt village. Approached by narrow, winding lane crossing ford, with 17th-century brick Estoft manor-house, and ancient motte beyond. Small brick, post-Gothic tower. Chancel rebuilt in Decorated times, with Recticulated E. window. Mutilated remains of Norman chancel arch, cut away and space above filled with screen-work by Temple Moore, 1893. Made-up W. screen of 18th-century woodwork. Estoft chapel on S. panelled, 1634, panels emblazoned with Estoft arms and those of family alliances. Wall monument to John Estoft, 1694 and chest-tomb with crude reclining effigy of Mary Moyser, 1633. S. Norman doorway cut away to incorporate later niche.

LONDESBOROUGH (All Saints)
12th–14th cent.; tower has Tudor belfry; funeral banners of Earls of Burlington; chrysom child of 1619; churchyard cross by Temple Moore, 1885.

LOWTHORPE (St. Martin)
Former collegiate church; 14th-cent. chancel in ruins; curious monument; signed brass by C. Mann, 1665 (see Rudston).

LUND (All Saints)
Mutilated monuments; 12th-cent. font.

LUTTONS AMBO (St. Mary the Virgin)
GR
G. E. Street, 1874–5; glass and triptych by J. Burlison and T. J. Grylls; screen by J. Potter.

MAPPLETON (All Saints)
14th and 15th cent.; badly restored; 14th-cent. octagonal font with heraldry.

MARKET WEIGHTON (*All Saints*)
Saxon and later tower with 17th-century top in brick; window stonework by Temple Moore, 1899.

MIDDLETON-ON-WOLDS (*St. Andrew*)
Fine 13th-cent. church; 12th-cent. font.

NAFFERTON (*All Saints*)
Rebuilt Norman chancel arch and font; old roofs and box-pews.

NORTH CAVE (*All Saints*)
Cruciform; Dec.; Elizabethan effigies.

NORTH DALTON (*All Saints*)
12th, 13th and 15th cent.; Norman font and arch; tower similar to Boynton and Carnaby.

NORTH FERRIBY (*All Saints*) GR
J. L. Pearson, 1846; Lillington monument N. of sanctuary by Edward Stanton, 1713.

NORTH GRIMSTON (*St. Nicholas*)
Norman chancel arch and font, with crude carvings of Last Supper, Descent from the Cross and St. Nicholas.

NORTH NEWBALD *(St. Nicholas*)
Austere aisleless 12th-century church situated beneath W. scarp of Wolds. Perhaps finest Norman church in E. Riding. Lower part of tower with its arches is Norman. To this Early English belfry added, surmounted by 15th-century battlements. In same century chancel rebuilt. S. doorway of four orders with vesica niche containing seated Majesty, mainly original. 13th-century circular font, carved with conventional foliage, and 17th-century cover. Wall monument to cavalier Sir Philip Monckton, 1679.

NORTON (*St. Peter, anciently All Saints*) GR
C. Hodgson Fowler, 1899–1911.

NUNBURNHOLME (*St. James*)
Setting in valley; Norman tower arch; modern tower.

OTTRINGHAM *(St. Wilfrid*)
At W. end of village street. Much rebuilding in 13th and 14th centuries, with clerestory added in 15th century. At W. beautiful 14th-century tower carries lofty broach spire, the broaches being very slight, and the whole having a very satisfying outline. The tower arch with zig-zag is 12th century. Stone Gospel lectern. Box-pews. 19th-century pen altar rails.

PATRINGTON *(St. Patrick*)
The 'Queen of Holderness'. Cruciform church of exceptional beauty with double-aisled transepts, and central tower, crowned by open corona from which rises lofty spire, a landmark for Holderness and N. Lincolnshire. Almost entirely in Decorated style, with Flamboyant tracery to aisle windows, and carved foliated capitals to nave. Slight indications of succeeding style in E. window. Rose window in S. gable. Unusual staircase, like crow-stepped gable over S. arch of crossing. Reredos to Lady Altar in central bay, with pendant, carved with Annunciation for lamp. Medieval screen restored by F. S. Brodrick, 1891. 17th-century pulpit. Easter Sepulchre. Modern gilded reredos by Harold Gibbons in memory of King George V, who was Lord of Manor.

PAULL (*St. Andrew*)
Cruciform; Perp.; stone gospel lectern; 14th-cent. glass.

POCKLINGTON (*All Saints*)
Cruciform; 12th–15th cent. Janus crosshead; monuments; stone gospel lectern.

PRESTON (*All Saints*)
Striking 15th-cent. tower; alabaster fragments of two medieval reredoses, shewing traces of colour.

REIGHTON (*St. Peter*)
Norman and E.E. exterior heavily restored; charming interior; floor of chalk cobbles under tower; square Norman font like Roman altar.

RICCALL (*St. Mary*)
Chiefly 12th and 14th cent.; Norman S. doorway of three recessed orders with unusual figure carvings on voussoirs; twin tower arches.

RILLINGTON (*St. Andrew*)
Pretty spire of Malton group; Trans. font with 17th-cent. cover; old roofs; 18th-cent. monuments to faithful servants.

RISE (*All Saints anciently St. Mary*) GR
R. D. Chantrell, 1844–5; good 18th-cent. wall tablets.

ROOS (*All Saints*)
Approach flanked by clipped yews; 13th–15th cent.; 14th-cent. sacristy with room over; old glass.

ROUTH (*All Saints*)
13th cent. and later; canopied brass, 1420.

RUDSTON (*All Saints*)
Norman and Dec.; restored by Fowler Jones 1861.

RUSTON PARVA (*St. Nicholas*) GR
Tiny Gothic fabric, dated 1832; box-pews.

SANCTON (*All Saints*)
15th-cent. octagonal tower; *cf.* Coxwold, N.R.

SCAMPSTON (*St. Martin*) GR
Small 19th-century 'Decorated' church by G. T. Andrews, the Railway King's architect.

SCORBOROUGH (*St. Leonard*) GR
Rebuilt 1859, J. L. Pearson; priest slab carved in low relief.

SCRAYINGHAM (*St. Peter and St. Paul*)
Rebuilt 1853; position at end of long village; churchyard contains tomb of George Hudson, the Railway King.

SEATON ROSS (*St. Edmund*) CL
18th-cent. Classic; tower dated 1788, restored by Temple Moore, 1908.

SETTRINGTON (*All Saints*)
Setting; Norman refashioned 12th–15th cent.; old glass; brass to John Carter, *d.* 1666, ejected Rector.

SEWERBY *(St. John the Evangelist)*
On fringe of park. 1847. Charming essay in Norman by Scott and Moffatt. Honey-coloured ashlar, richly and crisply detailed throughout. Nave, chancel and spire, with N. transept, formerly Squire's pew. Victorian Royal Arms in relief. 'Aylesbury' font. 'Gothic' box-pews. Interior recently lightened and coloured by Francis Johnson.

SHERBURN (*St. Hilda*)
Norman with late 13th-cent. arcades and 14th-cent. chancel; Norman chancel arch and S. doorway; much restored.

SHIPTONTHORPE (*All Saints*)
Norman and Perp.; restored by James Demaine, 1883.

SIGGLESTHORNE (*St. Lawrence*)
Chiefly 13th cent.; plate tracery in tower; good 18th-century wall monuments.

SKEFFLING (*St. Helen*)
15th cent. Interesting monuments to Holme family by J. Rushworth of Beverley; good roofs to nave and chancel.

SKERNE (*St. Leonard*)
12th cent. and later; Norman chancel arch and S. doorway; curious monuments built into N. wall. 17th-century roofs.

SKIPSEA *(All Saints*)
On mound backed by trees, in almost circular churchyard; built mainly of cobbles, away from brick and cobble village. S. aisle added in Perpendicular times of white Tadcaster stone. Church built on fringe of earthworks known as the 'Brough', among which motte of destroyed castle is prominent. Church principally 13th century with Reticulated E. window and Perpendicular clerestory to nave. Parapet of tower gives impression of slight hog's back. Monument by Earle of Hull. Restored by James Fowler, 1865–6.

SKIPWITH (*St. Helen*)
Lower stages of tower show 'long and short work'; restored 15th-cent. screen; modern glass by Nicholson studios, harmonizing with old.

SKIRLAUGH (*St. Augustine*)
Perp. chapel, scraped and gutted in 19th cent.; figured in A. W. Pugin's *Contrasts*.

SLEDMERE (*St. Mary*) GR
Temple Moore, 1898; medieval tower much restored; one of the best village churches in Yorkshire.

SPEETON (*St. Leonard*)
Austere and gaunt position in middle of field, near edge of high chalk cliffs; Norman chancel arch and font; medieval alms-box and crude niche.

STILLINGFLEET (*St. Helen*)
Norman S. doorway of five recessed orders with similar carvings to Riccall; very early decorative ironwork on door.

SWINE *(St. Mary*)
Quite lovely fragment of priory of Cistercian nuns. Chancel of former cruciform church, to which tower was added in late 18th century. Transitional arcades. Aisles have square-headed 14th-century windows. Important early 16th-century screen between Hilton chapel and aisle. Shows incipient Renaissance feeling in fenestration and has the pomegranate, the badge of Katherine of Aragon. Also carved misericords. Fine collection of alabaster altar tombs with five effigies. Very elegant rococo 'Gothick' font, contemporary with tower.

THWING (*All Saints*)
Sculptured tympanum to S. door with carved Agnus Dei.

TUNSTALL (*All Saints*)
Large village church of cobbles, interesting font.

WALKINGTON (*All Hallows*)
Spacious 12th-cent. church with Perpendicular detail; engraved chalice slab to Christopher Wilson; some late foreign glass.

WARTER (*St. James*) GR
W. G. Habershon & A. R. Pite, 1862/2.

WATTON (*St. Mary*)
16th cent. brick church.

WAWNE (*St. Peter*)
13th cent. with fine Perpendicular W. tower, built over most westerly bay of N. aisle. Perpendicular brick clerestory.

WEAVERTHORPE *(*St. Andrew*)
Early Norman church built by Herbert the Chamberlain between 1108 and 1121. Exhibits pre-Conquest features. Dedication together with that of several Wold churches suggests activities of Celtic missionaries. N. aisle added and rest restored by G. E. St. Street, 1871–2. Screen by T. Potter, glass and triptych by Clayton and Bell. Striking position on flank of Wolds overlooking mid-Wold valley.

WELTON (*St. Helen*)
Setting; almost rebuilt by G. G. Scott, 1863.

WELWICK *(*St. Mary*)
14th century remodelling of early Norman church to which clerestory was added in 15th century. 17th-century brick porch. Light, pleasing interior, with open space at W. end. Curious four-light window in chancel fitted beneath hood for three lights. Flamboyant tracery. Jacobean pulpit. Much restored chancel screen. Good, simple modern pewing. Brass to William Wright of Ploughland, brother of two Gunpowder Plotters. Tomb with effigy of medieval priest, beneath much patched canopy.

WETWANG (*St. Nicholas*)
12th and 13th cent.; very well restored with good modern woodwork.

WHARRAM-LE-STREET (*St. Mary*)
Interesting unrestored early Norman tower; 18th cent. altar table in N. aisle.

WINESTEAD *(*St. Germain*)
Situation amidst meadows in secluded position away from road and village. Tiny 12th-century chancel and nave, with remains of corbel table on S. aisle added S. of nave in 14th century. Strong resemblance to Barmston. Hildyard chapel on S. added in 17th century. Rebuilt 1893 by T. L. Moore who re-used Italianate panels bearing trophies of arms. Screened from church by panelling of former Hildyard pew. 18th-century pulpit and restored medieval screen similar to that at Welwick. Palimpsest brass to Sir Christopher Hildyard (Robin of Redesdale). Jacobean altar tomb to Sir Christopher Hildyard ii. 18th-century monuments in chapel.

WINTRINGHAM *(*St. Peter*)
Setting in dell of Wolds away from village of white-washed cottages. 12th-century chancel with later windows, and Norman corbel tables. 14th-century nave and aisles with W. tower and spire of Malton group. Arcades without capitals and windows of aisles have square heads, upper lights of which contain a galaxy of saints in 15th-century glass. Medieval altar slab in S. aisle. Perpendicular parclose screens at E. ends of aisles. Jacobean pewing, two-decker pulpit and alms box. Rhyming acrostic memorial to John Lister, d. 1651. Much heraldry on tower. Beautifully restored by T. L. Moore.

WITHERNSEA (*St. Nicholas*)
Good restoration, 1859, of derelict medieval church.

WOLD NEWTON (*All Saints*)
Untouched Norman S. doorway with carved tympanum; painted Victorian Royal Arms, 1839.

WRESSELL (*St. John of Beverley*) GR
1799; delightful brick Gothick exterior; interior refurnished and windows replaced 1873.

Yorkshire: the North Riding

and YORK CITY

INTRODUCTION

LIKE CAESAR'S Gaul, it divides into three parts: a central plain, bounded on either side by moorland sloping off into dales. Here is some of Yorkshire's noblest scenery. The western dales, Wensleydale and Swaledale, has each its own ruined abbey, castle and group of waterfalls. On the opposite side, moorland runs as far east as the sea, with villages few and scattered. Churches are isolated, and so often locked that the visitor needs to be adept at hunting for the key in unlikely places.

In the Riding generally there is much pre-Conquest work. Kirkdale has a Saxon nave and sundial. Fifty-two churches possess sculptured crosses, complete or fragmentary. Norman doorways and chancel arches have survived many a later reconstruction. Lastingham is a place of pilgrimage because of its Norman crypt and links with SS. Cedd and Chad. In the north-west, Wensleydale takes pride of place for churches as well as for cheese. Decorated is represented by Patrick Brompton and Ainderby Steeple, Perpendicular by Burneston. Old Malton has the nave of a Gilbertine priory serving as the parish church.

For grandeur it is the town churches which score – Bedale, Northallerton and Thirsk. There are few brasses (Wensley and Topcliffe have Flemish ones), but an abundance of 14th-century stone effigies. Admirers of 18th-century 'churchwarden' will enjoy themselves in Cleveland. Ingleby Arncliffe has been tidied up, but Yarm, Stokesley, and of course Whitby, must be allowed to stand as museum-pieces. At Kirkleatham the body of the church was rebuilt in 1763 and the magnificent almshouse chapel in 1742. Castle Howard, by Vanbrugh, is the Riding's conventional show-place. The chapel has memorable 19th-century decorations and glass.

The Victorian builders had their fling on Tees-side, with happier results than in Leeds or Sheffield. Thanks to Viscount Downe, Butterfield was commissioned to build an entire village, consisting of church, vicarage, schools and cottages, at Baldersby. Pearson may be studied in a French mood at Appleton-le-Moors. His friend and admirer, Temple Moore, did scholarly restoration work throughout the Riding, and new building in and around Middlesbrough. Of late, woodcarver Robert Thompson has been making Kilburn better known for mice than for white horses.

412

In York itself, twenty old churches survive from a 16th-century total of forty-one. For size they have nothing to compare with St. Margaret's and St. Nicholas', King's Lynn, or even with St. Peter Mancroft, Norwich, so completely is York overshadowed by the Minster. A forlorn atmosphere pervades them, nor is the hand of the philistine yet stayed. But they are all worth seeing, not least for their glass, which escaped destruction in the Civil War through the decency of Fairfax. In design the city churches show a certain uniformity; most are parallelograms with towers engaged inside the aisles. The best reconstruction of a medieval interior is at All Saints, North Street; with the possible exception of St. Mary's, Lowgate, Hull, no other church in Yorkshire so vividly preserves the spirit of medieval England.

D.R.

SELECTED LIST OF CHURCHES

by *George G. Pace*, F.S.A., F.R.I.B.A.

AINDERBY STEEPLE (*St. Helen*)
14th-cent. chancel restored in 1870; compare with Patrick Brompton and Kirkby Wiske.

ALDWARK *(*St. Stephen*)
Its architect, E. B. Lamb (1846) was the *bête noire* of the Ecclesiologists and is numbered amongst Goodhart Rendel's gallery of 'Rogue Architects'. The plan of the church is unusual yet effective both within and without. The external walling is rich in texture and colour, being a con-glomeration of pebble-stones, herringbone brickwork and freestone dressings. There is an elaborate roof of open timbering. The almost detached tower and spire form a composition typical of the architect.

ALLERSTON (*St. John*)
Well sited with moors behind; good 15th-cent. tower.

ALNE *(*St. Mary*)
The tower has a medieval ground stage and Renaissance upper stages in brick finished with obelisks at the angles of the parapet. The S. doorway with two orders of medal-lions, and the font, are good Norman work. Very odd reticulated tracery is found in the E. window of the N. chapel. The nave and N. aisle are mostly of 15th-century date and of the local wide and low proportions (compare Crayke). The yellow washed

plastered walls of the church form a good background to the Norman tower arch and the Jacobean pulpit. The ground stage of the tower, shut off behind an indifferent Gothic screen (20th century), contains pleasant 18th-century panelling, a homely brick floor and an exquisite cartouche (1695). The 20th-century screens are un-satisfactory, but the 19th-century tile flooring of the chancel, together with Kempe glass in the E. window and the S. side of the nave show a higher standard of design.

AMPLEFORTH (*St. Hilda*)
Sited on a steep hummock with fine view over the Vale of Pickering; 15th-cent. tower; military effigy, *c.* 1330.

APPLETON-LE-MOORS
  *(*Christ Church*)
A church finely conceived within and without by J. L. Pearson, 1863. The exterior is particularly satisfying, the W. front, the almost detached tower and spire and the apsidal chancel being its high lights. There is much competent French detail, but the tower up to belfry stage displays fully developed Pearsonic traits – which are best studied from the S.E. corner of the churchyard. Around the vestry door and the window of the N. chapel is much fanciful detail. The interior shows rich and effective use of ironwork and glass, quite

definitely of the 19th century and the work of a real architect.

APPLETON-LE-STREET (*All Saints*)
Good pre-Conquest tower.

APPLETON WISKE (*St. Mary*)
Good Norman chancel arch; inscribed board to woman churchwarden, 1687.

ARKENGARTHDALE (*St. Mary*) GR
1818; setting.

ASKRIGG (*St. Oswald*)
Mainly 15th and early 16th cent; heavily Victorianised.

AYSGARTH (*St. Andrew*)
Eviscerated in 19th cent., Green of Todmorden; 15th-cent. screen and stall ends (Ripon school?) brought from Jervaulx Abbey; 19th-cent. pews, font and glass; deadly 20th-cent. pulpit; some interesting headstones and yard tombs.

AYTON, GREAT: *see Great Ayton.*

BALDERSBY *(St. James*)
The whole hamlet – church, school and cottages – is the work of William Butterfield, 1857. Comparison with the architect's somewhat similar commissions for Viscount Downe at Hensall, Pollington and Cowick in the West Riding is inevitable. Without doubt Baldersby church is the finest. The churchyard is entered through a spidery lychgate. Many of the headstones follow the lead given in *Instrumenta Ecclesiastica.* The almost detached tower and spire is a development of the architect's work at All Saints, Margaret Street. For a Butterfield church the interior is elegantly detailed. The font and its cover, the pews, the dwarf wall at the entrance to the chancel, the clock face and the alabaster reredos all repay close study. In the impressive chancel floor is set the well-designed brass cross of the Founder's memorial. The chancel roof has a curious cusped arched principal reminiscent of St. Clement's, City Road.

BARTON (*St. Cuthbert with St. Mary*) GR
I. Bonimi, 1841; restored, 1910.

BARTON-LE-STREET (*St. Michael & All Angels*)
Perkin and Sons, Leeds, 1870–1; fine Norman stones from demolished church built into the structure; 19th-cent. 'Norman' has character of own.

BEDALE *(St. Gregory*)
The great semi-fortified W. tower of the church and the huge garden wall of the house opposite, hem in the road and form a striking termination at the head of the town's wide main street, with its cobbled sides and market cross. The S. entrance to the churchyard is through a gate flanked by well detailed 18th-century stone piers. In the churchyard are baluster table tombs of a local type and the particularly lush Neo-Grec. monument to Nancy Day. The W. tower with its deeply set windows and the masterly handling of the stair turret is impressive. The S. porch has a pointed ribbed barrel vault, covered externally with stone slabs. There are delicate 18th-century lead rainwater heads to the S. aisle and an interesting 20th-century wrought-iron gate to the crypt. The nave has a simple but effective clerestory. There are several 14th-cent. tombs; an 18th-century Creed and Lord's Prayer above the chancel arch and in the S. aisle a mural tablet by R. Westmacott to Henry Peirse.

BOLTON-ON-SWALE (*St. Mary*)
16th cent. restored; elaborate N. chapel.

BOSSALL *(St. Botolph*)
A cruciform church with central tower, mostly of 12th century. The chancel was rebuilt in the 13th century. Externally the stonework has scale and texture, but not so the interior, sadly stripped of plaster and the joints emphasized by bad pointing. There is a fine corbel course under the eaves of the nave and transepts. The domesticated early 19th-century S. porch floored with brick shelters a superb 13th-century doorway. Inside the church the arches and piers of the crossing are the outstanding feature, but the full effect is lost by the heartless treatment of the wall faces. In the N. transept windows there is very effective clear glazing. The Royal Arms (1760) has a marbled wood frame. There is a simple but effective 18th-century font cover, an exuberant 20th-century oak reredos and really good glass in some of the chancel windows (Kempe?). The church as a composition should be compared with Chipstead, Surrey, and Church Fenton (West Riding).

BOWES (*St. Giles*)
Saxon and Norman work; font rests on inscribed Roman altar stone.

BRAFFERTON (*St. Augustine or St. Peter*) GR
Nave rebuilt, 1832, J. P. Prichett; tower and chancel 15th cent.

BRANDSBY *(All Saints)
The church stands in undulating and well-wooded country. The architect was Thomas Atkinson and the builder Richard Scurr (1767-70). Outside, the classical detail is a trifle heavy, excepting the stone cupola poised imaginatively over the body of the church. Entry lies through a narthex in which stands an 18th-century baluster font. The door to the nave is protected by a wrought-iron grille. In the body of the church stand four Roman Doric columns connected by plaster cross vaults and forming the base supports of the cupola. The architectural effect is beyond praise. There is plenty of free floor space, a well-detailed W. gallery, good early 20th-century furniture and a successful brass lectern.

BROMPTON-BY-SAWDON (All Saints)
14th-15th cent. with broach spire; organ case by Temple Moore.

BROMPTON - IN - ALLERTONSHIRE
(St. Thomas) GR
Eviscerated in 19th cent.; magnificent collection of hogsbacks and pre-Conquest fragments.

BROTTON, OLD CHURCH (St. Margaret) CL
1778; Cleveland churchwarden classical.

NEW CHURCH (St. Margaret) GR
W. S. Hicks, 1888-91; 'Perp. manner'.

BULMER (St. Martin)
Late 11th-cent. core; notable texture of N. wall.

BURNESTON (St. Lambert)
Stately 15th-cent. exterior with good buttresses, pinnacles and clerestory range.

BYLAND, OLD: see Old Byland.

CARLTON-IN-CLEVELAND
(St. Botolph)
The church was built in 1896-7, the architect being Temple Moor. It is the conception of an architect at once alive to the needs of a small village church and sensitive to the local medieval regional characteristics. The tower stands within the body of the church. The vaulted ground stage carrying an open gallery is a fine conception. On a lesser plane, the furnishings are characteristic. The lychgate will be found to be full of subtleties in design and in the use of materials.

CARLTON HUSTHWAITE (St. Mary)
Pulpit with sounding board, 1678; 17th-cent. bobbin-ended pews.

CASTLETON (St. George) GR
Leslie Moore, 1925, with characteristic fittings.

CATTERICK (St. Ann)
Mostly c. 1412, the Master Mason being Richard of Cracall; brasses, 15th cent.

COVERHAM (Holy Trinity)
14th-15th cent. fabric; heraldic glass.

COWESBY (St. Michael & All Angels) GR
Setting; East Moors. Temple Moore, 1882.

COWTON, SOUTH: see South Cowton.

COXWOLD *(St. Michael)
The village street climbing a steep hill, with the church at its summit, forms a natural unity. With the exception of the chancel, rebuilt in 1777, the stately exterior is of 15th-century date. Regional characteristics abound. The tower is octagonal (compare with Sancton, East Riding). The buttresses and pinnacles are similar to those on the tower of St. Martin-le-Grand, York, and display an equally effortless subtlety in design. Inside, 17th and 18th centuries have left their delightful mark – the W. gallery, the plaster work on the E. wall of the nave, the box-pews, the pulpit and the monuments in the chancel. Owing to the narrowness of the chancel the communion rail is extended down its length, to leave room on either side for the enormous Fauconberg tombs (compare Fari Church, Venice). There is much fragmentary 15th-century glass.

CRAYKE *(St. Cuthbert)
Church and castle are at the top of a hill overlooking the Plain of York. The structure is mostly of 15th-century date. The wide and squat nave and N. aisle should be compared with Alne. Both nave and chancel have heavily timbered 15th-century roofs. There is a poor chancel screen (restored) of like date. The church has excellent pews, clerk's desk, churchwarden seats, pulpit (1637), font cover and chancel chairs all of 17th-century work.

CROFT *(St. Peter)
The church stands near the bank of the Tees. It is a long low building of a colourful stone of good texture and well weathered. The 14th-century chancel has good buttresses and tracery. Built into the S. wall is a piece of Romano-British sculpture representing a local deity. The interior is made interesting by the varying light in different parts and by the elevated

Milbank pew of the local family which provided Byron with a wife. The 14th-century piscina and sedilia, the monument of Sir Richard Clervaulx and the ostentatious Milbanke tomb should be studied.

DALBY (*St. Peter*)
Attractive plaster barrel vault to chancel.

DANBY-IN-CLEVELAND *(*St. Hilda*)
The church stands in an isolated position in fine rolling country. The detached 15th-century tower of warm stone is placed on the S. side. Its ground stage is a porch entered through an elegant white painted wood gate of early 19th-century date. The nave was classicised in the 18th century and medievalised by Temple Moore in 1903 – working with his usual imagination. The 18th-century W. gallery has been retained and is approached by external stone steps. The poor, mean chancel was built in 1848. There is a Royal Arms of George IV and a good series of 17th and 18th century monuments in the churchyard.

DANBY WISKE (*All Saints*)
Massive W. tower; 11th-cent. carved tympanum; 17th-cent. furniture.

DORMANSTOWN (*All Saints*) GR
Leslie Moore, 1932; personal gothic characteristic rood-screen – compare St. Hilda Shiregreen, Sheffield, before alteration.

DOWNHOLME *(*St. Michael*)
A small rural church perched high up on the south side of Swaledale. There is a stone-walled and grey stone-roofed building in the churchyard, possibly for stabling the worshippers' horses. The outside of the S. side of the church has suffered much in the 19th century but the 17th-century porch, the rood-loft window and a delightful domestic type window (like another in Marske Church dated 1638) remain. The fine texture and weathering of the N. wall and the plate tracery should receive more than a glance. Inside all is homely and yellow wash. The font is of interest. In the spandrels of the arcades are 18th-century painted texts. Many of the windows have clear glass in rectangular quarries. There are hatchments in the N. aisle, box-pews in the chancel, two stoves and a fearsome 20th-century pulpit.

EASBY *(*St. Agatha*)
The church is close to the ruins of the abbey, commanding a panoramic view of Richmond. On the hill above stands Easby Hall. In the churchyard notice some 18th-century monuments and a 20th-century bronze tablet. The church is long and low and of beautiful weathered stone. There is a double bell-cote, S. porch with a room over, an early 14th-century E. window and a 15th-century S. aisle. Within the S. porch the walls and plaster barrel vault are yellow washed. Inside the church has a lively atmosphere. Note the Norman font, the 19th-century nave roof with its unusual corbels, some excellent 19th-century nave pewing, the wall-painting (carefully restored by Scott) throughout the church, the hatchments and the 19th-century chancel arch. In the chancel the free floor space, the cast of the 7th-century cross, the glass in the E. window and the local needlework on the door curtain should be appreciated; together with the mid-19th century seating and other delights in the S. aisle.

EASINGWOLD (*St. John the Baptist & All Saints*)
15th-cent. arcades compare with Stillington and St. Denys, York; parish coffin.

EAST GILLING (*The Holy Cross*)
Setting; arcades Trans.; aisles and chancel 14th cent.; tower 15th cent.

EAST HARSLEY (*St. Oswald*)
Setting; double incised mural slab.

EAST ROUNTON (*St. Lawrence*) GR
R. J. Johnson, 1884; good 20th-cent. furnishings; Renaissance woodwork re-used in chancel.

EBBERSTON (*St. Mary the Virgin*)
Setting; restored by Ewan Christian, 1879; 12th–14th cent.

ELLERBURNE (*St. Hilda*)
Medieval; 17th–18th cent. fittings; careful restoration by W. D. Caröe, 1905.

FEETHAM (*Holy Trinity*) CL
Setting; rustic domestic type with cottage-like 'Narthex'.

FELIXKIRK (*St. Felix*)
Mostly 11th cent.; apse rebuilt; extensive restoration by R. H. Dykes; large German organ.

FOSTON (*All Saints*)
Norman doorways; Sydney Smith plaque.

GOATHLAND (*The Blessed Virgin Mary*) GR
Early 20th cent.; W. H. Brierley.

GREAT AYTON *(All Saints)
The church has been unloved since the building of Christ Church in 1876 (Ross and Lamb). The stonework of the old church is of the warm local stone beautifully textured and weathered. The tower was demolished, c. 1880. There is an altogether delightful mixture of Norman and of the 18th century churchwarden classical so popular in Cleveland. The furniture of 1790 included a three-decker complete with sounding board. If the insipidness of Christ Church, 1876, can be borne, fragments of three Saxon crosses may be seen.

GREAT THIRKLEBY (All Saints) GR
E. B. Lamb, 1850; amateur stained glass by Lady Falkland.

GRINTON *(St. Andrew)
A great grey, harsh church growing naturally out of Swaledale. The exterior is chiefly remarkable for its austerity and the almost domestic character of its windows. At the W. end of the nave there is an effective area of free floor, an early font carrying a 15th-century oak cover, with a sturdily moulded tower arch in the background. The internal face of all walls has been stripped of plaster with dire results to the effectiveness of the interior. The arcades are mostly of 15th-century date. The pulpit with sounding board is dated 1718. There is good clear glazing in the windows of the N. chapel, 15th-century parclose screens, a painted wood mural tablet to Dorothy Darcy, 1698, an oval framed Royal Arms (now banished to the vestry but obviously crying out to be sited as at Wensley), a cell on the N. side of the chancel with barrel-vaulted roof and domestic type 17th-century wood screen and door. In the S. chapel, Eliz. Blackburn's ledger stone (1688) has fine lettering and there are fragments of medieval glass in the E. windows and a domestic type 17th-century parclose screen.

GROSMONT (St. Matthew) GR
Setting; Armfield and Bottomley, 1875–84; recent furniture.

GUISBOROUGH (St. Nicholas)
Market town; chancel medieval; Bruce cenotaph 16th cent.; decent stained glass by H. J. Stammers; interesting headstones in the churchyard.

HACKNESS *(St. Mary the Virgin)
The church stands in a deep wood valley near the Hall. The tower and spire,

c. 1200, form a well detailed composition. The chancel of 15th-century date should be compared with Seamer. The finely conceived tower arch, the Saxon cross, the early 16th-century font cover, the fine series of mural monuments including one by Chantrey, the 17th-century domestic type window in the north chapel, the 15th-century stalls in the chancel and the unusual and exquisite candlesticks, the 17th-century vestry and the William and Mary arms are the high lights.

HAROME (St. Saviour) GR
Charles Barry, Junior, 1862; 'E.E. manner'.

HAUXWELL (St. Oswald)
Saxon herringbone masonry; brass of 1611.

HAWNBY (All Saints)
Setting; Tancred monuments.

HAWSKER (All Saints) GR
E. H. Smalls, 1876–7.

HEALEY (St. Paul) GR
E. B. Lamb, 1848.

HELMSLEY (All Saints)
Largely rebuilt c. 1867, by Charles Barry; 20th-cent. organ case, transept chapels; interesting altars and reredoses in transepts by Temple Moore, tall font cover G. G. Pace; fine 18th-cent. chandelier; pedestrian furniture in chancel.

HORNBY *(St. Mary)
The exterior is attractive due to the varying colours and textures of local stone used in its building. The campanile-type tower contains early work to which a belfry was added in the 15th century. The E. wall of the chancel is 19th century sham-Norman. Inside there is a genuine Norman arcade, an elegant 19th-century decorated font, a truly magnificent 19th-century mosaic chancel floor, medieval monuments and brasses in the S. chapel and some early 16th-century painted panels to the parclose screen of this chapel.

HOVINGHAM (All Saints)
Pre-Conquest tower; remainder mostly Victorian; 19th-cent. wood gates in churchyard; stained glass by H. J. Stammers.

HUNTON (St. John) CL
1794; rebuilt, 1894; Victorian Gothic.

HUSTHWAITE (St. Nicholas)
Setting; 17th-cent. pews.

HUTTON BUSCEL (St. Matthew)
Setting; Jacobean pulpit.

HUTTON RUDBY (All Saints)
Setting; pulpit, 1594.

INGLEBY ARNECLIFFE *(All Saints)
The little church stands below tree-covered slopes of the Cleveland Hills and adjacent to the 18th-century Hall (John Carr?). It was rebuilt in 1821 in Cleveland churchwarden classical, and has recently been restored by G. G. Pace. The interior is lighted by sash windows, the walls are white, the box-pews are painted a deep red and retain their original painted numbers; a Scandinavian ship hangs from the roof and on the W. wall are the arms of William III and George VI. The stonework of the E. window is probably of 14th-century date, re-used from the earlier church. In its glazing 14th-century glass fragments from Mount Grace Priory, 18th-century crown glass and new glass has been used. The chancel has two 14th-century effigies yet to be restored. The discordant oak altar rails replace a simple wrought-iron balustrade!

INGLEBY GREENHOW (St. Andrew)
Rebuilt, 1741; around 12th-cent. arcade; very attractive.

KILBURN (St. Mary)
Setting; Norman doorway.

KILVINGTON, SOUTH: see South Kilvington.

KIRBY HILL (All Saints)
Pre-Conquest work; traces of wall-paintings; benches with poppy heads; tower remodelled, 1870.

KIRBY MOORSIDE (All Saints)
Practically rebuilt by G. G. Scott, 1873–5.

KIRBY SIGSTON *(St. Mary)
The W. tower of early 19th-century date resembles Ingleby Arnecliffe nearby. Nave and chancel are Transitional with a Perpendicular E. window. The exterior is pleasant but not remarkable save for an early window head in the S. wall of the chancel. The lime-washed interior has character, and restoration in good hands (Temple Moore, 1890) has done much to heighten its good qualities. There is plenty of free floor space, a few chairs, oil lamps, a gilded and coloured rood-beam and cross but as yet no figures, a 17th-century pulpit incorporating earlier woodwork. The N. aisle, two steps lower than the nave, contains the font, 1662 (compare Northallerton). The narrow chancel arch is filled with a good 20th-century screen. In the chancel the built-up 14th-century arches have unusually good carved caps for this part of the county. There are 20th-century returned stalls and 18th-century altar rails.

KIRKBY FLEETHAM (St. Mary)
Massive tower with vaulted ground stage; monument by Flaxman; chancel rebuilt, c. 1871.

KIRKBY KNOWLE (St. Wilfrid)
Saxon carving; Kempe glass.

KIRKBY RAVENSWORTH (St. Peter & St. Felix)
Setting; massive tower, compare Melsonby and Manfield.

KIRKBY WISKE (St. John the Baptist)
14th-cent. chancel; heavily restored by G. E. Street, 1872.

KIRKDALE (St. Gregory)
Setting and texture; inscribed Saxon sundial.

KIRKLEATHEM *(St. Cuthbert)
The church, with the attached octagonal mausoleum on its plinth of rustic rocks and the gate piers and gates of the churchyard and Hall opposite, forms a satisfying 18th-century composition. The tower has a medieval core but was classicalised in 1731. The remainder of the church was rebuilt in 1763 by a local architect, Robert Corney, who is buried in the churchyard. Externally, the detail is good. Internally, in the nave two rows of stately Tuscan columns standing on pedestals carry the roof. There is a wealth of coeval furniture, marble pedestal font with earlier cover, cut-down box-pews, altar rails, pulpit and reading desk. There is also an array of ledger stones with superb lettering, the Turner monuments in the chancel and the 14th-century chest protected by an elegantly detailed 19th-century wrought-iron railing. The great octagonal mausoleum of the Turner family attached to the N. side of the chancel was built in 1740 and rebuilt in 1839. On the outside the robust lettering of the inscription will repay study. The interior, approached through a sort of Chippendale Gothic door, contains monuments by Scheemakers and Westmacott. Sir William Turner's Hospital, 1742, should be visited for the sake of its chapel with glass, originally by one of the Prices (now possibly a copy by Capronnier).

KIRKLINGTON (St. Michael)
Village; 15th-cent. tower with local type

turret stair; Jacobean pulpit; medieval tombs; restoration by C. Hodgson Fowler, 1890–3.

LASTINGHAM *(St. Mary)*
The village is set in a fold of the moors. Viewed from Spaunton, the basically 11th-century monastic church makes an unusual and very effective silhouette. At the W. end there is a thin 16th-century campanile-type tower. The design of the interior is on a simple yet grand scale, crowned with ribless groined vaults in stone by J. L. Pearson, 1879. The church ends in an apse. The poor apse by John Jackson, the local R.A., 1835, was taken away at the Pearsonic restoration. His copy of Correggio's *Agony in the Garden*, once an altar-piece here, is now banished to the N. chapel. The 18th-century Calvary and the electric lighting fittings should be observed. Abbot Stephen's crypt is entered from a staircase in the centre of the nave.

LEAKE *(St. Mary)*
Setting and texture; medieval; two 15th-cent. stall ends, possibly Ripon school.

LEALHOLM *(St. James)* GR
Temple Moore, 1902.

LEVISHAM, OLD CHURCH (supposed *St. Mary)*
Medieval tower; remainder rebuilt early 19th cent.

LEYBURN *(St. Matthew)* GR
C. G. Wray, 1868.

LIVERTON *(St. Michael)*
Norman walling and chancel arch; heavily restored.

LOCKTON *(St. Giles)*
15th-cent. tower; Jacobean pulpit.

LYTHE *(St. Oswald)*
This hill-top church with its tower surmounted by a short stone spire forms a prominent landmark near the sea. It was largely rebuilt in 1910–11 by Walter Tapper and ranks high in that architect's creations. The fittings and furnishings are fine down to the smallest detail. The placing and design of the rood-screen and of the organ case it carries do much to help in creating the atmosphere of this church.

MALTON, NEW: *see New Malton*

MALTON, OLD: *see Old Malton*

MANFIELD *(All Saints)*
Fine W. tower.

MARRICK PRIORY
The remains of the Benedictine nunnery, part of it now a farm-house, make an austere group on the banks of the Swale. The late 15th-century tower is of a local type. The chancel is in ruins. The nave was pulled down in 1811 and rebuilt. One 13th-century arch, two cylindrical piers and two half arches at this time were re-erected across the body of the new nave near its E. end. The reason for this is obscure, but there is no doubt as to its effectiveness. The yellow washed interior with its splashes of blue and terra-cotta, the fragments of medieval glass, the incised crosses, the varnished boarded ceiling, the Jacobean pulpit and the box-pews, all wearing an aspect of decay, make this interior a very ripe plum.

MARSKE - IN - SWALEDALE *(St. Edmund)*
Much altered in 17th cent.

MARTON - IN - CLEVELAND *(St. Cuthbert)* GR
Rebuilt, 1843, probably by amateur architect.

MARTON - ON - THE - FOREST *(St. Mary)*
The astonishing exterior with its crow-stepped gables, is due to a rebuilding, probably in 1540, using ashlar and worked stone from the Priory near by. The form was determined by the stones available. The cusped head to the tower is not what a first glance might deem to be an echo of Maids Morton (Bucks) but the economic re-use of a window head. The N. wall built of river stones remains in its 12th-century form. The S. door is of 15th-century date. The interior boasts an early chancel arch, 17th-century altar rails and benches, a 13th-century font and fragments of 15th-century glass. The effect of the exterior has been sadly destroyed by the electric power cable.

MASHAM *(St. Mary)*
The pleasant town keeping its green and market cross stands on the bank of the Ure. The lower part of the church tower is 11th-century work, without buttresses, and carries a 15th-century octagonal stage surmounted by a spire. About 1328 the body of the church was rebuilt with aisles and N. chapel by Sir Geoffrey le Scrope. There is a Saxon cross, 7 feet high, in the churchyard. Renaissance monuments abound.

MELSONBY (*St. James the Great*)
Fine W. tower.

MIDDLEHAM (*St. Alkelda & St. Mary*)
Village; chiefly 14th–15th cent.; some
medieval glass; part of font cover 15th
cent.; pretentious recent furniture.

MIDDLESBROUGH (*St. Alban*) GR
F. L. Pearson, 1902; now disused.

(*All Saints*) GR
G. E. Street, 1878.

(*St. Columba*) GR
Temple Moore, 1902–3; personal Gothic of
high order.

(*St. Cuthbert*) GR
Temple Moore, 1901; personal Gothic of
high order.

(*St. John*) GR
John Norton, 1894.

(*St. Martin*)
Poor inter-war period church; recent rood;
G. G. Pace and A. Durst.

(*St. Paul*) GR
R. J. Johnson, 1870–1; coffin-shaped.

MIDDLETON, Nr. Pickering (*St. Andrew*)
Pre-Conquest work in tower; collection of
Saxon crosses; restored by C. Hodgson
Fowler, 1884–6.

MIDDLETON TYAS (*St. Michael*)
Medieval; plate tracery in aisle windows;
restored and spire added by Sir G. G.
Scott, 1868.

NEW MALTON (*St. Michael*)
Norman arcades and font; eviscerated in
19th cent.; pretentious modern woodwork
in chancel and S. chapel.

(*St. Leonard*)
Norman arcades and font.

NEWTON-ON-OUSE (*All Saints*) GR
Early tower, remainder rebuilding of 1849;
poor Gothic Revival.

NORMANBY (*St. Andrew*)
Arcade and south doorway late 12th cent.;
Jacobean altar rails.

NORTHALLERTON (*All Saints*)
Setting; stately 15th-cent. central tower;
chancel 1884 by C. Hodgson Fowler; font
1662 (compare Kirby Sigston) with coeval
cover.

NUNNINGTON (*All Saints & St. James*)
Setting; font cover 18th cent.; Jacobean
pulpit; pedestrian 20th-cent. lectern and
screen.

NUNTHORPE (*St. Mary the Virgin*) GR
Temple Moore; personal Gothic of high
order.

OLD BYLAND (*All Saints*)
Setting; Norman chancel arch and font.

OLD MALTON *(*St. Mary*)
The present parish church is a fragment of
the Gilbertine Priory Church. The W.
front, lacking one tower and with the upper
part of the great 15th-century window
bricked up, would have delighted Cotman.
The S.W. tower is a magnificent creation
and strangely moving. The great W. doorway displays good late 12th-century detail.
In the churchyard are a whole series of
fascinating early Gothic Revival headstones, comparable in some respects with
those at St. Mary's, Whitby. The interior is
less impressive than the W. front but is full
of interest and has a tester at the E.
end, with stalls and organ case by Temple
Moore, 1887–8. The font of 19th century
is based on that at Holy Trinity, Hull. The
late 11th-century work at the base of the
S.W. tower and in the triforium is of a high
standard. The piers on the N. side were in
process of transformation in the 15th
century (compare Ripon).

OSBALDWICK (*St. Thomas*)
Restored J. O. Scott, 1877; 18th-cent.
altar rails; deplorable electric clock in
W. gable.

OSMOTHERLY (*St. Peter*)
Setting; medieval church 'churchwardenised'; further restored, 1892.

OSWALDKIRK (*St. Oswald*)
Jacobean pulpit; wood painted and gilded
1914–18 War Memorial.

OVER SILTON (*St. Mary or All Saints*)
Setting; medieval fittings.

OVERTON (*St. Cuthbert*)
Eviscerated in 1855; reredos by Temple
Moore, 1908.

PATRICK BROMPTON (*St. Patrick*)
Chancel 14th cent.; remainder eviscerated
in the 19th cent., but given a stately W.
tower.

PICKERING *(*St. Peter & St. Paul*)
Externally the long low lines of the church
punctuated with the spire (local type)

composes well with the market town. The 12th and 14th century church suffered a very thorough restoration in the 19th century. A more sensitive restoration is now (1955) in progress. In spite of the 15th-century wall-paintings (largely re-painted in the 1880s), which cover most of the nave clerestory walls, the interior is chill and antiseptic. There are many good details, the 20th-century Jacobean-type screen to the tower arch, the font cover (G. G. Pace), the verge on the wall near the vestry door, the 18th-century brass chandeliers and pulpit, the 20th-century chancel screen, the banner in the Bruce chapel, the white painted gates to the S. porch and the light fittings.

PICKHILL (*All Saints*)
Rich Norman work; font, 1686; restored G. E. Street, 1877.

POCKLEY (*St. John the Baptist*) GR
G. G. Scott, Jr., 1870.

RASKELF *(*St. Mary*)
The church is largely a 19th-century rebuilding around the 15th-century timber tower and pyramid cap (compare Shere, Surrey). The N. arcade is late 11th-century work. There is a Norman tub font with an elegant 17th-century cover. The oak chancel arch (renewed) and the oak arcades to the N. chapel are a reminder of the Forest of Galtres and should be compared with Sutton-on-Forest before its drastic restoration and with Eastrington in the East Riding. There is a 17th-century domestic-type baluster screen to the N. chapel, 18th-century altar rails, fragments of medieval glass and 17th-century seats at the W. end of the nave with coarse poppy heads.

RICHMOND (*St. Mary the Virgin*)
15th cent.; W. tower of local type; body of church eviscerated in the 19th cent.; 15th-cent. stalls from Easby Abbey; black Fosterley marble font with Jacobean cover; church restored by Sir G. G. Scott, 1860 and by C. Hodgson Fowler, 1892.

ROBIN HOOD'S BAY (*St. Stephen*) GR
G. E. Street, 1870, glass by Burne-Jones.

ROMALDKIRK (*St. Romald*)
Village; Arcades Trans.; S. transept 13th-cent.; chancel and N. transept 14th cent.; tower 15th cent.; furniture of various dates; fragments of wall-paintings; parabolic plaster roof in chancel; window tracery in S. transept (compare Easby and Bedale).

ROUNTON, EAST: *see East Rounton.*

ROUNTON, WEST: *see West Rounton.*

RUSWARP (*St. Bartholomew*) GR
C. H. Armfield, 1868–9.

SALTON (*St. John de Beverley*)
Mostly Norman.

SAND HUTTON (*St. Mary*)
Setting; rebuilt Salvin, 1839–42; recast by C. Hodgson Fowler, 1886; 19th-cent. glass, Kempe; ruins of old church surrounded by table tombs; an early vigorous but crude headstone.

SCARBOROUGH (*All Saints*) GR
G. F. Bodley, 1868.

(*Christ Church*) GR
Atkinson and Sharpe, 1826–8; apsidal chancel, 1873; Narthex 1950; G. G. Pace.

(*St. Columba*) GR
L. Moore, 1926; good massing on difficult site; dull but characteristic furniture.

(*Holy Trinity*) GR
Ewan Christian, 1879.

(*St. James*) GR
Austin and Paley; excellent massing on difficult site; very Edwardian.

(*St. Martin*)
One of G. F. Bodley's early churches, consecrated in 1862. The narthex and the Lady Chapel and the superb organ case are later Bodley. The church has excellent proportions both within and without and whilst still having a French flavour, it has none of the 'boyish antagonistic effort' of his slightly earlier, St. Michael's, Brighton. With his own hand he painted the patterns on the walling above the chancel and he made use of his pre-Raphaelite friends, Burne-Jones central panel of E. wall with side panels by William Morris, Spencer Stanhope side of organ case, chancel roof Morris and Philip Webb. Morris drew cartoons for the lower panels of the pulpit and a side panel is by Rossetti. The earlier glass was made by Morris from cartoons by Burne-Jones, Ford Madox Brown, Rossetti and Philip Webb. The reredos in the Lady Chapel is in Bodley's later style. More recent work is unfortunately below the Bodley standard.

*(St. Mary)

The church is perched high above the fishing village and under the lee of the castle. It suffered severe damage during the Civil War and is now without its great chancel and two W. towers. The loss of the chancel explains the E. tower (1669) which stands over what was once the crossing. The church went through a severe restoration under Ewan Christian between 1848–50 which made the fabric structurally sound but swept away the incredible character the interior had acquired and which may be studied in water colours hanging in the church and recreated in the mind after a visit to St. Mary's, Whitby. The most interesting medieval architectural remains are the piers, the arcades. the clerestory and the wall shafts in the nave (12th–13th centuries) and comparable with Bolton Abbey and Holy Trinity, York, and the range of chapels opening off the S. aisle with their ribbed barrel vaults, roofed externally with stone slabs. Ewan Christian's W. lancets (1850) are successful and so is the 19th-century glass which fills them. Other details to observe: the recent treatment of the 19th-century glass in the chapel windows, the excellent series of mural monuments including one by Roubiliac, the 20th-century bronze handle to the S. door, the 1939–45 war memorial casket and the magnificence of the 17th, 18th and 19th century yard tombs and headstones – many of the early Gothic revival type seen at its best at St. Mary's, Whitby. The E. window is by H. J. Stammers, 1958.

(St. Saviour)

J. T. Micklethwaite; W. window Francis Spear.

(St. Thomas)

Thomas Davidson, 1830; enlarged, 1859, by John and William Barry; 20th-cent. painted screen very near to crude vitality of medieval work.

SCAWTON (St. Mary)

Restored by C. Hodgson Fowler, 1888; High-Church fittings.

SCRUTON (St. Radegund)

Norman and E.E., but badly restored; E. window by Capronnier of Brussels, 1866.

SEAMER (St. Martin)

Chancel, 15th cent.; compare Hackness; tower rebuilt in 19th-cent Norman.

SHERIFF HUTTON *(St. Helen & the Holy Cross)

From the churchyard there is a good view across the Howardian countryside. The exterior is full of colour and texture due to the use of sandstone and limestone as rubble and as ashlar. The tower stands within the body of the church and before it is an early 19th-century W. porch of the greatest simplicity. The best view of the exterior is from the south-west corner of the churchyard which brings out to the full the interesting composition of tower and roofs and the good 15th-century work of the S. chapel. The interior is homely and intimate and full of good things. Brick floors, box-pews in which a good deal of medieval woodwork may be found, flat plaster ceiling in the nave, 17th-century altar table and rails, Gurney stoves, the 19th-century archaic glass in the E. window, the 15th-century oak door in the vestry, the 17th-century funeral achievements in the S. chapel, the Wytham brasses, the tombs in the N. chapel including that (recreated from fragments by G. G. Pace) to Edward, Prince of Wales, the son of Edward III, and the red painted organ case. The walls have been stripped of plaster and the great possibilities of this interior have been thereby largely ruined.

SHIPTON-BY-YORK (Holy Evangelists)

GR

1849; G. T. Andrews; screen and reredos by Temple Moore, 1891–1911.

SILTON, OVER: see Over Silton.

SINNINGTON (All Saints)

Carefully restored by C. Hodgson Fowler, 1904.

SKELTON *(St. Giles)

'Few ecclesiastical buildings of like dimensions will, I think, be found more perfect in harmony of parts, unity of design and purity of style' and in writing this Ewan Christian was not saying too much. The proportions and spatial relationships of the interior are quite remarkable and it is hard to realise that it is all within a rectangle of 44 feet 2 inches by 32 feet 8 inches. The church was completed prior to 1247. The great S. doorway is a 19th-century renewal and is already weathering. The font, gable crosses, bell-cote and buttresses should be closely observed.

SKELTON, OLD CHURCH (*All Saints*)
CL
1785 Cleveland churchwarden classical, with contemporary fittings.

SKELTON-IN-CLEVELAND (*All Saints*)
GR
R. J. Johnson; dull.

SNAPE (*St. Mary*)
Catherine Parr's chapel; Perp. panelling; richly painted ceiling.

SOUTH COWTON (*St. Mary*)
Late medieval; porch with barrel vault and room above.

SOUTH KILVINGTON (*St. Wilfrid*)
Texture; 12th and 14th cent.; the black Fosterley marble font is comparable with those at Richmond and Catterick.

SOWERBY (*St. Oswald*)
Mostly rebuilt by E. B. Lamb in 1842, restored and enlarged by J. H. Fowler, 1879–83.

SPENNITHORNE (*St. Michael & All Angels*)
Massive W. tower; medieval tombs; 17th-cent. wall-paintings.

SPROXTON *(St. Chad)*
The exterior of this small 17th-century church moved here from West Newton in 1879 is in a kind of domestic Jacobean in which pleasant windows, a grey stone roof and good entrance gate piers play their part. The interior is even better than the exterior. In particular, the free floor space in the chancel, the altar table and reredos, the glass in the E. window, the chancel screen by Temple Moore and the W. screens and font should be studied. This delightful creation is the work of G. G. Scott (II) and it is grievous to record that the interior has recently been ruined by a brutal electric-light installation.

STANWICK (*St. John the Baptist*)
Mostly 13th cent.; Jacobean font cover.

STILLINGTON *(St. Nicholas)*
The church forms a welcome break in the long village street with its well-kept grass banks covered with bulbs in the spring. The local warm stone is used for the walls and the windows follow a local regional type. The interior has considerable atmosphere. The whole is cream washed. There are late box-pews, arcades with the mouldings dying into the octagonal piers, red brick floors and clear glazing. The royal arms G.R.1739, is a spirited piece of painting for its date. Recent furniture does not succeed in capturing the highly individual qualities of this interior.

STOKESLEY (*St. Peter & St. Paul*)
Market town; 15th-cent. tower; medieval chancel; nave rebuilt, 1771.

STONEGRAVE (*Holy Trinity*)
Setting; pre-Conquest tower; Jacobean screen and pulpit.

SUTTON-ON-FOREST (*All Saints*)
Victorian around 15th-cent. tower; 18th-cent. pulpit; choir stalls, 1950.

TANFIELD, WEST: *see West Tanfield.*

TERRINGTON (*All Saints*)
Setting; late 11th-cent. core with 12th, 14th and 15th cent. refashioning.

THIRKLEBY, GREAT: *see Great Thirkleby.*

THIRSK *(St. Mary the Virgin)*
From a distance the tower calls to mind Bodley at Eccleston (Cheshire). The exterior is very stately and is helped by the under building to the chancel necessitated by the fall in the land. The body of the church, which is an essay in fully developed Perpendicular, probably more of the West Riding than the York regional type (compare Sherburn in Elmet, Ecclesfield, Bradfield), was built in 1420. The chancel followed in 1470. The interior of the nave is well designed both as a whole and in its various parts, and looking W. is very grand, but when looking E. there is an anti-climax in the chancel. The font cover is partly of 15th-century workmanship. There is medieval glass in one or two windows, traces of 17th-century paintings of the Apostles on the clerestory walls and a magnificent altar table. Restoration by G. E. Street, 1877.

THORMANBY *(All Saints)*
The isolated church has a squat brick tower and a domesticated S. porch. The external stonework varies much in size, texture and colour and is most attractive. The interior is homely and possesses atmosphere. The benches, the simple font cover and the limewashed walls in the nave are in contrast with the good early 20th-century furnishing and glass in the chancel. Recently a blocked window in the S. wall has been opened up and a panel of 15th-century glass inserted in good modern glazing.

THORNABY-ON-TEES, OLD CHURCH
(*St Peter*)
Village church; 12th cent. in origin; fine texture to external walling.

THORNTON-LE-DALE (*All Saints*)
Village; setting; heavy 19th-cent. restoration.

THORNTON STEWARD (*St. Oswald*)
Setting; medieval and 18th cent.; restored in 19th cent.

THORNTON WATLESS (*St. Mary*)
Victorian evisceration by G. F. Jones, 1868, around massive W. tower.

TOPCLIFFE (*St. Columba*)
Mostly 14th cent.; magnificent 14th-cent. Flemish brass; extensive 19th-cent. restoration by G. T. Andrews.

UGGLEBARNBY (*All Saints*) GR
C. N. Armfield, 1872.

UPLEATHEM (*St. Andrew*)
In ruins except for tower and fragment of nave; setting.

WATH (*St. Mary*)
Restored, 1873; brasses; Flaxman monument, 1814.

WELL (*St. Michael*)
Elegant 14th-cent. tower; 15th-cent. font cover; 18th-cent. frontal; Milbank monument by Westmacott.

WENSLEY *(*Holy Trinity*)
A church which is pleasant both within and without, but where the interest is in the parts rather than in the whole. Externally the buttresses on the N. side of the nave, the N. doorway with its pedimented hood mould and the cusping at the apex of the arch and the elegant white painted wood gates to the N. porch should be observed. Internally there is so much to note that only a catalogue is possible. Early benches and box pews, a magnificent 15th-century screen with Jacobean extras and a great banner and hangings forming the Bolton family pew (the screen was the Scrope parclose in Easeby Abbey), the oval frame hanging within the chancel arch and charged with coats of arms (compare with Grinton), the 1662 font and cover, the wall-paintings, the incised slab in the N. aisle wall, the Jacobean pulpit, the 13th-century sedilia, the 17th-century altar rails, the 15th-century stall ends with poppy heads and heraldic beasts (Ripon School?), the magnificent Flemish brass (1395) to the

priest Sir Simon de Wenselawe. The recent re-arrangement of the High Altar is to be commended.

WESTERDALE (*Christ Church*)
The church of 1838 embodied in the new church by W. Falkenbudge in 1874 and Temple Moore in 1911; restored by C. Hodgson Fowler, 1896.

WEST ROUNTON (*St. Oswald*)
11th-cent. font and chancel arch; glass in window H. J. Stammers.

WEST TANFIELD *(*St. Nicholas*)
From the river bridge a comprehensive view is obtained of the church on its romantic site on the high bank of the Ure with the 15th-century gate house of Marmion's Manor behind it. The church is chiefly 15th century but badly mauled in 1859 by unfeeling hands. There is a curious chamber in the N. wall of the chancel with traceried openings, but the glory of the church is the 14th-century Marmion alabaster altar tomb with its wrought-iron hearse. In the E. window on N. of aisle is some restored glass.

WHENBY (*St. Martin*)
Setting; 15th-cent. pews; Jacobean screen.

WHITBY (*St. Hilda*) GR
R. J. Johnson; a luxurious church; 1885; tower completed, 1938, G. E. Charlewood.

*(*St. Mary*)
The church stands on a hill high above the old town and looking down on the harbour. It has for near neighbours the Abbey ruins and Abbey House. The approach is by steps of formidable number with a cross erected in 1898 to the memory of Caedmon at their head. The tower and S. doorway are mid-12th century. The exterior is massive, even harsh, yet well suited to the site. It gives little indication of the delightful and amazing interior as re-modelled in the 18th century. The great rectangular nave is filled with box-pews and galleries which rise almost to the roof, and revolve around the high pulpit and reading desk. The nave appears light against the murk of the chancel, which is unspoilt 12th century. Between is the delicate crown of the pulpit's sounding board and the screen at the entrance to the chancel with its barley sugar Corinthian columns. The screen calls to mind the Dutch Colonial churches in Ceylon (perhaps there is a connection); whilst the precarious tiers of galleries echo

what Ewan Christian swept away at Scarborough. In the churchyard are a series of Chippendale-Gothic table tombs, lesser examples of which are found at Scarborough, Seamer and Old Malton. (*See Plate 51*)

(*St. Ninian*) CL
1778; Cleveland churchwarden classical.

WHITWELL-ON-THE-HILL (*St. John the Evangelist*) GR
G. E. Street, with a particularly successful tower and spire, 1860.

WHORLTON *(Holy Cross)*
The isolated church stands on a broken ground close to the Cleveland Hills. The approach lies through an avenue of yews. The nave, roofless since 1875, is 12th century, with an intact tower on the S. side, the upper part of which was rebuilt in 1722. The position of the tower in relationship to the nave is akin to Danby in Cleveland. The chancel is intact and is largely of 13th-century date. The interior is a ripe plum with attractive windows, corbels and an array of 14th and 15th century canopied wall tombs. New church by T. H. Wyatt, 1875–7.

WORSALL (*All Saints*) GR
Armfield and Moscrop, 1894.

WYCLIFFE (*St. Mary*)
Setting; 13th-cent core, recast *c.* 1350; small and aisleless; medieval glass.

WYKEHAM (*St. Helen or All Saints*) GR
Wm. Butterfield, 1855.

YARM (*St. Mary Magdalene*) CL
Except for W. end, rebuilt in 1730; William Peckitt glass of 'Moses Delivering the Law'.

YORK
(All Saints, North Street)
The exterior is pleasant but with exception of the tower and spire and the vestry is not remarkable. The tower stands within the body of the church (usual in York and common in Yorkshire) and its upper stage is a graceful octagon in two stages which has influenced St. Mary's, Castlegate. The early 20th-century vestry constructed in reinforced concrete and cladded with half timbering is ingenious. The interior is full to overflowing with every conceivable object from 14th-century glass to deal painted chests of drawers. This results in a considerable atmosphere akin to a medieval church interior. There is no structural chancel. The 13th and 14th century arcades run from end to end. Some of the piers have excellent caps very lithic in character which may well have inspired Temple Moore. The chancel and S. aisle have excellent 15th-century roofs. The medieval painted glass in this church is of outstanding interest. In the floors and walls are many incised stones. The 18th-century pulpit has simple and effective inlay. In 1906 Ridsdale Tate rearranged the chancel and N. chapel furniture, adding a rood and parclose screens. (*See Plate 37*)

(All Saints, Pavement)
A typical town church. The E. end was shortened for road widening in 1782 and now bears a strong resemblance to St. Peter, Sudbury. On the N. door is a metal knocker of 15th-century date (compare St. Gregory, Norwich). The W. tower rebuilt 1837, standing within the church, terminates with a tall open octagonal lantern and pierced parapet. Its beacon light has lately been restored. Inside, the tower is carried on fine 15th-century piers and arches. There is a large and fine 15th-century window in the W. wall with 15th-century glass from St. Saviour's. The arcades and clerestories are of 15th-century date. There is a notable pulpit (1634) and the medieval lectern from the demolished church of St. Crux is well known for its excellence. One of the church's early Gothic Revival safes is identical with that at St. Denys. Both the Lord Mayor's Boards and the Bequest Boards have good lettering. In the nearby church room many excellent monuments from St. Crux are preserved, together with an oak doorway of interest.

(St. Andrew, New Earswick)
The church lacks the intended S. aisle. Leslie Moore has seized upon the presence of an earlier building and the fall in the ground to create an unusual and highly successful arrangement. The earlier building forms a narthex or ante-chapel, from which steps lead down to the church proper.

(*St. Chad*) GR
Fragment of church in brick Northern Gothic, 1925, by Brierley and Rutherford.

(*St. Clement*) GR
W. Atkinson, 1874; an ugly red-brick Victorian church; contains Saxon cross-fleury, and 18th-cent. bread-board, mace-stands and charity-boards from St. Mary Bishophill Senior.

*(St. Cuthbert)

The churchyard has good trees, mown grass and even a path of herringbone brick. The small campanile-tower and the S. side of the church are simple well detailed 15th-century work. In the churchyard behind the 1914–18 War Memorial is a curious memorial chair conceived in a kind of attenuated Baroque. The church is a single cell building plus W. tower, S. porch (good 15th-century oak doors) and an 18th-century brick vestry with pantile roof. The body of the church has a 15th-century roof. In spite of good proportions, windows, and a well-arranged sanctuary, the interior is dull. There is a 17th-century altar table and pulpit, also hatchments and Lord Mayor's Board, Creed, Commandments and Bequest Boards with excellent lettering. In the vestry is an early Gothic Revival safe similar to that at St. Denys. The E. end has a kind of crypt below with some 17th and 18th century brass inscriptions.

*(St. Denys)

The church has suffered grievous truncation in the past and is now overshadowed by office blocks. The nave was destroyed in 1798, and the tower rebuilt in 1847. Mercifully the Norman S. doorway (cp. St. Nicholas and St. Margaret type) survived intact. The 14th-century tracery in the great E. window of the N. chapel may be compared with the W. window of the Minster and E. windows at Fishlake and Laxton. The interior is strongly reminiscent of the Norwich churches. The arcades are of notable span and dignity. The mouldings die into the piers (compare St. John's, Ousebridge and Stillington). The roofs are of 15th-century date and though the ribs shine with paint and varnish the effect is pleasantly in keeping. The 14th and 15th century glass in its chaotic arrangement has qualities which might be lost by re-arrangement. The brass monument to Mary Rose (1922), the Jacobean Pulpit, the wrought-iron riddle post of the High Altar (by Bainbridge Reynolds and comparable with his work at the Minster under Sir Walter Tapper), the early Gothic Revival safe, and the well-placed organ by Hughes should be observed. Excellent 19th-century gates.

(St. Helen)

Largely recast in the 19th cent. by R. H. Dykes; 12th-cent. font; 14th-cent. glass.

*(Holy Trinity, Goodramgate)

The church and churchyard are hidden from the street by buildings. At the street edge is a brick gateway (1786) with pleasant gates (1815) giving a glimpse of the churchyard with a weeping ash and a ledger stone – by far the most satisfactory entry to any York church. The exterior of the church is a delightful medley of different materials, colours and textures, many due to parsimonious repairs in the past; e.g. the much repaired tile roofs and the belfry stage of the tower. The pleasant square-headed 14th-century windows should be compared with Skipwith and other York churches. Internally, the church is one of the most picturesque in York, though without architectural pretentions. The effect is produced by the pews, of many dates, which heave and flow around the two-decker pulpit, 1785. There is a plain 18th-century font and cover, an altar piece of 1721 with the Holy Table covered by a dated 18th-century frontal. The rails follow a York pattern (compare St. Michael-le-Belfry and St. Martin-cum-Gregory). There is much excellent 15th-century stained glass of the York School. The arcades spring from very stumpy columns, some with the York corbel cap. The arches supporting the tower are of great vitality. The W. window should be compared with All Saints', Pavement.

*(Holy Trinity, Micklegate)

The present building contains a large fragment of the Benedictine Priory church. The W. front is an elegant 13th-century composition of deeply moulded main doorway, blind arcading and lancet windows. A scholarly restoration was undertaken in 1905 by Charles Hodgson Fowler. The tower at the N.W. corner was built over the W. bay of the N. aisle in 1453 using stones from the adjacent church of St. Nicholas. This accounts for the archaeological puzzles which at first glance seem unresolved. The doorway to the N. porch contains fragments of 15th-century woodwork. As the N. aisle has been destroyed the arches of the great arcade are built into the present wall. The window tracery is mostly 19th century but two windows of earlier date have been converted into quite surrealistic shapes. Traces of the 11th-century pier of the central tower may be seen near the chancel arch. Fisher and Hepper designed the rather dull 19th-century 'Perpendicular' chancel. Inside the nave the great scale and solemnity of the original nave arcades is seen (compare Bolton Abbey) and above the arch to St. Nicholas' chapel one bay of the triforium arcade remains intact. In the W. lancet of the nave is some excellent Kempe glass. The font and its magnificent cover have recently been brought from St. Saviour's Church and after careful restoration placed in their present position. The High Altar, reredos and Kempe window above form a composition of some richness reflecting the taste of their period. The early Gothic Revival monument to Dr. John Burton ('Dr. Slop' of *Tristram Shandy*) and the early 19th-century safe, now doing duty as a collecting box, should not be missed.

(St. John, Ousebridge)
Now an architectural institute (1955).

(St. Lawrence) GR
Campanile tower with 15th-cent. pierced parapet and 12th-cent. doorway from destroyed church of St. Nicholas (compare St. Margaret) remain in churchyard; present church 1880–3, J. G. Hall, Canterbury; bread-and-butter work.

*(St. Margaret)
The church and churchyard lie behind the buildings of Walmgate. Entrance to the sequestered churchyard with its ash trees and flagged path bordered by an avenue of limes, is through an early 19th-century cast-iron gate of considerable interest. The stone and brick tower was built in 1684. Apart from the exceptionally fine S. doorway (originally in the destroyed hospital chapel of St. Nicholas, c. 1160) the remainder of the exterior was rebuilt in 1852. The interior need not be quite so depressing.

*(St. Martin-le-Grand)
The church was gutted by incendiaries dropped in 1942. A scheme for restoring the tower and S. aisle and for creating a secluded garden on the remainder of the site is being prepared. The tower (completed 1437) and S. aisle (1443–50) in the fully developed local Regional type are of great subtlety and sensitiveness in detail. The Master responsible for the design (possibly Robert Couper) was an architect of ability. The tower buttresses should be compared with those at Coxwold and Sancton. The great glory of the church, the St. Martin W. window, probably by the

younger Chamber, was saved and will be incorporated in the restored portion of the church.

*(St. Martin-cum-Gregory)
Architecturally and archaeologically one of the most interesting churches in the city. Externally, the controlled decay adds colour and texture to the good architectural treatment of the N. and S. sides of the church. The E. end is of brickwork (1751) and the W. tower also of brick, rebuilt lavishly in 1667 and parsimoniously in 1844. In the base are stones thought to have been brought from the site of a temple which in Roman times existed on the other side of Micklegate. The S. porch is reputedly dated 1655. The interior is notable for its spatial relationships, perspective effects and the free floor space brought about by the removal of pews and organ. A catalogue will list the excellent details of this church but cannot convey the charm of the interior as a whole. The altar-piece and altar rails (1754) have recently been restored to their original state. The lettering should be compared with the lovely Poor Box. Then there are the sanctuary chairs, the altar table, the magnificent series of ledger stones, the pulpit, 1636, the 14th and 15th century glass and the 18th-century William Peckitt glass, including his memorial painted by his wife, the font cover (York type), the Bread Cupboard, the Royal Arms, the fire-buckets, the brass chandelier and the 15th-century roof timbers. In this church the fittings and accessories of worship made in accordance with the principles of the Book of Common Prayer survive in profusion.

*(St. Mary, Bishophill, the Elder)
One of York's declared redundant churches. It stands in an overgrown churchyard and the appearance of neglect would have astonished Cotman. The brick tower was built in 1659. The S. porch is good early 19th-century brickwork. The S. wall is of interest, archaeologically, and even more so aesthetically. The interior has been gutted and the contents removed to St. Clement's Church but a simple 15th-century roof remains. This is one of the oldest church sites in York and recent scholarly archaeological examination has discovered the remains of an 8th or 9th century church at the base of the W. wall of the nave.

(St. Mary, Bishophill, Junior)

The massive W. tower often illustrated in text-books has interesting Saxon work. The remainder of the exterior suffered from parsimonious rebuilding in the 19th century. The interior has atmosphere. The low, wide proportions, the lime-washed walls, the 15th-century ribbed and plaster-panelled nave roof (modern bosses), the tower arch of warm brown stone, the lithic font carrying an early 18th-century cover of the York type, the curious arches of the S. arcade, the simple dignity of the N. arcade, the openness of the chancel with its excellent 20th-century stalls, pulpit and reredos, the colour in the arches to the N. chapel and the finely designed 19th-century stonework of the N. chapel windows, combine to make a homely and satisfying interior.

(St. Mary, Castlegate)

A large freestanding church, heavily but well restored by William Butterfield in 1870. The tower stands within the body of the church (a local characteristic). It has rectangular lower stages carried on sturdy piers and arches within the church. The upper stage is octagonal with tall belfry windows on the cardinal sides, the remaining faces being unpierced and ornamented with slim buttresses (compare All Saints, North Street). The octagonal lantern terminates with a tall spire. The windows throughout the church have been faithfully restored and show forth many local characteristics. The interior is large, spacious and strangely chilly. Both arcades are well proportioned, the N. being Transitional Norman and the S. probably 14th century. To the 15th century belong the elegant arches in the N. and S. walls of the chancel with their ogee hood moulds and carved finials. There is good glass in the E. window of the S. chapel and a deeply cut ledger stone in the floor before it. The font is of Charles II's reign. Butterfield's pews are noteworthy and so is the dedication stone by Efrard, Grim and Aese of early 11th-century date.

(St. Maurice)

The church of 1878–86 designed by Charles Fisher is hardly worthy of an architectural glance, but it should be a place of pilgrimage to those whose first acquaintance with the evolution of window tracery was Parker's 'Introduction'. Alas! the famous Norman window of two lights with the pierced circle centrally above and the whole head contained in a semi-circular drip mould is no more.

(St Michael-le-Belfrey)

The siting of this church close to the W. front of the Minster and at an angle with it may not have been intentional, but visually it is most satisfying. St. Michael's is a good example of a Hall-type town church (compare St. Andrew Undershaft, London). It was built between 1525–36 and the Master responsible for the design was probably John Forman. In 1867 the W. front was largely rebuilt and the lower part re-designed by G. F. Jones. The exterior has a fine continuous clerestory, the aisle buttresses following a Regional type and the unusual bell turret on the W. front. The interior is remarkable for the masterly handling of spatial relationships, for the 14th and 15th century glass, the magnificent altar-piece and altar rails (1712) (compare Holy Trinity, Goodramgate and St. Martin-cum-Gregory), the series of 17th and 18th century tombs and mural monuments, the remains of 15th-century seating, the 18th-century Lord Mayor's Board and the Royal Arms on the West Gallery.

(St. Michael Spurriergate)

The exterior has suffered some lopping. The E. wall was set back 7 feet and the S. wall 5 feet in 1821. The 15th-century tower is a poor specimen, but the clock face on the S. side most decorative. Internally, the eye having grown used to the bilious yellow dado, the excellence of the 12th-century arcades may be appreciated, together with the 18th-century inner porch, reredos, altar rails and Lord Mayor's Board, the stamped leather altar covering framed on the E. wall of the S. aisle (Charles II), the 15th-century glass re-arranged by Dean Milner-White, and the 15th-century W. door.

(St. Olave)

The church is backed on the S. of the churchyard by the ruined N. aisle of St. Mary's Abbey, linked at the W. end to other Abbey buildings and attached at the E. end to a superb medieval wall. The N. side of the church is good 15th-century work. Between it and the road is a small garden with cobble bordered paths and a boundary wall with wrought-iron railings. The tower is a 15th-century campanile with the tracery missing from the belfry lights. The view across the nave from the N. door, through the open S. door protected by its delightful wirework and across the churchyard to the Abbey ruins has recently been improved by freeing the W. part of the church of pews and re-paving with stone. The nave arcades were rebuilt in the 18th century and the columns are a curious Gothicised Roman Doric. At the E. end of the N. aisle is a recent War Memorial Chapel (G. G. Pace). The chancel and S. chapel (1908) by James Francis Doyle are a rich and effective manifestation of the ecclesiological desires of that date. The glass in the E. window of the chancel is 15th century.

(St. Oswald, Fulford, Old Church)
This humble little church in its rural churchyard has been swallowed up by the York sprawl. The lack of self-consciousness of builders working in an alive vernacular and its happy results are thrown into sharp relief by the contrast between this church and the adjoining brutal new pumping station. At the W. end is a tiny brick tower, covered with ivy and capped with pyramidal tiled roof. The church-warden windows of the church are glazed in rectangular quarries. There are a few good 18th-century yard tombs. The well-textured stonework on the N. side of the chancel is pierced by early slit windows. This side of the building, with its overgrown churchyard is quite Piperesque. The interior is forlorn.

Yorkshire: the West Riding

INTRODUCTION

FOR CONTRAST of scenery, character and spirit, the West Riding has no equal in England. It is hard to believe that Wharfedale and the Dearne Valley could belong to the same land, still less the same Riding. And yet, considering its size, England's largest county is poor in ancient churches – 197 compared with Kent's 321.

Why? First because, until industry arrived, the Riding west of a line from Ripon to Sheffield was bleak moorland. Much of it is open country still. Down to 1850, the mother churches of Halifax, Dewsbury and Thornhill in the west, and Otley in the north, served vast areas with chapelries under them. To this day, no self-respecting dalesman would be married anywhere but in 't'owd parish church'.

In the second place, prosperity when it came was not accompanied by reverence for antiquity. So in pudding-time the old churches of Huddersfield and Keighley disappeared, and All Saints', Dewsbury, was given a Georgian new look. John Carr showed better taste at Horbury; his church might have strayed from Wren's London. But worse was to come. In Queen Victoria's reign, when large-scale building took place, the magnates of Leeds, Bradford, and Sheffield, stuck obstinately to their local architects. Scott, it is true, was given St. George's, Doncaster, to rebuild after a fire. Burges, disappointed of his hope in the towns, had to content himself with a kaleidoscope display at Skelton and Studley Royal.

The West Riding is distributed among five different dioceses. York keeps only a corner since Ripon reverted to cathedral status and the three parish churches of Wakefield, Bradford and Sheffield became cathedrals. Selby, Yorkshire's sleepiest town, has the one complete monastic building in use; Bolton and Nun Monkton are fragments.

The Craven churches come nearest to achieving a local style. Most of them are Tudor or late Perpendicular, with no division between nave and chancel. Two other peculiarities must be mentioned. Around Selby the landscape becomes strangely Dutch in character. The roof-tops of Snaith, Fishlake and Drax, are ablaze with channelled tiles, and below them glide barges on their way to the Humber. They could almost be in Middleburg or Gouda. The remaining area of interest lies west from Bradford: the Brontë country. In these moorland valleys around Haworth, with their gaunt churches and stone walls, one is made conscious of the spirit which underlies the pages of *Wuthering Heights*.

D.R.

SELECTED LIST OF CHURCHES

by John W. Shaw, the Rev. David Rutter and the Rev. B. F. L. Clarke

ABERFORD (*St. Ricarius*)
Early Norman tower.

ACASTER MALBIS *(Holy Trinity)*
Small cruciform Decorated church with spirelet (cp. Dunsfold, Surrey); unique external splaying of windows; slabs; low side windows, one with hinges of original shutter; old glass.

ACKWORTH (*St. Cuthbert with All Saints*)
Inscribed Restoration font.

ADDINGHAM (*St. Peter*)
14th–15th cent. aisle and arcade; rest pleasantly classicised in 18th cent.

ADEL *(St. John Baptist)*
Aisleless Norman church (cp. Birkin) among fields four and a half miles from Leeds. Magnificent S. doorway with carvings of Christ, four Evangelists and Paschal Lamb (symbol of patron saint). Much symbolism on capitals of chancel arch. Closing ring to S. door. Restoration by G. E. Street, 1879.

ADLINGFLEET *(All Saints)*
13th-century church on borders of Lincolnshire marshland; 15th-century tower, nave and clerestory; Transitional S. doorway; old-fashioned interior; altar-tomb of Haldenby family in N. aisle; huge classical monument in S. aisle to Mary Ramsden, benefactor of St. Catharine's College, Cambridge, 1745.

ADWICK-LE-STREET (*St. Lawrence*)
Norman, Perp. and Tudor; Elizabethan slab with Washington and Anlaby arms, 1580.

ALDBOROUGH *(St. Andrew)*
Roman city of Isurium, with considerable remains. Church is 14th century with 15th-century chancel, clerestory and tower and has good roofs, reredos, panelling, chairs, altar rail, etc., 16th century and 17th century pulpit incorporating part of medieval rood-screen. 14th-century glass. Brass of William de Aldeburgh, c. 1360. Roman statue of Mercury.

ALDFIELD (*St. Lawrence the Martyr*)
18th-cent. Gothick chapel-of-ease to Studley (q.v.); box-pews and three-decker pulpit; lovely 13th-cent. font admired by Flaxman.

ALLERTON MAULEVERER (*St. Martin*)
Cruciform 14th cent., churchwardenised in 18th cent.; hammer-beam roof to nave; alabaster and wooden tombs (cp. Thornhill) and brass of Sir John Mauleverer and wife, 1400, in transepts.

ALMONDBURY *(All Saints)*
Attractive late Perpendicular church, rather dark within. Roof with carved bosses dated 1522; restored rood and parclose screens; Jacobean font cover; 15th-century glass, including an Assumption, in Kaye chapel; painted heraldic shields in N. aisle. Communion cup with rare Leeds mark of the fleece, c. 1665, appears to have been copied from its companion, a cup of London make, 1631.

ALTOFTS (*St. Mary Magdalene*) GR
Adams and Kelly, 1873–90; lavish use of Caen stone; mosaics by Salviati.

ARKSEY (*All Saints*)
Cruciform Trans. with 14th and 15th cent. additions; heraldry; Jacobean pulpit and tester; 17th-cent. pewing; restored by Sir G. G. Scott, 1869–70.

ASKHAM RICHARD (*St. Mary*)
Dark little Trans. church spoilt in 1878; S. doorway mercifully spared.

ASTON (*All Saints*)
Trans., Dec. and Perp. church; Fane and Darcy monuments, 17th cent.

ATTERCLIFFE (*St. Bartholomew*) GR
J. D. Webster, 1891.

AUSTERFIELD (*St. Helena*)
Early Norman S. doorway and chancel
arch; N. aisle rebuilt by Americans in 1897
as memorial to Austerfield's Pilgrim
Father, Wm. Bradfield.

BADSWORTH (*St. Mary the Virgin*)
Mainly 14th cent. with 13th-cent. tower
built inside aisles (cp. Farnham); a little
heraldic glass; alabaster monument to
Cromwellian Sir John Bright, 1688.

BALNE, with POLLINGTON (*St. John
the Baptist*) GR
W. Butterfield, 1854.

BARDSEY (*All Hallows*)
Saxon tower; Norman S. doorway and N.
arcade.

BARNBURGH (*St. Peter*)
Trans. with 14th-cent. additions; remarkable oak effigy (cp. Worsborough) of Sir
Percival Cresacre, 1477, who is said to have
been killed by a wild cat.

BARNBY-ON-DUN (*St. Peter & St. Paul*)
Trans. nave arcades; Perp. tower; Dec.
piscina and sedilia; rood-loft stairs extending to roof; 17th-cent. monuments;
interesting glass.

BARNOLDSWICK (*St. Mary-le-Gill*)
13th-cent. chancel; Perp. nave and tower
dated 1524; 17th-cent. pulpit and pewing.

BARWICK-IN-ELMET (*All Saints*)
Norman chancel and rest mainly 15th cent.;
handsome tower of Somerset type, with
niche, dated 1455; Gascoyne and Vavasour
tombs.

BATLEY (*All Saints*)
Unrestored 14th and 15th cent. church;
screen with heraldry; 14th-cent. glass in S.
aisle.

BAYHALL (*St. John the Evangelist*) GR
W. Butterfield, 1852–3.

BENTLEY (*St. Peter*) GR
J. Codd, 1891.

BILTON (*St. John the Evangelist*) GR
Sir G. G. Scott, 1855.

BILTON-IN-AINSTY (*St. Helen*)
Late Norman chancel arch and nave
arcades; pre-Reformation wooden lectern;
all restored by Sir G. G. Scott, 1871.

BIRKIN *(*St. Mary*)
Almost unaltered Norman church consisting of W. tower, aisleless nave, chancel

and vaulted apse with later Decorated
tracery in E. window. Tower arch blocked
by organ. Restoration font. Monument to
17th-century rector, Robert Thornton.
Georgian pulpit and tester.

BIRSTALL (*St. Peter*)
Norman and 15th-cent. tower; shroud
brass of Elizabeth Popeley, 1632.

BISHOPTHORPE (*St. Andrew*) GR
C. Hodgson Fowler, 1900; contains Archbishop's throne from old church, and font
and bell from St. Crux, York.

BOLTON PRIORY (*St. Cuthbert & St.
Mary*)
14th-cent. choir and transepts ruined;
13th-cent. nave and N. aisle used as parish
church; W. tower begun in 16th cent. but
never finished; the whole a beautiful fragment.

BOLTON-BY-BOWLAND *(*St. Peter &
St. Paul*)
Coarse Perpendicular church, characteristic
of Craven; octagonal font; dated 17th-
century pews; Pudsey chapel S. of chancel
with brass of 1509 and monument of Sir
Ralph Pudsey who sheltered Henry VI
after Hexham field in 1464. Sir Ralph's
figure is carved in low relief, two wives on
right, one on left, and twenty-five named
children.

BOLTON PERCY *(*All Saints*)
Striking Perpendicular church; contemporary roofs, and glass of five archbishops
(restored) in E. window. The sedilia and
piscina are worthy of a cathedral setting.
Nave has Jacobean pewing and reading-pen.

BRADFIELD (*St. Nicholas*)
Well-proportioned Perp. church; old
roofs; 17th-cent. brasses.

BRADFORD† (*St. Clement*) GR
E. P. Warren, 1894.

(*St. John the Evangelist*) GR
T. H. & F. Healey, 1873.

(*St. Luke*) GR
1862; porch, etc. by Healey, 1900.

(*St. Peter*)
Parish church now cathedral; nave and
chancel, 1458; tower, 1508; 15th-cent. font
cover; 14th and 15th cent. sculpture;
monument by Flaxman to Abraham
Bulme, and by Noble to John Rand; extension planned by Sir C. A. Nicholson, 1926.

† Descriptions of the churches in Bradford by the
Rev. B. F. L. Clarke.

BRAITHWELL (*All Hallows or St. James*)
Norman tympanum over S. doorway;
15th-cent. tower; fine woodwork and
monuments; 19th-cent. chancel.

BRAMHOPE (*St. Giles*)
Quaint chapel of 1649, one of few built
during Protectorate.

BRAYTON (*St. Wilfrid*)
Norman tower with 14th-cent. octagon and
spire; superb untouched Norman chancel
arch and S. doorway with traces of colour;
Darcy slab in chancel.

BRODSWORTH (*St. Michael*)
Norman and E.E. with modern additions;
pulpit of 1696; slabs and cross-fleury.

BROUGHTON-IN-AIREDALE (*St.
Oswald or All Saints*)
Late Perp. church built by Tempests; two
Norman doorways and Norman font;
17th-cent. blue porcelain alms-dish in case.

BURGHWALLIS (*St. Helen*)
Unspoilt aisleless Trans. church; restored
Perp. chancel screen; brass of Sir Thos.
Gascoign, 1554.

BURNSALL (*St. Wilfrid*)
Coarse Perp. church of Craven type,
restored in 1612; pre-Conquest font and
carving in N. chapel.

CADEBY (*St. John the Evangelist*) GR
Sir G. G. Scott, 1856.

CALVERLEY (*St. Wilfrid*)
Dec. with traces of Norman work; Jacobean font cover; old heraldic glass in E.
window.

CAMPSALL *(*St. Mary Magdalen*)
A cruciform Transitional church recast in
14th century, keeping fine W. tower. Full
of interest: inscribed tablets with floor of
rood-loft; vaulted baptistry and chamber
above; wall monument by Flaxman to
Thos. Yarborough, 1772.

CANTLEY (*St. Wilfrid*)
E.E. with Perp. W. tower; N. aisle by Sir
Ninian Comper; treasury of Comper
work – altars, rood-screen, parcloses, seating, organ-cases, statues and font cover;
every window except one has his glass;
here was the first 'English altar'.

CARLETON-IN-CRAVEN (*St. Mary*) GR
F. H. Pownall, 1858–9.

CARLTON, NR. BARNSLEY (*St. John
the Evangelist*) GR
G. E. Street, 1879.

CAWOOD (*All Saints*)
Trans. or E.E. with Perp. additions; graceful E.E. nave arcade; restoration by
J. Oldrid Scott, 1887–8. Palace of medieval
archbishops of York nearby.

CAWTHORNE (*All Saints*)
Trans. core; Dec. additions and Perp.
tower; rest by Bodley & Hare, 1912; Saxon
crosses; Spencer-Stanhope mausoleum in
churchyard.

CHAPELTOWN (*St. John the Divine*) GR
1859–60, restored by W. J. Sykes of Hoy-
land.

CHURCH FENTON (*St. John Baptist*)
E.E. cruciform church; Perp. tower; Perp.
screen in N. transept; two altar slabs;
mosaic of 14th-cent. glass; curious female
effigy in chancel.

CLAPHAM (*St. Michael the Archangel*) GR
1814, restored by J. F. Curwen, 1899.

COLLINGHAM (*St. Oswald*)
Perp. W. tower; rest modern; Saxon inscription and cresset.

CONISBOROUGH (*St. Peter*)
Large Trans. church with Perp. additions;
carved Norman tombstone in N. aisle;
other monuments and brasses.

COPGROVE (*St. Michael & All Angels*)
Aisleless Norman church carefully restored
in 1900; brasses and slabs.

COWICK (*Holy Trinity*) GR
W. Butterfield, 1854; nave wall rebuilt and
chancel repanelled, 1910.

COWTHORPE (*St. Michael*)
Perp. with small W. tower built half into
nave (cp. St. Michael-le-Belfrey and St.
Helen, York); remains of founder's brass,
1494, in chancel; heraldic glass; Perp. canopied chest, perhaps an Easter sepulchre.

CROSLAND MOOR (*St. Barnabas*) GR
C. Hodgson Fowler, 1902.

DARFIELD (*All Saints*)
Big Dec. and Perp. church of complicated
evolution; alabaster altar-tomb and other
17th-cent. monuments and brasses; Jacobean pewing.

DARRINGTON *(*St. Luke & All Saints*)
Transitional church, enlarged in 13th and
14th centuries. Tower clumsily built inside

aisles. Exquisite Early English S. doorway; 12th-century stone crucifix on bracket in S. aisle. Unique Perpendicular gallery between chapel and N. aisle opening by three arches on either side. 17th-century brass inscriptions. Lych-gate by Sir A. W. Blomfield, 1894.

DARTON (*All Saints*)
Perp. church, chancel built by Cluniac monks from Bretton in 1517; old roofs and screens; brasses; pretentious 18th-cent. monument.

DENT (*St. Andrew*)
Late Perp. church of local type; 18th-cent. tower; quaint interior with box-pews; pulpit dated 1614.

DENTON (*St. Helen*) CL
1776; E. window by H. Giles of York, 1700.

DEWSBURY (*All Saints*)
Saxon cross-heads and tombstones; 14th-cent. glass. Restoration by G. E. Street and A. H. Kirk, 1884–5.

DEWSBURY (*St. Philip*) GR
Holton and Connor, 1878; frescoes by J. Eadie Reid of Paris.

DOBCROSS (*Holy Trinity*) CL
1770; restored, 1880.

DONCASTER (*St. Andrew*) GR
Teale of Doncaster, 1860–9.

(*Christ Church*) GR
Chancel by Sir G. G. Scott, 1858.

(*St. George*) GR
Big cruciform church by Sir G. G. Scott, 1854, replacing one burnt in 1853; a few stones and brasses saved; five-manual organ by Schultze (cp. St. Bartholomew, Armley, Leeds).

(*St. John the Divine*) GR
Penrice of Clapham, 1870.

DRAX (*St. Peter & St. Paul*)
Trans. tower and spire, nave and N. aisle; E.E. chancel and S. nave arcade; Dec. spire and N. chapel; large Perp. clerestory with parapets and gargoyles; Tudor benchends; carved bosses to roof, now successfully coloured.

EASTOFT (*St. Bartholomew*) GR
J. L. Pearson, 1855.

ECCLESFIELD *(*St. Mary*)
Called by Dugdale 'the Mynster of the Moores, being the fairest church for stone, wood, glase and neat keeping, that ever I came in of contry church.' Rebuilt, probably by Carthusians of Coventry, in late 15th century; old glass in N. aisle and in vestry; 16th-century screen and pewing in S. chapel; Renaissance monument by Swayne.

EDLINGTON (*St. Peter*)
Trans. chancel arch and S. doorway; Dec. N. chapel; Perp. tower, and Perp. screen in N. chapel; font dated 1599; Wharton monuments.

ELLAND (*All Saints*) GR
G. H. Fellowes-Prynne, 1901–3; interesting series of 15th-cent. glass pictures; oak panelling.

(*St. Mary the Virgin*)
Dull church, relieved by gilded modern screens and panelling; much old glass; E. window (restored) has scenes from the life of Our Lady.

EMLEY (*St. Michael*)
Perp. tower; Jacobean pulpit and tester; heraldic glass in E. window.

FARNHAM *(*St. Oswald*)
Transitional church, with late Perpendicular tower built, like so many hereabouts, inside arcades. Restored by Sir G. G. Scott, 1854. Barrel-organ of 1831 still working. Altar and standard candlesticks by Thompson of Kilburn; effective modern altar cross, silvered strap-work on ebony.

FELKIRK (*St. Peter*)
E.E. nave and chancel; Perp. tower on Norman base; Perp. N. and S. chapels.

FEWSTON (*St. Lawrence*)
Church rebuilt in 1697; medieval font and Jacobean cover.

FISHLAKE *(*St. Cuthbert*)
Fine church in dismal marshland surroundings. Transitional S. doorway. Flamboyant tracery in most windows; striking Decorated font with canopied statues in each of eight faces; Perpendicular rood and parclose screen.

GIGGLESWICK (*St. Alkelda*)
Perp. church of Craven type without chancel arch; medieval tombs; 17th-cent. pulpit and reading desk.

GOLDSBOROUGH (*St. Mary*)
Norman S. doorway; E.E. chancel with plate tracery in windows; Dec. nave and tower; monuments, including one by Joseph Wilton; restoration by Sir G. G. Scott, 1858.

GREAT MITTON (*All Hallows*)
Dec. nave; Elizabethan N. chapel; Perp. tower; all on different levels; choir screen inscribed and dated 1493, perhaps from Cockersand Abbey; monuments in Shirburn chapel.

GREAT OUSEBURN (*St. Mary the Virgin*)
Trans. W. tower, by same hand as Little Ouseburn, q.v.

GUISELEY (*St. Oswald*)
Norman S. arcade and S. doorway; E.E. chapel showing plate tracery in windows; Dec. N. arcade; Perp. tower.

HALIFAX (*Holy Trinity*) CL
1795.

***(St. John the Baptist*)
Large Perpendicular town church; dignified tower, 118 feet high; S. chapel built as chantry for Wm. Rokeby, abp. of Dublin, 1521–2; sedilia of three wooden stalls with misericords (cp. Darrington) and six other stalls in choir; extensive Jacobean pewing. Restoration by Sir G. G. Scott, 1878–80.

HALTON (*St. Wilfrid*) GR
A. Randall Wells, 1939.

HAMPSTHWAITE *(St. Thomas of Canterbury*)
Home of Thackeray. Church charmingly situated beside River Nidd; churchwardenised in 1821, Gothicised in 1901. Brass, c. 1350, re-used in 1570. Royal Arms and old clock-face at W. end. White marble tomb of Amy Woodforde-Finden, by Geo. Wade.

HAREWOOD *(All Saints*)
Secluded position in park. Perpendicular throughout; attacked in 1862 by Sir G. G. Scott, who crowded most of the fine 15th and 16th century monuments into S. chapel. Paten with Leeds mark, c. 1700. Heavy oak communion-rail in memory of George V.

HARROGATE *(St. Wilfrid*)
The finest of Temple Moore's churches, completed in 1935. 13th-century style is used with rare and refined taste. Clerestoried nave, aisles, chancel with triforium and clerestory and chapels; low embattled tower with pyramid rood built over crossing. The rood, glass, and wall reliefs by Francis Darlington, are all notable. Behind the church an arcaded cloister leads to parish hall.

HARTSHEAD (*St. Peter*)
Good Norman S. doorway and chancel arch; rest sham Norman; 16th-cent. Italian reredos and candelabra.

HATFIELD (*St. Lawrence*)
Big cruciform church; Trans. arcades, W. and S. doorways, and font; Dec. windows; Perp. transepts and central tower; screens, one with floor of loft; old roofs, chest and pewing; monuments.

HAZELWOOD (*St. Leonard*)
Castle chapel of Vavasours; Perp. or earlier, monuments; 18th-cent. fittings.

HEALAUGH (*St. Helen & St. John the Baptist*)
Trans. S. doorway and tower arch; Dec. and Perp. additions; Wharton tomb (cp. Kirkby Stephen, Westmorland) in chapel.

HENSALL (*St. Paul*) GR
W. Butterfield, 1854.

HICKLETON (*St. Wilfrid or St. Dennis*)
Late Perp. church, retaining Norman chancel arch and Trans. font; interior darkened by ornate modern furnishings.

HIGHFIELD (*St. Barnabas*) GR
Flockton and Abbot, 1876.

HIGH MELTON (*All Hallows or St. James*)
Trans. nave and S. aisle; chancel slightly later; Perp. S. chapel and tower; beautiful old parclose screens; Dec. glass of B.V.M. in W. window of aisle; other glass by Peckitt of York; reredos, rood-screen, stalls and glass by Comper.

HOLMFIRTH (*Holy Trinity*) CL
1787 'churchwarden'; altered in 1875.

HOOTON PAGNELL (*All Saints*)
Norman S. doorway (with original door), tower arch and chancel arch; E.E. additions; restored by J. L. Pearson, 1876; slabs; Georgian pulpit with marquetry work; dignified liturgical fittings.

HORBURY (*St. Peter & St. Leonard*) CL
Large and splendid in Adam style, despite Victorian furnishings; apses at E. and W. ends, fluted Corinthian arcades; Ionic S. porch; J. Carr, 1791.

HORSFORTH (*St. Margaret*) GR
J. L. Pearson, 1881–3.

HORTON-IN-RIBBLESDALE (*St. Oswald*)
Oblong Norman church without chancel arch; Perp. tower and windows; a little old glass.

HUBBERHOLME *(St. Michael & All Angels)*
One of the remotest of Yorkshire's churches, deep in Langstrothdale. Transitional, rebuilt in 16th century, well restored in 1863. Superb rood-loft (cp. Flamborough, E.R.) painted red, black and yellow, and dated 1558.

HUDDERSFIELD *(St. Andrew)* GR
W. H. Crossland, 1870.

(St. Thomas the Apostle) GR
Sir G. G. Scott, in Trans. style but with a pseudo-Gothic spire, 1858–9.

ILKLEY *(All Saints)*
Late Perp. of Craven type, keeping 13th-cent. S. doorway; five carved stones, one Roman; effigy of 13th-cent. knight in S. aisle.

(St. Margaret)
R. Norman Shaw, 1878–9; handsome carved reredos; fine chancel screen; notable modern glass.

ILLINGSWORTH *(St. Mary)* CL
1777.

INGLETON *(St. Mary the Virgin)*
Rebuilt church has fine carved Norman font.

KELLINGTON *(St. Edmund)*
Norman core; E.E. arcades and lancets; bosses to nave roof; medieval font re-dated 1663.

KILDWICK *(St. Andrew)*
The 'Lang Kirk' of Craven; medieval with Tudor elongation; heraldic glass; 17th-cent. woodwork.

KING CROSS *(St. Paul)* GR
Sir C. A. Nicholson, 1911.

KIRK BRAMWITH *(St. Mary)*
Aisleless Norman church (chancel arch and S. doorway) recast in churchwarden style; slabs; 17th-cent. glass.

KIRK BURTON *(All Hallows)*
E.E. nave; Perp. tower and clerestory; bosses to nave roof; glass; 17th-cent. pewing and chained book; striking modern font cover.

KIRKBY MALHAM *(St. Michael or St. James the less)*
Complete Perp. church; Trans. font; box-pews and other old woodwork; monuments; German glass of 18th cent.

KIRKBY MALZEARD *(St. Andrew*
E.E. church on Norman foundations;

Perp. tower built inside nave; modern woodwork by Thompson of Kilburn.

KIRKBY OVERBLOW *(All Saints)*
Formerly collegiate; 13th-cent. N. transept; tower of 1781; restored by G. E. Street, 1872.

KIRKBY WHARFE *(St. John the Baptist)*
Trans. arcades, tower arch and S. doorway; rest later; old screenwork; brasses; glass, some old, some enamelled, by Capronnier of Brussels.

KIRK DEIGHTON *(All Saints)*
Norman N. arcade, E.E. S. arcade; Perp. tower and spire; cross-fleury; monuments.

KIRK HAMMERTON *(St. John the Baptist)*
Good example of small Saxon church, though with modern additions; piscina and colourful reredos.

KIRK SANDALL *(St. Oswald)*
E.E. additions to Norman church; huge Rokeby chapel with monument, N. of chancel; screens; fragments of 16th-cent. glass.

KNARESBOROUGH *(St. John the Baptist)*
Originally cruciform E.E., rebuilt in Perp. period; tower with extinguisher spire of Herts. type; post-Gothic altar-tomb and other monuments to Slingsbys in N. chapel; 18th-cent. font cover; Burne-Jones glass. See also St. Robert's chapel by riverside.

LAUGHTON-EN-LE-MORTHEN *(A Saints)*
Blocked Saxon doorway in N. aisle; Perp. tower and spire, landmark; Trans. chancel, recast in 15th cent.; Trans. nave and N. aisle; Perp. stone chancel screen.

LEATHLEY *(St. Oswald)*
Early Norman tower and chancel arch; door has original ironwork; Perp. nave arcades; two fonts; pulpit and screen apparently made from old box-pews!

LEDSHAM *(All Saints)*
Saxon nave, chancel arch and lower stage of tower; 13th-cent. chancel; 14th and 15th cent. chapel and aisles; monument to Lady Eliz. Hastings, benefactor to Queen's College, Oxford, 'whom to love', declared Steele, 'was a liberal education'.

LEE MOUNT OVENDON *(St. George)* GR
Jackson and Fox of Halifax, 1878.

LEEDS† *(*St. Aidan*)
A Victorian red-brick church by one of the North's most prominent 19th-century architects, R. J. Johnson. The interior is probably the most impressive of any of the county's Victorian churches. Beautiful mosaic by Brangwyn. Outstanding font and pulpit, and more beautiful marble behind the altar in S. Chapel.

*(*All Souls*) GR
G. G. Scott, consecrated 1880.

*(*St. Hilda*) GR
1876–81, J. T. Micklethwaite. Red brick, with nave and chancel of the same height. Painted wooden reredos, screen, rood, loft and pulpit by W. H. Wood of Newcastle, in a Bodley-ish style.

*(*Holy Trinity*) CL
The only 18th-century church remaining in Leeds. In a busy shopping centre. 1721–7, by William Halfpenny. Doric without, Composite within. The tower was rebuilt by Chantrell.

*(*St. Margaret*) GR
Begun in 1905, still incomplete; Temple Moore; very simple and pleasing.

*(*St. Mary*) GR
1823–7, Thomas Taylor of Leeds; another Commissioners church. The exterior big, black and grim; very long lancet windows, and a shallow apse. Tall arcades, of no known Gothic form, but successful nevertheless: a plaster vault, and a Gothic canopy over the altar.

*(*St. Peter*)
Rebuilt in 1839–41 by R. D. Chantrell of Leeds. The style is ordinary Perpendicular of the period, but the planning is extremely interesting. It represents the ideas of Hook, who was an uncompromising High Churchman of the traditional type, but who also welcomed (more or less) the teachings of the Oxford Movement. There is room for a very large congregation on the floor and in the galleries: there are also stalls for the choir in the chancel. To the E. of the stalls is an empty space, for the communicants to 'draw near' and stand in; and the altar rails will hold forty people at a time. The interior is very impressive, with its dark varnished woodwork and bright glass. The E. window has glass from the Continent, put together by Wilmhurst of London: the W. window has armorial glass by David Evans of Shrewsbury. In the S.

† Descriptions of the churches, except St. Aidan's, in Leeds by the Rev. B. F. L. Clarke.

aisle is a window of St. Peter by Wright of Leeds, 1811. The memorial to Hook is by Sir G. G. Scott. Some brasses remain from the old church, and a cross of the early 10th century.

*(*St. Saviour*) GR
Built by Dr. Pusey: the foundation stone was laid in 1842, and the church was consecrated in 1845. Architect J. M. Derick, Middle Pointed, cruciform, tall and narrow: some contemporary glass.

*(*St. Bartholomew, Armley*) GR
By Walker and Atkinson 1872–7, taking the place of a smaller old chapel. Tower completed 1903–4. An admirable church. The best work of 19th-century provincial architects was quite up to the standard of the better-known masters. Schultze organ.

*(*St. John, Briggate*) GS
1631; Survival Gothic of twin nave plan; magnificent contemporary fittings, including screen, pews and pulpit with tester.

(*St. Matthias, Burley*) GR
1853–4, Perkin and Backhouse; Middle Pointed: very little altered internally.

*(*St. Matthew, Chapel Allerton*) GR
Begun in 1897, on a different site from the old church. G. F. Bodley. Nave and aisles under one roof; detached tower on S.; chancel and S. chapel. Painted waggon-roofs. Glass by Burlison and Grylls.

*(*St. Chad, Far Headingley*) GR
Designed by Sir Edmund Beckett (Lord Grimthorpe) and built under W. H. Crossland; consecrated in 1868. Solid early Middle Pointed. The apse was taken down, and a new chancel built in 1909. J. & J. H. Gibbons architects.

*(*The Epiphany, Gipton*) GR
1937–8, by N. F. Cachemaille Day. Parish Communion planning. The choir in curved balconies at the sides of the altar, reached by steps behind the altar.

*(*St. Michael, Headingley*) GR
J. L. Pearson, begun in 1884, taking the place of the old church, which had been rebuilt in 1837–8. Characteristic of its architect. Pearson's spires were often not completed. This one has been: it resembles St. Augustine's, Kilburn. Reredos (1905) by Temple Moore.

*(*St. Edward, Holbeck*) GR
By Bodley, 1903–4. A beautiful, devout church, nave and aisles, with the E. bay screened off to form sanctuary and chapels;

the altar in a recess. The E. wall is entirely
filled with a carved altar-piece, painted and
gilt. W. organ gallery.

*(St. Peter, Hunslet Moor) GR
1866–8, Perkin and Son architects. Uncompromisingly French Gothic, lined with
Pontefract white brick with stripes of red.
The W. end barbaric but impressive. (There
are several older churches of this type,
which have, fortunately, escaped 20th century purification – though churchmen of
the W. Riding still have a dangerous pre-
dilection for unstained oak panelling.)

(St. John, New Wortley) GR
1852, Dobson and Chorley. Camdenian
early Middle Pointed.

(St. John, Roundhay) GR
1826, Thomas Taylor; E.E.

(St. Clement, Sheepscar) GR
1868, George Carson, Grim, muscular
French Gothic, low.

(St. Mark, Woodhouse) GR
1825–6, R. H. Sharp architect.

LINTON-IN-CRAVEN (St. Michael)
Setting by Wharfe; Trans. pointed chancel
arch and two E. arches of nave arcade;
rest 14th cent.

LITTLE OUSEBURN (Holy Trinity)
Trans. W. tower, by same hand as Great
Ouseburn, q.v. old bench-ends in chancel;
chest in S. aisle, dated 1673.

LONG MARSTON (All Saints)
Late Norman church with Dec. and Perp.
windows; Trans. S. doorway (cp. Askham
Richard) brought here from Angram;
Caroline monuments.

LONG PRESTON (St. Mary the Virgin)
Unusual whitewashed interior; Dec. nave;
rebuilt chancel; slab dated 1445 in sanctuary; enamelled glass by Capronnier.

LOTHERTON (no dedication)
Norman chapel lovingly restored by Bilson,
1917; screen by Sir J. N. Comper; 15th-
cent. Venetian reredos now moved to N.
wall; Lutheran chest; Father Smith organ.

LOVERSAL (St. Katharine)
Late Perp. chapel of Wyvval family, with
tombs.

MARR (St. Helen)
Herringbone masonry in tower; rest Perp.;
Tudor brass of John Lewis and family,
1589.

MARSDEN (St. Bartholomew) GR
C. Hodgson Fowler, 1895.

METHLEY *(St. Oswald)
Has Perpendicular W. tower and spire;
Decorated nave; fine collection of monuments in Waterton Chapel, and 15th-
century glass (cp. St. Michael, Spurriergate, York). Altar-tomb of Sir John Savile
lately moved to W. end, thus exposing
beauty of this aisle. Monument signed by
J. Wilton to John Savile, 1778.

MIDHOPESTONES (St. James)
Small 17th-cent. chapel with earlier fragments; Jacobean pulpit, pews and gallery.

MILLHOUSES (St. Oswald) GR
J. D. Webster, 1910.

MIRFIELD (St. Mary the Virgin) GR
Sir G. G. Scott, 1871.

MITTON, GREAT: see Great Mitton.

MONK BRETTON (St. Paul) GR
Solaini of Liverpool, 1877.

MONK FRYSTON (St. Wilfrid of Ripon)
Saxon tower; E.E. nave arcades; Dec.
chancel; massive square E.E. font; 15th-
cent. clerestory.

MOOR MONKTON (All Saints)
Lonely 12th-cent. aisleless church; Slings-
by brass with emblems of mortality, 1667;
another monument under tower shows
infant in bed.

NETHER POPPLETON (St. Everilda)
Unusual dedication (cp. Everingham, E.
Riding); aisleless Norman church with
Dec. and Perp. windows; old glass; 17th-
cent. coloured monuments.

NEWTON KYME (St. Andrew)
Trans. N. aisle and chancel; 15th-cent.
tower; remarkable carvings in porch;
heraldic glass; Fairfax monument, 1725.

NORMANTON (All Saints)
Imposing church in dismal mining town;
Dec. chancel and nave arcades; Perp.
tower; panelled font; old glass, some of it
foreign.

NUN MONKTON *(St. Mary)
Is nave of vanished Early English nunnery
chapel, comparable with Skelton? (N.R.).
W. front shows transition from Romanesque to English Gothic. Nave windows
have peculiar, perhaps unique, recessed
arcades between them. E. end rebuilt in
1873, spoiled by vulgar modern lighting.

OAKENSHAW (St. Andrew) GR
Milnes and France, 1889.

OTLEY (*All Saints*)
Cruciform church; Norman windows; remainder Dec.; brass with family tree, 1598; Fairfax monument.

OULTON (*St. John the Evangelist*) GR
Thomas Rickman, 1827.

OWSTON *(All Saints)*
Well-kept church on edge of park. Transitional W. tower; Early English arcade in nave; Decorated chancel; restored by Sir G. G. Scott, 1873. Brass of Robert de Hatfield and wife, 1409, wearing SS collar and holding hands. Fine, well-preserved niche (?Easter sepulchre) N. of chancel, with watcher's seat to W. Monument by Chantrey to Mrs. Cooke.

PENISTONE (*St. John the Baptist*)
Nave arcades; Dec. chancel and S. chapel; Perp. clerestories; tower and N. chapel; old roofs with bosses; glass dated 1687.

POLLINGTON: *see Balne.*

PONTEFRACT (*All Saints*)
Cruciform, 15th-cent. nave and 14th-cent. chancel in ruins since Civil War; square central tower with octagonal lantern; transept restored by Chantrell, 1838.

(*St. Giles*) CL
1795.

RASTRICK (*St. John the Divine*)
Sir C. A. Nicholson, 1914.

(*St. Matthew*) CL
Grecian; 1796.

RAVENSTHORPE (*St. Saviour*) GR
C. Hodgson Fowler, 1901.

RIPLEY (*All Saints*)
Setting in model village of Ingilbys, Dec. church; Perp. clerestories and tower; brasses (one a chalice brass, cp. Bishop Burton, E. Riding, and St. Peter, Leeds); double piscina.

ROSSINGTON (*St. Michael with St. Luke*)
Fine Trans. S. doorway and chancel arch; 15th-cent. inscribed pulpit.

ROTHERHAM *(All Saints)*
Fine Perpendicular church in heart of busy industrial town. Choir has stalls with poppy-heads. Screen and base of rood-loft in Jesus chapel, S. of choir. 16th-century tombs. E. window by Peckitt of York tones in well.

ROTHWELL (*Holy Trinity*)
15th-cent. W. tower and S. doorway; Restoration font with canopy, dated 1662, and porch; rest modern; sculptured group by J. Towne of Guy's Hospital, 1842.

ROYSTON *(St. John the Baptist*)
Decorated church of character. Pentagonal oriel on W. face of tower (cp. Macclesfield). Roof with carved bosses in nave and aisles. Traces of wall-painting. 17th-century marble monument N. of chancel.

RUFFORTH (*All Saints*) GR
Demaine and Brierley of York, 1894–5.

RYTHER *(All Saints)*
Curiously shaped church by banks of R. Wharfe; Saxon chancel arch, Early English nave, Decorated S. aisle and chancel, all restored by C. Hodgson Fowler. 1898. Monuments to Ryther family. Four stone altar-slabs, the largest 7 feet long.

SANDAL MAGNA (*St. Helen*)
Cruciform, enlarged from Norman original; three E. windows (cp. Almondbury); screen and monuments in Waterton chapel; signed monument by E. Physick, 1836, in S. aisle.

SAVILE TOWN (*St. Mary*) GR
C. J. Ferguson, 1900.

SAXTON (*All Saints*)
Norman chancel arch; Dec. chapel and huge squint down to ground; Perp. tower; 17th-cent. ledger-stones to Hungate family; churchyard tomb of Lord Dacre, 1461; 18th-cent. chairs in sanctuary; woodwork by Thompson of Kilburn.

SCOTTON (*St. Thomas the Apostle*) GR
C. Hodgson Fowler, 1889.

SEDBERGH (*St. Andrew & St. Gregory the Great*)
Trans. arcades; Perp. windows and tower; brasses; bust by Flaxman to John Dawson, 1820; fine modern woodwork.

SELBY ABBEY *(St. Mary & St. Germain*)
Founded by the Conqueror for Benedictine monks. Norman Transitional nave (cp. Durham) and N. transept; Early English clerestories; Decorated chancel – perhaps the loveliest in N. England; twin W. towers built in 1935–6; restored 14th-century Jesse window. Scholarly restoration by J. Oldrid Scott, 1889–90. Central tower and S. transept rebuilt after fire of 1906.

SETTLE (*The Holy Ascension*) GR
Thomas Rickman, 1835.

SHEFFIELD†

The smallish old town of Sheffield had one parish church of no great size. As the town grew in the 18th century one or two new churches were provided, and the usual large Commissioners' churches were added in the early 19th century.

The town was almost untouched by the Oxford Movement, and the *Ecclesiologist* once lamented that there was no place which showed fewer signs of Church feeling. There were scarcely any churches of which it could approve: indeed, Sheffield is hardly mentioned in its pages.

In the 60's and 70's some large and expensive French Gothic churches were built, and some of the later 19th-century churches might qualify for the adjective 'handsome'. But, on the whole, it is a dull town for the church-hunter.

The architects are almost all local: T. J. Flockton, W. Flockton, Mitchell Withers, J. D. Webster, J. Mitchell, Joseph Norton, etc.

(St. George) GR
1821–5; a Commissioners' church, by Woodhead and Hurst of Doncaster; large, Perp.

(St. Luke) GR
1854–60; 15th-cent. glass brought from Spain, 1905.

(St. Mary) GR
1826–30; another Commissioners' church - architect, Potter of Lichfield; a more light-hearted, Gothick kind of Perp. than St. George and St. Philip. These three churches have all had the usual later alterations: choir stalls, electric light, reseating, oak war memorials, etc.

*(St. Peter)
Now the Cathedral. A 15th-century church with central tower and spire. The E. parts remain, more or less, but the walls were re-cased, and new tracery was inserted in the windows, c. 1772. The aisles of the nave were rebuilt and widened, and the W. wall rebuilt, in 1790–7. In 1800 the arcades were rebuilt and raised; the old roof was re-placed. Transepts 1878–80, and nave lengthened and reseated.

The Shrewsbury Chapel has several 16th-century monuments. This chapel has been replastered and whitened, and given a new altar and glass by Christopher Webb. Reredos by Temple Moore, 1919.

† Descriptions of the churches in Sheffield by the Rev. B. F. L. Clarke.

Sir Charles Nicholson prepared plans for the enlargement of this church, to make it more cathedral-like. It is hard to see why it was ever chosen as a Cathedral. St. Paul's, a noble 18th-century church by Platt of Rotherham, begun in 1720, would have made as adequate a Cathedral as St. Philip's, Birmingham, but St. Paul's was demolished in 1939.

(St. Philip) GR
1822–8; a Commissioners' church by Thomas Taylor of Leeds. Perp., but with peculiar Taylorian arcades.

(St. Silas) GR
Blackmoor and Mitchell-Withers, 1869.

(St. Swithun) GR
Flockton and Abbot, 1929.

(St. Mark, Broomhall) GR
1868–71; W. H. Crossland of Halifax.

(St. Bartholomew, Carbrook) GR
1890–1; J. D. Webster.

(All Saints, Ecclesall) CL
1788 – a poor 18th-cent. church: chancel and transepts by Temple Moore, 1906–8.

(St. Augustine, Endcliffe, Brocco Bank) GR
1897–8; J. D. Webster.

(St. Bernard, Parson Cross) GR
F. Etchells, of 18th-cent. brick from Clumber; planned for the Parish Communion, round a large central space.

(St. Paul, Pinstone Street) CL
Italian; 1720–1; bust by Chantrey; shamelessly demolished in 1939.

(St. John the Evangelist, Ranmoor) GR
E. M. Gibbs (of Flockton and Gibbs). Consecrated, 1879; burned, 1887; rebuilt, 1887–8; large and expensive; French Gothic.

(St. Andrew, Sharron) GR
1867–9; by Mitchell Withers; large, rather coarse French Gothic; reredos by C. Hodgson Fowler, 1913.

SHERBURN-IN-ELMET *(All Saints)

Hill-top site, visible for miles around. Late Norman nave arcades; Early English chancel with typical E. end - a vesica and three lancets; tower part Norman, part Perpendicular. Interior full of interest; 14th-century cross-heads and cross fleury; Foljame monument, 1618; old glass.

SILKSTONE *(All Saints)

13th–15th century church of charm in un-lovely mining area; buttresses with gargoyles (cp. St. Martin, Coney St., York);

screens across chancel and aisles; Wentworth monuments in S. aisle.

SKELTON *(Christ the Consoler)*
A lavish creation of Burges (cp. Studley Royal) built in 1871–2 by Lady Mary Vyner as memorial to her son killed by brigands in Greece. Profusion of multi-coloured marble, brass and windows; jewelled altar-frontal made by Lady Vyner herself. Immaculate churchyard.

SKIPTON-IN-CRAVEN *(Holy Trinity)*
Colourful setting by castle; rectangular church of seven bays with continuous arcades, Dec. and Perp.; old roofs; Perp. chancel screens, once dated 1533; Clifford tombs, restored, 1589; elaborate heraldry; Jacobean font cover; restoration by Sir G. G. Scott, 1870.

SLAIDBURN *(St. Andrew)*
Perp. church; Jacobean screen; coarse 17th-cent. pewing; glass; three-decker pulpit.

SNAITH *(St. Lawrence, originally St. Osyth)*
Dominates this old-fashioned town; massive 12th-century tower; church 170 feet long; Decorated chancel; brilliant modern glass of St. Lawrence; statue by Chantrey of Viscount Downe, 1832, in S. choir aisle.

SOUTH KIRKBY *(All Saints)*
Trans. aisles; Perp. tower, porches and S. chapel; Wentworth monuments.

SOWERBY *(St. Peter)* CL
1763; tower, 1781.

SPENBOROUGH *(St. Luke)* GR
Medland Taylor of Manchester, 1889.

SPOFFORTH *(All Saints)*
Trans. nave, chancel arch and S. doorway with beakheads; Perp. tower; sham Norman chancel.

SPROTBOROUGH *(St. Mary)*
Stands on a hillside above the Don. 14th and 15th century with older fragments; brass to William Fitzwilliam, 1474, and other incised slabs; chancel screen with seven return stalls; beautiful Decorated wall niche and figure in S. aisle; old pewing; Comper altars, screens, stalls, seating and glass.

STAINBURN *(St. John the Evangelist)*
Plain Norman Church in secluded position on moorside; Jacobean pewing; Trans. font with arcading.

STAINLAND *(St. Andrew)* CL
1778, with additions in Doric by W. S. Barber of Halifax, 1887–8.

STEETON *(St. Stephen)* GR
T. H. & F. Healey of Bradford, 1881.

STUDLEY ROYAL *(St. Mary)*
Sister-church to Skelton (q.v.) by Burges, 1871–8, and even more elaborate; built in 14th-century French style, with spire 152 feet high; multi-coloured marble, alabaster and mosaic again used; tomb of founder, Marquis of Ripon, 1909, in S. chapel. All sadly unkempt.

SUTTON *(St. Thomas)* GR
W. H. Crossland, 1869.

SWILLINGTON *(St. Mary)*
Late Dec. nave and chancel of white Tadcaster stone, untouched by soot; tower of 1884 black already!; brass; Royal Arms dated 1723 in vestry.

TADCASTER *(St. Mary)*
14th and 15th cent. church; imposing tower and gargoyled exterior; Norman fragments within; a little glass.

THORNER *(St. Peter)*
Perp. church; well-proportioned tower; monuments; traceried font.

THORNHILL *(St. Michael & All Angels)*
Perp. church, restored in 1879 by G. E. Street who destroyed 18th-cent. Georgian nave; rich in Savile monuments (one wooden) and glass.

THORNHILL LEES *(Holy Innocents)* GR
Mallinson and Healey, 1858.

THORPE SALVIN *(St. Michael)*
Pastoral setting. Norman S. doorway, inferior only to Adel in W.R., and font with carving of four seasons; 15th and 17th century monuments.

THURLSTONE *(St. Saviour)* GR
C. Hodgson Fowler, 1905.

TICKHILL *(St. Mary)*
One of the finest churches in the Riding. Core is probably early 13th century to which belongs base of tower and chancel. N. chapel is 14th century. Tower remodelled in last quarter of 14th century but upper part not completed until late when the nave was rebuilt and the S. chapel added. Large window over chancel arch. Early 16th-century table-tomb and late medieval glass in S. aisle. The tower retains old statuary on each face.

TODMORDEN (*St. Mary*) CL
1770; chancel 1896.

TONG (*St. James*)
Only five miles from centre of Bradford, but quiet in setting of lawns and trees; stocks and mounting block outside church-yard wall; Norman features, but church largely Early Georgian, with box-pews and three-decker pulpit.

UNDERCLIFFE (*St. Augustine*) GR
T. H. and F. Healey, 1877.

WAKEFIELD *(All Saints)*
Promoted to cathedral rank in 1888, but still the parish church; large cruciform building with spire 247 feet – tallest in county; rood-screen, lower part medieval, upper Carolean copied from St. John's, Leeds, q.v.; Classical pulpit with sounding board. Restoration by Sir G. G. Scott, 1858–74. Reredos by J. Oldrid Scott, 1896. See also chantry chapel (restored) on bridge.

(*St. John*) CL
1791.

WENTBRIDGE (*St. John the Evangelist*)
GR
Sir A. W. Blomfield, 1878.

WENTWORTH (*Holy Trinity*, *old church*)
15th-cent. tower, ruined nave, 17th-cent. chancel with important Wentworth-Fitzwilliam monuments.

(*Holy Trinity*)
J. L. Pearson, 1877.

WESTON (*All Saints*)
Old-fashioned church in park; Norman walls and chancel arch; interior unchanged since 17th cent.; Vavasour tomb and family pew.

WHISTON (*St. Mary Magdalene or St. James*) GR
G. G. Scott, 1883.

WHITKIRK (*St. Mary*)
Good Perp. tower with Herts. type spire;

Scargyll tomb, 1546; Irwin monument signed by Nollekens, 1778; another to Smeaton, builder of Eddystone lighthouse.

WHIXLEY (*The Ascension*)
Large Dec. church; Perp. tower; traces of pattern-painting in nave; Tancred monument, 1754.

WIGHILL (*All Saints*)
Trans. nave arcade and superb S. doorway with zig-zag, beak-head and grotesques; Stapleton monuments; 17th-cent. wood-work; modern glass by C. W. Whall.

WISTOW (*All Saints*)
Mixture of Dec. and Perp.; advanced tracery in E. window; glass; Jacobean pulpit; monuments, including canopied effigy of woman.

WOMERSLEY (*St. Martin*)
Cruciform; Dec. broach spire and elaborate porch; cross-legged military effigy in S. aisle; roofs repainted in medieval style.

WOOLLEY (*St. Peter*)
Perp. church (cp. Silkstone), keeping Norman tympanum; 15th-cent. glass in chapel; Wentworth monuments; fine carved screen and bench-ends; two chained books.

WORSBOROUGH (*St. Mary*)
Trans. core (window in sanctuary); Perp. enlargement; squint; extraordinary painted wooden monument to Roger Pockley, 1534, and family; old doors and roofs; brasses.

WORTLEY (*St. Leonard*) CL
17th and 18th cent.; Flaxman monument to Margaret Mackenzie, 1808.

WRAGBY (*St. Michael & Our Lady*)
Church in Nostell Park; 16th-cent. glass; other 17th and 18th cent. German-Swiss glass here since 1830; Norman font once in Auburn church, E. Riding; Italian pulpit hanging from pillar; Winn monuments by Flaxman and Chantrey.

GLOSSARY

AMBULATORY: semicircular or polygonal aisle enclosing an apse (q.v.).

APSE: vaulted semicircular or polygonal end of a chancel or a chapel.

ARCADE: range of arches supported on piers or columns, free-standing; or, BLIND ARCADE, the same attached to a wall.

ARCH: pointed, i.e. consisting of two curves, each drawn from one centre, and meeting in a point at the top; segmental, i.e. in the form of a segment; pointed; four-centred, see Fig. 1(a); Tudor, see Fig. 1(b); Ogee, see Fig. 1(c); round-headed, see Fig. 1(d).

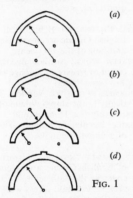

(a)

(b)

(c)

(d)

FIG. 1

ARCHITRAVE: lowest of the three main parts of the entablature (q.v.) of an order (q.v.) (see Fig. 3(a)).

ASHLAR: masonry of large blocks wrought to even faces and square edges.

ATTACHED: see engaged.

AUMBREY: recess or cupboard to hold sacred vessels for Mass and Communion.

BALDACCHINO: canopy supported on columns.

BALLFLOWER: globular flower of three petals enclosing a small ball. A decoration used in the first quarter of the 14th cent.

BALUSTER: small pillar or column of fanciful outline.

BALUSTRADE: series of balusters supporting a handrail or coping (q.v.).

BASILICA: in medieval architecture an aisled church with a clerestory.

BATTER: wall with an inclined face.

BATTLEMENT: parapet with a series of indentations or embrasures with raised portions or merlons between (also called Crenellation).

BAYS: internal compartments of a building; each divided from the other not by solid walls but by divisions only marked in the side walls (columns, pilasters, etc.) or the ceiling (beams, etc.). Also external divisions of a building by fenestration.

BELL-COTE: turret usually on the W. end of a church to carry the bells.

BILLET: Norman ornamental motif made up of short raised rectangles placed at regular intervals.

BLOCK CAPITAL: Romanesque capital cut from a cube by having the lower angles rounded off to the circular shaft below (also called Cushion Capital) (Fig. 2).

FIG. 2

BOSS: knob or projection usually placed to cover the intersection of ribs in a vault.

BOX PEW: pew with a high wooden enclosure.

BRACES: see Roof.

BRACKET: small supporting piece of stone, etc., to carry a projecting horizontal.

BROACH: see Spire.

BUTTRESS: mass of brickwork or masonry projecting from or built against a wall to give additional strength. *Flying Buttress:* arch or half arch transmitting the thrust of a vault or roof from the upper part of a wall to an outer support or buttress.

443

CABLE MOULDING: moulding imitating a twisted cord.

CAMBER: slight rise or upward curve of an otherwise horizontal structure.

CAMPANILE: isolated bell tower.

CANOPY: ornamental covering above an altar, pulpit, niche, etc.

CAPITAL: head or top part of a column.

CARTOUCHE: tablet with an ornate frame, usually enclosing an inscription.

CARYATID: human figure used instead of a column.

CEILURE: panelled and adorned part of a wagon-roof above the rood or the altar.

CENTERING: wooden framework used in arch and vault construction and removed when the mortar has set.

CHALICE: small cup used in the Communion service or at Mass.

CHAMFER: surface made by cutting across the square angle of a stone block, piece of wood, etc., at an angle of 45 degrees to the two other surfaces.

CHANCEL: that part of the E. end of a church in which the altar is placed, usually applied to the whole continuation of the nave E. of the crossing.

CHANCEL ARCH: arch at the W. end of the chancel.

CHANTRY CHAPEL: chapel attached to, or inside, a church endowed for the saying of Masses for the soul of the founder or some other individual.

CHEVRON: sculptured moulding forming a zigzag.

CHOIR: that part of the church where divine service is sung.

CLASSICAL: here used as the term for Greek and Roman architecture and any subsequent styles copying it.

CLERESTORY: upper storey of the nave walls of a church, pierced by windows.

COADE STONE: artificial (cast) stone made in the late 18th cent. and the early 19th cent. by Coade and Seely in London.

COB: walling material made of mixed clay and straw.

COFFERING: decorating a ceiling with sunk square or polygonal ornamental panels.

COLLAR-BEAM: see Roof.

COLONNADE: range of columns.

COPING: capping or covering to a wall.

CORBEL: block of stone projecting from a wall, supporting some horizontal feature.

CORBEL TABLE: series of corbels, occurring just below the roof eaves externally or internally, often seen in Norman buildings.

CORINTHIAN: see Orders.

CORNICE: in classical architecture the top section of the entablature (q.v.). Also for a projecting decorative feature along the top of a wall, arch, etc.

COVE, COVING: concave under-surface in the nature of a hollow moulding but on a larger scale.

CREST, CRESTING: ornamental finish along the top of a screen, etc.

CROCKET, CROCKETING: decorative features placed on the sloping sides of spires, pinnacles, gables, etc. in Gothic architecture, carved in various leaf shapes and placed at regular intervals.

CROSSING: space at the intersection of nave, chancel, and transepts.

CRYPT: underground room usually below the E. end of a church.

CUPOLA: small polygonal or circular domed turret crowning a roof.

CUSHION CAPITAL: see Block Capital.

CUSP: in tracery (q.v.) the small pointed member between two lobes of a trefoil, quatrefoil, etc.

DEC. ('DECORATED'): historical division of English Gothic architecture covering the first half of the 14th cent.

DIAPER WORK: surface decoration composed of square or lozenge shapes.

DORIC: see Orders.

DORMER (WINDOW): window placed vertically in the sloping plane of a roof.

DRIPSTONE: see Hood-mould.

DRUM: circular or polygonal vertical wall of a dome or cupola.

E.E. ('EARLY ENGLISH'): historical division of English Gothic architecture roughly covering the 13th cent.

EASTER SEPULCHRE: recess with tomb-chest usually in the wall of a chancel, the tomb-chest to receive an effigy of Christ for Easter celebrations.

EAVES: underpart of a sloping roof overhanging a wall.

ENCAUSTIC TILES: earthenware glazed and decorated tiles used for paving.

ENGAGED COLUMNS: columns attached to, or partly sunk into, a wall.

ENTABLATURE: in classical architecture the whole of the horizontal members above a column (that is architrave, frieze, and cornice) (see Fig. 3).

ENTASIS: very slight convex deviation from a straight line; used on Greek columns and sometimes on spires to prevent an optical illusion of concavity.

EPITAPH: hanging wall monument.

ESCUTCHEON: shield for armorial bearings.

FAIENCE: decorated glazed earthenware.

FAN VAULT: *see* Vault.

FESTOON: carved garland of flowers and fruit suspended at both ends.

FILLET: narrow flat band running down a shaft or along a roll moulding.

FINIAL: in Gothic architecture the top of a pinnacle, gable, or bench-end carved into a leaf or leaf-like form.

FLAMBOYANT: properly the latest phase of French Gothic architecture where the window tracery takes on wavy undulating lines.

FLÈCHE: slender wooden spire on the centre of a roof (also called Spirelet).

FLUTING: vertical channelling in the shaft of a column.

FLYING BUTTRESS: *see* Buttress.

FOLIATED: carved with leaf shapes.

FRESCO: wall painting on wet plaster.

FRIEZE: middle division of a classical entablature (q.v.) (*see* Fig. 3(*f*).

FRONTAL: covering of the front of an altar.

GALLERY: in church architecture upper storey above an aisle, sometimes opened in arches to the nave.

GARGOYLE: water spout projecting from the parapet of a wall or tower; carved into a human or animal shape.

GROIN: sharp edge at the meeting of two cells of a cross-vault.

GROINED VAULT: *see* Vault.

HAGIOSCOPE: *see* Squint.

HAMMER-BEAM: *see* Roof.

HATCHMENT: board with armorial bearings.

HIPPED ROOF: *see* Roof.

HOOD-MOULD: projecting moulding above an arch or a lintel to throw off water (also called Dripstone or Label).

IMPOST: brackets in walls, usually formed of mouldings, on which the ends of an arch rest.

IONIC: *see* Orders (Fig. 3).

JAMB: straight side of an archway, doorway, or window.

KEYSTONE: middle stone in an arch.

KING-POST: *see* Roof (Fig. 4).

LANCET WINDOW: slender pointed-arched window.

LEAN-TO ROOF: roof with one slope only, built against a higher wall.

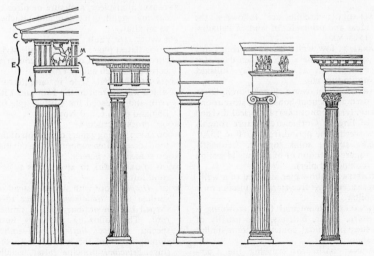

FIG. 3 ORDERS (*see over*)

Greek Doric   Roman Doric   Tuscan   Ionic   Corinthian
E, Entablature; F, Frieze; A, Architrave; M, Metope; T, Triglyph.

LINTEL: horizontal beam or stone bridging an opening.

LYCH GATE: wooden gate structure with a roof and open sides placed at the entrance to a churchyard to provide space for the reception of a coffin. The word lych is Saxon and means a corpse.

MISERERE: *see* Misericord.

MISERICORD: bracket placed on the underside of a hinged choir stall seat which, when turned up, provided the occupant of the seat with a support during long periods of standing (also called Miserere).

MULLION: vertical post or upright dividing a window into two or more 'lights'.

NARTHEX: enclosed vestibule or covered porch at the main entrance to a church.

NEWEL: central post in a circular or winding staircase; also the principal post when a flight of stairs meets a landing.

ORDER: *in classical architecture:* column with base, shaft, capital, and entablature (q.v.) according to one of the following styles: Greek Doric, Roman Doric, Tuscan Doric, Ionic, Corinthian, Composite. The established details are very elaborate, and some specialist architectural work should be consulted for further guidance (*see* Fig. 3).

PALLADIAN: architecture following the ideas and principles of Andrea Palladio, 1518–80.

PARAPET: low wall placed to protect any spot where there is a sudden drop, for example on a bridge, quay, hillside, house-top, etc.

PARVISE: room over a church porch. Often used as a school-house or a store room.

PERP. (PERPENDICULAR): historical division of English Gothic architecture roughly covering the period from 1350 to 1530.

PIER: strong, solid support, frequently square in section or of composite section (compound pier).

PILASTER: shallow pier attached to a wall.

PILLAR PISCINA: free-standing piscina on a pillar.

PINNACLE: ornamental form crowning a spire, tower, buttress, etc., usually of steep pyramidal, conical, or some similar shape.

PISCINA: basin for washing the Communion or Mass vessels, provided with a drain. Generally set in or against the wall to the S. of an altar.

PLATE TRACERY: *see* Tracery.

PLINTH: projecting base of a wall or column, generally chamfered (q.v.) or moulded at the top.

POPPYHEAD: ornament of leaf and flower type used to decorate the tops of bench or stall-ends.

PORTICO: centre-piece of a house or a church with classical detached or attached columns and a pediment.

PRESBYTERY: the part of the church lying E. of the choir. It is the part where altar is placed.

PRINCIPAL: *see* Roof (Figs. 4, 5).

PRIORY: monastic house whose head is a prior or prioress, not an abbot or abbess.

PULPITUM: stone rood screen in a major church.

PURLIN: *see* Roof (Figs. 4, 5).

QUARRY: in stained-glass work, a small diamond or square-shaped piece of glass set diagonally.

QUEEN-POSTS: *see* Roof (Fig. 5).

QUOINS: dressed stones at the angles of a building. Sometimes all the stones are of the same size; more often they are alternately large or small.

RAFTER: *see* Roof.

REREDOS: structure behind and above an altar.

RETABLE: altar-piece, a picture or piece of carving, standing behind and attached to an altar.

RIB VAULT: *see* Vault.

ROCOCO: latest phase of the Baroque style, current in most Continental countries between *c.* 1720 and *c.* 1760.

ROMANESQUE: that style in architecture which was current in the 11th and 12th cent. and preceded the Gothic style (in England often called Norman).

ROOD: cross or crucifix.

ROOD LOFT: singing gallery on the top of the rood screen, often supported by a coving.

ROOD SCREEN: *see* Screen.

ROOD STAIRS: stairs to give access to the rood loft.

ROOF: *Hipped:* roof with sloped instead of vertical ends. *Saddleback:* tower roof shaped like an ordinary gabled timber roof. The following members have special names: *Rafter:* roof-timber sloping up from the wall plate to the ridge. *Principal:* principal rafter, usually corresponding to the main bay divisions of the nave or chancel below. *Wall Plate:* timber laid longitudinally on the top of a wall. *Purlin:* longitudinal member laid parallel with wall plate and ridge beam some way up the slope of the roof. *Tie-beam:* beam connecting the two slopes of a roof across at its foot, usually at the height of the wall plate, to prevent the roof from spreading. *Collar-beam:* tie-beam applied higher up the slope of the roof. *Strut:* upright timber connecting the tie-beam with the rafter above it. *King-post:* upright timber connecting a tie-beam and collar-beam with the ridge-beam. *Queen-posts:* two struts placed symmetrically on a tie-beam or collar-beam. *Braces:* inclined timbers inserted to strengthen others. Usually braces connect a collar-beam with the rafters below or a tie-beam with the wall below. Braces can be straight or curved (also called arched). *Hammer-beam:* beam projecting

at right angles, usually from the top of a wall, to carry arched braces or struts and arched braces (*see* Figs. 4, 5, 6).

ROSE WINDOW (or WHEEL WINDOW): circular window with patterned tracery arranged to radiate from the centre.

RUBBLE: building stones, not square or hewn, nor laid in regular courses.

RUSTICATION: Ashlar-work of blocks with the margins only wrought and the faces rough or specially rock-faced: or ashlar-work of smooth-faced blocks with the joints greatly emphasized (smooth rustication). If only the horizontal joints are emphasized it is called banded rustication.

SADDLEBACK: *see* Roof.

SANCTUARY: area around the main altar of a church (*see* Presbytery).

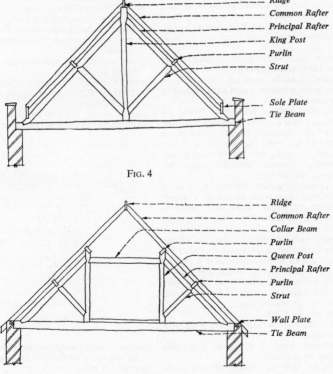

Ridge
Common Rafter
Principal Rafter
King Post
Purlin
Strut

Sole Plate
Tie Beam

FIG. 4

Ridge
Common Rafter
Collar Beam
Purlin
Queen Post
Principal Rafter
Purlin
Strut

Wall Plate
Tie Beam

FIG. 5

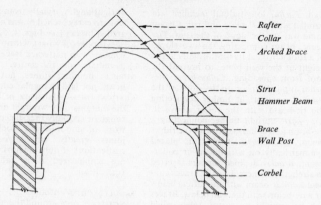

Rafter
Collar
Arched Brace
Strut
Hammer Beam
Brace
Wall Post
Corbel

FIG. 6

SCAGLIOLA: material composed of cement and colouring matter to imitate marble.

SCREEN: *Parclose screen:* screen separating a chapel from the rest of a church. *Rood screen:* screen at the W. end of a chancel. Above it on the rood-beam was the rood (q.v.).

SEDILIA: seats for the priests (usually three) on the S. side of the chancel of a church.

SEGMENTAL ARCH: *see* Arch.

SILL: lower horizontal part of the frame of a window.

SOUNDING BOARD: horizontal board or canopy over a pulpit. Also called Tester.

SPANDREL: triangular surface between one side of an arch, the horizontal drawn from its apex, and the vertical drawn from its springer, also the surface between two arches.

SPIRE: tall pyramidal or conical pointed erection often built on top of a tower, turret, etc. *Broach Spire:* spire which is generally octagonal in plan rising from the top or parapet of a square tower. A small inclined piece of masonry covers the vacant triangular space at each of the four angles of the square and is carried up to a point along the diagonal sides of the octagon. *Needle Spire:* thin spire rising from the centre of a tower roof, well inside the parapet.

SPIRELET: *see* Flèche.

SPLAY: chamfer, usually of the jamb of a window.

SPRINGING: level at which an arch rises from its supports.

SQUINCH: arch or system of concentric arches thrown across the angle between two walls to support a superstructure, for example a dome (Fig. 7).

SQUINT: hole cut in a wall or through a pier to allow a view of the main altar of a church from places whence it could not otherwise be seen (also called Hagioscope).

STALL: carved seat, one in a row, made of wood or stone.

STEEPLE: the tower or spire of a church.

STIFF-LEAF: E.E. type of foliage of many-lobed shapes.

STOUP: vessel for the reception of holy water, usually placed near a door.

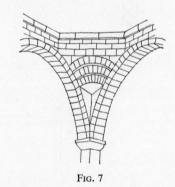

FIG. 7

STRING COURSE: projecting horizontal band or moulding set in the surface of a wall.

STRUT: *see* Roof.

STUCCO: plaster work.

SWAG: festoon formed by a carved piece of cloth suspended from both ends.

TABERNACLE: richly ornamented niche or free-standing canopy. Usually contains the Holy Sacrament.

TERRACOTTA: burnt clay, unglazed.

TESTER: *see* Sounding Board.

THREE-DECKER PULPIT: pulpit with Clerk's Stall and Reading Desk placed below each other.

TIE-BEAM: *see* Roof (Figs. 4, 5).

TIMBER-FRAMING: method of construction where walls are built of timber framework with the spaces filled in by plaster or brickwork. Sometimes the timber is covered over with plaster or boarding laid horizontally.

TOMB-CHEST: chest-shaped stone coffin, the most usual medieval form of funeral monument.

TRACERY: intersecting ribwork in the upper part of a window, or used decoratively in blank arches, on vaults, etc. *Plate tracery:* early form of tracery where decoratively shaped openings are cut through the solid stone infilling in the head of a window. *Bar tracery:* intersecting ribwork made up of slender shafts, continuing the lines of the mullions of windows up to a decorative mesh in the head of the window. *Geometrical tracery:* tracery consisting chiefly of circles or foiled circles. *Intersected tracery:* tracery in which each mullion of a window branches out into two curved bars in such a way that every one of them runs concentrically with the others against the arch of the whole window. The result is that every light of the window is a lancet and every two, three, four, etc., lights together form a pointed arch. *Reticulated tracery:* tracery consisting entirely of circles drawn at top and bottom into ogee shapes so that a net-like appearance results (Fig. 8).

TRANSEPT: transverse portion of a cross-shaped church.

TRANSOME: horizontal bar across the opening of a window.

TRIFORIUM: arcaded wall passage or blank arcading facing the nave at the height of the aisle roof and below the clerestory windows.

TROPHY: sculptured group of arms or armour, used as a memorial of victory.

TURRET: very small tower, round or polygonal in plan.

FIG. 8

TYMPANUM: space between the lintel of a doorway and the arch above it.

UNDERCROFT: vaulted room, sometimes underground, below a church or chapel.

VAULT: *Barrel vault: see* Tunnel vault. *Cross-vault: see* Groined vault. *Domical vault:* square or polygonal dome rising direct on a square or polygonal bay, the curved surfaces separated by groins (q.v.). *Fan vault:* vault where all ribs springing from one springer are of the same length, the same distance from the next, and the same curvature. *Groined vault* or *Cross-vault:* vault of two tunnel vaults of identical shape intersecting each other at right angles. *Lierne:* tertiary rib, that is, rib which does not spring either from one of the main springers or the central boss. *Quadripartite vault:* one wherein one bay of vaulting is divided into four parts. *Rib vault:* vault with diagonal ribs projecting along the groins. *Ridge-rib:* rib along the longitudinal or transverse ridge of a vault. *Sexpartite vault:* one wherein one bay of quadripartite vaulting is divided into two parts transversely so that each bay of vaulting has six parts. *Tierceron:* secondary rib, that is, rib which issues from one of the main springers or the central boss and leads to a place on a ridge-rib. *Transverse arch:* arch separating one bay of a vault from the next. *Tunnel vault* or *Barrel vault:* vault of semicircular or pointed section.

VENETIAN WINDOW: window with three openings, the central one arched and wider than the outside ones.

VOUSSOIR: wedge-shaped stone used in arch construction.

WAGON-ROOF: roof in which by closely set

P

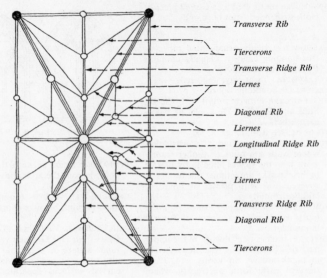

Transverse Rib

Tiercerons

Transverse Ridge Rib

Liernes

Diagonal Rib

Liernes

Longitudinal Ridge Rib

Liernes

Liernes

Transverse Ridge Rib

Diagonal Rib

Tiercerons

FIG. 9

rafters with arched braces the appearance of the inside of a canvas tilt over a wagon is achieved. Wagon-roofs can be panelled or plastered (ceiled) or left un-covered.

WAINSCOT: timber lining to walls.

WALL PLATE: *see* Roof.

WEATHER-BOARDING: overlapping horizontal boards, covering a timber-framed wall.

WEEPERS: small figures placed in niches along the sides of some medieval tombs (also called Mourners).

WHEEL WINDOW: *see* Rose Window.

INDEX OF ARCHITECTS AND ARTISTS

Figures in parentheses after page numbers indicate the number of references to a person on that page.

451

INDEX OF PLACES

A 11/58